MAJULAH!

50 Years of Malay/Muslim Community
in Singapore

World Scientific Series on Singapore's 50 Years of Nation-Building

The complete list of titles in the series can be found at
http://www.worldscientific.com/series/wss50ynb

World Scientific Series on
Singapore's 50 Years of Nation-Building

MAJULAH!

50 Years of Malay/Muslim Community in Singapore

Editors

Zainul Abidin Rasheed

Former Senior Minister of State for Foreign Affairs
and Community Leader

Norshahril Saat

ISEAS — Yusof Ishak Institute,
Singapore

World Scientific

NEW JERSEY · LONDON · SINGAPORE · BEIJING · SHANGHAI · HONG KONG · TAIPEI · CHENNAI · TOKYO

Published by

World Scientific Publishing Co. Pte. Ltd.

5 Toh Tuck Link, Singapore 596224

USA office: 27 Warren Street, Suite 401-402, Hackensack, NJ 07601

UK office: 57 Shelton Street, Covent Garden, London WC2H 9HE

Library of Congress Cataloging-in-Publication Data
Names: Zainul Abidin Rasheed, editor. | Norshahril Saat, editor. |
    Norshahril Saat. Progressive Malay/Muslim Singaporeans. Container of (work):
Title: Majulah! : 50 years of Malay/Muslim community in Singapore / editors, Zainul Abidin Rasheed,
    Dr. Norshahril Saat.
Other titles: Majulah! (World Scientific Publishing Co.)
Description: New Jersey : World Scientific, [2016] | Some contributions translated from Malay. |
    Includes bibliographical references and index.
Identifiers: LCCN 2015047281 | ISBN 9789814759861 (hardcover : alk. paper) |
    9789814759878 (pbk : alk. paper)
Subjects: LCSH: Malays (Asian people)--Singapore. | Muslims--Singapore.
Classification: LCC DS610.25.M34 M325 2016 | DDC 305.6/97095957--dc23
LC record available at http://lccn.loc.gov/2015047281

British Library Cataloguing-in-Publication Data
A catalogue record for this book is available from the British Library.

Front cover image: Courtesy of Sarafian Salleh © 2016. All Rights Reserved.
Back cover image: Courtesy of Tanoti Sdn Bhd © 2016. All Rights Reserved.

Desk Editors: Rhaimie Wahap and Karimah Samsudin

Typeset by Stallion Press
Email: enquiries@stallionpress.com

FOREWORD

Fifty years ago, we set out on our SG50 journey. We were determined to build a multiracial society where every citizen is equal, regardless of race, language or religion. It was the fundamental reason for our existence, the reason we left Malaysia to become a sovereign, independent republic. From that point on, we built a nation together. Our pioneers decided that there would be a Singapore, and that we would be a society where people are valued for their abilities and contributions, not the colour of their skin.

Fifty years on, against all odds, we have created a harmonious multiracial society, where each group maintains its heritage and culture, but all come together to share one Singapore identity. We journeyed from Third World to First as one united people. That is why we can celebrate SG50 together.

The Malay/Muslim community has played a vital role in this journey. They joined hands with other communities, tackled challenges together and achieved progress and prosperity together. These essays capture part of this SG50 journey from the perspective of the Malay/Muslim community.

We are now into the next phase of nation-building. I hope readers will draw valuable lessons from the past as we prepare for the future. Where Singapore goes from here will depend on each of us, and on whether we can come together to build a more united and prosperous Singapore. We must always be a society where minorities are confident of their place and proud of our nation, a city where every citizen has full opportunities to fulfil their potential and realise their dreams. Then Singapore will succeed, and all of us can celebrate together.

Majulah Singapura!

Lee Hsien Loong
Prime Minister

PREFACE

2015 was an eventful year for Singapore as it marked its 50 years of independence. On 9 August 1965, the country separated from Malaysia, after two years being part of the federation. The future was uncertain: the country had limited land, water and energy. Fifty years on, Singapore has moved from a third world to first. The same sense of achievement applies to the Malay/Muslim community in Singapore. On the eve of Singapore's independence, the community was in a dilemma: they had the option of moving to Malaysia, being part of the majority, with better job opportunities; and on the other, they could remain in Singapore, being a minority, and compete with other ethnic groups in a meritocratic setting. Many felt inadequate because they as a community was lagging behind economically. Undeniably, a number of Malay/Muslim professionals crossed over to Malaysia, but those who stayed on made Singapore a multiracial country.

Majulah! 50 Years of Malay/Muslim Community in Singapore traces the community's evolution in the last five decades. Although this book focuses on challenges facing the community after 1965, it does not deny its contributions before Singapore's independence. In other words, the country's history pre-dates 1965. The history of the Malays in Singapore has to include the Nusantara (archipelago). However, the last 50 years, during independent Singapore, have been significant for the Malays/Muslims in Singapore, as they made tremendous progress in the field of education, information technology, finance and thought, on top of contributions traditionally associated with the community, such as literature, music, the arts and Islam. Obviously it cannot be exhaustive but it will capture enough to portray the essential element of the community's growth or lack of.

Majulah! features reflections by academics, journalists, politicians, and practitioners. It begins with an article on the late president, Encik Yusof Ishak, detailing his vision for multicultural Singapore and progressive Malay/Muslim community. Chapter One is a personal reflection on the journey of the community through his eyes and experience. Education, self-reliance and multiculturalism remain strong in the Malay/Muslim journey in modern Singapore. We feel SG50 is a good moment for

Singaporeans to reflect on whether the community has achieved the ideals Encik Yusof envisioned 50 years ago, and what remains to be done as the nation moves towards SG100. This book includes articles which we hope are accessible to non-specialists. Articles range from serious academic pieces to short journalistic-style reflections. In between chapters, we also include quotes by both national and Malay/Muslim leaders which have historical significance. More importantly, we are also aware of balancing perspectives from our pioneer generations and the youth, as we think of future challenges.

One of the important highlights of this book is an interview with Dr Yaacob Ibrahim, Minister of Communications and Information, Minister-in-Charge of Cyber Security and Minister-in-Charge of Muslim Affairs, who candidly shares his views on the community's progress. It also includes an article by Mr Masagos Zulkifli, Minister for Environment and Water Resources. Due to space constraints, we regret not being able to capture views of all important personalities in the community. This is by no means discounting their contributions. The articles cover broad themes: such as national icons Encik Yusof Ishak, Pak Zubir Said and Syed Isa Semait; politics and civil society; education; moderate Islamic discourse; literature; and alternative discourses. This book also highlights how our national leaders perceive the community, and hence, we included comments and speeches by Singapore Prime Ministers which touch on the community. Some important speeches made by Malay/Muslim ministers, as well as those made in Parliament, have also been included. Lastly, this book provides the biodata of important icons and achievers in the Malay/Muslim community, as well as highlighting upcoming talents, as we approach SG100.

There are numerous people to thank for helping out in the completion of this book. We would like to express our gratitude to contributors of the articles, who obligingly sent in their drafts to us on short notice. We would like to also thank Mr Rhaimie Wahap and Ms Karimah Samsudin from World Scientific Publishing. A special thanks goes to Mr Aidi Abdul Rahim for helping out with the research work. Lastly, we would like to also dedicate this book to our family members. May this be an important contribution to existing literature on the Singapore Malay/Muslim community and we wish the community greater success in the years to come.

Editors
Zainul Abidin Rasheed
Norshahril Saat

EDITORS

Zainul Abidin Rasheed is the Former Senior Minister of State for Foreign Affairs and Community leader. He is currently Singapore's Ambassador to the State of Kuwait (non-resident) and the Foreign Minister's Special Envoy to the Middle East. Prior to his retirement from politics, he served as a Member of Parliament (MP) from 1997 to 2011. Mr Zainul has also held various key positions in government service and the media industry. He was Editor of *Berita Harian* for 20 years and *The Sunday Times* for five years, served as President of the Islamic Religious Council of Singapore (MUIS) and was Chief Executive Officer of the Council for the Development of Singapore Malay/Muslim Community (Yayasan MENDAKI). Mr Zainul's extensive knowledge and vast experience have contributed significantly to Singapore's international relations with the Middle East, Africa and Southeast Asia. Mr Zainul was also the Mayor of the Northeast Community Development Council District (2001–2009) and Chairman of the Malay Heritage Foundation (2003–2010).

Dr Norshahril Saat is a Fellow at ISEAS-Yusof Ishak Institute. In June 2015, he was awarded a PhD in International, Political and Strategic Studies by the Australian National University (ANU). He is a recipient of the Islamic Religious Council of Singapore (MUIS) Post-graduate Scholarship 2011. In 2015, he became the first recipient of the Syed Isa Semait Scholarship (SISS). His research interests are mainly on Southeast Asian politics and contemporary Islamic thought. In 2015, he published two books entitled *Faith, Authority and the Malays: The Ulama in Contemporary Singapore*; and *Yusof Ishak: Singapore's First President*. His articles have recently been published in journals such as *Contemporary Islam: Dynamics of Muslim Life*, *Review of Indonesian and Malaysian Affairs*, and *Studia Islamika*. He has also published numerous opinion and think pieces, including those in local newspapers such as *The Straits Times*, *Berita Harian* and *Today*; and international newspapers such as the *Canberra Times*, *Bangkok Post*, and the *Jakarta Post*. Dr Norshahril has a strong passion for music and was a member of the Singapore Police Force Band between 2002 and 2004. He is active in mosques, such as Al-Mawaddah and Al-Muttaqin, and helped out with Malay Youth Literary Association (4PM) Pre-University Debates judging.

LIST OF CONTRIBUTORS

Abdul Halim Kader, BBM
>President
>Taman Bacaan Pemuda Pemudi Melayu Singapura

Abdul Razak Maricar
>Chief Executive
>Islamic Religious Council of Singapore (MUIS)

Ahmad Fuad Abu Bakar
>President
>Singapore Malay-Muslim Group
>Dubai, U.A.E.

Aidi Abdul Rahim
>Independent Researcher

Aileen Tan Boon
>Managing Editor
>Suntree Media

Alfian Yasrif Kuchit
>Former President
>Syariah Court

Art Fazil
>Singer-Songwriter & Record Producer
>MORO Records

Azhar Ibrahim, Dr
>Lecturer
>Department of Malay Studies
>National University of Singapore (NUS)

Hadijah Rahmat, Dr
>Associate Professor
>Covering Head/Deputy Head of the Asian Languages
>   and Cultures Academic Group
>National Institute of Education (NIE)
>Nanyang Technological University (NTU)

Isa Kamari
>Poet and Writer

Jackie Yi-Ru Ying, Prof
>Executive Director
>Institute of Bioengineering and Nanotechnology

Joe Peters, Dr
>Ethnomusicologist
>Sonic Asia Music Consultants;
>Former Associate Director (Multimedia)
>National University of Singapore

Julina Khusaini (Ms)
>General Manager
>The Malay Heritage Foundation Ltd

Maarof Salleh
>Former President of the Majlis Ugama Islam Singapura (MUIS)

Marina Yusoff (Ms)
>Creative Director
>Sri Warisan

Masagos Zulkifli Masagos Mohamad
>Minister for the Environment and Water Resources

Masuri S. N. (Courtesy of Asas'50)
>Educator, Poet and Writer

Mohamed Ali, Dr
>Assistant Professor
>Studies in Inter-Religious Relations in Plural Societies (SRP) Programme
>S. Rajaratnam School of International Studies (RSIS)
>Nanyang Technological University (NTU)

Mohammad Hannan Hassan, Dr
>Vice Dean
>MUIS Academy

Mohammad Alami Musa
>Head of Studies
>Inter-Religious Relations in Plural Societies (SRP) Programme
>S. Rajaratnam School of International Studies (RSIS)
>Nanyang Technological University (NTU)

Mohd Guntor Sadali
  Former Editor
  Berita Harian/Berita Minggu
  Singapore Press Holdings

Mohd Raman Daud
  Senior Writer
  Berita Harian/Berita Minggu
  Singapore Press Holdings

Mohamed Latiff Mohamed
  Poet and Writer

Muhd Fuadi Rahmat
  Lecturer
  Lecturer Management/School of Media and Communications
    Management Development Institute of Singapore

Peter Augustine Goh
  Poet and Writer

Raja Mohamad Maiden
  Council Member
  Islamic Religious Council of Singapore (MUIS) and Secretary General
    Singapore Kadayanallur Muslim League (SKML)

Rasiah Halil
  Poet, Author, Translator and Educator

Sani Hamid
  Director
  Wealth Management (Economy and Market Strategy)
  Financial Alliance Pte Ltd

Sarafian Salleh
  Engineering Consultant
  Diagnos Veritas

Sharifah Mariam Aljunied, Dr
  Chartered Educational Psychologist
  British Psychological Society;
  Principal Educational Psychologist
  Ministry of Education (MOE)

Sher Banu A. L. Khan, Dr
    Assistant Professor
    Department of Malay Studies
    National University of Singapore (NUS)

Sidek Saniff
    Former Member of Parliament and Senior Minister of State (Ret)

Sujimy Mohamad
    Director
    ScreenBox Pte Ltd

Sumarleki Amjah
    Co-founder and President
    Macan Association, Singapore

Suratman Markasan
    Poet, fiction writer and essayist

Syed Farid Alatas, Dr
    Associate Professor
    Departments of Sociology & Malay Studies
    National University of Singapore (NUS)

Syed Muhd Hafiz Syed Nasir
    Assistant Curator
    National Gallery Singapore

Tuminah Sapawi (Ms)
    Chief Executive Officer
    Yayasan MENDAKI

Umar Abdul Hamid
    Co-Founder and Chief Operating Officer
    Charaku Pte Ltd, Portfolio Advisor of Asia Development Fund,
        Investment Advisor of Makara Capital

Wan Hussin Zoohri
    Chairman
    Board of Directors
    Al-Zuhri Institute of Higher Studies;
    Former Member of Parliament and Parliamentary Secretary
        for the Ministry of Health & Culture (Ret)

Yang Razali Kassim
    Senior Fellow
    S. Rajaratnam School of International Studies (RSIS)
    Nanyang Technological University (NTU);
    Former Chairman, Association of Muslim Professionals (AMP) and
    Founding Deputy Chairman of the Board and Founding Chairman
        Executive Committee AMP

Yatiman Yusof
    Former Member of Parliament and Senior Parliamentary Secretary
        for Foreign Affairs (Ret)

Zakiah Halim (Ms)
    Head of Malay Community
    Mediacorp

Zakir Hussain
    Deputy Political Editor
    The Straits Times
    Singapore Press Holdings

CONTENTS

Community and Nation-Building — Community of Excellence, Accommodation and Rallying Points

Part 2 — Icons, Pioneers and All

Conclusion

Appendix

INTRODUCTION

THE SPIRIT OF MAJULAH | Zainul Abidin Rasheed

Let the Journey Begin...

Majulah! Flourish! Onward! These simple words encapsulate the spirit of the pioneers of modern Singapore in 1965, and it is this spirit which has brought Singapore to where it is today as we celebrate SG50. We cherish the same spirit as we move forward to SG100.

Majulah! There is no single word that could be more apt for the title of this book on 50 Years of the Malay/Muslim Community in Singapore. *Majulah* is probably the one Malay word most recognisable to most, if not all, Singaporeans. *Majulah*, together with Singapura, form the title of our National Anthem, and I believe that *Majulah* represents exactly how the Malay/Muslim community of Singapore would like other Singaporeans to think of, reflect and remember its contributions to the Singapore story.

Furthermore, it also brings to mind the early history of the island from the time the Palembang Prince Sang Nila Utama set eye on what he thought was the legendary lion on the barren island and naming it Singapura or Lion City in Malay/Sanskrit. This could very well have been the reason why Singapore's founding Prime Minister, the late Mr Lee Kuan Yew, chose Sumatra-born Zubir Said's song "Majulah Singapura" as Singapore's National Anthem. Mr Lee said in his book *The Singapore Story*:

> The choice of the state anthem had proved easier [compared to the choice and symbolism in the state crest and flag, which needed reconciliation of different racial symbols and ideals].
>
> A Malay musician, Haji Zubir Said, had composed a suitable tune. The melody was of the region and the lyrics in Malay matched our motto Majulah Singapura.

The Malay community's early contributions to Singapore can perhaps be best reflected by the appointment and work of Yusof Ishak as the first President of the Republic of Singapore. Encik Yusof's strong belief in multiracialism helped create a strong foundation for a multiracial, multilingual and multireligious Singapore. His stately photograph continues to feature in our currency to this day. But does this symbolism merely attempt to hide the relegation of significance of our community in reality?

The Malay/Muslim community in Singapore evolved from being the indigenous majority, at the time Sir Stamford Raffles set foot in Singapore, into a minority, over time. And similar to many other such communities in other parts of the world, questions are always asked about whether our rights and interests are protected, whether we have benefitted equally from the nation's economic and social progress, and the ideals of democracy, peace, progress, justice and equality (as represented by the five stars on our national flag) have truly done us good? This calls for further scrutiny.

While the Malay/Muslim community would no doubt have experienced progress and greater prosperity over the years, the question remains whether such progress has permeated through all levels of the community, whether our role and stature in the wider Singapore community has been properly safeguarded and rewarded, and whether issues specific to our race and religion have been given due consideration. Many Malay Singaporeans still feel that more can be done with respect to issues like representation within the Armed Forces and the wearing of headscarf (*tudung*).

This book is neither an exhaustive compendium of historical events and facts, nor an analytical academic piece on the various issues affecting the Malay/Muslim community. Rather, this book encompasses a collection of personal reflections about the community's challenges and triumphs and anecdotal stories about our journey.

Much has been said and written about these issues prior to this book, and they will continue to be debated long after this book, but more importantly it is good to see divergent and diverse views, reflecting the variety of thoughts and perspectives about the community. Like the proverbial "the blind men describing the elephant", the issues are in fact often more complex than any one writer or commentator can fully account for, and therefore each point of reference can be expected to exude a different angle or feel, and seldom a truly comprehensive or complete outlook.

We hope that this book will encourage more to be written about the issues affecting the Malay/Muslim community and other communities in Singapore. As long as they do not serve to divide the community, but instead attempt to put forward the different ways forward and onward, they should serve the community well.

This reminds me of my personal experience and anecdotes as to how we should see the bigger picture. In 1981, the Council for the Upliftment of Education of the Malay/Muslim Community was established through the MENDAKI Congress. This was viewed by some as a significant milestone for the community; a sign that it was getting

The Spirit of Majulah | xxxi

its act together. At the same time, there were also divergent calls for alternative voices, with the biggest concern being that MENDAKI was too closely tied to the government and the Malay Members of Parliament, and therefore too pro-establishment, to be effective for the community. Some young Muslim professionals, in particular, had preferred an NGO-led organisation to lead the initiative.

These concerns were not new, and had been debated over and over again in various different contexts. Even in the early days of Singapore's independence and the 1970s, this issue was debated in the university campus, where I recall Professor Dr Sharom Ahmad of the University of Singapore then, calling for the Malay community to work within the national framework, including working closely with the government, in order to move forward.

Working then as Editor of the Malay language newspaper *Berita Harian* (BH), but more importantly, in the capacity of a concerned community activist, I had met the then Deputy Prime Minister Mr Goh Chok Tong, and persuaded him to give more serious attention to improving leadership and staffing at MENDAKI. I recall sharing with Mr Goh, "If you are serious about helping the Malay community, please help give MENDAKI stronger resources, backup and leadership," rather than allowing it to continue to operate like one of the old *kampung* Malay/Muslim community organisations, Mr Goh then challenged me to find him and MENDAKI a Chief Executive Officer (CEO) that would not only be strong but better accepted by the community. I had suggested Haji Ridzwan Dzafir, the top Malay civil servant then and head of the Trade Development Board. Mr Goh had told me that he too had thought of Haji Ridzwan (fondly called Pak Wan), but Pak Wan, who was already retired but recalled to serve further, would have to be persuaded. And so I met with Pak Wan to persuade him to give it a shot and help put MENDAKI on a better footing. Over lunch at the Istana with Mr Goh, the deal was clinched and Pak Wan agreed not just to be the CEO of MENDAKI, but also President of the Islamic Religious Council of Singapore (MUIS), on the condition that I would give him support on both MUIS and MENDAKI's executive committee and MENDAKI 's council.

I was therefore inducted into the MUIS council to support Pak Wan, together with a few others like Dr Yaacob Ibrahim and Haji Maarof Salleh, who both kindly agreed to help. Under the Chairmanship of the then Minister Dr Ahmad Mattar, MENDAKI formed an Exco to include community leaders like Mr Othman Haron Eusofe and Mr Rohan Kamis.

This was a tremendous shot-in-the-arm for the community, but it did not last long as Pak Wan wanted to step down after a short stint at MENDAKI. This was when Mr Goh challenged me to fill the big shoes of my mentor, Pak Wan, by taking on the role of CEO of MENDAKI. In believing that MENDAKI must succeed, I managed to convince the then Chairman of the Singapore Press Holdings, Mr Lim Kim San, to allow my secondment to MENDAKI, with the SPH bearing part of the cost. As expected, I found from the onset that the role of CEO of MENDAKI was a challenging one, and there was so very much to do.

Thus my surprise and disappointment when Mr Goh showed me his draft speech to the AMP Convention in 1990, where the Government would offer recognition and financial assistance to AMP. I must confess to feeling like the Government had pulled the carpet from under my feet. I had always felt the need for Malay/Muslim professionals to support and join forces with MENDAKI, in order to provide a solid platform for self-help for the community. I therefore disagreed with Mr Goh and asked him whether the Government was practicing a divide-and-rule approach to the Malay/Muslim community, which he of course denied. He felt that since the community was already divided, the Government should offer assistance to both groups so long as they were willing to work for the benefit of the community.

Realising how strongly I felt about the issue, Mr Goh said that I was free to express my views at the AMP Convention. I did exactly that, much to the chagrin of the AMP leadership. I had simply wished for more unity among the community's traditional and professional leaders under one roof (MENDAKI), to improve our chances of rallying the community to improve itself.

Years down the road, I came to the realisation that it was indeed better for the community to have multiple pillars of support through more self-help groups, so that more members of the community can benefit from more diverse programmes. This episode is a reminder to me of the importance of diversity of views, ideas and efforts.

This book, to a large extent, is a reflection of that spectrum of issues, concerns, efforts and institutions which envelops the development and growth of the community. Where there are gaps of information and reflection, we hope this book will inspire nonetheless to be just the beginning of that journey, to share and to reflect as we move on to the bigger challenges awaiting in SG60, indeed even more so in SG100.

The Journey Continues... Back to the Future

Indeed there was so much to be done and the community needed all hands on deck. Other than unity, or, lack of, in diversity, the last 50 years have also highlighted the essence of the importance placed on education (continuing education, and acquiring new skill sets), the spirit of self-reliance and a more inclusive approach to upliftment.

Allow me to share with you here my personal and community anecdotes which affirm these values and valuable assets.

To highlight how serious and backward the starting point was, to my mind, one needs to go back to the days before independence. I could still visualise the sad faces of my fellow school mates in primary school lining up for free milk. Many, if not most of them, had to attend school without breakfast. I was then in charge of the UNICEF Free Milk Programme when I was in Primary Three in Jalan Daud Primary School (now gone, having given way to the development of the Pan Island Expressway at Eunos Intersection).

Life then was full of challenges. Economics, social and political relations were not on our side. Communism, communalism threatened to tear the society apart. Chinese school riots and bus strikes initiated by the communists and communist-led trade unions preceded independence in 1965. I experienced my first curfew during those years and they made me understand the difficulties we had to face then. During curfew hours, we were even denied the 10 cents *prata* which we enjoyed in the village then.

Merger with Malaysia was deemed then as a way out towards achieving independence from the British and the threats from the Communists but the ugly head of communalism showed its fangs and did not help. The July 1964 riots that broke out during the Prophet Muhammad's birthday procession showed how fragile race relations were. I was almost killed during a subsequent riot in September the same year at Victoria Street where the Lavender MRT station now stands. I saw with my own eyes, innocent Malays (and Indians too, I suppose during the pandemonium, it can be difficult to differentiate the two) were killed or maimed during that riot. I escaped, only to see, when I reached the two racial "black areas" of Geylang Serai/JooChiat where I lived, Malays attacking Chinese trishaw riders. Senseless killings just because of a different skin colour.

A few years later in 1968, when I was with the People's Foundation (Yayasan Rakyat), we found there was still a need for free milk for the poor. Yayasan Rakyat, through its international network had obtained 20 tonnes of powdered milk from the Van Leer Foundation in Holland.

The Internal Security Department (ISD) had disallowed us to distribute the milk as they must have suspected that the NGO Yayasan Rakyat had motives to politicise the programme, possibly to show that the PAP Government did not do enough to help the Malay community or the needy. Thanks to a courageous but courteous letter to the ISD explaining our intentions, they allowed distribution through a third party, the Council of Social Service. I still remember the happy faces of the recipients when the milk was distributed at the old premises of the Malay Youth Literary Association (4PM) at Jalan Eunos.

Yayasan Rakyat (YR) did not stop at milk handouts. Its forward-looking leadership had even envisioned running a cooperative to facilitate the setting up of a preschool centre to emphasis sustainability in its self-help programmes and education, at its base level of pre-school education as the foundation. This was initiated more than 10 years before MENDAKI was born.

Another programme initiated by the YR to emphasis self-reliance was to send a group of volunteers to learn to grow mushrooms in the Philippines. This was with the Philippine Rural Reconstruction Movement programme in Nueva Ecija, north of Manila. I was among those who went there, funded by the Catholic Foundation Misereor, from Rome. YR felt then that growing mushrooms could be made sustainable in urban HDB living, but the startup plan to pilot the project in Tanah Merah was aborted after the Government acquired the land around the Changi Airport area for airport and industrial development. I was told then that the former Chief Minister, Mr David Marshall, who was close to the *kampung* folks at Tanah Merah, had agreed to offer a piece of his land for the pioneer mushroom-growing project. Even in the early days of community work, the community had been impressed by the need for emphasis by education, self-reliance and inclusive approach for networking with others for community development.

In 1973, the University of Singapore Muslim Society (USMS) was invited by the late President Muammar Gaddafi of Libya to attend an International Youth Conference to endorse his Green Book where he emphasised that capitalism was decadent and Communism was on the verge of collapse and that Islam was the answer to the world's woes. Interestingly, the youth conference rejected his vision of exclusivity and called on the Muslim youths then to work on an inclusive approach of working with others towards overcoming contemporary challenges. That had a strong impact on me and those who attended the conference on our outlook to life. Beyond the rhetoric, one has to be realistic about how one sees the unending challenges and the need to be pragmatic about how to tackle and overcome them.

Indeed, two years earlier, attending a leadership training programme invited by the National Association of Muslim Students in Malaysia (PKPIM), led then by Mr Anwar Ibrahim, in Kelantan, the Singapore delegation, when asked to present an impromptu paper, suggested that while the PKPIM leaders can go on thumping tables and shouting slogans (popular in those days), they should also embark on concrete programmes on community upliftment, especially in education. I believe the Yasayan Anda (Your Foundation) educational institution, started by Malaysia's Assembly of Muslim Youth (ABIM) and Mr Anwar then, was inspired by Singapore's mindshare.

After a couple of years at BH and learning on-the-job about running the sole Malay language newspaper for the Malay-speaking community, I found the daily was overwhelmed by social and political issues and was too sensational when it came to entertainment. I thought it lacked focus on economic issues which was the key to what Singapore was about. I attempted to place more emphasis and give more space and prominence on economics, business and financial news stories and features. Such stories which normally were not carried, or hidden in the inside pages, assumed prominence on page 1. The Malay readers and community, I thought, must learn to appreciate that. Even if they did not read them, I thought that more coverage on economic matters would make them realise their importance. Circulation dropped. The readers, indeed the community, were not ready for that. Such education had to be done in several steps, not at one go. An important lesson for me, no doubt: no point doing the right thing but losing the readership.

Change is not easy. Old mindsets linger and take time to change. One of the programmes I embarked on when I was Editor of BH, and given an opportunity to travel and learn from others and open my mind, was to look at Muslims and social change the world over. I chose this theme because I felt the challenge of social change was the cornerstone for the future. That took me to the Middle East (Saudi Arabia, Egypt, Jordan and other Gulf countries), Turkey, Iran, of course Malaysia, Indonesia, Brunei and other Southeast Asian countries, Europe, the Soviet Union and the USA.

Turkey was my first stop. Secular Turkey was then regarded as the leader among the modern Muslim world. It did not take me long to conclude that the Kamal Ataturk brand of embracing modernisation and social change in the contemporary world then was not the answer for Singapore to follow. In fact, many of the Muslim communities world-wide then, particularly in Indonesia and Malaysia, were suspicious of the kind of secularism preached by the Muslims in Turkey. Neither was the Middle East a model to emulate as each of the Middle Eastern countries had its own challenges of cultures, tribalism and political system which made them different from each other and what more with the Muslims in Southeast Asia, particularly Singapore.

Even Egypt, which provided the closest connection in terms of the Shafie school of thought and produced the most foreign-trained religious teachers (*asatizahs*) including our former and present *mufti*, had challenges too in meeting the needs of Singapore's answers to challenges of interpretation.

Even our close neighbours, Indonesia, Malaysia, Brunei (majority Muslim population), Thailand and the Philippines (the original six ASEAN countries closest in terms of regional relations) had unique differences.

Indonesia, the largest Muslim county in the world, is not a proclaimed Islamic State, where Islam is not seen as the official religion, like in Malaysia. Indonesia chose Pancasila (Five Principles) as the state ideology and is more akin to a secular state. Malaysia has Islam as its official state religion and the Sultans (as rulers) have power on the administration of religion in their individual states where they are the state's Sultans. Brunei has a system of Malay, Islam and Royalty (Melayu, Islam, Beraja) as its state ideology. Thailand is predominantly Buddhist, with a Muslim minority, while the Philippines has a Catholic majority with a Muslim minority. Singapore is about 75% Chinese (majority are Taoist and Buddhist) with minorities among them Malays/Muslims, Chinese Christians and Indians comprising mostly Hindus and some Muslims.

One can imagine the complex nature of its majority–minority ethnic/religious and cultural relations among and within each country. Both Muslim minorities in Thailand and the Philippines have problems, even secessionist tendencies in their relations with the majority populations, and Malaysia has had racial riots between the Malays and the Chinese.

Singapore too had its racial riots but since independence in 1965 (minus the spillover effects of the 1969 Malaysia riots), the Singapore Government had emphasised on protecting the special position of the Malays (Article 152/153 of the Constitution) but in ways unique to Singapore. No quotas in places of education at the university or polytechnic or in the school system, except for the ones started by the Malay MPs themselves. They had asked the Government to impose a ceiling for admission to primary school once the figure 20% was reached. The Malay MPs felt this would help the Malay students learn English better rather than stick to their own Malay language.

This was in contrast to the housing quota (30%) imposed on HDB dwelling initiated by the Government to ensure a better spread of Malays (and Indians) in the housing estates, facilitating better integration.

Even in politics, to ensure better multiracial, indeed minority representation in Parliament, the Government changed the Constitution in 1988 to introduce the Group Representation Constituency (GRC) concept where a number of group constituencies were designated as requiring Malay or Indian candidates, thus ensuring minority representation in Parliament, regardless of which political party wins the general elections. This also ensured that all political parties contesting the GE would have to practice multiracial politics.

When I was first approached to stand for the GE in 1976 by the ruling PAP, I had declined, thinking that I was not the political type. Moreover, I sensed then that the Malay/Muslim community was divided over its support for the ruling PAP. I had thought that it was better for me then to work from outside the political area of party politics to achieve better consensus in getting a majority of the Malay/Muslim community to work within the national framework. I had felt that it was not in the interest of the community to be on the fringes, worse to be against the popular ruling party then.

I had chosen to work from outside to bring about better unity. First through the media (*Berita Harian*), then after I was appointed President of the Islamic Religious Council of Singapore (MUIS) and then as CEO of MENDAKI, the Council for the Development of Singapore Malay/Muslim Community.

I recall, after about 20 years working and serving the community from the outside the political area, I was asked again to consider to stand as a PAP candidate. Having worked from the outside as I had wanted to, and to my mind, achieved what I could do to bring the society closer to mainstream, I agreed to stand as a PAP candidate, hoping to understand what it would be like to work from inside the political arena.

I remember asking PM Lee Kuan Yew then, why after saying "No" for over 20 years (after four General Elections); the PAP was still asking me to stand. Mr Lee's answer was simple and brief:

> *You have wanted to work from outside, you have done so, and there is now better unity of purpose, now join the team and work from inside. Help look after the Malays.*

I read that as a sincere effort on the part of the PAP to continue to work together to bring about better harmony and progress for the Malay/Muslim community, together in the mainstream of progress and prosperity of Singapore.

Whether through MUIS, MENDAKI and government support shown for other Malay/Muslim organisations, including the AMP, the setting up of the Malay Heritage Foundation and the GRC; to me, these were enough to show that the Government was sincere in wanting to ensure that the community remains an important part of an integrated Singapore. Yes, there are still areas which still leave sections of the community wanting to see more progress and better understanding; perhaps even more trust, for example, on the question of Malays/Muslims in the Singapore Armed Forces (SAF) and the *tudung* (headscarf) issues, but even then, the community acknowledges that there has been progress. As PM Lee Hsien Loong acknowledges, it is work-in-progress and we are glad we are still talking about bridging the gap of understanding and to bring about better trust.

Majulah, more than flourish, we need to move forward as one nation, one people as we continue to face the challenges of the future which are expected to be even more difficult. However, at least we are more experienced and more matured in facing these challenges together and we will be better prepared.

The *Majulah* spirit with which we started in 1965 is even stronger now as can be seen when we celebrated SG50. We should continue to be guided by this *Majulah* spirit as we prepare for the challenge of the next 50 years. The Malay/Muslim community will be an even stronger and more resilient part of this Singapore of the future.

Majulah Melayu Singapura, Majulah Singapura.

JOURNEY AS ONE PEOPLE

"We want every Singaporean to be able to connect through their personal stories with the broader Singapore story, and be a part of the anniversary celebrations. We should use this special occasion to come together to reflect on our past, to celebrate our past and our journey together as one people, as well as come together to imagine and create a better future together."

Heng Swee Keat
Minister for Finance
and Chairman of SG50 Steering Committee

PART 1

Malay/Muslim Community Matters

CHAPTER 1

PROGRESSIVE MALAY/MUSLIM SINGAPOREANS — THE THOUGHTS OF YUSOF ISHAK

Norshahril Saat

President Yusof Ishak with his medals conferred by Singapore (top), Brunei (right) and Malaysia (left). Yusof Ishak Collection, courtesy of National Archives of Singapore.

During the 2014 National Day Rally, Prime Minister Lee Hsien Loong called on Singaporeans to honour the country's pioneers, as Singapore celebrates its Golden Jubilee (50 years of independence) the following year. Among the pioneers singled out during the speech is Yusof Ishak, Singapore's first President. Lee also announced three initiatives to honour the late president. First, a mosque will be named Masjid Yusof Ishak. The mosque, scheduled for completion in 2016, will be located in Woodlands. The choice of the location of the mosque is significant because it is close to his final resting place: the Kranji State Cemetery. Second, the Faculty of the Arts and Social Sciences (FASS) at the National University of Singapore (NUS) will set up a professorship chair in his honour. The Yusof Ishak Professorship Chair will host prominent academics who research on multiculturalism, a value Yusof Ishak struggled for throughout his life. A committee, led by the Malay/Muslim community, was set up to raise $3.5 million for that purpose. So far, the committe has raised $7.6 million, exceeding its target. Third, the Institute of Southeast Asian Studies (ISEAS) will be renamed after him. Established in 1968, ISEAS is one of the oldest research institutes in Singapore which hosts academics who research on the region. On 12 August 2015, ISEAS, a statutory board under the Ministry of Education, was renamed ISEAS–Yusof Ishak Institute. On that occasion, the institute also launched a book titled *Yusof Ishak: Singapore's First President*.[1]

This chapter discusses Yusof Ishak's thoughts on the Singapore Malay/Muslim community. Adopting a sociological approach, the chapter examines the values and principles he considered necessary in spurring the community forward. What can the Malay community learn from Yusof Ishak's struggle in the 1940s to the 1960s? The chapter underscores three ways in which the community can emulate Yusof: embracing multiculturalism; understanding Islam beyond the worldly/otherworldly dichotomy (*dunia* and *akhirat*); and redefining success beyond academic achievements. The following section highlights Yusof's biography. This will be followed by a discussion of the three abovementioned aspects.

Close-up of the medal conferred by Malaysia to Yusof Ishak — Seri Maharaja Mangku Negara. Photo courtesy of Malay Heritage Centre Copyright © 2015 MHC. All rights reserved.

Close-up of the medal conferred by Brunei to Yusof Ishak — Darjah Kerabat Laila Utama Brunei, 1st Class. Photo courtesy of Malay Heritage Centre Copyright © 2015 MHC. All rights reserved.

Yusof Ishak (1910–1970)

Yusof Ishak was born on 12 August 1910. He grew up in Taiping (Perak), and received his primary education there. His father, Ishak Ahmad, is a descendant of Datuk Jenaton from Minangkabau, Sumatera (Indonesia). In the 18th century, Jenaton, a minister in the Minangkabau royal court, migrated to Kedah to escape a looming religious and political conflict between the reformists and traditionalists. The two camps disagreed on the position of Minangkabau *adat* (local cultural practices) in Islam. Jenaton sided with the reformists and called for the removal of innovations (*bid'ah*) in the community's religious rituals, and it was in this reformist orientation in which his descendants, including Ishak Ahmad, understood Islam and raised their children.

Ishak Ahmad received his education in the English stream, and worked as a civil servant in the Fisheries Department. In 1923, he rose up the rank to the Assistant Inspector of the department. With this promotion, Ishak Ahmad had to be transferred to Singapore. Yusof followed his father to Singapore and continued his primary education here. Yusof then did his family proud by entering Raffles Institution, a prestigious school in Singapore. In 1927, he topped his class and passed the Cambridge School Certificate Examinations.[2] During his student days, Yusof was active in sports and writing: he was a Second Lieutenant in the National Cadet Corp (NCC); represented his school in hockey, cricket, swimming, weight-lifting, water polo, basketball and boxing; and co-edited the school's magazine *Rafflesian.*[2] His active involvement in sports did not stop upon graduating from Raffles Institution. In 1932, he became the National Lightweight Boxing champion, and the following year won the Lightweight Weight-Lifting championship.

Yusof's ambition was to become a lawyer. However, his application to study law in London was turned down. Instead, he joined the Police Academy, and then relocated to Kuala Lumpur, as a trainee cadet. Having trusted Yusof's potential, capability and perseverance, the Police Commissioner promised that Yusof would graduate as an officer, a position normally given to sons of Malayan ruling elite. However, an incident happened which denied Yusof the promotion: Yusof criticised a member of the royal family, who was also a trainee at the academy, for mistreating his juniors. The commissioner refused Yusof's graduation as a police officer as promised. This was a blessing in disguise for Yusof, who then ventured into journalism. In 1934, Yusof joined *Warta Malaya*, a Malay language newspaper, as a clerk. His stint at the newspaper shaped his vision that one day, Malays could own their newspapers.

In 1939, Yusof Ishak's dream was realised with the founding of *Utusan Melayu*. He proudly declared the newspaper the "voice of the Malay community". Nevertheless, the founding of *Utusan Melayu* was not without challenges: funds, good journalists, printing equipment, and building were not easily available to him. In 1949, Yusof penned his reflections on the

> *"In September 1952 a tall, Indian looking Malay in his late 40s, with a long, thin, un Malay nose, arrived at my desk. Speaking English well but in a hesitant manner and with a slight stammer, he introduced himself as Yusof Ishak, owner, editor-in-chief and managing director of the Utusan Melayu.*
>
> Lee Kuan Yew
> *The Singapore Story: Memoirs of Lee Kuan Yew*

hardships when he started *Utusan Melayu*. He went door to door seeking for donations; gave public lectures in several villages, and persuaded the Malay elites to buy *Utusan Melayu* shares.[3] At one time, it was so difficult for him to convince Malays to buy *Utusan Melayu* shares that the authorities threatened to deregister the company. Yusof persevered, and on 29 May 1939, *Utusan Melayu* was officially opened. Yusof became the founding and managing editor of the newspaper and stayed on that position until 1959. During the Japanese occupation, Yusof had to return to Perak briefly because *Utusan Melayu* had to close. The Japanese desired to control information and only allowed newspapers that supported the occupation. As soon as the war ended, he returned to Singapore and revived the newspaper.

Yusof was a workaholic and did not give much thought into starting a family. It was only in 1949, at the age of 39, that he decided to tie the knot to Noor Aishah, a girl from Penang. He was introduced to Noor Aishah by his friend, H. M. Shah, and caught a glimpse of her through a photograph. He only met Noor Aishah in person three days before they were solemnised in Penang. Before meeting Noor Aishah, Yusof returned to Perak to obtain his mother's blessings. Noor Aishah was 16 years old when she got married to Yusof. After their marriage, the couple returned to Singapore. The couple raised three

Yang di-Pertuan Negara of Singapore Yusof Ishak and Puan Noor Aishah. Image courtesy of Puan Noor Aishah © 2015. All rights reserved.

children in all: Orchid Kamariah, Imran Yusof, and
Zuriana Yusof.

Multiculturalism

Articles published in *Utusan Melayu*
in the 1940s and 1950s may give an
impression that it is a pro-Malay
newspaper. For instance, on 2
September 1940, *Utusan Melayu* published an article advising Malay tailors to retain as much secrecy as
possible of their business operations.[4] The article urged the community to compete with Chinese tailors.
Utusan Melayu's pro-Malay stance
can also be seen in the company's
constitution, which states that only
Malays can own the newspaper. The
company's prospectus indicated that:

> With this aim in view, it is provided of
> Articles of Association of this
> Company that only Malays are enti-
> tled to be shareholders in the
> Company, that no shares shall be
> allotted to or registered in the name
> of any person who is not a Malay, and
> no shares registered in the name of a
> Malay shareholder may be held in
> trust for or be in any way under the
> control of a person who is not a
> Malay.[5]

"With the departure of the last British governor, we had to appoint our own head of state. We chose Yusof Bin Ishak, the managing director of Utusan Melayu, to be his successor, our first native Yang di-Pertuan Negara. We wanted a distinguished Malay in order to show the Federation that Singaporeans were willing to accept Malays as their leaders, and I knew him as a good man of simple habits who carried himself with dignity.

Lee Kuan Yew
The Singapore Story

Nevertheless, Yusof believed in multiculturalism all
his life and this is exemplified in several ways. First,
even though Yusof was the managing editor of the
newspaper, he did not write most of the articles, even
though it is fair to say that he oversaw the newspaper's
direction and determined the articles published. Most
of *Utusan Melayu's* articles excluded the author's name.
Second, Yusof's stand on wanting only Malays could

own *Utusan Melayu* was not because he was biased against other communities. He wanted Malays to have an equal voice in public discourse. In the 1930s and 1940s, the Arabs and Indian Muslims dominated the newspaper industry. Yusof felt these newspapers were not articulating Malay interests, but featured news from the Middle East, although the language used is Malay. *Utusan Melayu* was the vehicle for him to raise issues concerning the community's development. Third, when Yusof became the Yang Dipertuan Negara in 1959 and Singapore's President in 1965, he stood for multiculturalism. In 1966, just after Singapore separated from Malaysia, Yusof delivered a New Year's address in which he underscored his commitment for a multiracial Singapore.

> *Separation cannot deny us the right or deprive us [of] the power to demonstrate the correctness of our ideas within Singapore. I believe that we have a special responsibility to demonstrate the essential validity of our ideas because these ideas are relevant to the problems of not just Singapore but those of all multiracial societies which want to give a better life to its people.*[6]

In fact, when he was president, he made sure staff appointments under him were made based on merit, and not race, social status, or wealth. For example, he selected Winston Choo as his first *aide de camp* because Winston was able to speak several languages, and was willing to put the country's interests above personal ones. He learnt about multiculturalism since his Raffles Institution days. In 1961, Yusof delivered a speech at Raffles Institution (his *alma mater*), in which he recounted how the school taught him the importance of respecting other ethnic communities. He said, "It was a blessing in disguise because my association with these non-Malay pupils — Chinese, Indians, Eurasians, Jews — at Raffles Institution made me understand more and more what were in their minds and thus I could appreciate their good and weak points,

President Yusof Ishak signing roll of office after his swearing-in ceremony for his third term of office. Yusof Ishak Collection, courtesy of National Archives of Singapore.

their hopes and aspirations." He also told the audience he was a Malayan first, then a Malay.[7]

Singapore Members of Parliament (MPs) appreciated Yusof's belief in multiculturalism. In 1967, when the parliament debated about extending Yusof's presidency for another term, Prime Minister Lee Kuan Yew and three other MPs, S. Ramaswary, Rahmat Kenap, and Lim Guan Hoo, spoke up in support of the motion. For instance, Ramaswary pointed out that although Yusof is a Malay, no Singaporean considered him a Malay head-of-state because he was accepted as a Singaporean President.[8] Yusof, during his life, always believed that the nation should come first, and he instilled this value on his staffs.

Progressive Islam

While Yusof urged Singaporeans to respect the country's multicultural society, he was concerned about the Malay/Muslim community's progress. Because Yusof was educated in the English stream, he appreciated the value brought by modern education, and attempted to reconcile modern knowledge with religious values. The following paragraphs highlight the religious values that he struggled for.

Generally, Yusof was raised in a progressive religious tradition. Yusof's father raised his children to understand Islam beyond rituals, but to incorporate science in the study of the religion. He was interested in keeping Islam in sync with modern realities, especially how Islamic traditions could be used to solve modern problems. His friends, colleagues, and family members agree that Yusof was a religious person. He would make it a point to move from one mosque to another for his weekly Friday prayers. In 1963, he performed the *Haj* with his wife. *Haj* is the fifth pillar of Islam and an obligation.[a]

Even though Yusof was raised in Islamic modernist tradition, he allowed for open debate on religious matters in *Utusan Melayu*. For instance, in the 1930s and 1940s, there was an increasing *Kaum Muda* (modernist) influence on the Malay society. This camp called for a rethinking of religious traditions to suit contemporary needs, meaning that they were inclined to remove any forms of anachronistic practices: such as communal feasting, grave visits, and celebration of the Prophet's birthday. During this period, there was also the Kemalist influence. In 1920s, Mustafa Kemal Artarturk, a Turkish military leader, put an end to the centuries-old Ottoman Empire. He implemented an extreme form of secularism and modernism, which included issuing a law permitting only prayers recited in Turkish language, when normally, they are conducted in Arabic. Malaya also felt the impact of the Kemalist revolution, and *Utusan Melayu* played a crucial role in allowing this debate to be played out in the newspaper. One issue that was allowed to be debated was whether Friday sermons could be delivered in the Malay language, as opposed to

---

[a] The five pillars of Islam are: declaration of faith, five daily prayers, fasting during the month of *Ramadhan*, tithe, and *Haj*.

Arabic. Yusof did not take any sides in the debate, but he was progressive enough to allow the discussion to be carried out in the newspaper. Another issue which shows *Utusan Melayu's* progressive outlook was on education. The newspaper called on schools to give equal opportunity for girls. Previously, girls were discouraged from going to school because of their perceived role as homemakers. *Utusan Melayu* allowed the debate to be carried out.

In short, while Yusof had his own position on religious matters, he allowed *Utusan Melayu* to carry out these debates. Yusof did not take sides even though he had a strong position on educational

President Yusof Ishak praying at new mosque, Masjid Abdul Razak, at Jalan Ismail. Yusof Ishak Collection, courtesy of National Archives of Singapore.

matters. Rather than forcing Malays to accept his position, he led by example. His son, Imran, who graduated as a medical doctor, was one of the first few Malays of his generation to become one. Yusof's daughter, Zuriana, was accepted to study at Imperial College in London.

Redefining Success

Throughout his life, Yusof emphasised the importance of education. His father ensured that all his children receive the best education. In the early 20th century, Malays were reluctant to send their children to English stream schools, for fear that they will be converted to Christianity. Ishak, however, was educated in English schools and so were his children. And they did very well in their education: Yusof's brothers were all prominent politicians in Malaya. Aziz Ishak was a Minister of Fisheries in Malaysia and Rahim Ishak a founding member of the People's Action Party (PAP), the Senior Minister of State for Foreign Affairs. Yusof advised Noor Aishah that after he passed away, she must prioritise their children's education, and that if she faced difficulties to finance their studies, she should consider renting out their house.

Nevertheless, examining Yusof's student days demonstrates his belief in an all-rounded education that went beyond academic achievements. As mentioned earlier, Yusof engaged in sporting activities and excelled in them. As President of Singapore, Yusof was the Chief Scout for the scout movement, and he actively mingled with the members.

As Singapore's President, Yusof was also NUS Chancellor. He constantly reminded university students that education is not an end but a means to achieve greater things in life. In addition, he advised them not to neglect their social responsibility: to help the less fortunate and not just stay in the ivory tower. He reminded students to contribute to society in whatever means they could. What is most important, to Yusof, was that the Malays have the correct attitude to achieve success.

On the one hand, he struggled to combat racial stereotypes towards the Malays. During the *Utusan Melayu* years, he made the effort to debunk the notion of the lazy Malays. On the other hand, he urged the Malays to constantly continue to engage in learning. Thus, Yusof emphasised on the spirit to learn rather than the path one chose to take. To interpret Yusof's philosophy, one can become lawyers, footballers, teachers; but they must be the best amongst them and compete with the best in the world.

Conclusion

In the 1960s, there was an attraction for Malays to move across the Causeway. The main attraction was that Malays would become the majority, as a result, a number of Malay professionals, including artists, crossed over to Malaysia. Yet, Yusof stayed in Singapore because he believed in the system which the government upheld. He sent his children to Singapore schools, where they competed equally with other students without any preferential treatment.

Yusof made an important choice to believe in Singapore's principle of meritocracy and secularism, as opposed to Malaysian Malay supremacy (*ketuanan Melayu*). In this regard, he can be regarded as the first Singaporean.

I see three main contributions the Malay/Muslim community can draw from Yusof's life. First, the Malays should retain their cultural identity, but must not forget the broader goal of a Singaporean identity. For the last 50 years, the Malays have done well to integrate with the community at large, and they must continue living the spirit. Like Yusof, they have been loyal to Singapore, and will continue to defend its sovereignty.

Second, the Malays must not let their religiosity undermine the broader multireligious setting in Singapore. Yusof was a religious man, yet, he never isolated himself from the mainstream and mingled with other religious communities. He was sensitive towards the practices of other religious communities. During the racial riots in 1964, Yusof played the role of a statesman in not taking sides and was neutral towards all communities. The community should learn from Yusof's contributions when faced with two challenges: Islamic revivalism (since the 1970s) and Islamic extremism. The community must continue to show the beauty of the religion by not allowing extremist groups from hijacking its developmental agenda.

The new Yusof Ishak Mosque to embody the same values that former President Yusof Ishak often stressed: racial harmony and multi-culturalism. Besides serving as a place of worship for the Muslim community, it will also hold programmes that reach out to other communities and enhance understanding and social cohesion. Image courtesy of Majlis Ugama Islam Singapura © 2015. All rights reserved.

Mr Heng Swee Keat, the former Minister for Education presenting the book, *Yusof Ishak*: Singapore's First President, to Toh Puan Noor Aishah, wife of Encik Yusof Ishak at the ISEAS Renaming Ceremony: ISEAS–Yusof Ishak Institute. Image courtesy of ISEAS-Yusof Ishak Institute © 2015. All rights reserved.

For instance, the Muslim community here has been active in interfaith dialogue. They have also allowed

> *Singapore has come a long way. It is the work of generations, each standing on the shoulders of the one which came before and it started with one special generation — the Pioneer Generation (PG). And one outstanding member of the Pioneer Generation was Encik Yusof Ishak, our first President. Encik Yusof showed that in Singapore, you can rise to the top if you work hard. He stood for enduring values that underpin Singapore's success — meritocracy, multiracialism, modernisation. He was a President for all Singaporeans."*

Lee Hsien Loong
National Day Rally 2014

followers of other faiths to join their *iftars* (breaking of fast) during *Ramadhan*. This shows that the Malay community is inclusive and it should continue to be so.

Third, Yusof reminded Singaporeans of the need to redefine success. Yusof emphasised the importance of education and wanted his children to be successful in life. Yet, he did not neglect the less fortunate and talented individuals in non-academic fields. For example, he embraced sports throughout his life. For Yusof, life is not about academic certificates only. There are many talented individuals in the Malay community, and they include musicians, sportsman, artists and poets. The Malay community must continue supporting these talented individuals, though they must not lose sight on developing academic achievers in society. As Singapore approaches SG100, it is to people like Yusof Ishak that the community should seek inspiration from. Although the majority of Singaporeans today have not met the late president, one should honour him as the country's pioneer in developing a multicultural and multireligious Singapore.

Bibliography

1. Norshahril Saat. 2015. *Yusof Ishak: Singapore's First President.* Singapore, ISEAS-Yusof Ishak Institute.
2. Chew, Melanie. 1999. *A Biography of President Yusof bin Ishak.* Singapore: NSP Publishing.
3. Yusof Ishak. 1949. *Sepuluh Tahun Utusan Melayu.* Singapore: Utusan Melayu Press.
4. *Utusan Melayu.* 1940. *"Tukang jahit Melayu memodalkan China."* 2 September.
5. Zainuddin Maidin. 2013. *Di Depan Api Di Belakang Duri.* Kuala Lumpur: Utusan Publications and Distribution.

6. Ministry of Culture. 1966. "New Year Message by the President of the Republic of Singapore, Inche Yusof bin Ishak" 1 January.

7. *The Rafflesian*. 1961. 35, No. 1. November.

8. Parliament of Singapore Hansard. 1967. Election of President of Republic of Singapore, Vol. 26, 30 November.

"Indeed, the diversity of languages, religions, cultures and races can be a stumbling block to progress and prosperity. However, if we face these differences with goodwill and patience, and try to understand them, our success to overcome these differences will ultimately become our means to that progress and prosperity. It is this tolerance, among other things, that has made Singapore the dynamic and progressive city that it is today."

Inche Yusof Ishak
1968

Photo: Yang di-Pertuan Negara of Singapore Yusof Ishak
(President of Singapore from 9 August 1965) and Puan
Noor Aishah at the Istana, C1960S. Yusof Ishak Collection,
courtesy of National Archives of Singapore.

Singapore's first fully elected cabinet was sworn-in at City Hall on 5 June 1959. From left: Yong Nyuk Lin, Ong Pang Boon, Dr Goh Keng Swee, Dr Toh Chin Chye, Lee Kuan Yew, Ong Eng Guan, Ahmad Ibrahim, S. Rajaratnam and Kenneth M Byrne. Photo reproduced with permission from Ministry of Information and the Arts Collection, courtesy of National Archives of Singapore.

Serjeant-at-Arms Mahmood bin Abdul Wahab bearing the Mace as he heads the Speaker's procession at the opening of Singapore's first Parliament sitting on 8 December 1965. In the photo we can see Malay MPs, Mr Rahim Ishak and Mr Othman Wok standing in the front bench. At that sitting, the Yang Di-Pertuan Negara, Inche Yusof Ishak was designated as the President of Singapore. Photo reproduced with permission from Ministry of Information and the Arts Collection, courtesy of National Archives of Singapore.

CHAPTER 2

ZUBIR SAID — A SYMBOL OF THE MALAY IDENTITY*

Norshahril Saat

I n his lifetime, Zubir Said, or more affectionately known as Pak Zubir, was active in contributing academic papers relating to music and the Malay culture. His written works not only benefited historians and musicologists, but also sociologists who seek to do an in-depth research on the styles of thinking of the independence activists at that time.

Zubir Said's daughter, Datin Rohana Zubir, in a biography[1] written by her about her late father, mentioned her father's deep sense of patriotism for Singapore, as reflected strongly in the song *Majulah Singapura*, was a result of his earlier experiences of his younger days in Sumatra before he migrated to Singapore in 1928 at the age of 21. According to Datin Rohana, "through the trials and tribulations that her late father went through, he learnt a lot about freedom, independence and resilience."

The late Pak Zubir had that mental toughness to overcome all challenges. With all these experiences, he composed many songs on patriotism, among them *Melayu Raya*, *Tanah Bangsa dan Daulat* and *Ikatan Budaya*. However, his contribution in the approach towards tradition and modernisation is rarely made known. He had integrated Malay elements into his compositions used as scores or soundtracks for classical Malay films.

---

*This article is adapted from *Pak Zubir Pelestari Identiti Melayu* by Norshahril Saat, first appeared in *Berita Harian* on 30 October 2012.

Zubir Said (second from right) standing alongside the legend of the Malay film industry, P Ramlee (third from left). Image courtesy of Puan Rohana Zubir © 2015. All rights reserved.

Behind every successful man is a dutiful, loving and patient woman. Zubir Said and his wife, Tarminah Tario Wikromo. Image courtesy of Puan Rohana Zubir © 2015. All rights reserved.

This reminds us of an intense debate sociologists had in the 1990s on the role of tradition in modernisation. At that time, the heated debate was over the discourse on Asian and Western values. There exists a school of thought that equates modernisation with Westernisation. Essentially, Pak Zubir's works can be regarded as firmly opposing the correlation between modernisation and Westernisation. In fact, his works leaned more towards the strengthening of tradition according to what is being defined by sociology. Dr Shaharuddin Maaruf, former Head of the Department of Malay Studies, National University of Singapore, gave the view that "... tradition can be an integral aspect of social change. It fulfills this function by acting as the basis and foundation of social change, effectively combining permanence and the necessary adjustment demanded by new social conditions and requirements." Tradition need not be an impediment to modernisation nor be incompatible with it. It does not only strengthen the identity of a society; in fact, traditional values will allow the society to not dwell in the past and move forward, as imbued in a Malay saying "*buang yang keruh, ambil yang jernih*" (out with the old and in with the new). The Japanese for example had achieved good progress and modernisation while at the same time persisting with its own values. The strengthening of these values was integrated in the musical works of Pak Zubir.

Datin Rohana also mentioned in the biography that Pak Zubir was very protective over his musical works. For example, Pak Zubir would not agree to any changes to the melody as well as the lyrics without his permission. He likened the change without one's permission to "someone entering another person's home and changing the positions of the furniture as he or she pleases", as this ran contrary to the Malay and Islamic values of sincerity and honesty. Pak Zubir's works also refuted another current perspective that gives the impression that the Malay identity is a constructed one. It is an uncommon perspective to state how a Malay views the values and identity. We realise that although the Malays are not a homogeneous society, there will definitely be some basic elements that bind the identity of the Malays. Pak Zubir integrated elements of *gurindam*[a], words of advice, Islamic sentiments, and the daily life of the community in his works. These elements can be regarded as tradition in Malay music. Definitely, the community needs to renew itself but it must include progress in its thinking. It is the same with music — Malay traditions must be preserved. May all the contributions and good deeds of the late Pak Zubir be the catalyst for more research work to be done on his effort to preserve the Malay identity.

Puan Sri Datin Dr Rohana Zubir-Hamid, the third daughter of the late Pak Zubir. Image courtesy of Puan Rohana Zubir © 2015. All rights reserved.

---

[a] A type of irregular verse forms of traditional Malay poetry. It is a combination of two clauses where the relative clause forms a line and is thus linked to the second line, or the main clause.

Bibliography

1. Rohana Zubir, *Zubir Said: The Composer of Majulah Singapura*, ISEAS, 2012.
2. Shaharuddin Maaruf (1992). Some theoretical problems concerning tradition and modernization among the Malays of Southeast Asia," in *Asian Tradition and Modernization: Perspectives from Singapore*, Yong Mun Cheong (ed.), p. 258, Singapore: Times Academic Press.

Two national icons captured in a photo. Yusof Ishak and Puan Noor Aishah greeting Zubir Said's family at the Istana.

INCLUSIVE MALAY/MUSLIM COMMUNITY

The term Malays, Muslims, Malays/Muslims, the Malay/Muslim community and Malay–Muslim are being used throughout this book with deliberate intentions and connotations. While this book is about the Malays who are Muslims, you will notice the term Malay/Muslim community or Malays/Muslims are being used to reflect the choice taken by the community to be inclusive i.e., to include the Malays and also the non-Malay Muslims which include Arabs, Indians and others. However, when the term Malay–Muslim is being used, it is a specific reference to Malays who are by and large Muslims. As an illustration, while self-help groups like the Chinese Community Development Council (CDAC) and Sinda (Singapore Indian Development Council) cater purely for ethnic Chinese and Indians respectively, the Council of the Development of the Malay/Muslim Community (Yayasan MENDAKI) caters for both Malays and Muslims regardless of ethnicity.

CHAPTER 3

PAK ZUBIR SAID AND MAJULAH SINGAPURA — THE NATIONAL ANTHEM OF SINGAPORE

Joe Peters

It is not a film song. It is not a romantic song... It is a special kind of song... I had to consider the content of the lyrics. It should be in simple language, easy enough to sing and easy enough to understand by all races...know the policy of the government, the social life in Singapore and the wish of the people and how to progress to prosperity.

Zubir Said, His Songs (1990)

This statement is not just the ethos for a nation's anthem by the composer himself. It is a formula for musical creativity and inclusivity, the challenge all composers face at some point in their careers in a multiracial and multicultural independent nation. Singapore became a nation after more than a century of British colonial rule, trying to unify itself with a diverse tapestry of cultural, political, historical and social identities and imbedded realities.

The story of Singapore's national anthem was about a collective action but based on one man's creative energy and professional sincerity. Chew traces the song Pak Zubir wrote for the City Council in 1957 after Syed Ali Redha Alsagoff, a member of that council approached him to write a patriotic song for Singapore.[1] That song was titled *Majulah Singapura* (Onward Singapore). This was the first version. Pak Zubir took advice from the late Pak Mohd Ariff Ahmad, a Malay language teacher on the lyrics. Mr Paul Abisheganaden and the Singapore Chamber Ensemble performed the work in 1959 for the opening of the newly renovated Victoria Theatre.

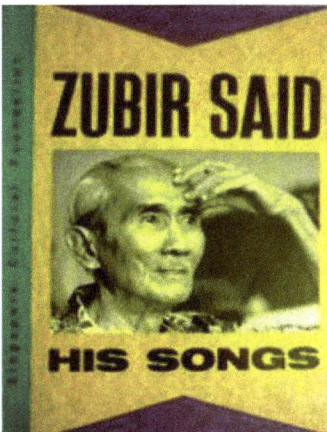

Figure 1: *Zubir Said: His Songs*, published for Singapore Cultural Foundation by Times Books International.

When Singapore obtained self-government in 1959, there was a search for a national anthem. All efforts led directly back to the song *Majulah Singapura*. Dr Toh Chin Chye, Singapore's Deputy Prime Minister, on the advice of a committee (made up of Paul Abisheganaden, Dick Abels, Aisha Ghows and leaders of the Military Forces Band, Radio Singapore Orchestra and the Berlin Chamber Orchestra), called for changes to be made to this song — to include shortening the tune, speeding up the tempo slightly, and making it reflect the multiracial character of the country. Chew states that the version done by the Berlin Chamber Orchestra was the one selected.

When Pak Zubir wrote the original *Majulah Singapura*, he was not a citizen of Singapore but a star in the world of film music and song-writing. Underlying this, we must remember, he had no formal musical training. He was a self-made talent who grew from his personal conviction and resolute sense of purpose to become a professional musician — to the point of even breaking traditional ties with his father who wanted him to observe an elite *status quo* in his Minangkabau homeland in Sumatra. What attracted Pak Zubir were the legends he heard about itinerant musicians who rose to heights plying the Asian Sea Trade Route. Singapore was an important part of that trade route and a special attraction for such musicians. Thus, he came here like the ancient *orang laut*[a] with a light bag on his back but a brain full of folk music knowledge. By the time he wrote *Majulah Singapura*, he was a master at churning a full spread of music for different uses using his own blend of East–West musical ingredients.

Figure 2: Zubir Said became a citizen in 1967. Image courtesy of Puan Rohana Zubir © 2015. All rights reserved.

The First Version of the Singapore Anthem

Majulah Singapura was first written in *cipta* notation — the notation of the solmization[b] system used in many of

---

[a] Sea gypsies.
[b] A system of attributing a distinct syllable to each note in a musical scale.

the traditional music of Asia at that time. It is based on numbers and solfa voicing. The key (as a Western music concept) is referred to as F = 1, which means that the anthem is in F major, and should be read as 1 (the solfa sound of "Doh". See, Figure 3).

Limited sets of the recording of this version were made on single floppy vinyl disks (R.M.P. 331/3). These floppies were usually used in the music industry then, to test releases on the market. Only a few such singles were made for *Majulah Singapura*. They are difficult to find today. I happen to know someone who had a copy but did not want to part with the actual disk. A photocopy copy of the record jacket of that single floppy can be seen below (Figure 4). The recording on this floppy can be heard at this site: https://www. youtube.com/watch?v=GtrZUMrXXS4

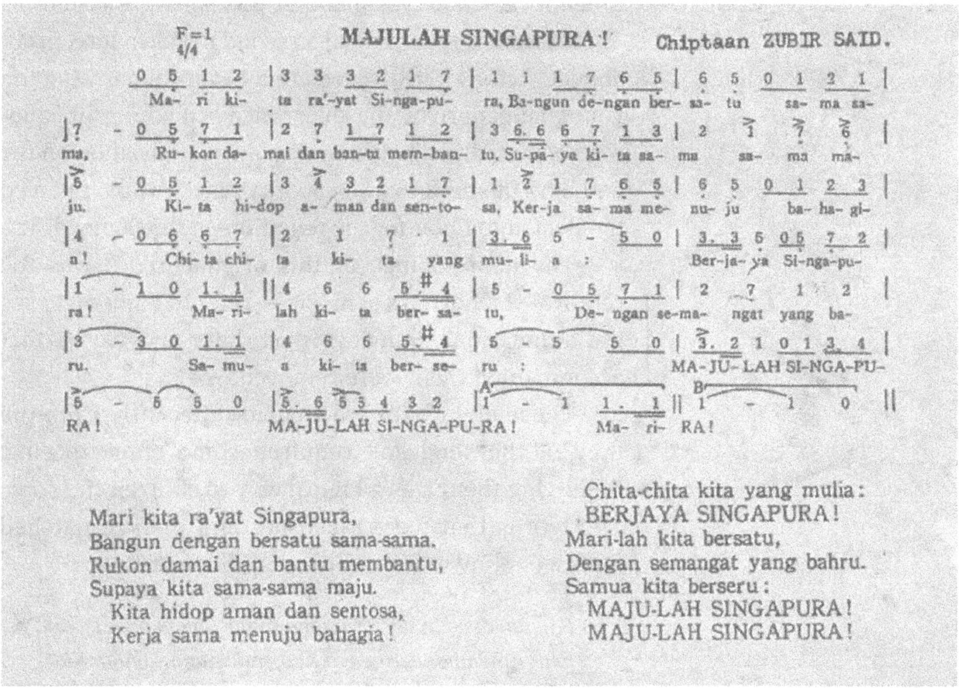

Figure 3: *Majulah Singapura* in *cipta* notation. A manuscript of Majulah Singapura written in the solmisasi number *notation* system. *Majulah Singapura* was originally composed as the official song for the City Council in 1957. When Singapore attained self-governance in 1959, upon the request of Deputy Prime Minister Dr Toh Chin Chye, the song was modified by Zubir Said to become our national anthem.

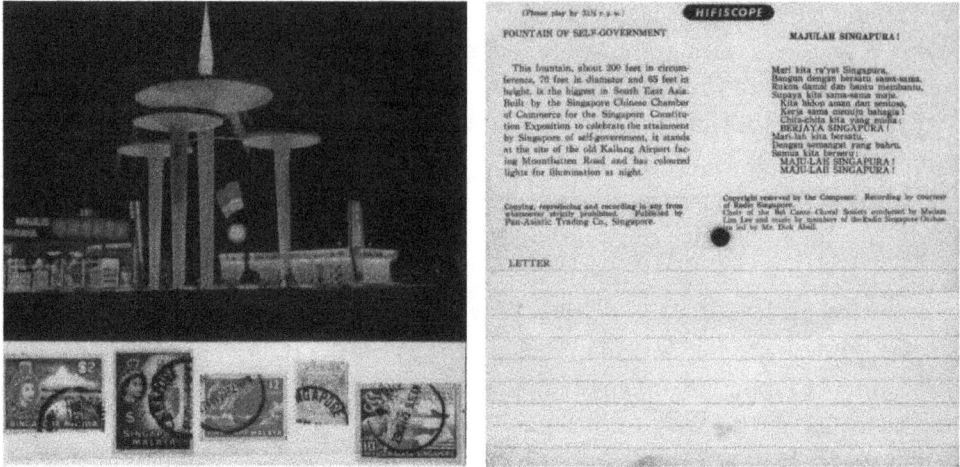

Figure 4: Floppy single vinyl jacket.

The recording is mounted on a "Timeline Music Annotation" software, and is described with graphics and text that change according to the indications on the timeline. A video was made of this software rendition. There is also a recording of a second performance, probably at Victoria Theatre, where a beautiful narration on young Singapore by the clear voice of a young Singaporean accompanied by a pianist playing a variation on the anthem's theme. Radio Singapore Orchestra accompanied the Bel Canto Choir for the rendition on the floppy disk.

The main change to this original score was the removal of eight bars of music — refer to Figure 3 to see the annotations showing which bars and words that accompanied them were removed.

These eight bars are shaped differently from the flow of the song and required some effort to sing. Removing them was a logical way to shorten the song. The words that were taken out and then re-patched (shown below in italics) needed more skill:

Bangun dengan bersatu sama sama. Rukon damai dan bantu membantu supaya kita sama sama maju. Kita hidup aman dan sentosa. Kerja sama menuju bahagia.

Which translates:

Renew life as one nation. With peace and effort we move forward together. We live in peace and cooperation to achieve happiness.

Original version in Staff Notation

Figure 5: Annotated score of changes to *Majulah Singapura*.

Pak Zubir had in those eight bars used a *Tanah Melayu* (*Asli*[c]) theme, as well as a common melisma connoted with Malay/Indonesian folk music, which he was quite good at because he used this melisma to great artistic lengths in *Sayang Di Sayang*, his most famous *keroncong*[d] song. Watch this video for a demonstration of how these motifs sounded: https://www.youtube.com/watch?v=Zush_LTX7cg

Pak Zubir was a music icon in Singapore by the time he wrote this anthem. He was never academic or possessive about his music in general. The removal of these eight bars is a timeless lesson from him to composers in Singapore: listen to your music through the ears of the common music listener.

Figure 6: Zubir Said after shooting a documentary — with producer Anwar Rashid and his technical crew. Image courtesy of Salleh Sariman © 2015. All rights reserved.

---

[c] One of the earliest forms of Malay music genres often characterised by its slow and gentle melodies and simple lyrics that often tell a moving story.

[d] Considered as one of the musical mainstreams of Indonesia, *keroncong* has its roots in Portugal. The genre was born when the Portuguese settlers played their own four-stringed ukuleles, called *macina* and locally known as *cak*, and the three-stringed *prounga* also known *as cuk*, in harmony with local sounds. Rather than plucking them, they strummed the instruments, creating the "crong, crong" sound that gave the genre its onomatopoeic name, keroncong.

The Final Version

Figure 7: The final version of *Majulah Singapura*.

THE SPEECH
of Mr Zubir Said,
Composer of National Anthem

I thank you, Principal, Teachers and students for inviting me to visit your school during this year's National Day Celebration. It's my pleasure to be with you today to enjoy the Celebration. I wish you luck and happiness.

For 26 years you and hundreds of thousands of school students have been singing the Singapore National Anthem every day in the morning and afternoon.

The anthem which is called "MAJULAH SINGAPURA" and not 'Mari kita' is actually a little prayer for the progress of Singapore and the unity of its multi-racial people, and should be sung with pride, dignity and national spirit!

It is wrong to call it 'Mari kita' instead of MAJULAH SINGAPURA and also wrong to call me Mr. Mari Kita as some people do.

My name is spelled ZUBIR SAID, 2 words and 4 Syllables:
1. ZU   pronounced as ZOO as in animal zoo.
2. BIR   pronounce as BEER as in a bottle of beer.

'MAJULAH SINGAPURA' was composed in 1958 at the request of the City Council Concert Committee. It was to be used at the opening of the City Council Concert.

Later in 1959 it became the National Anthem of Singapore.

Before I composed the song I asked first in what language the lyrics should be. The answer given to me was that the words should be in the National Language. So I composed the song with words as simple as possible.

In December 1959 the song MAJULAH SINGAPURA was sung for the first time as the National Anthem of Singapore. We Singaporeans should respect Singapore as our country and also respect the Flag and the National Anthem. It is the same as loving and respecting your parents and your family. Without your parents you won't be around today to sing Majulah Singapura. When you are grown up it will be your turn to care for and support them and similarly you should respect your school and your teachers because they give you education and knowledge so that you can become Singapore's intellectuals in your future.

Parents are able to care for 10 children but I'm not sure the 10 children can look after their parents.

I was born in Minangkabau in Central Sumatra. My education was only at my village Primary School. My father could not afford to send me to secondary school. Schooling at that time was not like the present days. There were no textbooks, no ballpens, no erazers and no school libraries.

You are lucky to have many proper schools and good teachers. You have school libraries and private libraries. You have all kinds of stationeries.

In Singapore today you can learn and study many languages, science and technology, engineering, medicines, trade & commerce, music and many more. I am 78 now. I wish I was born to-day!

I had a long 'crooked' way of learning, mostly from experience and self-teaching. I had no formal education in music.

My father was against my interest in music. He said it was against the religion. It was a sin to play music! But I had studied a lot of folk music and played the folk musical instruments too. I made my own bambu flute and later a guitar. I missed my further education in school. So there was no other choice for me but to carry on my own way of life. It was a big challenge for me of course. I had to face it if I wanted to be somebody in my profession of my own choice. So, after a long period of hard research and self-teaching (because there was no music teacher) I became a professional and landed in Singapore for the first time in 1928. I traveled round Malaysia in a Bangsawan troupe where I got more experience in different kinds of music.

When I settled down in Singapore in 1935 I made Singapore my country and later became a citizen. It was in Singapore that I reached the top of my ambition when my song composition Majulah Singapura was accepted unanimously as the National Anthem. My father who came here to witness the first Ceremony of Singapore Flag Raising Ceremony in 1959 and heard "MAJULAH SINGAPURA", he forgave me for my sin against him. I thank God!

Since then he became an ardent music lover until he died at the age of 103 years.

22

Figure 8: Zubir Said's Speech at Kong Yiong High School, 8 August 1985.
Image courtesy of Puan Rohana Zubir © 2015. All rights reserved.

Bibliography

1. Chew, Daniel (1990). *The Story of the National Anthem. His Songs.* Singapore Cultural Foundation, pp. 23–27.
2. Joe Peters (2012). *Zubir Said and his Film Music. Majulah: The Film Music of Zubir Said.* National Museum of Singapore, pp. 74–91.

THE SINGAPORE PLEDGE

As a way to promote national loyalty and consciousness among citizens following Singapore's separation from Malaysia on 9 August 1965, the idea of a pledge was mooted. The idea gained the support of then Minister for Education, Mr Ong Pang Boon.[a] The finalised version of the national pledge was largely drafted by then Minister for Foreign Affairs S. Rajaratnam in February 1966. The wording of the pledge was based on the belief that Singaporeans could overcome the divisions caused by differences of race, language and religion. On 24 August 1966, about 500,000 students at all 529 government and government-aided schools held the first daily recitation of the pledge of allegiance before the national flag.[b]

Our Pledge[c]

We, the citizens of Singapore,
pledge ourselves as one united people,
regardless of race, language or religion,
to build a democratic society
based on justice and equality
so as to achieve happiness, prosperity
and progress for our nation.

Ikrar Kita

Kami, warganegara Singapura,
sebagai rakyat yang bersatu padu,
tidak kira apa bangsa, bahasa, atau ugama,
berikrar untuk membina suatu masyarakat yang demokratik,
berdasarkan kepada keadilan dan persamaan untuk mencapai kebahagiaan,
kemakmuran dan kemajuan bagi negara Kami.

---

[a] Kwa, C. G., Heng, D. and Tan, T. Y. (2009). *Singapore, a 700-year History: From Early Emporium to World City*. Singapore: National Archives of Singapore, p. 194.

[b] http://eresources.nlb.gov.sg/newspapers/Digitised/Article/straitstimes19660825-1.2.99.aspx. Last accessed 23 April 2016.

[c] http://www.nhb.gov.sg/resources/national-symbols/national-pledge. Last accessed 23 April 2016.

CHAPTER 4

YAACOB IBRAHIM — IN CONVERSATION | Zainul Abidin Rasheed and Norshahril Saat

On 28 September 2015, Prime Minister Lee Hsien Loong announced his new Cabinet after the PAP's resounding victory in the 2015 general elections. He named several first time MPs as ministers, in the spirit of leadership renewal, but retained several senior PAP leaders, mainly to mentor the young ones. One of the senior politicians retained is Dr Yaacob Ibrahim, whom Mr Lee reappointed as Minister for Communications and Information (MCI) as well as Minister-In-Charge of Muslim Affairs and recently appointed as the Minister-in-Charge of Cyber Security. Dr Yaacob has been the Minister-in-Charge of Muslim Affairs since 2002, the post he assumed responsibility from Mr Abdullah Tarmugi. Before Dr Yaacob, there were only three Malay/Muslim MPs who held the position: they were Mr Othman Wok, Dr Ahmad Mattar, and Abdullah Tarmugi. The editors interviewed the man who has overseen the evolution of the community for more than 10 years. Dr Yaacob took over as Minister when the community was facing several challenges: post-9/11; the Muslim identity; compulsory education; and collective leadership. During this interview, Dr Yaacob gave us his insights into why he joined politics, the man who inspired him intellectually, how he dealt with the community's challenges, and his vision for its success.

Dr Norshahril: *You were doing well in academia, as an associate professor in Engineering in NUS. You also obtained a PhD from Stanford. What made you join politics?*

Dr Yaacob: I have always been involved in the community. I've been there since my student days (in Jamiyah) and then I continued in the university.[1] The association with the community is deep because I feel concerned. Being a part of the community, I have benefited from the leadership of the previous generation, and risen through the ranks. I want to give back. I thought politics in Singapore is not like what you see in other countries. I've been to America, it is back-biting pork barrel politics. Here [in Singapore], it is really about the welfare of the community or welfare of the state, welfare of the citizens. In a way, I see that as extending my contributions from the community to the nation. So I gave it a lot of thought, in fact, gave it one term to think about it. When 1997 came, and the question was asked again, (because it was asked in 1991 and I declined), I thought maybe I am ready because I also wanted to re-establish my connections with the community.

I see it as a community service. That's what you're supposed to do — look after the interests of the residents, look after the interests of the nation and to a large extent, also look after the interests of the community, because as a Malay MP, that's what you're supposed to do.

So when the opportunity came in 1997, I could not say "no" again to PM Goh Chok Tong twice. I decided to enter [politics] together with Zainul, Hawazi and Ahmad Magad because we thought this was an opportunity: If we can make a difference, contribute our ideas on policies that will make a difference not only for the community but at the national level. So that was my reason for joining politics because I see it as a community service. That's what you're supposed to do — look after the interests of the residents, look after the interests of the nation and to a large extent, also look after the interests of the community, because as a Malay MP, that's what you're supposed to do. So I see this as a continuation. It was just a matter of whether I was ready for it because it's a huge commitment and I was just starting a family at that time. My kids were very young and so I've always remembered when people asked me how long you have been in politics, I say my daughter's age plus one. She was born in 1997.

Zainul Abidin: *You were an activist during your university days. Who influenced you most on your thinking and direction to serve the community?*

Dr Yaacob: I became active in the Muslim Society there, rose through the ranks and became Secretary–General of the society. Our activism was of a different kind. While we were basically from the Muslim Society, we were more social activists looking into the issues of the community. I still remember joining a bunch of Malay/ Muslim undergraduates who started a tuition scheme at Onraet Road Mosque— free tuition, giving 'A' Level tuition. So I think there were instances of this that begin to shape my view. More importantly, I think the discussions with colleagues then. All these people, and together with Professor Syed Hussein Alatas (Head of Department of Malay Studies at the University of Singapore then), changed my life because [the discussions] allowed us to get a better handle of the developments of the society at a deeper level. That allowed me to then look at an issue not in isolation, but a lot more over time, and the impact. It was a very important exposure for me. I think that was the key defining moment in my adult life. In terms of my orientation, not only just towards how I see the community, but even towards Islam. Professor Alatas brought to our attention a view of Islam that were very counter-intuitive; it was not traditional, it wasn't extreme or conservative but it was more thoughtful. So that has shaped the way I see things and I have always felt that was a very important part of my life and my development.

> *All these people, and together with Professor Syed Hussein Alatas (Head of Department of Malay Studies at the University of Singapore then), changed my life because [the discussions] allowed us to get a better handle of the developments of the society at a deeper level.*

Zainul Abidin: *When you came back after your PhD and chose to serve in MUIS and MENDAKI, what was your orientation then, and what were your priorities?*

Dr Yaacob: The truth is that I was always concerned about people at the bottom rung of society. I feel sad when I see, even today, the struggles these families face, and I thought the reason we are there in both MUIS and MENDAKI was to really help the bottom 30%. And if we can make a difference to their lives, I think that would be a wonderful outcome. The middle class, the top, they know how to take care of themselves, they know how to manage the system, they know how to navigate their way through the complexities of society; I don't think that's a challenge. It is actually the low-income families, and I think if you can do that and do that well, I think we will solve the problem for a very long time to come.

At that time, the flavour of the month was to go for the top 10%. I felt that's not the right focus; we should go for the bottom 30%. When Zainul, who was the CEO then, offered me between the top 10% programme and the under-performers, I chose the latter. There was no template; you have to start from scratch, so I started the programme in Bedok South Secondary School. At that time, the principal was Mr Yusuf Zuhri. And we were really reaching out to the kids at the bottom of the academic ladder in secondary school. We were very creative then, we didn't have a name for it. So we called it S1, which means Secondary 1 project basically. And then when we went to Secondary 2, I say what do we call this programme? Then I came up with calling it LSP, Learning Support Programme. And the idea was to not so much to deal with the academic challenges because that we leave it to the MENDAKI Tuition Scheme (MTS), but it was really about supporting the learning process: the lack of environment, the lack of mentorship. So we created a programme out of the blue, where we had facilitators, really like the *abang angkat, kakak angkat* where young professionals gather five or six of them, keep in touch, go out with them, have a *makan* session, bowling. The idea is just to make sure that they are on an even keel and they can speak to somebody who, you know, can then talk about their challenges. So I chose the facilitators who are very close in age with the students — they were mainly NIE-trainee teachers.

> *At that time, the flavour of the month was to go for the top 10%. I felt that's not the right focus; we should go for the bottom 30%. When Zainul, who was the CEO then, offered me between the top 10% programme and the under-performers, I chose the latter.*

Dr Norshahril: *What were the challenges facing the community when you took over as Minister-in-Charge of Muslim Affairs from Mr Abdullah Tarmugi?*

Dr Yaacob: One of the biggest challenges was 9/11. There was the *tudung* debate in schools that started before that. There was actually another challenge, the Collective Leadership by AMP.[2] That took the attention of the community for well over two years. PM Goh then was trying to handle that. And when I came in 2002, we had to deal with the issues of terrorism and how to make sure that the community doesn't feel marginalised or isolated because of this incident. It's really about leadership. I believe the issue of leadership is not a matter that needs to be settled once-and-for-all but on a certain framework. We have to continue to think about it or refresh it, and get new people on board because we need to have also leadership renewal within the community.

Dr. Norshahril: *What are the highlights or the key progress made by the community in the last 50 years? In what areas do you think the community is still lagging behind?*

Dr Yaacob: Well I am an optimist, I look at the glass as half full rather than half empty. I think for the community in the last 50 years, by all accounts, you cannot deny that the community has progressed — housing, education, healthcare, employment — all the statistics are pointing in the right direction. So if you look at education, for example, in fact at the MENDAKI Anugerah Awards recently, we gave out 499 awards — highest ever number. They are students performing at national examinations — PSLE, 'O'-Level and universities.[3] So if you just plot that figure on the curve, it's a rising curve, which means our students are doing better. More students are going to post-secondary schools, and more students are going to institutions of higher learning. So to a large extent, from an education

Employment — we are now seeing Malay students or Malays in fields that I cannot imagine when I was growing up — IT professionals, cyber security, biosciences, genetics, genome — all of them are there, which shows that our talent-base has widened.

point of view, the trend is upwards. Housing, home-ownership, yes, we have a bit of rental problem, but it's [home ownership] close to 90%. And I think with Fresh Start (a programme by HDB to give second-timers with young children, staying in rental flats another chance at owing a home) that PM announced at the National Day Rally, we will be able to deal with our rental housing challenges. Employment — we are now seeing Malay students or Malays in fields that I cannot imagine when I was growing up — IT professionals, cyber security, biosciences, genetics, genome — all of them are there, which shows that our talent-base has widened. Fifty years ago, you either become a lawyer, doctor, engineer or teacher. Now, you have entrepreneurs, you have IT specialists. The other day we gave an award to a Malay girl for game design. She's going into game development, which is actually a job of the future. Because of the term, game development, some parents may see as just a waste of time But it's not actually just a game, it's what we call the gamification of application, which is important. Going forward when you develop apps, develop programmes, using IT of course, gamification is a way to attract people on board. You use games to develop apps which are attractive. She has that talent — that's great, and I am so happy that we gave her the Goh Chok Tong Youth Promise Award[4]

Dr Norshahril: *One alternative view, especially in the academia, is that when we discuss social problems, we have been racialising them. Do you think this is an effective way to tackle problems?*

> **We have to start somewhere. But I think, over time, the state recognises that there are some problems that you cannot see from a race point of view.**

Dr Yaacob: We have to start somewhere. But I think, over time, the state recognises that there are some problems that you cannot see from a race point of view. If you look at some of the challenges we face in public housing and transportation — these came about because in the early years of our independence we needed to build the infrastructure quickly in order to get the country going. No one can foresee challenges far ahead in time. But the responses then were right for those conditions. We needed to house a population who were then staying in dilapidated housing with no proper water and sanitation systems in place. So we build HDB flats where we can. Then we realised given new needs, we needed to move people elsewhere; and hence we have programmes like SERS (Selective En-bloc Redevelopment Scheme) where tenants are given new flats elsewhere and their flats demolished to make way for new facilities. To a large extent, when we deal with some of the problems, we didn't think far ahead. So "get the Malays together, organise and form MENDAKI to tackle these problems". But I think now that we have become a more matured society and a more matured economy, we recognise that looking at the problem from a race perspective will deny us other perspectives which will allow us to find solutions to that problem. Take education for example. There's a limit to what MENDAKI can do, there's a limit to what the community can do. That's an honest truth, I believe the solution lies within the education system, which I think the government recognises also. And that is why now there's an effort to bring student care across all the self-help groups together as a model rather than MENDAKI running one, CDAC, SINDA, because they recognise that a student care [programme] is a useful infrastructure to help students in dealing with homework and all the challenges of school — whether you are Malay or Chinese, you have to deal with that [same] problem.[5] And so let's provide it across the board, run by all the self-help groups so that everybody can benefit.

I think the government recognises that's the way to go. I mean, take for example SkillsFuture, which we are doing at MENDAKI.[6] And I keep telling my staff, you cannot run SkillsFuture. You don't have the resources to do that. But SkillsFuture is important for the community, right? So what do you do? You don't create a Malay SkillsFuture Department or unit, you basically help the Malay community to participate in SkillsFuture. That should be our role — to mainstream the community as much as

But I think now that we have become a more matured society and a more matured economy, we recognise that looking at the problem from a race perspective will deny us other perspectives which will allow us to find solutions to that problem.

possible. So I am forming this unit within MENDAKI, and I am getting MP Saktiandi Supaat to chair an advisory committee to see how we can encourage the community to be part of the SkillsFuture movement. There's no need to look at it from a race point of view. What we can do as a community organisation is to complement national effort, and I think that should be our job.

Dr Norshahril: *Who is the most important icon that defines your political career in Singapore?*

Dr Yaacob: The Prophet Muhammad (Peace be upon him) is the most important icon in my personal life. I take the cue from a lot of people. There are things I disagree with Mr Lee Kuan Yew, but a lot of things I agree with him and I follow him. So I don't have a specific individual that I look up to. I look more for what they represent, the values, the ideas that I can learn from. I learnt a lot, for example, from [the late] MM when he was in the Cabinet. In fact, I learn a lot from Dr Tony Tan when he was in the Cabinet and ESM [Goh Chok Tong] when he was Prime Minister. So I don't have an icon or something equivalent other than the Prophet (pbuh). I just keep an open mind and listen and see [what] I can learn from them. I also learned a lot from George Yeo who said a lot of things in Cabinet . So I don't necessarily look up to people, but I look up to what they have to contribute and I value those contributions.

Zainul Abidin: *What's the one thing that comes out strongly for you as far as the late MM Lee Kuan Yew is concerned?*

Dr Yaacob: His sense of discipline and focus of mind on doing what is right for Singapore. That is the thing I learnt a lot from him. And when you think about it, the things he did was not for personal interest; it's really for the long-term interest of Singapore. Singapore was his life project, and that came up in the discussions [he had] and that conviction to make sure that we did the right things. The dedication and commitment to Singapore's interests. That's what I learnt.

Dr Norshahril: *If I recall correctly after the 9/11 and Jemaah Islamiyah (JI) attacks, there was this spotlight put on the Malay community particularly on our madrasah[7] students, saying that they are not integrating. What is your view?*

Dr Yaacob: I will tell you that was the most difficult moment of my life. I mean, having to take over in 2002 at that point was not the best of times. It was after 9/11. There was the JI incident, all the things that happened in Bali and the 7/7 bombing in UK.[8] I was under the greatest amount of stress. It was difficult because the forces at play were very strong. On the one hand, you know your religion has been used to justify violent actions. But you know it's nothing to do with your religion. Yet at the same time, you know that religion, in a way, has a role to play because they used religious interpretations, they used religious text to interpret. So how you deal with that? On the other hand, you have the security concerns. From a security point of view, the easiest thing to do is to isolate the Muslims because they are the ones who are likely to produce the terrorists. You don't like that narrative because you said we [Muslims] are not, but you know that the state has to manage it somehow. If the state just ignored it and don't deal with it, I think we are lying to ourselves. We needed to assure the wider community. So it was a very difficult problem.

So I was happy that the RRG[9] was formed because it showed the willingness on our part to tackle some of these difficult issues that are bedevilling some members of our community. At the same time, I think the state understood that we cannot afford to marginalise the Malay/Muslim community at this point in time. Therefore the government created the IRCC.[10] We created new community institutions. And we have to thank our non-Muslim brothers and sisters for coming together for inter-faith dialogues and discussions. That really paved the way for us to not resolve, but at least, assure our non-Muslim brothers and sisters that we

> *And we have to thank our non-Muslim brothers and sisters for coming together for inter-faith dialogues and discussions. That really paved the way for us to not resolve, but at least, assure our non-Muslim brothers and sisters that we have nothing to do with this. I think one of the blessings of 9/11 is that we now have developed the ability to explain Islam to non-Muslims.*

have nothing to do with this. I think one of the blessings of 9/11 is that we now have developed the ability to explain Islam to non-Muslims. There is of course the curse that we are under the spotlight.

And then of course, *madrasahs* became the attention. The debate on *madrasah* occurred before 9/11. But I think we have done quite well in the way that we sort of got our act together. I see the issue of *madrasah*, not from a religious point of view, but from an education point of view. Now we are able to organise our *madrasah* sector quite well. We have the Joint Madrasah System (JMS). There is a clear conscious effort to ensure that our *madrasah* students remain employable in the economy. That's our responsibility. At the same time, we know that the *madrasah* is supposed to produce our religious leaders, and therefore now we have multiple pathways to allow that to happen without wastage of human talent. So those who find that higher Islamic learning is not for them can opt for Al-Arabiah[11] or, the polytechnics and eventually find employment in other fields. Those with the aptitude and interest to pursue higher Islamic learning, we groom them in Aljunied[12] and they go to Al-Azhar[13] and other institutions of higher Islamic learning, so that one day they will be our future *Mufti*, future Syariah Court judges or other leadership roles in the religious sector.

Zainul Abidin: *How do you see the challenges of living in a secular state, and the challenges of diversity?*

Dr Yaacob: The challenge of diversity will grow because of one very simple reason — the Internet. The Internet, with the social media, is a game changer. You can't stop it. The connectivity that we have now, which we enjoy, brings about not just the good but also the bad and unwarranted things. So people see a lot of things on the Internet. I look at some of the YouTube videos, some are fascinating. You cannot prevent that from spreading. No way can MDA[14] block all these sites. Every minute, a few sites are popping up. So the truth of the matter is, we are becoming very diverse

> *The challenge of diversity will grow because of one very simple reason — the Internet.*

primarily for two reasons — one, we are affluent, we travel a lot, we go to different countries and two, we are well-connected to the global world. So with that happening, how do you manage that? Today I can [easily] go online and get a *fatwa*?[15] Nothing to prevent that, but what does it mean for me to live as a Muslim in Singapore? So we can't say "don't do it", right, but at the same time, we must also try make sure that the reference points like the *Mufti* and the Office of the Mufti are heightened in terms of their credibility, so that people can see them as an important reference in one's life. So religious leadership is also very important.

Dr Norshahril: *Do we have any intellectuals in our community today, someone of Professor Alatas' stature?*

Dr Yaacob: We don't have an intellectual class yet. It is something which we debated with Alatas. He wrote his book *Intellectuals in Developing Society*[16] and we need an intellectual class. When we were in campus, we were hoping that one day we will be there, an intellectual class, but we got distracted, because to be a part of the intellectual class we need to pursue a life of the thinking mind, lead, and understand issues. I think that did not happen as much as I hoped for. It's a pity and we need to have a bit more of that. How that can happen, I am not so sure. But it's a matter of personal interest. I see it from two different point of views. I think it's a matter of standards and how the community approaches what is good and what is not. If you demand a higher standard, I think people will respond to that standard. But if you don't demand a high standard, that's what it is. So if I don't demand a high standard from a Malay organisation, they'll [continue to] be like that. But if I insist, that I demand them at a higher standard, they will respond positively.

References

1. Jamiyah Singapore was founded in 1932 by his Eminence, Moulana Abdul Aleem Siddiqui, the Roving Ambassador of Peace, from Meerut, India together with other religious leaders in Singapore and Malaya at that time. Jamiyah was then known as the All-Malaya Muslim

Missionary Society with branches in the various states of Malaysia. After the separation from Malaysia, the name was changed to the Muslim Missionary Society Singapore (Jamiyah) but ties with the former branches remain cordial. In 1970, Mr Abu Bakar Maidin and his colleagues were elected to join the office. Then it had $5.60 in the kitty and its membership was a mere 190. Over the years, its membership surged to 35,000 members.

2. It was during the 2nd Convention that AMP revisited its vision for a Collective Leadership for the community that was first proposed at the 1990 Convention. The underlying motivation for the Collective Leadership proposal from the start was to promote a sense of participation in the community's decision-making process through a more consultative and consensual leadership.

3. Anugerah MENDAKI celebrates the success of Malay/Muslim students who have done exceptionally well at the National Examinations and are in the top 10% of the national cohort.

4. Goh Chok Tong Youth Promise Award is an annual award mooted that recognises and seeks to support promising youths on their endeavours in non-academic fields.

5. Chinese Development Assistance Council (CDAC) was jointly set up on 22 May 1992 by Singapore Federation of Chinese Clan Associations (SFCCA) and Singapore Chinese Chamber of Commerce and Industry (SCCCI). CDAC was formally incorporated under the Companies Act and later granted the status of an Institution of Public Character by the Government. The Singapore Indian Development Association (SINDA) is a self-help group that works to uplift the Singapore Indian Community. SINDA's key thrusts are in education, family services and active collaboration.

6. SkillsFuture is a national movement to provide Singaporeans with the opportunities to develop their fullest potential throughout life, regardless of their starting points. Through this movement, the skills, passion and contributions of every individual will drive Singapore's next phase of development towards an advanced economy and inclusive society.

7. Arabic term generally to refer to educational institutions.

8. The 7 July 2005 London bombings (often referred to as 7/7) were a series of coordinated suicide bomb attacks in central London which targeted civilians using the public transport system during the morning rush hour.

9. RRG is an acronym for the Religious Rehabilitation Group. The RRG is a voluntary group formed by individual ulama and asatizah (Islamic scholars and teachers) community in Singapore, primarily towards performing counselling works on the detained Jemaah Islamiyah (JI) members. The main objective of the RRG is towards countering the ideological misunderstanding of the JI members through counselling.

10. The Inter-Racial and Religious Confidence Circles — better known as IRCCs — are local-level inter-faith platforms in every constituency, formed to promote racial and religious harmony. The work of the IRCCs is instrumental in strengthening our social cohesion and supports the Community Engagement Programme (CEP).

11. Madrasah Arabiah Al-Islamiah is one of the three madrasahs under the Joint Madrasah System in Singapore. It is an Islamic-inspired academic school that is focused on nurturing students who excel academically, are grounded in Islamic values, and are connected to the community with a keen sense of service.

12. Madrasah Aljunied al-Islamiah is Singapore's premier Islamic institution of learning. Of international repute, the school produces illustrious alumni who are key Muslim leaders in Singapore as well as in Southeast Asia.
13. Al-Azhar Al-Sharif in Cairo founded in 970 is the oldest university in the world and centre of Islamic scholarship.
14. Media Development Authority — A statutory board under the Ministry of Communications and Information.
15. A *fatwa* is an Islamic religious ruling, a scholarly opinion on a matter of Islamic law.
16. Published by Cass (21 January 1977).

"S'pore needs 'gotong-royong' spirit to do well."

PM Lee
1 September 2013

Malay - Village Pulo Brani

Photo credit: Art and Picture Collection, The New York Public Library. Malay - village Pulo Brani Singapore. Retrieved from http://digitalcollections.nypl.org/items/c2634d03-24af-f238-e040-e00a18061845

The phrases "gotong royong" and "kampung spirit" have been used side-by-side and at times interchangeably. The two phrases were widely used during the 1960s and 1970s and now making a comeback recently by community leaders, government bodies and local campaigns. What do these terms actually mean?

Etymologically, the phrase "gotong royong" comes from Javanese, "gotong" meaning foster and "royong" meaning together. *Gotong-royong* as a concept has two meanings:

- As a form of activity: a selfless effort and voluntarism by all members of the community, in their respective capacity, towards completion of a task for public/common interest.
- As a spirit: the attitude of mutual cooperation or assistance.

Though rooted in Javanese culture the spirit and principles of gotong royong and/or kampung spirit have been institutionalised in the whole of the Nusantara region.

Gotong-royong was the most significant aspect of living in a kampong during the 1960s and 1970s. Fresh from independence, Singaporeans were struggling with economy and national identity. Racial tensions were high with the horrors of riots and strikes. However the rural areas were relatively more peaceful and harmonious. With the kampung spirit well-rooted, multiracial neighbours lived harmoniously with each other and continued to look out for each other even during those turbulent years. The neighbours were able to share and help out one another based on trust and friendship, forging bonds and strong ties within the community.

SINGAPORE

SINGAPORE MUSLIMS — CONTRIBUTING TOWARDS NATION-BUILDING

"

Singaporean Muslims have always been integral
to the nation's progress. We have built Singapore together
with other fellow Singaporeans. Whilst we have faced many difficult
challenges in the past, we have overcome them in partnership with
the Government. This is because we are secure of our position and in our
belief that we will always have a stake in the country. With the trust
and confidence steadily built over the past 50 years, state–community
relations have strengthened and our community has thrived.

Partnership does not mean, however, that the state must accept
everything a community imposes. Partnership means that we accept
the norms of our multiracial and multireligious society. We share
our values but do not impose them.

Partnership also means recognising that in order to arrive at an
optimal solution, there must be a degree of openness, some measure
of give-and-take, as well as an appreciation of the concerns and constraints.
No doubt our socio-historical context, the choices we as a people had made,
and the accommodative nature of our multicultural society had influenced
this trajectory and allowed us to reap the benefits. As a result, we have become
more confident and more grateful for what life has given us.

For Singapore, since independence, our community and our
religious leaders have always approached issues with a view to find
meaningful solutions to concrete problems. Our community has a tradition
of being guided by the principles of moderation, inclusiveness, and respect
for diversity, and participating actively in our nation-building efforts.
This is the Singapore way and it is what we as a community and society
must cherish and protect zealously."

Dr Yaacob Ibrahim
Minister for Communications and Information,
Minister-in-Charge of Cyber Security and
Minister-in-Charge of Muslim Affairs
Excerpted from Speech at the S. Rajaratnam School of International Studies
Conference on Islam in the Contemporary World
28 April 2016

CHAPTER 5

50 YEARS ON: SINGAPORE'S MALAY/MUSLIM IDENTITY*

Masagos Zulkifli Masagos Mohammad

Following 50 years of independence, the Singapore Malay/Muslim community has forged a unique identity and shines as a role model for the Malay Archipelago. As we marked the nation's journey with milestone SG50 celebrations in 2015, I too would like to term this identity as the "SG50 Malay/Muslim Identity". The Malay/Muslim community stands out from their brethren in the Malay diaspora largely because the community took special effort in these 50 years to ensure a harmonious balance between national interests and racial/religious interests.

When Singapore gained independence on 9 August 1965, Singapore Malays became a minority overnight. However, instead of being boxed into a position of weakness, the community leaders worked together and chose to work with the Government to ensure that their religious and cultural interests were preserved and protected, even as the Government sought to rule a multicultural and multireligious society that was fraught with ethnic and religious conflicts in its history.

Indeed, for many countries around the world, a minority group's interests are often exploited to create conflict between themselves and the majority group. We witness this in Chechnya, Russia and in Xinjiang, China. Even minority migrant communities in developed countries like France and Britain may have never fully enjoyed the goodwill of their fellow citizens

---

* This article was translated from Malay. It first appeared in Mr Masagos Zulkifli's Facebook.

as the former often seek to preserve their special cultural practices or faiths and are confined to live in enclaves. Consequently, these minorities feel marginalised and oppressed by their countries' policies which do not recognise the need for respect and tolerance for the differences of a plural society.

In post-independent Singapore's early years, its founding Prime Minister, the late Mr Lee Kuan Yew, stressed the importance of equality for all Singaporeans, regardless of race, language or religion. However, it was important to assure Singapore Muslim leaders that their community's religious and cultural interests are to be safeguarded. The Government and community leaders, therefore, often had to find thoughtful solutions for the community to reconcile these seemingly contradicting outcomes. Ever so often, the community is faced with challenges that can potentially put them in conflict with those of the other or larger communities. Peace and harmony between communities were outcomes that both want; therefore avoiding conflict while resolving issues became a principle adhered to by these leaders. As peace was maintained, decade after decade, the position of the Malays/Muslims in Singapore strengthened even as they face and overcome challenges and could progress alongside their fellow citizens.

As peace was maintained, decade after decade, the position of the Malays/Muslims in Singapore strengthened even as they face and overcome challenges and could progress alongside their fellow citizens.

Fifty years on, these community leaders continue to play an important role in the Singapore Story. Three broad principles have guided the Malay/Muslim community leaders in ensuring that the interests of religion, race and country are in harmony. They are:

(i) In religion: practising Islam that preaches moderation and respects culture, heritage and context;

(ii) In culture: preserving Malay culture that embellishes Islamic values; and

(iii) In nation-building: joining fellow citizens to build a society which values meritocracy, self-reliance and integrity and living respectfully with others in a multireligious, multiracial society.

In Religion: Practising Islam that Preaches Moderation and Respect Culture, Heritage and Context

The Administration of Muslim Law Act (AMLA) and the formation of the Islamic Religious Council of Singapore (MUIS)

In 1965, Singapore's Malays were faced with the dilemma of moving across the Causeway to become Malaysians or to stay put amid the uncertainties of a new nation. To win the confidence and support of the Malays for the newly independent Singapore, the Singapore Government moved a few legislations to protect the special position of the Malays, the chief of which is enshrined in Article 152 of the Singapore Constitution. This was a pledge by the fledgling government that the cultural and religious position of the Malays will be protected even as Singapore will be a society of equals and embrace a multiracial and multireligious society.

This special position was demonstrated by the enactment of the Administration of Muslim Law Act (AMLA) in 1968 which was authored by the late Professor Ahmad Ibrahim. It was through AMLA, that the socio-religious life of the Malay/Muslim community was recognised with legal status and structure. In my opinion, the AMLA represents breakthrough thinking of Singapore's pioneer government leaders, both Muslims and non-Muslims. It was the cornerstone of a legal guarantee of the protection of the religious interests and needs of the Malay/Muslim community in Singapore.

In my opinion, the AMLA represents breakthrough thinking of Singapore's pioneer government leaders, both Muslims and non-Muslims. It was the cornerstone of a legal guarantee of the protection of the religious interests and needs of the Malay/Muslim community in Singapore.

AMLA was formulated with foresight and to implement it, the Islamic Religious Council of Singapore (MUIS) was formed.

In its early years, MUIS was fraught with many challenges to its leadership and legitimacy. In fact, the community took sides on many issues and there were even instances of Singapore Muslims celebrating Hari Raya on different days due to in-fightings among some community leaders. Nevertheless, with its unwavering determination, MUIS has earned the trust of the community.

MUIS through AMLA manages all the religious affairs and needs of the Muslim community in Singapore, including mundane yet important ones like determining the prayer times. Other major functions of MUIS include *haj* (pilgrimage) administration, halal food certification, *wakaf* (land donated and in trust) administration, inheritance, madrasah administration and mosque building.

AMLA was also fundamental to the formation of the Syariah Court and the Registry of Muslim Marriages (ROMM), which handle matters pertaining to the marriages of Muslims in Singapore and the family laws peculiar to the Muslims. The ROMM ensures that the State recognises Muslim marriages without requiring Muslims to undergo a civil marriage, as often practiced in secular states.

Mosque Building Fund (MBF)

The most visible of MUIS' achievements is its success to build mosque in all large housing estates. In the 1970s, the Government embarked on massive urban redevelopment projects and many mosques, temples and churches that had existed then had to be demolished to make way for new city plans. The Malays, whose economic status were still weak at that time, had to resort to going from door to door to raise funds for the construction of new mosques. The late Mr Lee Kuan Yew soon found that while most places of worship had been successfully rebuilt soon after, it was not quite the same for mosques and this position was not politically tenable.

After understanding the difficulties faced by the Malay community, Mr Lee proposed the use of the Central Provident Fund (CPF) to deduct from all salaried Muslim employees towards the Mosque Building Fund (MBF) in 1975. This too was enacted through AMLA. Slowly but surely, the MBF accumulated funds and the first mosque, Muhajirin Mosque along Braddell Road was completed in 1977. Today, after 50 years, the Muslims can now take pride of the 69 mosques island wide, with two more under construction (Maarof Mosque and Yusof Ishak Mosque) and another in the pipelines (Tampines North Mosque). Together, these mosques can accommodate more than 140,000 people at any one time.

It is also important to know that it was not only money that enabled these mosques to be built. Traditionally, mosque had to be built on *wakaf* land (land bequeathed to trustee for public use) which must be granted in perpetuity. This was not practical for such land were scarce and expensive. It was both MUIS' pronouncement (*fatwa*) that land with a 99-year lease was considered religiously acceptable for mosque to be built on that land and the Government agreement to grant a special 99-year lease concession for mosques that got the project to start. This was departure from the usual 30-year leases given to other premises of worship.

Today, after 50 years, the Muslims can now take pride of the 69 mosques island-wide, with two more under construction (Maarof Mosque and Yusof Ishak Mosque) and another in the pipelines (Tampines North Mosque).

Because MUIS was the sole administrator for mosques, land was purchased at offered price. This is notable, given that other religious groups had to secure land to build their places of worship via tender, in competition with others in the open market.

Over time, under MUIS' strong leadership and the active contribution of volunteers, mosques in Singapore have become not merely places of worship but are in fact thriving and busy Islamic centres. Many mosques house part-time *madrasahs* (religious schools) that conduct religious classes. They also provide a variety of social development assistance and other essential services to the community. Indeed, they have also begun to serve as a bridge between the Muslim and non-Muslim communities to engage each other.

As mosques are all administered by MUIS, they became important institutions that could disseminate information and instructions uniformly, consistently and effectively. This was instrumental in conveying guidance to the community on recent events of terrorism by religious extremists abroad and how they should react and perceive this phenomena.

Mosques have become catalysts for the development of the Malay/Muslim community. Their critical function in uniting the community should not be underestimated. Clearly, it was because MUIS succeeded in building and administering mosques effectively, that they became icons that attracted and then united the Malay/Muslim community. It was also a major feather in MUIS' cap that earned respect from the community.

The Madrasahs

The network of six local *madrasahs* is another collection of institutions that has long shaped Singapore's Malay/Muslim community and is also administered by MUIS. The Government recognises the need for local *madrasahs* to produce local religious leaders who are exemplary, moderate, and who understand how the teachings of Islam can be translated in a multiracial and multireligious Singapore. There are two important factors contributing to the community's resilience against extreme and foreign religious views that are now permeating and taking root in many Muslim minority societies around the world. Firstly, because Singapore had long had its own local religious scholars to help guide the community in context, and secondly, because mosques are built with local funds that do not have foreign influence or authority attached to them.

The story of the *madrasahs* in Singapore is not without controversy. In 2002, the Government moved on Compulsory Education so that every Singaporean child receives basic education from Primary One through to Primary Six and pass their Primary School Leaving Examination (PSLE — an examination which also measures how well schools and students do in basic subjects). In the process, it had to also consider the *madrasahs* which were admitting children affected by this new law. While the Government had no intention to stop the operation of *madrasahs,* the question drew the ire of the community alleging it was targeting to close down the *madrasahs.*

It was fortunate that the constant engagement of Government leaders with the community had long sowed goodwill with each other. Even if there were angry and irrational aspersions by some, the majority of the community leaders prevailed others to keep their calm. In the end, the *madrasahs* were allowed to operate with a limited intake of 400 students a year — enough to meet the demand for religious scholars — subject to these students passing a reasonable standard of the PSLE.

Many Muslim parents send their children to local *madrasahs,* largely to learn religion and later to become religious teachers. The Government has also put in resources to improve the learning of science and mathematics in *madrasahs* through funding and the training of teachers. It has allowed the application of Edusave to *madrasah* students and waived off examination fees for secular subjects at the national examinations.

MUIS today administers three of the *madrasahs*: Madrasah Al-Irsyad Al-Islamiah, Madrasah Aljunied Al-Islamiah and Madrasah Al-Arabiah Al-Islamiah, to work together to pool their resources to offer an integrated curriculum and provide students with clear educational paths under the Joint Madrasah System (JMS). A part of the fund collected for mosques (MBMF) are also allocated to the *madrasahs*.

Recognition of Wakaf and Zakat

One other important role of AMLA is that it safeguards *wakaf* properties owned by the Malay/Muslim community. It ensures that these properties are well maintained and developed in line with the country's vision, to reap benefits that can then be used to meet the needs of the community, as entrusted by *pewakif* (donors of *wakaf*).

AMLA also allows MUIS to develop and expand *wakaf* as Islamic endowment assets with new and innovative approaches. Since the late 1980s, many *wakaf* properties managed by MUIS have increased their yield and continue to benefit the Muslim community. If this was not done, the *wakaf* may be left unattended and unable to bring in any revenue. MUIS has successfully administered proceeds from the *wakaf*, and are used for charitable purposes. Similarly, *zakat* (tithes) paid by Muslims is granted tax relief by the Inland Revenue Authority of Singapore (IRAS).

MUIS have Done Well

Today, Muslim communities from other countries who visit Singapore are impressed with MUIS' leadership as well as the unity of our Muslim community. The Muslim community here is able to practice their religion in peace, are respected and respectful.

In Culture: Preserving Malay Culture that Embellishes Islamic Values

For centuries, Islam has served as a moral basis for Malay/Muslim Singaporeans. Malay culture and etiquette put a certain grace and context to morality enjoined by Islam. A former Brunei Minister once illustrated to me why religious morals and cultural etiquette must come hand in glove. He was once asked by a Saudi minister as to why Brunei adheres to the state ideology of Malay/Muslim Monarchy. The Saudi minister also asked him: "Isn't Islam sufficient without being consciously Malay?" to which the Bruneian replied, "Earlier, my passport was thrown back at me by the immigration officer. We Malays would have returned it with our right hands and warm smiles." Malay cultural values do not contradict Islamic values, even if remnants of Hindu and other cultural influence (including Chinese) exist in many of the Malay customs.

> *Malay cultural values do not contradict Islamic values, even if remnants of Hindu and other cultural influence (including Chinese) exist in many of the Malay customs.*

The Malay civilisation was always an open one and existed long before the arrival of Islam. Indeed, scholars opine that the Malay pre-Islam way of life and value systems facilitated the easy assimilation of Islam. Folk tales such as *Si Tanggang* illustrate the obedience of a child to his mother, and the ruses of Tun Perak[a] in Malay epics, teach the importance of wisdom and intelligence in governing a country. Similarly, practices such as walking with a slight bow in front of elders, not talking back to them, and kissing the hand of an older person as a form of respect upon meeting them all demonstrate a culture in which the young respect and appreciate the old.

Malay etiquette and kinship values are visible from the way they dress on festive days, taking great pride in their matching family outfits. Weddings are organised with the *gotong-royong*[b] spirit. They display values consistent with Islamic ones though practised in its unique and cultural ways.

Professor Naquib Al-Attas, a Malaysian scholar, opined that the Malay language was a major factor that facilitated the spread of Islam in the region. The language had long contained concepts and cultural nodes that allowed Islamic values and theology to be conveyed easily.

Si Tanggang**

Si Tanggang is a Malay folktale about retribution on an ungrateful son. A boy from a poor family sneaks onto a trading ship, eventually becoming rich, marrying a princess, and acquiring his own galleon. On his return to his home village, he is ashamed of his humble origins and refuses to acknowledge his elderly mother. She curses him, and when he sets sail, he and his ship are turned to stone.

** There are similar stories from Indonesia (Hikayat Maim Kundang) and from Brunei (Nakhoda Manis).

Role of Local Muslim Scholars

The establishment of the Islamic Republic of Iran in 1979 proclaimed as a theological state governed by Islamic laws was met with enthusiasm by Muslims around the world. However, this new state was swiftly rejected by Saudi Arabia because it threatened the latter's power in the Gulf region. The political conflict between these two major powers also reflected the ideological conflict between the official sects of Islam in these countries, Wahhabism in Saudi and Shi'ism in

---

[a] Bendahara Paduka Raja Tun Perak was the fifth and most famous *bendahara* (a rank similar to a prime minister in Malay rule) of the Sultanate of Malacca. He served under four sultans (Sultan Muzzafar Shah, Sultan Mansur Shah, Sultan Alauddin Riayat Shah and Sultan Mahmud Shah) from 1456 to 1498. Tun Perak started as a soldier-statesman for Malaccan rulers. In 1445, he led the Malaccan army to victory by defeating Siamese invaders. As a result, he was made *bendahara* in 1456.

[b] Malay for rendering mutual help and the sharing of burdens.

Iran. This was the beginning of the globalisation of these doctrines, spreading their influence around the world to check one another. These are done often through free scholarships to study in their respective countries and the funding of mosques and subsequent deployment of their scholars in these mosques.

In 1979 too, the Soviet Union invaded Afghanistan, and Islam was again used to enthuse the support of Muslims around the world to drive the Soviet troops out of Afghanistan as a *jihad* (religious war). Thus two Islamic doctrines at logger heads with one another also legitimised again a practice (war) long forgotten — the battlefield of the Afghans became precursors to many *jihadi* conflicts around the world. These conflicts (as well as the never ending Israeli–Palestinian issue) had significant impact on the Muslim world leading to the Taliban conflict in Afghan, Al-Qaeda fight against the US and recently the ISIS establishment of the caliphate in Syria and Iraq. In many ways, it affected the Muslim worldview in Singapore.

Insidiously, the events of 1979 indirectly brought about changes on how Singapore's Malay/Muslims practise Islam here. Colourful Malay traditional *baju kurung* made way for traditional Middle Eastern white or black long robes. Arabic words began to find its way in the Malay language (the plural of *ustaz* — religious scholar — was *ustaz-ustaz* and has now taken the form of the Arabic plural — *asatizah*).

Our local Muslim scholars should pause and comprehend what this means to our community and the impact they bring to our way of practising Islam. The infiltration of either Wahabism or Shi'ism on our community will not only further divide our small community, it will also import the disputes and conflicts which are alien to our region. Thus far, our local scholars have been valuable to the nation by corralling the support of the community and thus helped the Government address the problems of Islamic extremism, radicalisation and possible acts of terrorism by Al-Qaeda and Jemaah Islamiyah (JI) against the United States and Singapore, and on how we view the plight of the oppressed Muslims in the world like Palestine and Syria. They have also come forward to rally the community to reject the doctrines and calls to *jihad* and terrorism by ISIS both in the Levant as well as in Singapore. Evidently, our home-grown religious scholars are valuable in safeguarding the harmony of our multiracial and multireligious country. Without them, the voices of religious extremists would have quickly influenced our minority community.

We have seen their effects in Chechnya and Xinjiang where segments of the minority communities have joined forces with ISIS in Syria or have made attempts to overthrow their own governments.

Their roles in galvanising the community against these threats are well recognised. Our mosques are not only full on Hari Raya, but also during Friday prayers where both the old and young perform their prayers in the mosques. Yet the religiosity of the community has never been met with suspicion by others nor seen as a threat. Other communities know Singapore Malays/ Muslims are unique, peace-loving and do not subscribe to violence and terrorism.

Our community should therefore be judicious in allowing external elements to shape our beliefs given that their histories and contexts differ from ours. Our young may be eager to adopt changes after being influenced by what they see in foreign countries and from grazing the various opinions promulgated through the Internet. Those who post their religious opinions on the Internet are not always religiously knowledgeable enough in Islam, or worse, they may harbour ill intentions.

Our community must keep faith with our home-grown religious scholars who understand that religion must be practised in context and paced with the development of its own society and those around it. Thus far, they have proven to be mature and wise and value the peace and harmony arising from their guidance for the community. It is with this guidance, that Singapore Muslim women

Evidently, our home-grown religious scholars are valuable in safeguarding the harmony of our multiracial and multireligious country. Without them, the voices of religious extremists would have quickly influenced our minority community.

Yet the religiosity of the community have never been met with suspicion by others nor seen as a threat. Other communities know Singapore Malays/ Muslims are unique, peace-loving and do not subscribe to violence and terrorism.

who wear the *tudung* (headscarves) also project good character and not don the *tudung* merely to comply with the laws of the state or cultural demands, and behave to the contrary. At the same time, they have promoted interfaith and interracial mixing even while encouraging their flock to keep their faith deep.

It is important to note that the Malay/Muslim community life in Singapore is unique and is a model for other minority communities to study. Although Singapore is a pluralistic society, we Muslims are able to live peacefully and harmoniously with others of different faiths and culture. We have been able to keep the moral teachings of Islam alive and embellished it with our Malay culture. We know we are respected and our faith can be preserved. We know no matter how big a community in Singapore is, none can claim dominance and set the rules for others. Every individual in this country is able to practise his or her religion and culture peacefully and yet be respectful of others.

The Malay Language Council

The Malay language is thriving in Singapore. The Malay press, radio and television channels still have high followings despite the challenges posed by new media. When I listen to interviews on these media, I am proud of the effort shown by the young and old in conversing in proper and full sentences and avoid dotting them with English words they are more familiar with.

Although our community is very exposed to world cultures and mostly use the English language in our daily lives, we are proud that we have preserved our fluency in the Malay language. In fact, in Singapore, we still maintain the use of *"Bahasa baku"*,[c] or standard Malay in both its written and spoken forms while others in the region have begun to agree on a compromised standard. If you look closely, the crests of our uniformed services, be it the police or the armed forces, are

---

[c] The word *"baku"* is a Javanese word meaning true and correct. *Sebutan Baku* or standard spoken Malay was introduced in Singapore in 1993 by the Ministry of Education to be used in the teaching and learning of the Malay Language progressively beginning with the primary schools and followed by the secondary schools and junior colleges/centralised institutes.

still preserved with Malay words ("Polis Repablik Singapura" and "Yang Pertama dan Utama"). Our national anthem "Majulah Singapura" is also in the Malay language.

The Malay Language Council of Singapore (MLCS) was set up by literati and those concerned with the preservation of the language in 1976, first as a committee then formalised in 1992. Helmed by political leaders, MLCS ensures that the Malay language continues to flourish through the formal education system with sufficient funding for its promotion and monitoring of its frequency and quality of use in public. The Government remains committed to preserve all mother tongues and has channelled substantial funding, for example through the Lee Kuan Yew Fund for Bilingualism.[d]

> *If you look closely, the crests of our uniformed services, be it the police or the armed forces, are still preserved with Malay words ("Polis Repablik Singapura" and "Yang Pertama dan Utama"). Our national anthem "Majulah Singapura" is also in the Malay language.*

The Malay Language Council organises the Malay Language Month (*Bulan Bahasa*) annually to celebrate our mother tongue as a community. I doubt that other Malays in the Archipelago have such a national programme celebrated with such gusto. In fact, the annual event has become a source of pride of Malays in Singapore and attracts the interest of an audience who would usually use English in their daily lives. They participate to affirm their love for the Malay language.

Apart from the Malay Language Month, biannual Literature Awards (*Anugerah Persuratan*) are given to writers who produce various Malay language literature including dramas and novellas. The best Malay language teachers too are recognised with Arif Budiman Awards[e] annually. Parents are frequently roped in to play their roles in preserving our language. They are aware how

---

[d] The Lee Kuan Yew Fund for Bilingualism (the "Fund") was set up on 28 November, 2011, at the launch of Mr Lee Kuan Yew's new book, "*My Lifelong Challenge: Singapore's Bilingual Journey*". The Fund has been set up to supplement efforts by the Ministry of Education (MOE) in the teaching and learning of English and the Mother Tongue Languages.

[e] This award aims to recognise excellent Malay Language teachers in mainstream primary and secondary schools as well as pre-university teachers, who are exemplary in promoting and improving the use of the language, through teaching and learning.

the Malay language helps to inculcate Islamic moral values with a touch of cultural beauty.

Nation: Building a Multireligious, Multiracial, Meritocratic, and Self-Reliant Society which Values Integrity

MENDAKI

Singapore's policy of meritocracy has played a significant role in improving the standard of living of our Malay/Muslim community. The community has made progress by leaps and bounds over the past five decades. Many have achieved progress especially in education and employment. More have gone on to attain a university education, excelling in disciplines such as life sciences, information technology, law and medicine. This was rarely seen in the early days of Independence. More Malays/Muslims now hold high positions in private companies and are given important responsibilities in government ministries and departments in Singapore. Our community's status is improving, with most Malays/Muslims being able to own their homes. They have also learned the value of investing their savings for their children's future. This is the result of the community's efforts led by the Malay political and community leaders to continue to improve the standards of living of the community.

In the early days, the educational achievement trajectory of the Malays/Muslims was worrying. The MENDAKI Foundation was then formed in 1981 aimed at uplifting the educational standards of Singapore Malay/Muslim children. In 1984, the Mosque Building Fund (MBF) was expanded by law to allow it to support the educational and social programmes, managed by MENDAKI. Today, this fund has been renamed the Mosque Building and MENDAKI Fund (MBMF).

> *The MENDAKI Foundation was then formed in 1981 aimed at uplifting the educational standards of Singapore Malay/Muslim children. In 1984, the Mosque Building Fund (MBF) was expanded by law to allow it to support the educational and social programmes, managed by MENDAKI. Today, this fund has been renamed the Mosque Building and MENDAKI Fund (MBMF).*

MENDAKI also administers the funds allocated by the Government for the Tertiary Tuition Fee Subsidy (TTFS) which assists poorer Malay students to pursue their dreams through educational success virtually free. My siblings and I are very fortunate to have been beneficiaries of TTFS. We are fortunate that in Singapore, as long as one is willing to work hard to succeed in education, financial problems should not be an obstacle to success.

Singapore Malay/Muslim Leadership

For the Singapore Malay/Muslims to continue to achieve progress, it is important for us to identify and groom the next generation of leaders who are able to raise the community to a level where we are able to compete in an open but volatile world economy, while continuing to emphasise the importance of religion and culture as our moral compass. Although we have people with talent and leadership capabilities, it has never been simple for the Government or the community to identify and select those who will be entrusted to lead the community and nation in the future. It does not only take one with integrity and competency, but someone who will know how to steer the community against populist or extremist sways in order to safeguard their interests and the nation's long term security. It will indeed be a tragedy to our community if successful Malays only think of their own interests and forget how the spirit of *gotong-royong* of the community have helped them and for them not giving back to their community.

> *It will indeed be a tragedy to our community if successful Malays only think of their own interests and forget how the spirit of gotong-royong of the community have helped them and for them not giving back to their community.*

They should not forget that as hard as they have worked, the Malay/Muslim community worked together to contribute in their success too. When successful Malays contribute alongside the rest of our community, the benefits will be manifold and lasting. It will also preserve the spirit of our community. We will have produced bright individuals who will not only become the future leaders of our community but also understand why and how they should give back.

Some of the characteristics that these new leaders must possess are sincerity, honesty and trustworthiness, as well as the readiness and passion to serve the community. They should be sincere in helping the community, and not be motivated by position and status. We need capable community leaders who tirelessly contribute ideas to ensure that the needs of Singaporeans and their community are both met and safeguarded. They need to do this with great tact and wisdom to bring welfare and wealth to a multi-cultural and multireligious nation that can work together in spite of their diversity. This is a nation that has made our differences work for us, and not against us.

I wish to leave you with a quote by our first president of Singapore, the late Mr Yusof Ishak, in 1968:

Indeed, the diversity of languages, religions, cultures and races can be a stumbling block to progress and prosperity. However, if we face these differences with goodwill and patience, and try to understand them, our success to overcome these differences will ultimately become our means to that progress and prosperity. It is this tolerance, among other things, that has made Singapore the dynamic and progressive city that it is today.

Majulah Singapura!

FOCUS ON THINGS THAT UNITE

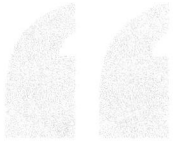

"Singapore is a multiracial, multireligious country and it's very important that we focus on the many common things we have together, rather than become obsessed with the differences between us. In this way, we can build an open and united society.

We started from a Singapore which was racially segmented, we live in different areas in Singapore and over the course of 50 years, we began to live together and integrated together. And over the next 50 years, again, it is a choice that we make: whether as communities and individuals we decide that we live together and integrate, or we decide we want to be separate and live apart. That will shape the Singapore of the future.

I came from an Edusave award ceremony this morning and, if you look around, the neighbours, the students — they come from all races and religions."

Teo Chee Hean
Deputy Prime Minister and
Coordinating Minister for National Security
23 January 2016

NATIONAL DAY RALLIES — TRACING THE DEVELOPMENT OF THE MALAY COMMUNITY (1990–2015)

Norshahril Saat

Singapore Prime Ministers have always been concerned about the development of the Malay/Muslim community. Central to their discourse on the community is their leadership, education and integration. Lee Kuan Yew's views on the community have been well documented, in newspaper reports as well as his writings. Before his demise in 2015, Lee candidly reflected on the Malays in his memoirs *The Singapore Story* and *The Hard Truths*. This chapter recaps the views of the other prime ministers: Goh Chok Tong and Lee Hsien Loong. Both Goh and Lee Hsien Loong have not written their memoirs, but their views on the Malays are captured during the National Day Rally. The annual National Day Rally (NDR) is the most important address Singapore's Prime Ministers make to the nation. It is akin to the State-of-Union address in the US. The Prime Minister uses the NDR to appraise society's progress for the past year, and to make important policy announcements for the following financial year. The NDR is generally held two weeks after National Day, 9 August. The Prime Minister will speak in three languages: Malay, Mandarin and English. The Malay speech will be the first speech, as a form of recognition it is the state's national language. The Malay speech normally provides an update on the Malay community.

The following provides some excerpts from the speeches made on the Malays during the NDR since the Goh Chok Tong era to the Lee Hsien Loong era. Highlighting these demonstrate a trend in the two leaders' thinking about the community. Undeniably, their views represent that of the government. But, such speeches also warrant a sociological study on how political, economic, and social context shape their worldview on the Malays, and what they see as the "Malay problem". Goh was concerned about the Malays underachieving in education. In his NDR speeches, he often reminded Malays to prepare for the Knowledge-Based economy (KBE). Moreover, while not touching on Islam *per se*, Goh raised concerns about the community moving away from the mainstream. Goh was shaped by the political context of the 1990s. The Malay/Muslim community then also raised several questions for the Goh administration, particularly the role of the Malays in the SAF, as well the quality of Malay Members of Parliament, whom they regarded as not championing enough Malay issues. There was also an international dimension to Goh's discourse. Singapore's relations with Malaysia, under the leadership of Mahathir Mohamad, was at its lowest. There were constant debates about which system works best for Malays: meritocracy or Malay special rights. In 2001, the issue of Malay collective leadership was raised again by the AMP, to the extent that Goh had to remind the Malays to be united and work closely with Malay MPs. After 9/11, the Malays again were seen under the spotlight, and they were constantly reminded to be part of the mainstream.

Lee Hsien Loong took a softer stance on the Malays, as compared to Lee Kuan Yew. Yet, he did not depart from Goh's concerns. His NDR speeches touched on the role of education and employability of the Malays in the challenging global economy. He highlighted several success cases of the Malays in which they should emulate. Lee also praised the efforts made by several groups to bring the community closer to the mainstream. For example, he praised the Religious Rehabilitation Group

(RRG) for their de-radicalisation efforts. Like Goh, Lee reminded the Malays to work together with the Malay MPs in the PAP, especially through the Community Leaders Forum (CLF). The following are the key points made by Goh and Lee on Malay education and employ-ability; national unity; and leadership.

Malay Education and Employability

The Chinese used to have very effective self-help organisations. Now, the Malays are setting the lead. MENDAKI, Majlis Pusat and Association of Muslim Professionals are amongst the leading Malay self-help organisations. Malay organisations and intel-lectuals have spent much time discussing ways to improve the Malay community's achievements. I urge the Malay community to support their programmes, especially their educational programmes. I am also heartened to see Malay leaders taking the lead in encouraging the community to tackle sensitive mat-ters. The recent campaign by the MUIS-initiated Muslim Kidney Action Committee to make Malays more aware of the plighht of those with kidney dis-ease, and to get more Malays support the idea of kidney donation, is a good example.

Goh Chok Tong 1992

In 1980, only 16% of Malays between the ages of 25 and 39 attained a secondary education and higher. In 1994, it was 46%. This is a huge achievement. Our next target is to get the Malay students do better, and the good students to excel. I am delighted that the Malay community has produced several top students recently. I would like to see more top Malay students.

I have spoken of my desire to level up Singaporeans. To help lower-income families, I am introducing a new scheme called 'Edusave Merit Bursaries'. This is to motivate and reward their chil-dren to do better in school.

Goh Chok Tong, 1995

The Government will continue to support MENDAKI and AMP. Soon we will be selling Singapore Telecom

(ST) shares to Singaporeans at a discount. We will also offer some shares to all the community self-help groups at preferential rates, to help them in their good work. We will be offering MENDAKI shares costing $4 million, and AMP shares costing $500,000, after discount. Their market value will be much higher. These ST shares will make good investments, and provide the two bodies more funds to carry out more programmes benefitting the community.

Goh Chok Tong 1996

As a father myself, I know that Malay-Muslim parents want their children to succeed in education, do well in their careers and become morally upright. At the same time, they also want them to learn and practise Islamic values. This is perhaps why some Malay-Muslim parents send their children to full-time madrasahs. These madrasahs provide religious education and aim to produce religious teachers and scholars. I understand their role. There are now 4,000 students in full-time madrasahs. Many of them dropped out annually. In fact, the majority of them did not get to tertiary levels. That's why I worry that these children may not be adequately prepared for the new economy. I am even more concerned because, over the last three years, an average of 65 per cent of madrasah students left every year without completing Secondary 4. This dropout rate is too high. They will have poor job prospects. What opportunities and prospects do these children have in future?

Goh Chok Tong 1999

The Malay MPs and I are most concerned that many Malay Singaporeans still do not fully realise the impact of the Knowledge Revolution on their children's future. They do not fully appreciate the need for their children to have some form of post-secondary education in the KBE. Not as many Malay students as we would wish are proceeding to post-secondary education. This is most unfortunate because the higher their educational level, the brighter their future.

Goh Chok Tong, 2000

I want to see more Malays occupy high positions in the public and private sectors. To do so, you must do even better in education, in particular, in IT, science and mathematics. You must acquire skills in new growth areas. You must be innovative and progressive. You must also have a broad outlook, and be well-integrated with others. At the same time, you should remain anchored in your culture and religion. If you get the right balance between traditional virtues and a cosmopolitan outlook, your community will do well in the New Economy.

Goh Chok Tong, 2001

Singapore is entering a new phase, and the Malay community too. We see many bright opportunities opening up ahead, and young Malays are poised to contribute in many fields of endeavour. We have the chance to take our whole country to a higher level.

You should continue to work with the government, Malay MPs, MENDAKI and MUIS to address current problems like economic downturn and dysfunctional families, and strive to further upgrade the community. Singaporeans must stay resolute, help one another and respond to our challenges as one nation. Then after the storm we will resume growing, and continue to build better lives for everyone.

Lee Hsien Loong, 2009

National Unity

Indeed, our Muslims must reject extremism. Extremists will split the community and tarnish its moderate image. The community, and especially MUIS, must continue to uphold Islam as a progressive, tolerant and peaceful religion. Also, isolate those who involve outsiders in our domestic affairs. These people will only create trouble for us. They will sow distrust and disharmony amongst the races. The second big challenge is economic. Our economy is being restructured to cope with globalisation and increased competition. Malay/Muslim workers, like other Singaporeans, will have to adjust. Given this difficult backdrop, you should work closely with the Malay political leaders to uplift your community. Yaacob Ibrahim and his team want to build a community of excellence for the Malays/Muslims. Such a community will be committed to education and life-long learning. It will focus on improving standards in all subjects, especially science and mathematics. It will draw upon Malay cultural traditions and Islamic values to improve itself.

Goh Chok Tong, 2002

Malay Singaporeans play an important role in shaping the future of our nation. Singaporeans of all races need to stay united in purpose, and work together as one national team. I am confident the Malay community will continue to hone your skills and build a Community of Excellence. Together, we will create a brighter future for the Malay community and for Singapore in this rapidly changing world.

Lee Hsien Loong, 2006

September 11 was a defining event for Singapore's religious harmony, and especially for our Malay/ Muslim community. Malays/Muslims in Singapore reacted to these events very differently, compared with some other Muslim communities elsewhere. You immediately and forthrightly condemned terrorism. Instead of feeling dispirited and psychologically "under siege", you resolved to become stronger. Instead of withdrawing, you reached out to engage other communities. Instead of becoming confrontational, you adopted an open and adaptive approach. This reflects a growing self confidence and progressive attitude when handling sensitive religious issues. We see the same spirit in issues like modernising madrasah education and organ donation.

Lee Hsien Loong, 2009

I believe all of us want Singapore to remain the best home for our families. We want our children and grandchildren to live well here and realise their dreams. We want a caring and compassionate society; an open city with a strong Singaporean spirit; and a multiracial society, maintaining harmony between the ethnic groups. To achieve all these goals, we must continue our multiracial approach to national challenges. You must know — through the television, newspapers or internet — how politics and society are often organised by race in other countries. Every issue is seen, and fought, in racial terms — which race gains, which loses. We should never let this happen in Singapore.

Lee Hsien Loong, 2012

Leadership

First is the bond between the new Malay leaders and the community. Like their predecessors, they will have to secure the trust and confidence of the community through their vision, deeds and service. Both of you, the leaders and your community, must work together to achieve your community vision, like the saying, 'berat sama dipikul, ringan sama dijinjing' ('shoulder heavy and carry light loads together').

Goh Chok Tong, 2003

In the last few years, through the Community Leaders' Forum, Malay/Muslim organisations have rallied around to support MENDAKI and work together to uplift the community. With the deep spirit of self-help, and the encouragement and support of the Government, you tackled difficult problems and gradually overcame them. As the Malay proverb says, "Water is shaped flowing through the bamboo; agreements are shaped by consensus". Whether in education, housing, socio-economic status, or in the fight against drug abuse, you have scored major successes. Improvements from year to year have been gradual, but the transformation over 25 years has been significant.

Lee Hsien Loong, 2007

Our Malays play an integral part in the Singapore story. You built strong institutions like MENDAKI and MUIS, which together with other Malay/Muslim organisations have helped to uplift the community. You created new platforms like the Community Leaders' Forum (CLF) to push the community forward. Our Malay MPs, together with other community leaders, led the community to identify and tackle key challenges. These include education standards, drug addiction and dysfunctional families. With these efforts, and the support of the government, the community has adapted to the globalised world, and continued to progress.

Lee Hsien Loong, 2009

Over the past year, Singaporeans have discussed our shared future in the Our Singapore Conversations (OSC). Malays have participated actively in this national effort. Besides the OSC, the Malay community also held the Suara Musyawarah, which focused more on issues specific to the community. But broadly Malay Singaporeans share the concerns of other Singaporeans in 5 areas (5P) — housing (Perumahan), healthcare (Penjagaan Kesihatan), education (Pendidikan), jobs (Pekerjaan), and opportunities (Peluang). This reflects how integrated our society is.

Lee Hsien Loong, 2013

Encik Yusof was a religious man, and at the same time had close and friendly relationships with non-Muslims. He strongly supported our multiracial policies. He believed in meritocracy — that everyone should have equal opportunities to advance themselves through their own effort. He had also advocated policies to modernise our society and which had enabled the Malay/Muslim community to make progress together with other communities. He had represented Singapore with dignity and distinction as President.

Lee Hsien Loong, 2014

LEE KUAN YEW:
IN HIS OWN WORDS

"

Over 100 years ago, this was a mud-flat, swamp. Today, this is
a modern city. Ten years from now, this will be a metropolis.
Never fear."

"But I say to you: here we make the model multiracial society.
This is not a country that belongs to any single community:
it belongs to all of us. You helped build it, your fathers, your
grandfathers helped build this."

Speech at the Sree Narayana Mission in Sembawang
12 September 1965

"If groups are left behind either on the basis of language, race,
religion or culture, and if these groups the line of division
coincides with the line of race, then we will not succeed in our
long term objective of a secure future."

National Day Rally Speech at the National Theatre
8 August 1966

LEE KUAN YEW*

Sidek Saniff

Paternalistic leaders like India's Mohandas Ghandi and Jawarhal Nehru, Indonesia's Sukarno and Muhammad Hatta, the Philippines' Dr Jose Rizal, Malaysia's Tunku Abdul Rahman and Tun Abdul Razak, and of course Singapore's Lee Kuan Yew have rightly earned a plethora of honorific titles: Fathers of Independence, Father of the Nation, Father of Development, among others.

For Lee Kuan Yew, three important characters must be conciously added to all these titles. He believed in meritocracy, pragmatism (not necessarily to always be politically correct) and a love for peace, the last trait making him one of the early world leaders to visit Israel and Jordan, helping to expedite the peace process between the Arabs and Jews. My understanding is that Mr Lee believed this was the area that needed the most urgent effort for lasting peace.

And then there is peace at home. For this, Mr Lee and like-minded colleagues such as S. Rajaratnam, Goh Keng Swee and E. W. Barker embarked on the following: leadership in the government and the civil service machinery; the trade union movement keeping pace with industrialisation, then modernisation, globalisation; and now, an intelligent nation, revamping the education system taking into account the latest developments in science and technology. He sent Mr Rajaratnam abroad to Russia, India, China and Japan, without forgetting our neighbouring countries, all to advance the identity of a new country, Singapore.

Politically, he invited on board all the like-minded Singaporeans with an interest in the country at heart, including those who held different views to his. He believed in an all-encompassing approach to the well being of the country. He even tinkered with the democratic system itself and introduced nominated MPs with different expertise to check our ministers, keeping them on their toes! He went further and invited candidates with the best results in the general election to parliament, true to his belief in pragmatism, meritocracy and openness. Let a thousand buds bloom.

He left his indelible mark on the system, fuelled by his experiences of the Japanese Occupation, self-government, the merger with Malaysia (and the shadow of communism) and then separation, the incoming danger of communalism and the urgent development of a new city–state.

* Article first appeared in *Asian Geographic*, No 113, Issue 4/2015. Reprinted with permission from writer.

"For Singapore, our
Founding Father Lee Kuan
Yew, left us with all the
ingredients for progress.
We should be selective
about our own present
needs. We can modify
the system if we must,
but keep in mind three
things that he disliked:
jejuneness, prevarication
and procrastination.
He is our icon."

Sidek Saniff

Image of the late Mr Lee Kuan Yew on
this page is reproduced with permission
from Collection of the National Museum
of Singapore, National Heritage Board.

CHAPTER 7

THE MAKING OF A MALAY/MUSLIM IN SINGAPORE: AN ANALYSIS OF HARI RAYA SPEECHES DELIVERED BY MINISTERS-IN-CHARGE OF MUSLIM AFFAIRS

Aidi Abdul Rahim

This question "Who were, are and will be the Malays?" has been and will be a recurring and an extremely significant one for the community and its thought leaders. During the pre-independence period, nationalist leaders such as Yunos Abdullah, Ibrahim Ya'cob, Burhanuddin Helmy and Yusof Ishak tried to define Malays and their role in the future independent nation of *bangsa Melayu* (Malay race). On 9 August 1965, Malays found themselves asking the same question but in a very different context.

Who are and will be the Singapore Malays?

What was the position of the Malay/Muslim community *vis-à-vis* other communities and what would be their issues and concerns in the making of a Singaporean Malay/Muslim community in the newly independent state? In 1965, two years after Singapore joined Malaysia, where the Malays/Muslims were a majority, they suddenly found themselves to be a minority again. Article 152 of the Singapore Constitution states that the Government "shall exercise its functions in such manner as to recognise the special position of the Malays, who are the indigenous people of Singapore, and accordingly it shall be the responsibility of the

Government to protect, safeguard, support, foster and promote their political, educational, religious, economic, social and cultural interests and the Malay language." As the Malays/Muslims ponder what their future would be after separation from Malaysia, the tentative steps of coming to terms of being a minority and facing the unknown future must have loomed large in their psyche. This essay examines the iconic Hari Raya speeches of the three Ministers-in-Charge of Muslim Affairs from 1981 to 2014 to map out the themes that were discussed with the goal to identify how the speeches projected the government's understanding in the making of the Malay/Muslim Singapore community.

1981–1993: Inculcating the Importance of Education in the Social-Spiritual Upliftment of the Community

Self-reliance and community involvement were seen as the key strategy to uplift the community. The decade of the 1980s was focused on the setting up of an institutional and the first community-based self-help group, Yayasan MENDAKI, to work towards addressing the educational challenges of the community. At each Hari Raya gathering, the community was exhorted to continue upgrading their education and training. Singapore was in the throes of economic restructuring, the ubiquitous impact of the computer and information technology in the work place with a future that focused more on brain than brawn. MENDAKI played a catalytic role in drumming into the thinking of Malay/Muslim parents about the importance of education. Parents were advised to encourage their children to pursue their education to the maximum level of their abilities. Their children were encouraged to attend the heavily-subsidised weekend tuition to provide extra coaching and remedial help to Malay/Muslim students.

We have been witnessing a gradual evolution in the thinking of Malay parents about the education of their children in the last two to three decades. Malay parents today place the enhancement of their children's future career and employment opportunities above all other rationale for education. Indeed most of the Malay children are now encouraged to pursue their education to the maximum level of their abilities.[a]

There were steady and rising numbers of Malays/Muslims from each cohort completing their secondary education; more Malay/Muslim students are getting more than five 'O' level passes in their General Certificate of Education (GCE) 'O' level exams and better performance at the Primary School Leaving Examination (PSLE) level. Naturally, it was conceivable to set higher goals; thus parents were told to encourage their children to aim beyond completing their primary or secondary education. Realistically though, not every Malay/Muslim student was academically-inclined. For such students, vocational training was an option.

While efforts were focused on educational upliftment, it did not escape the attention of the community that they were also facing other serious problems of drug offences among Malay/Muslim youths, high divorce rates and the high concentration of Malays/Muslims in less-skilled occupations.[b] Certainly, these were not new problems. The strategic thrust in alleviating these problems was to uplift and improve the socio-economic position of the community and the way forward was through a coordinated and total approach. At the turn of the new decade, MENDAKI saw its role and function widened to tackle these other serious problems, on top of educational upliftment and its registered society status changed to be a registered charity and an Institution of Public Character. Not unexpectedly, the community was encouraged to increase their monthly contribution in the Mosque Building and

---

[a] Speech by Dr Ahmad Mattar, Minister for the Environment and Minister-in-Charge of Muslim Affairs (1977–1993), at the Hari Raya Aidilfitri Gathering at the Istana on Saturday, 6 June 1987.

[b] Speech by Dr Ahmad Mattar, Minister for the Environment and Minister-in-Charge of Muslim Affairs (1977–1993), at the Hari Raya Aidilfitri Gathering at the Istana on Saturday, 21 May 1988.

MENDAKI Fund to support the additional activities and programmes.[c]

In his last Hari Raya speech, Dr. Ahmad Mattar broached the subject of what was a Muslim Singaporean.[d] According to the Minister, at the national level, the Muslim Singaporean could be described as being no different from the non-Muslim Singaporean: they have the same needs, they share the same circumstances and that life is not different just because they are Muslims. At the personal and community level, the Malay/Muslim Singaporean, could bring to Singapore's mainstream of life the "best qualities of an ancient heritage, the strengths of the Islamic tradition and cultural history, the important values of compassion, patience in hard times, the ability to face life's challenges with courage and humour and the strength of resilience". Above all, he emphasised unity within the community; he saw the strength of the Malays/Muslims here that they "shun tendencies and influences that split" them and elevated harmony as a higher communitarian value. Though he acknowledged that members of the Malay/Muslim community did progress at different speeds based on their abilities, he commended that the community had not stratified according to class or economic lines.

1993–2001 Forging the Singapore/ Malay/Muslim Spirit in a Globalizing World

In 1993, the community saw the appointment of Mr Abdullah Tarmugi as the second Minister in-Charge of Muslim Affairs. Like his predecessor, he too was concerned with the economic, social and spiritual upliftment of the Malay/Muslim community. He recognised

---

[c] Speech by Dr Ahmad Mattar, Minister for the Environment and Minister-in-Charge of Muslim Affairs (1977–1993), at the Hari Raya Aidilfitri Gathering at the Istana on Saturday, 20 April 1991.

[d] Speech by Dr Ahmad Mattar, Minister for the Environment and Minister-in-Charge of Muslim Affairs (1977–1993), at the Hari Raya Aidilfitri Gathering at the Istana on Saturday, 11 April 1992.

the strides made by the community and noted that the community was actively involved in improving themselves. The emphasis on the importance of education had had a positive response from parents who were paying more attention to the upbringing and education of their children. These were reflected in the performances at the PSLE, GCE 'O', and 'A' levels and up to the tertiary levels. Though encouraged, he expressed the concern that the community was not focused and responsive enough to the changing needs of education, where with the globalising economy, new knowledge and skills were always in demand. He emphasised the need to inculcate the culture of life-long learning. With the dawn of the Knowledge Economy and the on-going restructuring of the economy, the concern focused on the low-skilled Malay/Muslim workers losing their jobs and unable to find employment quickly. Nonetheless, he exhorted that by drawing on the community's core strength, the family as the basic foundation, the Malays/Muslims could strive for success and excellence was not an impossibility provided they put in the effort, perseverance, discipline and sacrifice.

In 1997, the role of religion in development was first explicated by Mr Abdullah. It was maintained that Singaporean Muslims, in observing their religious beliefs, did not prevent them from contributing to and deriving benefits from the country's national development. He continued:

> *Singapore Muslims have demonstrated that adherence to their religious beliefs has not prevented them from contributing to and deriving benefits from our national development. They do this by putting into practice the Islamic teachings that urge Muslims to seek the truth, to promote dialogue and consultation, to be moderate, to strike a balance between secular and spiritual needs, to be tolerant and to promote mutual respect among religions.[e]*

---

[e] Speech by Mr Abdullah Tarmugi, Minister for Community Development and Minister-in-Charge of Muslim Affairs (1993–2002), at the Hari Raya Get Together at Environment Penthouse on Saturday, 15 February 1997.

What it meant to be a Singaporean Muslim was put to the test after the 9/11 incident. This galvanised the Muslims here to showcase how Islam was practiced in Singapore. It was in response to this tragic turn of events that integrating the various communities became imperative to avoid suspicion or misunderstandings. According to Mr Abdullah, when the different communities are able to interact, live, work and play without emotional and physical barriers, there is the likelihood of at least understanding and appreciating each other's differences and interests. It is when these differences are accepted and the common space is deepened and widened, that cohesion becomes achievable. Obviously, it would be unrealistic to expect others to understand Singaporean Muslims if they limited their activities, movements and contributions to themselves only.[f] The community was spurred to reach out to other Singaporeans/faiths to open spaces for dialogues to promote understanding. Singaporean Muslims were again reminded that they are the ones who need to adapt to the changing environment and not demand that the environment changes to suit their circumstances.

The way forward for Singaporean Muslims to rise up to this challenge is to strive for excellence in whatever they do and treat knowledge acquisition as a religious duty. He regarded the good Singaporean Muslim as one who advanced the cause of Islam and effectively enhanced its image by displaying the previous traits and "by being a moral person, a model worker, neighbour, colleague, student, parent, employer, citizen".[g] Truly, the good Muslim "by deed and thought is also a good citizen of Singapore who is an asset and plays an integral part in Singapore's nation-building".

However, Muslims in Singapore are not isolated from events affecting the Muslim *ummah* (community)

---

[f] Speech by Mr Abdullah Tarmugi, Minister for Community Development and Minister-in-Charge of Muslim Affairs (1993–2002), at the Hari Raya Get Together at the Istana on Friday, 21 December 2001.

[g] Speech by Mr Abdullah Tarmugi, Minister for Community Development and Minister-in-Charge of Muslim Affairs (1993–2002), at the Hari Raya Get Together on Friday, 5 January 2001.

at large and they must be able to prepare themselves to face and adapt to the challenges and the opportunities afforded by a rapidly changing global environment. An oft-repeated reminder was the need to be cognizant about global and regional developments impacting the country and the community. They were encouraged to take a broader perspective of the world around them and not to be inward looking. Whilst cognizant of different orientations and ideologies, they were reminded that no one group has a monopoly over truth or the answers to the issues facing the community. As such, the community must avoid dividing themselves into factions, with each championing their narrow interests and concerns.[h] Worst still, they should not be distracted by trivial matters, matters that have traction only within the community or matters that are not beneficial.

What kind of a Singaporean Muslim community did Mr Abdullah envision? That would be one where the Muslim Singaporean is able to prepare his/herself to face and adapt to external challenges, but without having to shed and lose their identity as a Muslim and as a Malay.

2002–2014 Journey towards Excellence

A few months after 9/11, when Dr Yaacob Ibrahim took over the role as the Minister-in-Charge of Muslim Affairs in 2002, he not only had to turn his predecessor's vision into reality, he also inherited the challenges and was confronted with events that had an impact on the community's sense of unease. They include the 9/11 terrorist attacks which had raised untoward suspicion towards the community; a sense of resurgent Islam that motivated parents of four primary school girls to make them wear the *tudung* (headscarf) to school, thereby challenging the uniform policy of the state[i]; calming

---

[h] Speech by Mr Abdullah Tarmugi, Minister for Community Development and Minister-in-Charge of Muslim Affairs (1993–2002), at the Hari Raya Get Together on Friday, 18 March 1994.
[i] In 2002, four 7-year-old girls wore the headscarves to school along with their uniforms. This was against the Ministry of Education's no-headscarf rule for students attending government schools. The four girls were subsequently suspended.

community concerns about the *madrasah* issue in the context of Compulsory Education[j]; and the leadership debate[k] that ensued within the community.

Compulsory Education (CE) to Help Build Cohesion

CE was implemented in Singapore in 2003. The first cohort of pupils coming under CE are Singapore Citizen children born between 2 January 1996 and 1 January 1997 who are residing in Singapore.

The two key objectives of CE are to give our children:

- A common core of knowledge which will provide a strong foundation for further education and training to prepare them for a knowledge-based economy; and
- A common educational experience which will help to build national identity and cohesion.

On the issue of employability of *madrasah* students, the *madrasahs* have been revamped to focus on not only producing the community's future religious elite but to allow students who excel in academic subjects to go on to wider career options. For Islam to be of greater relevance and a living faith to Muslims here, the religious education curriculum has been reviewed by MUIS. An extensive and flexible system of religious instruction has been rolled-out to meet the varying needs and the different ages for the community. Parents

---

[j] This was raised by PM Goh Chok Tong in his 1999 National Day Rally speech. *Madrasah* education was discussed in the context of Compulsory Education and the drop-out rates and employability of madrasah students.

[k] The idea of an independent, non-partisan collective leadership for the Malay/Muslim community was first mooted at the First National Convention of Malay/ Muslim Professionals held in 1990. The second National Convention (in 2000) of Malay/Muslim Professionals Steering Committee proposed a Collective Leadership that reflects a desire to have a say in issues and developments that affect the community or the nation as a whole. The proposed system of Collective Leadership is meant to provide room and space for greater participation without having to negate the role of anyone, including the Malay/Muslim MPs.

and children have received positively the aLIVE[1] programme that offers learners to be a blessing to society
by excelling in whatever they do in their spiritual
motivation.

Before the turn of the new millennia, the decision-
making was led by the Malay/Muslim political leadership with inputs and support from leading Muslim
community leaders to mobilise the community to
confront challenges. The new millennia witnessed a
demand for other sections of the community to have
a greater say on issues that affect the community as a
whole. The proposed system of Collective Leadership is
meant to provide room and space for greater participation without having to negate the role of anyone, including the Malay/Muslim MPs. As the community entered
the second decade of the millennium, the response to
this demand was to move towards a less top-down
approach, which involved a wider cross section of community, religious and mosque leaders, professionals
and youths. The formation of the Community Leadership
Forum (CLF) had strengthened and synergised Malay/
Muslim organisations and institutions so that more can
be achieved for the community. The CLF has brought
together Malay/Muslim organisations to coordinate
and collaborate on the many needed programmes to
meet the challenges of the community. Unfortunately,
the CLF has turned out to be mainly operational —
organising social intervention programmes, youth
activities, and educational seminars — instead of
engaging in reflection and discussions with community
leaders and other thought leaders. The Suara
Musyawarah platform was another bottom-up initiative
led by community leaders and leading community personalities to gather views from across all segments of
the Malay/Muslim community about their aspirations
and make recommendations to address pertinent concerns. This independent committee was set-up to

---

[1] aLIVE (Learning Islamic Values Everyday) is a comprehensive Islamic Education programme
conducted by MUIS for children and youth between 5–24 years of age. Its primary objective is
to impart in young Muslims a religious education which is relevant and applicable to contemporary times.

collect feedback and suggestions[m] that are much broader in scope compared to the previous feedback and review exercises that were more organisation and programme-centric.

On the issue of a global resurgent Islam after 9/11, besides the negative impact on Muslims in general, the positive side effect of rising religiosity in the Malay/Muslim community manifests a very active religious life, with many stepping forward to help the under-privileged. Given the myriad understandings and manifestations of global resurgent Islam in the local context, could one posit a question whether there is such a thing as a "Singaporean Muslim"? Dr Yaacob thinks that there is, or at least he envisions that Singaporean Muslims should reflect a religious life that is inclusive, progressive and adaptable. When Malay/Muslim Singaporeans adopt a progressive mindset which allows innovation even in religious thinking, this enables them to reap the benefits of the modern world that does not entail abandoning one's faith but actually enhancing it. Singaporean Muslims must be able to demonstrate that Islam is compatible and relevant across time and space. The community must make the best of it without holding out for the right time and circumstances to show the importance of Islam. Elucidating further, Dr Yaacob states that:

> We cannot wait for another Andalusia to come by before we can make meaningful contributions to nation-building and humanity. What we need to do is to strive to make the spirit of Andalusia exist wherever we maybe. The spirit of inquiry, innovation, discovery, continuous learning, and contribution to public and community life is more important to Muslims than any move to construct or reconstruct institutions that pull Muslims away from the rest of the world.[n]

---

[m] The final report from this committee was delivered in July 2013 and available at http://suaramusyawarah.com in English, Malay and an executive summary in Tamil.

[n] Speech by Dr Yaacob Ibrahim, Minister for the Environment and Water Resources and Minister-in-Charge of Muslim Affairs (2002-present), at the Hari Raya Get Together at the Istana on Friday, 19 November 2004.

What he wanted to see is the community rooted in the values and fundamentals of Islam, operating confidently with a strong Singaporean Muslim identity. In this regard, the project to build a Community of Excellence° was overlaid by the Singapore Muslim Identity project. This identity project was to "give coherence and guidance to the development of this unique blend of being both Muslim and Singaporean".ᵖ For the Malay/Muslim Singaporean, his/her identity is closely intertwined with his/her identity as a Muslim. The Muslim Singaporean is not "any less a Muslim than any other Muslim or any less Singaporean than other Singaporean". As Singapore citizens, they supported the development of the nation and that their position as Muslims is recognised by the state. But this does not mean that the state must accept everything that the Singaporean Muslim believes in and just as well, it does not mean that everything that happens in Singapore is accepted by them. Singaporeans Muslims accept that they "live in a secular society with the general norms and the principles of good governance". Should there be conflicts or disagreement in values and ideals, the goal is to promote understanding and respect of each other's position. The community realises and accepts that Singapore is their homeland and they share this land with communities of other faiths and backgrounds. The ethos of the Singaporean Muslim is that they care to share their values but they in turn do not impose their values on others. This ethos is important because it relates to the idea of integration as part of nation-building. One misconception about integration is that, it requires the different communities to adopt a common set of norms. In Dr. Yaacob's view:

Integration does not mean homogeneity. Integration is about participating actively in the nation's life.

° Speech by Dr Yaacob Ibrahim, Acting Minister for Community Development and Minister-in-Charge of Muslim Affairs (2002-present), at the Hari Raya Get Together at the Istana on Friday, 13 December 2002.
ᵖ Speech by Dr Yaacob Ibrahim, Minister for the Environment and Water Resources and Minister-in-Charge of Muslim Affairs (2002-present), at the Hari Raya Get Together at the Istana on Friday, 18 November 2005.

*Integration is about being together, being a part of
the nation, and not being apart from the nation.*

Thus it was wrong to suggest that the Malay/Muslim
community wants to stand apart from the other communities. In fact, they want to work, build and protect
the common space with all Singaporeans. It falls on the
shoulders of our community leaders to continually
guard against fashionably and Islamically "correct"
ideas from abroad (or from the Internet) that the general Muslim community and particularly the youth may
be unduly influenced. It becomes important too that as
a Muslim minority community, they must not become
rigid and inflexible in their way of life and thus, are
unable to integrate into the wider community. This
myth that the Muslim community is "rigid and inflexible" is one they must be ready to dispel through act and
voice. The general Malay/Muslim community and our
youth must feel strongly the need for them to be partners with other Singaporeans in the building of a good
society here in Singapore. Hence, Muslims here must
also speak up against all forms of extremist and prejudiced views and stand with those who speak with reasons that seek peace and understanding and that cares
for humanity.

Singaporean Muslims here must recognise that
they live in an open, urban society which is multiracial,
multireligious and increasingly cosmopolitan in character. There is the realisation that the state is secular in
outlooks even though it recognises, the place religions
have in the life of each community. The formation of the
Inter-Racial and Confidence Circles (IRCC) showed the
Government's aim to strengthen the trust and understanding between Singaporeans of all races. Undeniably,
we cannot pretend or expect that everyone understands Islam and Malays/Muslims completely.
Misunderstandings and misconceptions can and do
exist. So it becomes incumbent on the community not
to shy away from coming forward to dispel myths and
correct misconceptions that may arise in the course of
public discussions about Islam or Muslims. In other
words, Muslims must not only speak out against actions

detrimental to Muslim interests, but also other forms of bigotry and hate speech that affects non-Muslims. Dr Yaacob adds:

> *Our community and our young must feel strongly the need for us to be partners with other Singaporeans in the building of a good society here in Singapore. As a result of all these, we reflect a religious life that is inclusive, progressive and adaptable — an Islam that lives and flourishes anywhere at all times.*

Clearly, the Singaporean Muslim community must make the best out of every situation. They will need to remain focused on tackling the issues of education, employability, family and youth, which have a long-term impact on the community, rooted in the values and fundamentals of Islam, operating confidently with a strong Singaporean Muslim identity.

On the other issues of social upliftment, many new community initiatives were rolled-out under his watch with the aim of building a "stronger and resilient community" and he observed that the community had changed, "displaying a progressive approach" through dialogues and discussions and "commendably moved-on after reaffirming their commitment to a multiracial and religious Singapore". According to Dr Yaacob, education still remained the approach to empower the community to uplift themselves. The community's efforts in education have seen Malay/Muslim students making discernible achievements in their studies. They have made the community proud in both the academic and other diverse areas such as the arts, sports and music. He noted young Malays/Muslims are also venturing into new fields such as jewellery design, fine arts, multimedia, IT, life sciences and languages. While commendable, he urged the young Malays/Muslims to be open and outward-looking, brave enough to seize opportunities abroad wherever these may arise. In doing so, the community expands their learning, experience and perspectives by bringing new impetus to the growth and survival of the community. He encouraged parents to ensure their children take advantage of

Singapore's world-class education system, which offers multiple pathways to meet their child's pace and talent to develop their full potential. To ensure the low-income families are not left out, a $10 million Malay/Muslim Education Trust Fund (ETF)[q] was setup to assist and support their children from pre-school and early years of school till upper secondary. The future looks positive as many Malay/Muslim parents have realised the value education brings to the individual; indeed the family, the community and all are ready to commit resources to give the best to their children. The next challenge for the community is to become life-long learners to ensure life-long employability.

Despite this undeniable progress in the educational field and the tangible success of Malay/Muslim students in the national exams, it was revealed that about 400 to 500 Malay/Muslim students dropped out of primary and secondary schools every year.[q] One of the reasons identified for this drop-out problem was that such students came from large families which, in the current context, do not allow parents to raise their children in a nurturing manner. In some families, it was found that those who "marry, divorce, remarry, and divorce again" are composed of young men and women who did not complete secondary education. The concern about the lack of stability in the family structure with different sets of siblings from different parents could result in an emerging underclass. Children from such families are disadvantaged educationally as they do not have a stable family structure. Such families may not be able to cope or those who are unaware of the changing environment face a "cycle of social deprivation" and will require assistance from the larger community. He advised that the community must avoid being the new poor, that is those who cannot and will not learn. Hence, a lot of resources and attention have been focused on the youth and family, on education and employability to develop positive life skills and instil a

---

[q] The Education Trust Fund (ETF) was launched in 2003 with the objective to help low income Malay/Muslim children who are in their critical educational years.

learning attitude. To undertake outreach and tackle the social issues faced by low-income and disadvantaged families, the community had in place a structured institutional support system. Leveraging on resource pooling and sharing, the Enhanced Mosque Cluster together with two MENDAKI@Heartlands centres and other Malay/Muslim organisations have been collaborating to provide community outreach and new programmes for this vulnerable group.[r] The community's key Islamic institutions *viz.* the mosques, the Syariah Court and the Registry of Muslim Marriages have also added new functions to assist and support the social and spiritual development of the community.[s]

Dr. Yaacob observed that Malay/Muslim Singaporeans have accepted the system of meritocracy. By meritocracy, he means that "every student or worker who does well knows that it is by his or her own merit."[s] One consequence of this personal success was the rising affluence that had afforded those who can perpetuate their status and sometimes, this may be at the expense of the less well-off. He urged successful Malay/Muslim Singaporeans not to abandon the less well-off in the community. He remains concerned with an emerging underclass where families with multiple problems grow from one generation to the next, and of successful Malays/Muslims who feel their responsibility is only towards themselves. If the better-off or middle class Malays/Muslims feel their success were achieved through their own efforts and decide to abdicate their responsibility to help the rest of the community, then the community as whole will be poorer as a

---

[r] Speech by Dr Yaacob Ibrahim, Minister for Communications and Information and Minister-in-Charge of Muslim Affairs (2002-present), at the Hari Raya Get Together at Sheraton Towers on Friday, 23 August 2013.
[s] Mosques have extended their role to link-up with community organisations, so that referrals and support can be arranged for people who need them (Speech by Dr Yaacob Ibrahim, Minister for the Environment and Water Resources and Minister-in-Charge of Muslim Affairs (2002-present), at the Hari Raya Get Together at Shangri-La Hotel on Friday, 17 September 2010). The latter two institutions now look into early intervention measures to save families and marriages to offer hope for a better future (Speech by Dr Yaacob Ibrahim, Minister for Communications and Information and Minister-in-Charge of Muslim Affairs (2002-present), at the Hari Raya Get Together at the Fairmont Singapore on Friday, 31 August 2012).

result. He cautioned Singaporean Malays/Muslims to avoid classifying segments in their community as "winners and losers". In the quest to raise attention to the issues and concerns of the community, he reminded those with a genuine desire to contribute, to do so in a civil manner with the understanding of the facts and not for the purpose of attracting personal attention. The community's unity and intra-group relationship should not be strained as a consequence.

The middle class and upwardly mobile must step forward to help and not abandon the less advantaged members of the community, as this would be worse for everyone. Indeed, there are strong signs that the community's spirit of *gotong-royong* is enjoying a revival. There is a strong sense of compassion to help those who are less fortunate. Harnessing this energy to affect transformation of the individual, family and community and to take greater ownership of solving the problems they faced gives them a sense of pride. Without this strong sense of pride and sense of shame that goes together, the community cannot progress.[5] This will strengthen the community's spirit of resilience and being less dependent on others.

Moving forward, a vision of a Community of Excellence[15] was mooted as a road map for the community to embrace the challenges and changing times. At its simplest, it is the idea of excelling at everything one does. To achieve this vision of excellence, the Malays/Muslims must become a learning community. Learning here implies an attitude of the mind that is constantly reflecting, searching for deeper understanding, exploring options and seeking out solutions and applying these principles to solve the underlying social challenges that confront the community. However, excellence does not mean winning at all cost. Instead it is about putting aside time and effort, possessing the ability to overcome disappointment and being resilient. It should be seen as an aspirational goal to realise our potential as a productive member of society by improving our contributions and helping others to uplift themselves. And neither was this vision to be achieved independent of what happens in Singapore. In a nutshell:

> *[E]xcellence is doing our best in what we do —*
> *whether we are students, parents, daily-rated work-*
> *ers or senior executives. If every one of us puts in our*
> *best as individuals, looks out for one another and*
> *works together as a community, we could achieve*
> *better outcomes for our community. As a nation we*
> *have risen against the odds, as a community we can*
> *too.*[t]

Conclusion

The Hari Raya speeches of the three Ministers-in-Charge of Muslim Affairs from 1981 to 2014, in a sense, do reflect the narrative of the making of the Singaporean Malay/Muslim. They chart a minority community faced with serious challenges of educational and social back-wardness at the dawn of independence, to a commu-nity that could rely on itself to compete in a meritocratic society. Undeniably, the Singaporean Malay/Muslim community "have painstakingly dealt with the twin challenge of problems and aspiration".[21] Exhorting on a change in mindset for self-reliance, life-long learning, community unity and a desire for excellence combined with institutional support, the Malay/Muslim leaders have managed to get a positive response from the com-munity, where tangible strides and successes can make the community proud. Most importantly, the Malay/Muslim community has developed and progressed in a uniquely Singaporean ethos of a secular, multiracial society, inclusive and cosmopolitan in character, where multiple identities are accepted and need not be exclu-sive where the Malay/Muslim is comfortable being Muslim and Singaporean. In the next 50 years, the main challenge of the Minister-in-Charge of Muslim Affairs

---

[t] Speech by Dr Yaacob Ibrahim, Minister for Communications and Information and Minister-in-Charge of Muslim Affairs (2002-present), at the Hari Raya Get Together at the Fairmont Singapore on Friday, 31 August 2012.

would be to forge a consensus and maintain community unity in an increasingly diverse and contested national and global space. If the future Malay/Muslim leadership continue to listen to alternative voices of the community and continue to chart a path in line with national and global developments, the values that have been inculcated in the first 50 years would indeed be invaluable.

REINFORCE MULTICULTURAL IDENTITY

"

The majority community should take keen interest in our Malay, Indian and other cultures.

We should instead evolve, adapt and strengthen our own cultures, and take a keen interest in each other's cultures. This will allow us to deepen our Singapore identity, and take real pride in multiculturalism in Singapore.

There is something in our cultural identities that was about the ethos of contributing to the community.

When I mean deepen our identity, I do not mean we dilute each of our cultural identity, I do not mean we fuse everything into one culture, I think if we try to do that I think we will end up with a weak and confused culture and a weak and a confused sense of identity among Singaporeans.

We must also take a keen interest in each other's cultures and participate wherever possible in each other's cultures.

We have to preserve and deepen our respective cultures ... take a keen interest in each other's cultures, and participate wherever possible in each other's cultures.

...but for all Singaporeans to learn about our evolving Chinese culture in Singapore, just as the majority community should take a keen interest in our Malay culture, our Indian culture, and the cultures of the regions around us."

Tharman Shanmugaratnam
Deputy Prime Minister and
Coordinating Minister for Economic and Social Policies
10 February 2016

HOW DID THE POST OF "MINISTER-IN-CHARGE OF MUSLIM AFFAIRS" COME ABOUT?

Historically, the Muslim minister in cabinet was entrusted with the additional responsibility of overseeing Muslim affairs in Singapore. Encik Othman Wok, the first Malay Minister in the post-independence cabinet[a] (as the then Minister for Culture and Social Affairs) was entrusted with that task.

The post of "Minister-in-Charge of Muslim Affairs" was non-existent until 1977, when Dr Ahmad Mattar, who was also the Minister of Social Affairs, was also appointed as the de-facto Minister-in-Charge of Muslim Affairs.[b] At a Press Conference to announce the new cabinet line-up after the 1984 General Election, it was announced that Dr Ahmad Mattar was to go to the Ministry of the Environment and S. Dhanabalan was to take over the Ministry of Social Affairs (subsequently renamed Ministry of Community Development). The First Deputy Prime Minister-designate (DPM) Goh Chok Tong, who chaired the Press Conference, was asked by one of the journalists, if Majlis Ugama Islam Singapura (MUIS)[c] will remain under Community Development or be transferred to Dr Ahmad Mattar's care. DPM Goh's reply was, MUIS will remain under Community Development but Dr Ahmad Mattar would be in-charge of the administration of MUIS.[d] In an interview the next day, Dr Ahmad Mattar said his appointment as the new Minister for Environment was a good thing for him. He was also glad he would still be responsible for MUIS as well as the affairs of the Muslim community.[e]

---

[a] The first Malay minister in the self-government cabinet in 1959 was Encik Ahmad Ibrahim.
[b] Between 1977–1984, there was still no Minister-in-Charge of Muslim Affairs. Dr Ahmad Mattar was then the Minister of Social Affairs and like his predecessor, Othman Wok, was entrusted with the responsibilities of looking after Muslim affairs.
[c] Islamic Religious Council of Singapore
[d] The Straits Times, 1 January 1985, *My two goals — by the striker*.
[e] Berita Harian, 2 January 1985, *Mattar: Pindah kementerian baik bagi saya*.

The title remains to this day, even though the designation was not in the Table of Precedence. The other Minister-in-Charge of Muslim Affairs was Mr Abdullah Tarmugi (who was also the Minister for Community Development) and currently, Dr Yaacob Ibrahim, who was the Minister for Community Development, before being appointed as the Minister for Communications and Information and the Minister-in-Charge of Cyber Security.

CHAPTER 8

Editors' Note

This text of the speech by Dr Yaacob Ibrahim, Minister-in-Charge of Muslim Affairs, is reproduced here in full because it reflected the thinking of the Minister about the community's vision and mission to establish the Community of Excellence for the Malay/Muslim community.

LEARNING TO BE A COMMUNITY OF EXCELLENCE — TEXT OF SPEECH BY DR YAACOB IBRAHIM, MINISTER FOR COMMUNITY DEVELOPMENT AND SPORTS AND MINISTER-IN-CHARGE OF MUSLIM AFFAIRS, AT THE HARI RAYA GET-TOGETHER, ISTANA, 28 NOVEMBER 2003

The many heart-warming stories that I have heard over the past year provide much hope that things are moving in the right direction for our community. Malays/Muslims — as individuals, families, and organisations — continue to show commitment towards learning, towards volunteerism, and towards nation-building and the community's progress. They reflect a spirit of excellence and a sense of achievement. Allow me to share with you some of the stories that represent the good that is happening in our community.

The Learning Community

Our community has been bitten by the learning bug. As an example, I would like to name three National Library Board employees who obtained their degrees even though it has been more than two decades since they left school. Madam Rohayah Mohd Lani, Madam Hameedah Ibrahim and Madam Marhama Mohamad, all mothers in their mid-forties, showed great perseverance in juggling work, family commitments, diploma and then degree programmes at night, and graduating with honours. I must also applaud the support given by their families.

For us to achieve our vision of a community of excellence, we must become a learning community. But we must not take it to mean that learning is only possible through books and at classrooms. Four years ago, MENDAKI (The Council for the Development of the Muslim Community) ran a programme to teach parents how to run a reading programme at home. When asked what reading materials they had at home, the parents said that they had none. When asked if they had newspapers and magazines, they said they did. They had thought that books, and only school textbooks, constituted reading material for their children. MENDAKI helped the parents realise that reading and literacy can be nurtured through various materials and activities almost anytime, anywhere.

> *For us to achieve our vision of a community of excellence, we must become a learning community.*

Learning implies an attitude of the mind that is constantly reflecting, searching for deeper understanding, exploring options and seeking out solutions. For this attitude to take root within the community, each and every one of us needs a learning curriculum. What do I mean when I say "a learning curriculum"? Essentially it is an awareness of our current situation and the things we need to learn to improve upon our current situation.

The story of Madam Roswati Kassim, the owner of RH Fashion, illustrates this attitude. Due to family circumstances, she had to stop work. But she soon started selling ready-made clothes from her home. In order to better understand consumer trends, she would frequently walk along Arab Street and other places to observe the latest styles and fashion. In modern parlance, she was doing market research. Or I would say she is learning by understanding her environment. Madam Roswati has a learning curriculum for herself. Over time she increased her business and is now the owner of five boutiques and a bridal house.

Consider the example of the low-income parents who were part of MENDAKI's pilot scheme to empower them to provide home support for their children in learning Mathematics. It was not the intention to train the parents to become Mathematics teachers. That would have been impossible. But it is possible, and, I dare say, MENDAKI succeeded in raising their awareness so that they could play a role in supporting and nurturing their children's learning process.

By giving the parents simple ideas on interactive games and asking them to observe their children's reactions, we helped them understand the challenges their kids face and the response needed to meet these challenges. In essence, we helped the parents learn the process by which their kids learn Mathematics. In the next stage of this scheme, we are giving parents further tips and skills.

Their children will enter primary school next year. Over time each parent should develop his or her own learning curriculum for supporting and nurturing his or her child. Every individual, family, and organisation should develop a customised learning curriculum.

Both MUIS (The Islamic Religious Council of Singapore) and MENDAKI have developed in-house processes to become learning organisations. MENDAKI has put in place research and information-sharing units, which seek to develop learning instincts in its entire staff. MUIS has embarked on a series of in-house consultations and retreats with various stakeholders to better understand the needs and demands of our religious life. As a result, a learning process is being embedded in everything that MUIS does.

I am also glad to announce that MUIS is now studying the key areas to focus on in the coming years, and these will be implemented either through new programmes or established ongoing programmes. MUIS should be able to make known its three-year plan in January. The call for learning is closely intertwined with the history of Islam.

After the Battle of Badr, the Prophet released those captives who agreed to teach the Muslims how to read

At their height, both Cordoba and Baghdad were international centres of learning, trade and culture. Within these great cities and their universities, learning was encouraged and supported by the rulers. Scholars — be they Muslim, Christian or Jewish — flocked to these places.

and write. At their height, both Cordoba and Baghdad were international centres of learning, trade and culture. Within these great cities and their universities, learning was encouraged and supported by the rulers. Scholars — be they Muslim, Christian or Jewish — flocked to these places. The diversity and multicultural atmosphere created an environment for learning and discovery. It was an inclusive atmosphere that formed an ideal setting for knowledge and ideas to flourish. It was truly a learning society.

Such an environment did not just produce Muslim scholars. From Muslim Spain came Moses Maimonedes or Ibn Maymon, the Jewish philosopher who was a contemporary of Ibn Rushd, and Avicebron or Ibn Gabirol, the Jewish poet and philosopher. Both studied and wrote in Arabic. Muslim thinkers such as Al Farabi, Miskawayh and Al Ghazali inspired many medieval Christian thinkers. It was a cosmopolitan world then where cultural exchanges and inclusiveness were the norm. Even Al Ghazali's works were peppered with quotes from the Christian epistles.

If we look back to such a time as an example of the world's glorious past, it is the idea of learning that will help us to build a glorious future. Many modern writers and thinkers have said that the new poor will be those who cannot or will not learn. Our community cannot afford to be the new poor. Our recent focus on youth and family, education, and employability reflects our concerns about whether we are using the ability we have within ourselves to learn from others and from our own past experiences, so as to move our community forward.

Many modern writers and thinkers have said that the new poor will be those who cannot or will not learn. Our community cannot afford to be the new poor.

Our community's battle against drug abuse is a long-standing one. The drug problem affects our young and hence our ability to grow as a community. In recent years, there has been some indication that we have seen the worst, and that things may improve. Indeed it has taken a long time and a tremendous toll on our families and community.

But there can be no let-up in our efforts; neither should the lessons learnt be forgotten. Can we learn from this experience and successfully address the underlying issues that surface in antisocial behaviour, juvenile delinquency and premature school-leaving? Can we draw lessons from the current unemployment situation that is a consequence of our pre-independence born generation having missed out on completing their formal education?

Similarly, can we look at the issue of young couples who go through marriage despite not being ready, and then ending up as dysfunctional families and weighing the community down? These are not new issues. But if we fail to learn from these as fathers and mothers, and, as community leaders, not evaluate, put in place, and see through long-term strategies that will help to reduce social ills, then we will become the new poor.

I urge all of us to work together to build a Malay/ Muslim community that forges ahead because of its learning culture.

Contributing to Nation-Building

In the midst of our efforts to secure a better future for our community, our contribution to nation building has continued unabated. When our nation faces a serious threat we rise to the occasion. Nurses Hamidah Ismail and Ashirdahwani Asmawi were among the many brave-hearted healthcare professionals who valiantly formed the frontline in our battle against SARS. Hamidah Ismail lost her life. When I visited her family, her mother told me amidst tears that Hamidah had just done her job. Hamidah's husband and children were very sad but also proud of her for having done the right thing — caring for her patients and helping to make Singapore a safer place for all.

When our nation faces a serious threat we rise to the occasion. Nurses Hamidah Ismail and Ashirdahwani Asmawi were among the many brave-hearted healthcare professionals who valiantly formed the frontline in our battle against SARS. Hamidah Ismail lost her life.

Similarly, in pitch-dark conditions and choppy waters, officers from the Police Coast Guard risked their lives to rescue survivors from the unfortunate RSS Courageous. Senior Staff Sergeant Mohd Ramli Mohd Shariff, Sergeant Mohd Faizal Ali and Corporal (NS) Sukiman Isnin were recognised along with their colleagues and awarded the Police Medal of Valour.

When we needed to restructure our CPF system in order to make our economy more competitive, our Malay/Muslim union leaders took on the role of explaining the rationale to our workers. It was an unenviable task given that many workers would have to face some financial difficulty. But we got the workers to understand through the efforts of such union leaders.

Similarly, when the war in Iraq brought about concerns within the community, leaders like Haji Wan Hussin Zoohri helped Malay/Muslims reflect our sentiments about the humanitarian impact of the war, without compromising the government's security perspective.

Our institutions, organisations and mosques continue to play important social roles within the community and nation. MUIS embarked on a worthy project this past Ramadan. Bridging from the norm of iftar-based events, MUIS launched three programmes aimed at seeding the idea of service to the needy as a pillar of our religious life.

MUIS's programmes showed that even as we fast in the holy month of Ramadan, society's interests and needs remain central and must be looked after. The community is also making strides in the areas of culture and heritage. MESRA has for the past two years organised Gentarasa — a commendable effort that showcases budding talent. The Malay Heritage Centre is fast developing at Sultan Gate and will be completed in the second half of 2004. Gedung Kuning will in fact be able to host Hari Raya gatherings next month. With all our cooperation and efforts, the Malay Heritage Centre can grow into cultural hub that all Singaporeans are proud of.

Meanwhile, PERDAUS successfully launched Mercy Relief — a humanitarian relief effort with roots within the community — as a national organisation. When the Bijani twins of Iran passed away, Ba'alwie Mosque came forward to organise special prayers for the sisters. People from all walks of life and all faiths who had keenly followed their tale of courage came to the mosque to pay their last respects.

As we gathered in shared humanity, our thoughts were with the twins; recognising that in their unfortunate passing lay not despair but hope of a better future.

Volunteerism — Our Part in Nation-Building

Our efforts have contributed to the building of a more compassionate and humane society. When MENDAKI made the call for more volunteers, many came forward. Mr Michael Koh came forward in 2002 to assist in MENDAKI's HELP or Home Enabling Learning Programme. He started by visiting and reading together with a lower primary Malay/Muslim student identified by MENDAKI. Over time he also assisted the student's younger brother with his homework and reading. He has now started helping a third student. He is doing this without being paid. Madam Endoon Omar is another example. She started out visiting and reading to a lower primary child once a month. But as her concern for the child grew, she visited him twice a week and for three hours at a time, way beyond the normal one hour. She would also buy books for the child with her own money. These two examples show that people do good work if the environment is supportive.

Yet another example is that of a mosque leader who uses his culinary skill to reach out and contribute to the good of society. As a mosque leader, he has built up a corps of young volunteers who diligently serve the community during the holy month of Ramadan. His earnest efforts have attracted the attention of donors of other faiths and they have contributed rice and ingredients for the *iftar* at his mosque. For two years in a row, he has put his skills at cooking briyani to a worthy cause, the President's Challenge. Indeed Haji Alla'udin Mohamed, Chairman of Khalid Mosque in Joo Chiat, is a shining example of a quiet but resolute man contributing to building the good society. By doing good he encourages others to do good too.

> *No matter how small the contribution, it is through the giving of our time, resources, energy, and skills that we help to build a good society here in Singapore.*

These are efforts worth emulating as we seek to define our community as a community of contributors. No matter how small the contribution, it is through the giving of our time, resources, energy, and skills that we help to build a good society here in Singapore.

Community Leaders' Forum — Update

Against the backdrop of these events, 40 community leaders came together to discuss and brainstorm strategic issues facing the community. The Community of Excellence Leaders' Forum with the Prime Minister took place on 11 October 2003, after five months of hard work by the leaders. The community leaders engaged in six focus group discussions to discuss three key issues, namely Employment and Employability, Education, and Youth and Family. Apart from these discussions, the Malay/Muslim MPs also organised six sessions to discuss the issues with various groups including students, workers, and families.

It was a comprehensive exercise to consult and gather useful insights into these issues and subsequently formulate strategic directions for the community. The process was supported by a wide cross section of the community with both SPH and Mediacorp news teams playing a valuable role in highlighting key issues and ideas.

Our Prime Minister has given his support to the strategic directions proposed by the leaders and suggested the formation of a Steering Committee to oversee the implementation of the key strategies. This will be done soon.

In fact, I am happy to report that work in identifying the key programmes has started. All the Malay/Muslim MPs are overseeing specific tasks to develop these programmes. MENDAKI has been providing the secretariat support. Two initiatives have emerged from this effort. The first is in the area of youth development where programmes are being designed for upstream intervention.

The underlying strategy is a simple one. If we equip our young with positive life skills, they will become more resilient and less prone to negative social behaviour in the future. Our hope is that our young will make the right life choices. To achieve this we need to build a supporting infrastructure within the community. We need a community of mentors who will help to guide our youths as they negotiate the demands of life. This will enhance their connectedness to the community.

If we equip our young with positive life skills, they will become more resilient and less prone to negative social behaviour in the future.

The second initiative is to provide opportunities for Malay/Muslim workers and other adults to engage in entrepreneurial activities as an option, apart from paid employment. Specifically, this initiative will look into the development of micro-business opportunities for our community. This is to address the issue of employability. But our efforts to encourage the more vulnerable workers to go for training and retraining will continue.

Apart from the above, efforts are underway to address the challenges of our community's educational performance. MENDAKI recognised a record number of five Malays/Muslims who achieved first class honours this year. Following the announcement of the PSLE results recently, Muhammad Haris and Norhaliim Putera shared the spotlight with Daniel Chew at St Hilda's Primary. In fact, in four out of the last five years, there has been a Malay/Muslim student among the nation's top 10. Generally, more Malay students are doing better at national examinations and tertiary institutions. However, a more long-term strategy is needed if we are to see more Malays do better academically on a sustained basis.

In this regard, we have identified two areas of concern: firstly, the school-readiness of our children; and secondly, the role of parents as learning mediators. Many studies have shown that going to pre-school or kindergarten helps to prepare our young for primary school. Having parents that are aware of and able to support their kids' learning processes will result in better performance.

Community of Excellence — On Track

The examples of Muhammad Salman who was named Senior Student of the Year at St Joseph's Institution; the three mothers getting their degrees while working and balancing family life; the Police Coast Guard officers who handled rescue operations of the RSS Courageous; the many professionals who assisted in containing SARS; the mother who volunteers to read to a primary school child so that he will have a better future; the mosque leader who tirelessly worked to raise funds for charity with his cooking skills; the community leaders who came together to forge a common cause — these are but a reflection of the spirit of a community wanting to do better.

Our challenge is to make this spirit a lasting legacy that our community bequeaths to succeeding generations of Singaporeans. The Quran urges us to race with one another to do good work. By competing to do good work and not building edifices, we leave behind noble values for all of mankind. Just like the early Muslims, who through their desire for learning and knowledge facilitated scholars from other faiths, our effort at doing good work will bring out the best in all. This is a tremendous contribution in shaping a national life that is compassionate and humane.

The legacy of the late Miss Hamimah Abu, the literature teacher who met with a fatal accident in Tasmania just after completing her Masters thus remains with us. She had touched the lives of her ex-classmates at RGS and NUS, her students and colleagues at Nanyang JC, as well as the many others she had come into contact with. This is a remarkable testimony of what a good Muslim and Singaporean we can all be.

CHAPTER 9

Editors' Note

Multiracialism is one of the pillars of Singapore's society. So is meritocracy. There lies a challenge of making this work in a dynamic Singapore. This speech was delivered back in 1995 when Singapore celebrated its 30th anniversary of independence and it reflected some of the concerns of multiracialism then. Indeed these concerns have been there since independence. Multiracialism cannot be taken for granted and deserves scrutiny and reflection as the Singapore society evolves. Founding Prime Minister, the late Mr Lee Kuan Yew, requested Zainul Abidin to send him a copy of this speech when he came to know about it. Apparently, he was interested to the reference about economic growth rates and its relation to racial harmony.

NEW DYNAMICS OF MULTIRACIAL SINGAPORE AS SEEN IN 1995 — TEXT OF SPEECH BY MR ZAINUL ABIDIN RASHEED, EDITOR, BERITA HARIAN, CEO OF MENDAKI AND PRESIDENT OF THE ISLAMIC RELIGIOUS COUNCIL OF SINGAPORE (MUIS) AT THE PEOPLE'S ASSOCIATION LECTURE SERIES, SATURDAY 21 JANUARY 1995 AT THE PEOPLE'S ASSOCIATION AUDITORIUM, KALLANG

This year we celebrate 30 years of independence. Beyond the grand celebrations in store, it will also provide us the opportunity to pause from our busy and bustling life to ask ourselves questions about nationbuilding and nationhood.

First, we need to understand what Singapore represents and who are we, the Singaporeans. Our Singapore has been described as not just another country. Ours is unique.

The economic miracle which we have made possible is a source of pride not only for us Singaporeans but also for those outside. Both in the developed and the developing world. From the days of the swamps of

Jurong to the Suntec City of today and beyond, success is more than just a question of inspiration. It calls for lots of guts and perspiration — hardwork and a collective sense of purpose. The gloss and glamour of development is one thing but what about nation-building? Nation-building in our multiracial, multilingual and multireligious Singapore? It's even more unique.

Senior Minister, Mr Lee Kuan Yew, once described Singapore as "a very unlikely country". Mr Lee cited Rupert Emerson, a Harvard professor, in his book *From Empire to Nation* to show how formidable nation-building can be.

I quote Professor Emerson:

> *The ideal model of the nation is a single people, traditionally fixed on a well-defined territory, speaking the same language, preferably a language all its own, possessing a distinctive culture, and shaped to a common mould by many generations of shared historical experience.*

Going by that definition, we will realise how difficult and challenging a task it can be for Singapore.

Another American scholar, Professor Robert Tilman, who had studied Southeast Asia for 25 years, wrote in his book *South East Asia and the Enemy Beyond* how "geography, history, language and culture have all conspired against the countries of Asean to make their task of nation-building and economic development more difficult." The Professor said that the future was pregnant with risks for every state in the region.

Professor Tilman said this of Singapore:

> *When Singapore was in the process of achieving independence, it was often commented that Malaysia needed a port and Singapore needed a hinterland. And to many it seemed apparent that Singapore needed Malaysia more than Malaysia needed Singapore. Logic suggested that a hinterland could develop its own ports, but a port could not create a hinterland. This, however, is precisely what Singapore had to do, and did, after it separated from Malaysia in 1965. By its trade policies and its*

development programmes, the world became Singapore's hinterland.

Yet some harsh primordial realities remained. The Republic of Singapore is literally a 641.4 sq km island, but it is also, figuratively, an island of ethnic Chinese in a sea of Malays.

The leadership of the newly-independent Republic had to create conditions to encourage the development of a Singapore national identity among an immigrant Chinese population, and they had to convince their Malay neighbours that this process was producing results. The task was formidable. The leadership faced a large proportion of the Chinese population who were very reluctant to part with their Chinese identity, and they faced an opposition leadership eager to exploit the alienation of the Chinese to achieve their own political ends.

Sometimes opposition leaders and followers went to considerable lengths, including shedding blood, to protect and defend a real or imagined Chinese heritage. Insofar as Singaporeans succeeded in defending their Chinese heritage, they provided further proof to their Malay neighbours that they were transplanted Chinese and not fellow South-east Asians.

Singapore leaders faced a delicate task. They had to push their constituents to shed their Chinese identity and acquire a Singaporean identity fast enough to convince their neighbours that Singapore was not a threat, but the process had to be slow enough to avoid a possible backlash that might wipe out their gains.

At the international level, the current state of relations with neighbouring Malaysia and Indonesia and at the national level, government programmes encouraging Singaporeans to rediscover their Confucian roots, suggest that the leadership is confident of its success in overcoming its major primordial obstacle to nation building.

Yet, the process is never complete, and retrogression is always a possibility. Moreover, Singapore despite its success in forging a nation from immigrants, remains a minuscule state, and no government policy can alter significantly this primordial fact.

We, of course, know that the situation is more complex than that. Yes, it is formidable and the task made even more difficult. In fact, all these point to the fact how vulnerable we are. However, it is not insurmountable.

The exercise in consensus-building when Parliament debated the Parliamentary Elections (Amendment) Bill and the Constitution of the Republic of Singapore (Amendments No. 2) Bill, culminating in the Select Committee report on Group Representative Constituency (GRC) is one important example of our efforts at trying to make multiracialism work. But first, allow me to go back into history to remind ourselves of the testing process of nation-building.

The roots of our nationhood go back more than 170 years. It was, however, only in the last two or three decades that we began moulding actively what we would like to see as distinctively a Singapore society. The baptism of fire our leaders and parents went through in those tumultuous '50s and '60s should constantly serve to remind us and future generations that while we did not suffer the pangs of great independence revolutions, it was not an easy birth either.

Communalism and communism were ever ready to puncture our fragile independence. Singapore's short-lived days in Malaysia from 1963 to 1965 proved long and rather nightmarish with the political leaders busy confronting the issues of communalism and multiracialism.

The what was seen as a "predominantly Chinese" People's Action Party's slogan of "Malaysian Malaysia" was considered as not only insensitive but provocative by most Malay Malaysian leaders. I'm not surprised if that was the main reason why the former Malaysian Prime Minister, Tunku Abdul Rahman, wanted Singapore out of the Federation. And I'm sure that the "Malaysian Malaysia" slogan would till today raise political goose pimples in many Malaysian politicians' mind. From a "political minority" position in Malaysian Parliament, the PAP fought for the concept of a Malaysian Malaysia society. When Singapore left Malaysia in 1965, the principle of "Singaporean Singapore" remains, as decided by a Chinese majority.

Dr Russel Henry Betts of the MIT wrote in his PhD dissertation *Multiracialism, meritocracy and the Malays of Singapore* that:

> *In the acrimony which resulted, and which ultimately led to Singapore's eviction from Malaysia, the Singapore Malay community became, in sequence, catalyst, pawn and intensely interested bystander in a dispute over fundamental questions of social, economic and political organization in plural societies.*

For the Singapore Malays, from a minority position they went on to achieve and enjoy a "majority" status in Malaysia, only too soon to be lost. Imagine the cultural and political shock they experienced when Singapore left Malaysia.

Singapore political leaders, realising the positions this sudden turn of event placed the Malays in, made reassuring pledges, including multiracialism as a policy, but not without meritocracy. The Prime Minister then, Mr Lee Kuan Yew, promised to do his best to develop and bring the Malays into the main stream. In short, Singapore Malays, which Singapore and the Malays themselves can be proud of. Perceptions as to how this would best be achieved, of course, differ. The secular, more modern and predominantly Chinese leadership saw it differently from the majority of the socially and economically-handicapped Muslim Malays.

I quote again Dr Russell Betts:

> *Since 1965, Singapore has attempted to realise its non-communal egalitarianism through a state experiment in accelerated social mobilization and modernization, the objective of which has been the creation in Singapore of a 21st-century multiracial meritocracy. As this process has proceeded, the Malay problem has become one of the more perplexing development/modernization/integration issues compelling the attention of the government and of the*

community itself. The logical imperatives of multira-cialism have dictated the increasing political unac-ceptability of community-specific considerations designed to enhance Malay competitiveness or to promote Malay integration while, in the face of the accelerating rate of general socio-economic develop-ment in Singapore, there is growing Malay concern that in the absence of such consideration the Malays are threatened with being left irrevocably on the periphery.

For the Muslims, however, having moved from the era of slogan shouting to self-help, culminating in this symbiotic relationship between the government and the community as manifested through MENDAKI (Council for the Development of Singapore Muslim Community), it has taken them more than two decades to finally convince the government to accept publicly that the Malay problem is a national problem. The early tumultous survival years of independence possibly did not allow the government to pay sufficient special attention to the problems of the Malays. Neither did the confrontational approach of some of the Malay organi-sations help. One perspective is achieving harmony through economic progress.

A Singapore economist once told me that as long as we are able to maintain the six percent annual growth, the superficially skin-deep racial harmony in Singapore will last.

When our economy was in the midst of a recession in the mid-1980s, way below the six percent growth bench mark, issues such as the controvery over the Israeli President's visit and the Malays in the SAF sur-faced, challenging, if not threatening, the stability of the multireligous fabric of our society.

It may have been a coincidence that this was to happen when we were grappling with our economic test. While the controversy over President Herzog's visit, the way it blew up, could well have been a "coincidence", certainly, the issue on the Malays in the SAF was not. It took the courage of the youngest Minister then, the Minister for Trade and Industry and the Second Minister for Defence (Service)

Brigadier-General (NS) Lee Hsien Loong, to broach the subject in public, for the first time with such openness and confidence. The subject itself is, however, not new. Behind the closed-door comfort of mutual confidence, trust and sense of direction and mission, the Senior Minister, Mr Lee Kuan Yew, and the Prime Minister, Mr Goh Chok Tong, have had discussions on this potentially explosive issue with Malay/Muslim leaders.

Some may question whether it was a mistake or not that BG Lee had decided to bring the issue to the "ground". We will let history be the judge for there are many who still feel that the issue was not ready for such an open airing. They fear that it would threaten harmony.

For me, any explosive issue, like TNT, has its risks, but if we are indeed mature, with the right Treatment and Timing (TNT), it should not generate more than the ordinary reaction. As for timing, after more than 21 years of independence then, should we have waited any longer? What better time to discuss it than when relations among the various communities in Singapore and that with our neighbours are relatively good?

The treatment chosen by BG Lee, unprecedented though, reflects the growing sense of maturity we see in ourselves, Singaporeans. It also reflects the leadership's growing confidence on the Malay/Muslim themselves. I am sure that if they thought otherwise, it would not have had the public airing. Collectively, we all would want to pass this test. We must, for the alternative is to move backwards to the turbulent years of the 1960s, in other words, retrogression. Not only in terms of racial harmony, integration and cohesion but also the economy which affects all Singaporeans regardless of race or religion.

We all know that Singapore will not lack the talent, the vision and the will to make it right — to make a continued success of the economic miracle. But like a typical Singaporean, we don't want to leave too many things to chance. We would rather tackle problems before they show their ugly head. Continued economic progress may or may not be adequate to completely resolve the problems our multiracial society present.

Dr Russell Betts' thesis spoke of this larger concern with the dynamics of communal interaction and integration in culturally heterogenous modernising societies. He said:

> *This concern derives its inspiration from scholarly evidence which suggested that communalism may be a persisting feature of social change and that, in contradiction of early theory and expectations, it may not be amenable to displacement as a society modernises.*

That brings me back to the question of the GRC. Much has been said about it. To some, perhaps, *ad nauseam*. But it certainly bears closer scrutiny. So please bear with me while I briefly draw out the pertinent pointers from the Select Committee debate on the GRC to emphasise certain points.

The concept of twinning and later the GRC brings us to another interesting, exciting and telling phase of multiracialism.

To some, it smacks of an admission of failure of what we have set out to achieve all this while. To others, it means being honest and pragmatic about the socio-political realities we face.

Mr Kirpal Singh, a lawyer who appeared at the Select Committee public hearing, said that the concept of twinning, the fore-runner to the GRC, reflects the nature of our multiracial society.

> *If we look at the twin proposal as made by the Prime Minister in 1982, it was not a razzle-dazzle idea let out of the air but a product of some very hard-thinking, some very caring thinking.*
>
> *What I think is more significant, and that the people in Singapore should understand, is that it was the product of a Chinese mind for the welfare of the Malay community.*

And this, coming from a Sikh, a member of another minority group. That's the beauty of our maturing multiracial society. But let not the example in Mr Singh lull us into complacency, thinking that everything is and should be all right. While most of those who gave their views are for the need of multiracial representation in Parliament, communal streaks still linger.

Of the 96 submissions, 78 supported the concept of a multiracial Parliament and the need to take immediate steps to ensure that our Parliament will always be multiracial. Most significantly, of the 59 submissions from Malays, Indians and other minority communities, 54 supported either the GRC concept or new provisions to ensure that Parliament will always be multiracial. A small minority of Chinese representors expressed concern about entrenching the rights of minorities in Parliament and giving them too much leverage over political parties. The GRC Select Committee report understands this concern as the Bill confers concessions on the minority communities, necessarily at the expense of the majority community.

The report, however, hastens to add that in a multiracial society, there is no way the majority can avoid making allowances for the minority communities so that they do not feel threatened or alienated. The Prime Minister then, Senior Minister Lee Kuan Yew revealed during the debate a very significant, if not telling, example of such a concession when he cited the case of his having to give choice land for a mosque project. Mr Lee was talking of a conflict of interest between the Malay community leaders' request for a piece of land near a new town centre and that of the Chinese for recreational purpose.

Mr Lee had decided to let it be a mosque because there wasn't one in the constituency but he said that wouldn't have been possible if there was a strong enough Chinese party which would have exploited the issue by accusing him of pandering to the needs of a minority whatever their dictates.

The process of educating our Singaporeans in politics of accommodation and compromises continues. I can go on but suffice it to say, that I hope the GRC concept will grow to be another pillar upon which we can build a stable multiracial society. There can be institutions like the GRC, but more importantly, the spirit behind it must be right.

Multiracial representation in Parliament is now enshrined in the Constitution but that may still not achieve the kind of racial harmony we need to continue to preserve if the spirit of understanding of each other is not taken seriously. Race relations in our multiracial and multireligious Singapore should not and cannot be taken for granted. Neither must each racial or religious group try to take the other for a ride. Any attempt to take the other for granted or worse, to undermine each other's beliefs, religion and culture, will only trigger disaster. We must come to grips with the realities of our multiracial and multireligious sensitivities.

We cannot allow race relations to cast any shadow of doubt on our efforts at integration and nation-building. There are still serious gaps of perceptions and expectations between the various races here. We cannot afford to leave such delicate matters to chance. The need for the Maintenance of Religious Harmony Act, passed by Parliament in November 1990 is another case worthy of mention.

Religious revival, worldwide, poses new challenges and problems too. There has been an increase in missionary zeal and religious fervour in recent years among the different religious groups in Singapore. Even the relatively "dormant" Hindu and Buddhist groups have now become more active. Competition for converts among the different religions is becoming sharper and more intense. Some even feel that the Chinese, who mostly ancestor worship, are fertile ground for conversion. Census statistics on religion will show us that if missionary zeal were to take its competitive course, there can be potential sparks for flare-up. Thus the need for caution, the Maintenance of Religious Harmony Act. We cannot assume that today's religious harmony, which we are proud of, will continue indefinitely.

Two issues which easily come to mind are the controversies over Israeli President Herzog's visit and the position of the Malays in the SAF. While President Herzog's visit, especially the demonstrations and the acrimony that followed across the Causeway, served as a good rallying point to unite most Singaporeans, it did make many Malays/Muslims feel alienated. So did the issue of the position of the Malays in the army. Many Malays still could not accept the thinking behind the policy. They feel that their loyalty should not be doubted and that they should be allowed to serve and to defend their country. There has been much movement and progress since. More doors have been opened. While creating new opportunities, they also pose new challenges, which if not properly handled, would create new problems.

Many Chinese, however, have serious doubts about possible divided loyalties of the Malays especially when it comes to their religion, and the state. Islam, if misunderstood, be it by the Muslims, or the non-Muslims, can pose serious credibility crises among Singaporeans.

Allow me to take a last fling at historical baggage, by referring to the book "Youth in the Army". It was so controversial that groups of Malays had wanted to burn them when it was first published. The book had published stereotype myths about Malays and that had angered many members of that community. Allow me to quote one example (page 43 of the book *Youth in the Army*):

> *Ah Nam was asked if he would elect a member of a different race, e.g., a Malay, to be Prime Minister of Singapore if he were the most able of all contenders. Ah Nam replied quite definitely that he would only elect a Chinese as leader of the state, even if he was inferior in ability to the others of a different race, for there might be favouritism for other races against the Chinese race (self-preservation again). 'But, anyway, Malays are always stupider'. He then gave his observation that Malays were lazy and would stay away from work after they had earned enough to last them for a short period of time.*
>
> *When forced to rank the four cases (Chinese, Malay, Indian and Europeans), in preference for marriage. Ah Nam came up with the order (1) Chinese (2) English (3) Indian (4) Malay. When asked for the criterion for his ranking, he said it was based on the fairness of skin.*

But aren't the Malays fairer than Indians? "At least Indians have a human sense. They are more tolerant than Malays who are aggressive and always answer back...' was the answer."

That was about 20 years ago. What about now?

Yes, the Malays will continue to "answer back" but Ah Nam and the others will be happy to note that the Malays today, and tomorrow, will be different. They are more self-confident, open-minded, progressive and more tolerant. There are less emotions too.

There is a greater sense of direction and a new momentum for progress. The Malays/Muslims are more willing to be open and practical-minded and sensitive to contemporary problems. They also realise there is a need to develop greater resilience to face the challenges of global 21st century Singapore. There is now a sense of vision, mission and the need for hard work in the pursuit of excellence. To top it all; there is always this sense of moral ballast provided by Islam.

Malays feel a greater sense of being Singaporean. Not that they were un-Singaporean before. There is a greater sharing of core values, aspiration and willingness to work hard for the Singapore we want. The Malays are commtited to making a success of multiracialism as a pillar of Singapore. But we must all realise that the dynamics of multiracialism has been changing and will continue to do so. We must continue to rise above the new dynamics of multiracialism to make it to continue to succeed. The ethnic approach to self-help (MENDAKI, Sinda and CDAC) is an example of the new dynamics. We have to manage them.

This is a subject which deserves greater scrutiny. We must manage those differing, if not conflicting, perceptions and expectations. They must be once and for all identified, and where possible bridged, if not resolved, before seeds of suspicion are destroyed and the shadows of doubts in the minds of our different racial groups sufficiently erased. The concept and principles of politics of accommodation are easier said than understood, appreciated and successfully applied.

We deserve and need to understand each other better as only then can we seriously work together for the vision we espouse. It is for people like all those gathered here, the grassroot leaders, the pillars of societies to work for it. It should not end with the rituals of dialogues such as these.

I was reminded of what the illusionist David Copperfield said motivated him to perform the act of the vanishing Statue of Liberty. It has been there for so long that it can easily lull the Americans into complacency and to take liberty for granted.

Multiracial harmony is no magic. We've got to work hard for it. We've worked hard for the economic miracle, we've got to work even harder to preserve it. Similarly for race-relations and harmony. Don't take each other for granted. Reach out. We need better integration to achieve more cohesion and progress.

"We use the term 'multiracialism' so often that we sometimes forget what it means. It does not mean that in becoming Singaporean we deny our heritage. A Malay-Muslim must not be forced to choose between being Malay-Muslim and being Singaporean. That is not acceptable. Part of the essence of being Singaporean is the right to retain our separate ethnic character. But that right carries a corresponding duty to accept that others of other races also have the same right.

On this shrinking planet, no race, no language, no religion is in the majority. Chinese are a minority in the world. Muslims are a minority. Christians are a minority. We are all members of minority groups in the world and we have to love with one another. In other words, we are not unique in having to worry about such problems in Singapore. These are problems of all mankind.

From a sociological perspective, multiracialism is a psychological complex which helps define our personality as Singaporeans. It is this complex which makes Chinese Singaporeans different from Chinese in China. It is complex which makes Malay-Muslim Singaporeans different from Malay-Muslims elsewhere."

Quotes exerpted from
Malay-Muslim Community in the Next Lap
George Yeo on Bonsai, Banyan and the Tao
Speech at the Association of Muslim Professionals Inauguration Dinner,
Westin Hotel, 31 October 1991

Former minister George Yeo after winning a prize in a *pantun* competition organised by 4PM, a Malay cultural organisation. Image reproduced with permission George Yeo © 2016. All rights reserved.

CHAPTER 10

Editors' Note

Issues facing the Malay/Muslim community will continue to evolve — understanding and interpretations too. Much has been said and shared by Malays/Muslims on those issues and concerns. We reproduce here two speeches by two non-Malay, non-Muslim Singaporean Minister/MPs reflecting on some of the issues.

Here is the first; a speech by George Yeo delivered at the Association of Muslim Professionals (AMP) inauguration dinner on 31 October 1991.

MALAY-MUSLIM COMMUNITY IN THE NEXT LAP* | George Yeo

On this shrinking planet, no race, no language, no religion is in the majority.

T he Malay-Muslim community in Singapore is going through a period of social and economic change. Such change is never easy. With good leadership and organisation, however, the result can be a stronger and a more dynamic Malay-Muslim community in Singapore. The Association of Muslim Professionals (AMP) can help bring about the transformation.

Three Major Tensions

There are three major tensions or three major opposing pulls which affect this transformation. These three tensions can have positive or negative effects depending on the way we respond to them. They are not avoidable. We cannot wish them away.

---

*Speech at the Association of Muslim Professionals Inauguration Dinner, Westin Hotel, 31 October 1991.

The first major tension is the one between being Malay and being Muslim. Hyphenating the two words does not remove the tension. Both MENDAKI and AMP have wrestled with this issue and will continue to do so. The idea of being Malay can be traced back to the early Malacca Sultanate and its encounter with the Portuguese. Malay nationalism became very strong after the Second World War over Britain's proposal to form the Malayan Union. Malayness became important as a political category.

To be Malay is to be Muslim and Malay *adat* has always taken this into account. For this reason, Indian and Arab Muslims have always found a special place in the Malay society. Perak *adat*, for example, has formal provisions for the recognition of Arab Muslims as Malays.

But to be Muslim is to be part of a larger community of believers, the *ummah*. Some Muslims believe that being Muslim is all that should matter. Being Malay is of secondary importance. Indeed, they decry some of the traditional practices of the Malay community as being un-Islamic. For them, the religious idea of being Muslim is of far greater significance than the political and cultural idea of being Malay.

This tension between being Malay and being Muslim can be creative and positive if well managed. A broader definition of the community can bring in more people to join in the common cause of uplifting those in need. Too strict a definition of Malayness will disqualify many who are now leaders and supporters. But it will also not do to move to the other extreme and drop the term "Malay" altogether because that is an inalienable part of the community. Malays are proud to be Malay and rightly so.

The second major tension which affects the Malay-Muslim community is that between the *kampong* and the city. Of all the ethnic groups in Singapore, the Malays are the least urbanised. Yet there is no choice but to participate in the economic life of the city, and by extension, of the world.

Mosque on Friday and *bersanding* on Sunday are occasions when Malays return back to the environment of the *kampong* and when they are physically together again. It is at such times that the emotional batteries are re-charged and news of the community exchanged.

The pressures of the city are, however, insistent. For many Malays, urbanisation puts great strains on family and other social relationships. The alienation of young people becomes common. In some ways, rapid urbanisation has contributed to the problem of drug addiction and the high divorce rate. For Indian and Arab Muslims, the problem is less severe because they have been urbanised much longer and so are better able to cope with the stresses of city life.

While we cannot go back to the *kampong*, we can build a social support network like those in a *kampong*, to help those who are less able to adjust to a city environment. Managing the tension between the *kampong* and city is not easy but it must be done. Malay-Muslim leaders face this tension all the time. On the one hand, they are expected to give special attention to members of the community. On the other, they are required to be national and multiracial in their approach. Malay MPs face this problem most acutely. AMP leaders will too.

The third major tension is that between cultural ties to Malaysia and cultural ties to Indonesia. Just as Chinese Singaporeans have cultural ties to China and Indian Singaporeans have cultural ties to the Indian sub-continent, so Malay Singaporeans have cultural ties to Malaysia and Indonesia. We cannot pretend that these ties do not exist. Before the Treaty of London in 1824, that is, before the British and the Dutch divided up our part of the world, Singapore's links were to all parts of the archipelago. Sang Nila Utama and Parameswara came from Sumatra. At different times, Singapore was part of Sri Vijaya, Majapahit and the Johore–Riau Empire.

Under British rule, our links were naturally much stronger with Malaya despite the fact that many Malays migrated to Singapore from Indonesia. From 1963 to 1965, we were part of Malaysia and had to fight off Sukarno's *konfrontasi*. It was only in the early 1970s that Singapore's relations with Indonesia warmed up.

With the growth triangle and the prospect of an ASEAN Free Trade Area in 15 years, Singapore's economic ties with Indonesia will grow dramatically. This will affect the way the Malay-Muslim community in Singapore sees itself. For one thing, new economic opportunities will be opened up. In many fields, there will be new points for comparison. Malaysia has a monarchy; Indonesia is republican. Islam is Malaysia's state religion; Indonesia has *Pancasila*. And so on. I am not suggesting that the Malay-Muslim community should subordinate itself psychologically either to Malaysia or to Indonesia. Far from it. What I am saying is that in discovering or re-discovering Indonesia, Malay-Muslims in Singapore will be stimulated by new ways of seeing themselves and the world. Indonesia will present an additional model to Malaysia for cultural comparison. In the process of learning from others, we will be better able to see ourselves and to develop our own uniquely Singaporean model.

I have described three major tensions which affect the development of the Malay-Muslim community. Let me now discuss how we can make them work in our favour. I would like to touch on three areas for action.

Three Areas for Action

The first is social infrastructure. The basic building block is the family which we must strengthen. We must never allow urbanisation to break up the family and alienate the young.

Beyond the family, we need a social support network of relatives, friends and civic organisations to replace the physical *kampong*. We cannot go back to the *kampong* but we can maintain the *kampong* spirit of *gotong-royong*. The fact that there are relatively few Malay-Muslims in old-age homes is an indication that such a network already exists. We need all kinds of organisations and we need leaders at all levels. Those who are more successful should help those who are less successful. The formation of AMP is therefore a very good sign.

Let me repeat that it is better to have a broader rather than a narrower definition of Malay-Muslim to enrich the pool of leaders available to the community.

And as I have mentioned earlier, Indian and Arab Muslims are already more urbanised and can help the others to urbanise more successfully.

The second area for attention is education. In the world we live, knowledge is the key to everything else. Malay-Muslim parents are becoming very anxious about the education of their children. This is extremely important because without the commitment of the parents, no progress is possible. We need a whole range of education programmes, from kindergarten classes to postgraduate scholarships, to help educate every member of the community to his full potential. Science and mathematics must be emphasised because they are very important in a modern economy. For those without the aptitude, we should find other fields in which they can do well and make a contribution to society. This has been MENDAKI's approach, which is why the government backs it fully.

We should aim high but we must not be unrealistic in our expectations. We need to put in a lot of hard work over many years. It will not be easy and there will be all manner of disagreement within the community over what to do. But it is an effort worth making. The government will help. Non-Malay Muslims will also help. But no amount of outside help will be of use if the community does not help itself.

We will have to strike a good balance between quantity and quality. We cannot just concentrate on those who are already doing well. We must also look after those at the bottom who are struggling. At the same time, we also need a few shining stars to inspire the rest. *Berita Harian* has done a good job of building up role models for the Malay-Muslim community. It is right to give full publicity to those who do well in examinations, business and public life.

But we must fight the temptation to always measure ourselves in relative terms against the other races. We cannot avoid comparison but we should concentrate on making steady progress year by year. Whether it is AMP or other Malay-Muslim organisations, our targets must be set realistically. In this way, we will not be disappointed. We must stay united and avoid pettiness. What is at stake is not our ego but our ability to raise the standard of living for as many members of the Malay-Muslim community as possible.

The third area for action is a continued commitment to multiracialism. We use the term "multiracialism" so often that we sometimes forget what it means. It does not mean that in becoming Singaporean we deny our heritage. A Malay-Muslim must not be forced to choose between being Malay-Muslim and being Singaporean. That is not acceptable. Part of the essence of being Singaporean is the right to retain our separate ethnic character. But that right carries a corresponding duty to accept that others of other races also have the same right.

The experiences of other countries show that ethnic differences can never be fully submerged. Look at the example of Yugoslavia or the Soviet Union or Canada today. The more ethnic differences are denied, the more they assert themselves, often with a vengeance. It is because we never try to remove ethnic differences that we have racial harmony in Singapore. It is only by acknowledging potential conflicts that we minimise them. We will never be able to stop worrying about problems of race, language and religion.

In reality, all countries face problems of race, language and religion, even countries like Britain and France. On this shrinking planet, no race, no language, no religion is in the majority. Chinese are a minority in the world. Muslims are a minority. Christians are a minority. We are all members of minority groups in the world and we have to live with one another. In other words, we are not unique in having to worry about such problems in Singapore. These are problems of all mankind.

But because we have always worried about such problems, we do in fact enjoy a certain advantage in the world. In Singapore, the races are mixed in our schools and housing estates, and in both the private and public sectors. From kindergarten all the way to university, from resident committees all the way up to the Cabinet, we are mixed. The Singaporean learns to be sensitive to others from a young age. We may be Chinese, Indian or Malay-Muslim but we learn very early not to take others for granted. This is why our national discussions on race, language and religion can be very beneficial. These discussions help us to find the optimal balance in our society. Sometimes we take; sometimes we give. We have to compromise; we cannot have everything our way. The desire to maintain overall peace and harmony is becoming ingrained in every Singaporean. To some extent, we have succeeded. Singaporeans are culturally sensitive in a way other people are not. We have a multi-channel facility and we know when to switch from one channel to another. This facility gives us a competitive advantage. Depending on whether we are dealing with Chinese, Javanese or Australians, we know how and when to adjust. It is our multiracialism which enables us to operate as a hub city and as an interphase for others. Dr Kenichi Ohmae made the same point to Singaporeans two weeks ago when he reminded us that Singapore's multiracialism helps us to be competitive in the borderless world of the future.

In other words, while we worry about our diversity, we also rejoice in it. From a sociological perspective, multiracialism is a psychological complex which helps define our personality as Singaporeans. It is this complex which makes Chinese Singaporeans different from Chinese in China. It is this complex which makes Malay-Muslim Singaporeans different from Malay-Muslims elsewhere. I therefore welcome the AMP's proposal to establish an award for Singaporeans who make a special contribution to multiracialism. I hope other ethnic groups will also join in. The proposal expresses the desire of Malay-Muslims to make the transition from the *kampong* to the multiracial city and from the multiracial city to the multiracial world. I also support the AMP's launch of a book prize for the best academic exercise by an Honours Year student on an area of study of relevance to the Malay-Muslim community.

Conclusion

Let me conclude. I started by saying that Singapore's Malay-Muslim community is going through a period of tremendous change. The community is challenged by three major tensions — between being Malay and being Muslim, the opposing pulls of the *kampong* and the city, and a shift from close cultural ties primarily with Malaysia to close cultural ties with both Malaysia and Indonesia. These tensions are in fact challenges which the community has to respond to. I mentioned three areas which deserve our special attention — building up a social infrastructure to support the urbanisation process, education and a continued commitment to the multiracial ideal.

It is in responding to the challenge of change that the Malay-Muslim community makes its transformation into a community that is uniquely Singaporean and into one that is urbanised, self-confident and tolerant of others. The process cannot take place overnight. We must be patient but persistent. Malay-Muslim leaders must expect to go through all kinds of difficulties. That a group like the AMP should spontaneously organise itself without government prompting augurs well for the future. That you have been able to attract the support of both Malay-Muslims and non-Malay-Muslims speaks well of your approach. That your publicly declared standpoint is national and not narrowly Malay-Muslim makes your Association truly Singaporean. I wish you every success.

CHAPTER 11

Editors' Note

Issues facing the Malay/Muslim community will continue to evolve — understanding and interpretations
too. Much has been said and shared by Malays/
Muslims on those issues and concerns. We reproduce
here two speeches by two non-Malay, non-Muslim
Singaporean Minister/MPs reflecting on some of the
issues.

Here is the second; a speech by K. Shanmugam
delivered in Parliament on 20 January 2003 on meritocracy with a heart.

TEXT OF THE SPEECH BY K SHANMUGAM, MP FOR SEMBAWANG IN PARLIAMENT, 20 JANUARY 2003

Strengthening Inter-Racial Ties

The events of the past year have shown that we are not immune from the phenomenon of radicalisation of parts of Muslim societies throughout the world. As I say that, let me make one point absolutely clear. We must not fall into the pattern of thinking that radicalisation has a special association with Islam. All religions and many societies have their extremists. They all abuse their religions and societies.

So, what do we do? Do we sit back suspicious of our Muslim Singaporeans and harbouring silent resentment? Or do we pretend that everything is all right, nothing is happening, and that life can carry on as it always has? Neither of these are sensible options. The only option which is in the enlightened self-interest of all Singaporeans is to reach across racial lines and build ties that bind us more closely while increasing our security measures. There is a need to build stronger ties because, at the end of the day, the battle is for the mind... One factor that will determine the fate of the ideological battle is the strength of our inter-racial ties. [W]e have to recognise that the battle is not easy and there can probably be no complete victory. It is not possible to always or easily triumph for our beliefs based on fate, but we must try. We have, as a society, always tried to increase the strength of our inter-racial ties.

Impact of Race Relations pre-September 11 and post-September 11

Pre-September 11, I felt that the relationship between the races was moving in the right direction, but the movement was slow. In particular, there were a number of psychological barriers between our Muslim Singaporeans and the rest. There were a number of reasons for this. I will deal with two. First, in our competitive society, by and large, our Muslim Singaporeans have done less well. That built in some defensiveness. Second, I think, it was ingrained in the psyche of many, though not all, non-Muslim Singaporeans that somehow our Muslim Singaporeans were less competitive, and less able. These feelings and reactions were reinforced by the relative insularity of the lives which many Singaporeans lead. Those who were involved in community work and had to reach across racial lines could overcome such reactions.

Our Muslim Singaporeans, of course, picked up on those feelings. And our Muslim Singapore society stood feeling that it was not adequately respected by sections of Singaporean society. I would add that these are only my personal views, and others may well disagree. We cannot prove or disprove these things. I believe that for these and other reasons, there was a degree of resentment among Muslim Singaporeans and a reaffirmation of links within the Muslim society.

Formal and Affective Disconnect But Things Are Changing

I do accept that, in formal terms, we have done most things correctly. The Constitution provides for equality, and we practise meritocracy, sometimes almost brutally. But societies are not built on such formal institutions alone. Feelings and attitudes are also important. And at that level, my view is that many of our Muslim Singaporeans did not quite feel that they were being accepted as equals. I believe that we have done better than many countries which have a mixed racial composition. But the fault lines and differences are still there.

But since September 11th, and more particularly since the JI arrests, there appears to be a change in mood both among Muslim and non-Muslim Singaporeans. Many of our Muslim Singaporeans appear to have been shocked into reacting. They want to make the point that they are loyal Singaporeans. There is greater openness. Malay organisations have come forward to denounce extremism and terrorism.

In this context, what should non-Muslim Singaporeans do? We have a serious opportunity to rejig the attitudes that are developing. We have to show, with sincerity, that we respect and value our Muslim Singaporeans and that we want to build deep links. Our own mindsets have to change. We must treat our Muslim Singaporeans in our heart of hearts with respect. We must show empathy for their problems but that must not mutate into disrespect.

Meritocracy

[I]t is a fact that our Malay Singaporeans have been performing better and better in many fields. But we need to catalyse that progress in the interest of a stable and inclusive society. It is in all our interest that there are Malay icons of success, wherever possible. The official policy is meritocracy and it is heresy to suggest anything else. But I will be mildly heretical. There must be opportunities, without affecting the core principle of meritocracy, for there to be some form of action which will see Malays in important positions in greater numbers than they are now.

[I]nitially, there could be a feeling that a person owes his position more to his race than his ability. But provided that he or she is, in fact, able, and the principle of meritocracy is not seriously prejudiced, these doubts can be overcome. More importantly, this will give considerable psychological boost to the rest of the Malay society, and the way non-Malays perceive Malays will also change faster.

I will also say this to our Malay Singaporeans: be realistic. Do not push beyond what society as a whole can accept. For example, I think the whole issue of Malays in the SAF is a red herring. Do not make that the litmus test for success. It makes for good political sound bite but is otherwise meaningless. Look at successful minority communities and other societies. Their success is based upon educational, cultural and economic achievements, not how many Generals they have. The issue of Malay performance in the SAF is one which really the Malay society should put on the back burner. The issue can be taken further only at the rate at which the whole society feels comfortable.

THE POWER OF ME WE

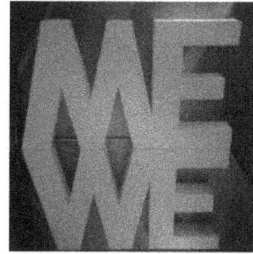

When we come together to play our part in Total Defence, the strength of "Me" is turned into the power of "We". "We" is the first word in our National Pledge, and it draws Singaporeans together as "one united people, regardless of race, language or religion". To capitalise on the power of "We", we have to continue building and investing in relationships, and having a proper understanding and trust amongst the different races and religions.

Dr Mohamad Maliki Bin Osman*
Senior Minister of State, Ministry of Defence and
Ministry of Foreign Affairs and
Mayor, South East District

*Dr Maliki is the first Malay-Muslim to be appointed as
Senior Minister of State for Defence

CHAPTER 12

AMP AND THE IDEA OF COLLECTIVE LEADERSHIP | Yang Razall Kassim

Amp — the Association of Muslim Professionals — burst onto Singapore's national scene in the early 1990s as a spontaneous movement of young professionals. It was brought about by circumstances at a critical juncture of national leadership transition in the first 30 years of nationhood. The significance of AMP's birth, however, has been much understated. In many ways, it was a major milestone, certainly for Singapore's Malay/Muslim community, but also for Singapore's evolution as a nation. Prime Minister Mr Lee Kuan Yew was stepping down in 1990, making way for his successor Mr Goh Chok Tong. Indeed, AMP was born as the new prime minister marked the rise of a generation of younger leaders. How Mr Goh related to AMP as PM encapsulated very much his approach and philosophy to the Malay/Muslim community and other minorities; to Singapore's civil society at large; and to the whole question of nation-building, post-Lee Kuan Yew.

Why AMP Emerged

AMP was born in 1991 as a ground-up response to a series of controversies in the second half of the 1980s: the unexpected visit of the Israeli President Mr Chaim Herzog; the airing of the issue of Malay loyalty by key government leaders; and the recasting of the long-standing policy of free education for the Malays. To be sure, all these were subsequently defused over the years, but at that point in time, these issues agitated the community. As a consequence, there was a sense of leadership vacuum in the community, as if its interests, aspirations and sensitivities were not being accommodated.

Against this backdrop, a group of young professionals came together to help forge a sense of direction for the community. Three key proposals were tabled at their ground-breaking convention in 1990. Firstly, Singapore's Malays/Muslims must be part of the larger Singaporean society and move from the fringe to the mainstream. They must engage in self-help and move up the socio-economic ladder through better education. Secondly, to help bring this about, the state must play its part. It must reduce the community's sense of alienation, such as that (being felt arising) from institutional restrictions on Malays/Muslims in the public service, especially in the armed forces; and the state must support the socio-economic advancement of the community more proactively through effective policies and programmes.

Mr Goh Chok Tong delivering the keynote address at the First National Convention of Singapore Malay/Muslim Professionals in 1990 which endorsed a resolution to form the Association of Muslim Professionals (AMP) the following year. Image courtesy of Association of Muslim Professionals © 2015. All rights reserved.

Thirdly, there must be a narrowing of the gulf between the community and the state. To facilitate this, the community's representation and participation must be felt at the level of national leadership, especially in the decision-making process that affected its aspirations. To this end, the professionals proposed what they called a system of Collective Leadership (CL). It was a Big Tent approach at forging an inclusive community leadership, broadly defined. It would bring together the Malay/Muslim leadership in government and in the community — including the civil society and NGOs — in a regular process of musyawarah and muafakat — a typically Malay process of consensus-building through mutual consultation. It was the conviction of the professionals that, if implemented, the CL would over time help shift the community from the fringe to the mainstream and strengthen the relationship between the community and the state.

Significance of the Idea of Collective Leadership

The emergence of AMP was significant. AMP was leading the community to see themselves as Singaporeans in as much as they were Malays and Muslims. It was a statement of identity that had never previously been so clearly articulated within the community. This growing sense of Singaporean identity required the state to respond in a way that would meet the community's aspirations to join the mainstream and to stand equal with other Singaporeans. AMP itself manifested the emergence of this new generation of Malay/Muslim elite who provided a new source of leadership for the community.

It should be noted that this new generation that AMP represented had emerged even as the Goh era was beginning. The new era promised to bring about a more consultative, participatory system to build a kinder and gentler Singapore, helping each other through "many helping hands". These were aspirations that resonated well with the young Malay/Muslim professionals, who were themselves products of the Singaporean system.

In a way, the idea of CL, just like the birth of AMP, marked a turning point in the community and came about in a period of significant change in Singapore's post-independence history. As a new generation, the Malay/Muslim professionals had their own ideas on how the community should contribute to the forging of

The First National Convention of Singapore Malay/Muslim Professionals, as it was officially called, proposed several breakthrough strategies to help propel the community forward. One of this was the formation of a movement of Malay/Muslim Professionals (MMP), which a year later was formally incorporated as the Association of Muslim Professionals (AMP). It was suggested that this association of Malay/Muslim professionals:

- Finalise a vision for the community;
- Mobilise Malay/Muslim professionals to play a constructive role in the transformation of Malay/Muslim society to face the 21st century;
- Be a think tank for the community;
- Play a leadership function within the community;
- Channel to the Government opinions and views of Malay/Muslim professionals on a broad range of issues affecting the community;
- Be role models for the young and be an inspiration for the community;
- Be a fountain and training ground for future leaders of the community with a view to systematically preparing various echelons of Malay/Muslim leadership in various fields; and
- Play a supportive role for existing Malay-Muslim organisations.

Source: Forging a Vision: Prospects, Challenges and Directions (1990)

The aims and objectives of AMP. Image courtesy of Association of Muslim Professionals © 2015. All rights reserved.

a multiracial nation. Mr Goh, as Prime Minister-in-waiting, gave his full backing for the formation of AMP, despite the initial objections of several Malay/Muslim MPs who were concerned it would undermine MENDAKI, the community's main self-help group. This fear was misplaced.

A decade later, at its second convention in 2000, the idea of CL was re-proposed by AMP. Surprisingly, this time, it was misunderstood. Mr Goh, now as Prime Minister, shot it down and accused AMP of attempting to undermine the leadership of the Malay MPs, who by then had formed the community's political leadership in government. The government's turn-around was perplexing to many in the community, not least the AMP leaders. An upshot was the formation of the Community Leaders Forum (CLF), spearheaded by the Malay MPs and MENDAKI, five years after the second AMP convention. There was a big difference: while the CLF was a top-down creation to steer the community's development, AMP's CL was the product of a spontaneous ground-up idea.

A panel discussion involving the author (fourth from right) at the Second National Convention of Malay/Muslim Professionals in 2000 which discussed the idea of Collective Leadership, first tabled at the 1990 Convention. Image courtesy of Association of Muslim Professionals © 2015. All rights reserved.

Community Leadership: Going Forward

The government's turn-around on the idea of CL was unfortunate. In the post-Lee Kuan Yew era, Singaporean society aspired for a more participatory system. The Goh era was much welcomed by Singaporeans at large, and with it, they saw the initial proliferation of civil society as the government gradually eased up on public engagement. But the negative response to AMP's CL idea in 2000 acted as a break on the extent to which the government was prepared to open up space for citizen participation. Prime Minister Mr Lee Hsien

Prime Minister Mr Lee Hsien Loong with some of the AMP leaders at the Third National Convention of Malay/Muslim Professionals in 2012. Image courtesy of Association of Muslim Professionals © 2015. All rights reserved.

Loong has inherited the system from the Goh era. Yet the civil society space, as seen from the people sector, has not really blossomed, with some such as the Roundtable even closing shop. The growth of civil society groups was marginal at best.

After 50 years of nationhood, Singapore is entering the maturing phase as a developed society, looking forward to SG100. The PAP's strong victory in the 2015 general election, in spite of the odds, shows that Singaporeans are prepared to stand behind a good government. A strong government should be a confident government. A confident government should be more embracing of the citizenry, and of civil society. Indeed, the people should be encouraged to take initiative and to come up with ideas on how to make Singapore an even better nation in the next 50 years. Initiatives like the Collective Leadership that manifest the people's aspirations should be encouraged, not just for the Malay/Muslim community but for the Singaporean society at large.

Important milestones for AMP.

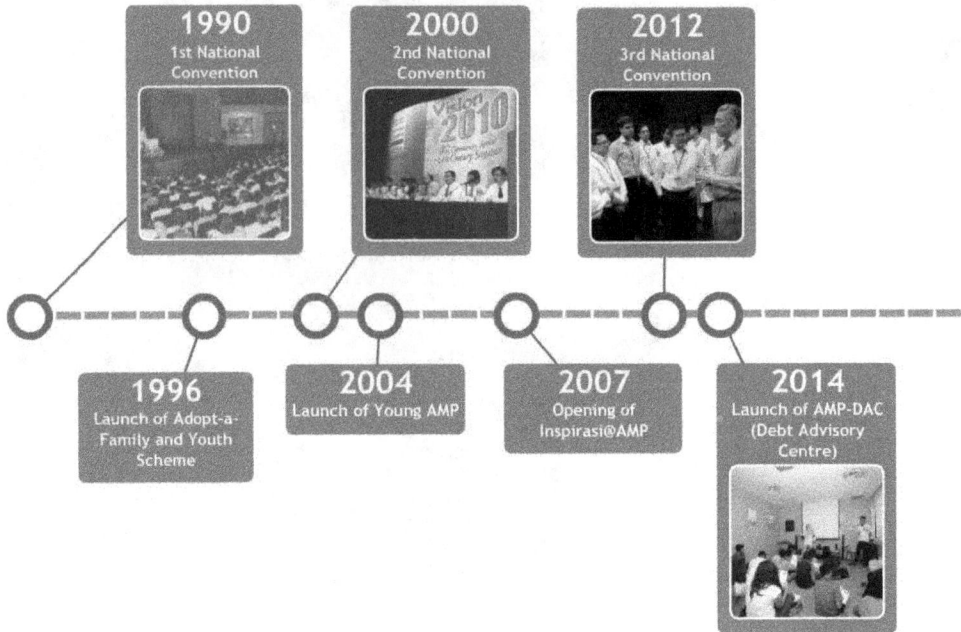

1990 1st National Convention

2000 2nd National Convention

2012 3rd National Convention

1996 Launch of Adopt-a-Family and Youth Scheme

2004 Launch of Young AMP

2007 Opening of Inspirasi@AMP

2014 Launch of AMP-DAC (Debt Advisory Centre)

ASSOCIATION OF MUSLIM PROFESSIONALS

Chairmen

Associate Professor Dr Hussin Mutalib	1991 – 1993
Dr Ahmad Mohamed Magad	1993 – 1995
Mr Mohd Alami Musa	1995 – 2003
Mr Ismail Ibrahim	2003 – 2004
Mr Yang Razali Kassim	2004 – 2006
Mr Imram Mohamed	2006 – 2009
Mr Mohd Nizam Ismail	2009 – 2012
Mr Azmoon Ahmad	2012 – 2015
Mr Abdul Hamid Abdullah	2015 – present

Executive Directors

Mr Mohd Alami Musa	1992 – 1994
Mr Ismail Ibrahim	1995 – 2000
Mr Muhd Nazzim Hussain	2001 – 2004
Mr Mohd Anuar Yusop	2005 – present

THE STORY OF FIVE BLIND MEN AND AN ELEPHANT — THE NEED FOR TRANSFORMATION | Maarof Salleh

You may have heard the story of five blind men identifying an elephant. Being blind, each man cannot define an elephant in full on his own. So, each one of them describes an elephant based on the part of the animal he so touches. For example, he who touches the elephant's leg describes the animal as a tree trunk, and he who touches its body defines it as a wall. They were unable to identify the elephant as a complete entity but instead, each one of them describes the animal differently and in fragmentation.

The story of the blind men and an elephant origi-nated from the Indian subcontinent, where the story has widely diffused and is interpreted in a variety of ways.

This story has often been used as an anology to describe how, in reality, a society could lose its sense of perception in identifying or describing an issue or a problem that it collectively faces. This often resulted in difficulties in resolving the actual problems. For example, in today's global context, how Islam is being identified and how Muslims are being looked at vary differently among scholars or among the common people.

Muslims are made of people of different races and nationalities. The different histories, customs, cultural practices and political systems they experience in the different countries they live in will influence their life-style and daily practices, which makes each community different from others. Such differences would, in turn, influence how non-Muslims understand Islam and the

Muslim practices, based on what they observe or experience through their daily interactions with Muslims.

In Western Europe, for example, with greater migration especially after World War II, Muslims immigrants are now forming a significant part of its population. In most cases, they form an enclave separate from the general population, and continue practising the social, religious and cultural rituals that they have brought with them from their countries of origins. Though this came about due to policies established in their new countries, this separation created the image that such Muslims were reluctant or not easy to integrate. Unfortunately, such segregation often puts the Muslim population in a bad light in the eyes of the general population of that country.

The understanding of Islam among scholars can often be influenced by the specific areas of their chosen research or studies about Islam or Muslims. It is no surprise that such studies have created various differing concepts on Islam. There are now Islamic economics, Islamic culture, Islamic politics, and even Islamic terrorism. These subsequently led to the development of specific but partial interests on Islam among scholars.

Being fragmented and by itself, such an understanding would make it difficult, if not totally impossible, for Islam to be identified and understood comprehensively (*shumul*) i.e., in totality. So, like the story of the blind men and the elephant, the understanding of Islam and Muslims based on a specific area of interest or

The many faces of Islam. Photo taken off a wall at the Harmony Centre located at An-Nahdhah Mosque. Image courtesy of Jamsari Ahmad © 2015.

study, or based upon the experience of living with a particular Muslim group, would be a distorted one. Such understandings or perceptions would be more confined to the person's limited observation and experience. At worst, it creates prejudices.

Prejudices against anything Islamic in the form of Islamophobia is real and happening right now, in particular in the West. The aftermath of the 9/11 attacks have further sparked debate on state–Muslim relations. There have been moves by some calling for the possible banning of the *azan* (Islamic call to prayer) from mosque minarets and the wearing of *burqa* (a one-piece veil that covers the face and body, with just a mesh screen for the wearer to see through) by Muslim women. I remember how a prominent Muslim scholar who lives in Europe, Dr Tariq Ramadan, strongly expressed his disappointment on the move to ban the

wearing of *burqa* for Muslim women in France. He argued that the *burqa* was not the main issue in Europe that should involve the relations between the state and its Muslim population. Rather, the main problem, he said, was the presence of general prejudices against Islam among the European population in the distorted way with which they look at and understand Islam. Such prejudices, Dr Ramadan insisted, was the main issue that must be comprehensively addressed. State intervention, he cautioned, would only further explode the existing prejudices, thus causing further tension not only in terms of inter-religious relations but also between the state and its Muslim population.

A man reading the Quran in a mosque. In Singapore, Islam is the religion of almost all Malays. Image courtesy of Jamsari Ahmad ©2016. All rights reserved.

This same analogy is still relevant when one discusses other social issues and problems facing the local Malay/Muslims in Singapore, perhaps also in the larger Malays/Muslim region comprising Indonesia, Malaysia and Brunei. One example is the prolonged debate regarding the need to quicken the pace of progress among the Malays *vis-à-vis* other ethnic groups or why, being the indigenous people, they remain relatively poor. There have been many debates mostly focusing on identifying factors for progress or otherwise, leading subsequently to debates on what are the appropriate planning and action plans to adopt. Different views, sometimes conflicting, emerged from different groups. As expected, each group identifiy the issues, and thus the problems, differently. As a result, each group would emphasise resolving it differently.

In Singapore, and likewise in Malaysia, Brunei and Indonesia, Islam is the religion of almost all Malays. Therefore, there is always the correlation between Islam and the Malays. The identifying of religion (Islam) as an issue as well as a factor in influencing Malay/Muslim progress is a clear example. There has always been a divide between those who want Islam to play a greater role in the society's progress (loosely referred to the Islamists) and those who do not think so (loosely referred to as the secularists). In Malaysia for example, this has been reflected in the political rivalry between its two largest Malay political parties — United Malays National Organisation (UMNO) and Parti Islam Se-Malaysia (PAS). In Indonesia, this debate is mainly reflected in the struggle between Nahdatul Ulama (NU) and Muhammadiyah, two of Indonesia's biggest social movements on one side and secular groups like Partai Golongan Karya (Golkar) and Partai Demokrat (PD) on the other.

Unlike in Malaysia and Indonesia, this divide is not too obvious among Malays/Muslims in Singapore. But there still exists those who strongly believe in

A Muslim man with a child. The image of Islam and Muslims in Singapore has been positive. Image courtesy of Sarafian Salleh © 2015. All rights reserved.

upholding Islam for the society's progress (or those who maintain that the lack of it is the cause for the community's slow progress). Conversely, there are those who think too much attention is paid to religion, causing the society to overlook other pre-requisites for progress. This divide is reflected in each group's approach to the issue of the society's progress and the solutions to overcome the problems they propose and undertake. Generally, the former stresses on the general neglect of Islam by Malays/Muslims as the main issue, arguing such neglect as contributing to their present state of affairs. According to this view, this neglect deprives Malays/Muslims of the true religious values and spirit needed for progress. Therefore, the call for the reviving of true Islamic teachings that would be compatible with modern needs and progress is pertinent. However, there is no consensus in identifying which aspect of Islam the Malays/Muslims have neglected.

Some attribute it to the general failure of Malays/Muslims to understand the true teachings of Islam, in particular on the understanding of *tawhid* (the concept of oneness of God). Some attribute it to over-emphasis on Islamic jurisprudence (*fiqh*), therefore the inclination to debate Islam more on *halal-haram* (allowable-forbidden) issues, while ignoring other Islamic aspects that would better prepare the society to deal with issues they will face in today's fast-changing world.

Like Muslims elsewhere, Malays/Muslims in Singapore are not totally free from the element of fanaticism, either fanatic towards a *mazhab* (school of thought) or to one's preferred ideology or thinking. One example is the debate on how Muslims should behave in today's challenging world, where Islam is facing growing criticism by the West regarding the attacks by militant Muslim groups.

Let us digress a little here.

One outcome of the aftermath of the September 11 attacks (9/11) has been the growing emergence of instant experts on terrorism mainly from

> *In Singapore, and likewise in Malaysia, Brunei and Indonesia, Islam is the religion of almost all Malays. Therefore, there is always the correlation between Islam and the Malays. The identifying of religion (Islam) as an issue as well as a factor in influencing Malay/Muslim progress is a clear example.*

among journalists and scholars in the West. Tracing the origins of Islamic terrorism has been a popular focus for them. Few writers have written alleging the role played by past and contemporary Muslim scholars in sowing the seeds of terrorism, currently committed to by groups that claim themselves Muslims. For example, Sayyid Qutb has been controversially alleged to be among them. Citing especially from his writing, *Milestones*, Qutb was proclaimed as the father of modern Muslim terrorists. There have been consistent attempts by the Western media to highlight similarities between what Qutb had said with those propagated by Osama Bin Laden and the Al-Qaeda. This view appears to gain acceptance when Muslim militant groups like the Takfiri and the Jihad Group associated their militancy with Qutb's doctrines.

As with Muslims elsewhere, such debates (and controversies) do affect Malays/Muslims here, at least through some of the sentiments expressed in mainstream media. Though their sentiments differ — some in agreement, some not — it often reflects how they react to challenges coming from the outside, especially from the non-Muslims.

In reality however, even among Western scholars, there are attempts to "rescue Qutb from misrepresentation". For example, in his book *Sayyid Qutb and the Origins of Radical Islam*, John Calvert traced the evolution of Qutb's thoughts within the context of his time, and concluded that "Lacking a pure understanding of the leader's life and work, the popular media has conflated Qutb's moral purpose with the aims of bin Laden and Al-Qaeda. He is often portrayed as a terrorist, Islamo-Fascist, and advocate of murder."

Prominent leaders of the Brotherhood (Ikhwan al-Muslimun) in the later years did the same. Sensing the dangers of the misrepresentation of Qutb by some militant groups, Hassan al-Hudaibi (1891–1973) wrote in 1969, *Du'at wa la Qudat* (Preachers, Not Judges), to tell Ikhwan and the state that the job of the Ikhwan was to preach, not to judge the faith of others. His aim was to help dampen the ardour of extremists and to salvage the reputation of Ikhwan in the eyes of the state. His approach was later followed by his successor, Umar al-Tilmisani (1904–1986).

Such sentiments have resurfaced with the recent Paris attacks. There are Muslims, globally as well as Malays/Muslims in this region, who expressed disgust as to why too much attention is given to the Paris attacks, but at the same time, the media is almost ignoring the sufferings in Palestine. The sentiment is understandable, yet it is a clear oversight of the main issue that Muslims, like other citizens of the world, must share — the rejection of terrorism!

On the opposite of the view that calls for Islam to be the thrust of the Malays/Muslims progress (or otherwise), there are those who attribute the slow progress of the society to too much (or over) attention given to religion. They argue that too much dependence on fate or *takdir* acquired from the religious teachings, may have contributed to the dampening of values or spirit necessary for progress, such as innovation and creativity.

In relation to this, some put the blame to the divide-and-rule policy of the past colonial governments. Claiming "to protect the Malays (indigenous)", such policies have put Malays at a disadvantage. Being protected, the Malays lost the opportunities to acquire skills that would help them to compete in the post-independent open economy. Unfortunately, the post-independent government, some argue, continues the colonial legacy, and are even supported by the Malay elites themselves. These, some claim, have caused difficulties for the Malays to climb the social and economic ladder. Many still feel the Malays/Muslims are still being discriminated in certain sectors of employment.

Added to this is the view that attributes the lack of Malay/Muslim progress to the poor or lack of educational acievements among Malay children. This view appears to be consistent in the overall Malay effort

Like Muslims elsewhere, Malay/ Muslims in Singapore are not totally free from the element of fanaticism, either fanatic towards mazhab *(school of thought) or to one's preferred ideology or thinking). One example is the debate on how Muslims should behave in today's challenging world, where Islam is facing growing criticism by the West regarding the attacks by militant Muslim groups.*

towards progress. Subseqently, in the late 1980s, this concern has led to the formation of Yayasan MENDAKI, a self-help group to raise educational awareness among Malay parents, as well as to increase the number of Malays acquiring tertiary education.

There is also a growing awareness to take another look into some aspects of the Malay cultures and traditions that would help boost the community's progress. Another area of concern is related to social problems that Malays/Muslims face and are affecting their progress. Such concerns lead to actions to rectify problems at the family level, including tackling drug addiction and reducing Malays/Muslim divorce cases.

To sum up, these are some of the different views expressed thus far, and are still prevalent today, on identifying the main issues of the progress of the Malays/Muslims here in Singapore. Some are complementing, some conflicting.

So, as expected, like the story of the blind men and the elephant, the different perceptions coming from people of different educational backgrounds and experiences, have resulted in different solutions proposed. Questions arise. How do you identify which perception is the right one, and therefore, which progress actions need to be given priority? How do you coordinate the different analyses and strategies, which at times can be conflicting?

This situation is understandable, though certainly would create its own difficulties. As it is now, each group may feel responsible to focus on its understanding of the main issues and to carry out the solutions its own way. But the situation is not always ideal, as groups engaging in championing the Malay progress are not equal in their resources. It is possible for the rise of a situation where the views of the most influential group that command the greatest resources become dominant, and therefore dictate the terms in which the Malays/Muslims issues are identified and determine the approach and strategy to be adopted for resolving these problems.

This group is of course the state or its representative, the politicians. But to what extent would this state intervention be considered acceptable and congruent with the society's wishes and aspirations?

This consideration would further delay the process of arriving at consensus to consolidate actions to quicken the pace of progress for the Malays/Muslims.

THE FUTURE IS US

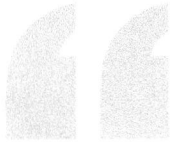

"

It is timely to cast our eyes forward. Our future is really
for all of us to continue to imagine, shape and strive
for together, based on our shared values."

Heng Swee Keat
Finance Minister
Speaking about The Future of Us exhibition
24 November 2016

CHAPTER 14

EDUCATION FROM 1959 TO 2014:
THE SEEDS OF THE FORMATION
OF MENDAKI

Wan Hussin Zoohri

The development of education in the Malay community from the post-colonial days to the present era has undergone an evolution. It would
indeed be voluminous to narrate this educational
development spanning over several decades (1959–
2014). In this paper, I provide snapshots of the main
events occurring during the different stages of the
Malays', educational development.

1959–1980

The PAP government came to power in 1959 with a
strong mandate from the electorates under the new
constitution. Singapore had control over her internal
affairs except in matters of internal security which was
under the purview of the Internal Security Council. The
British still had control over defence and internal
affairs. In the matter of education, the PAP government
had a 5-Year Plan (1959–1964). This plan had three
main objectives: equal treatment for the four streams
of education: Malay, Chinese, Tamil and English; the
establishment of Malay as the national language of the
new state; emphasis on the study of mathematics, science and technical subjects.[1] This new educational plan
was aimed at changing the colonial education system
into the national system of education.

It was during this period that the Malay schools saw
their expansion from the primary to the secondary level.
In line with its policy of equal treatment for the four

streams of education, the government took a bold step in setting up Malay secondary classes with an initial enrolment of 136 pupils. In 1960, the government set up the first Malay secondary school, Sang Nila Utama Secondary School[a]. In 1962, the second Malay secondary school, Tun Sri Lanang[b] was built.

There were two main challenges facing the Malay secondary education then. They were the shortage of teachers and the lack of Malay secondary level textbooks. To overcome the former, the

First batch of Singapore Teachers' Training College (TTC) teachers (Malay Wing), 1959. Seated left to right: Wan Hussin Zoohri, Alias Karsah, Khatijah Lasman, Abdual Karim Shariff (Lecturer), Kamarudin Ali, Abdual Rahman Ismail and Hassim Ahmad, Standing left to right: Effendi Kadir, Abbas Abu Amin, Ashari Alwi, Abu Zarim Abdullah, Baharul Yahya, Zainal Abidin Ismail, Abdullah Rahman and Ahmad Rahman. Image courtesy of Hassim Ahmad 2015. All rights reserved.

---

[a] Sang Nila Utama Secondary School was the first Malay-medium secondary school established in Singapore and the third secondary school built after Singapore achieved self-government in 1959. The school was officially opened in 1961 and ceased operation in 1988 due to dwindling student intake. Among its prominent graduates were former Members of Parliament Yatiman Yusof and Mohamad Maidin.

[b] Named after the Bendahara (Prime Minister) to the Sultan of Johor, who was largely credited as being the author of *Sejarah Melayu* or the *Malay Annals*, Tun Seri Lanang School was another Malay-stream school providing secondary education. It was officially opened in 1963 and closed about the same time as Sang Nila Utama Secondary School.

Ministry of Education transferred Malay teachers, who were trained in English from English schools to Sang Nila Utama and Tun Sri Lanang Secondary Schools. There were only 14 teachers who were bilingually-trained in Malay and English who graduated from the then Teachers' Training College in 1959.

As there were no Malay textbooks in science and mathematics in the initial years, the teachers had to personally translate the teaching contents from the English textbooks into Malay. The teachers had to depend on the Malayan Dewan Bahasa and Pustaka which was then translating the school science and mathematics textbooks for Malayan schools. These constraints did not deter the development of Malay secondary schools. From 136 pupils studying in four secondary classes, the number increased to 6500 studying in two single medium schools (Sang Nila Utama and Tun Sri Lanang) and six integrated schools (English–Malay) in 1964.[1] The Malay secondary school pupils sat for the Malaysian Certificate of Education in 1964 conducted by the Malaysian Ministry of Education. However, in 1969, they sat for the School Certificate Examination (Malay medium) conducted by the Singapore Ministry of Education.

When Singapore separated from Malaysia in 1965, it had its effect on the enrolment of Malay schools. With the gradual swing of pupils from the vernacular schools to English schools in 1970, there were no pupils enrolled in the Malay medium classes from 1976 to 1982.[1] This had its effect on the declining enrolment in Malay secondary integrated schools. Sang Nila Utama Secondary School (integrated) had to be closed in 1987. One year later in

"We're trying. Look, MENDAKI (Malay Muslim self-help group) and MUIS (Islamic Religious Council of Singapore) have been putting in a lot of effort and there's been incremental improved performance in mathematics and science. But I told the Malay leaders they will never close the gap with the Indians and the Chinese, because as they improve, the others also improve. So the gap remains. They are improving but they are not closing that gap. That's a fact of life. Sidek (Saniff) finally accepted that. He never believed it. When he came in he was the president of the Malay Teachers Union. So we brought him in. I said I'd put you in education, you just see it.

Lee Kuan Yew
Hard Truths to Keep Singapore Going

1988, Tun Sri Lanang Secondary School (integrated) was also closed.

> *The importance of education has been systematically emphasised by many societies: The Chinese by the creation of the "Mandarin" and the willingness of the rich to contribute generously to the institutions of learning. The pride of the Indians is measured by the educational performance of their sons and daughters. The Japanese, hundred years before the Meiji Dynasty, put supreme importance on the pursuit of knowledge. Muslims, even earlier. Since the revelation of the firs surah "Iqra" – READ – which also means comprehend, analyse and research, that finally benefited the whole mankind."*
>
> Sidek Saniff
> *Education and Singapore Malay Society: Prospects and Challenges*

The duration of Malay secondary school education was short-lived (1960–1988). This was quite understandable as the English language became economically important in the new independent Singapore. By the mid-1980s, the national system of education had replaced the vernacular schools with all pupils going to the national schools with English as the medium of instruction. The mother tongue languages (Malay, Chinese and Tamil) became the second languages. This showed that over the years, the multilingual system of education had evolved into single medium schools with the existence of only English schools.

The National System of Education

One of the discernable effects of Singapore's separation from Malaysia was the changing pattern of its multi-streams of education. As Singapore was searching for a policy and formula to ensure its survival after the separation, it had to plug itself to the world economic grid. This meant that the importance of the English language to Singapore's economy was paramount. As such, enrolment of students into the English medium schools began to outstrip the enrolment into the multi-streams or the vernacular schools. Although there was a gradual drop in the enrolment in vernacular schools, the decline in the Malay medium schools was quite drastic. This decline began to surface as early as 1967. By the 1970s and the 1980s, the Malay schools saw its rapid decline with the ultimate closure of the two Malay secondary schools, Sang Nila Utama and Tun Sri Lanang in 1987 and 1988 respectively.

This phenomenon in the declining enrolment of Malay schools caught the attention of the Singapore Malay Teachers' Union (SMTU). In the 1950s and 1960s, SMTU was regarded as the "custodian" of Malay schools championing the existence and advancement of the status of Malay schools. However, SMTU began to re-evaluate its role and function amidst the rapid decline of students in both the primary and secondary Malay schools. It had to decide between Malay education *per se* i.e., the existence of Malay schools or the education of the Malays. SMTU chose the latter. SMTU then was more concerned with the kind of education the Malay students received which would equip them with the desired skills that would enhance their employability in the job market. It, therefore, proposed the National System of Education (NSE) in 1971.

This proposal advocated the "merger" of all the multi-streams schools into a single or national system of education. This proposal had several advantages:

(i) It would remove the public's perception of the non-English streams being educationally inferior to the English stream as it would put all pupils on par educationally;

(ii) The products of this national system of education would be able to compete on equal strength for employment without being stigmatised as coming from non-English schools;

(iii) It would help the evolution of a stronger national identity as all students would go through a single national stream of education, experiencing a stronger integrative process, educationally and socially.[2]

The NSE curriculum would include the following features:

(i) The main medium of instruction would be English. This would be a pragmatic choice with the importance of English for the country's economy;

(ii) The National Language would be taught to all non-Malay students. This was a socio-political imperative based on the geo-political consideration of the region in which Singapore is located;

(iii) The students would learn their mother tongue languages including their own literature. This would ensure the preservation of their cultural roots.

The SMTU's proposal for NSE was its effort in finding a way out of the dilemma of Malay education. It considered its proposal to be educationally sound considering the changing pattern of the multi-streams of education then.

However, the NSE drew criticism from both the Chinese educated and the Government. The former saw the proposal as an attempt to close the Chinese schools. The latter saw the proposal to be chauvanistic and politically motivated. The climax of the Government's opposition to the proposal was reflected in then Prime Minister Lee Kuan Yew's statement when he said:

> By a remarkable coincidence, the Malay teachers were at the same time campaigning for a national type of school, using English as the medium of instruction... Malay compulsory as second language. All Chinese schools were to be closed. They were... playing someone else's game[3]

Sidek Saniff, the then President of SMTU rebutted the Prime Minister's critcism. He said that the only person behind SMTU's proposal was none other than God himself. It would be an insult to think otherwise.[2]

On hindsight, it was indeed ironic for SMTU to propose the NSE when it was itself pressing for the preservation of Malay education in the 1950s. It took intellectual courage on its part to voluntarily advocate the "abandonment" of the Malay medium schools. The NSE was in fact, an attempt to quicken the evolutionary educational process faster than it could endure. It was seen as ahead of its time. However, this evolutionary process took slightly over a decade to materialise. By 1987, all students were already attending a single or a national system of education with English as the main medium of instruction. The mother tongue was made compulsory as their second language. It could be said that the SMTU's NSE proposal which was 'still-born' in the 1970s was "reincarnated" in the 1980s into a system akin to its NSE.

Formation of MENDAKI: 1981–1989

The Malay community's socio-economic status was at its ebb in the early 1980s. This was because of the low educational achievements of the community in the 1950s to the 1970s. Such a situation was reflected in the 1980 Singapore Census of Population Report. The Report revealed the following dismal picture of the community: there were only 4.9% Malays in the professional, technical and related occupations as compared to 9.1% for the Chinese and 8.9% for the Indians; there was a higher percentage of Malays staying in the rented 1 and 2 room HDB flats as compared to the other races; it also revealed the low educational achievements of the Malay students — 36.38% had primary education, 8.95% had

The late Mansor Haji Sukaimi — one of the architects of MENDAKI. Image courtesy of Yayasan MENDAKI © 2015. All rights reserved.

secondary education, 1.80% had upper secondary education and only 0.17% had tertiary education.[2]

The Malay MPs saw the urgent need to address these issues. Having had their own internal discussion, the Malay MPs saw the need to involve the Malay community leaders and their organisations for a joint effort in addressing the socio-economic status of the community. This joint effort between the Malay MPs and the Malay community leaders would provide a common platform and give it a unity of purpose in tackling the socio-economic problems. It would also help strengthen the mutual understanding and trust between the two parties. Both sides would then be able to appreciate the extent of the possibilities and constraints facing them in trying to resolve the existing problem.

The Malay MPs led by the then Minister for the Environment and Minister-in-Charge of Muslim Affairs, Dr Ahmad Mattar, invited the Malay community leaders to its first historic meeting on 19 August 1981 at the then Ministry of Social Affairs. He informed the meeting that the purpose was to "discuss further efforts and cooperation in the upliftment of the education of Malay children in Singapore".[2] A discussion paper, prepared by the late Mansor Sukaimi, then MP for Kembangan, was presented at the meeting. The title of the paper was, "Towards a more integrated and effective education for the Malays". The meeting supported and endorsed the proposals set out in the discussion paper. The meeting also agreed to the formation of the Council on Education for Muslim Children (Majlis Pendidikan Anak-Anak Islam) or MENDAKI.

Opening of MENDAKI Congress by the then Prime Minister Lee Kuan Yew at the Singapore Conference Hall, 1982. Image courtesy of Yayasan MENDAKI © 2015. All rights reserved.

The early development of MENDAKI could be divided into two different periods: the pre-MENDAKI Congress and the post-MENDAKI Congress. The immediate task of the pre-MENDAKI Congress was to "sell" MENDAKI to the

Malay community for it to be accepted and supported. It therefore, made itself known to the public for the first time, by organising its inaugural ceremony on 10 October 1981 at the PUB Auditorium. The stage was then set for MENDAKI to garner public support through various educational activities prior to holding its educational congress in May 1982.

MENDAKI Congress

The MENDAKI Congress was a watershed in the development of the community's effort to improve its educational status. It had several new features. First, it saw between the symbiosis between Malay political leaders and the community leaders. Second, it was the biggest congress held — attended by 180 organisations representating different backgrounds — educational, social, cultural, economic and religious. Third, it was officiated by the then Prime Minister Lee Kuan Yew, who gave the keynote address.

At this juncture, it would be useful to remind ourselves of the salient points made by the Prime Minister in his keynote address:

(i) He reminded the Congress that "There is no quick fix-it" solution to the educational problems of the community;

(ii) He urged the Malay parents to start with their children's education as early as possible after the birth of their children;

(iii) He cautioned the leaders that while it was necessary to pay attention to the students at tertiary level, it was more crucial to direct their energies to the "overwhelming majority who do not make to the university";

(iv) The ultimate success of MENDAKI would be to increase the living standard of the majority and not only the minority who made it to the top.[2]

However, the most significant statement in the Prime Minister's keynote address was when he elevated the Malay problem from its communal plane. Hitherto, the Malay problem was seen purely as a Malay issue to be resolved by the Malay community alone. The Prime Minister widened the Malay problem as forming part of the national problem. He said, "The Malay problem is of concern to all Singaporeans and not just to Malay Singaporeans. It is in the interests of all to have Malay Singaporeans better educated and better qualified and to increase their contributions to Singapore's development".[3] The MENDAKI Congress was a resounding success. It received the "social mandate" from the community in translating MENDAKI's "educational blueprint" into reality.

A group photo of the participants of MENDAKI Congress I.
Image courtesy of Yayasan MENDAKI © 2015.
All rights reserved.

MENDAKI adopted a "total approach" philosophy in translating its educational blueprint. This approach widens the narrow interpretation of education from just being synonymous with formal schooling to its broader view of education. This requires the interplay of forces between the school, the home and the society. It is this total approach philosophy that became the educational mission of MENDAKI. It has to act as a social catalyst in enhancing and injecting a more vigorous educational motivations within the Malay community.

Between 1982 and 1988, MENDAKI organised educational activities for Muslim children: MENDAKI Tuition Scheme; computer courses; "Read with your child"; book on childcare; moral and religious education; MENDAKI Awards; bursaries and educational loans; and dialogue sessions.

The Present MENDAKI (1989–2014)

After nearly eight years of existence, the old MENDAKI was re-structured into the present MENDAKI. This idea was mooted by the then First Deputy Prime

Minister, Goh Chok Tong at a seminar in September 1984 organised by the Central Council of Malay Cultural Organisation, better known as Majlis Pusat (MP). This idea was taken up by an *ad hoc* committee formed by the then Minister-in-Charge of Muslim Affairs, Dr Ahmad Mattar. The *ad hoc* committee recommended the formation of a larger MENDAKI, which would focus not only on education but on the other related problems facing the Malay community such as its economic and socio-cultural development. This recommendation was endorsed at the second MENDAKI Congress in May 1989 attended by representatives from 113 Malay/Muslim organisations.

The new or the present MENDAKI would be known as Council for the Development of the Muslim Children (Majlis Pembangunan Anak-Anak Islam).[3] On 28 June 1989, the new institution was registered as Yayasan MENDAKI and as a company limited by guarantee.

The former Siglap Indah Primary School at Kee Sun Avenue, off East Coast Road, was chosen as MENDAKI headquarters, Wisma MENDAKI. The renovated school was leased to MENDAKI on a Temporary Occupational License and the Ministry of Finance has agreed to charge the MENDAKI a nominal rent. The other site taken under consideration was the Kota Raja School in Victoria Street but there were already redevelopment plans for that area.

Although the present Yayasan MENDAKI was expanded to address the development of Muslim children, education remains its main focus of concern. Building on the earlier foundation of its old MENDAKI, the present MENDAKI continues the "total approach" philosophy in addressing the education of Muslim children. It uses the term holistic approach.

MENDAKI Tuition Scheme (MTS)

MENDAKI's main thrust is still the MTS. Started in February 1982, it is now seen as MENDAKI's flagship programme. Its popularity is seen from its increased enrolment annually. Over the last five years, its enrolment increased from 6,808 students in 2010 to almost 10,000 students in 2014.[4]

Over the years, the MTS has been regularly reviewed and improved in terms of its teacher-pupil ration, enhancing teachers' delivery skills and related support facilities. A case in point is the setting up of the Homework Cafe. These Homework Cafes provide safe and conducive environment for students to complete their schoolwork under the supervision of trained personnel.[5]

One of MENDAKI's mentoring workshops in session.
Image courtesy of Yayasan MENDAKI © 2015.
All rights reserved.

The most recent review done by the Education Review Committee recommended that MENDAKI develop its signature pedagogy for MTS which would include a component on Social Emotional Learning (SEL) and motivation for MTS students. The other recommendation is for MENDAKI to place greater emphasis on early childhood education. MENDAKI's core focus on MTS is not only necessary but beneficial to the community.

(i) MTS provides financial assistance to poor deserving parents who cannot afford the tuition fees;

(ii) The tuition centres are easily accessible to the students as they are located at various places;

(iii) MENDAKI is in a better position to provide administrative support and professional expertise at these centres;

(iv) MTS strengthens the meaningful linkages with the parents to reinforce the importance of their children's education.

Related Programmes

In tandem with its MTS, MENDAKI conducts other education-related programmes for the parents. The aim is to get the parents involved and be partners in the education of their children. These include programmes such as Core Parenting Skills (CPS) and Family Excellence Circles (FEC). The parents are also empowered to be co-educators for their children through the Maju Minda Mathematika (Three M). They would be equipped with the skills to support their children's numeracy educa-tion. Reading programmes are also conducted to enhance the students' literacy level through creating conducive environment for reading at home.

The MTS and these educationally related pro-grammes form the inter-related holistic approach towards enhancing the students' learning ability.

MENDAKI–Community Symbiosis

As both the old and the new MENDAKI were overwhelmingly supported by the community at the 1982 and 1989 Congresses respec-tively, this symbiosis between MENDAKI and the community should be sustained and strength-ened. In the early years, informal dialogue sessions were held by MENDAKI to make known its objectives, roles and functions to the community at large. Now, after more than three decades, MENDAKI has managed to strengthen its image and standing within and beyond the community.

Some of the workshops conducted by MENDAKI involve both children and parents. Malay/Muslim parents are now giving more and more attention to their children especially in education. Image courtesy of Yayasan MENDAKI © 2015. All rights reserved.

Realising the importance of sustaining and strength-ening this emotional bond, MENDAKI has upgraded and finetuned its public relation effort through a more organised and structured strategy with the establish-ment of its Community Engagement Department (CED). This department adopts a two-pronged approach. First, to strengthen and break new grounds in building and sustaining relationships with the community. Second, to understand the community's aspiration and channel support for their developmental initiatives.[5]

In trying to fulfill these objectives, MENDAKI has redoubled its efforts by extending its Outreach Programme. In its effort to connect and extend its social services to the community, MENDAKI set up MENDAKI@Heartlands in two neighbourhoods, Pasir Ris and Woodlands. Finding these two centres were well received by the neighbourhood residents, MENDAKI further extended its outreach to four other satellite mosques at Assyakirin (Taman Jurong), Al-Muttaqin (Ang Mo Kio), Al-Ansar (Bedok) and Jamiyah Ar-Rabitah (Alexandra). These mosques where the "pulse" of the Singaporean Malay/Muslim community resides, allow MENDAKI to enhance its engagement effort and channel its social services to those who need them.[6]

Community Leaders Forum

To further involve the community in the effort to upgrade its educational and social-economic status, YM set up the Community Leaders Forum (CLF) in 2003. The primary objective is to bring in the community leaders of the Malay/Muslim Organisations (MMOs) to collaborate and partake jointly with MENDAKI in the development of the community. This would make them direct and positive stakeholders in the improvement of the community. With the secretarial support and the expertise provided by MENDAKI, the MMOs would be empowered in building their capacities to better serve their respective constituencies.

Achievement and MENDAKI Awards

Over the last decade, the academic performances of Malay/Muslim students have shown a steady progress. This is due to the tripartite partnership between the community (represented by MENDAKI), the homes and the schools. In this partnership, MENDAKI has been a strong and influential catalyst in producing the educational effervescence within the community.

The following statistics provide a positive picture of the academic landscape of our students:

1. Percentage of Malay students who passed the PSLE

2004	2008	2013
93.5%	91.2%	92.2%

Source: MENDAKI

2. Percentage of Malay students who scored A–C in English Language, Mathematics and Science

Year	English	Mathematics	Science
2004	95.2%	58.3%	78.4%
2008	94.4%	56.3%	74.8%
2013	92.0%	60.6%	72.0%

Source: MENDAKI

3. General Certificate of Education 'O' Level (GCE 'O') Percentage of Malay students with at least three 'O' Level Passes

2004	2008	2013
85.6%	85.6%	88.8%

Source: MENDAKI

Percentage of Malay students who passed English Language and Mathematics at GCE 'O' Level

Year	English	Mathematics
2004	76.7%	67.8%
2008	79.5%	66.4%
2013	84.9%	69.2%

Source: MENDAKI

4. Percentage of Malay students who passed General Paper at the GCE 'A' Level Examinations

2004	2008	2013
93.5%	86.6%	91.1%

Source: MENDAKI

5. Percentage of Primary One Cohort of Malay students admitted to Post-Secondary Education Institutions*

2004	2008	2013
79.0%	85.2%	90.1%

Source: MENDAKI

(*Figures included participation in junior colleges, pre-university institutions, polytechnics, Institute of Technical Education (ITE), LASALLE College of the Arts, Nanyang Academy of Fine Arts and private education institutions).[4]

These educational statistics of the past decade exceeded the performance of the previous two decades (1980s and 1990s). Although the present progress is incremental in nuture, it is understandable that any social change within a society would take a longer time to succeed. What matters most is for the community to ride on its momentum of progress and guard against any form of regression.

One of the earlier awards given by MENDAKI was the most improved student prize. Image courtesy of Yayasan MENDAKI © 2015. All rights reserved.

Anugerah MENDAKI

The educational achievements of Malay/Muslim students are recognised by MENDAKI by awarding the Anugerah MENDAKI (MENDAKI Awards) to the top 10% students who performed well in the various national examinations, PSLE, GCE 'O' and GCE 'A' Levels. Recently it has also included students who performed well in the International Baccalaureate Examinations.

The number of recipients for the Anugerah MENDAKI (including Special Achievement Award for Academic Excellence) has increased from 407 in 2012 to 466 in 2014. What is encouraging is to have 33 students from the *madrasahs* receiving this award.[5]

Students who are not academically-inclined, but instead excel in their respective talents are also recognised through the Goh Chok Tong Youth Promise Award (GCTYPA). A case in point is Mohammad Firdaos Mohammad who excels in footwear design, a career rarely pursued by many. He aspires to make a name in the international arena.[5] The number of recipients of GCTYPA has increased from five in 2010 to seven in 2014.[4]

Another award which recognises the potential of career professionals in the public and social service sectors to pursue post graduate studies in specialised fields is the Ridzwan Dzafir Community Awards (RDCA). Its first recipient in 2013 was Nureisya Saleha Abu Bakar, who is pursuing her Masters Degree in Health Administration from Johns Hopkins Bloomberg School of Public Health. Three other recipients were also awarded the RDCA in 2014.[4]

First Class Honours

An encouraging phenomenon in the last five years was the increasing number of Malay students receiving First Class Honours degrees at the university level. This trend augeus well for the pursuit of educational excellence in our community.

Year	Number of 1st Class Honours
2010	16
2011	19
2012	9
2013	21
2014	38

Source: MENDAKI

Conclusion

The development of Malay education during the colonial era was not only lamentable but ignominious. It was lamentable because throughout the colonial administration, Malay schools stagnated at the primary level. It was ignominious because it reflected the colonial policy of continued subjugation of the Malays, regarded as the native population of the country, to their traditional way of life without providing the opportunity for secondary or tertiary education.

MENDAKI now awards youths from the non-academic excellence as well. Image courtesy of Yayasan MENDAKI © 2015. All rights reserved.

From the time of the establishment of the first Malay school in Telok Blangah in 1856 until after the war, Malay schools remained at the primary level. It was not until Singapore achieved self-government in 1959, and later independence in 1965, that the Malay schools began to be expanded to the secondary level.

The growth of Malay schools at the secondary level was short-lived. After a brief period of accelerated expansion in the 1960s and 1970s, the Malay schools and enrolment began to decline drastically. Ultimately, in the 1980s there were no Malay schools in existence as all students preferred going to the English schools.

With the closure of the Malay schools, the focus of the education of Malay children shifted from Malay education, (i.e., Malay schools) to the education of the Malays. By this is meant how Malay students could receive the desired educational standard in the English schools which would enhance their employability in the job market.

From the 1980s, there was a discernable increase in the achievement of education of Malay students. Propelled by the catalytic effect of MENDAKI, and the growing awareness of the community on the importance of attaining good education, the community's educatoral level has shown tremendous progress over the past three decades. This is reflected in the increasing number of Malay professionals in the various public and private sectors. The emergence and the growing

---

[a] *Gotong* means foster and *royong* means together. As a spirit, it is the attitude of mutual cooperation or assistance. See page 49 for reference on *gotong-royong*.

numbers of Malay middle class is felt and seen in our present multiracial society. In short, the present Malays have come out of their traditional cocoon of traditionalism and conservatism. They are now better educated, more confident and self-reliant, and with a progressive world view of life within and beyond Singapore.

All these were made possible through the strong *gotong-royong*[a] spirit of the community in being partners with the various government and non-governmental agencies in striving for a positive social change.

As the African saying goes: "If you want to go fast, go alone. If you want to go far, go together."

It is this 'togetherness' that has made Singaporean Malays what they are today.

Bibliography

1. Lim Peng Han. An analysis of factors affecting the development of Malay secondary schools and Malay secondary school libraries within the multilingual school system during colonial and post-colonial rule in Singapore, 1819–1985 (Doctoral Thesis submitted to Laborough University, March 2012).
2. Wan Hussin Zoohri. *The Singapore Malays: The Dilemma of Development*, Singapore Malay Teachers' Union, 1990.
3. New Nation, 7 September 1971.
4. Yayasan MENDAKI. *Merai Tekad Tiga Dekad (Keluaran Khas Sempena Ulang Tahun YM ke-30, 2012)*.
5. Yayasan MENDAKI Annual Reports: 2012, 2013, 2014.

From Malay College to Singapore Institution to Raffles Institution

Sir Stamford Raffles conceptualised the idea of establishing a premier educational institution in Singapore where young men of Singapore and Malaya would be educated not only in their language and culture but also in the best English tradition. He had earlier proposed that Sultan Hussein Shah and Temenggong Abdul Rahman send their sons to Calcutta, India, to receive their education, but both the Sultan and the Temenggong were resistant to the idea. An institution in Singapore would therefore enable the sons of the Malay nobility to receive the education deemed good by Raffles without requiring them to travel out of Singapore.

In his memorandum on the establishment of a Malay College, Raffles had envisioned a full-fledged college with not only the Malay department but also departments of Chinese and Siamese, alongside with that of English. The institution will also be a centre for research and scientific enquiry. Raffles had also wanted the institution to provide the Europeans based in Southeast Asia at the time with instruction in the native languages.

On 12 January 1823, Raffles wrote a letter to his cousin, where he briefly mentioned that he had found a suitable location for the institution. It was decided that the institution would be located along what is known today as Bras Basah Road and Victoria Street. The laying of the foundation stone for the building took place on 5 June 1823. Raffles proclaimed the building to be the "Institution". It was subsequently referred to as the Singapore Institution. The Singapore Institution remained so named until 1867. In the school's annual report for 1868, the school was referred to as the Raffles Institution.

Background image shows a view of Raffles Institution, originally known as Singapore Institution, which was founded in 1823. It originally located in Bras Basah road, and then moved to Grange Road before being relocated to Bishan in 1990.

Bibliography

1. Doraisamy, T. R., *et al.* (1969). *150 Years of Education in Singapore*. Singapore: Teachers Training College.
2. Buckley, C. B. (1984). *An Anecdotal History of Old Times in Singapore*, 1819–1867. Singapore: Oxford University Press.
3. Wijeysingha, E. (1989). *The Eagle Breeds a Gryphon: The Story of Raffles Institution 1823–1985*. Singapore: Pioneer Book Centre.
4. Raffles, S. (1830). *Memoir of the Life and Public Services of Sir Thomas Stamford Raffles*. Singapore: Oxford University Press.

CHAPTER 15

RELIGIOUS LEADERSHIP IN SINGAPORE: FROM SUCCESS TO SIGNIFICANCE OF MADRASAH EDUCATION

Mohammad Hannan Hassan

PERGAS is a Non-Governmental Organization (NGO) that envisions "Religious Leadership that is Credible, Integrated and Contributing towards the Development of The Community". Founded in 1957, PERGAS was dedicated to raising the quality of Islamic Education and Welfare of the Islamic Religious Teachers (*asatizah*).

The *asatizah* fraternity has evolved over the past four decades. But this evolution is a story of a journey not a destination, a work in progress, and must continue to evolve from success to significance. As a young boy, I used to listen to my mother telling stories about her teachers Kiayi Ahmad Zohri Mutamim, Ustaz Daud Ali, Ustaz Ahmad Sonhadji Mohamad and her brother (my uncle) Ustaz Mustajab Shai'en, all of whom had dedicated their lives to helping fellow *asatizahs* and improving the Islamic education here. They were the founding fathers of the Singapore Islamic Scholars and Religious Teachers Association (Persatuan Ulama dan Guru-Guru Agama Singapura, PERGAS), founded in 1957 to support the welfare and well-being of the *asatizahs* and to disseminate Islamic teachings through *dakwah* and education. PERGAS has remained to serve the purpose for which it was founded till today.

I can recall as a young boy, my parents' house frequently became a meeting place for the *asatizahs* and community leaders. These were not just religious teachers of my parents, but also partners in their journey. Amongst them were luminaries such as Ustaz Daud Ali, Kiayi Ahmad Zohri Mutamim, Ustaz Embek Ali, Ustaz Mahmood Majid, Ustaz Zainal Arifin Sharbini and several others familiar to me. Watching and listening to them, discussing issues of their struggles, aspirations and dreams with my father had left indelible

Allahyarham hum Kiayi Ahmad Zohri Mutamim, Ustaz Mustajab Shae'in, Ustaz Embok, Ustaz Hj Daud Ali, Ustaz Said Ibrahim, Ustaz Mofradi Mohammad Noor, Ustaz Mohammad Amin Muslim, Ustaz Hafiz Hakim and Ustaz Idris Ahmad were amongst the protem committee that led to the formation of PERGAS. Image courtesy of PERGAS© 2016. All rights reserved.

Ustaz Peer Mohamed Rawther was a student of Raffles Institution with the late Mr Lee Kuan Yew.

marks on me. The old PERGAS at Jalan Damai was one of the places I used to frequent as a young boy.

Welfare, socio-economic survival, opportunities for the *asatizahs*, and contributions to the community and nation were among the issues extensively discussed. Some decided to seek greener pastures elsewhere, while some others remained in Singapore serving in various agencies: national schools, *madrasahs* and media, as well as in trade and business and as freelancers. My uncle, Dato Paduka Ustaz Mustajab, together with some of his colleagues left for Brunei in the late 1960s and early 1970s. He remained in Brunei as a teacher to the Royal Family until his passing in 2004. He continued to remain in touch with Singapore and his fellow *asatizahs*. Some returned to Singapore, like Ustaz Ahmad Sonhadji,[1] Ustaz Peer Mohamed Rawther[2] and Ustaz Syed Agil Othman. I remember vividly an *ustaz* who was considering migrating elsewhere discussing with my father and few other *asatizahs*. They then agreed that he should migrate with the intention of returning to Singapore when opportunities avail.

Opportunities to study in the renowned Al-Azhar University in Cairo were rare. The struggle of Sheikh Syed Isa Semait, the former Mufti, to complete his study in Al-Azhar is well told in his biography *Keeping the Faith*.[3] His good friend, Ustaz Syed Abdillah al-Jufri was not as fortunate as him. I can also recall the days when *asatizahs* left for Al-Azhar University or any other places to pursue their religious studies, I would always be there to send them off, or at least most of them. It was like a religious ritual to me — talked with them, bade them farewell and sought their prayers. These aspiring students are now serving the community and nation in various ways, the likes of Ustaz Salleh Sinwan, Ustaz Syed Ahmad Syed Mohamad, Ustaz Mokson Mahori, Ustaz Karim Ahmad, my elder brother Ustaz Mohamad Hasbi Hassan and many others. Pursuing Islamic studies then was not a desirable option; and many were not able to pursue their Islamic higher learning, much less their postgraduate studies. Not until recently, we could cite only the late Ustaz Abu Bakar Hashim and Ustazah Khadijah Jaafar as the two *asatizahs* with a Masters degree from Al-Azhar University. This, however, is no longer the case. The last two decades in particular have witnessed a substantial growth and new opportunities created both upstream and downstream.

Growth and Opportunities: Upstream

Upstream, *madrasah* education has seen significant development. Started purely as Islamic school that offered only Islamic sciences, *madrasahs* gradually started to offer non-Islamic subjects such as English, mathematics and science in the early 1970s at both primary and secondary levels. Subsequently, some *madrasahs* facilitated their students to take GCE 'O' and 'A' levels as private candidates.

In the early 1990s, parents saw *madrasah* education as a viable educational path for their children. Here, students were provided the opportunity to pursue their post-secondary studies in Islamic tertiary institutions as well as the conventional institutions.

Striking the right balance — the *madrasah* education system requires primary students to take five additional Islamic subjects on top of the four PSLE subjects. The *madrasahs* conduct admissions tests to ensure that students who they enrol will be able to cope well with the demands of the curriculum. Under the Joint Madrasah System (JMS), Madrasah Aljunied Al-Islamiah and Madrasah Al-Arabiah Al-Islamiah take in only secondary school students. Images courtesy of Majlis Ugama Islam Singapura © 2015. All rights reserved.

This rising expectation of the parents and community, in addition to several other factors, naturally provided an impetus for *madrasahs* to review and strengthen their curriculum: a perennial challenge in balancing between the national and Islamic curriculum. Since early 1990s, the Islamic Religious Council of Singapore (MUIS) initiated efforts to review the *madrasah* curriculum. In 1995, a Curriculum Development Committee was formed to study with an aim to propose an integrated curriculum for both the part-time and full-time *madrasahs*. In 2001, an integrated curriculum was proposed and subsequently a Curriculum Development Project (CDP) was initiated in 2001.

The debate on *madrasah* education in 1999 arguably could be regarded as a watershed event in the modern history of *madrasah* education in Singapore. In October 2000, the Compulsory Education Act was passed, and implemented in 2003.[4] The Compulsory Education aims to provide Singapore children with "a common core of knowledge which will provide a strong foundation for further education and training to prepare them for a knowledge-based economy; and a common educational experience which will help to build national identity and cohesion." *Madrasahs* are however categorised as designated schools whose primary level students are exempted but are required to

Since 2002, with support from MUIS and PERGAS, Al-Zuhri Institute of Higher Learning (Al-Zuhri) has been offering diplomas in Islamic studies. Private institutions like Al-Zuhri will provide alternative routes for those who are interested to pursue Islamic-based education. Image courtesy of Al-Zuhri © 2016. All rights reserved.

take the Primary School Leaving Examination (PSLE) and meet a certain benchmark for it to be allowed admission of new students.[4]

While the Compulsory Education provided a strong impetus to strengthening their curriculum, learning and teachers development, madrasahs were already putting in various initiatives and programmes to meet today's challenges. Nonetheless, the last decade witnessed significant growth. Since 2003, in human capacity development alone, more than $3 million were invested in developing teachers, heads of departments and principals. By 2013, 94% of teachers in *madrasahs* were professionally certified educators. Fifty-one graduated with a Diploma in Education from the Edith Cowan University, Perth, Australia; 119 teachers graduated from the National Institute of Education (NIE) with a Specialist Diploma in Teaching and Learning (SPECDip); and more than 20 *madrasah* management staff completed their training in the Management and Leadership in Schools Programme offered by NIE in January 2013.[5] This is made possible through a synergetic approach between the *madrasahs*, the community, MUIS and relevant national agencies.

Growth and Opportunities: Downstream

Downstream, *asatizah* development enjoyed what the pioneering generation did not, in terms of opportunities and growth. The former Mufti of Singapore, Sheikh Syed Isa Semait recollected in his biography the challenges he encountered to pursue his studies at the Al-Azhar University in 1961. Together with his peers, Ustaz Hassan Salim and Ustaz Mashor Awi, they struggled to cover their sea passage to Cairo. They had to seek assistance from the Muslim Advisory Board (MUIS was not yet established at that time) and the Asia Foundation to cover their sea fare. Syed Isa recalled a panelist of the latter asked, "Why don't you Muslims start a foundation like this?" Syed Isa then could only wish that such a body would exist. However, "it would take time but would see fruition in the Islamic Religious Council of Singapore's scholarships and bursaries for a different generation of students, nurturing their desires to pursue their own studies in religion." MUIS was eventually established in 1968, but it took many more years before it was able to offer financial assistance to students in Islamic studies. In my conversation with Shaikh Syed Isa, he narrated

The MUIS Postgraduate Scholarship identifies budding scholars and supports their further studies at graduate level (Masters and PhD), either locally or at international universities.

Images courtesy of Majlis Ugama Islam Singapura © 2015. All rights reserved.

the early days in MUIS when aspiring students would seek financial assistance from MUIS. The available resources were insufficient. MUIS had to spread thin the limited resources. Sheikh Syed Isa kept secret a wish to himself that one day he could offer better assistance. His wish became a reality.

As MUIS gained greater trust from the community, with better *zakat* collection and working closely with other community institutions, budding students could find support for their aspirations. MUIS granted funds to the Lembaga Biasiswa Kenangan Maulud (LBKM)[6] to provide bursaries for students wishing to pursue Islamic studies. MUIS also offered undergraduate scholarships to top students to pursue Islamic studies. Together with the mosques, the Religious Officers Scholarship Scheme (ROSS) was introduced in the early 2000 with an aim to supply mosques with quality religious officers. And since 2005, MUIS has been offering its Postgraduate Scholarship (PGS) Scheme to produce local experts and specialists in the area of Islamic studies and Muslim societies.

Many of the *asatizah*, graduates of established Islamic learning institutions such as Al-Azhar University and the International Islamic University of Malaysia, return to serve the community at MUIS or institutions such as Pergas and the National University of Singapore. Image courtesy of Majlis Ugama Islam Singapura © 2015. All rights reserved.

Today, support for Islamic studies at both undergraduate and postgraduate levels has been made accessible. In addition to providing bursaries, LBKM is now offering scholarships for *asatizah* wishing to do postgraduate studies at prestigious universities. Pergas too has been awarding grants to *asatizah* for postgraduate studies. Similarly, Muhammadiyah offers the Ibn Sina and Ibn Taymiyyah Awards to encourage multidisciplinary studies in Islamic sciences and Muslim societies. Through its' PGS scheme since 2005, MUIS has awarded scholarships and grants to 24 outstanding Masters and Doctoral candidates in various specialisations on Islam and Muslim societies studies. The most recent was a scholarship for an *ustaz* who is venturing his Master of Philosophy in Islamic theology and history at the University of Oxford in the United Kingdom. His is a story of the new opportunities created to nurture future *asatizah*. He rose up from *madrasah* education, selected into the year-long MUIS-Madrasah Scholars Programme in 2006, pursued his studies in Cairo University, emerged as among the top students of his batch, and now is granted the scholarship to Oxford. And his, apparently, is not the only story of *asatizah* climbing up the ladder, venturing new opportunities, and assuming various roles and functions in the Muslim community and the Singapore society at large.

More *asatizah* are pursuing post-graduate degrees. Currently, more than 50% of *asatizah*, and rising, possess at least a Bachelor degree from numerous centres of Islamic studies in the Middle East and North Africa (MENA) such as in Egypt, Libya, Jordan, Saudi, Syria and Turkey; as well as in the Southeast Asia (SEA) such as Malaysia, Brunei and Indonesia. These graduates are also contributing through various public and private sectors such as the ministries, embassies, hospitals, social agencies, academia, and certainly the religious sectors. No less of them who ventured into business and social entrepreneurship.

Designed to place *asatizah* under the tutelage and mentoring of Islamic scholars of international standing, the Overseas Attachment Program (OAP) began its first run in January 2013. Image courtesy of Majlis Ugama Islam Singapura © 2015. All rights reserved.

Beyond academic, professional and career development, *asatizah* are continuously contributing to Islamic discourse, actively engaging in various platforms with local and international scholars and thinkers in the face of emerging issues, and complex and multi-faceted challenges. They publish research articles, commentaries and analysis. They present papers at international conferences. They sit in national committees and Government Parliamentary Committees (GPC). They lead national projects such as the Harmony Centre, the Religious Rehabilitation Group (RRG) and some Inter-Racial and Religious Confidence Circles (IRCC). And they head departments in MUIS and ministries. At his acceptance speech of the Anugerah Jauhari 2015, the highest award in the Muslim community of Singapore, Hj Mohd Alami Musa, the President of MUIS, expressed his honour in serving the community and the nation. He duly acknowledged that developing the Singapore Muslim Identity (SMI) project, working closely with the *asatizah* within and outside MUIS, was indeed the most valued and cherished contribution.[7] *Asatizah* were key contributors to the SMI project: as interlocutors, reviewers, and drafters of the SMI document Risalah for the Building of Singapore Muslim Community of Excellence.

Mosque Officers Development Scheme (MODS) is a compulsory part-time mosque management certification programme for all full-time key appointments and executive positions in our mosques. This includes Mosque Religious Officers (MRO), Social Development Officers, Youth Development Officers and aLIVE administrators. Image courtesy of Majlis Ugama Islam Singapura © 2015. All rights reserved.

From Success to Significance

This is an evolving story of new opportunities being created for *madrasah* graduates. We should aspire higher and expect deeper and more significant contributions beyond the Muslim community, beyond legal issues that concern the Muslims, and beyond Singapore shores. The untapped potential for pro-active and leading contributors are tremendous in shaping religious lives and thoughts of the Singapore Muslim Community, the nation, and

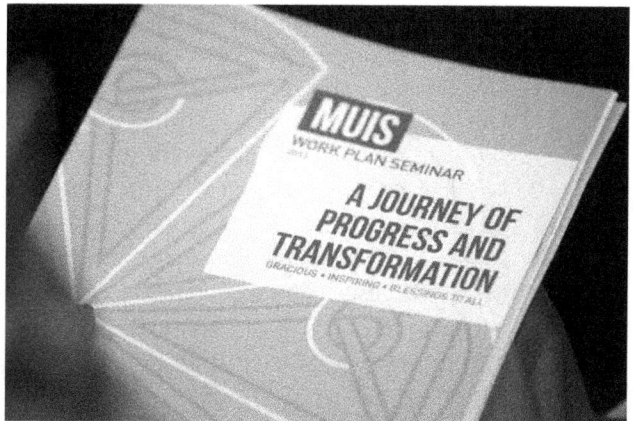

MUIS Workplan Seminars highlight MUIS' 3-year workplan amongst others in the following areas (1) Enhancing and increasing the reach of Islamic Education; (2) Improving and increasing delivery of social assistance to needy families; (3) Expanding and improving mosque space and infrastructure; and (4) Strengthening the *madrasah* sector. Image courtesy of Majlis Ugama Islam Singapura © 2015. All rights reserved.

beyond. Numerous international scholars and thinkers who visited Singapore, and engaged with the society and the *asatizah* in particular acknowledged that Singapore is not short of potential. These potentials could be harnessed, and the humility demonstrated by the *asatizah* be laid accordingly at the right and appropriate place.

The pioneering and founding generation, such as Ustaz Daud Ali, Kiayi Ahmad Zohri Mutamim, Ustaz Embek Ali, Ustaz Mahmood Abdul Majid, Ustaz Syed Ahmad Semait, Maulana Muhammad Abdul Aleem Siddique, Maulavi M. H. Babu Shahib and numerous others have passed on, and could not witness this evolution to what it is today. However, their earlier contributions to the ideas and initiation to plans that made ways for the subsequent generations will remain and are considered as bricks to the building, chapters to the evolving story, and landmarks on this journey.

Bibliography

1. A prolific author, teacher and scholar, Ustaz Ahmad Sonhadji then became the Principal of Madrasah Aljunied, published numerous books, and the most important of all is his *Tafsir Abral Athir*, the only complete book of Tafsir in the Malay language.

2. Few know that Ustaz Peer Mohamed was a student of Raffles Institution with the late Mr Lee Kuan Yew, who later decided to do Islamic and Arabic studies at Madrasah Aljunied.

3. Syed Zakir Hussain, *Keeping the Faith — Isa Semait, Mufti of Singapore 1972-2010*, Straits Times Press, 2012.

4. For the background and recommendations on Compulsory Education, see the report of the Committee of Compulsory Education in Singapore available at http://www.moe.gov.sg/initiatives/compulsory-education/

5. See http://www.MUISMUIS.gov.sg/documents/Annual_Reports/MUISMUIS-html/edit-institution.html

6. LBKM was the brainchild of another pioneering religious leader, Ustaz Syed Ali Redha Alsagoff in 1963, and was officially launched in 22 August 1965 just after Singapore's separation from Malaysia.

7. Hj Mohd Alami Musa said, "*Saya amat bertuah kerana diberi peluang berkhidmat kepada masyarakat dan negara. Bagi saya, sumbangan yang menyentuh diri saya ialah usaha membentuk Identiti Muslim Singapura (SMI) bersama asatizah di dalam dan di luar MUIS.*" See http://beritaharian.sg/setempat/alami-pingat-hasil-kerjasama-semua-bina-harmoni-pupuk-identiti-muslim#sthash.Rpo7m2Mt.dpuf Accessed on 25 Aug 2015. Hj Mohd Alami Musa was the Executive President of MUIS from 2003–2013, before he became the Non-Executive President of MUIS.

CHAPTER 16

SCIENCE, TECHNOLOGY AND THE MALAY/MUSLIM YOUTHS* | Jackie Yi-Ru Ying

S cience and technology form the basis of various industrial sectors. Over the past 50 years, Singapore's industries have evolved substantially. We not only have manufacturing capabilities, but also R&D expertise. This has led to the creation of many high value-added jobs, and drawn multinational companies to Singapore for manufacturing as well as research.

Public investment in research has increased dramatically from $2 billion in the National Science and Technology Plan 2000, to $6 billion and $13.55 billion in the Science and Technology 2005 Plan and 2010 Plan, respectively. The bold investment in research by the Singapore government allowed for major infrastructure to be established in Biopolis and Fusionopolis, with A*STAR not only drawing world-class researchers to Singapore, but also offering a large number of overseas and local scholarships to nurture our own young scientists and engineers. In the local universities and hospitals, greater emphasis has also been placed on research. While the percentage increase in the budget is not as high for the Research, Innovation and Enterprise 2015 Plan and 2020 Plan, the overall public investments are very sizeable at $16.1 billion and $19 billion, respectively.

---

* This article was written in the author's personal capacity. The opinions expressed in the article are the author's own and do not reflect the view of the Institute of Bioengineering and Nanotechnology.

As we move forward, it is critical to not only grow research and development capabilities, but to also nurture innovative enterprises. The key to all these advances lies in creating the appropriate talent pool. The Malay/Muslim organisations should proactively encourage more young people to pursue science and engineering in their studies, and research and entrepreneurship as a career choice. While there are some young Malay and Muslim researchers in Singapore, the number is disproportionately small. Science and technology can make a tremendous impact to the nation and the society, and young people should not miss this golden opportunity to make a difference, especially when the government is devoting major resources to the growth of these areas.

Professor Ying is executive director of the Institute of Bioengineering and Nanotechnology (IBN), which comes under the Agency for Science, Technology and Research, or A*Star. Image reproduced with permission from Institute of Bioengineering and Nanotechnology © 2016. All rights reserved.

Professor Ying with her daughter Hsi-Min. Image reproduced with permission from Jackie Ying © 2016. All rights reserved.

In particular, over the past decade, research investment has successfully brought in pharmaceuticals, biologics and medical technology industries to Singapore. This sector is driven by a large demand for better medicine and diagnostics. It invests heavily in research, and offers high value-added jobs. Our young people may want to note however, that there is an oversupply of graduates and PhDs in biology, and a shortage of graduates and PhDs in chemistry, pharmacy and engineering. In particular, engineering students with interdisciplinary training are needed for the biomedical sector. Also, students with entrepreneurship background are lacking.

Globally, many innovations in this growing sector are driven by startup companies. Hence, if Singapore is to fully capture the value of research in this sector, it should create an environment that would really foster the growth of spinoffs. These high-tech spinoffs would need greater support than the traditional SMEs that are manufacturing based, as biomedical technologies need to go through a long gestation period for validation and clinical trials before commercialisation. In Boston, San Francisco and San Diego, startups strive on having great ideas and technologies spinning off from the top universities and research institutes. They receive strong financial support from the government (through the ample Small Business Innovative Research grants), as well as investments and business guidance from venture capitalists and angel investors. In Singapore, there is the need and potential for more spinoffs. The young people that would be driving such spinoffs would ideally have both research expertise with a major in science/engineering and a minor in business administration.

Highly impactful research is accomplished by those who know which problems are important to address, and have superb capability and creativity to tackle those complex problems successfully. Hence, even the entry-level research positions would require excellent PhD and post-doctoral experience. This career path demands many years of studies and training and should be taken on only by those who are first-rate and committed.

Hence, Singapore as a whole and the Malay/Muslim community in particular would need to nurture more young people who are really interested in and passionate about science and technology. If they are not truly driven and creative, their research would not be cutting-edge. The Government needs to ensure that more young people become interested in science by further improving the quality of teaching and shifting much greater emphasis to laboratory work. A dry curriculum that is based on textbook teaching

Professor Ying with research staff and Youth Research Programme (YRP) students. Image reproduced with permission from Institute of Bioengineering and Nanotechnology © 2016. All rights reserved.

with little hands-on exposure turns away many young people and does not prepare them well for further studies in science, which are focused on tackling open-ended questions and conducting experiments. The schools should also partner with research institutes and universities to establish more research internship opportunities for pre-university students so that the latter can gain experience in and appreciation for research.

The Malay/Muslim community has certainly done better both in education and professional development over the years, but there is still a lot of room for improvement. For example, there is a decreasing trend in the number of young Malays and Muslims attending the top secondary schools and junior colleges and the number of Malay/Muslim scholarship holders remains disappointingly small. It is important for more young people in our community to attend the top secondary schools and junior colleges as they often offer the best resources for academic pursuits. These schools would also help to open the doors for further studies and scholarships in the top universities.

Professor Ying and her daughter Hsi-Min at the Mustafa Prize award ceremony. The Mustafa Prize is a top science and technology award granted to the top researchers and scientists of the Organization of Islamic Cooperation (OIC) member states biennially. Image reproduced with permission from Jackie Ying © 2016. All rights reserved.

The community must ask itself if it has done everything to inspire, encourage, mentor and financially support those who are highly talented to make it to the top. We should also find out why some of the small number of qualified students did not choose to enter the top schools. Some families may be worried because of financial reasons and that their children may not fit in as minorities. These are concerns that the schools can address if the Malay/Muslim organisations can help to identify the top minority students so that the schools can reach out to them. There are also a number of girls who are excellent in their studies who choose to go to *madrasahs* and polytechnics because they really want to be able to wear the *hijab*. This is a more complex issue that needs to be examined by the Malay/Muslim leaders and organisations along with the government.

As we look ahead, we see the exciting potential to contribute to Singapore economically and socially through research and entrepreneurship. As we celebrate the nation's golden jubilee, it is also timely to remind ourselves of our responsibility to nurture the next generations of young people so that we have future leaders in every field, including science and technology.

CHAPTER 17

A VISION FOR MALAY STUDIES | Syed Farid Alatas

I n the different fields of study in the arts and social sciences, there are some which are concerned with specific regions of the world. These include Asian Studies, Southeast Asian Studies, Middle Eastern Studies, Central Asian Studies and so on. Malay Studies is one of these so-called area studies. At the National University of Singapore, the Department of Malay Studies adopts a broad definition of the Malay world. The geographical scope of interest is the entire Malay–Indonesian Archipelago consisting of Indonesia, Malaysia, Brunei, southern Thailand and the southern Philippines. The department is also interested in areas with substantial Malay minorities such as Singapore, and countries to which the Malay diaspora had spread such as Sri Lanka, Madagascar and South Africa.

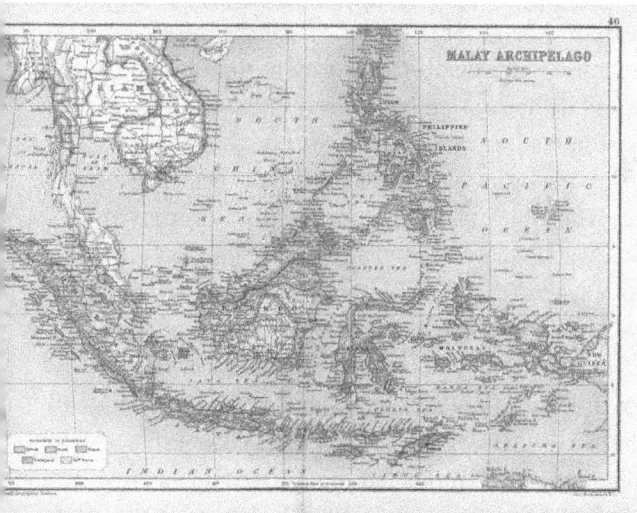

"Malay Archipelago" by the Edinburgh Geographical Institute, published in an atlas by John Bartholomew & Co., about 1880. Chromolithographic map. Image is in public domain.

The Department of Malay Studies at the National University of Singapore has an interesting history. Upon the recommendation of the Commission for University Education in Malaya, a department dedicated to the advancement of the study of the Malays was established at the University of Malaya, Singapore during the 1952/53 academic session. The first head of department was Za'ba (Zainal Abidin Ahmad). He was succeeded by R. Roolvink. Following the independence of Malaya and the establishment of a separate, autonomous University of Malaya in Kuala Lumpur, the Department of Malay Studies was transferred to Kuala Lumpur. Meanwhile, on 1 January, 1962 the Singapore Division of the University of Malaya was re-established as the University of Singapore, later to be renamed the National University of Singapore in 1980. On 1 March, 1967, the Department of Malay Studies was re-established in Singapore with Professor Dr Syed Hussein Alatas as Head of Department.

More important and interesting is the direction that the department has taken over the years and the perspective in the study of the Malays that it takes. Indeed, the Department of Malay Studies had presented a somewhat new and creative approach to the study of the Malays. Differing from Malay Studies in Malaysia and Indonesia, where the approach tends to be more language- and literature-based, Malay Studies in Singapore takes a decidedly more social scientific approach to the study of the Malays. While literature is by no means ignored by the teaching staff in the department, students are also given a great deal of exposure to sociological and historical perspectives with which they can study the Malay society. Furthermore, since the department was established in 1967, it promoted a critical perspective for the study of the Malays. This meant that the research and teaching of the department did not simply accept perspectives that were dominant in British or other Western studies of the Malays. Nor did the department simply accept without question perspectives that were promoted by governments or politicans in the region.

The first head of the department, Syed Hussein Alatas, pioneered this critical perspective. Before Alatas had moved to Singapore, he spoke of the problem of intellectual imperialism or the "wholesale importation of ideas from the Western world to Eastern societies".[1] Alatas also suggested that the way of thinking of colonised peoples paralleled political and economic imperialism — hence, the expression academic or intellectual imperialism.[2] Tham Seong Chee, a member of the Department of Malay

Studies as well as its head from 1989 to 1997, referred to such colonial thinking as being informed by "a false consciousness about values, person and goals. It is a mode of seeing one's society — its workings and the direction of its movement — by super-imposing on it another reality, that is to say, the reality of a foreign society".[3] The idea of the colonial mentality was developed by Syed Hussein Alatas in the form of the concept of the captive mind.[4,5]

Because of this tradition of being conscious of intelletual imperialism, Malay Studies in Singapore has for several decades produced scholarly works that "swim against the tide" or *melawan arus*, as the Malays say. Examples of such writings include Alatas' research on colonial ideology which focused on (i) the political philosophy of Raffles[6] and (ii) the myth of Malay, Javanese and Filipino laziness.[7]

In his work on Raffles, Alatas presents a critique of the philosophy of the colonial administrator at a time in Singapore scholarship when there was hardly any critical assessment of the man. In fact, Raffles had been presented by the independent Singapore state as a hero of sorts, one of the rare instances in history of a colonial administrator serving as a national icon. Alatas' task was to present a critical and not Eurocentric account of the thinking and deeds of Raffles. Specifically, he had set out to examine the status of Raffles as a hero through an assessment of his political philosophy and his conduct. Alatas concluded that the silence among scholars about Raffles questionable political philosophy and conduct was strange in that even by colonial standards, he fell short of the humanitarianism that was attributed to him.[6] In Alatas' *The Myth of the Lazy Native*,[7] the colonial view that the Malays, Javanese and Filipinos were inherently lazy was critiqued and explained in terms of the economic interests of colonial capitalism.

Other scholars of the department also worked on the critique and reconstruction in history and the social sciences. They include Shaharuddin Maaruf,[8,9] who headed the Department of Malay Studies for several years until he left NUS in 2007, Sharifah Maznah Syed Omar,[10] and Noor Aisha Abdul Rahman. Shaharuddin, also took a critical approach in his research. For example, his book, *Malay Ideas on Development* critiques commonly held

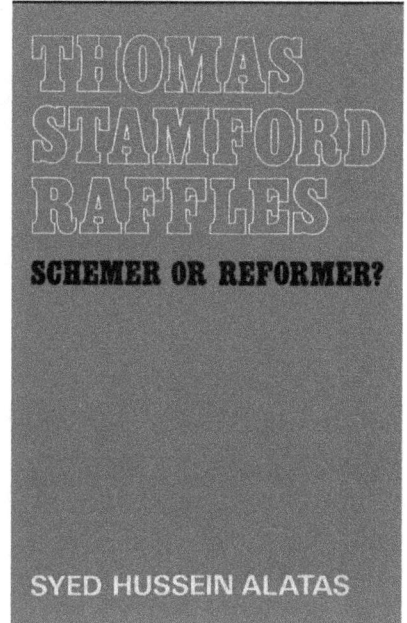

THOMAS STAMFORD RAFFLES

SCHEMER OR REFORMER?

SYED HUSSEIN ALATAS

An account of Raffles' political philosophy during his colonial career in Java, Sumatra and Singapore. *Thomas Stamford Raffles — Schemer or Reformer?* Angus and Robertson, 1971.

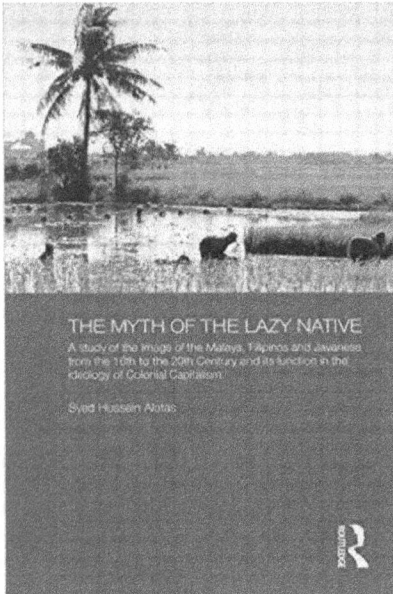

THE MYTH OF THE LAZY NATIVE
A study of the image of the Malays, Filipinos and Javanese
from the 16th to the 20th Century and its function in the
Ideology of Colonial Capitalism.

Syed Hussein Alatas

Syed Hussein Alatas began pondering the question of why Western colonialists had, for four centuries, considered the natives of Maritime Southeast Asia to be generally lazy. His research eventually produced. *The Myth of the Lazy Native — A Study of the Image of the Malays, Filipinos and Javanese from the 16th to the 20th Century and Its Function in the Ideology of Colonial Capitalism.* Frank Cass & Company Limited, London, 1977.

ideas about Malay thinking on development, showing that what often appeared to be progressive thinking was actually conservative or even regressive. The current head of the department, also the first woman head of the department, Associate Professor Noor Aisha Abdul Rahman, is an expert on sociological perspectives on Muslim law.[11] She has also contributed much to critical thinking about the Malays. One of her areas of concern has been the religious orientations to be found among the Malays. Her works discuss what we may call progressive orientations as well as those that are backward and are unable to constructively deal with the problems of Malay society.[12] Noor Aisha has played a very important role in nurturing younger scholars and students who have adopted the critical bent that informs Malay Studies in Singapore. This nurturing takes place not only in the classroom but also through informal sessions that she often holds or is invited to speak at.

Throughout his time as head of the Department of Malay Studies, Syed Hussein Alatas was concerned with the role of the intellectual, whom he defined as a "person who is engaged in thinking about ideas and non-material problems using the faculty of reason". Furthermore, "knowledge of a certain subject or the possession of a degree does not make a person an intellectual although these often coincide. There are many degree holders and professors who do not engage in developing their field or trying to find the solution to specific problems within it. On the other hand, a person with no academic qualifications can be an intellectual if he utilizes his thinking capacity and possesses sufficient knowledge of his subject of interest".[13] One of the roles of intellectuals is to think about the direction a society should take. Regarding my own personal view about this, I would like to make some remarks on the role of the Malay language and what intellectuals should push for.

There is a view among the Malays themselves that the efficiency, capability and productivity of those for whom Malay is a first language and who are not proficient in English is lower than that of the workforce of those who are proficient in English. Such a view assumes that the Malay language is linguistically handicapped as far as being a conveyor of scientific knowledge is concerned. This view is based on a lack of understanding of the development of languages. For example, that we have borrowed many scientific terms from English does not mean that Malay is an inferior language. Many European languages themselves contain loan words, terms, and phrases that have their origins in Greek and Latin, Arabic and even Malay. Do we conclude that English, French, German, Italian, and Spanish are not up to the task of scientific discourse?

In fact, Malay is an extremely rich language. Its system of prefixes and suffixes enables the speaker to switch tenses, shift back and forth from the active to the passive voice, and to convert verbs to nouns. Its grammatical tools are sufficient for its user to express herself in any scientific or literary endeavour. Those who are not able to express themselves scientifically in Malay ought not to denigrate Malay. More than likely, it is they who need upgrading in order that they may learn to use Malay more fruitfully. The development of the Malay language is dependent upon the intellectual and scientific development of the Malays and their seriousness in utilising the language as deeply and widely as possible. It is clear that a balance must be struck between English and Malay. For obvious reasons, the Malays must attain a certain degree of proficiency in English. On the other hand, the further development of Malay must not be neglected if it is to become a conveyor of scientific concepts and ideas.

References

1. Alatas, Syed Hussein. 1956. "Some Fundamental Problems of Colonialism", *Eastern World* (London), November 1956.
2. ———. 1969. "Academic Imperialism", Lecture delivered to the History Society, University of Singapore 26 September.
3. Tham Seong Chee. 1971. "Intellectual Colonization", *Suara Universiti* 2 (2): 39–40.
4. Alatas, Syed Hussein. 1972. "The Captive Mind in Development Studies", *International Social Science Journal* 24(1): 9–25.
5. ———. 1974. "The Captive Mind and Creative Development", *International Social Science Journal* 26(4): 691–700.
6. ———. 1971. *Thomas Stamford Raffles 1781–1826: Schemer or Reformer*, Sydney: Angus and Robertson,

7. ———. 1977(a). *The Myth of the Lazy Native: A Study of the Image of the Malays, Filipinos, and Javanese from the Sixteenth to the Twentieth Century and its Functions in the Ideology of Colonial Capitalism*, London: Frank Cass.

8. Shaharuddin Maaruf. 1989. *Malay Ideas on Development: From Feudal Lord to Capitalist*, Singapore: Times Book International.

9. ———. 1992. "Some Theoretical Problems Concerning Tradition and Modernization Among the Malays of Southeast Asia", in Yong Mun Cheong, ed., *Asian Tradition and Modernization: Perspectives from Singapore*, Singapore: Times Academic Press, pp. 241–265.

10. Sharifah Maznah Syed Omar. 1993. *Myths and the Malay Ruling Class*, Singapore: Times Academic Press.

11. Noor Aisha Abdul Rahman. 2004. Traditionalism and its impact on the administration of justice: the case of the Syariah Court of Singapore Inter-Asia Cultural Studies 5(3): 415–432.

12. ———. 2006. *Colonial Image of Malay Adat Laws: A Critical Appraisal of Studies on Adat Laws in the Malay Peninsula during the Colonial Era and Some Continuities*, Leiden: Brill.

13. Alatas, Syed Hussein. 1977(b). *Intellectuals in Developing Societies*, London: Frank Cass.

CHAPTER 18

SAYANG ANAKKU SAYANG | Sharifah Mariam
(MY BELOVED CHILD) | Aljunied

There is a strong-held belief among Malay/
Muslim families in Singapore that children are
rizki (providence) from God. Even today, when
one hears about an Encik Ahmad with six children,
the typical response would be to say "Your *rizki* will
be plentiful, God-willing". And when we receive the
good news that an Encik Ali has received a big pay
rise, we congratulate him by saying "Alhamdulilah,
this is your children's *rizki*".

We love our children. Children are
the core of a Malay/Muslim family,
and even today, most couples would
say that the reason for getting married
is to start a family, i.e., to have children. Today, although less common, it
is not unusual to find Malay/Muslim
families in Singapore with four children or more. Following the trend of
other families in Singapore, the average size of a Malay/Muslim family has
gotten smaller, but it is nonetheless
larger than that of other races.[1]

Forty years ago, growing up and
going to school near Tanjong
Katong, I knew of several families
with more than 10 children in one
household. My parents, who had "only" four children,

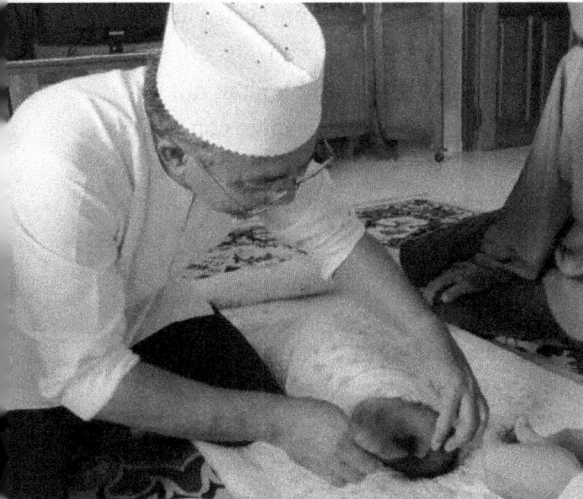

Loving tender care for a Malay/Muslim child starts
from birth. A newborn Malay/Muslim baby undergoing
the "cukur rambut" (hair shaving) ceremony. Photo
courtesy of Aminur Rasid © 2015 All rights reserved.

were considered to have a "very small" family. In my younger days, I simply appreciated the fact that when I make a new Malay/Muslim friend, I instantly gain several more, i.e., their siblings. This makes for a very good social investment in my circle of friends! Over the years, as I interacted and forged close relations with many of these families, I better appreciate and understand the complex factors that encouraged them to have big families, even though it was against economic imperatives and the then prevailing government policies.

One of my best friends in primary school was Raihan; an eighth child in a family of 12 children. Like me, Raihan had the opportunity to study right up to university. Raihan's dad held two jobs — a night security guard, and an odd-job labourer by day, while her mum made *kuih* at home to be sold at the market.

I know her two eldest siblings well. Kak Siti, who was like a mother to her, was the one who fetched Raihan to and from school every day, and attended to all school matters. For all finances related to school, e.g., school fees and textbooks, she relied on her elder brother, Abang Mat. Later on when Raihan needed money for "floppy disks" for her computer use at NUS, Abang Mat helped out. Abang Mat was a whiz at mental calculations, and often helped me and Raihan out with our math homework. Abang Mat never quite completed Primary 6 and Kak Siti never went to school. Abang Mat started work at 13 years old as an assistant in a car-repair workshop, and through long apprenticeship and dedication, he became the lead mechanic in the workshop. Kak Siti helped their mum to sell and make *kuih*, and at 12 years old, started work as a domestic helper with a Eurasian family that lived in Katong. Kak Siti picked up English through interactions with her "madam", and taught herself reading and writing. After school, Kak Siti would often grill me and Raihan on our spelling list.

Raihan's family was not unique. In large families like hers, very often, the elder siblings had to sacrifice their education so that they can help out in providing care and additional finances to support the rest of the family. It is not because that her parents did not know the value of education; instead, they felt they had to prioritise. They felt the urgency to first ensure that there was food on the table for all the children. Many hands make the task light: so having large families meant that you can have more just than the mum and dad to shoulder parental duties and responsibilities. The younger children, like Raihan, stood to gain in this arrangement, and consequently had more opportunities for education. In turn, they shouldered the family's hope for a better future life and security for old-age. Throughout the years that I knew her, there was never a doubt in Raihan about her reasons for studying hard: she needed to take care of her parents, as well as her siblings.

While the formula worked for Raihan's family, it did not do so well for another classmate of ours, Iskandar. Raihan and I used to sit near Iskandar in school and copied his work during mental sums, as he seemed to get all the answers right. We lost touch with him in secondary school. Last I heard of him, he was in jail for the second time for drug abuse and trafficking. His parents were separated and two of his siblings were in drug rehabilitation centres.

Table 1: Total abusers by ethnic group for 2011–2014

	2009	2010	2011	2012	2013	2014
Chinese	1036	1050	1109	1099	1259	946
Malay	1158	1376	1603	1773	1710	1586
Indian	374	403	539	567	541	497
Others	48	58	75	68	71	56

Source: MHA (Public).

Table 2: New abusers by ethnic group for 2011–2014

	2009	2010	2011	2012	2013	2014
Chinese	543	531	379	327	411	299
Malay	496	588	577	568	513	585
Indian	136	173	141	166	155	146
Others	25	35	31	31	31	28

Source: MHA (Public).

Both Raihan and Iskandar contributed to the statistics that we often read about Malay/Muslim children in Singapore over the first 20 years of Singapore's independence: low educational participation, high rates of divorce and drug abuse. While some struggled and succeeded, others crumbled.

Malays form the largest group, about 51.4% of the total drug abusers caught in 2014. Malays are also over-represented among new abusers.

I recalled a conversation I had with my late father over breakfast one day when I was in secondary two. He read the *Berita Harian* headlines about the forming of Yayasan MENDAKI, a self-help organisation aimed to improve the education of Malay/Muslim children in Singapore. The messages resonated with my dad. Education is a necessity; it is not a luxury item that is "good-to-have" if one can afford it. The best and most effective antidote to poverty is education. The best social investment is education. The most valuable gift that we can bequeath to our children is education. My father reflected, "They should have done this 20 years ago! Inshaa Allah, it is not too late".

In the subsequent years, a glimmer of hope began to arise, as seen in the steady increase in the number of our children that completed primary and secondary education, and a small but notable number of Malay/Muslim undergraduates in the university. However, while educational participation has improved, the quality of educational attainment of our children continued to lag behind that of others. In the early 1990s as I first entered the education service, the pattern was too obvious to go unnoticed: while the percentage of Malay/Muslim children that completed primary and secondary education had increased by leaps and bounds, and were close to national averages, our percentage of passes in subjects like Math and Science did not show a similar trend.[2] In many schools, one could see that a large number of children from poor families were identified for learning support in Primary 1 because they lacked the requisite skills for basic literacy and numeracy. More needed to be done.

A slew of programmes targeting educational support for Malay/Muslim students were initiated by several Malay/Muslim organisations, including academic tuition programmes, financial assistance schemes, outreach and parent training. These efforts were labour-intensive and did not yield immediate outcomes. Instead, they were aimed at creating impact that would be seen in the longer-term; making a difference to the lives and quality of learning of our children, one child at a time.

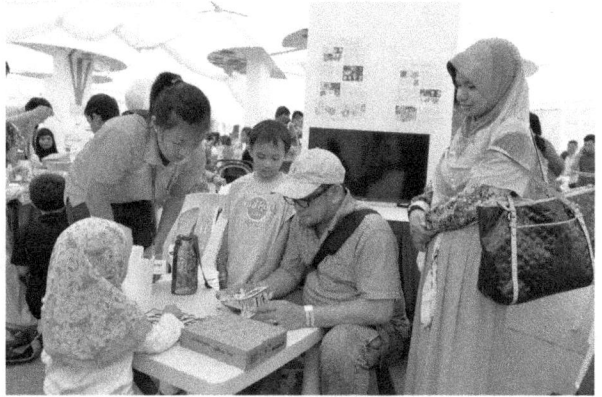

Participants of the various MENDAKI educational programmes. Image courtesy of Yayasan MENDAKI © 2015. All rights reserved.

I had been a volunteer with MENDAKI for some time, and had the blessed opportunity to develop and spearhead a parent coaching programme on mathematics for parents of Malay/Muslim pre-school children from the lower SES.[3] My Sunday afternoons in 2002 were well spent at a community centre (CC) in Boon Lay with 16 pre-schoolers and their parents. I vividly remembered what one particular participant, Puan Noor, shared with me at the end of the first pilot of the parent training programme known as "Tiga-M" or *Maju Minda Matematika* which means "progressive minds in mathematics". She candidly shared:

The Maju Minda Matematika (Tiga M) (progressive minds in mathematics) programme is targeted at parents with pre-school children (four–six years old). This free programme started after a survey in 2002 found that primary school children from low-income families did better in mathematics if their parents were involved in teaching mathematics skills. Tiga M has three objectives: (1) To increase parents' knowledge and understanding of the development of basic numeracy concepts. (2) To boost the confidence level of the parents and at the same time improving their skills in engaging their children in home-based activities. (3) To empower parents in creating a home environment that is conducive to the development of children's mathematical skills. Image courtesy of Yayasan MENDAKI © 2015. All rights reserved.

To be honest, I don't usually like to come for workshops like this. I only passed Primary 6. When I was in school, math was my worst subject. Once I went to a talk at my elder son's school. The person spoke English too fast, I could not keep up. He shared many ideas and information. But when I came home, I did not know what to do and where to start with my son. For this Tiga-M, to be honest, the first day I came was because I know MENDAKI will give me a grocery voucher if I attend. But I continued to come for the 10 sessions because I learnt something here. Here, I can see what you do and how you teach my son. Then you make me teach my son, and you guide me and tell me what I did well and how I can do better. Each session, I feel more

Maju Minda Matematika (Tiga M)   MENDAKI

- Maju Minda Matematika or Progressive Mathematical Minds conceptualised and piloted in 2002; rolled out in 2004

- Targets low-income Malay/Muslim families and their pre-school children aged 4 to 6 years old

Maju Minda Matematika (Tiga M)   MENDAKI

Objectives:

- To increase parents' knowledge and understanding of the development of basic concepts in mathematics

- To increase parents' confidence and skills in engaging their children in home based activities that would develop problem-solving and numeracy skills

- To empower parents in creating a home environment conducive to the development of children's mathematical skills

confident. I see that my son also enjoys learning math with me.

From one CC in Boon Lay, the Tiga-M programme has now been expanded to other CCs, mosques and HBD void-decks, and has helped more than 4000 Malay/Muslim preschool children from underprivileged homes and their parents. Based on longitudinal tracking of these children, MENDAKI found that children who had undergone the Tiga-M programme were less at-risk of being identified as needing learning support at Primary 1.[3]

Debates will continue about whether the quality of educational attainments of our Malay/Muslim children today is "good enough". Different views arise because we may be looking at the same issue with different lenses and different benchmarks. Compared to 20 years ago, our children are attaining better results in all subject areas, and more of our children are getting better quality grades across all levels. However, our children's attainment in selected subjects like math is still below national averages.[4] We can and should continue to do more.

Nonetheless, what is clearly evident is a marked increase in parental engagement in our children's education. Malay/Muslim parents today are deeply committed to their children's education. Many make personal sacrifices to ensure that their children get the best opportunities in education. Many take personal interest and participate actively in their children's education, both at home and in school. In the Parent Support Groups (PSG) across many schools, the presence and participation of parents of Malay/Muslim children are

> "Parents are the most important teachers. Because from young, you are first person that they see. So if the parents are not able to be a good teacher to the child, what will happen to the child?

keenly seen and felt. Madam Faridah Din, Chairperson of the PSG in her child's secondary school, summed up well the reasons for her active involvement[5]:

Throughout the 50 years, what remained constant is the strong love that Malay/Muslim parents have for their children and their desire to giving their best for them. What has markedly increased is the commitment shown towards the education of their children, and the strong desire to take an active participation in their children's learning, both in school and at home. The love and commitment that we have for them are the pillars of strength that will help our children overcome future challenges.

References

1. Association of Muslim Professionals (2010) Demographic Study of Singapore Malay/Muslims. Retrieved from URL: http://www.amp.org.sg/edisi/data/Publications/3rd%20Convention%20Journal/Section%209%20-%20Demographic%20Study.pdf

2. Ministry of Family and Social Development (2003). Progress of Malay/Muslim Community Since 1980. Retrieved from URL: http://app.msf.gov.sg/portals/0/Summary/publication/ProgressofMalay/MuslimCommunity.pdf

3. Yayasan MENDAKI (2012) Community Leaders Forum Convention Report (2012) Retrieved from URL: http://www.clfprojects.org.sg/CLF/upload_files/cuteeditor/1/document/CLF%20Report%202012.pdf

4. Ministry of Education (2013) 10-Year Trend of Educational Performance 2004–2013. Retrieved from URL: http://www.moe.gov.sg/media/press/2014/11/10-year-trend-of-educational-performance-2004-2013.php

5. Ministry of Education (2015) Workplan Seminar Video — Every Parent A Supportive Partner. Retrieved from URL http://www.moe.gov.sg/work-plan-seminar/

CHAPTER 19

KEEPING THE FAITH, WHILE LOOKING
FORWARD — SHAIKH SYED ISA
SEMAIT, MUFTI OF SINGAPORE
FROM 1972–2010

Zakir Hussain

W hen the Majlis Ugama Islam Singapura (MUIS) or Islamic Religious Council of Singapore was formed in 1968 to help administer the religious affairs of the Malay/Muslim community, none of its first seven staff members had much experience.

They took a leaf from their counterparts across the Causeway and elsewhere. Early MUIS staff recalled calling up friends who worked in Muslim councils in various states on the Peninsula for advice on how to organise the collection of *zakat*, and visited villages around Singapore to collect *zakat fitrah* during the fasting month of *Ramadan*.

But what about establishing when *Ramadan* begins and ends? The Islamic calendar is a lunar calendar and, for generations, Muslims throughout the world have relied on sighting the new moon, a practice known in Arabic as *rukyah*, to determine these dates.

In Singapore, the Chief Kadi[a] would often trek up Mount Faber or set out by boat to Sultan Shoal, off the main island's western tip, to try and sight the new moon. Often however, it could not be seen with any certainty, and thus, a check with religious leaders in the various Malaysian states would have to be made to

---

[a] A *kadi* is a judge ruling on matters of Islamic religious law. In the Singapore context, a *kadi* oversees marriage registrations.

be sure the moon had indeed been sighted, and the important date had arrived.

Many Muslims in Singapore either stayed at home to wait for the formal announcements over the radio to signal the start of *Ramadan*, or its end, or congregated at the mosque nearest their homes to wait for an announcement. However, this method lent a degree of unpredictability to what some felt could be determined accurately by scientific calculation. A solution was found in the early 1970s, after the appointment of Syed Isa Semait as Mufti.[b]

Syed Isa took on the job in 1972 at the age of 33, succeeding the first *mufti*, 62-year-old Haji Sanusi Mahmood. In Muslim communities around the world, the role of a *mufti* is to provide religious rulings or guidance on various matters based on his understanding of Islamic law and jurisprudence. He should have a good understanding of religious texts, be able to draw on the expertise of earlier scholars and, most importantly, consider the context and requirements of his society.

In Singapore, the *mufti's* position was laid down in the Administration of Muslim Law Act (AMLA) passed in 1968, which provides for the establishment of MUIS to advise the Government on Muslim affairs, and look after the community's interests.

But the 1970s were a challenging time for MUIS. Many Malay/Muslims felt demoralised after the Separation, as overnight, they had become a minority once more. At the same time, many old villages, and with them their places of worship, mosques and prayer houses, had to be demolished to make way for new housing estates and industrial developments — and community funds

After working as a typist, a translator, a bookseller, a marriage registrar and even a welder, Syed Isa's experiences and exposure to people from all walks of life here and abroad helped shape his progressive outlook on faith. Image courtesy of Majlis Ugama Islam Singapura © 2015. All rights reserved.

---

[b] A *mufti* is chief Islamic scholar who interprets and expounds Islamic law and is deemed qualified to give legal opinions and religious rulings or *fatwa*.

were short for new mosques to take their place in these new towns.

Syed Isa himself was upset but he understood that such development was vital for a country that had to fend for itself. He went back to core religious principles, consulted the work of past scholars as well as present-day ones, sought to formu-late decisions based on consensus — and worked to convince the wider community of the merits of a posi-tion, taking into account the reli-gious requirements and interests of the Muslim community, as well as the context of Singapore's multiracial, multireligious society and the overriding need to pre-serve harmony.

By the time he stepped down from the role at the end of 2010, he was the longest-serving senior Muslim government official who not only witnessed first-hand, but also helped to shape key developments. This chapter aims to capture a sense of his thinking through key mile-stones over the years — determining the dates of Muslim festive days in the 1970s, handling issues to do with land such as the demolition of mosques and redevelopment of endowments in the 1980s and 1990s, as well as endorsing the inclusion of Muslims under the law on human organ transplant in the 2000s, based on the needs of the times.

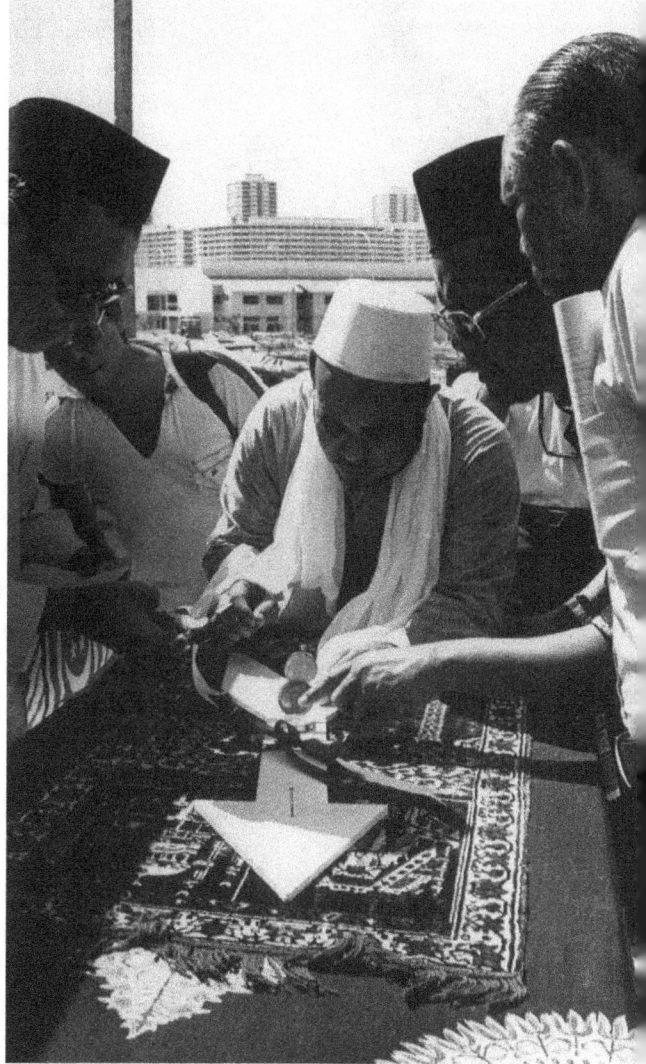

Syed Isa setting the *qibla* (the direction for prayer) for Al-Muttaqin Mosque at Ang Mo Kio. Image courtesy of Majlis Ugama Islam Singapura © 2015. All rights reserved.

Date Dilemma

Syed Isa was barely two years into his job as *mufti* when he came across a sight that moved him to tears. It was January 1974. He was on his way to the mosque to perform the Hari Raya Haji prayer when he saw a Muslim cleaner sweeping the streets. While many Muslims were celebrating the day by wearing their best clothes and sacrificing sheep to mark Prophet Ibrahim's devotion to God, the sweeper was hard at work as he could not get the day off in time.

The fact that Hari Raya fell on that particular day was made known only a week or so earlier, after the moon had been sighted on the Malay Peninsula. However, public holidays are gazetted almost a year in advance based on preliminary calculations. As a result, the date set aside for Hari Raya was a day later than it should have been. This meant that many workers could not get the day off, although many were able to get time off to go to the mosque instead.

Relating this anecdote about his predecessor, current Mufti Dr Fatris Bakaram said: "He realised that if the community did not make use of astronomical calculations to determine the dates of the Islamic calendar in advance, there was no way it would be able to make adequate preparations for its holidays."

That encounter strengthened Syed Isa's resolve, and one of his most critical early decisions as *mufti* was to depart from the prevailing method of sighting the moon to determine Islamic calendar dates, especially for the start of Ramadan and the days for Hari Raya days.[c] Syed Isa, who returned to Singapore in 1969 with a degree in Islamic jurisprudence from Egypt's renowned Al-Azhar University and had served as an assistant registrar of Muslim marriages, began studying how to make these calculations from an expert in Johor, Malaysia. When that expert moved to the state of Perak, he would travel up to learn from him there.

Custom is often hard to undo, and when Syed Isa departed from the practice of moon-sighting, there was considerable opposition from religious leaders and those who felt the new *mufti* had cast aside tradition. He kept his calm, and persuaded the public that the method of calculation was based on what Prophet

---

[c] The Hari Raya days include Hari Raya Puasa (Aidilfitri) and Hari Raya Haji (Aidiladha).

Muhammad had taught his followers about determining the start of Islamic calendar months. His conviction was grounded in the fact that astronomy is a precise science; relying on it was the better option, especially when it seemed that the precise new moon had never been sighted in Singapore.

He was also humble when defending his decision to adopt the practice before senior religious leaders, deferring to their judgment in the matter. They agreed with his arguments, and it won him their approval, and respect.

Fortunately for Syed Isa, and Singaporean Muslims, religious administrators in Malaysia and Indonesia felt the need for the region to adopt a unified position on this issue. In July 1974, the Indonesian Ministry of Religious Affairs invited its Malaysian counterpart and MUIS to a meeting in Jakarta, Indonesia, where all three parties agreed to cooperate and use calculations to determine the Muslim festive dates.

The grouping evolved into MABIMS, the council for religious ministers from Brunei, Indonesia, Malaysia and Singapore, which now meets yearly to discuss matters of religious administration. One key achievement has been to synchronise the festivity dates for Muslims across all four countries till this day.

Syed Isa was also one of the founding members of Yayasan MENDAKI. Image courtesy of Yayasan MENDAKI © 2015. All rights reserved.

Development Dilemma, and Singapore-style Solutions

Although Syed Isa had built close ties with his counterparts in the region, he was clear that Muslims in Singapore should find their own solutions to the challenges they faced as a minority community in a small, multiracial country open to the external influences from the outside world.

Many were particularly upset by the Government's policy of acquiring land for development and resettling villagers in flats, which they felt was destroying not just their homes, but also their places of worship. Even the dead were not spared, with graves having to be exhumed and relocated. MUIS officers spent many evenings visiting villages that were about to be resettled to deal with issues like clearing mosques and exhuming Muslim graves. They spent hours persuading and explaining the issues. Still resentment lingered, even as the Government allocated land in new housing estates for mosques — and other places of worship — to replace those that were demolished.

Syed Isa was clear as to the permissibility of mosques and *suraus*[d] making way for the greater good of the community. "There was no way to progress without the redevelopment of rural areas to make way for industrial land and so on. The government would have studied the need to improve the situation of the entire country at the time, and the early leaders felt the way for Singapore to survive was through major redevelopment. It would be difficult otherwise," he recalled.

Indeed, many resettled residents soon demanded mosques in their new estates. But the community lacked the financial resources to build them, causing considerable anxiety among many. In December 1974, Syed Isa was among eight Muslim community leaders called by then Prime Minister Lee Kuan Yew to the Istana for a discussion with Social Affairs Minister Othman Wok and other Malay Members of Parliament to talk about the matter. The late Mr Lee proposed collecting some 50 cents from every working Muslim for a fund for mosque building through the CPF mechanism.

The meeting was made public the following month, in a statement from the Prime Minister's Office that noted all eight MUIS leaders "acknowledged that with the redevelopment of Singapore, it was inevitable that places of worship, among other buildings, will have to give way to high-rise buildings." It added: "The few

---

[d] A *surau* is a building or space used for worship and religious instruction, similar to a mosque but usually smaller in size.

exceptions will be those of historic value. They agreed that the building of one new mosque for each new town was the most practical way to meet the needs of Muslims as they are resettled in these new towns."

Wakaf Redevelopment

Land acquisition also affected another key institution of the community — *wakaf*, or religious endowments. The institution of *wakaf* is a key vehicle by which Muslims of means dedicate their properties or put them into trusts to be used for pious, religious and charitable purposes within the wider community. Often, the endowment generates income that can then be continuously used for charitable purposes.

The *wakif*, the individual who decides to put his or her property in trust, has to state clearly how the income generated should be used — for instance, to build and maintain a mosque, *madrasah*, school or hospital. Trustees are also usually appointed to ensure that the earnings are used according to the wishes of the *wakif* and not for other purposes. Often, benefactors would also buy properties near a mosque they endowed, whose rental yield would provide a steady revenue stream to maintain the mosque and fund part of its activities.

In Singapore, a considerable body of *wakaf* land and properties had been built up by wealthy Muslims from more than a century ago to just after the Second World War. Their trustees generally administered the *wakaf* properties before MUIS was formed. However, a good number of them were under financial strain, as many of the shop houses and properties in the endowment were rent-controlled and were consequently in poor condition.

Wakaf Kassim consists of its mosque, the surrounding residential areas and a burial ground in Siglap Road. It was developed for the maintenance of the Kassim Mosque and to ensure that the burial grounds at Siglap were well-kept. Image courtesy of Majlis Ugama Islam Singapura © 2015. All rights reserved.

Under the Administration of Muslim Law Act (AMLA), the ownership of all *wakaf* property was vested in MUIS, giving it the legal rights to these properties on behalf of the community. As MUIS lacked the capacity to manage *wakaf* in the earlier years, it had to bide its time.

The wake-up call for a more active role in *wakaf* management came in 1986, when MUIS received a notice from the government to demolish and clear buildings that stood on three *wakaf* plots: Wakaf Jabr on Duku Road in Katong, Wakaf Kassim on Changi Road and Wakaf Masjid Abdul Hamid on Gentle Road. MUIS was given the option to redevelop the land if it so chose, and was given a two-year timeframe to do so, with the rider that the government could take over the land after that two-year timeframe if there was no development.

Under Islamic law, *wakaf* cannot be destroyed. There were few comparable precedents from recent times on whether redeveloping *wakaf* land was permissible, and the Fatwa Committee Syed Isa chaired had to consider this and provide guidance on the issue. Several factors hung over the issue. There was the possibility of losing properties and failing to safeguard whatever the *wakif* had created. This drove the need to develop *wakaf* management. And there was, too, perhaps a lingering unspoken sentiment that the eternal nature of *wakaf* implied that anything to do with it should be left untouched.

Syed Isa recalled: "Originally, *wakaf* should not be sold, shifted or used for alternative purposes. But given the present situation, such a condition would create difficulties, for what if redevelopment proceeds apace? Whereas the original aim of *wakaf* is to safeguard and ensure its benefits continue to accrue to the community."

The Fatwa Committee studied the matter and the condition of *wakaf* in Muslim countries elsewhere facing similar problems, such as Turkey. Its members found that the restrictions on selling *wakaf* strictly stipulated that the value of an endowment had to be preserved. However, jurists from the Hanafi school of thought acknowledged that selling a *wakaf* was allowed if the intention is to improve the condition of that endowment, such as developing it by buying other properties with higher yields.

The committee thus decided that if a *wakaf* is forced to be sold due to reasons that cannot be avoided, such as the prospect of land acquisition, then the proceeds of the sale must be used as stipulated by the *wakif*; for a mosque, school, welfare home or a worthy charitable purpose the religious authority deemed fit. It also ruled that a portion of the *wakaf* could also be sold on a specified lease, say 99 years, especially if the proceeds provided a stream of income that could be channelled towards the *wakaf*'s original purposes.

The committee's ruling paved the way for a 1990 amendment to AMLA, which allowed MUIS to erect any building on any property vested in, belonging to or acquired by the council. This meant it had the power to develop *wakaf* land.

When work started on MUIS' first *wakaf* redevelopment in 1991, the combined value of the 53 *wakaf* it managed stood at some $40 million. By 2001, the redevelopment of 15 *wakaf* properties under MUIS in the past 10 years had boosted their combined value to $87 million. The once controversial decision to pull down and rebuild *wakaf* properties, and in some cases relocate them altogether, had proved beneficial to the community, and MUIS proceeded with plans to continue enhancing the value of these community assets. In 2001, it set about creating a wholly-owned subsidiary, Warees Investments Pte Ltd, which is an endowment asset management company to manage and develop its *wakaf* portfolio. *Wakaf* with poor returns due to their bad locations were sold off, and proceeds from the sale, or combined sales, are used to buy property in a better location, one that had potential for bigger returns.

Syed Isa explained: "The Land Acquisition Act had impinged on *wakaf*, and while we were compensated for them, the amount was often very small. At one stage, we had so many small properties so what we decided to do was group them together and use the proceeds to acquire new property that was much larger. The income from this new property was far greater than income from previous *wakaf*, so we rented them out. The *wakaf* need not be fixed, but what is key is that their objective is met."

Singapore's longest serving *mufti* (perhaps the world too) of nearly 40 years (1972 to 2010). He was instrumental in making several crucial changes to local interpretations of Islamic laws, some of which were controversial, for example the *fatwa* to give Muslims the option of donating their organs without the consent of their family members. After his retirement, he plays an active role towards building bridges of understanding between different religious groups. In 2015, he was appointed as one of the new members of the Presidential Council for Minority Rights (PCMR) — a body to reassure our minorities that laws passed by Parliament will not discriminate against them. Image courtesy of Majlis Ugama Islam Singapura © 2015. All rights reserved.

Fatwas and Flexibility

Medical advances in the 1970s meant the issue of human organ transplants came into question. In one of the earlier rulings of the Fatwa Committee led by Syed Isa, organ transplants were ruled impermissible in 1973, as Islam required that no part of the body should be detached on death. Moreover, there were few successful transplants then.

By the 1980s however, such transplants had become feasible and were seen to be able to save lives. Syed Isa viewed this as an equally important religious consideration.

This issue came to the fore when the Government proposed the Human Organ Transplant Act (HOTA) — under which a person is assumed to have agreed to donate his kidneys, heart, liver and corneas when he dies, unless he has signed an opt-out form.

The Fatwa Committee deliberated the issue again, and they invited 60 leading religious leaders to explain the matter and solicit their views. Some 43 turned up, and all but one backed the committee's move to allow transplants. The panel of five senior religious leaders then ruled that organ transplants were permissible. However, strict conditions must be adhered to: there had to be an emergency and the transplant should be done to save the life of the recipient. Also, the donor would have to give his consent actively, and his next of kin had to agree with the donor's decision.

Even when this position was made public, many in the community could not accept it. There was much heated debate, and so, community leaders proposed that Muslims be excluded from HOTA but be allowed to opt in if they so wished. Thus when HOTA was introduced in 1987, Muslims were exempted unless they opted in.

To set an example, Syed Isa himself became the first person to opt in and pledge his kidneys. Still, the number of Muslims who opted-in remained low, despite changes to the law that made pledging easier.

Some 20 years after the exemption, calls for a review of the community's exclusion grew as the plight of Muslim kidney patients became more dire. The exemption had resulted in many Muslim patients waiting longer for desperately needed organ transplants, as pledgers get priority in the queue. The plight of these patients on the transplant wait-list prompted the Fatwa Committee to re-look its earlier stand on HOTA.

This time in 2007, the *fatwa* committee ruled that as HOTA was a well-known law to many people, and the time for including Muslims was right, it was religiously permissible for Muslims to come under the law like all others. Those who wished to opt out could still do so.

Setting out its religious justification, it noted that Islam does not forbid organ donations or transplants. Muslim jurists worldwide also agree that organ donation is allowed, as Islam stresses the importance of protecting and saving human life.

As for the main stumbling block — the issue of "presumed consent" — as Islamic jurists agree that the decision to donate organs must be expressly made — the committee decided that HOTA gives a Muslim enough opportunity to opt out during his lifetime, and that this approach to obtaining consent is in keeping with Islamic law.

Syed Isa's approach and thinking on these issues evolved over time, but they were in keeping to his key principles. As Minister-in-Charge of Muslim Affairs Yaacob Ibrahim noted, Syed Isa's main preoccupation as *mufti* "has always been to find ways to ensure that Muslims in Singapore live full lives as good Muslims."

"He has approached issues with a view to find common ground and searched for meaningful solutions that will enhance our lives. His legacy is not one of confrontation and advocacy but of deeper understanding and conciliation based on Islamic principles that have helped Muslims be more Singaporean and not less," Dr Yaacob said in a 2011 speech to recognise Syed Isa's contributions.

> His keenness in wanting to find solutions that help Muslims to be a part of the larger Singaporean family has also contributed to the harmonious relationship among our various communities in Singapore."

In his own quiet way and through his persuasive leadership, Syed Isa shaped the religious well-being of Singaporean Muslims on various issues. Today, Muslims from countries where they are in the majority continue to approach and visit Singapore to learn more about MUIS and its rulings, which in no small way were shaped by Syed Isa himself.

The synergy between old and new leaders can help an organisation move with the times. Dr Mohamed Fatris Bakaram, seen here on the right shaking the hand of his predecessor, Shaikh Syed Isa. Dr Mohamed Fatris became the new *mufti* of Singapore on 1 January 2011. His appointment came after the President of Singapore's consultation with the Islamic Religious Council of Singapore (MUIS). The role of the *mufti* is significant not only does he provide spiritual guidance to the Muslim community; he also needs to advise the Government on Islamic matters. Dr Mohamed Fatris began his career as a teacher in Madrasah Aljunied. He later worked as a MUIS Executive Officer and then went to become the Principal of Madrasah Al-Irsyad Al-Islamiah for six years. In 2004, he was designated the Deputy Mufti. He completed his doctoral thesis for a PhD in Islamic studies at Britain's University of Birmingham. He also has a master's in educational administration and management from Malaysia's International Islamic University and a degree in Islamic theology from Al-Azhar, Islam's most prestigious university. Image courtesy of Majlis Ugama Islam Singapura © 2016. All rights reserved.

CHAPTER 20

LIVING AS FAITHFUL MUSLIMS | Mohammad
IN SECULAR SINGAPORE | Alami Musa

In Harmony with Secular State

Muslims celebrated 50 years of Singapore's independence as a secular nation together with their compatriots. As daughters and sons of the soil, they are fully committed citizens who accepted the founding values of secularism and multi-racialism.[1] Their identity as Muslims within the secular context was never an issue. It is only lately that there has been some discussion centring on the *hijab* (headscarf for Muslim women) issue which iconises the encounter between Islam and secularism. In the case of Singapore, the issue of *hijab* within the broader question of identity politics surfaced in 2002.[2]

The emergence of the *hijab* issue could be attributed to the rise in religiosity amongst Muslims and this generated interest in the question of Muslim existence in secular states. The increase in religiosity was coupled with the conservative Islamic orientation in Singapore (and the region) which became stronger in the 1980s and 1990s. There were several reasons to explain these religious trends and they included the rigid

Madrasah students observing National Day. There's no issue of being faithful as a Singaporean and a Muslim because Muslims were taught that part and parcel of being a good Muslim is being a good citizen. Image courtesy of Majlis Ugama Islam Singapura © 2015. All rights reserved.

interpretation of Islam preached to the community; the influence of conservative Islam on the increasing number of Singaporean *haj* pilgrims when they came into contact with Muslims from other countries, and the intensification of Islamisation fuelled by events in the Middle East. The rise of conservative–traditional religiosity manifested itself in many ways including the introduction of new institutions like Islamic banking and a visible increase in the number of women donning the *hijab*.[3]

The *hijab* issue begs more fundamental questions which pertain to the relationship of Muslims with the secular state, their subjugation to codes of law other than *Syariah* laws, and the role of Islam in the public square. The old discourse on Muslim identity in the 1980s and 1990s generally shaped by fundamentalist ideas is no longer useful as path-finders as the Muslims seek for a solution that allows them to be faithful to Islam and at the same time, good citizens.[4]

Hence, there is a need to re–evaluate old thinking. The centre of gravity of recent Islamic scholarship on issues of Muslim identity in secular, non-*Syariah*-based states is shifting away from centres of Islamic dominance to Muslim communities in non-Islamic countries.[5] The current thinking and discourse take into cognizance the unique historical context, different experiences of Muslim communities in secular states and the non–homogeneous interpretation of Islam.[6] This trend of contextualising Islam is gaining momentum. We have Imam Feisal Abdul Rauf writing about Islam the American way,[7] Tariq Ramadan speaking about how to be a European Muslim,[8] Tahir Abbas discussing the idea of the British Muslim[9] and Abdullah Saeed about living as a Muslim committed to Australian fundamental values.[10]

This chapter discusses the idea of the Singaporean Muslim community keeping their Islamic faith within the context of living in a secular state.[11] The discussion will also draw upon some of the findings of a religious outlook study to better appreciate the attitudes and behaviours of Singaporean Muslims in their socio–religious life within the secular environment.

Singaporean Muslims' Unique Context

The Muslim community in Singapore lives within a unique context where survival instinct dominates the national narrative since independence. Till today the narrative is loaded with the *politics of survival*, even after Singapore has achieved the status of a first-world economy.[12] The *politics of survival* entails society to be well disciplined to live in harmony. The potential threat of religion to divide society and give rise to conflicts was neutralised in the early days of nationhood. The ruling elite's painful experience with the politicisation of religion before independence shaped their world-view and the philosophy upon which the new state was founded.[13] One of the pillars of this philosophy is secularism. It was resolved in the pre-independence years that religion must not feature itself in public and national life. Legislation, policies and decisions cannot be made along faith lines. The Constitution guarantees that all religions are recognised by the state and given equal standing, in spite of the reality that the Chinese religions (Buddhism and Taoism) are embraced by about 44% of the citizens.[14] To further strengthen the commitment to secularism, the state declared that religion should not prejudice the ethos of equal recognition and treatment in society.

It is important to keep working on multiculturalism and safeguard our unique multiracial harmony.

The Singapore Constitution protects the rights of religious communities. It is the manifestation of the social compact that regardless of race, language or religion, all have equal standing as citizens.[15] It also

guarantees freedom to practice religion so long as it does not create conflicts or "breach any other laws relating to public order, public health or morality."[16] The practice of secularism moderates the situation and holds religions at bay to exclude them from public domain and politics. Lee Kuan Yew (founding leader of modern Singapore) stated emphatically in his speech in 1987 that:

> ... religion must not get mixed up in politics; otherwise a clash of views can easily turn into a clash of religious beliefs. Then there will be deep enmity between our different religious communities and our society will come to grief."

In 1990, he re-affirmed the belief in secularism by saying that:

> Religion cannot be a force for national unity. Indeed, secularism is essential for inter religious harmony for our multireligious community."[17]

After five decades of nationhood and the introduction of a number of social and political structures, Singaporean Muslims have accepted the imperatives of living within a secular state. They are cognizant of the socio–religious space given and the limits to be observed. The *hijab* issue, first surfaced as a "public show of defiance" in 2002 and resurrected a few times since then, is perhaps the last bone of contention in the encounter between Islam and secularism in the Singapore context.

Living Islam in a Secular State

Muslims fall into two categories, according to Abdullah Saeed, in their attitude and conduct of living in secular states. "Participants" are those who adopt the enlightened and contextualised approach in practicing Islam within a secular state environment while "Isolationists" are those who choose the rigid as well as rejectionist approach.[18]

The mainstream response of Singaporean Muslims is to accept the status, believing that it is in the right spirit of Islam to be participants in the secular context. They accept the position that in Islam, religion and state can be separated. They believe that the Prophet's mission was not to establish the Islamic state; otherwise God would have made him a king like Prophet Solomon. But the Prophet was sent as the "worshipping" prophet to establish the moral community or the Islamic community.[19]

The minority view that prevails amongst some segment of Singaporean Muslims is that they cannot be completely faithful Muslims if they live in a secular state. They are inclined to be isolationists as they embrace a view that Islam cannot be separated from state and to believe otherwise is sacrilegious because it implies that Islam is not a perfect religion as well as a complete way of life. These Muslims believe that Islam can function as a pervasive force in all aspects of life without the religion–state separation. Their utopian vision is to establish the Islamic state which they regard as a religious obligation. They are closed to the idea that there are secular states which are not against religion and where they can live their faith. It is therefore important that Muslims carefully evaluate their secular context to make a fair conclusion.

Singapore is considered a non-religious secular state that does not allow religion to have a role in public or political life. However, it can take a positive view on religion; even to lend support in its role in the private space. It therefore differentiates itself from other types of secular states, namely the irreligious and anti-religious secular states. The irreligious secular state is one that does not tolerate the existence of religion in any form of expression. It will want to see religion vanish from the lives of people. In this case, religion can only be strictly practiced in the privacy of the home, prayer house and religious buildings. An anti-religious secular state is one that is not only irreligious but also shows hostility and enmity towards religion. It will initiate actions to confront religion.[20] Islam does not object to Muslims living in a secular state that provides freedom of religion within the life of communities.

Muslims in Singapore, like their other co-religionists, enjoy a number of privileges within the ambit of the secular state. There are many examples of this. The state is conscious of the need for public places of worship and hence parcels of land are allocated for this purpose when town planning is done. Religious Advisory Boards are set up by law to act as custodians of religious endowments. Malays, who constitute about 85% of Muslims, enjoy special privileges under the Constitution (Article 152) which is a carry-over from the Malaysian Constitution when the two countries separated in 1965. Furthermore, there are special legal provisions uniquely for Muslims. These are embodied in the Administration of Muslim Law Act (AMLA) which gave birth to several religious institutions, namely the Islamic Religious Council of Singapore (MUIS), the

Minorities and special position of Malays

152.—(1) It shall be the responsibility of the Government constantly to care for the interests of the racial and religious minorities in Singapore.

(2) The Government shall exercise its functions in such manner as to recognise the special position of the Malays, who are the indigenous people of Singapore, and accordingly it shall be the responsibility of the Government to protect, safeguard, support, foster and promote their political, educational, religious, economic, social and cultural interests and the Malay language.

Article 152 of the Singapore Constitution.

Registry of Muslim Marriages (ROMM) and the Syariah Court.[21] Special legal provisions are given to Muslims under AMLA to facilitate the performance of their religious obligations through the licensing of *haj* operators, *halal* food providers and collection of tithe. Even contributions of *zakat* qualify for tax exemption. Positively speaking, secularism has given society a lot of good things.[22]

Nevertheless, there are also policies that are not favourable to religious communities. No religious symbols are allowed in public schools or uniformed services and programmes over broadcast media cannot project any religion. The *hijab* issue is also a case in point. There was a campaign to pressure the Government to allow Muslim women working as nurses and in front–line, uniformed services to be allowed to don the *hijab*. The Government viewed the issue with deep interest and the Prime Minister himself conducted a dialogue with community leaders to explain that the existing restriction has to be maintained but its position is not static.[23] In spite of a number of examples to illustrate the non-religious attitude of the state, religious communities see that Singapore on the whole is a religiously friendly secular state.

Civil Laws Embody *Syariah* Spirit

A key feature of a secular state is the religious neutrality of its laws so that they can equally apply to all citizens regardless of beliefs. Singapore adopts the civil code of laws that are meant to protect all citizens, their rights, promote their well–being and guide them towards the path of justice, equality as well as fairness. These end goals or moral goods delivered through civil laws are also the objectives that *Syariah*-based laws are intended to achieve. Hence, one may conclude that civil laws that govern Singapore embody the spirit of the *Syariah* in almost all aspects and religious leaders found no issue for Muslims to live and abide by civil laws.

In the case of Singapore, there is also an added safeguard which requires any piece of new legislation to go through a Presidential Council of Minority Rights before the President ratifies it.[24] This is to ascertain that no law that is passed by Parliament will prejudice the rights or interests of minorities.[25] Furthermore, it is a practice that draft laws which clearly bear ethical

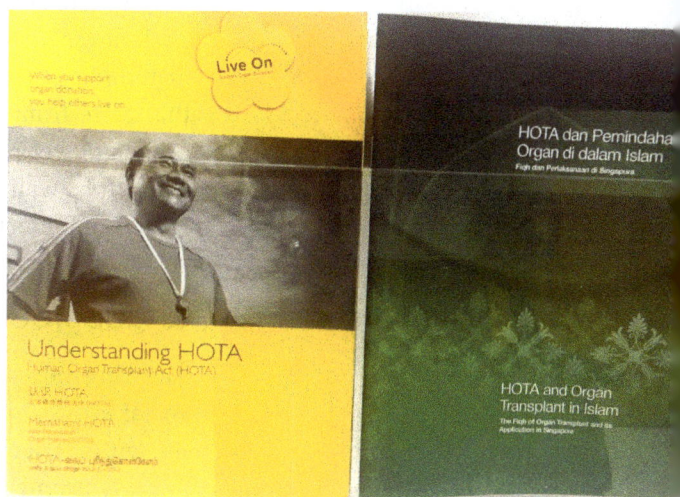

Booklets distributed by the Ministry of Health on HOTA.
On the right is the version by MUIS

implications are referred to religious advisory boards, including MUIS for comments. Concerns will be raised if such laws contravene religious principles and a dialogue with the state will take place. There had been cases where Muslims were exempted from laws that could not be accepted in Islam. An example was the Human Organ Transplant Act (HOTA), enacted in 1987, which allowed the state to harvest organs specified in the Act from individuals who died due to unnatural causes. This was the consequence of the *fatwa* (religious ruling) at that point of time that disallowed the transplantation of organs.[26] However, the *fatwa* was reviewed in 2007 to allow organ transplantation and consequently, Muslims were all included in HOTA, since then.[27]

Not all civil laws are in consonance with Islam. A good example is the law that legalises casino gambling. Muslims cannot accept it. They exercised their freedom of conscience and civic rights to express their disagreement and distance themselves from it. Notwithstanding this issue, Muslims, according to Abdullah Saeed, should continue to discharge their duty of citizenship by upholding the general body of civil laws.[28] Muslims Singaporean are successfully negotiating their religious life around the challenges that arise from such non–Islamic laws by adopting a pragmatic yet principled approach with the guidance of *mufti* as well as other Islamic leaders, so that their faith is not affected.

Singaporean Muslim Identity

The Singaporean Muslim Identity embodies a set of social ethos that enables the community to embrace life within a secular state governed by the civil code of laws. It promotes the values of progressiveness and adaptability which are necessary tools to bridge the application of Islamic text to the reality of socio-political context. Abdullah Saeed's category of "Participant" has been expanded to include sub-categories of *adaptive–participant* and *progressive participant,* to further describe Muslim response to issues of living in a secular state.

A study was conducted by MUIS in 2010 to determine the social behaviour of Singaporean Muslims living in a secular state. It involved a sample size of 1000. 47% of respondents were males, 48% were above 40 years old and 16% had tertiary education. The sample used in the field–work was a good representation of Muslims in Singapore. The study looked into the social ethos and social behaviour of Singaporean Muslims. The findings are good measures of how Muslims identify themselves in secular Singapore.

The Singaporean Muslim Identity

Holds strongly to Islamic principles while adapting itself to changing context

Appreciates Islamic civilisation and history, and has good understanding of contemporary issues

Appreciates other civilisations and is self-confident to interact and learn from other communities

Morally and spiritually strong to be on top of the challenges of modern society

Progressive, practices Islam beyond forms/rituals and rides the modernisation wave

Well adjusted as contributing members of a multi-religious society and secular state

Inclusive and practices pluralism, without contradicting Islam

Believes that good Muslims are also good citizens

Be a blessing to all and promotes universal principles and values

Be a model and inspiration to all

Almost all respondents (95.5%) felt that they could live as good Muslims under civil laws in Singapore. By conducting themselves as *progressive–participants,* Muslims are able to conform to these laws yet remain faithful to Islam. They endeavour to understand the spirit of the *Syariah* and through the faculty of *ijtihad,* determine its congruence with the intent of civil law. This can be illustrated through three pieces of legislation to show how Singaporean Muslims as progressive-participants function under secular laws. They are the Joint Tenancy Law, the Central Provident Fund (the national pension fund) Nomination Law and the Revocable Insurance Nomination Law. All these three pieces of civil law can be applied to protect the interests of women. There had been many cases when Muslim women were left in the lurch with no roof over their heads or with little means to support themselves, upon demise of their husbands.

This happened when family members used the religious argument of *faraid* (Islamic inheritance laws) to dispose of assets of the deceased husbands for distribution. The Fatwa Committee of the MUIS Council realised the seriousness of the problem. They issued three *fatwas* that enable Muslims to apply the abovementioned civil laws and protect the interests of the affected women. The fatwas recognised that the civil laws are in fact aligned to the spirit of the *Syariah* to protect those who may be susceptible to injustice or unfairness. The *fatwas* are based on a re–interpretation of the concept of ownership found in classical Islamic text. The concept of property ownership in the Singapore context has significantly changed and because of this, its classical definition in Islam needed to be reviewed.[29]

In the area of adaptive religious life, the scores were high (25.3% — very adaptable and 73.5% — adaptable). This orientation of being *adaptable–participants* has been helpful in guiding Muslims to adapt their Islamic way of life to suit Singapore's secular context.[30] For example, they have no qualms to limit the calling of the *azan* (call to prayer) to within the mosque compound so that the sound emitted will not cause a discomfort to nearby non-Muslim residents, especially during the *fajar* prayers. This is the unique social context whereby mosques in Singapore are located within residential estates with high concentrations of non–Muslims. In turn, Muslims successfully negotiated with the state to allow *azan* to be punctually aired over the national radio station for every prayer. Another challenge is the need for all faith communities to refrain from open proselytisation. Muslims who are *adaptable–participants* have no issue with this. They abide by this code of conduct because this will contribute to harmonious living amongst all people of religion. Open proselytisation in the past had created friction between religious groups.

There are also manifestations of isolationism but these only occurred minimally, in some aspects of life. For example, there are a handful of Singaporean Muslims who reject the modern financial system because they believe that it is based on *riba* (usury). Hence, there is an initiative to introduce an alternative system based on the *dinar* and *dirham* currency. There are also those who refuse to take conventional bank loans because of interest payments. They prefer to rent a house instead of purchasing their own home. They also reject the education system as one that is not Islamic and enrol their children in either madrasah or schools abroad. These are a few examples which illustrate the rejectionist mindset of *isolationists.* Nevertheless, they do not undertake *hijrah* (migration) but choose to remain in the secular state to take advantage of the benefits of living in a developed economy and technological society. Furthermore, they avoid as far as practicable, engagements with non–Muslims and do not support inter-faith dialogue and outreach efforts to non-Muslims.

Secular Model of Singapore — Not Anti-thesis to Islam

The well-being of religious communities can only be ensured if the state guarantees their liberty of conscience, equal treatment to all regardless of faith, public order in society and positive civic relations amongst its citizens. The state that can best provide these guarantees according to a global scholar on secularism, Bhiku Parekth, is the secular state.[31]

Singapore has generally provided the above guarantees although its model of secular state has evolved uniquely in its short history of 50 years. In this sense, Singapore has never been ideological in its embrace of secularism. It adopts a pragmatic model of the secular state, one that merely provides "the rules of the game" as mentioned by Olivier Roy, a French scholar on Islam.[32] The uniqueness of Singapore's secularism lies in its clever application of the principle of being equidistant in accommodating the special needs and interests of the various religious

The enlistment of Malays into the Singapore armed forces has evolved over time. Image courtesy of Erfi Anugrah © 2015. All rights reserved.

groups, as well as giving some space to religion in the public square without causing disharmony.[33]

Therefore, Singapore's model of secular state does not neatly fall into either one of the two categories, referred to by a global scholar of religion, Rowan Williams, that is *programmatic secularism* (typified by the French *laïcité* model) or *procedural secularism* (exemplified by the Indian model).[34] Programmatic secularism believes that for a society to function well, religion needs to be off the map and there is a strictly defined secular space — in short, there is the exclusive demarcating of the public space. Singapore's practice of secularism is not uncompromising as programmatic secularism nor is it too lax as in procedural secularism, where religious issues are discussed publicly and that religious identity is not exclusively a private matter.

Singapore's secularism recognises that religion can bring benefits to the state. It has also forged a positive relationship with religion. Singapore is a *secular state with a soul* and its brand of secularism cannot be an anti-thesis to Islam or any other religion.

Bibliography

1. Stanley S Bedlington, The Singapore Malay Community: The Politics of State Integration, (Thesis presented to the Faculty of the Graduate School of Cornell University for the Degree of Doctor of Philosophy, 1974) 72–73, pp. 3–4.

2. Kam Yee Law, "The myth of multiracialism in post 9/11 Singapore: The tudung incident" (*New Zealand Journal of Asian Studies*, 5.1, June 2003), p. 53.

3. Fred R von der Mehden, "Islam in the 21st Century" in *Asian Islam in the 21st Century*, ed. by John L Esposito *et al.* (Oxford: Oxford University Press, 2008) pp. 13–14.

4. Feisal Abdul Rauf, *Moving the Mountain A New Vision of Islam in America* (New York: Free Press, 2012) pp. 13–14.

5. John L Esposito, "The Muslim diaspora and the Islamic world" in *Islam, Europe's Second Religion*, ed. Shireen T Hunter (Westport: Praeger Publishers, 2002) pp. 245–246.

6. Azyumardi Azra, "Islamic thought: Theory, concepts and doctrines in the context of Southeast Asian Islam" in *Islam in Southeast Asia — Political, Social and Strategic Challenges for the 21st Century*, ed. K S Nathan and M Hashim Kamali (Singapore: Institute of Southeast Asian Studies, 2005) pp. 3–4.

7. Feisal Abdul Rauf , op. cit., pp. 179–200.

8. Tariq Ramadan, "To be a European citizen" in *To be a European Muslim* (Leicester: The Islamic Foundation, 1999) pp. 162–179.

9. Tahir Abbas, *Muslim Britain — Communities Under Pressure* (London: Zed Books Radical International Publishing, 2005).

10. Abdullah Saeed, "Commitment to fundamental Australian values" in *Islam in Australia* (Australia: Allen & Unwin, 2003) pp. 198–208.

11. M Alami Musa, "Keeping with the times while remaining faithful to Islam", *The Straits Times*, Singapore, May 7, 2005, Review, S12–S13.

12. World Development Indicators Database, "GDP per capita, PPP (current international $)" http://data.worldbank.org/indicator/NY.GDP.PCAP.PP.CD?order=wbapi_data_value_2013+wbapi_data_ value+wbapi_data_value–last&sort=desc

13. Stanley S Bedlington, *op. cit.*, pp. 81–84.

14. Singapore Department of Statistics, "Census of Population 2010: Statistical Release 1 on Demographic Characteristics, Education, Language and Religion" http://www.singstat.gov.sg/publications/publications_and_papers/ cop2010/census10_stat_release1.html

15. Parliament of Singapore, "Speech by Minister of Law and National Development, E W Barker, December 1965", cited, Raj K Vasil, Governing Singapore (Singapore: Eastern University Press, 1984) p. 99.

16. Bureau of Democracy, Human Rights & Labour, US Department of State, "International Religious Freedom Report", October 2009; http://www.state.gov/j/drl/rls/irf/2009/127287.htm

17. Lee Kuan Yew, National Day Speech, 8 August 1987, National Archives of Singapore, www.nas.gov.sg/archivesonline/data/pdfdoc/ lky19870808.pdf, last accessed 2 November 2015.

18. Abdullah Saeed, Muslims in Secular States: Between Isolationists and Participants in the West (Singapore: MUIS Occasional Papers Series — Paper No 1, 2005) p. 5.

19. Ahmad B E Hassoun, *Islam's Enduring Values for Humanity*, The MUIS Distinguished Visitors' Programme lecture, 8.

20. Azzam Tamimi, "The Origins of Arab Secularism" in *Islam & Secularism in the Middle East*, ed. A Tamimi & John Esposito (London: Hurst & Company, 2000) pp. 14–15.

21. Stanley S. Bedlington, *op. cit.*, pp. 177–180.

22. Mahmoud Ayoub, Basis for Inter-faith Dialogue–Prospects & Challenges, (Singapore: Islamic Religious Council of Singapore (MUIS) Occasional Paper Series No 9, 2011) pp. 8–9.

23. Lee Hsien Loong, "Government position on tudung not static", *The Sunday Times*, January 26, 2014, p. 1.

24. Eugene Tan, "Norming Moderation in an Iconic Target: Public Policy & the Regulation of Religious Anxieties in Singapore" in *Terrorism & Political Violence* (Singapore: Routledge Taylor & Francis Group, 2007) p. 446.

25. Stanley S Bedlington, *op. cit.*, pp. 173–175.

26. Office of the Mufti, MUIS. "Fatwas issued by the Islamic Religious Council of Singapore", 42 http://www.muis.gov.sg/cms/uploadedFiles/MuisGovSG/Religious/OOM/Resources/Muis%20kidney%20book%20ENG.pdf

27. Office of Mufti, MUIS. "Science & Medicine–HOTA (2007) http://www.muis.gov.sg/cms/oomweb/fatwa.aspx?id=14698

28. Abdullah Saeed, *op. cit.*, pp. 9–10.

29. Office of the Mufti, MUIS, "Fatwa on Joint Tenancy, CPF Nomination, Revocable Insurance Nomination", http://www.muis.gov.sg/cms/ oomweb/fatwa.aspx

30. Islamic Religious Council of Singapore, MUIS, Survey report on Religious Outlook of the Singapore Muslim Community (unpublished, May 2011) pp. 46–47.

31. Bhiku Parekh, Secularism & Managing Religious Diversity, Seminar organised by Centre Of Excellence for National Security, S Rajaratnam School of International Studies (RSIS), 15 September 2015 https://www.rsis.edu.sg/ event/cens-seminar-on-secularism-and-managing-religious-diversity- by-professor-lord-bhikhu-parekh/#.VjhssdIzfGg

32. Olivier Roy, "Islam and Secularization" in *Secularism Confronts Islam* (New York: Columbia University Press, 2007) p. 38.

33. Scott Morrison, Equidistance *in Secularism Revised: Arab Islam, Religious Freedom and Equidistance* (Malaysia: The Other Press Sdn Bhd, 2013) pp. 148–151.

34. Rowan Williams, *Faith in Public Square* (London: Bloomsbury Publishing Plc, 2012) p. 2.

CHAPTER 21

MODERATE ISLAM IN SINGAPORE — IN CONVERSATION WITH HABIB SYED HASSAN AL ATTAS

Zainul Abidin Rasheed and Norshahril Saat

In May 2015, President Tony Tan Keng Yam presented the IRO (Inter Religious Organisation) Award to Habib Syed Hassan Bin Muhammad Bin Salem Al-Attas from the Baalwie Mosque. The award recognises his contributions in fostering religious harmony in Singapore. Syed Hassan's father, Habib Muhammad Al-Attas, was a prominent Sufi who came to Singapore in 1936. The Al-Attas family originated from Hadramaut (Yemen), and brought to Singapore the tariqah Alawiyah.[a] After his father passed away, Habib Syed Hassan became the Imam of the Baalwie mosque. To this day, he continues to lead the recitation of Ratib Al-Attas[b] every Thursday evening.[c] Habib Syed Hassan is a respectable ulama, progressive in his outlook and an advocate of peaceful and harmonious Islam. On 30 December 2015, Habib Syed Hassan shares his observations with Mr Zainul Abidin Rasheed and Dr Norshahril Saat on Malay/Muslim community's progress and future challenges. The following paragraphs highlight some aspects of the discussion.

---

[a] A *sufi* (Islamic mysticism) order.

[b] A form of *zikir* (devotional acts in Islam in which short phrases or prayers are repeatedly recited silently within the mind or aloud) specific to followers of the *tariqah* (a *sufi* order).

[c] Norshahril Saat, *Faith, Authority and the Malays: The Ulama in Contemporary Singapore* (Singapore: Select Publishing; Malay Heritage Foundation, 2015), pp. 74–76.

Habib Syed Hassan opines that over the last 50 years, Singapore Muslims have demonstrated good progress in so many fields, and praises Singapore leaders for doing a commendable job. Giving the example of the Association of Muslim Professionals (AMP), the Association of Muslim Lawyers, he reflects on how well-organised the community is today. He also says that Malays are becoming specialists in all medical fields. Compared to minorities in other countries, Singapore Malays are doing better.

He however expresses his concern about how Islam is understood and practised by some Malay Muslims. Singapore has about 700–1000 *asatizahs*[d] in Singapore, and many receive their religious education from the Middle East. He is worried that these teachers import Middle Eastern culture and politics into Singapore. "If they cannot answer them [theological queries], they [religious teachers] will ask their mentors and teachers [from the Middle East]". And many, although not all of their teachers will interpret according to the situation of their country," he expresses candidly. He adds that many Middle East countries are in crisis.

If they cannot answer them [theological queries], they [religious teachers] will ask their mentors and teachers [from the Middle East]". And many, although not all of their teachers will interpret according to the situation of their country," he expresses candidly. He adds that many Middle East countries are in crisis.

Moreover, he acknowledges that the Internet has a huge influence on the religious discourse in Singapore. He suspects that many learn more about Islam from the internet. He is sceptical about relying on providing good textbooks to prevent misinformation; instead, he believes in producing good teachers: "We can have texts, but the teachers will bring in their minds and their thinking."

The conversation then moves on the notion of diversity in Islam. While diversity of views is welcomed in the Quran, he has a different outlook on what diversity means, and warns the community to be cautious of the term. He accepts diversity is part of Islam, but wants the community to reject extreme

---

[d] Religious teachers.

ideas. He gave an analogy: "In a farm, we have chickens and ducks, but then we place a snake, the snake will destroy all the other animals. Just like in religion, extreme and dangerous ideas will destroy the sanctity of the faith." He reiterates that Muslims should foster good relations with the Christians and other non-Muslims, but they must shun teachings that destroy Islam.

He then speaks about another problematic religious orientation: the [over]emphasis on rituals. Today, most of the classes talk about the rituals but less of Islamic philosophy or *mantiq* (logic). The problem originates from how religion is taught in the Middle East. It is unsurprising, according to him, that some universities in the West produce better leaders and thinkers.

He feels that intra-faith diversity must also be respected. Other views that worry him include the prohibition of wishing Christians "Merry Christmas", or Hindus "Happy Deepavali". He points out: "For hundreds of years, we have been doing that. Look at Muslims under Ottoman Empire, Muslims in Spain, they have no problems." Instead, he believes that there are terrorists among Sunnis, even those who claim to practise the correct Islam. This is the group that must be rejected.

> *He feels that intra-faith diversity must also be respected. Other views that worry him include the prohibition of wishing Christians "Merry Christmas", or Hindus "Happy Deepavali". He points out: "For hundreds of years, we have been doing that. Look at Muslims under Ottoman Empire, Muslims in Spain, they have no problems." Instead, he believes that there are terrorists among Sunnis, even those who claim to practise the correct Islam. This is the group that must be rejected.*

He feels that very likely the source of one of the problems lies with inviting popular preachers, not knowledgeable ones. The community needs to distinguish between information and knowledge, he says. Quranic verses and Hadith are easily available in mobile devices, but to him, real knowledge of Islam is to be a good person; it is the *akhlaq* (morality).

He concludes the conversation by speaking about the Paris attacks. He elaborates on the works the Muslim community did to calm the angst non-Muslims have towards the community and to correct misconceptions about Islam. He said, "We approached the French Embassy in Singapore to convey our regret of the Paris attacks. The Singapore Muslim organisations then condemned the Paris and other terrorist attacks. The steps made by us to convey our condolences to the French Ambassador in Singapore helped to calm the situation and correct misconception about Islam especially among the French and Europeans living in Singapore. We took this initiative because non-Muslims in general are no longer blaming terrorists but Islam and the Quran."

It is hoped that more young religious teachers could follow Habib Syed Hassan's footsteps in building trust among religious groups in Singapore. He does not seek popularity and is firm when discussing community's problems. One trait our religious teachers should learn from him is his ability to discuss problems in a diplomatic and sensitive manner. Most importantly, he broadens the understanding of Islam, more than just rituals, but to include morality and values.

CHAPTER 22

THE RELIGIOUS REHABILITATION GROUP (RRG): A COMMUNITY-GOVERNMENT PARTNERSHIP IN FIGHTING TERRORISM

Mohamed Ali

Introduction

December 2001 marks a significant event in the history of Singapore's security. It witnessed the first wave of arrests of Jemaah Islamiyah (JI) members in Singapore. JI is an active Islamist militant organisation operating in Southeast Asia which aims to create an Islamic state in this region through means of violence.

The existence of JI in Southeast Asia came to the attention of the governments in this region after 11 September 2001. In December 2001, Singapore's Internal Security Department (ISD) disrupted a plot against US, British, Australian, and Israeli diplomatic missions as well as other targets planned by JI in Singapore. The law enforcement, security and intelligence agencies of Malaysia, the Philippines and Australia collaborated with Singapore in that year to dismantle JI.

JI was known to be an Al-Qaeda associate. It was believed that Al-Qaeda had funded JI to attack the region's best-known tourist resort, Bali, in October 2002, killing 202 people, including 88 Australians. Although the Indonesian authorities targeted JI, the

The Religious Rehabilitation Group (RRG) logo. Image courtesy of Religious Rehabilitation Group © 2015. All rights reserved.

group survived and revived in Indonesia, conducting intermittent attacks. The threat of ideological extremism and operational terrorism persists. Singapore's global profile and its affiliation with Western countries such as the US have made it a legitimate target among extremists and terrorists in the region.

Although acts and incidents of violence and terrorism are not new phenomena in Singapore, the arrest of JI members demanded a need for a new strategy in dealing with ideologically motivated movements. Using Islamic concepts such as *jihad*, these JI members portray a sense of exclusiveness in religion by claiming to act under the banner of Islam.

For Singapore, the threats and acts of terrorism are more than just in terms of potential destruction to lives and properties. Extremism and radicalism could endanger the harmonious multiracial fabric of Singapore society which is the cornerstone of the nation's progress. Any friction could lead to distrust and discord among the peoples of the different faiths living here.

> "Let me be clear. Terrorism is not inherent in Islam. That is what Muslim scholars and religious leaders tell us. That is what my Muslim friends tell me. That is my own experience with our Muslims. Fifteen percent of Singapore's population are Muslims. They live harmoniously with Singaporeans of other races and religions. The Mufti of Singapore, the highest religious authority on Islam, has strongly condemned terrorism and terrorist acts. He emphasised that the actions of JI suicide bomb-maker Azahari Husin were a complete deviation from the teachings of Islam, which forbid anyone from committing suicide. He added that the teachings of the Koran call for peace in multireligious societies. If only more Muslim scholars (*ulemas*) and religious teachers (*asatizah*) all over the world would state their positions so openly and courageously."
>
> Senior Minister Goh Chok Tong speaking at the opening ceremony of East-West Dialogue on 16 Nov 05 in Barcelona, Spain

Formation of the Religious Rehabilitation Group

Realising the threat of religious extremism and terrorism as a very challenging one, the Singapore government implemented a comprehensive counter-terrorism and rehabilitation programme. Fortunately, the Singapore authorities moved in quickly and competently in dealing with the JI threat. Uncovering that these JI members share a deep ideological motivation, assistance from the local Muslim community, especially the *asatizah* (religious scholars), were initially sought to delve deeper into the minds of these arrested individuals.

Singaporean leaders understood quite early on that they had the structures in place to fight the threat of terrorism but not the threat of ideological extremism. They knew that Singapore's Muslim community was under threat of radicalisation by the vicious ideology imbibed by violent extremist groups. As these threat groups were active outside Singapore and were not within the reach of Singapore, the government had to incorporate the participation of the Muslim community to deal with the threat. The government in partnership with the community create programmes to reach out to vulnerable segments of the Muslim population. With regards to those involved in JI, a very small number of Singaporean Muslims that had either joined terrorist groups or planned terrorist attacks were detained. They could not be held indefinitely. Singapore had to develop strategies to meet the contemporary challenge of ideological extremism that was radicalising and had radicalised a segment of its community.

Prime Minister Lee Hsien Loong presenting a plaque to Co-Founders and Co-Chairmen of Religious Rehabilitation Group Ustaz Ali Haji Mohamed and Ustaz Mohamad Hasbi Hasan (fourth and fifth from left). Image courtesy of Religious Rehabilitation Group © 2015.

We find that the Islamic teachings have been misinterpreted by a portion of the Muslim community who call themselves the Jemaah Islamiyah. They (the radicals) put forth an understanding of Islam that is too extreme. There should be an effort to portray the understanding of Islam

"Because they (terrorists) were motivated by a religious creed which is based on their misinterpretation of the Quran, either they were taught by their leaders or read from the Internet or whatever. We got to get people who can speak with authority to counter that.

The late Mr Lee Kuan Yew

*as taught by Prophet Muhammad (pbuh) which is
moderate in nature. It is not extreme as displayed by
the group in question which involve murder, armed
war and so on.*

Ustaz Mohamad Hasbi Hassan,
Co-Chairman RRG

Prominent Islamic scholars like Ustaz Ali Bin Haji Mohamed, chairman of Khadijah Mosque and Ustaz Mohamad Hasbi Hassan, President of PERGAS, were among those who were invited by the Singapore security agencies to have an initial dialogue with the JI members. In their assessment, both *ustazs* concluded that the religio-ideological component of the JI movement needed to be dealt with to achieve a longer term strategic response to this type of terrorist threat. According to them, the grave danger of JI's religio-ideological inclination is a concern to Singapore's security which needed to be addressed, hence the formation of RRG was initiated.

The Religious Rehabilitation Group, or RRG as it is widely known, was officially inaugurated in April 2003. It originally had 11 members, though the number now has grown to more than 38 members today. These members consist of mainly *asatizahs* of diverse age groups, careers and educational backgrounds. Apart from the religious scholars, the RRG also comprises of a secretariat, whose members are from both the *asatizah* and non-religious backgrounds to provide the administrative support to the RRG.

As the name suggests, RRG's main and initial task is provide religious counselling to the JI members in detention, those placed under Restriction Order (ROs) and their family members. Today, counselling efforts by the RRG have been extended to include self-radicalised individuals and individuals deemed to possess radical and extremist views. A second and equally important objective for its formation is to assist the Singapore security agency to study JI's ideology and provide an expert resource panel to assist the government and community towards understanding Islam in relation to any misconceptions and misinterpretations of the religion.

"The RRG aims to counter radicalisation and extremism with the ideals of moderation *(wasatiyyah)* through the spirit of loving, caring and sharing for a cohesive Singapore."

RRG's role was later expanded to include misinterpretations promoted by self-radicalised individuals and those in support of ISIS. The RRG's mission is to correct the misinterpretation of Islamic concepts and dispel the extremist and terrorist ideologies they have been indoctrinated with. Image courtesy of Religious Rehabilitation Group © 2015. All rights reserved.

There is no doubt that the counselling of the JI detainees is a long term process that requires time and perseverance. Today, while the counselling efforts are still ongoing, RRG has broadened its activities to include educational and social programmes. This programmes aim to proactively educate the wider public on the dangers of extremist ideologies and prevent the Muslim youth from being persuaded into the lures of deviant teachings.

Although the *asatizah* of the RRG are qualified Islamic scholars and teachers, understanding and dealing with the religious ideology of JI is still a great challenge. This is particularly because JI's worldview, their understanding and interpretation of Islamic concepts are alien to the Islam and thus, it was something that the *asatizahs* were not taught of during their studies.

On the RRG's strategy, Ustaz Ali Haji Mohamed said that when it started the rehabilitation work, it did not have any model or example to follow. He said: "This rehabilitation approach to extremists and radicals is possibly the first of its kind. Not much research had been done then."

Ustaz Dr Mohamed Bin Ali briefing President Tony Tan Keng Yam during the official Opening of the RRG Resource and Counselling Centre (RCC). Image courtesy of Religious Rehabilitation Group © 2015. All rights reserved.

We started with an in-depth research. We went back to history, to look at the causes of extremism. We analysed and compared different patterns of extremism and radicalism. We returned to our revered sources and our Islamic intellectual tradition and heritage.

We engaged our ulama (religious scholars) and dwelt on the need to open the gates of ijtihad (reasoning) specifically on this issue of terrorism and radicalism. Simply put, all RRG members had to become 'students' again.

Former President S. R. Nathan showing support for the RRG. Image courtesy of Religious Rehabilitation Group © 2015. All rights reserved.

In order to ensure a smooth and effective counselling session for the JI detainees, the RRG needed to conduct research on Islamic concepts misconstrued by Islamist militants in general and JI's ideology in particular. This research effort has lead the RRG to produce their first counselling manual entitled *Islam Agama Salam & Damai: Langkah Hayati Erti Jihad Sebenar* (Islam Religion of Peace: Steps towards Understanding the Real Meaning of *jihad*) which is used by the asatizah as a guide in the counselling process. Last year, RRG has produced its second counselling manual, which consists of broader and current issues, like the threat of self-radicalisation and religious extremism to name a few.

In counselling the JI detainees, RRG members, coupled with their religious knowledge, voluntarily provided their time to sit and talk with the JI members. Initial counselling sessions with the detainees centred on explaining the correct understanding of concepts like *jihad*, *hijrah*, *bai'ah*, *ummah* and *daulah Islamiyah*. Apart from discussing these concepts, RRG members have a greater role to educate the detainees on the peaceful and moderate message of Islam, universal Islamic and moral values that are deemed important in order for the detainees to have a wholesome understanding of Islam. Reflecting on the fruits of the religious counseling, the late Ustaz Mohd Ibrahim Mohd Kassim who was the most senior member of RRG said:

"Today, RRG has grown in confidence and outreach, and has stepped up efforts to engage the community in mosques and public forums. Their work remains of crucial importance and will be even more so in the future with the growing threat of self-radicalisation.

Prime Minister Lee
Hsien Loong
Excerpted from Winning Hearts and Minds, Embracing Peace.

I found great satisfaction when a detainee expressed his deep gratitude for my help and guidance through a mutual friend. The detainee, who has been released, had asked the mutual friend to convey this message to me. "Please convey my salaam to him and tell him that I am very grateful for the lessons he taught me.

Today, the concept of religious rehabilitation, particularly for Islamist militant, has gained wide acceptance locally and internationally. Singapore is not alone in this effort — similar concepts of rehabilitation can be found in countries like Saudi Arabia, Yemen, Egypt, Malaysia and Indonesia. Today, many governments have realised that religious rehabilitation is an important component to formulate a more effective counter extremism and terrorism strategy. In particular, Singapore's approach to religious rehabilitation has gained the interest of many governments and scholars. Professor Bruce Hoffman of Georgetown University, Washington states that:

The path-breaking work of Singapore's Religious Rehabilitation Group (RRG) provides a model and inspiration for counter-radicalisation efforts everywhere. The RRG's outreach efforts, not only to radicals but to their families, are a seminal example of the most innovative and novel approaches to addressing this phenomenon. Most importantly, it proves that there is no war on Islam, as the radicals often claim, and that communities can indeed co-exist peacefully and harmoniously.

Due to the importance and interest of such effort, RRG members have travelled widely to share Singapore's approach of detainee rehabilitation with the authorities in many countries including Malaysia, Indonesia, Saudi Arabia, United Kingdom, United States, Germany, Belgium, Austria and Denmark.

Responding to the Ideological Threat of ISIS

Although the threat of JI has been diminished today, RRG continues to play its role in curbing extremist ideologies particularly those of ISIS (Islamic State of Iraq and Syria) — an extremist and terrorist group operating in Iraq and Syria. Today, we are living in a very challenging period — a period of great upheaval. Every day, we hear news of the atrocities and brutalities of ISIS. ISIS poses not only security threats in Iraq and Syria, but its ideological influence has infected the entire world. This is particularly due to the strong use of technology and especially social media by ISIS.

The recent arrest and detention of two young Singaporeans who have been swayed by ISIS to support their radical ideology and violent tactics, is an example of how vulnerable our youth are, and how easily influenced they are. One of the youth revealed that he intended to carry out violent attacks and was prepared to do it even within Singapore. Our youths rely heavily on the Internet for religious guidance. However, without a strong foundation in religious knowledge, these youths are unable to discern correct Islamic teachings espoused from traditional sources, from misconstrued Islamic ideals imparted from the likes of ISIS.

ISIS justifies its radical narrative by using and mis-contextualising Islamic teachings and concepts. These include concepts such *as jihad, hijrah, bai'ah, shari'ah* and several others. They claim their actions are in line with Islamic teachings and called Muslims to migrate to the so-called Islamic Caliphate or Islamic State they have established. ISIS also calls upon Muslims to pledge allegiance to their self-proclaimed leader Abu Bakar Al-Baghdadi. What ISIS has done is totally against Islamic teachings that always call for peace and harmony. Their actions are no doubt a disgrace to Islam and are crimes against humanity. Members of ISIS are completely ignorant about the faith they proclaim.

There is a dire need for the Muslims to be convinced of the illegitimacy of ISIS. Their actions do not represent Islam and the Muslims. They are a terrorist group. Their ideology, which has generated concerns, must be rejected and debunked. Any form of violence against innocent civilians or prosecution of minorities contradicts the principles of the Quran and the traditions of the Prophet.

Singapore is not spared from the ideological threat of ISIS. Singaporeans, Muslims and non-Muslims stand united in condemning ISIS. RRG has initiated several efforts to counter ISIS's ideological threat. In July 2014, RRG established the RRG Resource and Counselling Centre or RCC. The RCC aims to chronicle the work of RRG over the past decade, and to enhance RRG's capability and capacity to meet with the evolving challenges of radicalism and terrorism. It also provide training and resource materials to the RRG counsellors, *asatizah* and others who are interested to do research on issues related to religious and violent extremism.

The RCC is seen as an important addition to Singapore's overall efforts to counter radical and extremist ideologies. It will further augment RRG's positions as an authority in the field, as well as promote greater awareness, knowledge and assurance to the public that a concerted effort in counter-ideology is

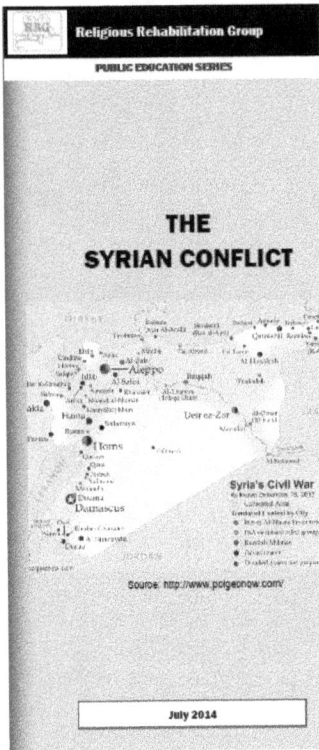

Excerpted from the pamphlet:
Dr Mohamed Fatris Bakaram, the Mufti of Singapore warned that jihad could not be determined and declared by any individual or organization, but should be endorsed by the highest Islamic authority. He added that it is a big mistake for Singaporeans to help the Syrians through participating in the armed conflict in Syria.

currently being undertaken to prevent Singaporeans from falling prey to violent extremism.

With the establishment of the new centre, RRG continues to strive in countering extremist ideologies and radicalisation in Singapore. Since 2014, RRG has published several pamphlets and booklets as part of its Public Education Series. The first pamphlet entitled *The Syrian Conflict* aims to inform the public on the nature of the conflict in Syria and debunk the allegations made that the fight in Syria is an act of *jihad* that requires the participation of all Muslims. The second pamphlet entitled *The Fallacies of ISIS Islamic Caliphate: A Brief Introduction*, which was published in early 2015 to explain the illegitimacy of the Caliphate. Through this publication series, RRG hopes the public will be well informed on ISIS, its threat and atrocities and more importantly, not be influenced by any of their narrative and propaganda.

RRG has also produced short video clips as part of its community outreach against religious extremism and terrorism. The videos featuring RRG members speaking on a variety of issues related to religious extremism have been uploaded on YouTube and Facebook. These initiatives are hoped to delineate any misunderstandings of Islamic teachings and help the community to better understand the threat of extremism and terrorism.

RRG has also produced its third counseling manual to counter the ISIS ideology. The manual provides arguments to debunk the ISIS Islamic Caliphate, obligations of *jihad* and several other narratives of ISIS. It discusses important topics such as Muslims living in a secular environment and the need for critical thinking to evaluate religious sources. The manual is used by RRG members as a guideline to re-educate individuals and youths who have been influenced by ISIS narratives and especially for RRG public education purposes.

Another initiative of RRG is the setup of a helpline for the public to call if they have questions related to issues on radicalisation, or aspects of religion which can potentially lead one to be radical. This initiative aims to provide the public another access to a legitimate reference point on radicalisation matters, rather than being left in a lurch without any religious guidance, or turning to non-credible sources on the Internet for clarification. RRG has also embarked on short religious talks before the weekly Friday Prayers to raise awareness about the threat of radicalisation in the community. This is to leverage on the large gathering of the Muslim community (i.e., the Friday prayers) to spread counter-ideology messages on a big scale.

> *The Government appreciates the efforts of the community to counter the spread of radical ideology. It is very important that our religious leaders and teachers not only have a deep understanding of the religious tenets, but also how we can all live together peacefully and harmoniously in a multiracial, multireligious society*

> DPM Teo at the launch of the new RRG helpline
> on 29 June 2015

Conclusion

The efforts made by the Singapore government and the community to fight terrorism and mitigate the threat of ideological extremism have been strong and robust. Nonetheless, though the threat has been diffused, there is no guarantee that Singapore will not suffer a terrorist attack. The story of the RRG is a fine example of the importance of government–community partnership in dealing with the threat of terrorism and extremism.

However, to ensure the strength of an effective response to terrorism and extremism in the future, continued action will be necessary. The threat of terrorism remains cogent and the best efforts and necessary resources have to be channelled towards an efficient and effective strategy. Singapore's success is a direct result of leadership at all levels, the allocation of sustained resources to train manpower and the building of infrastructures to ensure its security, and at the strategic level is the support and intervention of the community and religious organisations.

The discovery of the JI network in Singapore, the phenomenon of self-radicalisation and the ideological threat of ISIS has taught us invaluable lessons. The recognition by the government and the Muslim community that defeating terrorist and extremist groups requires an ideological weapon is an important step. It is not a war against Islam, but a war against any misrepresentation and misunderstandings of Islam. It is not a clash of civilisations, but a clash of ideas that has divided the world into peace and war.

As part of its outreach programme, pamphlets explaining the phalacies of ISIS Islamic Caliphate were printed by RRG in the four main languages and disseminated. Image courtesy of Religious Rehabilitation Group © 2015. All rights reserved.

A CAREFULLY CALIBRATED APPROACH

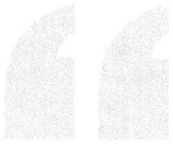

"
I have been impressed by the commitment of the RRG members. They knew it was to be a challenging task from the start. Religious rehabilitation/counselling is not a science, and there are no easily measurable benchmarks that can be used to gauge the success (or otherwise) of the programme. Moreover, the RRG members had to overcome the initial scepticism that greeted the news of the group's formation back in 2003. Yet they persisted, and on a voluntary basis."

K. Shanmugam
Minister for Home Affairs and Minister for Law
Excerpted from *Winning Hearts and Minds,
Promoting Harmony — A Decade of Providing Care and Support
Commemorating the 10th Anniversary of the
Religious Rehabilitation Group*

FIGHTING TERRORISM: PREVENTING THE RADICALISATION OF YOUTH IN A SECULAR AND GLOBALISED WORLD

Abdul Halim Kader

Since the September 11, 2001 terror attacks, terrorism has swiftly brought Islam and Muslims under close scrutiny from local, regional and global communities. Terrorist groups are also leveraging on the exponential growth of the Internet and social media to swiftly spread their ideologies. Reports have shown that terrorist groups are using a host of creative ways to recruit sympathetic individuals via online platforms such as social media, blogs and chat rooms. These are the very platforms that many of today's youth spend a significant amount of time on.

But it is not just disgruntled or marginalised youth who are at risk. Recent terrorist incidents in Europe show that the terrorists have also managed to persuade well-educated youths from good family backgrounds to believe in and fight for a misinterpreted cause of Islam. In light of this, Muslim communities need to develop safeguards and strong defences against the threat of online radicalisation.

It is a real tragedy when we begin to see youths completely indoctrinated into extremist thought to the extent that they consider the destruction of innocent human lives as a noble and justifiable act. The radicalised individuals are willing to use violence not just in far-flung lands where battles are being fought, but in the very communities that they live in.

Terrorists are able to persuade young minds because a number of these youths have a very narrow perspective of values in Islam and other major religions, as well as a limited and skewed understanding of international politics and world history. There is widespread consensus among Muslim scholars and academics that the arguments put forward by terror groups such as ISIS have no foundation in Islamic tenets.

Singapore, like any other country, is not immune to the threat of self-radicalisation, as a handful of local cases have shown. Extremist rhetoric, therefore, cannot be allowed to go unchallenged but must be countered at every level of our community. Muslim organisations such as the Religious Rehabilitation Group (RRG),

Islamic Religious Council of Singapore (MUIS) and the Inter-Agency Aftercare Group (ACG) have the responsibility to continually mould a Singapore Muslim Identity (SMI) that is free from subversion by extremist elements, whether from within or outside of Singapore.

Our approach to tackling extremist ideology must be based on both security measures and community efforts. The aim should not simply be to stop people from committing violence, but also to actively challenge the ideology that drives them. We cannot rely solely on security agencies to defend us against terrorist threats; we also need the collaborative effort of our society to do this effectively.

Despite our diversity, Singaporeans share the same values of respect for the law, freedom and equality of opportunity, as well as responsibility towards our fellow human beings. These values are the backbone of our society. It is imperative that we resist the viewpoints of a misguided few in our society who seek to undermine these values by propagating hatred and division.

We have done this relatively well over the past few decades. The challenge for us now is to reach out to our youths, especially those who are vulnerable to extremist views. Some will say that this is a task for the Muslim community alone. However, putting an end to the terrorist threat is a national responsibility. Everyone has a role to play in countering any ideology that breeds intolerance and violence, regardless of race and religion.

Where terrorists seek to drive us apart, we must strive to stand firm and through our collective strength show that the spectre of terrorism will not dampen our resolution to work together for our common good. It is this cohesion that is the best defence against the terrorist threat and the best means to ensure our continued peace and prosperity.

The ACG has worked hard in reaching out to our youths to provide them with the right knowledge so that they will be able to discern legitimate information from extremist ideology. But our efforts alone are not enough. The youths themselves must step up to tackle the dangers of extremist ideologies on the Internet. They must actively rebut the distortions of Islam, and perhaps even produce their own contents to challenge the extremist ideas, writings and videos that are circulating online. It is vital that they have the support and encouragement of the community in doing this.

Moving forward, while a number of organisations and individuals from the community have been actively engaged in countering the extremist ideology, it is timely to establish a shared platform to reach out to our youth in a targeted way. It is indeed the ACG's hope that in our renewed fight against radicalisation, we band together as a community to form a strong support structure for our youths.

CHAPTER 23

MUSLIM INSTITUTIONS WITH STATUTORY POWERS IN SINGAPORE: THE ADMINISTRATION OF MUSLIM LAW ACT (AMLA)

Alfian Yasrif Kuchit

Background

On 30 December 1965, the then Minister for Culture and Social Affairs, Mr Othman bin Wok, moved to read the Administration of Muslim Law Bill in the Singapore Parliament a second time.[1] The Bill, if passed, would "repeal and re-enact law relating to Muslims and to make provision for regulating Muslim religious affairs and to constitute a Council to advise on matters relating to the Muslim religion."[2] This Bill was built upon past colonial efforts which gave recognition to Muslim institutions.[3] On 1 July 1968, the Administration of Muslim Law Act (AMLA) finally came into force.[4]

AMLA led to the creation of three major institutions relating to the administration of Muslim law. They are:

(i) Majlis Ugama Islam (hereinafter "the Majlis"),
(ii) the Registry of Muslim Marriages (hereinafter "ROMM"), and
(iii) the Syariah Court.

However, it must be noted that AMLA did not specifically mention the institution of the Registry of Muslim Marriages. Rather, what is mentioned in AMLA is the office of the Registrar of Muslim Marriages.

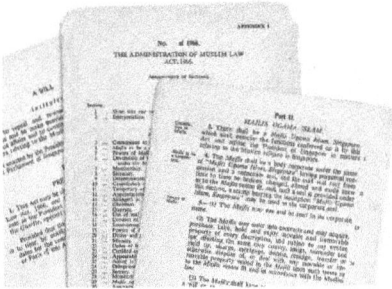

ADMINISTRATION OF MUSLIM LAW ACT (AMLA**)** — An Act relating to Muslims to make provisions for regulating Muslim religious affairs and to constitute a council to advise on matters relating to the Muslim religion in Singapore and a Syariah Court.

This article does not purport to provide a historical narrative[5] although it is certainly useful to understand that these institutions evolved from a colonial setting[6] and a distinctly colonial idea of "Anglo-Muhammadan" law. An appreciation of these institutions will help form a basis for understanding the contemporary application of Muslim law in the Singapore legal system.[7] The article will also not trace the development of AMLA throughout its years of existence as it should be noted that the AMLA has gone through several rounds of amendments. However, what this article purports to do is to provide a cursory study of the functions of Muslim institutions by focusing on the current statutory provisions.[8]

Before a brief study of these three major institutions can be carried out, one must first understand the roles of the Constitution of the Republic of Singapore, the President of Singapore and the Minister-in-Charge of Muslim Affairs. As such, I will deal with these roles in turn.

The Constitution of the Republic of Singapore

When Singapore separated from Malaysia in 1965, the republic made a pragmatic decision to retain the existing Singapore State Constitution, albeit with some necessary changes, and to address the needs of racial and religious minorities.[9] Muslims in Singapore form about 15% of the total population.[10] Unlike Article 153 of the Federal Constitution of Malaysia, the Singapore Constitution (hereafter "the Constitution") does not entrench any notions of special rights. Nevertheless, the Constitution recognises the needs of racial and religious minorities.[11]

Besides the Constitution, the President of Singapore and the Minister-in-Charge of Muslim Affairs also play crucial roles.

The President of Singapore

Under AMLA, the President of Singapore has the power to appoint[12] the following positions: President of the Majlis; Council Members of the Majlis; Vice-President of the Majlis; Mufti of Singapore; Members of the Legal (Fatwa) Committee; Presidents of the Syariah Court; registrar of the Syariah Court; Registrar of Muslim Marriages; *Kadis*[a] and *Naib*[b] *Kadis* and nominate members of the Appeal Board. Apart from the powers to appoint or nominate, AMLA also specifically empowered the President of Singapore to cancel the following appointments: the President of the Majlis; Council Members of the Majlis; the Vice-President of the Majlis; Mufti of Singapore; Registrar of Muslim Marriages; and *Kadis* and *Naib Kadis*.

However, it is curious that AMLA did not specifically mention that the President of Singapore could cancel the following appointments or nominations:

- Members of the Legal Committee;
- Presidents of the Syariah Court;
- Registrar of the Syariah Court; and
- Members of the Appeal Board.[13]

AMLA also empowered the President of Singapore to use his discretion to "call for the record of any proceedings before the [Syariah] Court, the Registrar [of Muslim Marriages], *Kadi* or *Naib Kadi* and may refer such record to the Majlis for its consideration".[14] What is curious is that AMLA did not specifically empower the President of Singapore to call for the records of Appeal Board proceedings. After all, the Appeal Board hears appeals against the decisions of the Syariah Court as well as decisions of a *Kadi* or *Naib Kadi*. A plausible explanation is that aggrieved parties have a choice of two avenues to address their grievances i.e. either appeal to the Appeal Board or seek the President's consent to refer the matter to the Majlis.[15] If this is so, then

---

[a] An official of religious standing to consider, solemnise and register Muslim marriges.
[b] Deputy

it is submitted that the President of Singapore cannot exercise revisionary powers against the Appeal Board. It is also curious why it is necessary for the President of Singapore (or the Majlis) to have such powers since the High Court has the jurisdiction to grant leave to aggrieved parties for judicial review of a decision of a public authority.[16]

Other than the powers listed above, the President of Singapore also has the power to make rules "necessary or expedient for the purpose of carrying out the provisions of this Act"[17] and to "delegate the exercise of all or any of the powers vested in him by this Act to the Minister or the President [of the Majlis]".

The Minister-in-Charge of Muslim Affairs

Even though the three Muslim institutions are under the administrative purview of the Ministry of Culture, Community, and Youth (MCCY), the Minister responsible for these institutions is the Minister-in-Charge of Muslim Affairs. The current Minister is Associate Professor Dr Yaacob Ibrahim who is also the Minister for Communications and Information and Minister-in-Charge of Cyber Security. Before 1977, the designation of Minister-in-Charge of Muslim Affairs did not exist.[18] (See also p. 100.)

Under AMLA, the Minister has, among others, the power to (i) appoint the Secretary of the Majlis; recommend not more than seven members to be appointed by the President of Singapore as members of the Majlis; consider appeals against *halal* (Arabic word which means lawful or permissible) certification decisions made by the Majlis; approve the estimates of all income and expenditure of the Majlis; approve the rules made by the Majlis; approve the Majlis' decision to form or participate in the formation of any company, or enter into any joint venture or partnership; approve the Majlis' decision with regard to the property and assets of *wakaf* (endowment) or *nazar am*[c]; provide directions; and vary the amount of contributions to the Mosque

---

[c] An expressed vow to do any act or to dedicate any property for a specific purpose allowed by Muslim Law.

Building and MENDAKI Fund.[19] The Minister is also the approving authority for any initiatives and policies implemented by the three Muslim institutions mentioned in AMLA. Apart from these statutory functions, the Minister also charts new paths and provides strategic directions for the Malay/Muslim community.[20]

Majlis Ugama Islam

During the Third Reading of the Administration of Muslim Law Bill on 17 August 1966, Mr. Othman bin Wok, highlighted that "no political influence will be made to bear on [the Majlis]. All that the Government is interested in is to see that the affairs of the Muslims in Singapore are entrusted to a wise, forward-looking and stable organisation."[21] The idea for a supreme Muslim body was mooted by Singapore's first Attorney-General, Mr. Ahmad Ibrahim.[22]

The Majlis advises the President of Singapore in matters relating to the Muslim religion in Singapore; administers matters relating to the Muslim religion and Muslims in Singapore including any matter relating to *Haj*[d] or *halal* certification; administers all Muslim endowments and funds vested in it; administers the collection of *zakat* (tithe) and *fitrah* (tithe given to the poor at the end of the fasting in the month of Ramadan) and other charitable contributions; administers all mosques and Muslim religious schools; and to carry out such other functions and duties as are conferred upon the Majlis.

For the purposes of this article, attention is drawn to two important statutory establishments. They are the Legal Committee of the Majlis and the Appeal Board.

Legal Committee of the Majlis

AMLA empowers the Mufti as the chairman of the "Legal Committee of the Majlis" to issue a ruling (*fatwa*).[23] The Mufti can only do so if a unanimous

---

[d] *Haj* literally means, "to continuously strive to reach one's goal." The *haj*, or pilgrimage to Mecca, is a once-in-a-lifetime obligation for those who have the physical and financial ability to undertake the journey.

decision is reached. In the event the Legal Committee is unable to reach a unanimous decision, the question "shall be referred to the Majlis, which shall in like manner issue its ruling in accordance with the opinion of the *majority* of its members [emphasis added]."[24]

Under AMLA, the membership of the Legal Committee is made up of

(i) the Mufti;
(ii) two members of the Majlis (who after from having been appointed as Council Members of the Majlis by the President of Singapore must have also been appointed by the President of Singapore to the Legal Committee), and
(iii) not more than two non-members of the Majlis. As such, AMLA allows for a minimum of four members in the Legal Committee and a maximum of five.

However, a quorum is formed when the Mufti, a member of the Majlis and a non-member of the Majlis are present. It should be noted that the members of Legal Committee (with the exception of the Mufti) are not salaried officers of the Majlis. Under Section 33, the Majlis and the Legal Committee in issuing any ruling "shall ordinarily follow the tenets of the Shafi'i school of law"[e] although the Majlis "may follow the tenets of any of the other accepted schools of Muslim law as may be considered appropriate".

Appeal Board

The Majlis also provides administrative and secretariat support to the Appeal Board as Appeal Board hearings are carried out in the Majlis' office building. Under Section 2 of AMLA, Appeal Board means "an Appeal Board constituted under Section 55".

The Appeal Board hears appeals from the decisions of the Syariah Court. On any appeal, "an Appeal Board may confirm, reverse or vary the decision of the Syariah

---

[e] The Shafi'i madhhab is one of the four schools of Islamic law in Sunni Islam.

Court, exercise any such powers as the Syariah Court could have exercised, make such order as the Syariah Court ought to have made or order a retrial, or award costs if it thinks fit". Similarly, the Appeal Board can also hear appeals from the decisions of a *Kadi* or *Naib Kadi*.

The President of Singapore, at least once in every two years, "nominates at least seven Muslims to form a panel of persons from among whom an Appeal Board of three may be constituted from time to time by the President of the Majlis". The wordings of AMLA suggest that the Appeal Board is meant to be an *ad-hoc* committee of three people (where one of them shall chair the Appeal Board) constituted by the President of Majlis. As such, the composition of the Appeal Board varies from time to time.

Unlike the phrase "Legal Committee of the Majlis", it is interesting to note that the phrase "Appeal Board of the Majlis" cannot be found in AMLA. This suggests that the Parliament intended for the Appeal Board to be separate from the Majlis. None of the members of the Appeal Board are salaried officers of the Majlis. However, unlike the members of the Legal Committee, there is no statutory provision that enables a member of the Appeal Board to enter a dissent.

The Registry of Muslim Marriages

The provisions of Part VI of AMLA (which relates to marriage and divorce) apply only to "marriages, both of the parties to which profess the Muslim religion and which are solemnized in accordance with the Muslim law".[25] This should be compared to Section 3(1) of the Women's Charter which states that "[e]xcept otherwise provided, this Act shall apply to all persons in Singapore and shall also apply to all persons domiciled in Singapore" although Section 3(4) of the Women's Charter provides that "[n]o marriage between persons who are Muslims shall be solemnized or registered under this Act." This means that where one party is a Muslim and the other, a non-Muslim, the marriage will be registered under the Women's Charter and not AMLA.

As mentioned earlier, the name "Registry of Muslim Marriages" was not specifically mentioned in AMLA. Instead, Section 90 mentions the office of the Registrar of Muslim Marriages. Under AMLA, the Registrar keeps the Register of Marriages, the Register of Divorces and the Register of Revocation of Divorces. However, in 1990, AMLA was amended and the Registrar no longer keeps the Register of Divorces.[26]

To assist the Registrar, the President of Singapore appoints "suitable male Muslims of good character and position and of suitable attainments to be Kadis or Naib Kadis".[27] Under Section 92(1), every *Kadi* and *Naib Kadi* "shall be a Deputy Registrar of Muslim Marriages". Every *Kadi* and *Naib Kadi* shall within one week of the registration of a marriage or revocation of divorce, send a copy of the certificate of marriage or revocation of divorce, as the case may be, to the Registrar. Apart from the solemnisation of marriages,[28] a Kadi or Naib Kadi may also hold an inquiry into wali's refusal to consent under Section 95(3) of AMLA.[29] However, only a Kadi may hold an inquiry regarding an application for a polygamous marriage.[30]

AMLA provides for the regulation of polygamous marriages.[31] It also provides for the regulation of minor marriages[32] as a Kadi may under Section 96(5) of AMLA "solemnize the marriage of a girl who is below the age of 18 years but has attained the age of puberty". The Appeal Board can hear appeals from the decisions of the Kadis and Naib Kadis.[33]

As AMLA does not purport to validate a Muslim marriage, the Act does not render "valid or invalid merely by reason of it having been or not having been registered any Muslim marriage, divorce or revocation of divorce which otherwise is invalid or valid." This is consistent with the statement by Mr. Othman Wok that AMLA "does not seek to deal with the Muslim law itself but only with its administration".[34] Therefore, a Muslim marriage contracted overseas would not be considered invalid just because it was not registered in Singapore. The onus is on the Muslim couple to prove that the marriage is indeed valid according to Muslim law.

The Syariah Court

Unlike the Majlis, there was an additional step involved before the Syariah Court came into existence. According to Section 34 of AMLA, the President of Singapore "may by notification in the Gazette constitute a Syariah Court for Singapore". In July 1968, the then President, Mr. Yusof bin Ishak, made a notification in the Gazette[35] and the Syariah Court of independent Singapore was born.

The Syariah Court, however, is not part of Singapore's judiciary. As noted earlier, the Syariah Court is a creature of AMLA and only came into being by an executive act of the President of Singapore.

The Syariah Court has jurisdiction to hear and determine all actions and proceedings in which all the parties are Muslims or where the parties were married under Muslim law and which involve disputes relating to

(a) marriage;
(b) divorces;
(c) bethrotal, nullity of marriage or judicial separation;
(d) the disposition or division of property on divorce or nullification of marriage; or
(e) the payment of emas kahwin (nominal payment of marriage), hantaran belanja (marriage expenses), maintenance and mutaah (consolatory gift pursuant to divorce).[36]

As such, in the absence of a dispute, the Syariah Court would not have jurisdiction. In deciding these disputes, the rule of decision "shall .... be the Muslim law, as varied where applicable by Malay custom."

The Syariah Court has, among others, the following powers:

(a) to procure and receive evidence and to examine all such persons as witnesses;
(b) to require the evidence of any witness;

(c) to summon any person to attend before the Court;

(d) to issue a warrant of arrest to compel the attendance of any person and to order him to pay all costs which may have been occasioned in compelling his attendance; and

(e) to exercise the powers of a Magistrate's Court for the purpose of giving effect to a warrant of arrest.

The Court is also statutorily mandated to issue a certificate of presumption of the death of the husband; an inheritance certificate to certify its opinion as to the persons who are entitled to share and as to the shares of the estate; and to make such decree or order regarding the revocation of a divorce in the event the *Kadi* is not satisfied that both parties have consented to the revocation.

In Malaysia, the exclusive jurisdiction of the Syariah Courts is conferred by Article 121(1A) of the Federal Constitution. In Singapore, the exclusive jurisdiction of the Syariah Court is indirectly conferred under Section 17A(1) of the Supreme Court of Judicature Act (Cap. 322) which states that " ... the High Court shall have no jurisdiction to hear and try any civil proceedings involving matters which come within the jurisdiction of the Syariah Court under Section 35 (2) (a), (b) or (c) of the Administration of Muslim Law Act (Cap. 3) in which all the parties are Muslims or where the parties were married under the provisions of the Muslim law." However, it should be noted that Section 17A(2) provides concurrent jurisdiction to the High Court "to hear and try any civil proceedings involving matters relating to (a) maintenance for any wife or child; (b) custody of any child; and (c) disposition or division of property on divorce". Under Section 35A of AMLA, even in the absence of consensus between both parties to the dispute, the Syariah Court may grant leave for a party to proceed to the civil courts to adjudicate claims relating to the (a) disposition or division of property on divorce or (b) custody of any child.

The Syariah Court generally does not enforce its own orders.[47] Rather, Syariah Court orders are enforced by the civil courts. Previously, Syariah Court orders needed to be registered at the civil courts before it can be enforced. This additional step costs time and money. However, in 2008, AMLA was amended and Syariah Court orders are deemed as District Court orders for the purpose of enforcement.[37] Furthermore, Syariah Court orders for *nafkah iddah* (maintenance) and *mutaah* are considered as maintenance orders which will enable Muslim women to use the Family Court enforcement mechanism.

Under Section 39 of AMLA, parties to the dispute must appear in person or be represented by an "advocate and solicitor or by an agent, generally or specially authorised to do so by the Court".[38] Unlike other provisions which make explicit mention that the office holder has to be Muslim,[39] this provision does not. As such, non-Muslims lawyers have appeared before the Syariah Court.

Conclusion

This article provides a brief overview of Muslim institutions with statutory powers in Singapore. It takes a somewhat reductionist approach in studying the statutory provisions as it omits other important considerations e.g. colonial and common law influences on AMLA, the impact of AMLA on Singapore, the areas of Muslim life beyond those regulated by AMLA, as well as the contestation within the Muslim community. These questions should be addressed though they are not within the scope of this short essay. What is important is to note that these institutions have continued to adapt to serve the needs of the Singaporean Muslim community.

References

1. Othman Bin Wok: Singapore Parliament Report (Administration of Muslim Law Bill), 30 December 1965.
2. "Public views invited on Muslim Bill", *The Straits Times* (Singapore) 5 January 1966, p. 5.
3. For the definition of institutions, see Roff's definition i.e. bureaucratic or corporate structures which embody and constrain law, administration, education, economic behaviour, and some similar features of Islamic social organisation. See William R. Roff, "Patterns of

Islamization in Malaysia, 1890s–1990s: Exemplars, Institutions and Vectors" in *Studies on Islam and Society in Southeast Asia* (Singapore: NUS Press, 2009) p. 97.

4. AMLA was passed by Parliament in 1966 after extensive deliberation by a Select Committee and came into operation on 1 July 1968. See Select Committee Report on the Administration of Muslim Law Bill (Parl. 3 of 1966, 31 March 1966). See also "Call for a Pure Muslim Law is Absurd", The Straits Times (Singapore) 9 November 1966, p. 5.

5. See e.g., William R. Roff, "The Origin and Early Years of the Majlis Agama Kelantan" in *Studies on Islam and Society in Southeast Asia*, (Singapore: NUS Press, 2009) for a historical study of a Majlis Agama.

6. Ahmad Ibrahim, *Towards a History of Law in Malaysia and Singapore*, (Kuala Lumpur: Dewan Bahasa dan Pustaka, 1992). See also s. 6 of AMLA which vested all property, rights, powers, duties and liabilities vested in or imposed on the Board established by the Muslim and Hindu Endowments Ordinance (a colonial legacy) to the Majlis.

7. For a brief introduction to the Singapore legal system, see Eugene Tan & Gary Chan, *The Singapore Legal System*, at http://www.singaporelaw.sg/sglaw/laws-of-singapore/overview/chapter-1 (date accessed: 20 Oct 2015).

8. The law stated is as of 20 October 2015.

9. Li-ann Thio, "The Passage of a Generation: Revisiting the Report of the 1966 Constitutional Commission" in Li-ann Thio & Kevin YL Tan, eds., *Evolution of a Revolution: Forty Years of the Singapore Constitution*, (Oxon and New York: Routledge-Cavendish, 2009), pp. 7–8.

10. See para 13 of the press release issued by the Singapore Department of Statistics, http://www.news.gov.sg/public/sgpc/en/media_releases/agencies/singstat/press_release/P-20110112-1/AttachmentPar/0/file/C2010%20R1%20Press%20release.pdf (date accessed: 20 Oct 2015).

11. *Halsbury's Laws of Singapore, Vol. 1* (Singapore: Butterworths Asia, 2008 reissue) at para 10.829.

12. Under s. 2 of the Interpretation Act, appoint includes re-appoint.

13. Presumably, there is no need to have this power mentioned explicitly in AMLA as s. 28 of the interpretation states that the power to make appointments shall be construed as including a power to dismiss.

14. See s. 56.

15. The author is unaware of any case which has been referred to the President of Singapore.

16. See Mohamed Yusoff bin Mohd Haniff v Umi Kalsom bte Abas (Attorney-General, non-party) [2010] SGHC 114.

17. See s. 145.

18. See Anthony Green, *The MUIS Story: 40 Years of Building a Singapore Muslim Community of Excellence*, (Singapore: Majlis Ugama Islam Singapura, 2009).

19. s. 78(5). The Mosque Building and Mendaki Fund "facilitates Muslim employees to make regular, monthly donations towards mosque building. Established in 1975, it was expanded in 1984 to inject MENDAKI (a self-help group for the Malay/Muslim community) with much-needed funds to run some of its programmes". See Yaacob Ibrahim: 85 Singapore Parliament Report (Administration of Muslim Law (Amendment) Bill), 17 November 2008, at col 727 (hereafter "Yaacob").

20. Othman Work, Press Statement, Hari Raya Message, 20 Jan 1966, available at http://www.nas.gov.sg/archivesonline/data/pdfdoc/PressR19660120.pdf (date accessed: 20 Oct 2015);

Ahmad Mattar, Speech, Hari Raya Puasa Reception at The Istana, 7 August 1981, available at http://www.nas.gov.sg/archivesonline/data/pdfdoc/am19810807bs.pdf (date accessed: 20 Oct 2015); Abdullah Tarmugi, Speech, Hari Raya Aidilfitri Get Together at The Istana, 29 January 1999, available at http://www.nas.gov.sg/archivesonline/data/pdfdoc/at19990129c.pdf (date accessed: 20 Oct 2015); Yaacob Ibrahim, Speech, Hari Raya Get-Together at the Istana, 2 October 2009 available at http://www.nas.gov.sg/archivesonline/speeches/view-html?filename=20091009006.htm (date accessed: 20 Oct 2015).

21. Othman Bin Wok: Singapore Parliament Report (Administration of Muslim Law Bill), 30 December 1965.

22. Ibid, at p 31.

23. See s. 32(4). See also s. 31(5) where the President of Singapore may appoint another person recommended by the Majlis to be the chairman where the Mufti has recused himself.

24. See s. 32(5) read together with s. 31(1).

25. S. 89. See also Yaacob, *supra*, note 19. The amendment removed the provision allowing the Registry of Muslim Marriages to register marriages between Muslims and the *kitabiyah*, or People of the Book.

26. Ahmad Mattar: 56 Singapore Parliament Report [Administration of Muslim Law (Amendment) Bill], 18 July 1990, at col 322; see also S. 100(3).

27. S. 91(1).

28. Rule 3 of the Muslim Marriages and Divorce Rules (hereafter "MMDR").

29. Rule 4 of MMDR.

30. Rule 5 of MMDR.

31. Othman Bin Wok: Singapore Parliament Report (Administration of Muslim Law (Amendment) Bill), 30 December 1965, at p 770.

32. See Yaacob, *supra*, note 19.

33. For a compilation of ROMM cases from 1973–1987, see Salbiah Ahmad (1989), *The Administration of Muslim Family Law in Singapore*, unpublished thesis, International Islamic University Malaysia, Petaling Jaya (hereafter "Salbiah"). See also ss. 105 and 106.

34. Othman Bin Wok: Singapore Parliament Report [Administration of Muslim Law (Amendment) Bill], 17 August 1966, p. 239.

35. Government Gazette Subsidiary Legislation Supplement No. 54 (12 July 1968) p. 401.

36. S. 35(2). For a compilation of Syariah Court cases from 1973–1986, see Salbiah, *supra*, note 33, at pp 258–453. For a study of the Syariah Court, see Noor Aisha Abdul Rahman (1999), *The Syariah Court and the Administration of the Muslim Law on Divorce in Singapore*, Unpublished Ph.D dissertation, National University of Singapore, Singapore. See also Noor Aisha Abdul Rahman, "Traditionalism and Its Impact on the Administration of Justice: The Case of the Syariah Court of Singapore", Dec. 2004, Vol. 5, Issue 3, Inter-Asia Cultural Studies, pp. 415–432.

37. See Yaacob, *supra*, note 19.

38. See also Rule 2(1) of the Muslim Marriages and Divorce Rules where the word "solicitor" is defined as an "advocate and solicitor of the Supreme Court".

39. See, for example, ss. 7(5), 8(1), 90(1), and 91(1).

THE ISLAMIC RELIGIOUS COUNCIL OF SINGAPORE (MUIS) JOURNEY: CONTINUING THE PURSUIT OF EXCELLENCE — LEGACY FROM THE PAST

Abdul Razak Hassan Maricar

MUIS'[a] transformation from its humble beginnings to its present position as a key institution in the Muslim community as well as an established statutory board parallels the nation's 50-year post-independence journey. It started off responding to the disruptions and crises triggered by the early pangs of a young nation still finding its way while undergoing rapid change. Nevertheless, MUIS had the fortune of being under the stewardship of forward-looking pioneering leaders who had the foresight and well-grounded understanding of their social realities. Their wisdom and insights have shaped the approach of subsequent generations of leaders who continued the legacy of a progressive outlook to drive MUIS and the community towards excellence. MUIS has since evolved into a more proactive institution with clarity of vision and well-defined processes to achieve its goals. At the heart of this developmental ethos are three key principles which remain constant

(i) Shaping a Progressive Religious Outlook;
(ii) Forging Trust and Confidence;
(iii) Investing in Assets to Drive Change.

---

[a] Majlis Ugama Islam Singapura (MUIS), also known as the Islamic Religious Council of Singapore.

Shaping a Progressive Religious Outlook

The former mufti Syed Isa Semait's perseverance to push for the introduction of mathematical calculations over moon sighting to determine the start and end of *Ramadan* despite strong resistance from the community was a good example of the embodiment of the progressive religious outlook. Unlike some other Muslim communities elsewhere which are still saddled by this perennial problem, we had the benefit of resolving such disputes early in our development which has allowed Singapore Muslims' to observe their religious rituals peacefully without being embroiled annually in meaningless conflicts. Together with Ustaz Ahmad Sonhadji, Ustaz Abu Bakar Hashim, Ustaz Syed Abdillah Aljufri, Ustaz Ibrahim Kassim (all of them have passed on) and many others, Syed Isa and members of the Fatwa Committee have a deep appreciation on the need for the community to quickly adjust to Singapore's economic demands and not be distracted by such concerns. Such contextual appreciation has inspired and guided our succeeding religious scholars in finding new solutions to emerging challenges like the inclusion of Muslims in the Human Organ Transplant Act (HOTA), joint tenancy, CPF Nomination, etc.

After more than four decades, the respect and support of the community for MUIS and its leaders has strengthened. Image courtesy of Majlis Ugama Islam Singapura © 2015. All rights reserved.

Beyond *fatwas*[b] and religious guidance, this progressive outlook forms the essence of the religious content and curricula which inform the religious learning delivered through various programmes and platforms for different levels in the community. Religious scholars and teachers are being systematically and comprehensively developed to embrace

---

[b] Islamic legal ruling.

this progressive ethos through our *madrasahs* as well as mentoring, engagement and developmental programmes driven by the MUIS Academy. The inculcation of religious ideas has evolved into a living ecology which will continue to be sustained and enhanced as it responds to changing socio-religious landscape.

Forging Trust and Confidence

MUIS recognised from the beginning that it could not succeed without the support of the community. The community's psychological trauma of losing its majority status with the separation from Malaysia and familiar spaces like the *kampong* mosques due to urbanisation formed a significant mental barrier which hindered full confidence and trust in MUIS. The introduction of the Mosque Building Fund (MBF) and the eventual building of the first phase of MBF mosques aided in breaking that mental barrier which made MUIS gradually more endearing to a larger segment of the community.

From being functional spaces for worship and religious learning, the mosques have evolved into important institutions serving the many aspirations of the community. They have become well-integrated into the national social assistance fabric and work in tandem with various community and national agencies to deliver relevant services to the community. The mosques have helped MUIS to be even closer connected to the community and foster stronger ties and understanding. This contributed to a virtuous cycle of greater trust and confidence, not only within the community but also with the larger Singapore society.

Muhajirin Mosque was the first mosque to be built under the Mosque Building Fund. It was completed in April 1977 with a capacity of 1400 people and serves Muslims of all ages living in Toa Payoh and surrounding estates. Image courtesy of Majlis Ugama Islam Singapura © 2015. All rights reserved.

Some of the old mosques and *suraus* that had to give way to modernisation. Image courtesy of Majlis Ugama Islam Singapura © 2015. All rights reserved.

Investing in Assets to Drive Change

Without the resources, MUIS would not have been able to grow and do more for the community. The centralisation of zakat[c] and the subsequent advancements in MUIS' zakat management practices were pivotal in injecting adequate resources for MUIS to bring in better talent and deliver new programmes. However, a quantum leap in its asset accumulation was achieved through MUIS' foray into wakaf[d] development. This was driven by a combination of the progressive religious outlook of religious leaders like the late Ustaz Muhammad Kamil Fadhlullah Suhaimi and the inclusion of professional Muslim talent which gave birth to the early wakaf development projects which provided substantial yield for the community's assets.

Alias Villas, Singapore's first Islamic endowment villas located along Jalan Haji Alias off Sixth Avenue, have a 99-year lease, and are expected to be ready by 2017. The development is part of an ongoing revitalisation scheme to enhance the asset value of wakaf properties. Image courtesy of Majlis Ugama Islam Singapura © 2015. All rights reserved.

The establishment of Warees Investments[e] in 2002 as a wholly-owned subsidiary of MUIS was a significant milestone which contributed to more resources for MUIS and the community. Through creative and innovative design of financial instruments like the Musyarakah Bond, MUIS has been able to undertake various development projects. This led to MUIS

---

[c] Islamic concept of tithe and alms; spending a fixed portion of one's wealth to give people who meet the criteria for receipt of zakat, such as the poor or the needy. al-Zuhaili, Wahbah, al-Fiqh al-Islami wa Adillatuh. Damascus: Dar al-Fikr, 1985. Vol 1, p. 819.

[d] The literal meaning of this Arabic word is to detain or prevent. When speaking about buildings or structures, it means that the normal worldly transactions — the buying and selling of the building or structure — have been stopped and the property has been "given over" to be used for the work of God. Apart from buildings, other things, such as books and equipment, can also be dedicated for this purpose. Wakaf is an unalienable endowment for a charitable purpose that cannot be given away or sold to anyone. al-Zuhaili, Wahbah, al-Fiqh al-Islami wa Adillatuh. Damascus: Dar al-Fikr, 1985. Vol 8, p. 155.

[e] Warees is the acronym for WAkaf REal EState. Waris, as pronounced in Malay, means "heritage" and "beneficiary", both of which are closely related to the management of trust properties.

attaining international accolade like the International Sheikh Mohammed bin Rashid Al-Makhtoum Award in 2006 by the Ruler of Dubai for Innovative Solutions in Islamic Finance.

Moving Into the Future

Those three principles will stay relevant and central as MUIS advances into the future. MUIS will remain focused in shaping a Muslim persona which is confident, well-adjusted and contributing to the modern world. MUIS will also continue to address the evolving religious needs of the community as well as work hand in hand with the larger Singaporean society to benefit humanity so as to embody the prophetic attribute of *rahmatan lil alamin.*[f]

A gracious Muslim community of excellence that inspires and radiates blessings to all. Image courtesy of Majlis Ugama Islam Singapura © 2015. All rights reserved.

Bibliography

Anthony Green, 2009. Honouring the Past, Shaping the Future: The MUIS Story: 40 Years of Building a Singapore Muslim Community of Excellence, Majlis Ugama Islam Singapura, Singapore.

---

[f] A blessing for the whole world.

PAST AND CURRENT MUIS OFFICE BEARERS

Presidents:

1. Hj Ismail Abdul Aziz (1968–1972)
2. Mr Mahmood Hj Yusof (1972–1974)
3. Hj Buang Siraj (1974–1980)
4. Hj Ismail Mohd Said (1980–1986)
5. Hj Ridzwan Dzafir (1986–1990)
6. Hj Shafawi Ahmad (Acting President Jan–Jun 1991)
7. Hj Zainul Abidin Rasheed (July 1991–1995)
8. Hj Maarof Salleh (1995–Aug 2003)
9. Hj Mohammad Alami Musa (Sept 2003–Present: Non-Executive President)

Muftis:

1. Hj Sanusi Mahmood (1968–Jan 1972)
2. Syed Isa Mohd Semait (Feb 1972–2010)
3. Dr Mohamed Fatris Bakaram (2011–Present)

Secretaries:

1. Hj Jamil Dzafir (1968–1971)
2. Hj Musa Yusof (1971–1987)
3. Syed Haroon b Mohamed Aljunied (1987–May 2007)
4. Hj Abdul Razak bin Hassan Maricar (June 2007–2013)

Chief Executive:

1. Hj Abdul Razak bin Hassan Maricar (Aug 2013–Present)

The first MUIS Council, with President Yusof bin Ishak (first row, fourth from left). Standing on the President's right is Haji Ismail Abdul Aziz, President of MUIS. On the President's left is Mohamed Sanusi Mahmood, Singapore's first Mufti. Image courtesy of Majlis Ugama Islam Singapura © 2015. All rights reserved.

OF MOSQUES AND MOSQUE BUILDING FUND

The mosque is a religious institution that is the foundation of the Malay/Muslim community's religious life. The 1970s saw Singapore undergoing rapid urbanisation and with the state's emphasis on pragmatism and developmentalism, the relocation and demolition of religious buildings[a] were inevitable — mosques and *suraus*[b] included. Between 1974 and 1987, 23 mosques and 76 *suraus* were acquired and cleared.[c] Despite the issue of acquisition and clearing being contentious, the process went ahead and the urban change was being presented as inevitable, as shown from the extracts from two speeches by Mr Othman Wok (then Minister for Social Affairs):

> *"Progress in Singapore cannot be achieved without change. The numerous development schemes such as oil refinery, public housing, etc. have necessitated the reciting of burial grounds and religious institutions. These have affected all sections of the community. It is not a deliberate policy of the Singapore Government to demolish places of worship. The process of urban renewal has necessitated the moving of population from one area to another. However, every effort has been made to ensure that the way of life of the people concerned is not adversely affected both economically and spiritually. In fact, the object of development is to upgrade the living standards of the population as a whole. In the process of development, the old must make way for the new and demolition of some masjids, temples and churches affected by redevelopment is inevitable. Such action has only been resorted to when absolutely necessary and unavoidable."[d]*

---

[a] Included under the acquisition and clearing et were 700 Chinese temples, 27 Hindu temples and 19 churches (Press statement from Prime Minister's office, 9 October 1987).

[b] A small mosque.

[c] Kong, Lily, 1993, Environment and Planning D-Society & Space, 11, no. 1: 23–46, DOI:10.1068/d110023.

[d] Othman Wok, 1974a, "Speech delivered at the Pasir Panjang Koran Reading Competition", 17 July, in Ministry of Social Affairs: Speeches, Statements, Press Conferences and Interviews, 1971–1973 (Information Division, Ministry of Culture, Singapore).

> *"Development projects which are for the benefit of Singapore society as a whole must go on, and if any building is in the way of such development, obviously it will have to go if this is unavoidable."*[e]

In 1974, the then Prime Minister Mr Lee Kuan Yew invited a few Malay/ Muslim community and religious leaders to the Istana for a discussion.[f] In the discussion, Mr Lee expressed concern about the ability of the Malay/Muslim community to raise funds to build mosques in new housing estates without a stable source of income. He then proposed that every Muslim worker contribute to mosque development through the deduction of their pay using the CPF mechanism.

Mr Othman Wok recalled, "He (Lee) said he would instruct the Civil Service to prepare a circular for all Malay/Muslims working in the government service to donate voluntarily to the mosque building fund, and the deduction will be through CPF. That was a good idea. Readily, they gave 50 cents."[g]

The meeting led to the establishment of The Mosque Building Fund (MBF)[h] the following year. It resulted in a more effective system of fundraising and has allowed the community to develop the mosques in an efficient and well-organised manner. Between 1977 and 2015, a total of 24 mosques have been built in housing estates under Mosque Building Programme since 1975.

The latest mosque is Al-Islah Mosque which was built in Punggol in 2015. Two new mosques are being built — Maarof Mosque and Yusof Ishak Mosque. Together with the completion of Al-Islah, these mosques will collectively add 13,000 new prayer spaces throughout Singapore.[i]

---

[e] Othma Wok, 1974b, "Speech delivered at a meeting with new members of the Majlis Ugama Islam Singapura, 25 October, in Ministry of Social Affairs: Speeches, Statements, Press Conferences and Interviews, 1974–1976 (Information Division, Ministry of Culture, Singapore).

[f] The meeting on 10 December 1974 was attended by officials such as then Minister for Social Affairs Othman Wok, then MUIS president Buang Siraj and Mufti Syed Isa Semait.

[g] http://tblet.todayonline.com/rememberinglky/pla e-bl, la te cessed 30 November 2015.

[h] The Mosque Building Fund (MBF) was established in 1975 as a means of gathering funds for the building of mosques in new public housing estates. After the formation of the MENDAKI Foundation in 1984, the MBF was integrated with the MENDAKI Fund and renamed the Mosque Building and MENDAKI Fund (MBMF). Muslims voluntarily contribute to this fund by having a fixed amount deducted from their salary every month through the Central Provident Fund (CPF).

[i] MUIS Annual Report 2014, Moving Forward with the Community, http://www.muis.gov.sg/About/a nual-report.html, la te cessed 30 November 2015.

In 1981, the MBF was expanded in scope when it was used to partly fund self-help efforts by MENDAKI to give assistance to needy students and disadvantaged families. It was subsequently renamed Mosque Building and MENDAKI Fund (MBMF).

This year, MUIS announced a revision to the monthly contributions — the first since 2009. Muslims will each have to pay $1 to $10 more in monthly contributions to the MBMF from 1 June. The expected increase in annual contributions to the fund will go a long way to improving the socio-religious life of the Malay/Muslim community.

Total Monthly Wage of Muslim Employee	Current Monthly Contribution	New Rate Change	Revised Monthly Contribution
≤ $1,000	$2.00	+ $1.00	$3.00
> $1,000 to $2,000	$3.50	+ $1.00	$4.50
> $2,000 to $3,000	$5.00	+ $1.50	$6.50
> $3,000 to $4,000	$12.50	+ $2.50	$15.00
> $4,000 to $6,000	$16.00	+ $3.50	$19.50
> $6,000 to $8,000	$16.00	+ $6.00	$22.00
> $8,000 to $10,000	$16.00	+ $8.00	$24.00
> $10,000	$16.00	+ $10.00	$26.00

Source: http://www.mbmf.sg/About/What-Is-The-New-Contribution-Rate. Last accessed 22 April 2016.

Typology of Phase 1 Mosques (1976–1980);

Pioneers – Grand Mosques

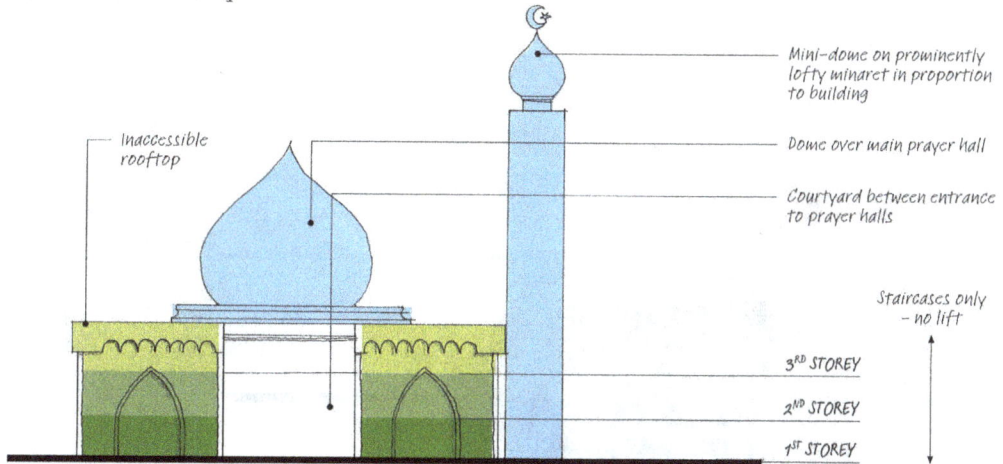

- Mini-dome on prominently lofty minaret in proportion to building
- Dome over main prayer hall
- Courtyard between entrance to prayer halls
- Staircases only – no lift
- Inaccessible rooftop
- 3RD STOREY
- 2ND STOREY
- 1ST STOREY

- Huge prayer halls
- Small administration office / committee meeting rooms
- 'Jenazah' room
- Open terraces / courtyards as extended prayer areas
- Monolithic structures
- Rigid spaces (No proper demarcation of iktikaf & maslahat areas)

Typology of Phase 2 Mosques (1980–1995)

Nusantara Mosques

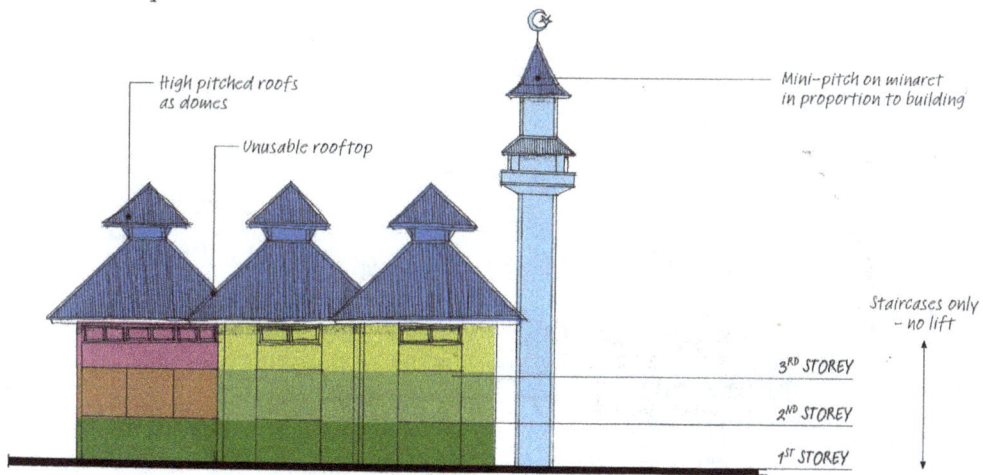

- Mini-pitch on minaret in proportion to building
- High pitched roofs as domes
- Unusable rooftop
- Staircases only – no lift
- 3RD STOREY
- 2ND STOREY
- 1ST STOREY

- Main prayer halls / female prayer Halls
- Small administration office / committee meeting rooms
- Multipurpose halls (auditorium)
- Classrooms accommodate part-time madrasah
- Southeast Asian-Malay architectural features
- Rich designs, hand-crafted architraves
- Sacred spaces maintained

☐ Minaret & dome   ☐ Main prayer hall (male)   ☐ Main prayer hall (female)

Typology of Phase 3 Mosques (1996–2005)

Compact Urban Mosques – Contemporary Singapore Model

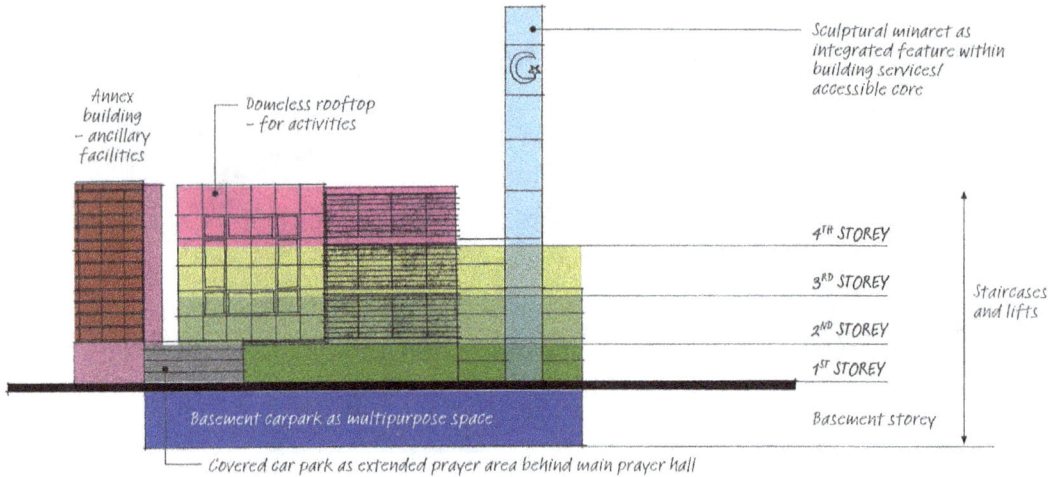

Annex building – ancillary facilities

Domeless rooftop – for activities

Sculptural minaret as integrated feature within building services/ accessible core

4TH STOREY

3RD STOREY

2ND STOREY

1ST STOREY

Staircases and lifts

Basement carpark as multipurpose space

Basement storey

Covered car park as extended prayer area behind main prayer hall

- Main prayer halls / female prayer halls with better accessibility
- Complete ancillary facilities (beyond worship; mosque as Islamic Centre)
- Multipurpose halls (auditorium) & special rooms for counselling etc
- Adequate classrooms for madrasah & kindergarten
- Contemporary, minimal and universal design
- Clear demarcation of iktikaf & maslahat areas

Typology of Phase 4 Mosques (2006–2010)

Post Mosque Convention 2005 Mosques – Performance-Friendly Urban Mosques

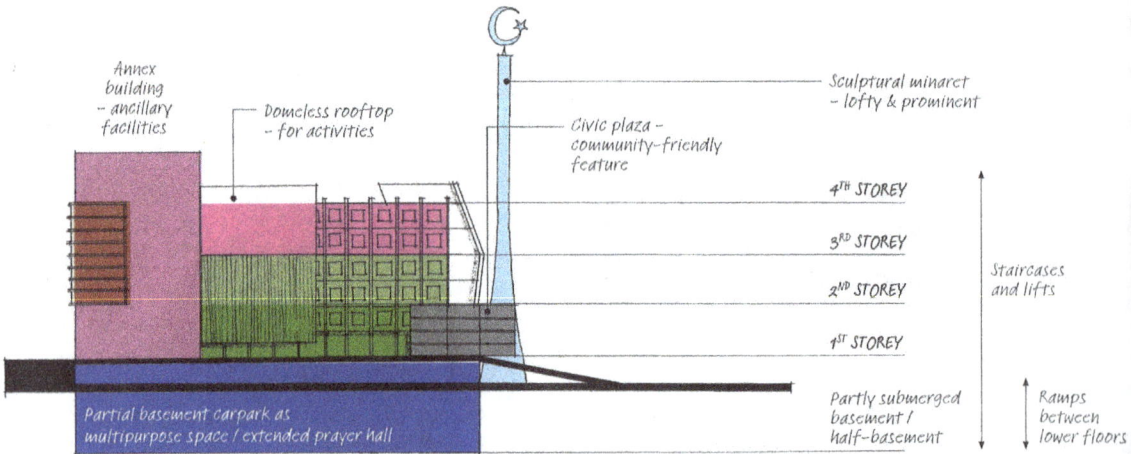

Annex building – ancillary facilities

Domeless rooftop – for activities

Civic plaza – community-friendly feature

Sculptural minaret – lofty & prominent

4TH STOREY

3RD STOREY

2ND STOREY

1ST STOREY

Staircases and lifts

Partial basement carpark as multipurpose space / extended prayer hall

Partly submerged basement / half-basement

Ramps between lower floors

- Main prayer halls / female prayer halls with better accessibility
- Complete ancillary facilities (beyond worship; mosque as Islamic Centre)
- Family-, youth- and elderly-friendly facilities/designs
- Flexible classrooms for madrasah & kindergarten
- Modern universal design with clean look
- Cost-conscious development
- Clear demarcation of iktikaf & maslahat areas

| | Extended prayer hall | | Classrooms/multi-purpose halls | | Offices/multi-purpose rooms |

CHAPTER 25

GENESIS OF MENDAKI AND MILESTONES | Tuminah Sapawi

The year 2015 marks the 33rd anniversary of Yayasan MENDAKI. Though officially registered with the Registrar of Societies as Yayasan MENDAKI on 10 October 1982, it has its beginnings as early as August 1981 with the formation of the Joint Action Committee on Malay education by the then Malay/Muslim Members of Parliament.

MENDAKI or the Council for Education of Muslim Children was formed as a task force looking into ways and means of improving the educational levels of Malays in Singapore. This was in response to the comments made by then Prime Minister Lee Kuan Yew who called on the community to look into improving the academic attainment of its population. The late Mr Lee cited 63% of the community as without GCE 'O' Level, of which slightly more than 40% having failed at the PSLE.

The arrival of the late Mr Lee Kuan Yew being greeted by community leaders at the opening of the MENDAKI Congress, 1982. Image courtesy of Yayasan MENDAKI © 2015. All rights reserved.

Following a series of discussions and dialogues with the various Malay/Muslim organisations and education institutions, as well as conducting research and surveys, the MENDAKI Weekend Tuition Scheme was piloted in 1982 with a group of 60 students sitting for their 'A' levels in the

I promise you that the government will give every assistance by making premises available, and by appealing to non-Malay teachers to join in this exercise. This problem is of concern to all Singaporeans and not just to Malay Singaporeans. It is in the interests of all to have Malay Singaporeans better educated and better qualified and to increase their contribution to Singapore's development."

You can reach them through their hearts, not just their minds. You have the motivation, the dedication and commitment. This emotional/ psychological support can make a vast difference, between a student who tries, fails, and tries again, and another who fails and gives up."

The late Mr Lee Kuan Yew
Mendaki Congress I
28 May 1982

same year. The programme was strongly supported by the community with the various grassroots coming out in full force. Haji Shafawi Ahmad, MENDAKI'S first Executive Officer for Education called it, "a new phenomenon in our society." Such was the support the community gave that the programme was soon expanded to include more and more students across the various levels.

Over the years, the programme has undergone several reviews and in 2012, the MENDAKI Tuition Scheme (MTS) underwent a rebranding exercise signifying its evolvement. It is now the largest community-based academic support programme with an enrolment exceeding 10,000 students per year. The programme currently serves those from Primary 1 to Secondary 5 involving the services of more than 800 tutors.

But MENDAKI is more than just a tuition provider. Following the first MENDAKI Education Congress held in May 1982, MENDAKI also organised a series of congress and conventions; notably the Singapore Malay/Muslim Economic Congress (KEMAS) in 1985, the MENDAKI II Congress in 1989 and the KBE (Knowledge-based Economy) Convention for Malay/Muslim Community in 1999.

Two important milestones also took place in 1989. Firstly, MENDAKI became a company with IPC status, allowing it to receive tax deductible donations. This allows MENDAKI to enhance its fund building capacity especially with the government support of a matching grant. Secondly, the acronym was also enhanced to now read Council for the Development of the Malay/Muslim Community — symbolising a more holistic approach when looking at the progress of the community as a whole.

Many papers were presented and recommendations made at these conventions and conferences. Whilst education remains as its key focus, these early conventions also highlighted the need to look into other factors that contributed to the poor academic

The late Mr Lee Kuan Yew delivering his speech at the opening of the MENDAKI Congress, 28 May 1982. Image courtesy of Yayasan MENDAKI © 2015. All rights reserved.

The Mendaki Tuition Scheme started off with only 880 students in 1982. To date, about 200,000 Muslim students have benefitted from the scheme. Classes are conducted in more than 50 schools around the island. Image courtesy of Yayasan MENDAKI © 2015. All rights reserved.

The Malay community has made signifi-cant progress. If some of those who make it to the university and polytechnics can afford to pay some fees, then maybe they should vol-unter do so, and thereby help other in their community who cannot afford to pay ... The scheme could work like this: the direct Government subsidy to Malay tertiary stu-dents in the form of fee waiver could be given instead to MENDAKI. MENDAKI will then administer a separate financial assistance scheme for Malay students in the university and polytechnics." How do low-income families cope? How do children of broken homes cope? How do single parents work, raise a family and play the role of father and mother all at the same time? When they cannot afford to pay the HDB rentals and PUB bills, who helps them? Do they live in the dark and on the charity of neighbours? How do their children perform in schools? Do they go to schools or do they drop out prematurely? These are the questions to which we do not quite know the answers."

Former Prime Minister Mr Goh Chok Tong
Mendaki Congress II
19 May 1989

performance of the community. On the recommendations of the various work groups, MENDAKI expanded its work to also include, among others, the setting up and management of the Amanah Saham MENDAKI, the setting up of a department to look into the social and cultural needs of the community including the drug issue plaguing the community in the 1980s, and taking over the administration of the Tertiary Tuition Fee Subsidy (TTFS) from the government.

This process of engaging the community leaders, professionals, academics and the community in general continues to this day. A Research department currently oversees these engagement sessions by organising forums, dialogues, presenting research papers and scanning the environment on policies that affect the community. A Community Outreach and Engagement Department ensures that the organisation is grounded in its approach and that families with school-going children are supported in their educational journey.

The backbone of the MTS — its volunteers. The success of any educational programme relies on the quality of its teaching staff. Image courtesy of Yayasan MENDAKI © 2015. All rights reserved.

The Malay/Muslim Voluntary Sector is fast evolving. The changes in the operating landscape give rise to different kinds of challenges for the community. In 2003, the Community Leaders Forum (CLF) was launched with MENDAKI as the secretariat. Its main objectives were to provide a platform to address the gaps within the community, and to enhance the capacity and capability of the Malay/Muslim Organisations (MMOs), whilst optimising the use of community resources and minimising duplications in our efforts to address the gaps.

The CLF now boasts more than 100 partners including national agencies, grassroots organisations such as the Malay Activity Executive Committees (MAECs), and Family Service Centres (FSCs)

The then Prime Minister Mr Goh Chok Tong at the MENDAKI Congress II, 19 May 1989. Image courtesy of Yayasan MENDAKI © 2015. All rights reserved.

Dr Ahmad Mattar spearheaded the formation of Yayasan MENDAKI to look into the educational and welfare needs of the Malay/Muslim community. Image courtesy of Yayasan MENDAKI © 2015. All rights reserved.

conducting educational and developmental programmes to support the student's educational journey.

MENDAKI conducts regular programme reviews and evaluations to ensure their relevance and effectiveness. Over the years, programmes and services have been enhanced, replaced, or terminated to meet the current needs of the community.

One of the services that have been enhanced is the provision of more scholarships, bursaries and awards to support Malays/Muslims in their pursuit of excellence. With more Malay/Muslim students performing well academically, MENDAKI embarked on expanding its scholarship and bursary schemes by collaborating with institutes of higher learning to provide scholarships and bursaries for those seeking diploma and degree courses at these institutions. To encourage working adults to take up skills upgrading, the interest-free study loan scheme was extended in 1997 to provide loans to help defray the course fees.

With increasing needs and limited resources, MENDAKI with the support of community leaders and Malay Members of Parliament, set up the Education Trust Fund (ETF) in 2003. Though initially set up to ensure all pre-schoolers have access to a pre-school education by subsidising the preschool and childcare fees for low income families, it now includes the provision of stationery vouchers for primary and secondary school students, as well as start-up fee schemes for ITE students in selected courses.

MENDAKI continues to seek innovative ways of engaging and supporting the community as part of its mission to navigate, empower and position the community at the forefront of excellence. In keeping abreast of the diverse pathways available, and recognising the talent and potential among the young, MENDAKI

Mr Abdullah Tarmugi (second from left) was the second Chairman of Yayasan MENDAKI, taking over from his predecessor in 1993. He is seen here meeting five students at the "MENDAKI meets the 1994 Top 10% PSLE pupils and parents session". The event was held at Temasek Junior College on 28 January 1995. Image courtesy of Yayasan MENDAKI © 2015. All rights reserved.

Recipients of the Goh Chok Youth Promise Award and Special Achievement Award 2015.
Image courtesy of Yayasan MENDAKI © 2015. All rights reserved.

has introduced new awards to encourage and celebrate these talents. The Goh Chok Tong Youth Promise Award was introduced in 2005 to award youths with potential to excel in non-academic fields. Since its introduction, it has awarded a total of 55 young talents as diverse as sportsmen, film makers, shoe designers, graffiti artists to musicians. Other awards such as the Special Achievement (Non-Academic) Awards were also introduced to give recognition and moral support to talented school students.

Other recent milestones include the setting up of its social enterprise arm SENSE in 2004 and the setting up of six satellite centres in 2013 and 2014.

Prime Minister Lee Hsien Loong in his address at MENDAKI's 25th Anniversary Celebrations, said, "we see a new Malay/Muslim community, confident that it is progressing with the others, and succeeding through its own efforts." Indeed MENDAKI has grown with the community. Though results cannot be measured by the number of programmes and schemes, nor can it be measured by the numbers of attendees in those programmes and schemes, we can proudly say that MENDAKI has significantly played a role in making the community "understand the paramount importance of education as the key to progress in many other areas."

As what the late Mr Lee Kuan Yew had foretold, that MENDAKI would need stamina and perseverance and that we would have to wait for years before distinct improvements in performance levels were registered. The community's labour is beginning to bear fruit. We see many successes across all sectors, at schools, institutions and at the workplace.

This achievement is mirrored in the number of award recipients receiving the Anugerah MENDAKI. This year the community celebrated the performance of 501 students with 40 receiving first class honours from both the local and overseas universities.

Over the last 25 years, MENDAKI has grown and matured, together with the Malay/Muslim community. We can see the achievements across many indicators. But beyond the statistics in the report, there is a new mood and confidence in the community. It is willing to seize opportunities and move ahead, and just as ready to recognise problems and tackle them openly and objectively, even when they are sensitive and difficult. That is why the community has made progress, and is in a strong and confident position today."

PM Lee Hsien Loong at MENDAKI's
25th Anniversary Dinner
2 September 2007

Though these successes speak volumes on how far the community had progressed, the journey has not ended as we enter a new phase in the community's journey towards excellence. In 2014, a dedicated team was formed to look at enhancing the internal processes whilst a committee comprising academics and professionals was set up to review the education programmes and initiatives.

MENDAKI will continue to play a central role in charting the future and progress of the community as it rides the global and technological challenges that lie ahead. As reiterated by MENDAKI's Chairman, Minister Yaacob Ibrahim, "Our community members are our greatest asset. MENDAKI recognises that engaging, collaborating and nurturing relationships have become increasingly important to catalyse and realise the full potential of the community."

The culmination of its 10th year in promoting lifelong learning and enriching workers with relevant skills saw MENDAKI SENSE open its doors at WIS (Work In Style) @ Changi. This location at the heart of the Malay/Muslim community in Geylang allows easy access to more of our workers and students. Image courtesy of Yayasan MENDAKI © 2015. All rights reserved.

As part of its strategy, MENDAKI will put in measures to address the needs of the community based on three key areas; getting our students to be school-ready, ensuring that our community is able to perform well at school and at the workplace, and preparing our community to be future-ready.

MENDAKI is confident that together with the support of the Malay/Muslim organisations and the community as a whole, in the spirit of *gotong-royong*, we will realise our vision of a community of excellence.

YAYASAN MENDAKI PROMINENT MEMBERS

Founding:

1. Dr Ahmad Mattar
2. Mr Abdul Latiff Hj Taris
3. Mr Abbas Abu Amin
4. Mr Abdul Halim Kader
5. Mr Abdullah Musa
6. Mr Ahmad Thani Hj Ahmad
7. Mr Embek Ali
8. Mr Mansor Hj Sukaimi
9. Mr Hassan Mutalib
10. Mr Hussain Suradi
11. Mr Ismail Mohd Said
12. Mr Jalil Haron
13. Mr Juri Wari
14. Mr Maarof Hj Salleh
15. Mr M. K. A. Jabbar
16. Mr Musa Yusof
17. Mr Mohd Yusof Ahmad
18. Mr Mohd Maidin Packer Mohd
19. Mr Othman Haron Eusofe
20. Mr Rohan Kamis
21. Mr Rahim Ishak
22. Mr Saidi Shariff
23. Mr Shafawi Hj Ahmad
24. Mr Samat Mohd Yusof
25. Mr Sidek Hj Saniff
26. Mr Suratman Markasan
27. Mr Syed Ali Redha Alsagoff
28. Mr Syed Isa Mohd Semait
29. Mr Wan Hussin Hj Zoohri

Individual:

1. Mr Abbas Abu Amin
2. Mr Abdullah Tarmugi
3. Dr Ahmad Mattar
4. Mr Ibrahim Othman
5. Mr Maarof Hj Salleh
6. Mr Othman Haron Eusofe
7. Mr Ramli Osman
8. Mr Ridzuan Abdullah Wu
9. Mr Ridzwan Dzafir
10. Mr Rohan Kamis
11. Mr Sidek Hj Saniff
12. Mr Shafawi Hj Ahmad
13. Mr Wan Hussin Hj Zoohri
14. Mr Yatiman Yusof
15. Mr Zainul Abidin Rasheed
16. Mr Zulkifli Muhammed

Chairman:

1. Dr Ahmad Mattar
    (Jun 1989–May 1993)
2. Mr Abdullah Tarmugi
    (May 1993–Feb 2002)
3. Dr Yaacob Ibrahim
    (Mar 2002–present)

CEO:

1. Mr Ridzwan Dzafir
    (Jun 1989–Sep 1990)
2. Mr Zainul Abidin Rasheed
    (Oct 1990–Sep 1993)
3. Mr Sumardi Ali
    (Oct 1993–Dec 2001)
4. Mr Rozlan Giri
    (Jan 2002–Dec 2004)
5. Mdm Rashidah A. B. Rasip
    (Jan 2005–Dec 2006)
6. Mdm Zuraidah Abdullah
    (Jan 2007–Dec 2009)
7. Mdm Moliah Hashim
    (Jan 2010–Dec 2013)
8. Mdm Tuminah Sapawi
    (Jan 2014–present)

THE MALAYS AND NATIONAL EDUCATION

Sidek Saniff

"... We, in the Singapore Malay Teachers Union (SMTU), had suggested the total over-hauling of our education system into a single stream, national type school where every subject were [sic] to be taught in English. In order to ensure Cultural Ballast, we emphasised the importance to include Mother Tongue languages, Literature and religious or faith-based learning into the curriculum. This would put us in good stead in facing the future with the vigorous burgeoning era of science and technology dawning upon us and the English language becoming of paramount importance.

Further, the teaching on the National Language, that is the Malay language, for all students, perhaps two periods in a week. It would be good for non-Malays to learn the language as Singapore is part of the Malay Archipelago.

Shamsuddin Tung of Nanyang Siau Pau was imprisoned, because he was harping about Chinese language, Literature and Culture. Thereafter, all eyes were on SMTU and me as its President after the then PM was quoted in the New Nation on Tuesday 7th September as saying,

'Singapore are getting a little on the soft side. This will not do. We are all aware that a new situation is likely to develop in the region. We must nip some of these problems in the bud. Take the recent Nanyang Siang Pau agitation, heating up the Chinese Language and Culture issues. We acted. By "national type of schools", using English as the medium of instruction. Malay, compulsory as a second language. All Chinese schools were to be closed! They were both playing someone else's game. They both stopped, but only after they knew we meant business. By the time we were prepared to act against the majority, everyone else got the message.'

My parting words were, 'Jangan jadikan Singapura tempat orang-orang jujur ter-bujur, jangan jadikan bumi ini tempat orang-orang jujur terkubur'. (Don't allow Singapore to be turned into a land where the honest and sincere citizens are pun-ished for their convictions or beliefs.)

I delivered those words at a farewell gathering organised by SMTU for two of our members, the late Mamat Samat and Wan Hussin Zoohri, before they continued with their studies in the United Kingdom. Both confided in me that should the fate of Shamsuddin Tung were [sic] to befall me, they would terminate their studies and return home. 'Don't!' I told them and ask them to complete their further studies as this would further motivate me to pursue my law degree in prison. They are my true friends. I will never forget that episode in my whole life.

The late Mr Lee was a tough taskmaster. Never succumb to jejune and prevarication. Be very open. Be attentive, firm but, above all, be polite. These ingredients make it easier for issues to be discussed, especially the most sensitive matters concerning race and religion. And, of course, education. His advice was to concentrate and dedicate ourselves in looking after the progress of our children in this vital area as we believe in meritocracy. This would ensure that our children would become trustworthy trustees of our nation.

He even asked that MOE release the results of the PSLE for all ethnic groups. If I were reluctant, one of the officers could do it. I readily accepted it without a moment's hesitation. It is significant to note that Mr. Lee himself opened the first MENDAKI Congress on 10 October 1982."

Community leaders of the past posing for a picture at the Istana. Image courtesy of Zainul Abidin Rasheed © 2016. All rights reserved.

CHAPTER 26

THE ROLE OF *BERITA HARIAN* IN THE DEVELOPMENT OF THE MALAY/ MUSLIM COMMUNITY IN SINGAPORE

Mohd Guntor Sadali

The Internet has made our world borderless, with information travelling across the globe at lightning speed. Mobile phones have become cheap and an effective tool to communicate, allowing users to share news and visuals in real time. In the early years after our independence in 1965, the world was completely different. The source of information then was mainly the so-called mainstream media — newspapers, radio and television — and they played a critical role in shaping our people's attitude towards nation-building.

Berita Harian, being the only Malay language newspaper, was part of the mainstream media which played an important role, especially in helping the Malays fit into the mainstream life in Singapore, as the country's separation from Malaysia had left them feel insecure as from a majority, they are now a minority. As the new country grappled with a number of critical issues to survive and develop, the Malay/Muslim community too had to endure some sensitive issues. It was a daunting task to pacify the community as some of these issues could easily be exploited by irresponsible elements and cause instability to the country. Race and religion would always remain sensitive subjects in a plural society like Singapore thus they are not to be taken for granted. This could be seen in the racial riots that

The first mosque to be completed using the Mosque Building Fund, Masjid Muhajirin, was opened in Toa Payoh. It was completed in April 1977 with a capacity of 1400 people and serves Muslims living in Toa Payoh and surrounding area. Image courtesy of Majlis Ugama Islam Singapura © 2015. All rights reserved.

Masjid Muhajirin's new look after completion of its upgrading programme in 2009. Image courtesy of Jamsari Ahmad © 2015. All rights reserved.

erupted in the 1960s[a] that triggered our separation from Malaysia.

One of the most challenging issues that emerged in the early 1970s was the need for some mosques and *suraus* to give way to development. It was a very contentious issue and touched the nerve of the Muslim community. *Berita Harian* saw its critical role in putting the issue in perspective and helping the community understand the rationale behind the policy. Through its news coverage and commentaries, it explained why a young and land-scarce country like Singapore needed to prioritise the use of its land. The community was also made to understand the move was not meant to deny them of having their own mosques, as the affected mosques would be replaced by newer and bigger ones with modern facilities. The other equally important point *Berita Harian* put across was that Muslims were not being singled out and the policy also applied to places of worship of other religions, with the Buddhist temples being the most affected. This fact helped calm the community, as did discussions held by the Islamic Religious Council of Singapore (MUIS) with the various mosque committees. The community had something to cheer when the Government agreed that MUIS set up a Mosque Building Fund (MBF) to allow Muslim workers to contribute 50 cents a month, using the CPF (Central Provident Fund) check-off system. Within two years of its introduction in 1975, the first modern mosque was opened in Toa Payoh satellite town, followed by another

---

[a] Three racial riots took place in the 1960s — two in 1964 and one in 1969. http://eresources. nlb.gov.sg/infopedia/articles/SIP_45_2005-01-06.html, last accessed 4 November 2015 https://www.hometeam.sg/article.aspx?news_sid=20150202aB5mDqxcamZJ, last accessed 4 November 2015.

> *... the Muslims had to be convinced that any changes to their public call for prayer were not aimed at curbing the practice of their religion. The changes were also made incrementally. First, the loudspeakers were tilted inwards and away from nearby houses, and limits were set on their volume levels. Later, a radio frequency was allocated to allow the call to prayer to be broadcast over the radio. In this way, all Muslims who wished to receive the call to prayer could just tune in to their radio. Over time, the mosques did away with loudspeakers. This showed the pragmatism of our Muslims and their sensitivity to the feelings of non-Muslims."*

Goh Chok Tong
Speaking at the MUIS International
Conference on Muslims in Multicultural
Societies, 14 July 2010

in Queenstown a few months later.[b] By 2012, within a span of 38 years, the Muslim community was able to build 24 mosques worth more than $170 million all over the island. The MBF has become a source of pride for the community.[c]

Another sensitive religious issue that surfaced was the *azan* (call to prayer). It is a common practice for mosques to make the call to prayer five times a day, the earliest being at dawn. Traditionally, this was done through a loudspeaker placed at the minaret, facing outwards from the mosque, to allow Muslims to hear it. However, in a multiracial and multireligious society, this practice could easily cause unhappiness and misunderstanding among non-Muslims. There was a proposal by the Government for loudspeakers to be turned inwards towards the mosque's prayer hall rather than outwards. Some Muslims interpreted this as an attempt by the Government to curtail their freedom to practise their religion. However, the unhappiness eased when it was suggested that in addition to this move, the *azan* could be broadcast through the radio for all prayer times. Many Muslims saw this as an advantage as the *azan* could now be heard anywhere, as long as there was a radio.

The other issue that *Berita Harian* had to grapple was the question of Malay loyalty to the country. The Malays had been unhappy with the Government over its National Service policy since its inception, as many Malays were exempted. Even when Malays were enlisted, they were assigned insignificant duties. This unhappiness reached its peak when the then Prime Minister Lee Kuan Yew made a comment[d] that was interpreted

---

[b] Masjid Muhajirin was officially opened by the then Minister for Social Affairs, Mr Othman Wok in April 1977. This was followed shortly by the opening of Masjid Mujahidin by Dr Ahmad Mattar, who took over the portfolio of the Minister for Social Affairs in October the same year.
[c] http://www.mbmf.sg/about.html#Mosque_building_33_years.
[d] *Straits Times*, 30 September, 1999.

by the Malays as questioning their loyalty to the country. *Berita Harian* gave extensive coverage to this debate, but in a controlled manner. The paper saw it as an opportunity to air the frustrations of the community which had been ingrained for quite a while. As a result, a heart-to-heart dialogue was held with the Malay/Muslim leaders. The dialogue helped cool things down and created a better understanding on the issue.

There were other issues that cropped up from time to time that required careful handling by the media, including *Berita Harian*. One such issue was when the Government decided to introduce Compulsory Education (CE). Some members of the Malay/Muslim community were concerned that the policy would have serious ramifications on the *madrasahs* (Islamic religious schools).

Madrasah students' morning ritual include supplications and the national anthem. Image courtesy of Majlis Ugama Islam Singapura © 2015. All rights reserved.

The aftermath of the terrorist attack in the United States in September 2001 and the discovery of the Jemaah Islamiah[e] group too affected the Malay/Muslim community here as they again became the focus of attention. Whilst reporting these issues, *Berita Harian* worked very closely with the Government to ensure that Singaporeans remained united.

The Malay/Muslim community, like other communities in Singapore, had its own set of problems to deal with — high divorce rate, school dropouts and drug abuse were some of them. Believing in self-help, the Malay organisations such as MUIS, MENDAKI, Association of Muslim Professionals (AMP), Jamiyah and Pertapis, to name just a few, chartered their own programmes to tackle them. *Berita Harian* was always there to lend support by working closely with these organisations and providing ample editorial space for their activities.

---

[e] Jemaah Islamiah is a Southeast Asian terrorist network with links to Al-Qaeda.

While some of these problems still exist, there is no doubt that over the years, the Malay/Muslim community has made tremendous progress. It has produced many doctors, dentists, architects, engineers, lawyers, magistrates and other professionals. Some of them hold senior positions and have played important roles in multinational companies (MNCs), not just locally but also overseas as well.

In business, there is a growing number of Malay businesses seizing opportunities abroad. Progressively, more of them are using our neighbouring countries, especially Malaysia and Indonesia, as well as the Middle East, as their new bases to do business and this trend is likely to continue as our businessmen are more willing to take risks.

In 2015, out of the 280 Singaporean Primary 6 students who sat for the PSLE, 275 students (or 98.2%) are assessed suitable to proceed to secondary school.

MUIS
Media Release, 25 November 2015

While Facebook, WhatsApp, Instagram, Twitter and blogs are the in-thing now, the "mainstream" and "official" media comprising newspapers, radio and television will continue to remain relevant as they are able to re-invent themselves by going digital, and most important, by being responsible and reliable in their reporting. They will continue to play a critical role in disseminating news and interpreting events, to help readers and viewers to have more informed views and a better understanding of issues confronting the society and country. The bilingual policy that Singapore has adopted will also ensure that the vernacular newspapers, including *Berita Harian*, will continue to be in demand.

BH All-in-One	BH Print	BH iPad	BH Smartphone	BH Online
(Print • Online • iPad • Smartphone • HTML5)			(iPhone • Android • HTML5)	
$18.99*/month	$14.45*/month	$16.45/month	$16.45/month	$16.45/month

Berita Harian/Berita Minggu is now available in multiple platforms to cater for a more IT-savvy Malay/Muslim community. Image screen grabbed from http://beritaharian.sg/

Communist revolution unlikely as it must come from Malay peasantry and not urban Chinese

MALAYA'S REAL DANGER IS COMMUNALISM NOT THE REDS, SAYS PREMIER

The Straits Times
17 September 1959

THE immediate danger to Malaya was not Communism but communalism, said the Prime Minister, Mr. Lee Kuan Yew, at a dinner of the Foreign Correspondents Association tonight.

"There can be no Communist Malaya until there is a Ma-

SINGAPORE, Wednesday

lay-led Malayan Communist Party," he said.

"This follows from the hypothesis that it is the Malay peasantry and not the Chinese urban proletariat who can and will decide the pace of the Socialist revolution in Malaya."

But there could be no Malay-led M.C.P. until there was a disgruntled Malay educated elite to lead a discontented Malay peasantry, he added.

These were events unlikely to happen in the foreseeable future because for many years to come there will be more important and valuable jobs than there were Malay candidates for them, said Mr. Lee.

Exploit

There were groups which were bound to emerge and which would exploit the natural desire of the Malay to be dominant in his own country in the political, economic and social fields. The country could easily drift into communal conflicts.

"Does the existence of a left-wing Government elected by a largely urban Chinese population in Singapore aggravate or alleviate the situation?" he asked.

"I suggest the answer depends upon how the Government in Singapore conducts its affairs.

"If a pandering to Chinese chauvinism and use to position to give encouragement and expression to Chinese greatness, then it is bound to aggravate the situation."

Mr. Lee said that whatever the differences of political philosophy or ideology between the Federation and Singapore Governments, both desired a national and not a communal solution.

"For that reason we can look confidently to the problem being tackled in a firm and courageous manner on both sides of the causeway."

Mr. Lee had always thought that a country faced prominently in the World Press mainly when it was in trouble.

Nobody bothered about Laos until it was reported to be in difficulties. Nobody outside heard much about Singapore until there were riots in 1955 and 1956, in the course of one of which two persons were killed.

He had come to believe that so far as the foreign Press was concerned, no news was good news. For he news meant either that there was quiet, steady progress, at the least, to grave or sensational difficulties.

"Apart from the first month following the elections in May we have not been in the news," he said.

Imagination

Nobody had been literally kicked to death, as was reported in 1956, and the pages of the English and Australian papers had been free from the "more vivid flights of imagination or narrative that appears from time to time."

Mr. Lee said he had no headline material to offer tonight. "In fact, I believe that the art of government is, in part, the art of not creating headlines in the world Press.

"But I thought perhaps you might be interested in some observations on the general trends of the forces at play in the midst of the Malayan situation, so that if one day the strange, the exotic or the sensational does crop up, you may find it easier to do a post-mortem."

In the 14 years since the end of the war, the political face of Asia had undergone more changes than during any other equivalent period on Asian history.

"Events have taken place which are likely in the next few decades to shift the centre of world gravity from Europe and the West to Asia and the Far." he said.

"The massive potential greatness of India and China dominates the Asian scene.

"Events in Malaya must be looked at in this background if we are to see them in proper perspective. What happens to the rest of

Tensions

"But in the meantime, the communal tensions can easily increase. The Chinese urban population may chafe at what they consider a slow pace determined by a Malay peasantry. And there are bound to be groups who are prepared to exploit the dissatisfaction of the urban Chinese by making communal appeals.

"Those of you who watched the elections in some of the large towns in Perak will know how easily this can be done.

"On the other hand, the Malay sector is equally open to exploitation by communal and, this is more serious, by religious appeals. Groups are bound to emerge who will exploit the natural desire of the Malay to be dominant in his own country not only in the political but also the economic and social fields.

"A government which

Asia is bound to affect Malaya.

"With one exception, the problems that we face are the problems common to the whole region—the problems of under-developed territories seeking ways of rapid industrialisation and progress.

"The one exceptional problem is that caused by the plural society of the Malaya.

"It was because the Malayan Communist Party misjudged the situation caused by this plural society that their revolt failed. And other political movements, besides the Malayan Communist Party, ignore this factor at their own peril.

Answer

"Put briefly it means this—that the pace of the social revolution in Malaya is as fast or as slow as the Malays in the kampongs want it, and as the Chinese in towns desire it.

"The towns can act as a catalyst on the kampongs, but it is the kampongs that decide the pace.

"If there is a free-for-all in Malaya, it may be possible that a movement of the Chinese urban proletariat can assume power and dictate the course of the revolution." Mr. Lee said.

Impossible

But this is impossible. For the British and the Americans will never allow a free-for-all in Malaya.

"Now if the Chinese People's Republic and the Russians were prepared to intervene as in Indo-China and throw their weight on to the Communist side, then the position would be different and a small militant party might succeed in capturing power. But they are not and will never be so stupid as to intervene.

"They want to win over 90 million Indonesians and many more millions of the uncommitted people in South-East Asia.

"And nothing is more likely to make the South-East countries more anti-Communist than the spectacle of the China might coming to the aid of Chinese minorities in South-East Asia. The fact that the Chinese are numerically only a minority in Malaya does not alter the position.

"There can be no Communist Malaya until there is a Malay-led Malayan Communist Party," he said. "That follows from the hypothesis that it is the Malay peasantry and not the Chinese proletariat who can and will decide the pace.

"There can be no Malay-led Malayan Communist Party until there is a disgruntled Malay educated elite to lead a discontented Malay peasantry.

"But there is no likelihood of any significant Malay educated elite becoming disgruntled anywhere in the foreseeable future.

"For many years there will be more important and valuable jobs than there are Malay peasantry so long as the Federation Government keeps up social advance and progress in the kampongs.

openly declares its desire to foster inter-racial co-operation and makes concessions to the Chinese in economic, cultural or educational issues can be accused by communal-minded groups of selling out Malay rights."

And so the country could easily drift into communal conflicts, he continued. Unlike Communism, whose dialectics had to be taught and learned before loyalties to it can develop, communalism made a direct primitive appeal to emotional loyalties whose response can be immediate and spontaneous.

"Anyone who lived through the Maria Hertogh riots of 1950 and the Hock Lee riots of 1955 can remember the difference in the intensity of the emotional hysteria, generated in the first as against the second.

Good effect

"For this reason, if the Singapore Government conducts its affairs as to convince the Malays in the Federation kampongs than the Chinese in this big city like Singapore are prepared to be assimilated as one Malayan people and to convince the Federation Chinese in the towns that there can be a happy medium between the tempo of the Malay kampong revolution and the Chinese urban revolution it cannot but have a healthy effect on the whole Malayan situation."

Mr. Lee said he would end on a note of optimism.

"Whatever the differences of political philosophy or ideology between the Federation and Singapore Governments, both are acutely conscious of this problem.

"Both desire a national, not a communal solution to it. For that reason, we can look confidently to the problem being tackled in a firm and courageous manner on both sides of the causeway.

"If we succeed there will be no headlines for the foreign Press. But these are the headlines we can well afford to miss."

will still be the case, whether or not the Press produces different editions in the two territories or the radio news is separately and differently presented by Singapore and Kuala Lumpur.

"For there is no possible way of ensuring that the Singapore situation can be isolated from the Federation.

The Straits Times
29 April 1965

Premier Lee: Target is a Malaysian Malaysia

SINGAPORE, Wednesday

SINGAPORE'S Prime Minister, Mr. Lee Kuan Yew, last night said that the PAP together with other like-minded groups in Malaya, Sabah and Sarawak would lead the people of Malaysia towards the realisation of a truly Malaysian Malaysia.

Mr. Lee declared: "We know this is a long and relentless struggle, We are prepared to fight for it constitutionally to the last."

Mr. Lee, who is also PAP Secretary-General, was speaking at a dinner for members of citizens' consultative committees, goodwill committees and artists who had helped in performances organised by the Ministry of Culture during the past year.

Outdated

He said certain people still could not shake off their old political habits and propaganda tactics, which were effective electorally in the old Malaya but were now no longer valid in the broader context of Malaysia.

He said: "These are the people who are not helping the country's progress to national unity and solidarity.

"They still believe that a certain racial group could dominate the political scene and that all other communities must be satisfied with their activities confined to making money in business. Unfortunately not many can find satisfaction in business success.

The crux

"Malaysia has been formed out of a necessity to uphold and safeguard the mutual interests of the people of different racial origins who have struck roots into this country and are irrevocably Malaysians."

Mr. Lee stressed that the PAP had never been opposed to Malay privileges, and he could not see any contradiction between these special privileges for Malays and the concept of a Malaysian Malaysia.

He said: "Our approach to the problem is different from those who keep on stressing Malay rights.

"While we uphold special privileges for Malays in the constitu-

tion, we believe that the crux of the problem is how to raise the living standards of the rural people, who are mainly Malays.

"Their standards of living are not advanced by special rights for a small number of special Malays, and that is why the problem still remains, waiting to be solved.

"Special privileges will only help a small group of Malay bourgeoise to become capitalists, who will later exploit the poorer section of the people of all races.

The problem

"Therefore, special privileges will not help solve the problem. The more difficult problem is how to ensure that the Malay have-nots, mostly farmers and fishermen, begin to increase their earning capacity at the same time as the workers in the towns also advance their living standards."

Mr. Lee saw hope in the faces of the mixed young audience before him.

He said: "Though some of the older generation still refuse to re-orientate their thinking to fit in the new Malaysian context, the younger people are beginning to gather a consciousness of being together as Malaysians.

"Race is not a barrier among the young, and mixing freely as workers and, sharing the same problems, they will learn that they must benefit by collective action for common advancement."

The Straits Times
16 March 1967

Singapore Parliament

Success... that's when a minority doesn't feel it's a minority: Lee

MR. LEE

Multi-racial society ideal to be perpetuated in Constitution

Safeguards for the minorities

By JACKIE SAM   SINGAPORE, Thursday

THE present Singapore Government's ideal of a multi-racial society is to be perpetuated in the constitution, the Prime Minister, Mr. Lee Kuan Yew, announced today.

Special aid for Malays

The Straits Times
13 August 1965

SINGAPORE, Wednesday.

THE Prime Minister, Mr. Lee Kuan Yew, said in Parliament today that if 10 years from now Singapore was still making exhortations of religious tolerance and the virtues of a multi-racial society, then the Government would have failed.

QUOTE

Factors that can influence social progress

The problem

Accepted

Contrary

Reluctant

Lee: My pledge to all of you

'No race riots' promise

By R. CHANDRAN and N.G. KUTTY

MR. LEE KUAN YEW last night pledged that there would be no more racial riots in Singapore. "This is a pledge I give, whatever your colour, language or religion," he told a rally at Geylang Serai car park.

Malays told: A common destiny if you decide so

Brass tacks

PAP rally at Geylang Serai last night. — Picture by Tan Wee Him.

The Straits Times
31 August 1972

The Straits Times
11 December 1962

Lee: Difficult to get Malays to leave kampong

SINGAPORE, Monday.

THE Prime Minister of Singapore, Mr. Lee Kuan Yew, today told a gathering of United Nations urban development experts that the authorities here had found great difficulty in persuading the Malays to give up their traditional forms of kampong society.

Mr. Lee was declaring open the first Asian seminar on urban community development sponsored by the United Nations Economic Commission for Asia and the Far East at the Victoria Theatre.

The Prime Minister said that an interesting feature in Singapore's urban community was the difference between the high mobility and adaptability of the Chinese and Indian immigrants as against the indigenous Malays.

Reluctant

"The Chinese and Indians, being immigrants were people who had psychologically prepared themselves for change, and they took to the urban life in Singapore easily and without tears.

"The Malays, on the other hand, being a settled rural community in Singapore are reluctant and resistant to sudden change in their living habits.

"They still prefer to live in 'kampongs' or villages in the country."

He explained this attitude of the Malays; "With the Malays it is not just an economic adjustment between a cheap attap hut and a great city flat.

"The greater problem is the psychological one of making them willing and happy to give up their traditional forms of kampong ...

MR. HOMJI

praise for the Prime Minister

... delegates will learn from the wealth of expertise that so many of the distinguished delegates bring to this conference."

At a press conference later Mr. H. B. M. Homji of Pakistan, the programme director of the 11-day seminar, praised the Prime Minister's speech as one reflecting expert knowledge.

Mr. Homji said that Singapore was fortunate to have such a Prime Minister whose Government could justifiably be proud of the tremendous housing development that had and was taking place in the State.

He has made the grade: PM

RISE OF THE NEW MALAY

TODAY's Malay Singaporean displays g r o w i n g self-confidence and pride, feeling and thinking more and more as a Singaporean than as a Malay. This is the portrait painted by Mr. Lee Kuan Yew in his Hari Raya Puasa message.

Malay Singaporeans know they are making the grade in modern Singapore, according to the Prime Minister. They are contributing towards the nation's economic and social progress.

Says Mr. Lee:

"Today, there is little talk of Singapore Malays being left behind in the process of modernisation and industrialisation. Most have made the grade. Yet only 16 years ago, many Malays felt most uncertain of their future in a fast changing Singapore.

Self-confidence

"At that time, my colleagues and I urged and encouraged Malay Singaporeans to acquire new skills and disciplines for industry and to break out from the confines of traditional jobs and studies. Gradually, but increasingly, the Malays in Singapore ...

"Never have we had Malays working in factories as semi-skilled jobs, as supervisors, as we had thousands have sworn courses at the Polytechnic Technical College and Ing Board.

"In the universities, are no longer confined but are to be found doing law, accountancy, business, sociology and psychology.

"I can sense the growing self-confidence and pride among the Malays. They know they are making the grade in modern Singapore. They are contributing towards economic and social progress. I also sense that this younger generation is feeling and thinking more and more as Singaporeans, rather than as Malays.

Satisfying

"There is another healthy development as seen in discussions on ways and means to cope with problems of high-rise living, and seminars on ways and means to generate and facilitate group cultural and recreational activities in the new towns.

"It is immensely more satisfying to solve these new problems, which are the result of economic development, than to be stuck with the old problems of stagnation, poverty and unemployment.

"Many have become vulnerable to social problems of drug addiction. Others have campaigned for the blood bank. Everyone is conscious that there are problems which affect all things, persons, and not just the Malays. All recognise that they are the result of our industrialisation and urbanisation.

The significance of the words in our national anthem is clear for all, that we are working progress together.

— The Prime Minister in his Hari Raya message

The Straits Times
4 September 1978

The Prime Minister's National Day Rally speech

Reports by Paul Jacob, Bertha Henson, Salim Osman, Irene Ngoo and Leong Weng Kam

Malays will be in the national mainstream in one generation

PRIME Minister Lee Kuan Yew has expressed confidence that Malay Singaporeans would be in the national mainstream in one generation.

He said this was because many Singaporeans today interact among themselves at HDB new towns.

"There is hope that in one generation, there will emerge a common feeling among all of us to be Singaporeans who are just and united," said Mr Lee in his Malay speech at Sunday's National Day Rally.

On the Malay community's desire to be part of the national mainstream, Mr Lee said: "They want to get into the mainstream of life, which is to be encouraged because they want to be Singaporeans."

But being a part of the mainstream really boiled down to the question of one's feelings and emotions as a Singaporean, "not the amount of money or status which one has".

"In your heart, you must feel you are a Singaporean," he said.

As this was difficult to measure, the Government relied on the changes taking place within the community, how the community behaved and what was said within it.

Speaking in English later, he said the Malay community was concerned with keeping pace with the Chinese and the Indian communities.

But Mr Lee cautioned: "It is going to be a tremendous effort to keep pace because as they make their advances in education, the Chinese and the Indian are not going to stay put.

"They are not going to stay at today's level. They are going to go further ahead. So it's a constant effort to keep up."

Mr Lee said he thought the Malays could keep up, as they were now living in the same Housing Board new towns as other Singaporeans.

Producing data on home-ownership, he said that more than 70 per cent of the Malays now lived in HDB new towns.

Projections of home-ownership patterns in 1997

Referring to projections of home-ownership patterns in 1997, he said that the Malays — as well as other Singaporeans — could see what they would get in 10 years' time if they worked together and, at the same time, also competed with one another.

The need to balance co-operation and competition in striving for progress and excellence was a major theme of the Prime Minister's address.

During his Malay address, Mr Lee also touched on the difficulties in moulding a cohesive nation.

Singapore, he said, had a delicate problem, in that its people were young and the level of inter-racial understanding was not yet mature enough to ensure stability.

To illustrate how difficult the process was for a multi-racial, multi-religious nation such as Singapore, Mr Lee cited the example of Arab countries such as Saudi Arabia, Kuwait and Bahrain.

Despite having a single race, a single religion and a single language, these countries had problems too because of differences between the Sunni and Shi'ite schools of Islam.

"In countries like Saudi Arabia, Kuwait and Bahrain, the people are of one race — Arabs, (they have) one language — Arabic, and one religion — Islam.

"But the people are aware of the differences. There are differences in the Islamic faith, one group belonging to the Sunni school, while another, the Shi'ite school," he said.

He added that the situation there was "not that stable".

Mr Lee hoped that gradually, Singaporeans would be persuaded to be cohesive, to use a common language to communicate with each other and to work together in one spirit.

... immigrants and their descendants as against the more settled and conservative kampong-dwellers.

"I am sure the Singapore ...

The Straits Times
18 August 1987

Berita Harian's interview with the Prime Minister

We need time to forge stronger bonds

Unity of Singaporeans 'shaken' after Herzog invite

An issue that highlighted clashing loyalties ... report in ST, March 1.

[Article text in small print, largely illegible]

From 1965 to today — taking big strides

At the National Day parade.

The Straits Times
7 July 1987

SINGAPORE'S TASKS AHEAD

Towards a more integrated society

MR. LEE

EVERY serious political party sets out to achieve certain ideological, economic or social objectives. To achieve these objectives, it must achieve power.

[Article text in small print, largely illegible]

The game

Doctrine

Break-up

Perspective

Vietnam

Japanese

The Communists

Africa

PAP's role

Policies

By LEE KUAN YEW

★ See Page 19—Col. 3

Kuan Yew: We're prepared to concentrate more than our average share...

Singapore to launch massive plan to advance Malays

Mr Lee

The Straits Times
12 June 1967

SINGAPORE, Sun. —A massive programme to alleviate the educational, social and economic position of Singapore Malays is in the offing.

The hint came from the Prime Minister, Mr Lee Kuan Yew, today when he went to the sprawling Geylang Serai Malay settlement. He was there for almost six hours, his first visit since 1963.

He assured the Malays: "The Government, with the support of the non-Malays, are prepared to concentrate more than the average share of our resources on our Malay community.

"We want our Malay community to have every opportunity to train and equip themselves for the industrial Singapore of tomorrow."

Requests

He then announced the formation of a committee of senior Malay officers in Government to advise him on ways and means of accelerating Malay advance in the educational, social and economic fields.

Anyone interested in having his views considered can get in touch with his secretary for oral and written presentation of such views, Mr. Lee said.

Preceding this was an on-the-spot consideration of five requests for social development.

First was the question of three community centres for the area, Mr. Lee said one would be built almost immediately. For the other two, time would be needed to look for sites.

Mr. Lee explained the predicament of development in an area of 595 acres of privately-owned land and the desire to cause as little inconvenience as possible in the event of re-settlement of people who might have to make way for such projects.

Mr Lee agreed that a traffic light for the Changi-Joo Chiat-Geylang junction was necessary. He also told them an over-head bridge costing $26,000 would be built soon at the same junction.

To requests for flood alleviation and flood drainage, Mr. Lee explained that these would have to be thoroughly studied as the area was low—below sea-level— and water could not flow into the sea.

A promise

But he gave a firm promise that every possible remedial action would be taken.

He reminded the kampong people that there were other areas in Singapore subject to worse flooding. But reading the Malay newspapers, he added, one would imagine that only

Quote

SLOWLY we are going to deal with these Barisan Sosialis chaps, but first the people must understand that hooliganism and destruction of public property means loss to e v e r ybody.

— MR LEE

Geylang Serai suffered from floods.

Complaints of heavy timber lorries destroying the roads secured the Premier's promise that such vehicles would be required or the roads built up to necessary specifications for heavy duty traffic.

Since his last visit, the Government has already spent almost $4-million in road, drainage, electricity, water, educational and health projects. Other projects costing $263,340 are either in progress or on planning boards.

At mass rallies at Jalan Alsagoff and at Geylang Serai Flats car park, the Prime Minister warned that "something for nothing" never solved anything.

Training and equipping the Malay community for the industrial Singapore of tomorrow was the only possible way the Malays enter into the challenge to work, learn and train, so that they can increase their earning capacity.

A pity

Mr Lee said it was a pity that the progress in Geylang Serai was not as much as he had wished for. The speed of progress in the four years from 1959 to 1963 was better.

What had happened in 1964 and 1965 has left its mark on the thinking and feeling of our people. They have also affected the course of subsequent events. They have given us a deeper appreciation of the techniques and methods used in communal politics.

However, one good result was that everybody understood that in multi-racial Singapore no one can derive any advantage from the exercise of communal politics.

It had taken two years after separation for feelings to subside and a saner rational thinking atmosphere to be restored.

He was now convinced that both Malays and non-Malays in Geylang Serai wanted to make a fresh start in cooperative and constructive endeavour and that the Government intends to take steps to improve the social conditions in housing, roads, drainage lighting, sanitation and community services.

But to those who still believed that Singapore owes them a living or that Singapore belongs to them or that they could force the Government into making concessions, Mr Lee said he could only tell them the PAP Government is always sensitive to public opinion, and will respond quickly to reason and logic, but it was not impressed by obscure and odious hints, however vehemently repeated.

Equal part

Mr Lee also said that past ways of living and earning a living will no longer adequate in the modern world of which Singapore is a part.

Let those who wish to be a part of this modern world come and talk quietly and seriously about the plans that we have to make Geylang Serai a living equal part of the new Singapore you can see growing up and symbolised in what is being built in Queenstown and Jurong.

The Prime Minister also warned that all things cost money, such as the traffic lights requested for the area. These lights, he said, cost about $3,000.

The people must understand that each time the Barisan Sosialis went round and smashed them up, they must be repaired which meant diverting money from other projects.

Slowly we are going to deal with these Barisan Sosialis chaps but first the people must understand that hooliganism and destruction of public property means loss to everybody.

Mr. Lee said he expected a tightly-knit society is evolving between three to four years time and lawlessness of this sort would have no place in such a community.

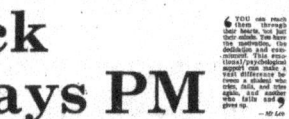

More cocaine victims

Mendaki can make the difference, but...

No quick fix-it, says PM

YOU can reach them through their hearts, but just their minds. You have the motivation, the dedication and commitment. This emotional/psychological support can make a vast difference between a student who tries, fails and tries again, and another who falls and gives up.
— Mr Lee

THE Prime Minister last night pointed out the massive scale of the task of raising the educational level of Malay Singaporeans, and proposed a number of ways the job can be done.

He told Malay parents, Mendaki (Council on Education for Muslim Children) and all Singaporeans have a part to play in the exercise which will take a long time because there is no quick fix.

The job, he said, had to be done from the very beginning — from the day a child began his education if his surroundings.

Parents, he said, must realise that their attitude to life was as important as that of the teacher in terms of results.

KNOWLEDGE IS A DIVINE 29-30 MEI 1982

MENDA

"Parents have to decide to be forceful believers for results, capable of making sacrifices of travel or school or a place in school because he failed in examination," he said.

He said past ways of doing things no longer applied. "You must think through these things in a calm way, decide what you have to do and do it," he said.

Mankind, he said, could go through the ages using their minds through their brains. Since the beginning of time and civilisation mankind had improved.

Mendaki's support can mean the difference between a child who tries, fails and tries again — from the very beginning to the child taught quietly through his school's surrounding.

Full support

Singaporeans, he told, can help by realising that the purpose of education is to make a better man and how these men will help us to live in a better world.

It is in the interests of us to have Malay Singaporeans better educated and better qualified and to increase their ability in Singapore's development.

MR LEE: Kuan Yew speaking at the Mendaki congress.

I PROMISE you that the government will give every assistance by making premises available, and by appealing to individual teachers to join in this exercise. This problem is of concern to all Singaporeans and not just to Malay Singaporeans. It is in the interests of all of us to have Malay Singaporeans better educated and to increase their ability in Singapore's development.

Attention

To do this, Mendaki will go down in the schools to reach Malay parents, and convince them to give more attention and respect to their children's progress.

To Malay parents, Mr Lee said, what is help their children and guide them. They have to exert their efforts for the very beginning. With attention from day the child begins to get conscious of his surroundings, he learns better. With support from his mother and father, the child learns how to perform. He is able to learn.

"In other words, these we guide the child, teaching the middle end of the wisdom. Training him on how to study to pass their out of our examinations can give better."

The Straits Times
29 May 1982

The full text of the Prime Minister's speech at the opening of the Mendaki Congress last night

Education is the road to success

WHEN I received the invitation from Dr Ahmad Mattar, as Chairman of Mendaki (the Council on Education for Muslim Children), to speak at the opening of this congress, I paused to reflect for sometime before I decided to accept. That this is an important occasion is beyond doubt.

Seven leading Malay/Muslim organisations have got together to discuss ways and means of improving the educational levels of Malays in Singapore. Four more organisations have been co-opted. Two hundred Malay/Muslim organisations will take part in this three-day congress.

Why did I reflect? My reflection springs from my reservations as to whether the organisers know how much stamina and perseverance is required of them, as leaders and sponsors of this movement.

Do well

Let me explain. Before a student gets into university, he must have passed his 'A' levels well enough. Before he gets into junior college to do 'A' levels, he must have done well in his 'O' levels. Before he gets to do his 'O' levels, he must have passed his Primary School Leaving Examination (PSLE).

To improve the percentage of students to get into the university, you have to improve the performance, ie interest and effort of all potentially able students, as early as Primary One if you can identify them. In other words, there is a 12-year time lag before an exercise, starting in 1982 with Primary One students, produces better results at 'A' levels.

To start with Primary Six students, and try to get them to pass the PSLE is a short cut which may not work with the slow or late developers.

For the effort to achieve full success, you have to start right from the very beginning, which means, from the day the child begins to be conscious of his surroundings, to learn to recognise sounds from his mother and father, to learn to vocalise, to learn to interact with his brother or his sister. In other words, there is no quick fix-it.

Solutions which start towards the middle or end of the education process, with special classes for PSLE, 'O' and 'A' levels students to pass their end of year examinations, can produce better results only at the margins.

In the nature of such movements, the organisers of Mendaki have to go for quick achievable goals, hoping to produce early results. Thus their concentration on students sitting for PSLE and 'A' level examinations.

However, the nature of education requires a long, comprehensive and sustained effort to encourage students at kindergarten, even before Primary One, and throughout their school career, to achieve their full potential. Table One shows the numbers and the percentages of Malay students in English and Malay streams who passed their PSLE, 'O' and 'A' levels in the last 10 years.

‘Language is the key to acquisition of knowledge. If a student is unable to understand a language, then he is unable to receive information or knowledge in that language. It is therefore crucial that a breakthrough must be made in the English language and as early in life as possible.

Parents have to decide on the trade-off between the convenience of speaking Malay or the mother tongue at home with their children at the cost of EL1.’

It has shown gradual improvement. Those who graduated from the university in the last six years, range from 22 in 1976 to 27 in 1981. (See Table Two). They represented a small fraction of their generation of around 8,000 in 1976, and 10,000 in 1981, who had entered Primary One at the same time as these graduates.

Your responsibility is as great, if not greater, to this overwhelming majority who do not make it to university. They must be encouraged and helped to become skilled craftsmen, Polytechnic technicians, computer programmers and in large numbers.

Performance in examinations depends upon two factors: Nature and nurture — nature being the natural intelligence of the child, nurture being the training and education. Or to use computer language, it depends on hardware and software, the hardware is the size or capacity of the computer, and the software is the teaching or educational programme.

What weightings are alloted to hardware as against software, or nature against nurture, is a matter of deep controversy between the experts, the psychologists and doctors. The fact is, individuals are born with different capacities.

Encourage

What we must set out to do, therefore, is to help students achieve the maximum potential of whatever nature has endowed them with. In other words, to nurture them, to give them the software, to encourage, support and help them to achieve their fullest.

Table Three sets out the results of Malay pupils in 1981 in the PSLE English as First Language (EL1) examinations. It shows that the smaller the percentage of Malay pupils there is in a school, the better their standards of English and Science.

It is not the case with Malay as Second Language (ML2). There may be a lesson from this on the effect of nurture, or the environment, on performance. Principals have reported to the Ministry of Education that when a school has large numbers of Malay students, they tend to speak Malay among themselves.

The less able ones, feeling uncomfortable in English, discourage the more able ones from speaking English to them. So the English of all suffer.

From this table, where there are less than 5 per cent of Malays in a school, their mean score for English language is 73. When there are 75 to 95 per cent in a school, their mean score goes down to 58. It is valuable to know that when the Malays are forced by their smaller numbers in school to speak in English with their fellow students, their scores improved.

A study on the correlation between home language and mean score at PSLE for Malay pupils (Table 4) has shown that the more English is used at home, the better the performance in EL1. Where only Malay is used at home, scores for EL1 are low.

A study at PSLE for Chinese pupils (Table 5) also shows that the more English is used at home, the better the performance in EL1. The more dialect is used at home, the worse the performance, both in EL1 and CL2.

Language is the key to acquisition of knowledge. If a student is unable to understand a language, then he is unable to receive information or knowledge in that language. It is therefore crucial that a breakthrough must be made in the English language and as early in life as possible.

Parents have to decide on the trade-off between the convenience of speaking Malay or the mother tongue at home with their children at the cost of EL1.

Formidable

If they want their children to do well in EL1, their children must also, besides Malay, speak in English at home. If parents cannot speak English, then their children should use English with brothers, sisters and neighbours.

The task therefore is enormous and formidable. To reach out to as many Malay pupils in school as possible, the resources Mendaki has mustered by way of volunteers, are not enough.

Results will be slow to come, limited to the few who can be reached. But with perserverance and determination, you can increase the number of volunteer teachers especially if you ensure that they will not be out of pocket. They may not be paid market rates for private tuition, but comparable recompense, for their travel and time, will draw out many of the 679 Malay university graduates and 3,677 'A' level graduates (1980 Census figures).

Their biggest contribution is the tremendous psychological boost they will give to the Malay students who are motivated enough to attend these special tuition classes.

I promise you that the government will give every assistance by making premises available, and by appealing to non-Malay teachers to join in this exercise.

Our concern

This problem is of concern to all Singaporeans and not just to Malay Singaporeans. It is in the interests of all to have Malay Singaporeans better educated and better qualified and to increase their contribution to Singapore's development.

However, we have to recognise the nature of Singaporeans. They are aware of the market rates for private tuition. To expect teachers to do this for free is to be impractical.

What Mendaki must do is to build up an organisation which, besides tapping the altruistic and charitable impulses of the educated and the successful Malays, can also marshal funds to pay those who are not stirred by such high sentiments. When enthusiasm is not strong, there must be enough material inducement.

For more than 2,000 years, off and on, as dynasties rise and fall, the Imperial examinations in China offered every Chinese the chance of becoming a magistrate and a high official through scholarship. So the importance of performance in examinations has become part of the culture of Chinese.

For over 180 years in India, the British ran competitive examinations for entrance into the Indian Civil Service. Hence the Indians too are keenly aware of the importance of studies and examinations as the road to success.

A virtue

I am told by Muslim MPs that Muslims can draw similar lessons from Islamic teachings and culture. Mendaki must strive to make the striving for success through scholarship universally accepted and admired as a virtue. There are no easy or quick solutions. The attitudes of Chinese and Indian parents to learning as the road to progress are the result of historical experience.

However, the basic values of parents take a long time to get established. These basic values have a profound influence on their children. A government-run scheme cannot achieve a quarter of the results of this voluntary, spontaneous effort by Malays/Muslims to help themselves.

You can better succeed because you will be more effective with Malay/Muslim parents than government officers or school teachers and principals. You can reach them through their hearts, not just their minds. You have the motivation, the dedication and commitment. This emotional/psychological support can make a vast difference, between a student who tries, fails, and tries again, and another who fails and gives up.

It is more important now not to give up. With our economic restructuring, every student must be encouraged to achieve his maximum, whether it be to the Vocational and Industrial Training Board, the Certificate of Secondary Education, 'O' levels or 'A' levels, Polytechnic or university.

Mendaki's real achievement will be to raise the educational levels, and thus the living standards of the majority, and not only of a minority who make it to the top.

Behind the Headlines and Down Memory Lane are on page 13.

Table 2

FEW MALAY PUPILS BECOME GRADUATES

	No. of Pr. 1 Malay pupils	No. who graduated 15 years later
1961	8471	22
1962	9050	28
1963	9443	40
1964	9593	41
1965	10,254	38
1966	10,658	27

• Based on tables accompanying Mr Lee's speech

Table 3

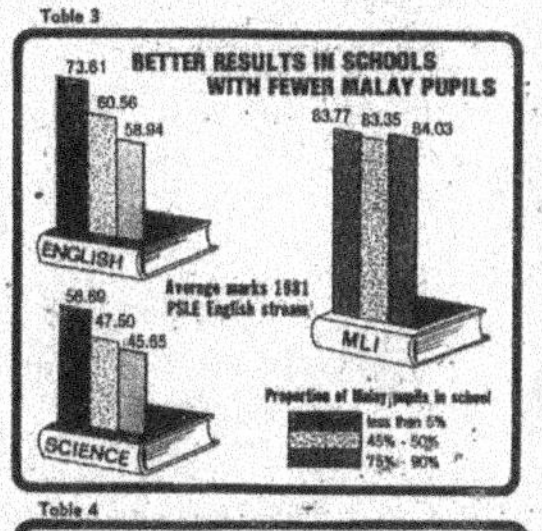
BETTER RESULTS IN SCHOOLS WITH FEWER MALAY PUPILS
73.61
60.56
58.94
ENGLISH
83.77
83.35
84.03
MLI
Average marks 1981 PSLE English stream
58.69
47.50
45.65
SCIENCE
Proportion of Malay pupils in school
less than 5%
45% - 50%
75% - 90%

Table 4

BETTER RESULTS WHEN ENGLISH IS SPOKEN AT HOME

Mean T-scores* –1981 PSLE English stream

Mostly ENGLISH Some Malay		Only MALAY
50·9	ENGLISH	42·4
45·3	MATHS	39·5
49·1	SCIENCE	42·9

*T-scores are calculated based on the performance of all students who sat for the examination.

‘For the effort to achieve full success, you have to start right from the very beginning, which means, from the day the child begins to be conscious of his surroundings, to learn to recognise sounds from his mother and father, to learn to vocalise, to learn to interact with his brother or his sister. In other words, there is no quick fix-it.

Solutions which start towards the middle or end of the education process, with special classes for PSLE, 'O' and 'A' levels students to pass their end of year examinations can produce better results only at the margins.’

The Straits Times
29 May 1982

Berita Harian

KHAMIS, 25 JUN 1987

MENDAMPINGI IBU BAPA

USAHA Mendaki menganjurkan siri lima seminar yang lebih tersusun untuk membantu ibu bapa Islam mendidik anak-anak, bulan depan, adalah langkah menarik dan bernas. Tidak seperti ceramah dan bengkel pendidikan yang pernah dianjurkannya sebelum ini, kali ini Mendaki menampilkan rancangan lanjutan selepas seminar. Selepas mengikuti penerangan yang lebih bersifat teori, ibu bapa yang menyertainya berpeluang berbincang dengan para konvenor yang akan melawat mereka di rumah. Sekaligus, pendekatan ini membolehkan ibu bapa memahami dengan lebih mendalam masalah pelajaran anak-anak mereka bukan sekadar pada permukaan tetapi mengupasnya dengan lebih mendalam dan menilai peranan mereka sendiri.

Pada mata kasar, bayaran sebanyak $50 untuk pasangan ibu bapa atau $30 bagi peserta perseorangan adalah mahal. Namun, pada hakikatnya Mendaki akan membiayai sebahagian besar kos seminar tersebut. Pokoknya, mutu perkhidmatan itu yang perlu menjadi pertimbangan utama. Ibu bapa Islam yang kini lebih sedar akan tugas mereka dalam mendidik akan berpeluang menyelami kaedah yang lebih berkesan untuk membantu anak-anak mereka membesar dalam suasana yang sihat dan mengejar kemajuan. Namun, mereka akan hanya dapat pelajaran dan menikmati manfaat sepenuhnya daripada seminar itu jika mereka bersungguh-sungguh mengambil bahagian dan mengamalkan apa yang dipelajari.

Kejayaan pendekatan baru Mendaki ini bergantung kepada sejauh mana eratnya hubungan ibu bapa dan para penyelenggara yang terdiri daripada pengajar kelas bimbingan. Lazimnya rancangan kemasyarakatan seperti ini tidak akan berjaya sepenuhnya tanpa usaha-usaha lanjutan. Ertinya, setiap tahap program itu harus diteliti kesannya, disesuaikan dan dipermaju dari masa ke masa sehingga tercapai matlamat. Kaedah mendampingi ibu bapa ini memanglah akan mengambil masa yang lama untuk melahirkan hasil yang diharapkan. Ia memerlukan tenaga konvenor atau penasihat tetap yang berdedikasi agar ibu bapa dapat membincangkan masalah pendidikan anak mereka pada waktu yang fleksibel. Bagi ibu bapa Islam, seminar seperti ini adalah peringatan sekali lagi akan tanggungjawab mereka untuk memastikan bahawa generasi Islam hari muka akan dapat maju dengan lebih cepat lagi.

▬ Mutiara Kata ▬

UMAT yang berjaya dianugerahi oleh harapan tinggi.

Iqbal

Berita Harian

SELASA, 13 JANUARI 1987

HASRAT BESAR BIAYA BESAR

SEJAK diasaskan hampir lima tahun lalu, peruntukan perbelanjaan Yayasan Mendaki terus meningkat. Tahun ini ia berjumlah kira-kira $1.5 juta, iaitu satu kenaikan 25 peratus berbanding dengan biaya tahun lalu. Kegiatan-kegiatan Mendaki akan berkembang dan bertambah sejajar dengan pelan induknya. Oleh itu, besar kemungkinan peruntukan Yayasan Mendaki akan terus meningkat pada hari muka. Namun, perkembangan ini telah mengurangkan kumpulan wang untuk disalurkan ke dalam dana simpanan korpusnya yang dirasakan perlu untuk memantapkan kewangan yayasan itu bagi jangka masa panjang. Moga-moga dengan perhatian terus masyarakat, kedua-dua keperluan itu akan tercapai.

Tidak dapat dinafikan, masyarakat Islam telah menjadikan Mendaki semacam lambang kegigihan dalam matlamat meningkatkan pencapaian pelajaran anak-anak Islam. Sejauh mana Mendaki maju ke arah matlamatnya itu akan mempengaruhi semangat dan sokongan yang diterimanya dalam bentuk kewangan dan tenaga daripada masyarakat Islam. Dengan peruntukan yang bernilai jutaan dolar itu dan ditambah dengan harapannya untuk terus meluaskan skop kegiatannya, Mendaki menghadapi cabaran yang besar untuk memenuhi hasrat masyarakat.

Untuk memastikan rancangannya berhasil, Mendaki perlu mendapatkan lebih banyak tenaga pemimpin, termasuk karyawan, bagi mengatur, melaksana dan menilai program-programnya dengan teliti dari masa ke masa demi memastikan kejayaannya. Mendaki juga bergantung kepada sokongan penuh dan ikhlas masyarakat. Untuk terus meyakinkan masyarakat terhadap hasrat nurani Mendaki itu, yayasan ini perlu memastikan bahawa maklumat tentang kegiatan dan pencapaiannya bukan sahaja disebar luas tetapi dihayati ramai. Walaupun Mendaki diperlukan untuk menerbitkan laporan dan penilaiannya dalam tempoh tiga tahun sekali, namun ia juga sedar tentang perlunya laporan dan penilaian tahunan dibuat. Tidak kurang penting juga adalah laporan-laporan semasa berhubung dengan projek-projeknya. Menerusi maklumat sedemikian dan diperteguh dengan usaha Mendaki untuk lebih mesra dengan masyarakat, umat Islam setempat, insyaallah akan lebih yakin untuk terus memberi, malah menambah, sumbangan ikhlas mereka kepada Mendaki.

▬ Mutiara Kata ▬

KEIKHLASAN pemberian datangnya tanpa diminta-minta.

Kahlil Gibran

Wanted: A Muslim of impeccable character, well-versed in Islam, a top-notch administrator, able to earn the respect of his community and deal with Government on sensitive matters of religion. The job: President of Muis, the supreme Islamic body. **ZURAIDAH IBRAHIM** of the Political Desk asks community leaders what qualities are needed in the man who will succeed incumbent Ridzwan Dzafir.

Muis looks for new Islamic leader

Ridzwan who juggles other commitments, hopes a successor will be found

A Muis President should be:

The Straits Times
24 August 1990

Benta Mingsu
17 November 1991

The Sunday Times
24 August 1990

Pres Wee: Anak muda Islam positif mengenai S'pura

MAJLIS PENJALIN HUBUNGAN: Presiden Wee Kim Wee, bersama (dari kiri) Encik Zainul Abidin, Haji Abdul Khair, Haji Muhammad Arif, Haji Shubasi, Haji Rohan dan Dr Ahmad Mattar.

The Sunday Times, January 19, 1992

Mendaki to pool efforts to uplift Malay community

Education programmes to be co-ordinated under one banner

MENDAKI is planning to co-ordinate its education programmes under one banner to speed up the development of a total approach to uplift the Malay/Muslim community, Environment Minister Dr Ahmad Mattar said yesterday.

He noted that since its inception in 1981, Mendaki, the Council for the Development of the Singapore Muslim community, had focused on education. "But latterly it has been looking to the big picture," he said.

This bigger picture meant Mendaki was also looking at programmes to improve the professional achievements, economic successes and social stability of the community, he said.

But in order for this total approach to work, there was a need to co-ordinate activities.

"We cannot talk about a strategy for total development if our activities are scattered and isolated. There is therefore a need for Mendaki to co-ordinate these programmes under one banner," he said.

Dr Mattar, who is also the Minister in charge of Muslim Affairs, was speaking at the launch of this year's Mendaki Enrichment Programme for top PSLE students.

Mendaki's Chief Executive Officer (CEO), Mr Zainul Abidin Rasheed, later confirmed that the chairmen of the council's five main education committees will meet regularly to co-ordinate efforts and share resources.

As the CEO, Mr Zainul will chair this co-ordinating committee.

In addition to the Enrichment Programme for top students, Mendaki has a tuition scheme for middle-level students, and another for under-achievers.

Two other committees take care of child and family development, and pre-school education.

In his speech, Dr Mattar said the opening of a Fast Forward basic skills training centre for workers at the Mendaki headquarters in Siglap, and Mendaki's entry into the business world with the establishment of its Growth Fund, were examples of the wider approach to uplift the community.

Similarly, the Enrichment Programme, which organises leadership camps, workshops on interview and communication skills and other programmes, and also gives career guidance was also a step in the right direction.

"Clever school children do not develop into useful or even happy adults without those other skills that enable them to cope with the realities of later life," he said.

The Enrichment Programme, which was launched last May, is a six-year programme for the top 10 per cent of PSLE students. Programmes are designed to help them continue to do well from Secondary 1 to Pre-University 2.

A Malay/Muslim professional is also assigned as "big brother" or "big sister" to these students.

Last year 134 students and 52 mentors took part in the programme.

Another 80 professionals have signed up as mentors to this year's batch of 113 students.

Berita Harian's interview with the Prime Minister

Malay S'poreans: Coping with the dynamic times

Education one of the keys to better jobs for community

The Straits Times
7 July 1987

In conjunction with its 30th anniversary, Berita Harian interviewed Prime Minister Lee Kuan Yew. Subjects discussed included the progress of the Singaporean Malays, how more and continuing progress can be achieved in the national milieu and the strengthening of inter-racial bonds.

We reproduce the interview, which was conducted by Mr Zainul Abidin Rasheed, Berita Harian Editor, and published in the Malay newspaper on Sunday and yesterday.

How to help the students

Parents and community leaders

Parents are the best people to motivate their children.

Be realistic and objective

Teachers

Develop strong points

> **QUOTE**
>
> Group comparisons are a misleading measure of the real progress made by Malay students. Within each group there is an imbalance between talented and less talented individuals.
>
> — Prime Minister Lee Kuan Yew

The Prime Minister with Berita Harian editor Zainul Abidin ... Malays should measure their progress against their performance five and 10 years ago.

Pada ceramah sulung Jalinan Budi 2015, baru-baru ini, Hj Wan Hussin Hj Zoohri merumuskan bahawa kemajuan orang Melayu di sini kian teguh dan mantap, walau masih ada kepincangan sosial.

'Kemajuan kita kian mantap'

MOHD RAMAN DAUD
raman@sph.com.sg

HATI KE HATI... Hj Wan Hussin Zoohri dan pengerusi ceramah Siti Jalinan Budi, Prof Madya Dr Hadijah Rahmat, cuba memedangkan isu kemajuan Melayu secara bersama-sama. - Foto MOHD RAMAN DAUD

ASAL DILEMA

ILMU DAN AKHLAK

FEUDAL MELAYU

ZAMAN MERDEKA

MOHD EUNOS ABDULLAH

Haji Wan Hussin guru, pemimpin dan ilmuwan

THE SINGAPORE MALAYS
The Dilemma of Development

Berita Harian
2 March 2015

SOAL JAWAB DENGAN PAK WAN

Masih perlu dialog belakang tabir

▶ Kepupusan aliran Melayu

▶ Desakan atau dialog

▶ Masa depan minoriti

▶ Dua atau tiga tonggak

Bersama Menteri Pembimbing

Melayu
harus tumpu
pendidikan
dan
keluarga

U NTUK terus maju, masyarakat Melayu Singapura perlu terus memberi penekanan kepada pendidikan dan memperkukuh institusi keluarga.

Dua bidang ini memainkan peranan penting dalam usaha orang-orang Melayu melangkah lebih jauh dalam era globalisasi.

Pandangan ini disuarakan oleh Menteri Pembimbing, Encik Lee Kuan Yew.

Menurutnya, pasangan Melayu muda tidak harus terburu-buru bernikah kerana kelangsungan kehidupan mereka bercerai adalah besar.

"Bidang-bidang kritikal bagi masyarakat Melayu Singapura ialah penekanan terhadap pendidikan ilmu dan mengekalkan kestabilan keluarga, iaitu pasangan tidak harus tergesa-ge-

ENCIK LEE KUAN YEW: BH berperanan membantu dan menggalak masyarakat Melayu agar menyertai pembangunan negara dan mengekalkan keharmonian kaum.

oleh Azahar Mohd
(azahar@sph.com.sg)

sa bernikah, kahwin cerai dan kemudian bernikah lagi.

"Keluarga yang bercerai menyebabkan anak-anak menjadi keliru dan mereka berkemungkinan besar berasa terganggu dan kurang keyakinan diri," kata Encik Lee dalam wawancara khas sempena menyambut jubli emas BH.

Encik Lee juga menyentuh pelbagai isu, termasuk penga-

nasan, peluang pekerjaan dan perniagaan di Timur Tengah dan sumbangan BH kepada pembangunan negara.

Beliau berkata respons masyarakat Melayu terhadap ancaman pengganasan adalah positif dan proaktif.

Golongan asatizah dan imam daripada Kumpulan Pemulihan Keagamaan (RRG), katanya, telah sama-sama membantu memulihkan anggota Jemaah Islamiyah (JI) yang diserapi fahaman menyeleweng akibat salah tafsir agama.

Beliau turut menyentuh peranan BH dalam membantu dan menggalak masyarakat Melayu supaya mengambil bahagian dalam pembangunan negara dan mengekalkan keharmonian kaum.

Dalam hal ini, Encik Lee memberi contoh bagaimana masyarakat Melayu menerima langkah untuk merobohkan kampung-kampung Melayu dan masjid lama bagi memberi laluan kepada pembangunan bandar baru lengkap dengan masjid yang besar untuk kepentingan semua.

Masyarakat Melayu juga menerima langkah untuk menghalakan suara azan ke dalam masjid demi mengekalkan keharmonian kaum, tambah beliau.

"Selepas perpisahan daripada Malaysia pada 1965, 42 tahun lalu, *Berita Harian* secara beransur-ansur memberi tumpuan kepada masyarakat Melayu di Singapura. Kini masyarakat Melayu/Islam boleh menjadi sebahagian masyarakat yang lebih besar di Singapura, dan bukan di Malaysia. Menjelang 1990-an, *Berita Harian* membantu menyesuaikan pembacanya untuk menjadi sebahagian daripada Singapura yang sekular, berbilang bangsa, berbahasa Inggeris dan bersifat antarabangsa dari segi pandangannya."

— MM Lee tentang penilaiannya terhadap peranan *Berita Harian* dalam sekitaran moden yang pesat berubah.

"Dasar dwibahasa dengan bahasa Inggeris sebagai bahasa kerja bermakna bahasa Inggeris mengambil 70 peratus daripada masa kurikulum di sekolah rendah, 80 peratus di sekolah menengah, 100 peratus di institusi pengajian tinggi. Bahasa Inggeris merupakan bahasa yang fasih digunakan oleh sebahagian besar warga Singapura yang berbilang bangsa. Kita menggunakannya di tempat kerja. Namun, adalah penting bagi setiap bangsa mengekalkan penggunaan bahasa ibunda, yang penting bagi jati diri dan identiti kebudayaan. *Berita Harian*, *Zaobao* dan *Tamil Murasu* serta pelbagai saluran TV termasuk *Suria* memainkan peranan penting."

— MM Lee tentang sama ada BH perlu memainkan peranan lebih aktif menggalak pembelajaran bahasa Melayu

Berita Mingsu
1 July 2007

The Straits Times
4 October 2014

THE SUPPER CLUB | USTAZ MOHAMED ALI

Battle to protect Islam from untruths of 'jihad'

Ten years ago, a group of Islamic religious leaders came together to begin rehabilitating terror detainees and counter their misinterpretation of certain concepts. In August, the Religious Rehabilitation Group (RRG) received the Berita Harian Achiever of the Year Award. As countries around the world grapple with a resurgent terror threat, RRG vice-chairman, Ustaz Mohamed Ali, 41, talks to **Tham Yuen-C** about the group's work.

ST PHOTO ILLUSTRATION: RUDY WONG & MANNY FRANCISCO

■ How did the founders of the RRG hit upon the idea of using rehabilitation to counter extremist ideology?

When some Jemaah Islamiah (JI) members were arrested here in 2001 and 2002, Ustaz Ali Haji Mohamed and Ustaz Mohamed Hasbi Hassan (RRG co-chairmen) were given the opportunity to talk to the detainees. They discovered these individuals used religion to promote their political objectives, and had misunderstood religious narratives. When asked why they wanted to attack Singapore, the detainees said: "This is my jihad."

As religious scholars, it is our duty to correct them and reflect upon such extremist ideology. The best way is to talk to them, to guide them, and re-educate them, to clear any confusion they may have. That is why the idea of counselling and rehabilitation was mooted.

■ How are the counselling sessions carried out?

We have a three-step process.

First, we talk to the detainees to identify the misinterpreted religious concepts they hold. Then, we provide the correct and proper understanding of these concepts. Last, we try to help them understand and appreciate living within Singapore's multiracial, multi-religious society.

■ Are they receptive?

In the earlier sessions, they generally don't trust us. They perceive us as "government ustaz". So we explain that we are volunteers. If our religion is being threatened, hijacked, used wrongly, then it is our duty to correct it.

Usually, slowly, after months and sometimes years of counselling, they begin to be receptive and understand we are there to help them, and they request more advice.

■ How can you tell someone has been successfully rehabilitated?

Ideology, thinking, and orientation are something non-physical and unseen. So, to be honest, we cannot be 100 per cent sure.

But we make an assessment using several indicators.

For example, these individuals previously believed that Islam required hate and violence of its adherents. After counselling, they must demonstrate resilience against these ideas, and realise that terrorists have been misinterpreting Islam.

We also look for whether an individual has reflected on his past actions and understood that the move by the JI members to create chaos in Singapore tarnished the good name of the Muslim community here.

You can tell by the way they speak, and their actions. They integrate well, they begin to speak positively, and better understand what it means to be living in a multicultural Singapore.

They are also part of a supervision program by the authorities which stops them from going back to

■ So, can they really change?

No one is born a terrorist, a radical or extremist. It's through a process of radicalisation that these people become like that. They think they are doing something good, because they are led to believe that. From our experience, extremists can be rehabilitated. However, some people may need a longer time to be rehabilitated.

■ What experiences of the RRG are relevant in stamping out the threat of extremism posed by the Islamic State in Iraq and Syria (ISIS)?

We learnt that a robust and innovative counter-ideological approach is required to deal with such threats. The community, ticipation are key, and, fortunately, this is our strength in Singapore. This approach is a huge hurdle and challenge for many countries. ISIS ideology developed from Al-Qaeda. What ISIS is doing today is not something very different from Al-Qaeda in Iraq. Beheadings are not something new. In 2004, Al-Qaeda was doing it in Iraq.

But ISIS has become very brutal, very extreme. This July, RRG came up with a pamphlet to explain the Syrian conflict. Now, we are working on the ISIS phenomenon. RRG has formed a research team to discuss this. We will soon come up with the counter-narratives to provide the public with clear explanations to counter ISIS.

■ RRG also has to help detainees come to terms with living in a multiracial and multi-religious society. Why is this so?

I think, thereotion. Ideology plays an important role in shaping the action. But the act of planning to bomb, in the case of the JI detainees, also arises from hatred towards Singapore, the United States, and its allies.

Ideology provides some kind of justification. We need to understand the psychological aspect too.

That's why in the Singapore rehabilitation programme, there are three major components: religious, psychological and social. The RRG is involved in only the religious component.

■ Everyone can look at the same verses and give a different spin. How do you convince them your interpretation is right?

You can have a different orientation, but when it comes to religious fundamentals, you have tised well without any problems.

We have Muis (Islamic Religious Council of Singapore), we have a minister for Muslim affairs, the Syariah Court (for family law) and Amla (Administration of Muslim Law Act).

Islam also promotes integration among the different religious communities. In the Quran, there is a verse that says God created human beings in different tribes, different religions, languages so that we can get to know one another.

the scholars. You cannot have your own interpretation.

■ But these groups have their own scholars and preachers, so how would people know their teachings are not legitimate?

It's very clear in Islam that violence cannot be accepted. There are many orientations, and even if you want to pray, there are several versions of prayer, every version is correct. But Islam condemns and forbids violence.

■ So, why do the people who join ISIS believe that their actions are sanctioned by their religion?

It is because they are misinterpreting the verses in the Quran. If you refer back to the interpretation of the scholars, you will see that these verses are not about the killing of non-Muslims. They speak about the battlefield or war fought by Prophet Muhammad during his time. That is a legitimate battlefield.

But how can you put on a suicide vest, blow up yourself in public, killing yourself, killing others and call it a jihad? Is that a jihad?

Obviously it's not. That's violence. Islam forbids you to kill yourself and others.

They believe that what they do is jihad, a holy war, and it's a religious obligation. But Islam and the Prophet did not teach that.

■ There have been reports of Singaporeans travelling to Syria to join ISIS. Why are they attracted to the conflict there when they are not directly affected by it?

Many people do not understand the nature and context of the conflict in Iraq and Syria. But it has been widely portrayed as jihad and a religious duty of Muslims, thus helping attract many foreign fighters from across the globe.

In addition, many also believe the conflict in Iraq and Syria is a prelude to the anticipated end of time (Judgement Day) and feel anxious – that they need to be "better Muslims now". Hence, they feel they need to respond to the ISIS call for "jihad".

The truth is far from this. The conflict is very tribal and political and there is no religious requirement for anyone to get involved. Those who support it are confused about their religious obligations. They fail to seek proper advice or clarification and are too impulsive in making their decision.

■ You said people who become radicalised are often those wanting to be more religious. What is the difference between a holy person and an extremist?

The difference is crystal clear. A true holy man will never commit any indiscriminate and unjustified violence and will use religion to bring peace in himself, his family, community and the world.

Militants, on the other hand, justify violence and attempt to attract people to their way of them are not radicals and know what shallabout religion.

Bersama Mufti Syed Isa Semait

Sama-sama bentuk identiti Muslim

oleh Halifi Hussin (mdhalifi@sph.com.sg)

SOALAN (S): Mengapakah Majlis Ugama Islam Singapura (Muis) melakarkan 10 ciri masyarakat Islam cemerlang?

Jawapan (J): Ia bersangkutan dengan usaha membangun dan membina keupayaan dan pemikiran masyarakat Islam Singapura. 10 ciri ini melambangkan identiti Muslim Singapura (SMI). Ia mengariskan cara kehidupan masyarakat Islam yang berusaha untuk terus berpegang teguh pada prinsip dan dasar agama, pada masa yang sama, mampu menyesuaikan diri dengan konteks kehidupan masa kini. Tentu sekali kita memerlukan kepimpinan keupayaan yang mampu memandu kita untuk terus melayari bahtera kehidupan di Singapura sebagai Muslim yang baik lagi berjaya dan bijak serta matang menangani cabaran-cabaran yang mendatang.

S: Apakah peranan BH dalam menyebarkan mesej Muis?

J: Peranan BH adalah untuk meningkatkan pemahaman dan memberi kesedaran kepada masyarakat. Ia juga menyediakan wadah penting bagi menyebar luas dan mengwar-warkan program dan inisiatif Muis dan badan-badan Islam lain kepada masyarakat. BH menyediakan ruang khas setiap Jumaat mengulas 'Masjid Kita' menyokong kupon rakat setiap tahun dan bekerjasama dalam projek membentuk SMI.

S: Sejauh manakah peranan BH dalam membentuk SMI?

J: BH wadah penting dalam hal ini. Selain laporan perihal usaha dan program Muis mengenai projek ini, BH juga menyiarkan komentar pengamat dan pemimpin masyarakat mengenai SMI. Ruang forum juga menyiarkan pendapat masyarakat dan memberi peluang bagi Muis menjelaskan maksud dan contoh SMI.

S: Apakah langkah seterusnya menangani cabaran global?

J: Muis akan sentiasa meningkatkan khidmatnya kepada masyarakat dan menyesuaikan pendekatannya dengan cabaran baru. Antara ciri SMI-ga adalah sifat inklusif, bererti masyarakat Islam dapat menerima perbezaan dengan hati terbuka. Seperti kita maklum, dunia global akan melihat lebih banyak interaksi antara budaya dan agama berbeza.

Kita harus bersedia menghadapi cabaran itu, yang tidak semestinya tidak baik. Bahkan, ia akan menambah kemakmuran kita, sebagai masyarakat maju.

Berita Harian
1 July 2007

ItChangedMyLife

Warm, Fuzzie feeling after surgery

After overcoming a host of health problems, Farhan Noor could hit pay dirt with new app

Wong Kim Hoh
Senior Writer

In 2011, Mr Farhan Noor was one semester shy of graduating with two first-class honours degrees – one in life sciences, the other in economics – from the National University of Singapore when he was beset by an avalanche of health problems.

Among other things, he experienced intense pain in his ears, and found it hard to breathe. "At night, I found myself waking up every hour or so gasping for air," he says.

He developed allergies to food which never used to give him problems, and also began stuttering.

Visits to various specialists did not help, scans and tests yielded no clues either. "None of the doctors could put the pieces together."

It took a couple of years before he found a neurosurgeon in private practice who told him his spine was severely damaged.

"He said it was very serious and that I had to have emergency surgery," says Mr Farhan, 30, who reckons he hurt his spine during a biking accident several years earlier. "He said that if I had waited for one more week, I could have been paralysed from the waist down."

A ceramic disc with a titanium rod was implanted into his spinal cord to replace his damaged disc at cervical spine level C4-5.

By then, he was convinced that he did not have long to live.

"I decided to give up my studies. I felt it was not important and I wanted to make the best use of my time and leave behind a legacy and some money for my parents," says Mr Farhan who, as it turned out, had completed enough modules to earn a degree in Life Sciences with a minor in Economics.

He hatched a couple of business-es which did not quite take off.

But he may have hit pay dirt with Fuzzie, a mobile gifting app which he conceived. To be launched before year-end, it allows users to send gifts - vouchers in different denominations from fashion retailers to spas and hip cafes and restaurants - to family and friends.

Besides angel investors, his start-up Fuzzie, with a team of 11, has already caught the attention of venture capitalists and corporations including Singapore Press Holdings. It is the first start-up to receive a Collaborative Industry Projects grant from Spring Singapore, given to encourage collaborations between enterprises and industry partners.

Happily, Fuzzie's flight dovetailed with his recovery. "It's only in the last two months that I stopped stuttering," he says.

Mr Farhan grew up in Bukit Batok, the third of seven children. His father works in a printing company; his mother is a masseuse specialising in antenatal treatments.

At Bukit View Primary, he was a bright but non-conformist kid who always challenged teachers and questioned rules.

"I remember we could not fill up our water bottles at the water cooler. How dumb was that?"

He continued his education at Gan Eng Seng Secondary, where he was, he sheepishly confessed, a "dirty prefect".

Recalcitrant students needed only to bribe him with a Snickers bar if they wanted to puff away in peace.

"I guess that was the start of my entrepreneurial journey," he says with a hearty laugh.

He then had "two phenomenal years" in National Junior College.

"I fell in love with biology, spent a lot of time in labs and took part in national-level science competitions," says the straight-A student.

National service beckoned next. But just one week before entering the army, he got involved in a nasty accident, one which changed the course of his life.

He had gone to the Bukit Timah Bike Trail to test out his new mountain bike, not knowing it was a challenging trail. To make matters worse, he wore neither a helmet nor other protective gear.

While careening down the trail, he accidentally pressed the brake of his front wheel as the bike went over jutting roots. Thrown into the air, he landed face down, tearing his lips and injuring his legs and back.

Since he could still walk, it did not occur to him that he could have injured his spine. At a polyclinic, he did not take up the doctor's suggestion to undergo a scan. One week later, he entered the army.

"I didn't know I was harbouring an injured disc. Two and a half years in the army training probably took a toll."

While in the army, he applied to study life sciences at the prestigious Imperial College in London.

"I applied for three consecutive years, and succeeded each time. But I could not take up the offers because I could not find a bond-free scholarship," says Mr Farhan, who did not want to be tied down to a six-year government bond.

He finally settled on a bond-free scholarship offered by his father's employers to study in NUS.

The go-getter set himself an ambitious goal: to graduate with two degrees in five years. "Pursuing two radically different degrees meant that I would have to do two final-year projects. I told myself there had to be a smarter way of doing it so I decided I would combine both."

His thesis proposal? Cellular economics which uses economic principles to explain cell behaviour.

"Does nature follow the principles of economics when it comes to evolution? Does it follow the path that requires the least amount of resources to get maximum results?" he says, adding with a grin that his proposal got the green light from both NUS' Life Sciences and Economics departments.

His schedule and workload were gruelling. While most students averaged five modules, he took seven in the first semester. On top of that, he also rented a space and ran a tuition centre tutoring 20 students. "I could pull in between $5,000 and $8,000 a month. It was very good money but I got burnt-out very quickly," he says, adding that he gave up the centre after one year.

The savings he amassed, however, came in very handy when his health issues cropped up.

The constant whirring in his ears, his food allergies and breathing problems drove him bonkers and led him to quit university.

"I was losing my mind. I was resigned to my fate and thought I might not live very long," he says.

Desperate to make money, he launched two business ideas – a stylish but functional lab coat and a fund to help families invest in stocks and options – but these did not have the legs he had hoped for.

Mr Farhan then conceived Don't Tell Teacher, which sought to produce animated educational videos to explain science in a fun way.

The idea was to set up a platform to cover three subjects – physics, biology and chemistry – which schools could subscribe to.

He hammered out a script to explain enzymes, and found some talents in New York - from animators to code writers - to help him make a five-minute animated video for just $1,500. The vice-president of Magic Lantern – one of Canada's biggest distributors of educational videos – was so impressed she agreed to a collaboration. "She figured we could easily make a million dollars in sales in the first year. The company has access to over 30,000 schools in North America and they have sales agents who could push and market the products. The investment was $500,000. If each school paid $1,000 in subscription a year, the business could bring in $30 million a year," he says.

Science North, an interactive science museum in Canada, was keen to come on board as investor and producer. "They were willing to provide the content; I just had to raise half of the investment amount."

Thinking that he had a winning formula, he pitched it to a senior officer at the Media Development Authority of Singapore, who rejected his application for a grant. Mr Farhan learnt later that the officer was jailed last year after being found guilty of corruptly obtaining loans from applicants in return for facilitating grants.

He could not proceed but loaded the video Enzymes: A Fun Introduction on YouTube, where it has been viewed more than 330,000 times.

The business plan for Fuzzie was drawn up while he was on his way back from Florida after a meeting with Science North executives.

In the US, he was struck by the sheer array of gift cards – from Starbucks to H&M – sold in convenience stores. The industry, he soon discovered, was worth US$130 billion (S$180 billion) in the US alone.

"The market in Asia hasn't been tapped; it's easily worth $300 billion," he claims. A mobile app, he decided, would be perfect because it does away with distribution channels.

"The challenge is to make the experience fun and throw in lots of cool features - reward programmes, promotions and other killer features I can't tell you yet."

It was only after his trip that Mr Farhan would find the neurosurgeon who diagnosed his problems and performed his life-changing surgery. "I thought my Florida trip was my last trip before I die."

After his operation, he began to develop Fuzzie in earnest.

His experience with Don't Tell Teacher taught him that talents can be sourced globally and operate remotely. Among his team of 11 are a French designer and an American developer. There are three Singaporean handling marketing, graphic design and administration.

"If you can convince people you have a great concept, they will work for you at low cost. It's not just about making money but making a difference," he says.

It took his team about 1½ years to develop Fuzzie, which initially drew investors such as the owners of Mad Men Attic Bar and The Batter Factory. But now, big corporations have expressed interest in the app, which has landed more than 50 brands, including Fred Perry and hip cafe Carpenter and Cook as partners. A prototype has been launched and Fuzzie has landed several millions in sponsorship programmes with brands like Topshop and Mothercare.

He is convinced he is on the cusp of something big. "We want to make gifting easily accessible to people so that whenever they want to, they can just send an appreciation to someone by simply pushing a button. And we have just scratched the surface with Fuzzie."

kimhoh@sph.com.sg

Mr Farhan Noor at the office for Fuzzie, a mobile gifting app he conceived which has attracted big corporations, including Singapore Press Holdings.
ST PHOTO LIM SIN THAI

(From left) Mr Farhan Noor with younger sister Nur Nazira, father Noor Mohamed, mother Amirjan and younger brother Luqman Nol Hakim. Mr Farhan had undergone an operation for a damaged spine. PHOTO COURTESY OF FARHAN NOOR

SUPPORTED BY

Standard Chartered

Look out for Wong Kim Hoh's upcoming book commissioned by Standard Chartered Bank.

It Changed My Life is a compilation of inspirational stories from this series, and is part of the bank's initiative to celebrate Singapore's Golden Jubilee.

Farhan Noor on his struggles with spine injury
http://str.sg/ZBfT

The Rise of the New Malay/Muslim

Against all odds Farhan Noor has developed a mobile gifting app, Fuzzie, that has attracted angel investors and venture capitalists and secured partnerships with more than 50 brands. Fuzzie is also the first start-up to receive a Collaborative Industry Projects grant, an initiative by Spring Singapore that supports collaborations between enterprises and industry partners. His resilience and tenacity are qualities that Malay/Muslim youths need to emulate in order to compete not only with fellow Singaporeans but the rest of the world.

CHAPTER 27

SINGAPORE MALAY RADIO
BROADCAST SERVICE — AN
OVERVIEW OF THE LAST 50 YEARS
AND A WAY FORWARD

Aidi Abdul Rahim

U ndoubtedly, radio played an important role to many homes by providing listeners with entertainment, information and education. The Malay radio broadcast service in Singapore started in 1936 but was interrupted during the Japanese interregnum. The service resumed immediately after the war with a limited number of hours of service, until in 1977, when the Malay radio service began to operate on a 24-hour daily basis. In 1965, Radio Television Singapore (RTS) was formed and continued until it was corporatised into a statutory board as the Singapore Broadcasting Corporation (SBC) in 1980. Currently Malay radio broadcasting services in Singapore are undertaken by Warna 94.2FM and Ria 89.7FM[a] — both owned by Mediacorp Singapore.

Key personalities from the education and literary fields were recruited into or had a hand in contributing to the early days of the Singapore Malay radio broadcasting service. Zaharah Za'ba, the first female trainee teacher accepted into the Sultan Idris Teachers College (SITC), was the first female head of the Radio Singapore Malay Services from 1958 to 1973. Ramli Abdul Hadi, the man who initiated the formation of the Malay Language Council and the Permanent Congress Council, head of the News Unit and a prolific scriptwriter of radio

---

[a] Warna 94.2FM caters for the older generation while Ria 89.7FM is aimed at youths.

dramas. Mahmud Ahmad, a former Head Master and President of the Malay Cultural Association, was another prolific radio scriptwriter on Malay culture in the 1960s. His programme was subsequently published into a book, *Kebudayan Sepintas Lalu* (Culture, a Quick Glimpse) in 1963. Other language and literary activists who were involved in the Malay radio broadcast service included Masuri Salikun, the 1980 Southeast Asia Write Award winner for Malay poetry, and Muhammad Ariff Ahmad, the 1987 Cultural Medallion winner.

This year Mediacorp is marking 80 years of radio broadcasting in 2016. Radio transmission first started in Singapore back in June 1936 with one radio station operating from a Government building in Empress Place. Now, there are 13 FM stations that broadcast mainly in the four national languages. Radio stations play an integral role in the lives of Singaporeans reaching out to more than 80% of the population.

Generally, about 60% of the programmes aired play popular and traditional Malay music and the rest of the air time is filled with information about local and world news, general medical issues, health and legal advice; information and quizzes about language usage and literature, news about cultural events, interviews with personalities and talks on Islamic history and *fiqh*[b] and Quranic exegesis. There are also programmes catered for children and youth, as well as news about local and international sports. In the last two decades, listeners participated in radio shows by having to call in, but now smartphones and social media apps are the "new" alternatives to interact with the radio deejays and other listeners at large. It used to be common back in the 1970s and 1980s for traditional Malay music like *keroncong, dondang sayang, ghazal, joget* and *gambus* to be commonly heard on the airwaves at specific times of the day. Nowadays, this genre of Malay music is rarely heard. Malay music has had its fair share of external influences, and in the 1960s; *Pop Yeh-Yeh* was very popular with Malay listeners.

A staple of the Malay radio service are the radio dramas, and this can be either of the traditional types

---

[b] Islamic jurisprudence.

viz. bangsawan[c] or Malay opera and contemporary drama. *Bangsawan* programmes were aired from 1957 to the early 1990s. The *bangsawan* programmes aired by the Singapore Malay Radio had high production values and were well-known throughout the region. After each *bangsawan* programme, the recording was copied and shared with the Radio Brunei Darussalam as part of their broadcast sharing collaboration framework. The *bangsawan* reflects court etiquette, *matters that intrigue and to stir listeners'* imagination and immersion. Singing, music and sounds played an integral role and the application of court language augmented the story line. Scripts were written by *bangsawan* actors and promoters themselves. One of the prolific *bangsawan* radio scriptwriters was Abdul Hamid Ahmad, a *bangsawan* enthusiast and leader of a *bangsawan* club. Other *bangsawan* legends were Shariff Medan, S. Kadarisman and M. Saffri A. Manaf.

Another much-loved programme for language and cultural enthusiasts and listeners of all ages was the *pantun* and *puisi* programmes. *Pantun* is a traditional oral expression that invites participation to either tease, answer a riddle, or a give witty rejoinder, and usually attracts listeners to phone in and respond, or on other occasions, to spontaneously participate if the programme is held outside the studio. *Pantun* was a firm favourite among listeners

Suara Singapura (Voice of Singapore) was the fourth radio service to be provided by Radio Singapore. It was headed by Zain Mahmood and supported by a team of announcers. They were Ian Hope (English), Hayattee Yusof and Seah Cher Seck (Malay), Foo Hua Lim (Chinese) and Ramyah (Tamil). The new service contained programmes that included news bulletins in Malay, Chinese, English and Tamil but the continuity links were in the national language — Malay. The service was launched by Inche Yusof Ishak, the Yang di-Pertuan Negara of Singapore, and took place at the Victoria Theatre. A multicultural performance followed thereafter. Image courtesy of Mun Chor Seng © 2016. All rights reserved.

---

[c] The term literally means "of good birth, noble" — *bangsa* (rasa) and *wan* (royal lineage) has come to collectively refer to Malay opera.

and especially during the *Aidilfitri* celebrations where Singapore and Brunei hosts this much anticipated radio programme. On the other hand, *puisi* or poetry recitations usually attract a younger crowd and those interested in literature. In the past, as part of the station's public outreach and connection with their listeners, *puisi* recitations in public have been organised with local poets participating at the Singapore Botanical Gardens, The Padang, East Coast Park and Changi Beach.

Discussions and understanding about the nuances of the Malay language is an important educational function that the Malay radio services offer to their listeners. Having been fortunate to have access to language experts such as the late *Pendeta* Muhammad Ariff Ahmad and regional experts as studio guests, like the Malaysian linguist (*bahasawan*) Professor Asmah Hj Omar, Dr Awang Sariyan from the Malaysia Dewan Bahasa dan Pustaka and Dr Tunas Effendy from Riau, listeners learnt and became acquainted about the intricacies of the Malay vocabulary, grammar and common usage mistakes in speaking and writing in *Bahasa Melayu*. In the mid-1990s, the Malay Radio service adopted the use of standard spoken Malay or *Sebutan Baku*, taking up the recommendation of the Malay Language Council. With the cooperation of the Malay Language Council and expert help from the Malaysia Dewan Bahasa dan Pustaka, the two Malay language radio stations Warna and Ria and the television channel TV12 (now renamed Suria), slowly and steadily rolled out among their radio deejays, presenters and news readers the use of *sebutan baku* or standard spoken *Bahasa Melayu*. During the early days, listeners and radio presenters reacted awkwardly to this new form of pronunciation of standard Malay and

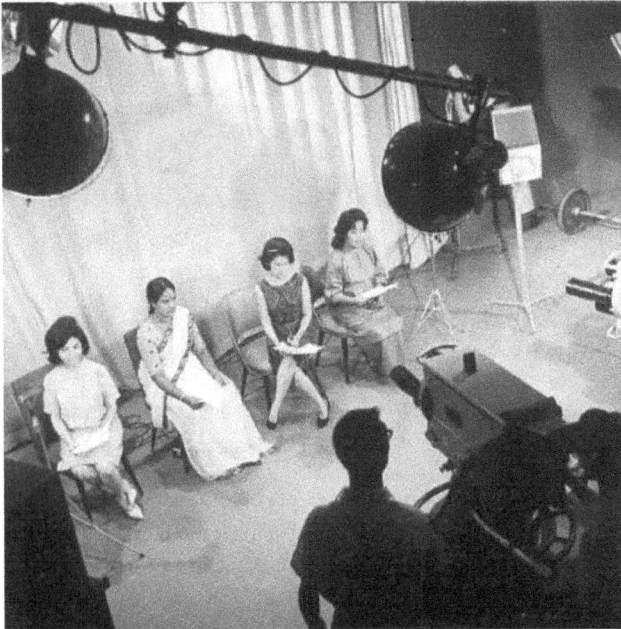

Radio presenters Joan Chee, Naragretnam Suppiah, Alice Chong and Asmah Laili Image courtesy of Mun Chor Seng © 2016. All rights reserved.

even to this day, the older listeners who were used to the non-standard pronunciation still voiced misgivings about this change. Indeed, the attempt to speak standard Malay on radio was tried in 1963 when the news in Malay was read but it was stopped because of listeners' unfavourable reactions.

In the current environment where social media has a pervasive hold on the wake-time of the individual, the Malay radio broadcast service like other media platforms that connect to the masses is in an intense competition to retain and win in the marketplace of entertainment, education, information and interactivity. While music, drama, news and information will be the staple of radio services, changing demographics, changing tastes and preferences and higher education levels of listeners will determine if radio will still be a constant companion, like the relation radio had in the last half of the 20th century. But it cannot be denied that the Malay radio service plays an important role in keeping alive and fresh and engaging publicly the use of the Malay language in the personal and public spheres. Importantly, the role of radio presenters will be critical in that they remain disciplined, and realise their public role in maintaining the high standards of Malay language communication over the air waves. Just as important, the programmes that are offered and presented will have to keep pace with the changing profile of a more educated and literate Malay listenership. More time should be devoted, for example, to the exploration and discussion of the difficult issues and challenges confronting the community that have been raised by the various contributors in this book.

Inche Yusof Ishak and Mr S. Rajaratnam meeting members of the Radio Singapore Orchestra at the auditorium. Image courtesy of Mun Chor Seng © 2016. All rights reserved.

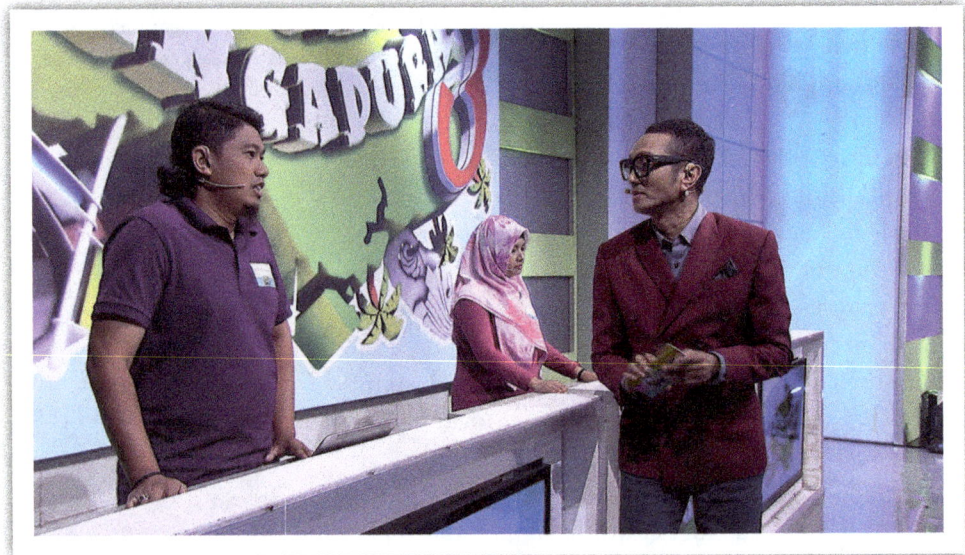

Hosted by Najip Ali, popular gameshow *Kita Orang Singapura* garnered strong following and viewership on Suria. Season 3 aired in 2016 featured a celebrity special finale episode where a total accumulated prize money collection of $16,400 was donated to Rainbow Centre Margaret Drive School. Image courtesy of Mediacorp © 2016. All rights reserved.

CHAPTER 28

THE ROLE OF MALAY MEDIA | Zakiah Halim

Introduction

The year 2016 marks the commemoration of 80 years of radio broadcasting in Singapore (also known as Radio80). Since its launch in 1936, this *Grand ole Dame* has continued to rule the airwaves, capturing the imagination of listeners for the past eight decades in spite of predictions that television (when it was first launched in 1963) and later on new media (in the 2000s), will kill the medium.

The year 2013 was a milestone for television as it celebrated its 50th Golden Jubilee. The older generation may recall the beginning of television in Singapore as a communal activity where the whole village flocked

Warna 94.2FM and Ria 89.7FM celebrated Radio80 with two events, an outdoor family carnival, *Viva Karnival* and a sold-out *Rentak Singapura — Anda Mau Rock* concert on 26 March 2016 at Mediacorp's new campus (1 Stars Avenue). Both events are supported by Suria and *Manja*. Image courtesy of Mediacorp © 2016. All rights reserved.

over to that one house with a TV set, until a period in time where the goggle box became a household necessity and watching TV became a favourite family activity. There was also great buzz and excitement when colour TV made its debut in 1974.

Television became a portal for the commentary of social issues in the 1980s and 1990s, when locally produced dramas graced the screen. The tears of the audience were matched with the smiles and laughter induced by a number of iconic music and entertainment-centred shows like *Pak Awang Temberang, Mat Yoyo, Hiburan Minggu Ini, Kelab Dondang Sayang* and *Adubakat. Seni Asli* was the first Malay info-ed programme on Malay culture. Since then, viewers have been entertained with a host of infotainment programmes like *Potret Keluarga, Selamat Pagi Singapura* and *Semarak Budaya*. Today, dramas, talk shows and variety programmes continue to be staples on TV. TV has certainly been like a friend, accompanying the audience through the good and sad times.

Riding on the success and popularity of the hit children show in the 1980s of the same name, *Mat Yoyo*, Mediacorp brought back the show to the screen in 2012 with four versions — English, Mandarin, Malay and Tamil — which were telecast on Okto, Channel 8, Suria and Vasantham channels respectively. Image courtesy of Mediacorp © 2016. All rights reserved.

Radio Malaya (Bahagian Melayu), as it was called then, with Programme Head, Zaharah Za'aba at the helm, aired many popular radio programmes. Over the years, listeners tuned in to programmes such as *Pentas Radio, Bangsawan, Suara Mahasiswa, Aslirama, Senda Mesra,* as well as current affairs programmes like *Berita dan Peristiwa* and *Tumpuan* that had kept listeners updated on important current issues. *Tumpuan* was radio's pride and joy when it won "Most Outstanding Radio Station" in the Asia Pacific Region at the 1986/87 Pater International Broadcasting Awards held in Australia.

The only Malay-language lifestyle and entertainment monthly magazine, Manja, has also been a must-read for 16 years by the community. Manja is packed with celebrity updates and discerning tips for the urban Malays.

The Malay media have certainly come a long way in being part of Singapore's history.

Mediacorp Malay Community

The Malay media has been serving the Malay community to inform, entertain and update the public through its different platforms. These include TV channel, Mediacorp Suria, radio stations Warna 94.2FM and Ria 89.7FM as well as lifestyle magazine, Manja, that are collectively a one-stop entertainment hub and home to popular local programmes and thought-provoking current affairs series.

Pater Award Winners, Inon Salleh, Zakiah Halim, Surtini Sarwan with Malay Radio Controller, Hashim Yusof , Radio Director, Raymond Huang at a celebratory lunch with then Minister for Communications and Information, Dr Yeo Ning Hong. Image courtesy of Mediacorp © 2016.

Manja's covers featuring local artistes, and its Open House event at Jurong Point Mall. Image courtesy of Mediacorp © 2016.

Since the merger in 2015, Suria, Warna, Ria and Manja have grown even stronger and closer with the Malay community, providing a convenience for the community to stay in touch with reliable news, progressing with them in good and challenging times, as well as significant milestones such as the General Elections, the National Day Parade, the launch of key organisations like MENDAKI, the Association of Muslim Professionals (AMP) and the passing of our national icon, Mr Lee Kuan Yew.

The Malay media have also given their best support for many charitable organisations and worthy causes including non-profit organisations like Tabung Amal Aidilfitri (TAA) through charity concert *Sinaran Hati* and Ain Society through *Projek Kasih*.

Suria

Since its inception in 2000, Suria has kept its audience informed on the latest information from around the world with *Berita* and its current affairs series such as *Detik* and *#ForumSG*. Suria holds the pulse of the Malay community in all its local programmes. From skilfully crafted dramas that become instant hits, to fun and entertaining variety shows, staged with top local and international artistes, Suria has continued to progress and is capturing more eyeballs today.

Its tagline "Suria, Sinar Bersama Anda" (Suria Shines with You) reflects the channel's commitment to be the heartbeat of the Malay community. With its diverse offerings of programmes, Suria hopes to reflect the affluent new breed of Malay Singaporeans.

Left: *Rapsodi 2015* marked the 25th anniversary of Memorandum of Understanding (MOU) Concerning Co-operation in the Field of Broadcasting and Information between Singapore and Brunei Darussalam. Co-produced by Mediacorp Suria and Radio dan Televisyen Brunei (RTB), *Rapsodi* is an annual gala variety show jointly produced by the two TV stations with Singapore and Brunei taking turns to host the event. Right: Mediacorp Suria and Radio Televisyen Malaysia (RTM) jointly present the 10th instalment of MOU variety special, *Muzika Ekstravaganza* in 2016. The concert was broadcast 'live' from Kuala Lumpur and paid tribute to the late well-loved icon of the Malay entertainment industry, Tan Sri P Ramlee. Image courtesy of Mediacorp © 2016. All rights reserved.

Suria has also opened doors and produced some of Singapore's brightest talents through its popular reality shows such as *Anugerah*, *Anugerah Skrin*, *Ratu* and *SG Mania*.

At the regional level, Suria has collaborations with counterparts from Brunei, Malaysia and Indonesia, staging programmes like *Sukmairama* (which is now called *Rapsodi*), *Muzika Extravaganza* and *Fiesta Muzik*.

Warna 94.2FM and Ria 89.7FM

Warna and Ria are the most popular Malay radio stations in Singapore. Engaging the community in new and exciting ways through its lifestyle magazine programmes, the radio stations also offer infotainment and often reminisce the past through evergreen songs. Listeners could enjoy a wide range of music programmes, from Malay rock hits, to pop and contemporary genres, anchored by popular radio deejays who have become household names.

Radio has progressed through time with more interactivity for better engagement with the listeners. Since the 1980s, it has started to have "live" call-ins via phones and also interacted with the listeners via SMS, inviting them to send requests or taking part in contests or just to have a chat like good, old friends. The 1990s was also the period where Warna and Ria started featuring its personalities, bringing them out to on-the-ground events and getting closer with the fans instead of just

Left: Anugerah Planet Muzik 2014's big winners; from left Sufie Rashid, Taufik Batisah and Aisyah Aziz. Right: Sharing the same stage at APM 2014 — Cakra Khan, Sufie Rashid and Hazama. Image courtesy of Mediacorp © 2016. All rights reserved.

Left: Local band A. Ramlie & The Rhythm Boys that set the 1960s *Pop Yeh Yeh* phenomenon was awarded the Planet Music Special Award at *Anugerah Planet Muzik 2015* as a tribute for their involvement and contribution to both the local and regional Malay music industry. Right: Established band, NOAH, received their Best Band and APM Most Popular Artiste awards at *Anugerah Planet Muzik 2014*. Image courtesy of Mediacorp © 2016. All rights reserved.

Anugerah Planet Muzik is a worldwide Twitter-trending event and for more than a decade, it has been a platform for artistes and musicians from Singapore, Malaysia, Indonesia and Brunei to showcase their talents. Left: Opening of *Anugerah Planet Muzik 2015* by Siti Nurhaliza. Right: Anggun receiving the International Breakthrough Artiste award at the same event. Image courtesy of Mediacorp © 2016. All rights reserved.

being "voices behind the microphones". Warna and Ria has also successfully produced an annual mega concert featuring local and regional artistes through *Anugerah Planet Muzik* (APM), with sold-out tickets, worldwide trending and massive viewership and coverage from Singapore, Indonesia, Malaysia and Brunei.

Summary

Suria, Warna and Ria have established a strong trans-media presence as we continue to engage our viewers and listeners on various social media platforms and Toggle online, with audience engagement, webisodes, exclusive footage and 360° media campaigns — enriching their experience from on-air, online and on-the-ground. Local programmes are now in High Definition (HD) and can be viewed online at any time.

The Malay media is also geared towards making media and entertainment more robust, creatively more vibrant and socially more meaningful with the strong alignment and merger of transmedia platforms. Committed to being the heartbeat of the Malay community, Suria, Warna, Ria and Manja hope to continue to be the integral part of the community, engaging them in new and exciting ways.

In 2015, Ria 89.7FM organised a youth forum, *Tanya AP Anda — Edisi Belia (Ask Your MP — Youth Edition)*. This special forum provides a platform for junior college and tertiary students to interact with the Malay Members of Parliament and share their concerns on national and Malay/Muslim community issues. The forum was an extension of the successful radio series that was aired on Warna 94.2FM. Image courtesy of Mediacorp © 2016. All rights reserved.

Kasih Berbisik is a drama series produced under a joint venture agreement signed between Suria and Malaysia's Media Prima. Filming for the 13-episode series took place in three countries —Singapore, Malaysia and Indonesia. Image courtesy of Mediacorp © 2016. All rights reserved.

Rudy & Rilla is another of Suria's talkshow that is well-received by the Malay viewers. It has become a household name and is now into its sixth season this year. The programme highlights social issues faced by the Malay/Muslim community, and apart from an encouraging increase in viewership season-to-season, more importantly, it has managed to have a stronger audience engagement and participation especially through Facebook and Twitter. From these responses, we can see that the community is now more receptive and willing to share their laments and opinions with the rest of the community. Image courtesy of Mediacorp © 2016. All rights reserved.

CHAPTER 29

SINGAPORE MALAY MEDIA INDUSTRY SHINES | Muhd Fuadi Rahmat*

B ack in the 1960s, every household was glued to their black and white television watching *Pak Awang Temberang*, the series that provided some backdrop on the Singapore landscape. The main actor, the late Salim Bachik, became a household name and because of its huge popularity, it even set the trend for a successful drama format then. Pak Awang's furniture also became a must-have for many Malay families back then. Other famous series include *Kalong Senandong* and *Keroncong*, where talents such as Datin Paduka Julie Sudiro, the late Datuk Ahmad Daud and Kartina Dahari became famous. The early directors of the Malay media industry include the late Bani Buang, Mockram Kassim and now retired Wahidah Jalil, Rohayaton Rohani and Fatimah Arpah (Variety/Info-Educational/ Children), all of whom were well respected by industry players. Apart from television, both *bangsawan* and *sandiwara* on radio also attracted quite a number of followers. With her unique and expressive voice, the late radio deejay Faridah Hanim together with Hamid Ahmad became the talk of the town. The Singapore Malay media industry has since shone since the days of *Pak Awang Temberang*. From black and white to

* Contributor was previously the Deputy Head of Suria and former Business Development Manager with MediaCorp TV 12. He is also a member of the Programme Advisory Committee for English and Malay Content (PACE, MPAC), Media Development Authority. This article was contributed in his personal capacity. The views expressed are his own and do not necessarily represent the views of Suria, PACE, MPAC and MDIS.

colour, analog to digital and standard to high definition, here is a recap of some of the talents and programmes that added colour and zest to the Malay media in Singapore.

Talents

Previously, talents for television came from theatre and dance groups such as Sriwana, Sri Warisan, Perkumpulan Seni and Sri Anggerik, just to name a few. Many veterans such as Madam Ponisah Bachik, the late Zulkassim Daud, and many more started from both theatre and radio. Other veteran radio personalities with their very own unique voices include the late Hamid Ahmad, M. Safri A. Manaf and radio's very own DJ, Mohd Asyik. Their evergreen presence on screen and on air had indisputably set the standard for many budding talents to follow, even till today. Current award winning actors such as Rafaat Hamzah, Azhar Noor Lesta, Muhammad Najib Soiman, Khairuddin Shamsuddin and actresses Seri Wahyuni, Wahyu Rahman as well as Mastura Ahmad also started with theatre before making it big on television.

Mat Yoyo at the Singapore Zoological Gardens, one of the few venues that the show travelled to, meeting fans and viewers on the ground. Photo circa 1985. Image courtesy of Samri Badi. Copyright © Samri Badi.
All rights reserved.

For the young, Madam Nona Asiah was a mother figure and she was instrumental in producing many young prodigies who excelled in singing, hosting and acting. Celebrities such as Djohan Abdul Rahman, Rilla Melati, Khairuddin Samsudin and Faisal Ishak all had emerged from her talent development initiative *Bengkel Kanak-Kanak*. Arguably, the *Mat Yoyo* series was one of the most successful children's programme since independence. Having the well-known comedian Mat Sentol as their elderly mentor, the cat icons, Yoyo and Yaya, and their fun personalities attracted much interest from both children and their parents. The winning formula of singing and dancing added excitement and curiosity to the growing mind of a child. The producers weaved in many social values in the scripts such as respecting the elders, appreciating culture/arts and helping the needy. The show was revived recently and produced in other languages — English, Chinese and Tamil for their respective channels. With similar concepts and treatment, other kids programme, *Ya Aliff* and *Krayon*, also garnered above average ratings from both the Malay and non-Malay audiences. Perhaps for many children now, they do not need to learn to read as early to develop their imagination. All their fantasies, bedtime stories, fairy tales and dreams are now shown in the exciting and wonderful living colour on television. *Krayon*, *Ya Aliff* and *Mat Yoyo* are clear examples of such winning formula, which also became platforms to identify young talents.

There were also many talent competitions that were produced to identify and showcase budding talents for both young and old. These include the *Juara* and *Anugerah* series. Fauzie Laily, a second runner-up winner in Singapore's Malay channel annual singing competition *Anugerah*, is an example of such a success story, having many singing and hosting stints, as well as acting roles in local productions on both Suria and the English channel in Singapore, Channel 5. Many who came from the series have launched their own albums. They included Sarah Aqilah and Aliff Aziz, among many others. The recent *Anugerah Skrin* series iden-

Special 10th Anniversary Celebration of Mat Yoyo show held at Sentosa's Amphitheatre in 1992. Attended by more than 20,000 fans, the show had to be re-staged in the afternoon, as many could not be seated for the morning show. Image courtesy of Samri Badi. Copyright © Samri Badi. All rights reserved.

tified many raw diamonds in the acting and hosting arena. Auditions were often held in the heartlands, providing a more engaging platform between Suria and the community. Previous winners include Huda Ali,

Shah Iskandar and Nurul Aini, celebrities who had opportunities to act in large-scale Malaysian productions for television and film. They had managed to captivate many fans, both in Singapore and from the region.

In the 1990s, Haney Hadad and Zarinah Safuan were the eye candies of the MTV generation. As hosts and MTV V-jays, they were considered the teen idols of the Malay media industry, and had introduced many Malay songs to the region. In fact, many youths were driven to the MTV Channel because of its more unique and creative approach on programming. This proves that local talents do have quality and is on par with international standards. Some local talents did make it big across the Causeway, where the industry is bigger. Artistes such as Aaron Aziz, Adi Putra, Hisyam Hamid and Shah Iskandar are perfect examples. Their professionalism is acknowledged and appreciated with the accolades they have received there. Others who had ventured successfully include actress Norish Karman, rapper-songwriter Daly (formerly with Ahli Fiqir), and singing duo Sleeq, having collaborated with Malaysian singers Najwa Latif and Ramlah Ram. Without a doubt, singer-songwriters M. Nasir and Ramli Sarip are the most recognised Singaporean talents who have established themselves as strongholds in the Malaysian music and media industry. Both were conferred the title "Datuk" in recognition of their contributions to the music industry.

Programmes

For Suria, with Basir Siswo at the helm, much of the programming reflected a lot on the community. From an initial emphasis on news and information, it shifted to a more balanced scheduling, with more variety in genres including drama, info-educational (info-ed), children, variety and also culture. MediaCorp's in-house production arm, Eaglevision led by Suhaimi Jais, with its strong pool of talented producers and directors provided the regular staple programming for the Malay channel. Tear-jerking drama series such as *Jeritan Sepi*, *Gerimis Di*

Hati and *Rahsia Perkahwinan* received overwhelming ratings in the history of the industry.

Selamat Pagi Singapura was Suria's signature Sunday morning info-ed programme, and it generated high ratings consistently for more than five seasons from 1998 to 2004. Its earlier hosts were Sujimy Mohamad and Ainah Embit, and were later replaced with Sharon Ismail and Khairuddin Saharom. Both pairs of hosts had perfect chemistry with each other that related well to the audience. Complete with interesting segments and comic relief from the late Ishak Ahmad, the show became a must-watch for Singaporean Malays to keep them updated and informed over the morning weekend.

Public adherence is what empowers the media's intent and overall impact, depending on what is being portrayed in it. The controversial series, *Anak Metropolitan* and arguably *Bara*, had the Malay audience involved in endless debates over the portrayal of delinquent youths and issues such as drug abuse, gangsterism and teenage pregnancy. The highly-rated programmes were well-researched but created much debate on the responsibility of the media in portraying the situation and raising awareness for certain pockets of the community, without resorting to sensationalising for dramatic effect. With the previous success of the earlier two seasons, *Anak Metropolitan 3*, produced in

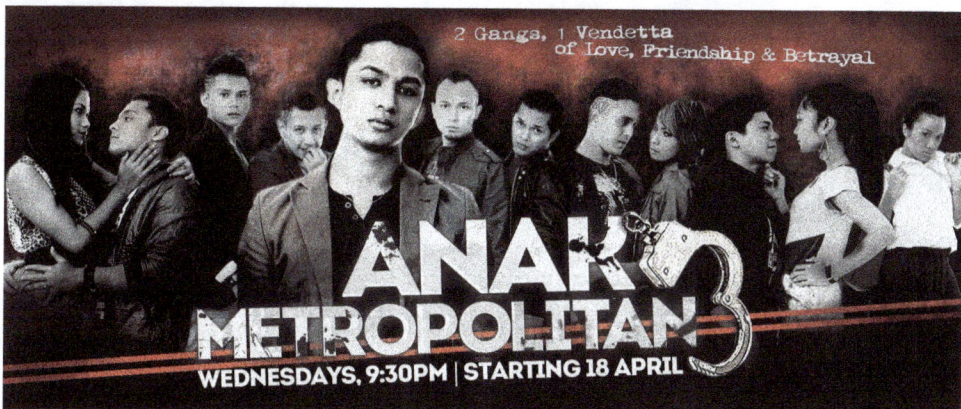

Poster promotion for *Anak Metropolitan 3*. Image courtesy of Mediacorp © 2016.

2012, garnered another respectable rating. Real life admissions of ex-convicts, who had turned over a new leaf, were included at the end of each episode and that added credibility to the issues raised.

With *Tetangga*, a series that promoted neighbourliness and social cohesion, it had a multiracial cast that added colour to the series. Malaysian actress and comedian Sheila Rusly was paired with a local comedian, Suhaimi Yusof, and generated much interest from non-Malay viewers. Veteran executive producers Khamaliah Salleh and Azizah Malik portrayed Singapore's very own real-life heartlanders and their antics with good scripts that reflected very well on relationships between the multiracial neighbours.

Within the variety or entertainment genre, the regular festive special shows were something many Singaporean Malays looked forward to. Often glamorous, well-produced and structured, there were also comedy segments that provided many talking points even after the shows were over. One of the shows, *Salam Lebaran*, celebrated our Malay culture and heritage garnered high ratings including reaching out to many non-Malays. Executive producers Sabariah Ramilan and Amiruddin Abbas from Eaglevision often pushed boundaries and kept viewers occupied in the final preparations on the eve of Hari Raya's.

Much was also done on the news and current affairs genre, which often had a more mature and well-informed target audience. *Detik* and *Berita* are key programmes that provided in-depth insights on many issues that affect the community. Often seen as the provider of first-hand news on and for the community and to the community, many issues were addressed. Experts and community leaders were often

Phua Chu Kang (Gurmit Singh) and the late Ishak Ahmad appearing in a skit in *Muzika Ekstravaganza*, the first show of the yearly co-production between Mediacorp and RTM, held at Mediacorp TV Theatre in 2004. Image courtesy of Mediacorp © 2016. All rights reserved.

invited to provide a more balanced perspective. The appreciation of news has also migrated from the television screen to the social media platforms where the same issues were often discussed more actively.

Suria also showcased many high quality and credible info-ed programmes. Series such as *Digit, Jalan, ReTV, Jus, ForumSg, Kembara Kasih* and *Secupak Harapan* were well-researched info-ed, documentaries and magazine series, with excellent hosts and good narratives that helped stimulate learning and acquiring of knowledge.

To add variety, there were also experimental initiatives for a more creative treatment with series such as *KOTT* (*Kopi O Teh Tarik*), *Gerek* and *Cinta Bollywood*. The unique approach of *KOTT* and the *Gerek* series with the animated and evergreen Najib Ali as its host attracted promoted the Singapore spirit and attracted more youthful viewers. The initial idea of having a legendary Bollywood star featured in a Malay drama series was something to look forward to by the network. *Cinta Bollywood* featured Aaron Aziz and Suhaila Salam, and was directed by the talented Faisal Ishak and Chetan Shah. The series was subsequently acquired by NTV7, a free-to-air terrestrial television channel in Malaysia. It took the honour as the first Singapore-made Malay programme to be distributed regionally. The theme song sung by then newcomer Lynn Nasir became one of the most downloaded ring tone.

With the expansion of Suria programming hours, it attracted many independent production houses to provide media content for the channel. The likes of MYI, Comm 2000, IMO productions, FLIP Creatives, ScreenBox, Dua M, Cokelat Productions and Shortman Films, just to name a few, and with their very own specialties, had provided many good alternative programmes for viewers. Both independent production houses and Eaglevision had provided a multitude of genres to whet the appetite of the Malay audience. Additionally, quality foreign programmes were also acquired to provide a wider range of relevant content.

Awards

To acknowledge the contributions of those in the media industry, the award show *Pesta Perdana* was introduced in 2001. The show aimed to recognise, acknowledge and honour the best talents in the Malay television industry. Suria celebrated the 13th edition of this prestigious biannual awards show that took viewers down the memory lane with the 50s theme.

The rock group Wings from Malaysia was awarded the Planet Music Special Award for their contribution to the region's music industry. Image courtesy of Mediacorp © 2016. All rights reserved.

In 2001, MediaCorp Radio, introduced a regional award show *Anugerah Planet Muzik* (APM) which gathered musicians from around the region and introduced Singapore as a potential Malay Music hub. Often grandiose and also glamorous, the show brought together the region's best musicians and composers. Many local talents, including heartthrob Taufiq Batisah and Hardy Mirza had the opportunities to compete with the best including Datuk Siti Nurhaliza, Anggun and many more. There was also a 'live' simulcast — the result of a collaboration between the Malaysian cable Broadcaster ASTRO and Suria.

Memorandum of Understanding (MOU)

Other than reaching out to the Singapore community, broadcasters need be more proactive to compete in the region and globally. Through government initiatives, there are now many collaborations and partnership between broadcasters and networks. Joint MOUs in the area of broadcasting between Singapore and its neighbours Brunei, Malaysia and Indonesia, help to build better working relationships. These further encouraged the sharing of ideas and skills that will help to raise the quality and standards of the industry in the region. *Sukmairama*, *Rapsodi*, *Muzika*

Extravaganza and *Fiesta Muzik* were some of the variety programmes that showcased talents from participating countries. Other interesting collaborative programmes among these countries include *Titian Minda*, a debate in collaboration between youths from Singapore and Brunei, and *Xpedisi Siswa*, an experiential learning collaboration in the form of a reality TV programme involving undergraduates from Singapore and Brunei.

Challenges — Present and Future

Future challenges in the Malay media industry in Singapore are on talent development, raising the standards of professionalism, channel aggregations and rising up to equal opportunities across other channels in the industry. Engagement between all stakeholders including broadcasters, talents, education institutions, independent production houses, as well as the authorities would aid in raising the standards of professionalism and quality of the Malay media industry. Often driven by passion, the majority of the talents are amateurs or freelancers in the industry on a part-time basis. For the sustainability of the local Malay media industry, such talents should be supported and groomed further for a more vibrant industry.

Muzika Ekstravaganza is an annual gala variety show featuring artistes from Singapore and Malaysia, with the two countries taking turns to host the event each year. It is co-produced by Mediacorp's Suria and Radio Television Malaysia (RTM). The show underscores the close bilateral ties and provides a platform for collaboration between officials, broadcasters and artistes from both countries. Image courtesy of Mediacorp © 2016. All rights reserved.

The much-needed upgrading of skills include the development of individual talents to more than just the practical knowledge, but also towards a holistic understanding of the industry. It would be useful for all talents to appreciate and develop themselves in other areas within the industry, such as production management, understanding media laws and financial planning. Independent production houses should also explore more co-productions across regions that will indirectly develop more business opportunities, encouraging more new ideas and fostering creativity.

There are already some who are bold enough to explore and venture to new platforms; from television to the more challenging big screen, such as Papahan Films. Its Creative Director, M. Raihan Halim constantly pushes the boundaries with new narratives and storytelling in Papahan Film's first feature film released in 2014, *Banting*. The controversial film tells the story of Yasmin, a young woman in hijab and raised in a strict Muslim household who finds her passion in life when she begins to secretly take professional wrestling lessons. The feature film has successfully penetrated the Malaysian media industry when it screened in Malaysian cinemas in 2015 and was also offered on Malaysian on-demand channel Astro First.

One of the most talented directors Singapore has ever produced; Sanif Olek is also constantly pushing for new ideas. In 2013, his very own short film, *Sayang Di Sayang*, travelled across the globe and won the Jury Award in the Philippines. The film was also showcased in many regional film festivals. There should be more of such individuals who are constantly chasing their dreams and breaking barriers.

The representation of Malays on other channels, other than Suhaimi Yusof, is now more prominent, where Elfaeza Ul Haq, Fauzie Laily, Syirah Jusni, Mastura Ahmad, Rahman Rahim, as well as Hatta Said are already featured in the Channel 5 series *Tanglin*, a more than 100-episode local drama production on the lives of multiracial and multigenerational families of a middle-income neighbourhood in the Tanglin area of Singapore.

More could be done to collaborate with other Malay/Muslim organisations (MMOs) for a more holistic and integrated approach towards developing the community. Collaborations with Ain Society's *Project Kasih*, TAA's *Sinaran Hati* and 4PM's *Bahas* are a few of such initiatives. It is important that Suria remain relevant and attuned to on-the-ground needs. This could further provide a much needed effort or push towards better awareness, and drive to support the needy and minimise gaps within the community. Consistent and regular engagement with the relevant authorities, associations, ministries, unions and also statutory boards such as MENDAKI or MUIS could provide fresher and more current media content.

Media can also play an important role to help promote the development and preservation of arts and culture as well as the proper usage of the Malay language. More collaboration with various arts and culture group locally and regionally could enhance the appreciations of such unique and colourful practices. In fact, platforms such as Malay Heritage Centre and the future Wisma Geylang Serai could be the ideal platforms for Media to have joint productions or partnership.

The future however, cannot just rely on past successes. Raw diamonds need to be identified and polished. There should be more opportunities for youth or budding talents to showcase their works. More could be done to encourage professionals to mentor and guide these young minds before they embark into the challenging Media industry. Ideally, there should be a separate independent hour within the transmission hours that allow students and new talents to present their quality works. Broadcasters should take the initiative and provide platforms by collaborating with educational institutions for a more concerted effort to tap into the already available sources of creative talents and minds of the future. Creativity cannot be something routine and done repeatedly from an old formula but it needs development from minds that are more adaptive, flexible and relevant.

Success for broadcasting should be measured, not by the number of viewership or high ratings, but also by the ability to move and elevate the community to the next level of success. With creativity within its programmes, there are ample opportunities to reach, educate and inform.

For sustainability and recognition, more could be done to promote Singapore-made programs globally. With more than 20 years of experience and its many high quality productions, Suria could consider distributing its whole channel and reach to a much wider audience. This will bring the Singaporean Malay media to a global stage, and in turn, raise the quality of its productions. Cable channels such as 'Sensasi' on

Starhub, ASTRO Singtel Mio and other Indonesian Channels are clear examples of aggregated platforms with Malay content which Suria could emulate.

As highlighted by the PSB review panel committee in 2012, in many countries including Singapore, a lot of emphasis is being placed on Public Service Broadcast or PSB, as an essential tool to shape and reflect their very own unique national and cultural identity. Often, these include catering to the increasingly demanding and many diverse viewing needs and interests. Especially so in an affluent society like Singapore, with its vast heterogeneous population, PSB aims to help promote the growth of a common identity and shared heritage, while at the same time, also celebrating Singapore's multicultural and multiracial society.

The review further added that Singapore is currently facing something similar. A growing proportion of the population, especially the young who are "digital natives," is turning to online platforms for multimedia content. Global sites like Netflix, Vimeo, Facebook, and YouTube rank among the most-accessed multimedia sites in Singapore. There are already huge followers of Singapore Press Holdings very own Razor TV and the controversial STOMP. Print media including Berita Harian are already gaining momentum and popularity in their interactive online platforms to cater to the digital native's generations.

Fortunately, there are also now online platforms such as Mediacorp's Toggle to help introduce PSB content. Suria needs to create all the available platforms to reach out and market itself. Talents need to learn to adapt and constantly embrace new skills in the ever-changing landscape. New technology, the YouTube phenomena and the constant push for more liberalisation will challenge the initial values created by the founding leaders to nurture and protect Singapore citizens. Media was constantly used as a platform to educate and inform. Leadership within the industry must be vigilant to ensure the key principles are protected. These include protecting the vulnerable and providing balanced directions without being seen as too reactive, restrictive or prescriptive. The integrity of our value system that is often guided and influenced by religion and cultural practices that placed community first, should remain protected. Adapting does not necessarily mean compromising on our value system, but instead, for more inclusivity broadcasters should actively engage all its stakeholders and deliberate for that important and necessary change or changes.

Undoubtedly, there are still many more milestones for broadcaster to achieve. It needs to remain creative, resilient, forward looking and adaptive. Funding and talents will remain limited, and may not necessarily be exclusive. However, no matter what the limitations and challenges are, change will be constant and the broadcaster cannot lose itself in its endeavour (of flame) to reach out to the community and shine.

Suria's latest blockbuster is a four-episode drama *Bunga Tanjong* set in the 1950s and 1960s. Image courtesy of Mediacorp © 2016. All rights reserved.

Bibliography

1. Public Service Broadcast (PSB) Review Panel Report, 2012.

"My hope is that Malay TV productions in this region will move in tandem with the rest of the world. I am glad that with new technology, viewers are able to find the contents they desire via traditional sets, online and social media. However, technology can't by itself create good content. The demand for high standards of TV programmes continues to be a challenge for all programme makers. Great television programmes are created by teams with soft skills, those with rare and precious talents — story makers, performing talents and producers and directors with a special gift. Only a selected few have the ability to connect with audiences and tell great stories. My wish is that the business in creating TV stories in Singapore will flourish further for our broadcast industry to continue to have that cutting edge."

Sabariah Ramilan
Vice-President
Eaglevision

CHAPTER 30

GLIMPSES OF 50 YEARS OF MALAY TV | Aidi Abdul
AND ITS FUTURE | Rahim

O n 2 April 1963, President Yusof Ishak officially inaugurated the regular service of *Television Singapura*. It began broadcasting from 7.15 pm to 11.15 pm every day, showing programmes in Singapore's four official languages. On 23 November 1963, a second channel, Channel 8 was inaugurated. It took over Chinese and Tamil programming, while English and Malay programming remained on Channel 5. This essay brings the reader down memory lane of Malay TV programmes over the last five decades providing a brief background of some of the iconic TV shows and explores briefly the challenges of Malay TV broadcast in the new millennium.

Malay TV Dramas through the Years

The famous Malay programme on 5 in the early days of TV was the *sandiwara* (drama), *Pak Awang Temberang* (Bombast of Pak Awang). The show depicted how the family of Pak Awang adapted to living in the high-rise public housing flat upon their shift from their *kampung* house. The show was very popular and lasted from 1966 to 1968 and was shot mainly in the studio. The two lead actors were Salim Bachik as Pak Awang and Zainon Ismail as Mak Oteh. The popularity of this show led to other new Malay dramas such as *Mama Sayang Papa* (Mum loves Dad), *Pahit-Pahit Manis* (Sweet and Sour) and *Masa* (Time). To meet with the strong viewer interest of TV dramas, 5 had set aside two time slots each week. Every Sunday, Malay drama fans were satisfied with a 30-minute household drama and a one-hour drama on either a Tuesday or Wednesday. It was not unexpected that viewers found the studio scenes to be monotonous and many made their views known in the local Malay paper, *Berita Harian*. Readers had commented that while drama shows need to step up in the quality of the storylines and dialogues, there were praises for dramas like *Hilang Kabus Nampaklah Ia* (1970) that portrayed the hypocrisy of the elites that were obstructing the community's progress.

Colour TV came to Singapore in 1976 and the first Malay programme to be shown in colour was a *purbawara* (ancient drama) *Jejak Kembara* (Wandering Steps) written by Nadiputra and Ramli Ahmad. It told the story of two powerful district chiefs fighting over resources and had the dramatic elements of *pencak silat*, traditional costumes and lyrical dialogues.

On 1 February 1980, Radio and Television Singapore, which was under the Ministry of Culture, became partially privatised by an Act of Parliament and was launched as Singapore Broadcasting Corporation (SBC). The Malay drama unit was created and for the first-time had a full-time scriptwriter instead of depending on part-timers to do the job. Drama script writing and acting workshops were organised to develop a pool of writers. During this early period, the dramas reflected themes about the adjustments from *kampung* living to living in a high-rise flat, the importance of education for a better future and the usual stories about family love and bonding. There was the introduction of a novel drama format — the serial drama — *Sepanjang Jalan* (The Long Road) and *Dedaun Masa* (Leaves of Time), both lasting 14 episodes each. In the 1980s, scriptwriting for Malay TV dramas saw new blood injected as permanent scriptwriters (Nadiputra, Hamed Ismail, Anwar Hassanuddin, Maznah Hj Abdul Hamid, Nik Fatimah Ismail and Hartinah Ahmad) were exploring themes with startling twists in the plot, writing sit-coms and adapting foreign books to local TV drama. *Asap Peluru Bunga Cinta* (1986) was a love story set during the Japanese

Occupation in Singapore but ended in tragedy because the male lover was shot by his girlfriend when he professed to wanting to return to his fiancé rather than marry her when the war was over. There were also book adaptations that were turned into dramas; one that caused viewer outrage was *Sketsa Cinta Biru* (1991), adapted from a Japanese novel by Y. Kawabata, whereby a young man slept with the ex-lover of his father. Hamed Ismail was the proponent and scriptwriter of these book adaptations for Malay TV dramas.

Interestingly too, sensitive topics like homosexuality was explored despite Singapore's strict censorship policy. The dramas were *Laut Tak Bertepi* (A Sea Without a Shore) and *Birat Gincu* (Lipstick Scab) with the latter directed by Khamaliah Salleh. SBC also pleased the appeal of *bangsawan* enthusiasts with the TV dramatisation of *Iskandar Jauhari* (1984), *Bispuraja* (1988), *Puteri Sakdung* (1989) and *Sang Rajuna Tapa* (1990) that was scripted by the *bangsawan* veteran Abdul Hamid Ahmad.

In a significant development, on October 1994, SBC was privatised as Television Corporation of Singapore (TCS), Radio Corporation of Singapore (RCS) and Singapore TV12 (STV12). All Malay television programmes came under STV12 under the channel Prime12. SBC's Malay Drama Unit saw a name changed to Eaglevision. With this new development, Malay viewers had high expectations in the variety Malay programmes shown on TV. Malay TV drama was no longer the single drama episode. Instead viewers were presented with serial dramas as the new norm. Another novelty at that time was to invite local Malay drama groups to stage comedy shows under the *Teater Komedi* programme. The response from drama groups to do comedy was very encouraging in the initial years but in the third year, it became difficult to obtain quality comedy scripts and hence the permanent writers in Eaglevision (formerly the Malay Drama Unit) had to step in to accomplish this role.

On January 2000, Suria was launched to replace STV12 under the Mediacorp Group. The new free-to-air channel targeted about 504,000 persons who identified themselves as Malays in the population census. According to Kwek (2011), Malay Language programming more than doubled from 23 hours to 56 hours with the launch of Suria. Suria as a Malay TV channel operates almost as a monopolist and is dependent on TV advertising and sponsorship revenue. This operational model has consequences in terms of meeting Malay viewership needs and demands, fans, ratings, audience as commodity for advertisers and target for state propaganda.

With the launch of Suria, there was more broadcasting hours that needed to be filled with Malay programmes. New opportunities were also created with the sprouting of new productions houses to meet the supply for new Malay TV programmes. In this new broadcasting environment, scripts for Malay drama, info-educational and variety shows could be submitted by any interested parties (or production houses) other than Eaglevision. Competition was strong among the production houses but the quality of the story proposals and scripts was not of a high standard because of inexperienced writers and the unfamiliarity of the viewing preferences of the local Malay TV audience. From time to time, viewers were presented with TV shows from Malaysia and Indonesia that were acquired by Suria.

Children's Programmes through the Years

The first children's programme in the Malay during the early days of TV was *Teropong Si Mamat* (Mamat's Telescope) that covered the adventures of Mamat with his telescope. Another related programme targeted at kindergarten kids is *Intan,...Oh Intan* (1971) that had an adult as the "mother" to a group of young children learning the alphabets, numbers and learning basic general knowledge. Another children's programme that received positive public response was *Suara Adik-Adik* (Little Voices) that showcased young talents of their acting, singing, dancing, story telling and palying musical instruments. Many parents had auditioned their children for this programme to uncover any hidden talents of their children might have which no other organisations or private companies were doing then. The most iconic kids programme in the 1980s was *Mat Yoyo* later known as *Aksi Mat Yoyo*, a Malay children's programme that was screened in the mid-1980s and which ran for 12 years. In 2012, this programme was revived as *Mat Yoyo, the Next Generation*, which was fashioned into English, Mandarin and Tamil versions. This Malay children's TV show generated a lot of interest among non-Malay viewers as well.

Children's programmes in the present Suria era covered a wider genre in terms of objectives, concept and format. According to the 2000 and 2010 census, more Malay children are speaking less Malay in the households; the Suria producers planned Malay language learning and enrichment programmes to address this problem. Quiz shows that developed the vocabulary, grammar and spelling of the Malay language and words for young viewers and school children were commissioned. These programmes include *Tahu Nahu* (2007); *Pantas Pintas* (2008) and *Cepat Tepat* (2009) and were conceptualised with inputs of Malay language experts from the Ministry of Education and the Singapore Malay Teachers Union.

The TV medium was also used to promote and engage young minds about Malay literature. Usually these programmes had an adult character that acted as the story teller and supported by young talents acting out the story. In 1980, the show *Datuk Harimau* was helmed by comedian Samad Ayob as the adult story teller, and later in 1986, Zulkassim Daud, a drama actor, as the adult story teller in a children's literature-based programme *Tok Selampit*. In *Tok Selampit*, stories and folktales from *Kisah Sang Nila Utama*, *Hikayat Panji Semirang* and *Badang* among others were acted out by children from the SBC TV workshop. In the new millennium, the children's programme *Almari Ajaib* (Magic Cupboard) stood out, bringing viewers to relive the time of that era when three friends discovered an antique cupboard that acted as a time tunnel. The storyline depicted and enabled the three young friends to experience the day to day things of the past like catching fish with a net and using baits, playing pulling the coconut frond and understanding the importance of the river to the lives of people in the past. Altogether *Almari Ajaib* ran for 13 episodes depicting old Malay stories such as *Mahsuri, Tun Fatimah, Si Luncai, Hang Tuah and Puteri Gunung Ledang* — which are some of the more familiar Malay historical and folk characters.

Future of Malay TV Broadcast

A more educated community, declining usage of Malay as a spoken language; a growing retiree or silver generation; people more connected to social media, the many options and wide availability of pay TV channels; rising religious piety and the increasing demand to voice and access to alternative points of views are factors that will have an impact on the viewership of Suria and other free-to-air Malay language channels. Viewership attrition of local Malay shows will be the elephant in the room. While novelty grabs early interests, it is quality scripts and compelling story lines, good acting, credible presenters and articulate guest speakers that will determine a programme's viewership and memorability. This requires programmes to be well-researched and produced, put in resources to meet the standards of similar programmes found on other pay TV channels and cover matters and social issues or community-based events that resonate with the Malay community's way of life, values, interests and aspirations. The Malay Television and Radio Programmes Advisory Committee (MPAC) had indicated that there is progress in the quality of programming over the years, but definitely more can be done. Local Malay broadcasters need to continuously improve and offer innovative styles and formats to the different TV genres. Suria has been repeatedly urged by the MPAC to ensure that their shows are not overly youth-centric and must also cater to the older generation. More can be done for the elderly with info-educational programmes on lifestyle tips, health information and inspiring stories which could encourage them to enjoy their golden years. The cultural diversity of the Malays around the region and the history of Nusantara are themes that have not been given sufficient attention by TV producers and these can be collaborated with local historians and cultural anthropologists. Such programmes have not been produced by cable channels and being Suria can take the opportunity to produce such programmes. At the same time, while negative characters usually makes stories compelling, good wins over evil or prohibiting what is wrong reflects a morally positive learning point that is more powerful with Malay TV viewers.

Commissioning editors and producers must be brave to challenge accepted beliefs of what and who is the average Malay TV viewer. It is a sad reflection of the Malay community if watching Suria shows is a "no brainer" (see Kwek 2011, p. 209) even though this may be the preference of the Malay viewer. Would it be timely for concept testing, test screening and a pilot is rolled out so as to avoid unnecessary waste of resources and being described as "not up to standard" and "lack of credibility" labelled at the drama, *Satu Jam*? (See MPAC Report 2006–2008, p. 8). This drama showcased different scenarios that took place within one real-time hour that received those descriptions). Some in the Malay community and in the industry view Malay TV programmes as not intellectually stimulating or plain boring. According to Kwek (2011, pp. 207–213), Malay TV producers are hemmed by a Malay TV audience that is described as being "Malay-Malays" with "a resistance to change", avoidance of conflict, "restricted by our [Malay] culture, the way we [Malays] look at things. While, on the other hand, the "Malay but not too Malay" TV producers who distinct themselves as "supposedly more progressive and open" to produce shows that can, according to the then Deputy Prime Minister Lee (2000), form "a national outlook and identity".

Conclusion

This essay provides an overview of the types of TV genres that was broadcasted over the last 50 years with glimpses into the different dramas, children's programmes, current affairs and info-educational programmes that were iconic. Variety shows that showcased established and budding local talents (*Pop Agenda, Hitz. sg*) remains the staple of a multi-genre TV channel like Suria and usually attract high viewership. Indeed, Suria has a dual function: meeting TV consumers' needs and also in "forming a national outlook and identity". Whatever genre of TV programmes, these create perceptions and generate reactions in viewers. At the January 2000 launching ceremony, Lee Hsien Loong highlighted that Suria was to "equip [its viewers] with the attitudes, values and instincts that make them culturally-vibrant and proud citizens of Singapore." This is achieved when broadcasters are in-tune with the viewers' changing preferences to be entertained, educated and informed. But at the same time, broadcasters must put in the resources and do the research to entice and engage viewers to new TV formats and themes. This threads a fine line between balancing communal sensibilities and comfort zone and trying out new things that are awkward initially. Unless local Malay TV production challenges the "no-brainer" mould of the Malay TV viewer, with the rapidly evolving media landscape, the viability and permanence of local Malay TV programmes will remain relevant to only some in the Singaporean Malay community.

Bibliography

Amanah Mustafi, "*Menyusuri Setengah Abad Rancangan Kanak-Kanak di TV Singapura*" in Yang Terukir — Bahasa dan Persuratan Melayu: Sempena 50 Tahun Kemerdekaan Singapura, Hadijah Rahmat, ed. Majlis Bahasa Melayu SIngapura: Singapura, 2015.

Hamed Ismail, "*Perkembangan Skrip Drama TV Sejak 1965*" in Yang Terukir — Bahasa dan Persuratan Melayu: Sempena 50 Tahun Kemerdekaan Singapura, Hadijah Rahmat, ed. Majlis Bahasa Melayu SIngapura: Singapura, 2015.

Kwek, Ivan, "*Malayness as a Mindset: When Television Producers Imagine Audiences as Malay*" in Melayu: Politics, Poetics and Paradoxes of Malayness, Mohamad Maznah and Syed Muhd Khairudin Aljunied eds., NUS Press: Singapore, 2011.

Lee, Hsien Loong, English translation of speech by DPM Lee Hsien Loong at the launch of Suria on Sunday, 30 January 2000, at TCS TV Theatre, Media Division, Ministry of Information and the Arts, 2000.

MediaCorp TV 12

IFTAR Kita Kita Kita Aje!!!
5 Oktober 2007

The big and happy family of then Mediacorp's TV12 in an annual Ramadan Iftar (Breaking of Fast) celebration. Staff and artistes from Suria and Eaglevision. Image courtesy of Mediacorp © 2016. All rights reserved.

ROLE OF THE MALAY TELEVISION AND RADIO PROGRAMMES ADVISORY COMMITTEE (MPAC)

Aidi Abdul Rahim

Since August 1995, the Malay Television and Radio Programmes Advisory Committee (MPAC) had been evaluating the content and quality of Malay TV and Radio programmes, commenting on the impact of these programmes on the Malay community and making suggestions on how these programmes can be improved. MPAC members were appointed by the Minister for Information, Communication and the Arts on a two-year term. MPAC reports are published at the end of the two year term that provides the committee's observation of programmes that attracted their attention and concerns and a section that sets out MPAC's expectations and recommendations on improving future programming. The MPAC undertook to:

- Provide advice and feedback on the range and quality of broadcast programmes on Suria, Sensasi, Warna and Ria as well as make recommendations for their improvement;
- Provided advice and feedback on the broadcasters' compliance with guidelines on programmes and advertisements;
- Provided advice to the Media Development Authority (MDA) on the validity of public complaints on programming; and
- Review and provide inputs on the MDA's review of guidelines for TV and radio content.

Overall, MPAC (2006–2008; 2008–2010; 2010–2012) observed that Malay programmes on TV have served their viewers well. The Malay dramas that depicted and reinforced positive family relations (*Rahsia Perkahwinan*) and the harmonious co-existence of multiracial neighbours (*Tetangga 2*) received high praises from members. Dramas that looked into the challenges facing youths (*Cinta Ixora, Ratna*) were commended for their fresh story lines. However, *Jeritan Sepi* was admonished by members and public feedback about disturbing scenes where alcohol was served in the presence of a minor (and other similar themes about promiscuity, infidelity, tattoos and teenage pregnancies) should be handled with care. Not unexpectedly,

MPAC advice was to present such scenes sensitively and not gratuitously so as not to offend the sensibilities and level of comfort of viewers. Similarly, *Anak Metropolitan 3*, a gritty portrayal of the social challenges faced by the lower-income group was red-flagged because there were no Helplines or telephone number included in the show to assist viewers who may be in similar circumstances. In fact, some viewers had written to the press to express their concern about the crude language used in the dialogue and the very realistic portrayal of problems faced by the drama characters. Suria's response was that the usual practice for previous dramas included Helpline telephone numbers but for *Anak Metropolitan 3*, advice was delivered through interviews with real-life past offenders and gang members who gave their opinions on the issues protrayed and what the drama characters could have done differently. While such personal accounts of real-life past offenders offer insights of what they would have done differently, it begs the question of whether an expert or a counsellor could have offered a more optimal solution instead?

It was suggested that current affairs programmes on Suria does not reach a wide viewership (although no figures were published in their MPAC Reports). Naturally, such programmes would attract lower viewership compared to entertainment and info-educational programmes (such as *Pantas Pintas, Singapura Syok, Kpak Bing Bing*) because current affairs programmes require a different type of viewer cognitive involvement. Weaving important information and facts in dramas and variety shows for the general audience if not handled well may somehow trivialise the significance of the issue. Apparently, Malay PMEBs (professionals, managers and executives and business persons) do not watch Malay language current affairs programmes; it was thought that they have access to other sources of information or the 8.30 pm prime slot timing was not convenient. When Suria wanted to shift the programmes *Detik, Bicara* and *Akhir Kata* from 8.30 pm to 10.30 pm later in the evening, the concern was that the general audience may have less access to watch such shows even though it was presumed that the later timeslot fitted nicely for the PMEBs. However, the challenge of attracting more viewership usually lies with the quality of the show and this means inviting quality and knowledgeable panellists and guest speakers. Quality interactions between the presenters and guest speakers presumes that speakers can engage at a level of discussion that goes beyond the obvious, raise ideas that challenges the orthodoxy and provide different perspectives. For serious issues to be discussed in an interesting manner boils down to the quality of the studio guests. MPAC members alluded to these issues when they highlighted in their 2010/2012 Report the "views of invited studio guests were often similar and this did not add value to the discussion".

Bibliography

1. 2006/2008 — Report by the Malay Programmes Advisory Committee.
2. 2008/2010 — Report by the Malay Programmes Advisory Committee.
3. 2010/2012 — Report by the Malay Programmes Advisory Committee.

CHAPTER 31

FROM RADIO TO TELEVISION — MY STORY | Sujimy Mohamad

I entered broadcasting in 1985. I was 16 then. A young radio producer, Zakiah Halim, auditioned me for a radio show and she took me under her wings and along with Suhaimi Yusof, Siti Rahimah and Rabaah, introduced us to the world of broadcasting and became our mentors.

Ever since then, I never looked back. The media and broadcasting industry resonated with me and I felt completely at home and at ease with it. Not many people then had that chance and I knew I was privileged and lucky. With the given opportunity, I was determined to understand its processes and get a helicopter view of the industry by connecting with as many broadcast professionals as possible. The mingling and networking led me to another door of opportunity when another producer/newscaster in Mediacorp, Sujadi Siswo, gave me a big break on television. He mentored me to read news on TV. In later years, Sujadi's brother, Basir Siswo, offered me a job as a TV Producer/Broadcast Journalist in

ScreenBox had won a number of awards for the Best Information Programme in Pesta Perdana[a] among them *647 km²* and *Hanyut* (Adrift). All images in this article courtesy of Sujimy Mohamad © 2016. All rights reserved.

---

[a] *Pesta Perdana* is the highly anticipated local award show which showcases quality local programmes with regional reach.

a current affairs programme *Tinjauan*. I am forever grateful to both Zakiah and the Siswo brothers for giving me the opportunity to be in the broadcast industry. Alhamdulillah.

When I joined Singapore Broadcasting Corporation (SBC) as a full-time Broadcast Journalist, TV was very much the only mass audio-visual platform consumers had. It was easy to get people's attention through television and it was the most powerful tool at that time. The challenge was only to produce captivating content and, if the content managed to land itself on TV, we will be able get many people to watch and be moved by the intended message.

My wife, Haslinda Ali, and I left the TV station and set up ScreenBox because we knew how to produce engaging content that could reach to the hearts of the viewers. Moreover, there was a stark gap in the market that no one was serving back then in 1999. At that time, there were only two Malay radio stations and a spanking new full Malay TV channel that was about to be launched. We saw that there were no Malay content providers and advertising experts then. So in a leap of faith, both of us left our stable, well-paying jobs to provide the industry what it needed badly then — Malay media experts. The company ScreenBox stood out well among advertisers and agencies with its niche services. The challenge we faced then was manpower and media talents. We could not find enough qualified Malay content producers and writers so we had to train new recruits from scratch.

My wife, Haslinda Ali, and my daughters, Qistina (13), Qasrina (11) and Qadisah (7).

In 2003, when SARS hit Singapore, our company faced the longest dry season ever. Advertisers stopped spending advertising dollars. For a period of eight months, we did not have any jobs. This was the toughest period of our business. We knew we had to do something new.

While TV and content business was affected, something else was brewing in the market. It was social media. We went online to create our Malay video contents through an entertainment portal called sungguh. com — it was then a paid website. The response for the online infotainment portal was overwhelming until Facebook came into the picture. Celebrities no longer needed websites like ours to post content or market their shows, movies or projects. So we had to innovate again.

Through the years, I observed that the media landscape has changed tremendously. It is so fragmented now that it has become harder to pinpoint the right audience and what they truly prefer to consume. But the fragmentation of media gave us a huge opportunity to reach out to a variety of new audience.

I believe if we can focus on our core competence in today's media landscape, we can make this big change work for us. As for ScreenBox, we decided to improve our story-telling capabilities, get-

From top-left (clockwise): An interview with Prof. Jackie Ying, filming a docu-drama with Taufik Batisah, the day ScreenBox, Channel NewsAsia and 47 other artists broke the Guinness World Records for Longest Anamorphic Pavement Art and conducting an interview with Prime Minister Lee Hsien Loong.

ting experienced producers and look for opportunities beyond Singapore and beyond the Malay domain. With technology and social media, the world has become smaller. We decided that we have to think INTERNATIONAL. This has proven to be a right move especially when we secured documentaries and lifestyle programmes for international distribution in the United States, Asia and Europe.

In the last few decades, the Malay media in Singapore too faced the same challenges. There are now numerous Malay TV channels in the region that one can access online. Due to the multi-device-multi-platform environment that a Malay consumer is exposed to, it gets even easier today for Malays to receive content that might also harm them. For example, the recent threats of ISIS[b] online recruitment videos that have been reported to reach our young. These threats could be the reason for us to take a relook at our mixed media platform for the Malays. In my personal view, it will not be too long before someone completely harnesses the power of social media and influences its algorithm to present to our young undesirable content seamlessly. In fact, this is already happening.

Filming intensively for 11 days. ScreenBox was installing and documenting the Longest Anamorphic Pavement Art. We broke the Guinness World Record (December 2015).

Today, I see another gap. The Malay media is in need of more experts in the field of content creation, technology enables and digital forensic and marketers. The explosion of multi-device environment calls for immediate action in order to ensure we have the experts ready to face the challenges that lie ahead of us. In the next few decades, we need to put these experts together and help create a much more wholesome media approach that will be engaging and safe, yet attractive enough for our young to consume.

In one of the live transmission of Sunday morning show, *Selamat Pagi Singapura*. The iconic show debuted around mid-1998 and made a come back in 2014.

---

[b] The Islamic State of Iraq and Syria or Islamic State of Iraq and al-Sham is a radical and violent group that desires the creation of an Islamic Caliphate.

CHAPTER 32

THE MALAY HERITAGE FOUNDATION | Julina Khusaini

The façade of Istana Kampung Gelam. Photo courtesy of Malay Heritage Centre Copyright © 2015 MHC. All rights reserved.

The establishment of the Malay Heritage Foundation (MHF) on 28 July 1999 was an important milestone for the Malay community in Singapore. For the first time, a non-government, non-profit organisation has been formed as a steward and champion for the heritage of the Malay community in Singapore. Its objectives are to promote research and study, and public understanding and knowledge of the history and socio-cultural development of the Malay community in Singapore.

To achieve its mission and as a strategic enabler and facilitator for the community in the arts and heritage sector, MHF focusses on three key strategies.

Enhancing Awareness and Deepening Appreciation

First on its agenda is to enhance awareness and deepen the appreciation for heritage of the Malay community and its contribution to nation-building. Many platforms are being used to achieve this. Working in partnership with the National Heritage Board (NHB), it aims to make one of its heritage institutions — the Malay Heritage Centre (MHC), into an iconic historical landmark that is a must-visit destination for all visitors — both locals and non-Singaporeans. MHC is made up of a museum housed inside the former *istana* (royal palace) known as the Istana Kampung Gelam, its surrounding grounds, a black box and several annex buildings used for temporary galleries and offices. The displays inside the museum had been revamped twice, in 2005 and 2012, in order to keep the content relevant with the changing times. Wherever possible, interactive exhibits, including dramatised historical characters and sections in the galleries that come alive with a "live" traditional music and *wayang kulit*[a] performances, were incorporated so that visitors could have a more experiential and immersive museum-going experience. Stories shared by our volunteer docents helped to deepen the engagement with visitors during the daily guided tours.

New and more interactive programmes that appeal to the public from all walks of life are introduced to bring the Malay culture and heritage more up close and personal with the wider Singapore society. These include heritage hunts for families with young children and monthly cultural performances on the streets of Kampung Gelam precinct. Malay CultureFest, the annual signature programme featuring indoor and outdoor performances from various cultural groups — both local and from the wider Nusantara (Malay-Indonesia Archipelago), is a crowd favourite drawing hordes of visitors to the MHC every October/November.

Snapshots of the myriad of activities during the Budi Daya Special Exhibition. Photo courtesy of Malay Heritage Centre Copyright © 2015 MHC. All rights reserved.

To celebrate and further deepen the awareness of Singaporeans on the rich and diverse culture and heritage of the Malays in Singapore, two alternating

---

[a] A type of puppet shadow play performed around the Indomalayan archipelago.

exhibitions occupy the temporary galleries every five to six months. In 2014, a co-curated community exhibition series known as SeNusantara (Of the Same Archipelago) was introduced. Each exhibition showcases a specific sub-ethnic community that make up the Malay community in Singapore. The Baweanese and Minangkabau communities took centrestage in 2014 and 2015 respectively. Other sub-ethnic groups including the Javanese, Bugis and Banjarese will take their turn in consecutive years.

Alternating with the SeNusantara exhibition series are special temporary exhibitions based on annual themes such as *bahasa* (language), *adat* (customs and tradition), *nilai* (values) and *bangsa* (nation) were put up to enable a deeper exploration of various aspects of Malay heritage. In addition to artefacts and objects from yesteryear, there are also opportunities to explore how ancient practices and traditions have evolved in order to remain relevant in modern and contemporary times. In the Budi Daya special exhibition (2014) for example, contemporary works of art from young and emerging artists were juxtaposed with traditional objects and artefacts as if they are "in a conversation".

To widen its footprint and continue these "conversations" with the wider Singaporeans, mobile exhibitions featuring our early Malay pioneers and their contribution to nation-building, and the customs, traditions and religious significance of fasting during the month of *Ramadan* and the *Eid* celebrations (*Hari Raya Aidilfitri*), travelled to many public libraries, shopping malls and schools.

All these efforts have paid off as visitorship to MHC had been increasing over the last three years, surpassing more than one million visitors. In August 2015, in conjunction of Singapore's Golden Jubilee SG50 celebrations, the 172-year old former *istana* gained the honour of being gazetted as the 70th National Monument.

Next to MHC is Gedung Kuning (Yellow Mansion), another historical landmark that has been conserved since the historic district of Kampung Glam was

Each year, the Malay Heritage Centre will collaborate with community organisations to present an exhibition on one of the ethnic groups from the local Malay community. The Se-Nusantara Series [meaning 'From the Same (Malay-Indonesian) Archipelago'] aims to celebrate the ethnic diversity and richness of the Malay community in Singapore as well as to enable audiences to become more deeply acquainted with network of relations between ourselves and the wider Malay communities throughout the Archipelago. Photo courtesy of Malay Heritage Centre Copyright © 2015 MHC. All rights reserved.

gazetted as conservation area in 1989. Today, it houses a fine dining restaurant that focuses on traditional Malay cuisine. In addition to its traditional offerings, the current tenant has upped the ante by also introducing some innovative approaches to traditional Malay cuisine to appeal to a wider market. In recent years, it has also hosted several school learning journeys to introduce students to Malay culinary art and heritage.

Documenting our Heritage

Another key aspect to enhancing awareness and deepening appreciation is to ensure that our heritage is properly documented so that it can be used for future reference. MHF had identified that there is a lack of information and resources that is currently available on the Malay community in Singapore and saw the need to bridge this knowledge gap. This led to the launch of its heritage publication series, "Singapore Malays: Our Heritage and Legacy" in 2014. Written from the 'insider perspective' by local researchers and writers, three books have been published under this series which cover topics such as the social history of the Malay community, development of Malay poetry and the role of religious authority in Singapore. Apart from the publications, seminar-styled workshops were also held with post-secondary and tertiary students to share and discuss the issues raised in these publications. Digital versions are available for online purchases and translations into either English or Malay are also being considered, to extend the outreach and discourse. Other topics such as the contribution of Malay artists to the development of the visual arts landscape of Singapore and the legacy of our entrepreneurial heritage are currently being developed for the publication series.

The first three books published under the heritage publication series, Singapore Malays: *Our Heritage and Legacy: (left to right) Faith, Authority and the Malays: The Ulama in Contemporary Singapore* written by Dr Norshahril Saat, *Potret Puisi Melayu Singapura* written by Isa Kamari and *Narrating Presence: Awakening from Cultural Amnesia* written by Dr Azhar Ibrahim. Photo courtesy of Malay Heritage Foundation Copyright © 2015 MHF. All rights reserved.

With the rise of the Internet and social media changing the way we interact with one another, MHF has also taken the initiative to ride on these developments and extended these "conversations" into the cyberspace. In January 2015, MHF developed and launched a mobile-friendly portal www.warisansg.com to make information on the heritage of the Malay community in Singapore, more accessible, available every time, everywhere — literally at the palm of your hands. It also launched the first-ever Malay heritage-themed puzzle mobile game app, Warisan Enigma, featuring Malay artefacts from the National Collection that are displayed at MHC, the Asian Civilisation Museum and the National Museum of Singapore. MHF has also embarked on a digital engagement strategy by putting up regular postings and relevant links to Malay heritage-related news and articles on its social media Facebook page to widen outreach and enhance awareness among the netizens in cyberspace.

Building Capacity for the Arts and Heritage Sector

Another key strategy for MHF is to value-add to the arts and heritage sector by nurturing emerging talents and building capacity for the sector. Internship programmes for tertiary students had been introduced since 2012 to enable student participants to apply classroom knowledge to real-world context and be exposed to more current content as they acquire work-life skills and be more work ready upon graduating from their courses. To date, 35 students from the Republic Polytechnic's School of Technology and the Arts, and the Department of Malay Studies, National University of Singapore have benefited from these internship opportunities.

Students from Republic Polytechnic undergoing an internship programme for video production and transmedia with MHF in collaboration with industry partner Reta Transmedia Storytelling Pte Ltd. Photo courtesy of Reta Pte. Ltd © 2015. All rights reserved.

Complementing such efforts, MHC piloted the Arts Incubation Programme in 2013 to provide the much needed space for two up-and-coming arts practitioners to hone their skills and performance of their craft. The founders cum artistic directors of these groups have gone on to win many accolades and awards at both the national and international level. Riduan Zalani, co-founder and Artistic Director of NADI Singapore was conferred the National Youth Award (2013), ASEAN Youth Award (2013) and the Young Artist Award (2015). Norisham Osman, founder and Co-Artistic Director of a multidisciplinary collective of artists, known as The Kaizen M. D., was awarded the Goh Chok Tong Youth Promise (Merit) Award in 2015.

Strengthening Partnerships

Finally, MHF continues to build and strengthen its partnerships with various stakeholders to promote of Malay culture and heritage to the wider Singapore community. For instance, it participates actively in the place management discussions of the Working Group for the Kampung Gelam precinct set up by the Urban Redevelopment Authority (URA) to ensure that the quintessential heritage character of the area is maintained, despite the competing demands for commercialisation and frenetic development happening in the surrounding area. It continues to give its feedback and guidance to the working committee working for the annual *Hari Raya* light up at Geylang Serai so that the Malay character of the annual festive lighting continues to be celebrated. As one of the key members of the Wisma Geylang Serai (WGS) Workgroup project and chair of the Programming Sub-Group for WGS, MHF provided valuable inputs and views that have been taken into consideration in the decision making process for this landmark project for the Malay community.

Conclusion

Moving forward beyond SG50 and as Singapore continues its trajectory to be the arts and cultural hub of the region, it can be envisioned that arts and heritage landscape in Singapore will also continue grow. So too will be the interest on Malay heritage as it forms one of the important component our shared heritage and what makes us Singaporean. MHF looks forward to further enhancing its contribution and strategic role in this sector.

MALAY HERITAGE OF SINGAPORE

Aileen Tan Boon

The book *Malay Heritage of Singapore* originated from an idea that sprung while researching for another project which covered seamen's welfare and unions.

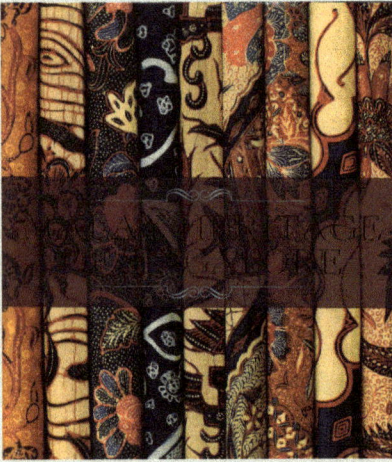

Malay Heritage of Singapore, Lau, Aileen T. and Dr Bernhard Platzdasch (Eds.), Suntree Media (2010).

It was a topic that opened a window into the Malay community, early Singaporean seamen and their lives. Notwithstanding numerous academic papers written on various aspects of Malay culture, I then realised that little existed to capture this very rich culture lavishly illustrated in a large-format book.

S. R. Nathan, the then President of the Republic of Singapore, gave full encouragement. He linked me to the late Ridzwan Dzafir and Zainul Abidin Rasheed, both leading figures from the Malay Heritage Foundation and the Malay community to explore ways using such a book to benefit the newly opened Malay Heritage Centre in Kampung Gelam and the Malay Heritage Foundation.

The passage from conception to realisation of the book proved a most interesting journey into the Malay world. I sought and worked with contributors of diverse backgrounds to contribute on thematic aspects of Malay life, which were to be illustrated by numerous and wonderful images. Needless to say this editorial journey was not easy. The purpose was to convey descriptions and documentation at a popular level, while satisfy the highest standards of accuracy and credible research findings. The range of these thematic chapters was diverse as it was exciting to shape and illustrate.

As a result, the rich cultural tapestry found in *Malay Heritage of Singapore* reflects a diversity of content and rhythm, which in turn

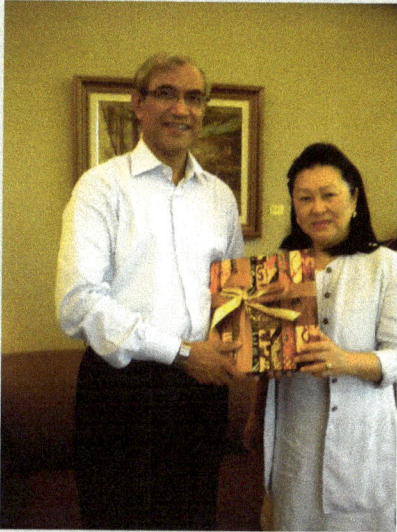

Senior Minister of State (Foreign Affairs)
Mr Zainul Abidin Rasheed being presented
with a copy of the book *Malay Heritage
of Singapore* from Aileen T. Boon.

points to the vitality and richness to be found in a culture we must claim and celebrate as our own, albeit much of its origins may be traced to the rest of the Southeast Asian region.

Personally, it was an enriching experience to be immersed in the construction of this book, not least for the friendships made with many fellow Singaporeans from the Malay community. Undistracted by skeptics in my position as a non-Malay looking into the Malay world, and at times commended for courage and nerve, I can only hope that I have acquitted myself in the process.

A group photo of the contributors of the book.
Photo courtesy of Malay Heritage Centre
Copyright © 2015 MHC. All rights reserved.

Former President S. R. Nathan and wife being welcomed with a pencak silat performance. Photo courtesy of Malay Heritage Centre Copyright © 2015 MHC. All rights reserved.

The idea of setting up the Malay Heritage Centre first came up when Mr George Yeo, then Minister for Information and The Arts (now Communication and Information) took an afternoon walk with the former editor of Berita Harian, Mr Zainul Abidin Rasheed around the Kampung Gelam area. The Minister said either the Istana Kampung Gelam or Bukit Chandu could be possible venues for a Malay heritage centre. Mr Zainul Abidin recalled it was drizzling at that time. It was finally decided that Istana Kampung Gelam to be the Malay Heritage Centre.

THE MALAY HERITAGE CENTRE — MILESTONES

1822 — Stamford Raffles allocated Kampung Gelam to the Malays, Bugis and Arabs.

14 March 1823 — a total of 56 acres of land was allotted to the Sultan.

2 August 1824 — Sultan Hussein Mohamed Shah later ceded Singapore to the British East India Company.

5 September 1835 — Sultan Hussein Mohamed Shah never lived in the building then known as Istana Kampung Gelam, as he passed away on this date in Malacca.

1840 — His eldest son by his second wife, Tengku Mohammed Ali Iskandar Shah, came to Singapore to claim his father's estate as rightful heir. Tengku Ali built the then Istana Kampung Gelam.

1855 — Tengku Ali was only recognised as the Sultan of Singapore by the British in this year.

1896 — There was a succession dispute in the royal family. Sultan Ali's three wives took to court the dispute regarding who had the rights to the estate.

1897 — The court ruling repealed the privilege of land ownership, and ruled that no one could claim to be the successor. Therefore, the estate belonged to the colony of Singapore, although the Sultans descendants were allowed to use it.

1 January 1905 — In accordance with Section 2 of the 1904 Sultan Hussain Ordinance (Cap. 382), the land at Istana Kampung Gelam was reverted to the state of Singapore, and became state property.

7 July 1989 — The district of Kampung Gelam was gazetted as a conservation area.

1993 — The Singapore government announced plans to develop the Istana Kampung Gelam as it was located in the 16-hectare Kampung Gelam conservation area.

12 March 1999 — The Singapore government announced that the Istana Kampung Gelam would be converted into a Malay heritage centre.

June 2005 — The Malay Heritage Centre was officially opened by Prime Minister Lee Hsien Loong.

2008 — The Ministry for Information, Communications and the Arts announced that the Malay Heritage Centre would be repositioned as a platform to showcase key aspects of the community, alongside the Sun Yat Sen Memorial Hall and the then proposed Indian Heritage Centre.

2009 — The National Heritage Board (NHB) was appointed as the operator of the Malay Heritage Centre, conducted under a co-funding framework between the government and the Malay community, established under a memorandum of understanding (MOU) signed with NHB.

April 2011 — The Malay Heritage Centre was officially closed for redevelopment and upgrading works.

1 September 2012 — The Malay Heritage Centre was officially re-opened. The new heritage centre features six permanent galleries spread over two levels of the building. There were also two exhibition galleries to host seasonal and travelling exhibitions

6 August 2015 — Istana Kampung Gelam/The Malay Heritage Centre is gazetted by the NHB as Singapore's 70th National Monument.

NATIONAL MONUMENT
Gazetted on 6 August 2015

ISTANA KAMPONG GELAM

Istana Kampong Gelam was commissioned by Sultan Ali Iskandar Shah, the heir of Sultan Hussein Shah. Completed in 1843, this building exhibits both European and Malay architectural features. It was the palace of Malay royalty when Singapore was the seat of the Johor Sultanate during the 19th century.

Pembinaan Istana Kampong Gelam telah dititahkan oleh Sultan Ali Iskandar Shah, putera mahkota Sultan Hussein Shah. Disiapkan pada tahun 1843, bangunan ini memaparkan ciri-ciri seni bina Eropah dan Melayu. Ia adalah istana kediaman keluarga diraja semasa Singapura menjadi pusat kerajaan Johor pada abad ke-19.

National Heritage Board

UNLOCKING THE COMMUNITY'S POTENTIAL THROUGH PROPER MANAGEMENT OF ITS ASSETS AND LIABILITIES

Sani Hamid

When I look into the future of the Malay/Muslim Community the next 50 years, I feel very encouraged. I base this optimism on the community's demographics: our huge youth base. As of October 2015, we are a community of 520,923, of which 46% are below the age of 30. This is significantly higher when compared to the Chinese (33%) and Indian (39%) communities.

I do not think it is an exaggeration to say that this demographic phenomenon is the community's best opportunity to economically move to the next level. In 10 to 20 years' time, these youths will become our middle class and if we can imagine a relatively large, well

Table A1.3 Singapore Residents by Age Group, Ethnic Group and Sex, June 2014

Number

Age Group (Years)	Total			Chinese			Malays			Indians			Others		
	Persons	Males	Females	Persons	Males	Females	Persons	Males	Females	Persons	Males	Females	Persons	Males	Females
Total	3,870,739	1,902,410	1,968,329	2,874,380	1,403,927	1,470,453	516,657	257,036	259,621	353,021	181,359	171,662	126,681	60,088	66,593
0 – 4	181,369	92,528	88,841	126,663	65,120	61,543	30,899	15,869	15,030	17,378	8,530	8,848	6,429	3,009	3,420
5 – 9	205,790	104,588	101,202	135,766	69,555	66,211	32,837	16,864	15,973	26,878	13,285	13,593	10,309	4,884	5,425
10 – 14	220,796	112,959	107,837	148,099	76,144	71,955	38,395	19,789	18,606	24,969	12,534	12,435	9,333	4,492	4,841
15 – 19	247,337	126,514	120,823	172,689	88,722	83,967	44,424	23,006	21,418	22,579	11,241	11,338	7,645	3,545	4,100
20 – 24	263,918	132,902	131,016	186,771	94,189	92,582	49,165	25,206	23,959	22,452	11,075	11,377	5,530	2,432	3,098
25 – 29	265,659	129,304	136,355	193,787	94,600	99,187	42,597	21,596	21,001	23,161	10,907	12,254	6,114	2,201	3,913
30 – 34	292,287	138,954	153,333	211,976	101,060	110,916	35,985	17,966	18,019	32,386	15,296	17,090	11,940	4,632	7,308
35 – 39	302,029	144,959	157,070	220,906	104,419	116,487	29,430	14,083	15,347	35,755	19,363	16,392	15,938	7,094	8,844
40 – 44	316,023	154,320	161,703	234,352	111,470	122,882	32,636	15,803	16,833	32,716	19,086	13,630	16,319	7,961	8,358
45 – 49	308,533	153,194	155,339	227,540	111,126	116,414	39,787	19,363	20,424	28,494	16,192	12,302	12,712	6,513	6,199
50 – 54	315,503	158,734	156,769	237,697	118,717	118,980	43,038	21,462	21,576	25,726	13,716	12,010	9,042	4,839	4,203
55 – 59	288,392	144,316	144,076	227,374	113,178	114,196	34,819	17,271	17,548	20,447	10,655	9,792	5,752	3,212	2,540
60 – 64	231,502	115,217	116,285	188,427	93,875	94,552	24,415	11,686	12,729	14,953	7,494	7,459	3,707	2,162	1,545
65 – 69	161,198	78,285	82,913	134,123	65,144	68,979	14,944	7,044	7,900	9,759	4,686	5,073	2,372	1,411	961
70 – 74	106,815	49,438	57,377	90,889	42,164	48,725	8,841	3,883	4,958	5,807	2,687	3,120	1,278	704	574
75 – 79	76,294	33,753	42,541	63,831	28,394	35,437	7,200	3,132	4,068	4,292	1,767	2,525	971	460	511
80 – 84	48,418	19,515	28,903	40,331	15,940	24,391	4,386	1,754	2,632	2,996	1,505	1,491	705	316	389
85 & Over	38,876	12,930	25,946	33,159	10,110	23,049	2,859	1,259	1,600	2,273	1,340	933	585	221	364

Source: Monthly Digest of Statistics Singapore, October 2015.

educated, fully employed and successful one, I believe we would have reached our goal of being a community of excellence. This stratum of our community can provide a strong backbone as a whole to the community and secure the future of generations to come.

However, with this opportunity comes the community's greatest threat — the failure to harness the full potential of our youths, which will not only be seen a missed opportunity but also leave it in a weakened and vulnerable situation. Therefore, if there has been a time in our community's history where destiny is in our hands to secure our very future, I believe it is now.

Inspiring youths and harnessing their potential is the way forward to build a better future and a better community leading to a better Singapore. Photo reproduced with permission from 4PM © 2015. All rights reserved.

One of the key things I see as vital in securing our community's future is to measure it differently from how we have been doing for the past 50 years. I believe there is an urgent need to adopt a new perspective on measuring the community's progress: the Net Worth Approach. This is important because over the years, when one speaks about economic challenges facing the community, the focus has often been on issues relating to education/skills, employment, entrepreneurship and globalisation. To this effect, a lot of effort and resources have been put into these areas, and with very good results to show for. Today, no one can argue that we have better skilled and educated workers and more children doing very well in school. However, these present measures of the community's progress do not provide us with a holistic picture.

While we can say that our children are increasingly better educated, our workers are earning more and are better skilled, and the community collectively owns more assets than before, these measures admittedly only focus on issues relating to improvements in the community's 'assets'. Instead, in the coming years,

"Thus, unless we become a net income surplus community and pare down our liabilities, no matter how much progress we make on the 'income' or 'assets' fronts, we will always remain vulnerable to economic shocks.

I believe the community's Achilles' heel will be the flip side of this: its 'liabilities'.

By adopting the Net Worth Approach, we are recognising the fact it is not only the management of the community's assets that is important but also its liabilities. Like corporations or individuals, the overall standing of the community should be measured by its net worth. This is vital as I believe if there is anything which could unravel many of the gains made over the past few decades it is the community's prudently inability to manage its liabilities.

Take for example the latest 2005 General Household Survey. They show that the community's household net income was a small negative balance, based on the income and expenditure figures of $2830 and $2844 respectively. This deficit in the community's net income would imply that households would have had to either sell their existing assets or increase their liabilities (take on debt), to finance this shortfall. If not reversed, this underscores a key threat to the community over the long run as it weakens our ability to weather economic downturns.

To understand the above further, the community's position could be akin to an individual who has put in a lot of effort to boost his income, for example, through improved education or skills training. With his better income, this individual can now afford, via credit or debt, to purchase assets like household appliances, a car or even a property. However, this same individual spends more than he earns every month and finances his monthly deficits by drawing down on his savings (an asset) and also by increasing his credit card balances (a liability).

So clearly, based on one measure (income/asset), this individual is successful but based on another set of measures (expenditure/liabilities), he is not. What really matters is when we put these two together to get a measure of an individual's net worth. In this case, the picture we get is that of an individual who spends more than he earns and thus, has liabilities exceeding his assets or a negative net worth.

In my view, it is this net worth approach which is more holistic and in fact, challenges us to relook some data underlining the community's progress over the past couple of years. For example, data on the community's ownership of consumer durables, which has increased over the past few years. Statistically, more Malay households presently own cars, air conditioners, mobile phones, personal computers, and laser/VCD players than ever before. But do we know how much of these have been bought on credit? What about data showing that more Malay households are living in bigger homes? Do we know how many can realistically afford these bigger dwellings? How many have fully utilised their CPF Ordinary Accounts and thus are dependent on being employed as the only means to pay their installments? How many are in arrears on the HDB loans, especially after this crisis?

In the years ahead, our community — and for that matter, all other communities too — will face a major

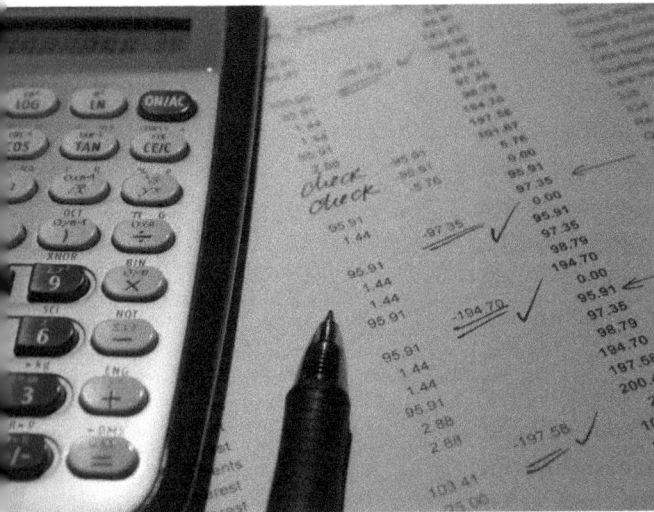

In 2013, the Debt Advisory Centre (DAC) was set up by the Association of Muslim Professionals (AMP) to address debt problems among Malays here. The DAC was expected to help about 200 people in the Malay community struggling with debt in the first two years of its existence; instead, it has seen a significantly higher 580 cases in the first year alone. The three-hour workshop (conducted in Malay) is designed to help participants appreciate and practise the value of being thrifty and also to understand the importance of managing their finances, differentiating between needs and wants and living within their means. (Source: http://www.amp.org.sg/subindex.asp?id=A005_14)

challenge: managing its debt amid a volatile economic environment. The continued rise in consumerism and the availability of easy credit will encourage many to spend and be indebted. In fact, this has sadly become a way of life. In addition, we are also living in an increasingly volatile world where crises have become more commonplace. Already, in the past decade alone, we have had three: the Asian financial crisis of 1997, the Dot Com crisis of 2001 and the recent Global Financial Crisis of 2008. I would be the least surprised to see more of such shocks in the coming years.

Thus, unless we become a net income surplus community and pare down our liabilities, no matter how much progress we make on the "income" or "assets" fronts, we will always remain vulnerable to economic shocks. At a micro level, there is strong evidence that one of the leading issues facing broken families relates to the mismanagement of finances. To better protect our youth, individual families and collectively as a community, have to ensure that they manage their finances diligently and have a positive net worth.

Encouragingly, we now hear of public education programmes like *Projek Bijak Belanja*[a] and many more discussions in the media on financial planning, both of which play a key part in educating the community. In 2013, the Debt Advisory Centre (DAC) was set up by the Association

Since the first development of the *wakaf* at Duku Road in the early 1990s, MUIS has gained valuable experience and made significant progress in *wakaf* development in Singapore. The Wisma Indah complex was a ground-breaking achievement for MUIS's *wakaf* developmental efforts. The $25 million project to redevelop Wakaf Kassim not only increased the annual income of the *wakaf*, but also that of the beneficiaries and the whole Muslim community. Image courtesy of Majlis Ugama Islam Singapura © 2015. All rights reserved.

---

[a] This programme is designed to help participants deal with financial worries in an easy-to-follow and interactive format. It has been customised to take into consideration the current economic situation, and its direct effect on most people's lives. The programme involves both Core and Elective Modules to ensure that participants are equipped with the essential information as well as have the choice to learn the appropriate workshops of their interest.

of Muslim Professionals (AMP) to address the debt problems facing individuals especially among Malays here. In its first three years of existence, over 2000 individuals have walked through the door of the centre to seek advice on their debt problem. Today, the DAC actively manages at least half of these cases and believes that there may be many more individuals and families out there that are mired in this debt trap.

Despite all of these efforts, in my view, there is still a lot more to be done and a serious need to tackle this on a much larger scale if we, as a community, are going to effectively face the challenges that lie ahead.

Having touched on the liabilities side, is there anything on the asset side that the community needs to take need of? Yes. I believe that there is a need for the community to look into setting up a *wakaf* infrastructure fund. Today, we already have a *wakaf ilmu* (knowledge fund) and our existing *wakaf* properties are being managed by Warees, a subsidiary of MUIS. However, from the economic standpoint, there is an important need for the community to actively secure assets for its future, more so, assets that are deemed strategic for the community's future.

Such strategic assets would refer to land, commercial and even industrial buildings that would be purchased using *wakaf* money that is accumulated via a fund. Why is this important? With land becoming scarce in Singapore as time passes, it is clear that one of the major challenges for any entity operating here in the future will be higher rentals. These entities will also include those seen as essential to the community, for examples, our Islamic learning institutions, key *halal* industries and others. By securing such assets, the community will be able to ensure that these entities are able to continue to operate to serve the community's interest despite the fact their operating environment has become challenging.

Securing strategic assets such as land or buildings also provides the community with the ability to take advantage of opportunities which may occur in the future. For example, if ever there was an opportunity to set-up Singapore's first Islamic university, we would have the necessary funds to do so without having to depend on the government or other parties. It would truly be a proud effort by the community, for the community. How such a *wakaf* fund is to be structured is left to be seen but one simply along the line of the Mosque Building Fund that we have presently, where individuals make monthly contributions, would be a good start.

In all, as mentioned earlier, I hold high hopes with respect to the community's future. There is a saying that in order to get different results, one needs to do things differently. I hope that by evaluating itself differently, the community will in the next 50 years, for exceed the success of the past 50 years.

The latest *wakaf* development is the iconic Red House at Katong. The residential-retail-lifestyle development is set to revive the old Katong charm and local legacy but with a twist — part of the retail wing of the Red House project is a new commercial bakery run with a social mission. Image courtesy of Majlis Ugama Islam Singapura © 2015. All rights reserved.

FIVE THINGS YOU MAY NOT HAVE KNOWN ABOUT *WAKAF*[a] IN SINGAPORE

1. Long history in Singapore

This practice of religious endowment originated in the Middle East and it was introduced to Singapore by Arab traders almost 200 years ago. The first *wakaf* documented in Singapore was Omar Mosque off Havelock Road and was endowed by Yemen-born businessman Syed Omar Ali Aljunied in 1820. The mosque is also the oldest in Singapore. Many of the *wakaf* were given by Arab and Indian Muslim merchants and a number of important *wakaf* were established in the 19th century.

2. *Wakaf* properties

There are more than 100 *wakaf* properties; most are managed by MUIS while a number are managed by trustees. The properties were valued at $584 million as of December 2013 and they include residential properties, serviced apartments and commercial properties. There are also *wakaf* mosques such as Masjid Haji Md Salleh, Masjid Khalid, Masjid Khadijah, Masjid Kassim and Masjid Bencoolen.

3. Where does the money go?

The money goes to eight *asnaf* (beneficiaries); the largest beneficiaries are the mosques. Sixty-two per cent of *wakaf* funds are distributed to them, and nine per cent to madrasahs. Other beneficiaries include the poor and needy, as well as

---

[a] *Wakaf* is the dedication of properties by a Muslim, through a will or otherwise, for purposes recognised by Islamic law as pious, religious or charitable. Once this is done, the ownership is transferred to Allah (God). The dedicator is called the wakif and the person he appoints to manage the properties to ensure that the purposes are carried out is called the *mutawalli* or trustee. The income derived from these properties is used in accordance to the *wakif's* wishes for the benefit of the beneficiary. Since 1968, under the Administration of Muslim Law Act (AMLA), these properties must be vested with MUIS. MUIS' role is to manage *wakaf* properties which have no trustees and to monitor other *wakaf* properties with trustees to ensure that the *wakif's* wishes are carried out.

charitable organisations. Some funds are disbursed to foreign countries according to the donors' wills.

4. Revitalisation of *wakaf* land

Warees Investments, the real-estate development arm of MUIS, was formed in 2001 to find ways to enhance the value of *wakaf* properties. Recently, it has embarked on a *wakaf* revitalisation scheme to rejuvenate properties in its care. The Red House Bakery in Katong is its first project under the scheme. The integrated heritage development project, called The Red House, will consist of 42 residential units and six shophouses. It will be completed in 2016. The second project in the pipeline is the Alias Villas. There will also be another project in the city centre.

5. Overseas expansion

To explore joint-venture opportunities abroad, Warees signed a memorandum of understanding with property management firm CPG Facilities Management in 2005. It will offer its expertise and services in property management and development to Muslim countries in the region and the Middle East.

CHAPTER 34

THE SINGAPORE MALAY CHAMBER OF COMMERCE AND INDUSTRY (SMCCI) — HISTORY AND MILESTONES

History

The Singapore Malay Chamber of Commerce (SMCC) was founded in 1956 and was set up by a group of enterprising businessmen — Abdul Hamid, Yusof Ishak, Mohd Mahmood, Raja Mohd Yusof Ahmad, Mohd Tom Manas, Habib Mohd Shah and Syed Haron Abdul Rahman Alhabshi — in an effort to uplift the Malay/Muslim business community.

SMCC managed to garner 15 companies within the first year, its membership increased to 48 the following year. Their first office was at 500 Victoria Street, shifted to 72A Bussorah Street in 1997 and relocated to its current location, 15 Jalan Pinang, on 14 August 2009, a move that proved to be beneficial for its members, many of whom had business connections in the Kampung Gelam district.

In November 1995, SMCC changed its name to the Singapore Malay Chamber of Commerce and Industry (SMCCI) to reflect on its wider scope and was officially inaugurated in February 2001. Since its inception, SMCCI has served to facilitate its members' trade activities by providing communication

Led by Chairman Abdul Hamid Allwie, industrial and commercial delegates from Singapore and Malaya visited Taiwan in July 1957 where they attended a product showcase and a seminar on Singapore–Malay trade. Image courtesy of The Singapore Malay Chamber of Commerce and Industry © 2016. All rights reserved.

facilities and acting as a liaison body between domestic and overseas sellers and buyers. Like other chambers of commerce, SMCCI is also authorised to endorse certificates of origins as needed by exporters.

Mission and Objectives

This year marks the 60th anniversary of SMCCI. SMCCI started with seven companies in 1956 and has since grown to 512 members in 2016. SMCCI continues to meet the changing needs of its members and is spearheaded by a capable board of directors representing the various industries.

Management Committee of Singapore Malay Chamber in 1986. Image courtesy of The Singapore Malay Chamber of Commerce and Industry © 2016. All rights reserved.

SMCCI's mission is to nurture a vibrant entrepreneurial culture amongst Malay/Muslim enterprises and is engaged in activities that would benefit and safeguard their interests while fostering good relations with other Chambers of Commerce and trade bodies. Based on an estimated 15% of 187,700 Small and Medium Enterprises (SMEs) in Singapore (Singstat, 2014), Malay/Muslim businesses contribute up to $14 billion to the economy, at an average $0.5 million turnover per company.

SMCCI's key thrusts include:

(a) Marketing Members to Market
(b) Financial Access
(c) Customised Solutions and
(d) *Halal* and Internationalisation

Key Milestones and Activities

- **Malay/Muslim Business Conference (MMBC)**

MMBC is aimed at showcasing successful Malay/Muslim entrepreneurs though the sharing of industry knowledge and expertise. Since 2010, MMBC has garnered participation from more than 1000 local and overseas delegates. In 2014, the theme was "The Art of Collaboration in Business: Fostering Ties Within Asia; the event was attended by Guest-of-Honour Prime Minister Lee Hsien Loong and Dr Yaacob Ibrahim, Minister for Communication and Information and Minister-in-Charge of Muslim Affairs.

Guest-of-Honour Prime Minister Lee Hsien Loong and Dr Yaacob Ibrahim, Minister for Communications and Information and Minister-in-Charge of Muslim Affairs (10th and 14th from right, respectively) attended the Malay/Muslim Business Conference in 2014 with SMCCI Board of Directors. Image courtesy of The Singapore Malay Chamber of Commerce and Industry © 2016. All rights reserved.

• **Industry Cluster Approach**

SMCCI has set up industry clusters to strengthen Malay/Muslim businesses through collaboration. This is achieved by the sharing of resources for profitable opportunities, raising industry standards through accreditation and providing a bigger voice in addressing issues facing specific industries. Currently, SMCCI has six active clusters — SMCCI-Wellness, SMCCI-Wedding, SMCCI-Learning, SMCCI-Tech, SMCCI-Halal F&B and SMCCI-Hospitality & Tourism.

• **Seed Funding & Scholarship Support**

In its inaugural year in 2015, the *Protégé Kita* Competition saw 42 aspiring entrepreneurs undergo rigorous training based on the Business Excellence Framework. The top five aspiring businesses received seed funding of $5000 each while the grand winner won a $30,000 cash prize to contribute to spur further growth. The programme was spearheaded by the Young Entrepreneurs Network (YEN@SMCCI) and supported by the Community Leaders Forum (CLF) Fund.

After an intensive business programme, top five teams of *Protégé Kita* received $5000 cash each, while the grand winner walked away with $30,000 cash prize to further harness their spirit of enterprise. Image courtesy of The Singapore Malay Chamber of Commerce and Industry © 2016. All rights reserved.

SMCCI also awarded 15 scholarships at a total value of $75,000 to outstanding students in the field of business-related studies, in support of the future pillars of the business community. This was only made possible though generous contributions from members and supporting corporations though fundraising efforts like SMCCI's bi-annual Charity Golf.

Guest-of-Honour Minister Masagos Zulkifli, Minister for the Environment and Water Resources, attended SMCCI's 3rd Scholarship Award Ceremony where eight outstanding students received scholarships in support of the future pillars of the business community. Image courtesy of The Singapore Malay Chamber of Commerce and Industry © 2016. All rights reserved.

• **Singapore and Beyond**

Over the years, SMCCI has broadened its efforts to prove members the opportunities to venture overseas through conducting business missions regionally and internationally. SMCCI has conducted business missions to China, Vietnam, Jakarta, Malaysia, Philippines, Bangladesh, Turkey and Japan.

• **SME Centre@SMCCI**

SME Centre@SMCCI was established in 2006 with the support of SPRING Singapore to provide a one stop centre for SMEs. In 2014, SME Centre@SMCCI assisted 2,110 SMEs with complimentary one-on-one business advisory, 94 companies with business needs analysis to identity and plug critical gaps, and assisted with $363,000 worth of support from Government assistance schemes towards productivity. SMCCI together with its subsidiary SME Centre@SMCCI, advocate strengthening core competencies while increasing knowledge and

Mr Zainul Abidin Rasheed, business advisor of SMCCI (first row 4th from left) and Dato Zain Abdullah, former President of SMCCI (5th from left), led a business mission in Izmir, Turkey with delegates from Singapore to gain insights into the global market. Image courtesy of The Singapore Malay Chamber of Commerce and Industry © 2016. All rights reserved.

enhancing internal capabilities to achieve growth and success for their businesses.

LIST OF PRESIDENTS OF SMCCI

1. Mr Haji Abdul Hamid Allwie (1956–1960)
2. Messrs. Salleh Basharahil (1963–1966)
3. Mr Zainal Haji Alias (1968–1969)
4. Mr Mohd Ghazali Caffoor (1970–1980)
5. Mr Haji Abdul Jalil Bin Haron (1980–1984, 1988–1992, 1994–1998)
6. Mr Umar Marican (1999–2003)
7. Mdm Nooraini Nordin (2003–2005)
8. Dato Mohd Zain Abdullah (2005–2009)
9. Mr Abdul Rohim Sarip (2009–2013)
10. Mr Zahidi Abdul Rahman (2013–present)

"Malay companies cannot afford to stick to old ways of doing business especially now that wage costs have gone up. They must take steps to improve their skills upgrading. Wage increase must, in future, be commensurate with productivity. We cannot expect to be paid more than our worth. Malay companies should also take positive steps to mechanise, automate and adopt new management styles."

Dr Ahmad Mattar

13–15 September 1985

KEMAS: Singapore Malay Muslim Economic Congress, Dewan Persidangan Singapura

Photo: Industrial and commercial delegates from SMCC visited Taiwan in 1957 where they networked with government officials and attended a seminar on Singapore-Malaya trade. The mission was led by Chairman Abdul Hamid Allwie. Image courtesy of The Singapore Malay Chamber of Commerce and Industry © 2016. All rights reserved.

SUSTAINING THE COMPETITIVE EDGE FOR MALAY/MUSLIM BUSINESSES — LESSONS FROM AN AUTOMOTIVE WORKSHOP

Stepping into a clean motor vehicle workshop during operating hours is unthinkable but keeping your workspace clean was one of the important lessons workshop owner Mr Hanip Abdul learnt from his industrial training attachments with Toyota in Japan. It taught him discipline is everything, not only in business but in life.

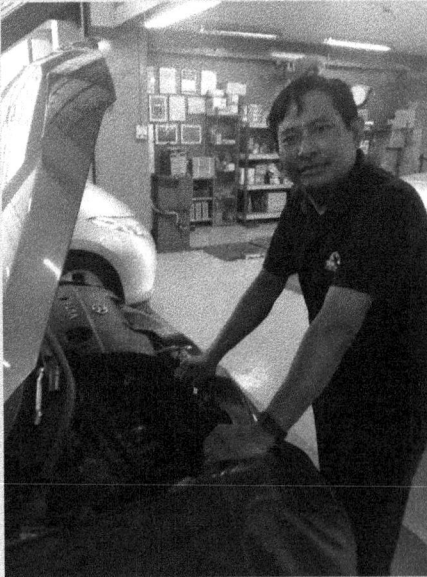

All images in this article are courtesy of Hanip Automobiles © 2016. All rights reserved.

Hanip started his career in the automotive industry at the bottom — as a greaser at Borneo Motors back in 1984 and now, more than three decades later, he is the owner of Hanip Automobiles who recently was awarded the Star Merchant Award 2015[a] — an award given to outstanding companies in the automotive aftermarket industry for their market leadership and service excellence. To be the only Malay/Muslim car workshop owner to receive the honour made it more meaningful. The award is given annually by SGCarmart, Singapore's leading car site. This was not the first time he had the honour. He received the same award back in 2013.

However, the road to success was not an easy one and to still survive and thrive

[a] The award is open to all automotive merchants that fulfill the following requirements:

- Business, Partnership or Company Registered in Singapore.
- Have at least 30% local ownership.
- Have a minimum staff strength of three employees.
- Has automotive aftermarket retail/service as its primary business activity.

in an industry where not many Malay/Muslim entrepreneurs venture, according to Hanip, requires discipline, hardwork and most importantly — knowledge. The three will be the driving force to propel any business forward. But his venture into the automotive workshop business was fortuitous.

It was his late father, Haji Abdul Hashim who first saw Hanip's potential and suggested he open a workshop. Hanip then was already in a comfort zone and the decision to strike out on his own was a difficult one. In 1998, after 14 years with Borneo Motors, with partial funding[b] from his late father, he took a huge risk and opened Hanip Automobiles. As a start, he already has the credential of the few workshops owned, run and operated by a former diagnostic specialist and master technician. Reputation is an important asset and with that he earned the trust of many of his initial pool of clients — many of them Chinese who form the majority of car owners here in Singapore. Gaining trust is an important initial step for any new business. His experience and decades of training and gaining pertinent knowledge at Borneo Motors were his other assets. Pre- as well as post-service consultation is done by him to ensure that customers are kept well-informed. Assuring customers is important as his target is not only first-time customers, but returning ones and referrals. To be able to compete with the best, he incorporates the latest technologies and constantly upgrades himself and his staff.

Having technical competency is still not enough. In order for him to run and develop the business, a different set of knowledge, skills, aptitude and attitude is required. Due to his busy schedule, Hanip has no time to read books on business improvements but he learns by talking to people. By talking, asking and exchanging ideas with those in the same line, especially industry leaders, he can gain valuable insights and keep himself abreast of the latest trends and technology. Communication skills are very important, not only to clients but to partners and everyone else. Anyone can be a potential client or a business partner. At the same

---

Winners are selected among the list of eligible merchants on a weighted-average computation based on the following:

- Popularity in sgCarMart.com based on page views   20%
- Attractiveness of products/services based on number of enquires   15%
- Quality of products/services offered   15%
- Comfort of retail/services area   10%
- User Rating & Reviews on sgCarMart.com   40%

[b] In order to come up with the other half of the capital, Hanip had to sell his five-room flat. It was a huge but necessary risk to take. Unfortunately before the start of the business, his father passed away, but that motivated him even more to succeed.

time, being humble is important too because with that, people are more open to share their thoughts, he said. A friendly disposition will help in networking and especially in the automotive industry; building and expanding networking is the single most powerful marketing tactic to accelerate and sustain success as your business rely on many partners from spare parts distributors to spray painters. The relationship with them may make or break your business. Sincerity and honesty are important values too but are often overused in the automotive industry.

SGCARMART
Annual Awards
2015/16

STAR
MERCHANT
2016

CONGRATULATION TO
HANIP AUTOMOBILES PTE LTD
SPECIALTY WORKSHOP - JAPANESE & KOREAN CARS

On behalf of sgCarMart. We would like to congratulate all winners of Star Merchant Awards 2016!

According to Hanip, let your work speak for both. Customers will definitely come back if you provide quality work and the right pricing.

Automotive industry, just like any other knowledge-based industry, is everchanging. Many factors determine its path and no one can ever predict its future and therefore it is important to diversify. Besides making your core business stronger, the Malay/Muslim business community needs to diversify their business, according to Hanip. The expression "never put all your eggs in one basket" is a calling for him. While Hanip Automobiles is already an established brand name, his latest venture is into motor trading. With proper management of liquid asset, his goal for diversification is to reduce risk. He urges those who are already thinking of starting a business to plan well their business plans. Although his formula seems simple — discipline, hardwork and knowledge — the real challenge will come from the actual implementation of the formula and to sustain them in order to enjoy a smooth ride in any business venture. Overcoming the psychological barrier is all that matters.

Prominence Motors is Hanip's latest venture.

CHAPTER 35

ARE THE MALAYS READY FOR THE NEW ECONOMY?

Umar Abdul Hamid

Within a span of 50 years, Singapore has enjoyed an income per capita gain of more than 100 times from US$516.29 in 1965 to US$53,604 in 2015, and the real median wages of Singaporeans have grown 600% since 1965. The economic strategies to achieve such stellar achievement were implemented in phases moving from a low-value manufacturing industry to a high-value-added manufacturing and services industries. Globalisation promotes borderless economic activities where financial and human capital can move seamlessly allowing many countries in the region to replicate Singapore's strategies for their economic development. To maintain the wage rate increase, Singapore has begun to lose its competitive advantage and experience difficulties in attracting multi-national corporations (MNCs) to set-up their Overseas Headquarters (OHQ) in Singapore. The tax incentive offered to the MNCs is no longer attractive when competing countries are amenable to extend whatever benefits and privileges for the MNCs to invest and create employment. Singapore can no longer compete on the same platform and need to progressively shift from a value-add economy (borrowed market) to a value-creation economy (owned market).

The construction of value-creation economy involves the development of innovative entrepreneurial companies employing the available resources and infrastructures. One of the key resources will be the human capital in the workforce and learning institutions. The new economic strategy resets the level playing field for every Singaporean and it is the biggest opportunity for members of the Malay/Muslim community to create and capture values through innovation in technology or business processes for domestic and global markets. The millennial generation (those born in the year 1981 onward) is the largest consumer or user of products and services with technological innovation. Being a relatively younger community with a median age of 31.4 years as compared to the national median age of 37.4, the Malays have an advantage to understand the needs and even possibly offer solutions to the large millennials market especially in the fast-growing regional market created by the Trans-Pacific Partnership (TPP).

Charaku is a Singapore startup that builds an Internet-of-Thing (IoT) application for digital media technology. Image courtesy of Umar Hamid © 2016. All rights reserved.

On 4 February 2016, Trade Ministers from Australia, Brunei Darussalam, Canada, Chile, Japan, Malaysia, Mexico, New Zealand, Peru, Singapore, United States, and Vietnam signed the TPP Agreement, where the thrust of the accord was to promote free trade and facilitate movement of talent among member countries. The TPP free trade agreement[a] being the largest regional accord in history making up 40% of the world economy will boost trade and investment and the creation and retention of jobs for Singaporeans. In the

[a] The Trans-Pacific Partnership ("TPP") is a Free Trade Agreement ("FTA") between 12 countries: Australia, Brunei Darussalam, Canada, Chile, Japan, Malaysia, Mexico, New Zealand, Peru, Singapore, the United States and Vietnam. All 12 TPP countries are members of the Asia-Pacific Economic Cooperation (APEC). The TPP was concluded on 5 October 2015 in Atlanta, Georgia, USA.

near future, we can expect more Malays having to travel extensively to these countries for work and business especially for those who have the skills and experience in the various innovative industries.

The areas of opportunity for innovation promoted and funded by the government include Advanced Manufacturing/Robotics, Biomedical Sciences and Healthcare, Information and Communication Technology, Transport Engineering/Engineering Services, and Clean Technology. To be involved in any of these areas of innovation, the Malay community will need to equip themselves with the basic technical or engineering skills that can be acquired either at the ITEs, polytechnics, or universities. A study commissioned by the Association of Muslim Professionals (AMP) in 2011 revealed that the relevant major field of study by Malays as of 2010 was as follows: 12.2% in Statistics/Computer Studies, 6.6% in Natural/Physical Sciences, 5.4% in Medical/Dental/Health, and 13.5% in Engineering. The figures demonstrated that the community possessed the talent pool that could be tapped onto be part of the developing innovative ecosystem that is growing exponentially in Singapore. As for those who lack the relevant skill, they have the opportunity to use the SkillsFuture[b] grant to either retrain or upgrade themselves vertically in one of the spaces of the future innovative industry.

> *"The TPP embodies what Singapore sees as the future of the Asia–Pacific. It will transform the region by reducing tariff and non-tariff barriers substantially for both good and services, encouraging greater investment, and addressing new trade challenges in the modern economic. The TPP has also been deliberately designed to be more inclusive, so that small and medium-sized enterprises can take full advantage of its benefits.*
>
> — Minister Lim Hng Kiang, Minister for Trade

---

[b] SkillsFuture is a national movement to provide Singaporeans with the opportunities to develop their fullest potential throughout life, regardless of their starting points. Through this movement, the skills, passion and contributions of every individual will drive Singapore's next phase of development towards an advanced economy and inclusive society.

The major barrier to entry in the innovative industry is the availability of strong and vertical technical skills that are applicable to find the solution to a specific problem existing in the global market today. Apart from the need for technical skills in searching for a solution, creative design capability is paramount. The Malays have, for a long time, been respected as the creative lot and the moment has come for us to start applying it. The ability to aggregate designing and computer programming skills will make an individual to be sought after globally as a co-founder of a startup or a member of a design team in large firms like Google, Facebook and Amazon. And the good news is that there is no pre-qualification of the innovator's age, ethnicity and location to be part of the global and continuously growing ecosystem of the innovative industry. Everyone can get a shot at the opportunity if they are willing to take the chance and it will have to start with the changing of the mindset that the global economic paradigm has shifted for the better future.

The future offers many opportunities for the Malay/Muslim community as Singapore moves towards the value creation economy through innovation and we have the ability to be part of it to complement and compete with other global communities on a new level playing field. Let us ride on the innovative bandwagon as we strive towards and celebrate the next SG75 and SG100.

Malay street vendor with two boys, c. 1914. Public domain.

The upward trend of entrepreneurship among the Malay/Muslim youths is encouraging. A survey conducted by the Singapore Malay Chamber of Commerce and Industry (SMCCI) in 2014 has reported an exponential increase in the number of Malay/Muslim businesses — 14 times higher than that of the national average. (http://berita.mediacorp.sg/mobilem/singapore/pekerja-melayu-boleh/2693052. html — last accessed 15 April 2016.)

SKILLSFUTURE AND THE MALAY/ MUSLIM COMMUNITY — OPPORTUNITIES FOR THE FUTURE

Aidi Abdul Rahim

SkillsFuture — A Mindset, An Action, A Passion for Lifelong Learning

Launched in November 2014, SkillsFuture is a national movement to encourage Singaporeans to develop their fullest potential and instil within themselves the ethos of pursuing knowledge and skill mastery throughout their life. The wide range of SkillsFuture programmes and initiatives cater not only for those still in school but for almost anyone from a fresh job-seeker, those in mid-career, or even recently retrenched or newly retired. Importantly, it is a mindset and an action towards skill mastery, by keeping abreast with new practices, and learning new techniques. SkillsFuture fits perfectly with the needs of the Malay/ Muslim community as it prepares itself for the challenges of the future.

Lifelong Learning is in the Malay/Muslim Community's DNA

The Malay/Muslim Singapore community welcomes this movement wholeheartedly because in their religious ethos, the pursuit of knowledge is incumbent upon every Muslim, male and female and in another *hadith* (sayings of the Prophet), Muslims are encouraged to acquire knowledge and impart it to the people. This mantra has been imbibed in the community since the setting up of MENDAKI in 1989 which acted as a catalyst to re-orientate the community's attention on the importance of education. Even MENDAKI's logo is embellished with the word *iqra*, the first word of the holy Quran, meaning "read". Ten years later, in December 1999, when Prime Minister Mr Goh Chok Tong launched the Malay/Muslim KBE (Knowledge-Base Economy) movement, the community was urged to fully understand the implications of the new economy. Mr Abdullah Tarmugi added, "It is just not enough being hardworking, disciplined and efficient. To remain relevant and employable, a worker has to become a learning worker". He added "[g]earing the community for the new knowledge-based economy is a long haul that requires a mindset change" (Speech at Launch of Mendaki–Accord CREST programme, 28 December 1999).

In 2004, MENDAKI Social Enterprise Network Singapore Pte Ltd (MENDAKI SENSE) was set-up to enhance the competitiveness and confidence of the students and workforce through Continuing Education and Training, Employment Facilitation, Social Enterprise and Education services in Singapore. For the Malay/ Muslim community, MENDAKI SENSE will play a pivotal role to inspire and encourage the community to continue towards their learning journey in the SkillsFuture movement.

SkillsFuture Initiatives

There are many SkillsFuture programmes and initiatives that have been rolled out; these include Education and Career Guidance, Enhanced Internships, on-the-job training SkillsFuture Earn and Learn programmes, SkillsFuture Qualification Award (SQA) for completing the Singapore Workforce Skills Qualifications (WSQ) levels full qualifications, subsidies for skills-based modular courses, P-Max, a Place-and Train programme to help PMEs better acclimatise to the SME work environment and the SkillsFuture Credit.

In particular, the SkillsFuture Credit gives all Singaporeans 25 years and above, an initial $500 credit into their SkillsFuture Credit account. The credit can be used to pay for any of the 12,500 and more approved skills-related courses, ranging from basic computing to web design, digital animation, to HR management. The financial aspect of training is almost covered; what the individual has to invest is time, willpower and discipline to complete the course and the desire to improve for himself/herself and the family.

Many Singaporeans are IT-savvy and would not have problems accessing the SkillsFuture Credit portal. But for the Malay/Muslim community, the challenges lie with those in the lower-income group where they may not have a personal computer or laptop in the house and may not be familiar in navigating the internet. MENDAKI has formed the Future Ready Unit to help the community to be aware and understand how SkillsFuture can benefit them (*Berita Harian*, 1 April 2016).

An Opportunity for a Fulfilling Future

Lifelong learning is not something new, nevertheless it still needs to be stressed and reinforced. It is up to the Malay/Muslim individual to explore their passion and interest and take advantage of the various SkillsFuture initiatives to develop to their fullest potential, regardless of their starting point. For those who feel they had missed out on the educational and skills learning opportunities when they were younger, they must not miss the SkillsFuture train. Career guidance and assistance about employment opportunities and career path in the different economic sectors and the types of courses suitable will mitigate the risk of making the wrong choice. For the Malay/Muslim community, the pursuit of knowledge in itself is a noble effort — a *fardhu kifayah* or a communal obligation; the outcome can only be positive. It will strengthen their economic resilience and improve the future well-being of their families. The SkillsFuture Credit is a nudge to help people get started on the lifelong learning journey. Together with the other SkillsFuture initiatives, the Malay/Muslim community will be assured of a fruitful progression to develop to their fullest potential.

Image reproduced with permission © 2016 SkillsFuture. All rights reserved.

CHAPTER 36

SOME THOUGHTS ON GLOBALISATION AND THE MALAYS: LESSONS FROM THE PAST

Sher Banu A. L. Khan

Globalisation — signifying inter-connectedness and inter-dependence on a transnational scale, has become a phenomenon that no state could escape from, certainly not Singapore. Focusing the lens of globalisation on the Malay community in Singapore, the important question here is whether the current globalisation poses a threat or an opportunity and should the Malays be worried? In regard to the popular Malay saying *"Takkan Melayu hilang di dunia"*[a], would the Malays be swept away by the tide of globalisation? My short answer is 'no' and this is why.

Contrary to popular understanding, globalisation is not new. Where the current globalisation constitutes the third wave, two earlier waves already connected the world on a global scale though not as intense, varied and fast paced as the present. From the 7th to 13th centuries, the Islamic Caliphate stretching from Spain to Tunis to Sumatra already formed a cultural and linguistic ecumene followed by the Mongol Empire in the

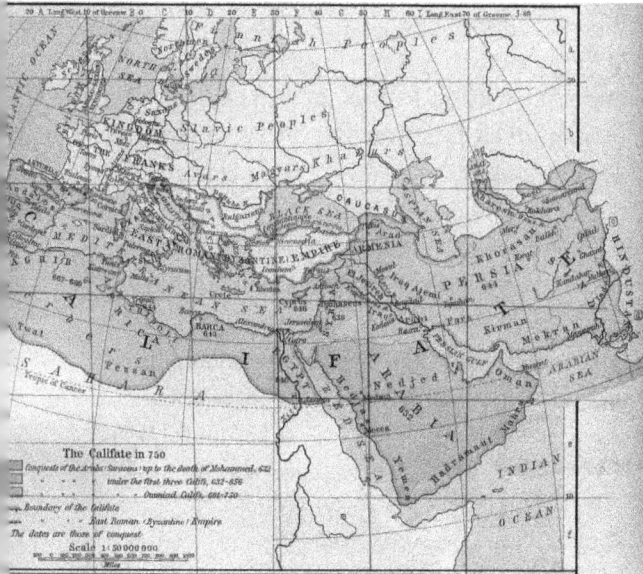

Map of the Umayyad Caliphate in 750 CE. Image extracted from The Historical Atlas by William R. Shepherd, 1926. Public domain.

---

[a] Trans. "The Malays will not vanish from this earth".

12th–13th centuries stretching across Central Asia to Southeast Asia. The first wave of globalisation could be traced to 1571, with the establishment of Manila by the Spanish, truly connecting flows of silver from Europe, Asia and America. The second wave of globalisation was in the 19th century in the form of European colonialism and imperialism. The third wave was ushered in 1991 with the fall of the Soviet Union and American power became hegemonic worldwide.

Situated in Southeast Asia, the crossroads between East and West, the inhabitants in this region have been exposed to global forces since time immemorial. The Malays, originating from Bukit Seguntang in Palembang, Sumatra, have responded to earlier global waves of Indianisation, Islamisation, Westernisation and Modernity in the form of European colonialism and have adopted, adapted and rejected these influences in various capacities where by the end of European decolonisation, the Malays have emerged as a community with its religion, culture and identity intact, albeit evolved.

One main reason why the Malays "*takkan tenggelam dalam gelombang global*[b]" is precisely because of the counter-tide of globalisation — "glocalisation"[c]. According to the sociologist Roland Robertson who is credited with popularising the term, glocalisation describes a new outcome of local conditions toward global pressures where there exists the simultaneity — the co-presence — of both universalising and particularising tendencies. The global ecumene itself is a diverse one, not homogenised and monolithic, characterised by diversity of organisation and autonomy and boundedness of cultures should be understood in terms of degree. More importantly, the influx of new and alien cultural forms do not enter into a vacuum, a cultural *tabula rasa*, but enter into various kinds of interaction with already existing meanings and meaningful forms resulting in a "creolising" of

---

[b] Trans. "Will not perish/be swept away by the waves of globalisation".
[c] Discussions of the respective globalisation concepts can be found in Lechner, Frank J. and Boli, J. (eds.), *The Globalization Reader*, 4th Edition, (UK, Wiley-Blackwell, 2011).

global forces. Foreign influences could be hegemonic and invasive and the cultural flow could be unilateral determined by the power balance between the power centre and the periphery. However, the periphery could exercise agency and most cultures are involved in selective cultural borrowing based on local needs where foreign influences are rarely wholly imitated or rejected.

Indeed, the Malays of the past survived waves of cultural globalisation because they were adept at localising these forces and adapted them to their own way of life. Tensions between global and local of course exist, so do differences between local groups in their responses to global forces and their varied nature and degree of impact. Citing examples and lessons from the Malay past, I will illustrate that the Malays today could be assured that they have the capacity to deal with the forces of current globalisation. Contrary to the perceived dominant narrative that Malays are generally parochial, communal, inward-looking and rooted to the land, a glimpse of the Malay past shows that the Malays were commercially mobile and diasporic, Malay societies generally were open, inclusive, plural and cosmopolitan in nature where Malay identity was dynamic consistently evolving, synthesising global influences with local traditions forming "hybrid" cultures. These attitudes of mind and orientation are critically relevant in today's context where the Malays have to deal with new ideas and the continued cultural flows of Westernisation, Americanisation and more recently "Arabisation" where selective adaptations are necessary to balance between multiple identities and loyalties, innovation and tradition.

The Malays were exposed to global commercial, missionary–scholarly and literary networks and were engaged in cross-cultural encounters as early as the Srivijayan period of the seventh century. Using the example of global Islamic literary networks, there was an exchange of shared texts, including stories, poems, genealogies, histories as well as readers, listeners, authors, patrons, translators and scribes who not merely translated Islamic texts from the centres of the

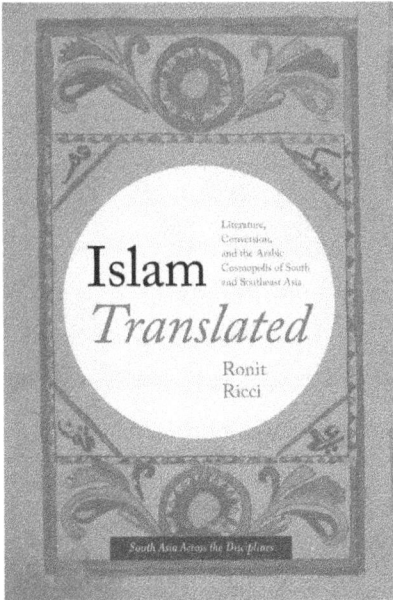

Ronit Ricci, *Islam Translated: Literature, Conversion and the Arabic Cosmopolis of South and Southeast Asia*, (Chicago, The University of Chicago Press, 2011).

Muslim world but locally adapted them creating new localised forms and transmitted them playing a vital role in establishing both local and global Islamic identities. "Arabisation", a term gaining prominence now, already took place centuries ago. Ronit Ricci's study on the "Arabic cosmopolis" stresses the importance of Arabic as a trans-local language of authority and dignity recognised by the global *ummah* and became adopted into local literary genres such as *syair*, *serat*, *hikayat* and *kitab*. Sanskrit and local languages became Arabised. Arabic entered into everyday language and life in the form of greetings, epitaphs in tombs, in the mosques, and terms of endearment. However, in her study of the Arabic text *One Thousand Questions*, she showed that the dynamic process of literary interactions revealed that far from being simply Arabised by contacts with speakers and writers of Arabic, Malays vernacularised Arabic itself through literary translation, adaptation and transmission.

Other Arabic cultural influences were adapted into other domains of life such as dressing, music and food, but these influences were not hegemonic but heterogeneous since innovative forms were created and became part of Malay culture, such as the *zapin* dance and *nasyid*.[d] So were other global influences such as from India in terms of wedding rituals and *dangdut* music. The craft of indigenous *batik* printing and manufacturing perhaps embodies this cultural infusion with batik motives embodying Indian, Islamic, Chinese and European motives reflecting the different cultural influences.

Islam from the Middle East, India and China made its way to Southeast Asia, in their varied orientations, but rarely were these imitated lock, stock and barrel. As in most cultures, the religion was syncretised/indigenised (or glocalised) taking on the culture and traditions of that society and the responses from locals were just as varied and contested. For example, in the 17th century, intense religious debates took place in Aceh

---

[d] Choral singing.

(an important Islamic center of the Malay world) between the orthodox Gujerati-born Nurrudin al-Raniri and Syekh Shamsuddin, the student of the local mystic Hamzah Fansuri. In the early 19th century, the influence of Wahhabi ideology brought back by returned local scholars and pilgrims from the Hejaz-inspired the Padri Wars (1821–1837). This uprising failed partly because they were defeated by the Dutch, but also because this puritanical strain of Islam was rejected by the locals and seen as alien to Minangkabau culture. In general, the history of Islam in this region shows that extreme, fanatical orientations have been rejected by the Malays. Islam in this region generally exhibits moderation in practice and outlook as manifested in what is called "Islam Nusantara".

Pre-colonial Malay identity was not based on race (which is a colonial construct by the way), but was based on an inclusive form of Malay way of life signified by the use of Malay language and Islam. The term "*masuk Melayu*[e]" demonstrates the ease in which foreign traders, travelers and scholars assimilated into Malay society and was accepted as part of the community. "Malays" as a fluid and flexible category could include Javanese, Bugis, Makassarese, even Chinese, Indians and Arabs if they had inter-married and adopted a Malay way of life forming hybrid cultural identities such as the Jawi-Peranakan.[f] Identities were diverse and multiple where a sense of belonging could be to something as fluid as a commercial diaspora or a place. Malay-constructed identities continued to evolve where during the colonial period, allegiance

An episode of the Padri War. Dutch and Padri soldiers fighting over a Dutch standard in 1831. Public domain.

---

[e] Trans. Literally, "Enter into Malayness".
[f] Offspring of Indian men who marry local Malay women.

to the sultan was transferred to the *bangsa* and then to the post-colonial nation states of Indonesia, Malaysia, Brunei and Singapore.

Before the advent of nation–states with its attendant bounded territorial and national identities, the pre-colonial Malay world was made up of urban city centers or port polities (such as Banten, Makassar, Aceh and Johor) which were cosmopolitan in nature. These port-polities had diverse subjects, fluid and shifting populations very much subjected to the tides of international trade. These urban cosmopolitan centers were attuned to the latest global, ideological, political and cultural influences from the Eastern and Western metropolitan centers of power of the time, be it the Ottomans, Mughals, Ming and Tang dynasties and later London and Amsterdam. Sultan Iskandar Muda of Aceh (r.1607–1637) and his daughter Sultanah Safiatuddin Shah (r.1641–1675) established and institutionalised Acehnese law codes and fashioned court culture after the Mughals and Ottomans. Their reigns witnessed a proliferation of Aceh's Malay literary works adapted from Arabic and Persian texts.[g] Her predecessor husband, Sultan Iskandar Thani (r.1637–1641) was very much into fashion and ordered jewels and diamonds in local design but cut and custom made in Amsterdam. Sultan Abu Bakar of Johor (r.1885–1895) was well-travelled and hobnobbed with Queen Victoria of England and adopted European military fashion into formal royal court dressing.

Cosmopolitanism as drawing on traces and residues of many cultural and ethical systems connotes the ability to stand outside one's life scripted by any one community (whether it is faith, tradition or culture) to draw selectively on a variety of discursive meanings. A more genuine cosmopolitanism is first of all an orientation, a willingness to engage with others. It is an intellectual and aesthetic stance to openness and divergent cultural experiences, a search for contrast rather than uniformity; a state of readiness to make one's way to other cultures through listening, looking, intuiting and

---

[g] Some examples are the *Hikayat Aceh* and *Adat Aceh*.

reflecting. Pre-colonial Malay world exhibited these characteristics in a sense due to geographical and practical needs of trade. However, this plural cosmopoli of Southeast Asia was transformed into a more distinctly European space during colonialism and later this space was dominated and controlled by the independent states which succeeded the colonial states. These states (Singapore, Malaysia, Indonesia) tend to dominate and control this space in their effort to create a national identity based on what the state deemed as local values that could define the state's identity. However, with globalisation, these states are finding it increasingly difficult to find a consensus since these states cannot control new ideas, ways of life, new faiths, allegiances and loyalties resulting through global contacts and networks. Globalisation has changed traditional ties and also challenged the relative boundedness of the constituents of the nation–state. Now, new ties can be forged and broken by almost anyone.

Fast forward to the present, the main question is how do the Malays in Singapore balance global and particular forces such as the need to juggle between global, national and communal/familial identities and loyalties, the need to adapt forces of global Islam with its varied and complex orientations of Wahabism, Salafism, Sufism to a local secular and multi-cultural context and the need to retain Malay culture and language from being diluted by Westernisation, Americanisation, even the recent Korean wave in the form of pop-culture and consumerism? One extreme is to take on a disembedded form of humanistic universalism with the notion of world citizenry whilst the other is to try to remain closed, pure and authentic, free from any outside influences. The former is perhaps unrealistic, considering the resilience of nation–states and their continued pursuit to build and embed national loyalties in its citizens, especially one as diverse ethnically as Singapore; the latter is impractical if not impossible given the current stage of globalisation (perhaps with the exception of North Korea). The alternative is "grounded cosmopolitanism" or "national cosmopolitanism", a space where someone can be open to the world and at the same time be at "home". The Singapore government plays a critical role here in providing the framework to work out its nation-building projects based on secular and developmental foundations providing space for individual agency, liberal and progressive features of society in a fair and equal context. Another possibility is to open space from the ground-up i.e., "popular cosmopolitanism" or "everyday cosmopolitanism" where the citizens exercise agency to build a space for diversity and respect for others' differences[h].

Singaporean Malays found themselves a minority and in a uniquely Singaporean ethos of a secular, meritocratic and multicultural state since independence. New spaces for dealing with other communities and new identities and loyalties need to be forged. New waves of globalisation had to be dealt with together with its attendant threats and opportunities. The challenges are indeed great and complex. Singapore's nation-building project will continue to need the concerted efforts of both the government and its citizens, however, after 50 years,

Malay youths in *baju kurung*[i] during Hari Raya in the 1960s (top) and the new millennium (bottom). They still do wear the *baju kurung*; an indication the Malay identity is still very strong 50 years on. Top image courtesy of Salleh Sariman © 2015. All rights reserved.

---

[h] For a discussion on the different types of cosmopolitanism, see Gerhard Hoffstaedter, *Modern Muslim Identities: Negotiating Religion and Ethnicity in Malaysia* (Nias Press, 2011).

[i] A distinctive Malay dress worn by both men and women. The term *baju kurung* is loosely translated to mean "concealing dress" in Malay. It is a loose-fitting outfit that covers the wearer's body without showing its form. A typical *baju kurung* consists of a loose shirt with a rounded neckline, although there are variants that come with a collar. The outfit is usually worn as a top over a *sarong* (for women) or a pair of pants (for men). Occasionally, men also wear the *baju kurung* over a *sarong*. Norwani Md. Nawawi. (2010). Malaysia. In J. Dhamija (Ed.), *Encyclopedia of World Dress and Fashion* (Vol. 4). Oxford: Oxford University Press.

the Malays have evolved and developed a new Singaporean Malay/Muslim identity, just like the Malays of the past had transferred their allegiance from a sultan to *bangsa* Melayu to *bangsa* Singapura. Malay culture and language continue to evolve absorbing and synthesising external influences — English words have been adopted, hip-hop, Korean-pop, Bollywood, Hollywood found their way into Malay movies and songs. The Malays too, just like other communities in Singapore, are subject to other current global forces such as consumerism and popular culture. As in the past, the Malays have glocalised and made these their own. Popular culture has been Islamised and the burgeoning *halal* market is another example where the Malays have participated in a global capitalist market.

Other global challenges still need to be confronted; one of which are new variants of global Islamic forces — puritanical, fanatical and extremism threaten to once again split the community. However, the Malays today could draw important lessons from their commercially peripatetic ancestors who had survived earlier waves of globalisation. The attitude of mind, the moderate, tolerant, inclusionary and open Malay way of life where external influences were not shunned but adapted and localised and made into their own are critical in today's global context as well. Far from diluting Malay identity and culture, selective borrowing of foreign cultures and ideas enrich them. The Malay hybrid and cosmopolitan past could be used as a source of inspiration and as bases for future endeavours as Singaporeans and as responsible global citizens.

| BREAK NEW GROUND AND BE THE MALAY/MUSLIM ICON | Sumarleki Amjah |

My hope for the Singapore Malay/Muslim community come SG100 is that we will be a progressive community in Singapore contributing beyond its numbers. That we will excel in business and professions that we focus on. That we will be a community with a significant number of global business leaders, entrepreneurs, lawyers, doctors, architects and all fields that can contribute significantly towards Singapore's competitiveness in the global arena as the future challenge is not within but beyond.

We may not continue to grow in numbers but certainly, we can grow in quality. Our children will study abroad, in professional courses, in Ivy League schools, Oxbridge and top Chinese universities using our community funds. MENDAKI's core mission should not only be to alleviate the overall educational standards (aggregate level) of the community but to produce global Malay talents. In private equity ownership, our community should be over-represented, not only in business and property investments in Singapore but more so in the region. We can be the Malay elites of "Nusantara Melayu", one with a global worldview, traversing freely within the region and beyond. We will be a knowledge community specialised in specific fields which we can excel. We will own businesses across the region — Singapore, Malaysia, Brunei, Indonesia, Cambodia, Southern Thailand and Mindanao. While we continue to build strong social ties with the wider Singapore community, thus enhancing our social equity domestically, we expand our network deeper into the region, to regions where we will own properties and businesses, to the ASEAN hinterland, where we will dispense our professional expertise. We take control of the "Nusantara Melayu" with our sharpened skills, knowledge and expertise.

However, all these aspirations, no matter how noble, cannot be achieved without a strategic roadmap to surmount the obstacles. Given the current challenges facing our community, discrimination (institutionalised or otherwise) being at the core of it all, our community should stay focused in pursuing targeted interests, in the pursuit of being a community of excellence. Contrary to popular belief that education can be the "cure-all" remedy to our community's malaise, we should instead specialise in specific (identified) fields of excellence. *Opportunity is key*. We start by competing within our own community to harness our strengths and build a competitive ecosystem before competing broader at the national and global levels. We should specialise in certain business fields and professions and not spread ourselves too thinly. We have seen how the Jews succeed in global finance, media and entertainment. In Singapore, we see a disproportionate number of Indians in the legal profession. The Singapore Malay/Muslim community can excel by using the same approach. We focus and specialise, using all the resources at our disposal. We should focus our efforts and allocate maximum resources on the Malay/Muslim middle class to produce future talents. We should strengthen the core middle class so as to produce more regional and global talents of the future.

While the aspirations to being regional (and ultimately global) talents are appealing, there must be political will to ensure an equal playing field for all, regardless of race, language, or religion. Ultimately, we are competing against common global competitors. The government should take the lead in ensuring fair employment practices in all government sectors so that the private sector can follow suit.

At the core of it all, a democratic nation such as Singapore must be single-minded in its pursuit to attain a just and fair society. This we must pursue at all levels, be it the community, the government and the private sector.

The community meanwhile recognises that a growing number of its professionals is now engaged in the region — in the Middle East, Australia, perhaps even Europe and America. It might be worthwhile to develop a network of such talents and benefit from their experience and grow on them. I realise the Singapore Muslim Group in Dubai/UAE is already extending their "wings" back home, helping those who want to venture out, but more could be done and achieved. Here back in Singapore, we are always on the lookout for new external wings and for the Malay/Muslim talent to ride those wings better and further.

CHAPTER 38

GOING GLOBAL

AHMAD FUAD ABU BAKAR

Ahmad Fuad first arrived to the United Arab Emirates (UAE) in 1985 to work with Dubai Petroleum. With only about 200 Singaporeans in Dubai at that time, Ahmad Fuad collaborated with some Malaysians in UAE to form the Malaysia–Singapore Club and organised a Malaysia–Singapore night. This was the forerunner of Singapore's own Community Club and *Malam Singapura*. He also helped with the formation of other clubs like the Singapore Business Council, Singapore Women's Group and Singapore Malay/Muslim Group, to cater to the different interests of the larger Singaporean community.

Ahmad Fuad's quiet leadership is appreciated by many Singaporeans. With an affable disposition, he works with all groups to bring Singaporeans closer and foster a Singapore identity away from home. He will always be actively involved in all the events and has even volunteered his house as the venue for some of the events and gatherings. He has hosted visiting Singapore students to Dubai and even provided shelter for student interns, domestic helpers and whoever who is in need. During the 1990 Gulf War, Ahmad Fuad acted as the *de facto* Consul in Dubai when he organised evacuation for Singaporeans.

For all his efforts throughout the years, in pioneering the Singapore Club, helping fellow Singaporeans and organising various activities for the Singaporean community in Dubai, he was presented the "Outstanding Singaporean in Dubai" award by the Singapore Consulate-General.

Since his arrival in 1985, he has made Dubai his home for the last 30 years. And to make Dubai a home away from home, he and his wife opened an eatery in 2002, Singapore Deli, to offer home-cooked Singaporean and Asian cuisine.

ANITA SARAWAK

Born in Singapore on 23 March 1952, Ithnaini Mohamed Taib, better known as Anita Sarawak, is a professional entertainer famous for her showmanship, powerful vocals and energetic performances.

As the daughter of celebrated Malay film actor, director and film producer the late S Roomai Nor, and actress the late Siput Sarawak, she was exposed to the performing arts at a very young age. After her parents divorced, she grow close to her stepmother Umi Kalthum, also a veteran Malay film actress, and step-sister Noorkumalasari, who is a model, actress and singer. When she was 12 years old, Anita Sarawak returned to the care of her mother, Siput Sarawak. Siput was strict with Anita and rarely allowed her to play outdoors, so she spent most of her time at home practising ballet.

When she was 14, Anita Sarawak acted in her first film *Dua Kali Lima*. She also frequently performed at weddings and school functions, and her first professional job was singing Mandarin and Chinese-dialect songs at a Chinese restaurant. Soon, she performed in other venues such as the Neptune Theatre Restaurant and the Hilton Hotel. When she was 19, she was dubbed a "singing cyclone", and by the time she was 30, Anita Sarawak was dubbed Singapore's "First Lady of Song".

An EMI Records employee spotted her television performance on the then-Radio and Television Singapura and offered her a record deal. Anita Sarawak has since released numerous English and Malay records and albums.

Anita Sarawak was recruited to be a singing ambassador for Singapore from the mid-1970s. She was sent by the then Singapore Tourist Promotion Board (now known as the Singapore Tourism Board) and Singapore Airlines to countries such as the United States of America, West Germany and Brunei, to promote Singapore as a tourist destination. She performed at an international convention in Monte Carlo, Monaco in 1976 to boost Singapore's bid to host the next general meeting of the International Congress and Convention Association. She also represented Singapore in the Yamaha Music Festival held in Tokyo, Japan and the World Music Festival held in Seoul, South Korea in 1980.

Anita is a versatile and talented artiste, having performed in film, on television and on stage. She also set her sights on establishing her career beyond Singapore, and took on an offer at a club in Las Vegas. Despite her huge success in Southeast Asia, she had to encounter a lot of hurdles, and put in hard work and much effort to establish herself in the new environment. In the 18 years she was in Las Vegas, she worked her way up, from performing at lesser-known nightspots to Cleopatra's Barge at the famed Caesars Palace.

ASHLEY ISHAM (ESHAMUDDIN ISMAIL)

Ashley Isham is one of Singapore's most prominent figures in fashion and is well known worldwide. His career was sparked by his interest in watching and helping his seamstress mother with her sewing. He started designing his own clothes as he was dissatisfied with the limited designs in local shops.

Moving to London in 1996, he then pursued a diploma in fashion design at the Central Saint Martins College of Art & Design, and continued his further education at the London College of Fashion and Middlesex University. Ashley's debut collection launched in

November 2000 to critical acclaim, and his collections has since continued to be featured at the London Fashion Week. He has also showcased his works at various international fashion shows such as the Singapore Fashion Festival, the Audi Fashion Festival, Jakarta Fashion Week, Malaysia International Fashion Week and Singapore JewelFest. He has designed over 100,000 commemorative bottles and 1,000,000 cans of Coca Cola light for the Audi Fashion Festival held in Singapore in 2009, and also collaborated with Lee Hwa Jewellery to produce special designs for the jewellery brand in 2010 and 2012.

His collections are stocked in stores worldwide including London where he is based, Russia, China, and the Middle East, with a few stores in Singapore located at the Fullerton Hotel, Mandarin Gallery and Orchard Central.

Ashley has dressed some of the big names in the film, television, music and fashion industry such as Angelina Jolie, Keira Knightley, Kylie Minogue and Lady Gaga, as well as British and international royalties.

He was awarded the Berita Harian Achiever of the Year Award in 2007 for his achievements in his profession as a fashion designer.

EIRLIANI ABDUL RAHMAN

Eirliani is co-founder and Executive Director of YAKIN (Youths, Adult survivors & Kin In Need), which works in the area of child rights and child protection. YAKIN, which is a member of Twitter's Safety & Trust Council, organises creative writing workshops for children, as well as rock climbing camps for children from abused and/or disadvantaged backgrounds, and youths-at-risk.

From 1999 to 2003, Eirliani organised trade missions to Russia and Kazakhstan whilst at the then Singapore Trade Development Board (TDB), and was a member of the secretariat, partnering with Bain & Company, on the TDB's restructuring to the International

Enterprise Singapore. In 2004, she worked closely with Harvard Business School's Prof Michael Porter on the Kazakhstan Competitiveness Programme, where she was responsible for mapping out the strategies for the oil and gas machinery, and the transportation clusters at the national level. From 2005 to 2015, she was in the Singapore Foreign Service, where she served as First Secretary (Political) in Berlin and then as Political Counsellor in Delhi. She conceptualised and secured funding for the inaugural Singapore Film Festival in India. Working in concert with the Youth Olympic Games' Organising Committee, she played a role in the organisation of the celebrations in Berlin during the Olympic flame's journey across five continents.

In 2015, she won the BMW Foundation Responsible Leaders Award for her work on child sexual abuse in India. The social media campaign, called #FullStop to #childsexualabuse, which she led on behalf of Nobel Peace Prize laureate Kailash Satyarthi, reached 16 million people over six weeks. She writes for the Huffington Post and the India Today Group's DailyO on the issues of child abuse and child online safety. She is currently working on a book to be published by HarperCollins India, chronicling the true stories of survivors of child sexual abuse from around the world — Canada, Germany, India, Myanmar, Singapore, South Africa and the United States. Eirliani is a member of the Advisory Council of the Global Diplomacy Lab, a platform for exploring a new and more inclusive diplomacy which goes beyond traditional politics. She is an Asian Forum on Global Governance Fellow, co-sponsored by the Die Zeit newspaper and the Delhi-based Observer Research Foundation.

A graduate of the London School of Economics and Warwick University, Eirliani was a British Council Pathfinder scholar and was awarded the University of Warwick Singapore Scholarship. She won the MENDAKI Award in 1993, given to top Malay/Muslim candidates at the national level examinations. An avid rock climber and mountaineer, she regularly climbs in the Himalayas, and blogs for the Outdoor Journal on her adventures. She divides her time between Berlin, Delhi and

Singapore. Eirliani speaks English, Malay and German fluently, and has a rudimentary understanding of Arabic, French, Hindi, Mandarin and Russian.

HARDI KAMSANI

Hardi Kamsani is an Audio Engineer with All Mobile Video, Inc., a New York-based company that provides end-to-end video and audio solutions. Mainly, he is responsible for audio signal flow from inception to transmission. Twenty years of experience — from stage, studio and remotes, was recognised when he was awarded the TEC Award.[a] The TEC Award is presented annually by the National Association of Music Merchants (NAMM) Foundation at The NAMM Show. The NAMM TEC Awards recognises the individuals, companies and technical innovations behind the sound of recordings, live performances, films, television, video games and other media.

However his path to success was not without its challenges. To start a career at an unfamiliar terrain, one needs to be independent and know one's immediate responsibilities fast. Balancing account at that initial point is an immense challenge in itself as one needs to deal with the exorbitant rent and other expenses. Unfamiliar working landscape means one needs to play catch-up with his peers with regards to music catalogue who grew up with that sort of environment. One also needs to adapt to the work force and culture there. Knowing the lingo, references to an older piece of equipment or gear, cultural icons seem mundane but substantial enough, so as to get the right feel for the audio and video industry there.

One of the key traits to have is professionalism. For example, it is hard not be star-struck when working alongside one's musical heroes. Imagine he said, "Here I am second day at work and I'm standing next to ...."

---

[a] The TEC Awards is an annual programme recognising the achievements of audio professionals. The awards are given to honour technically innovative products as well as companies and individuals who have excelled in sound for television, film, recordings, and concerts. "TEC" is short for "Technical Excellence & Creativity".

Some of the concerts and live recordings he was involved in were performances by groups like U2, Linkin Park and The Rolling Stones, just to name a few. He was involved in recordings of some of the television programmes like the Survivor series and award shows like the Grammy Awards[b].

One piece of advice Hardi has if one wants to succeed as a global Malay one has to evolve as one's career goals become achievements, then repeat the process.

MAIMOONAH HUSSAIN

Maimoonah Hussain is the Group Managing Director of Affin Hwang Capital, a major integrated investment banking powerhouse which today ranks among Malaysia's largest. She is responsible for leading the combined Investment Banking, Securities and Asset Management businesses. Prior to her current position, Maimoonah had successful stints with Affin Investment Bank, Standard Chartered Bank Malaysia and Standard Chartered Bank Singapore and Morgan Grenfell (Asia) Limited. When she was the Managing Director of Affin Investment Bank in 2007, she successfully executed a turnaround and growth strategy. She successfully led and won the bid for the purchase of HwangDBS investment banking, asset management and futures businesses in January 2014 amid intense competition from other industry players such as AMMB Holdings, Alliance Financial Group and K&N Kenanga Holdings. In September 2014, she again led and successfully merged the investment banking, securities and asset management businesses of Affin Investment Bank with HwangDBS. The RM1.36 billion merger led to the formation of Affin Hwang Capital. Under her leadership, the Affin Hwang Investment Bank was ranked the number one brokerage by both traded volume and traded value by Bursa Malaysia and was also named Best

---

[b] https://www.discogs.com/artist/406211-Hardi-Kamsani.

Equities Investment Bank and the Best Institutional Equities Investment Bank for 2014 at the Bursa Malaysia Broker Awards. For her leadership and passion in growing a medium-sized niche investment bank into a major integrated player in the Malaysian financial industry, she was awarded the Outstanding Chief/ Senior Executive (Overseas) Award at the Singapore Business Awards (SBA) 2015. The award recognises an outstanding Singaporean who works overseas and definitely for her achievements, she is a perfect role model for Singaporeans working overseas.

M F MAJEED

Mr M F Majeed has been in private practice in Sydney, Melbourne, Perth, Brunei, USA, UK and in Asia–Pacific Rim region as a consultant. He has more than 25 years experience in all aspect of investment management in real estate development, fund management, business management, legal management and contract management of projects using softwares like Estate Master, Edwards, Buildsoft and Cost X. He has been partner, director, senior consultant to various USA multinational corporations, and leading fund management, project management, contract management and cost management consultancy firms like EG Fund Management, Rawlinsons, Mott McDonald Franklin and Andrews, Atkins Faithful and Gould, Wilde and Wollard, Assetlink and property developers like Frasers Property, City Development, Singapore Land, Hong Kong Land, AllGreen Development and Regent Development and financial institutions like Standard Chartered Bank, DBS Bank OCBC and others. He has participated in more than 100 major projects such as apartments, serviced apartments, hotels, residential, health care, hospitals, commercials, educational, banks, retail and industrial. Having completed the various cost engineering and project management courses in the United States, he is in the panel of Arbitrators and Mediators in CDRLS[c] in the United States. Currently, he is a Senior Consultant with a leading residential property developer based in China, developing the renowned $228 billion Forest City project in Malaysia.

NOOR IMAMBECK

Noor Imambeck left Singapore for Bahrain in 1989 to be the Manager of the Arab Banking Corporation. He left Arab Banking Corporation as Executive Director in 1999. Prior to this appointment, he was a cheque clearing clerk with the First Chicago Bank Singapore branch (1972–1983). He rose to become the Head of Administration culminating as the General Manager of Abu Dhabi Islamic Bank in 2006 and in 2008, Executive Vice President/General Manager until 2012. Noor Imambeck is a perfect example of a Singaporean Malay/Muslim who had done well internationally. He was the first Chairman of the Singapore Business Council and the Singapore Malay/Muslim Group in Dubai. After his retirement, he was appointed Advisor to the Singapore Malay/Muslim Professional and Entrepreneur Group, United Arab Emirates. He is currently serving the Board of Director of Warees Halal and Investment Committee Member of the Basel Property Fund.

NUR AMALI IBRAHIM

Nur Amali Ibrahim is an Assistant Professor of Modern Islam in the Department of Religious Studies and the Department of International Studies at the Indiana University Bloomington. He graduated with a degree in 2001 from National University of Singapore with First Class Honours in Southeast Asian Studies. He then did his Masters and Ph.D in Anthropology at New York University. Prior to his appointment at Indian University Bloomington, he worked as an Academy Scholar at the Weatherhead Center for International Affairs in Harvard University from 2011 to 2013.

---

c Contract Deliverables Requirements List.

As an anthropologist of Islam who specialises in Indonesia, his research interests include Islam in the modern world, theories of pedagogy and socialisation, contests of scriptural interpretation, social movements as well as religion and media. His current project examines two rival student groups of university students in contemporary Indonesia — Islamists who hold a puritanical religious view demanding the implementation of the Sharia (Islamic law) in Indonesia, and liberal Muslims committed to pluralism and the secularisation of the polity.

RAIHAN MOHAMMED NAWAWI

Raihan Mohammed Nawawi is an example of a Global Malay who has established roots in Melbourne, Australia, and is actively involved in volunteering and contributing to the growth and development of Malays/Muslims in Australia.

Before moving to Australia, he graduated from Nanyang Technological University (NTU) with a bachelor in Electrical Engineering in 1996. He then worked as an Engineer at PCR Engineers Pte Ltd for four years (1996 to 2001). In 2002, he graduated from National Institute of Education (NIE) with a Postgraduate Diploma in Education, and then went on to become a teacher with the Ministry of Education for six years from 2002 to 2008.

He moved to Australia in 2008 to pursue his Master's in Education from the University of Melbourne, and graduated in 2011. While in Australia, he also pursued a Graduate Diploma in Management from Victoria University (2008 to 2009), and gained a Certificate in Training and Education from Southern Cross Training, Melbourne in 2012.

He was a Marketing Team Leader for the Federation of Australian Muslim Students and Youth (FAMSY) from 2010 to 2012, and worked as a design teacher at the Minaret College (2010 to 2014), the largest co-educational Islamic school in South-eastern Melbourne. Since 2012, he is the manager for

mybookstore, a leading online Islamic bookstore owned by FAMSY. He is also a casual broadcaster for the Suara Melayu Melbourne since 2013, a radio station that is part of the Ethnic Public Broadcasting Association of Victoria, where he introduced a new segment on Malay culture and values based on the late Dr Muhammad Ariff Ahmad's book titled *Nilam: Nilai Melayu menurut Adat*. Since 2014, he is also a religious teacher at Mt Hira College, a co-educational Islamic College for students in Grade 1 to Year 12, with the aim of developing confident students who are proud of their Islamic identity, and are committed, passionate and hardworking citizens who are ready to contribute positively and productively to the Australian society.

ROSANA GULZAR MOHD

With more than 10 years of experience as financial journalist and banker, Rosana is currently pursuing her Master of Science in Islamic finance at INCEIF, Malaysia. As an MSc candidate at INCEIF, her research interest is in finding a feasible framework for equitable financing and investment arrangements in banking. She had also completed Chartered Financial Analyst examination level 1.

A Singaporean Muslim, she graduated from Nanyang Technological University (NTU) with a Second Upper Class Honours in Communications Studies in 2003. Following stints with several business newspapers, she was headhunted to join Hongkong Shanghai Banking Corporation (HSBC) in Singapore. Her work, which involved investment communications for retail bankers, included helping the bank manage raging customers during the 2008 global financial crisis. In 2010, she joined HSBC's global Islamic banking business in Dubai. She headed the HSBC Amanah's corporate communications efforts across their retail, commercial and investment banking businesses in Southeast Asia, the Middle East and the UK.

SHAFIE SHAMSUDIN

Shafie Shamsudin is the Chief Executive Officer and President of Board of Director at PT Trans Retail Indonesia, a franchisee of Carrefour and a subsidiary of Chairul Tanjung Corporation, an Indonesian-based holding company. As CEO of PT Trans Retail Indonesia, Shafie leads an organisation of approximately 20,000 employees and 100 stores across 35 cities in Indonesia. He is also sits on the Alumni Advisory Board of Nanyang Technological University (NTU)'s Nanyang Business School.

Before joining Trans Retail in Indonesia, he was the Executive Director of Global Talent Management and Organisational Development of the Carrefour Group based in Paris. He also served as the Managing Director of Carrefour Singapore, Carrefour Malaysia, and Carrefour Indonesia, prior to his appointment in Paris.

He began his career as a trainee for Carrefour, and then became the chain's first non-Frenchman to hold a top position. He made history when he became the first Asian expatriate staff from Carrefour to be posted to Indonesia first as the Non-Food Merchandise Manager and then the Managing Director.

In 2010, he was given the Berita Harian's Anugerah Jauhari (Achiever of the Year Award) for his excellent corporate achievements.

SHAHRIN ABDOL SALAM

With a career spanning over 18 years, Shahrin has accumulated extensive experience in the railway industry. He started his career in SMRT in the Maintenance Division, specialising in Environmental Control Systems as a Maintenance Engineer. His portfolio expanded as he progressed in the organisation to become a Section Manager in 2000 and in 2005, taking on the role of a Senior Manager, Facilities and Building Management; responsible for all MRT and LRT stations in the North-South, East–West Lines and Bukit Panjang LRT.

In 2008, Shahrin was seconded to Dubai as General Manager of SMRT Engineering Middle East; the first overseas subsidiary for SMRT to spearhead the team in providing railway consultancy during the construction phase and thereafter, the operations and maintenance services for the Palm Jumeirah Monorail System — the first of its kind in the Middle East. In 2009, Shahrin was appointed as Managing Director of SMRT Engineering Middle East and SMRT International (Abu Dhabi). He was responsible for business development and operations covering the United Arab Emirates. He played a pivotal role in supporting the certification and operationalisation of the first in the region, the Personal Rapid Transit (PRT) in Abu Dhabi's Masdar City.

Shahrin returned to Singapore in 2010 to helm various senior leadership roles in SMRT's Rail Operations Division. He was the Director of Station Operations between 2010 and 2011; and Director of Train Operations till 2012. In November 2012, he was relocated to United Arab Emirates to join Dubai Government's Roads and Transport Authority (RTA).

In 2014, he was appointed as Chief Engineer, Rail Operations where he facilitated the mobilisation and inauguration of Dubai's first Tram system. In 2015, the Director–General of Roads & Transport Authority appointed Shahrin as the Subject-Matter-Expert (SME) for Railways Operations. Shahrin's last held appointment in RTA was Rail Expert & Advisor to the CEO, Rail Agency where he provided strategic advice on matters relating to railway operations, maintenance and projects. Shahrin was a member of Dubai Railway System Operations & Maintenance Management Board. In May 2016, Shahrin will be returning to Singapore and be appointed as SMRT's Vice President, Trains Planning and Capability Development. He has been tasked to oversee the strategic and operational planning and build-up of core capabilities to deliver robust rail reliability and service excellence. He is to synergise the activities in SMRT Trains and engage key stakeholders such as Land Transport Authority (LTA) to achieve the strategic and operational outcomes for train services under SMRT.

Work aside, Shahrin has been an active grassroots leader since 1989; starting with People's Association Youth Executive Committee (YEC) where he held various positions, including Chairman of Bukit Timah CC YEC and Member of PA Regional Youth Council (West). When he was stationed in the Middle East, Shahrin supported the Singapore community in the UAE through his involvement in the Singapore Malay–Muslim Group (SMG) and Singapore Business Council (SBC). Since 2012, Shahrin has been a member in the Executive Committee of the SMG and participated in the various initiatives to forge a strong Singapore community spirit in the UAE.

DR SHAMSIAH ABDUL KARIM

Dr Shamsiah Abdul Karim is currently the Chief Operating Officer (COO) of the Albukhary Foundation, a personal charity of Malaysian businessman Syed Mokhtar Albukhary that is focused on programmes aimed at eradicating poverty and fostering racial harmony that spans Asia, Europe, Africa and Australia.

Previously, she was with the Islamic Religious Council of Singapore (MUIS) and managed the Assets Development division in the area of *zakat*, *wakaf*, mosque building, Islamic education fund, *fara'id* and other voluntary funding programmes.

With more than 20 years of experience in revenue management and administration, she has delivered many talks at conferences and seminars on Islamic finance, *wakaf*, *zakat*, *fara'id*, real estate, accounting and marketing, as well as having several scholarly publications on *wakaf* and *zakat*.

She graduated from the International Islamic University of Malaysia with a First Class Honours in Business Administration. She also has a post-graduate diploma in Islamic Banking and Finance from the same university, as well as Doctor of Philosophy (PhD) in Islamic Finance from the University of Durham, United Kingdom.

SUMARLEKI AMJAH

Sumarleki has more than 20 years of general management, sales and marketing experience in the consumer goods space at a regional level, specialising in Southeast and South Asia. His career started at Prudential and went on work as head of international marketing (consumer products) at Sime Darby. In 2008, he joined Del Monte, an integrated global branded food and beverage company. As Head of S&W Processed Business and Business Development (Asia), he crafted strategic plans charting new business frontiers and accelerated growth for the company in the region. His career path then took him to World Kitchen LLC — a global market leader in the houseware industry with a turnover of almost US$800 million. They market iconic brands such as Corelle, Pyrex, Corningware, Visions, Snapware, Revere and Chicago Cutlery. He held the position of Managing Director — South Asia covering the full business operations of Southeast Asia and South Asia (Indian sub-continent), managing four P&L clusters.

UMAR ABDUL HAMID

Umar is a serial entrepreneur and an angel investor actively investing in startups in fintech (financial technology) and media industry in the United States and Singapore. He invests at an early stage and works closely with founders and co-founders to build startups beyond the idea stage. He was involved in startups four years ago when his son and other young and smart entrepreneurs of various nationalities in New York, presented him with game-changing ideas in the fintech industry. Throughout the four years of investing and managing several startups, he had built the ecosystem in the United States and has been tapping on it to launch and develop a new ecosystem in Singapore. Within the next three years, he plans to setup an accelerator in Singapore

focusing on Internet-of-Things (IOT) and Artificial Intelligence (AI).

Prior to his startup journey, Umar has been for the past 18 years deeply involved in managing, acquiring and divesting public and private companies. He has in-depth experience in renewable and conventional energy, infrastructure, manufacturing, technology, food and services industry. Equipped with many years of operational business acumen, Umar usually takes an active role as Executive Chairman or CEO in most companies in which he has invested.

His past appointments include serving as Chairman and Member of the Board of Directors of several public companies, namely KFC Berhad, QSR Brands Berhad (Malaysia's only fully-integrated food operator and dominating the country's retail food industry), First Engineering Ltd (a leading manufacturer of ultra-precision mold and plastic components for high-technology engineering applications with operations in Singapore, Malaysia, China and India) and ZingMobile Ltd (a pioneer for publishing value-added mobile content, services and applications). He also served as CEO of Reed Group Holdings Ltd (renamed as China Entertainment Sports Ltd) and Executive Director of Strike Engineering Ltd (providing a fully integrated range of mechanical and electrical engineering services, re-named as Magnus Energy Ltd). Prior to that, Umar was a Project Engineer with Alstom Group (France), where he managed power distribution projects, installing high-voltage switchgears in Saudi Arabia, Bahrain and France. He also served as a Manager of Industry Development at the Singapore Polytechnic, supporting technology and knowledge transfer from engineering institutions to companies.

Umar has served as elected Member of Parliament in the Republic of Singapore as well as both Vice-Chairman and Chairman of Middle East Business Group at Singapore Business Federation. He has been an Advisor to several non-profit and non-government organisations, supplementing social, educational, and economic development initiatives.

A Fulbright Scholar, Umar earned his Master of Business Administration from the University of Chicago Booth School of Business, his Master of Education focused on Administration, Planning and Social Policy from Harvard Graduate School of Education, and his Bachelor of Science in Electrical Engineering from the University of Arizona. He was a participant of the Owner–President Management Program at Harvard Business School. He writes and speaks fluent English, French, and Malay.

ZACK ZAINAL ABIDIN

Zack Zainal Abidin started his career in the security field as a Police Inspector with the Republic of Singapore Police Force at the age of 19. He was among the first batch of AVSEC Professional Managers certified through the alliance between AACO (Arab Air Carriers Organisation) and ICAO (International Civil Aviation Organisation).

In his current position as Divisional Vice President of Group Security, Emirates Airlines, Emirates, he reports to the Divisional Senior Vice President (Group Security). The scope of work covers:

- General management and operations of the Emirates Group Security (EGS) Division,
- Operation of aviation security and security risk management of Emirates Airlines' network and EK Group on the whole with a total workforce of about 64,000 employees
  (a) Number of Aircraft (on order) — 257
  (b) Number of stations/routes — 150
  (c) 171 Nationalities
- As well as general security spectrum of the other business streams within the group which also includes dnata operations.

He is also immensely involved in the integration of new security solutions, aviation security training and development and quality drive in the realm of AVSEC. A firm believer of continuous improvement process and that "Security is Everybody's Business", he is very much involved in initiatives towards increasing and enhancing safety-related education.

He has been instrumental in steering Emirates Group Security to be among the few in the world to be certified with ISO 2001, ISO 2800, TACSS, and such. Hence Emirates Group Security was accorded with the distinction of receiving the Dubai Quality Award (Appreciation) in 2012.

Despite his busy schedule, he still gets himself involved in numerous community and social activities. Every now and then, based on his experience in the media, he will help with the small-scale productions for the Singapore community in UAE and also for his children's school. An active sportsman, he also heads several portfolios for sporting events/clubs.

SMG leaders with Guest-of-Honour Zainul Abidin Rasheed (in blue *baju kurung*) and Consul-General Dileep Nair (third from left) at the SMG-organised Nusantara Aidilfitri with fellow members of the ASEAN community — Brunei Darussalam, Indonesia and Malaysia. Image courtesy of The Singapore Malay/Muslim Group (SMG) © 2016. All rights reserved.

Desert outing organised by SMG-Youth for the Singaporean community in the UAE. Image courtesy of The Singapore Malay/Muslim Group (SMG) © 2016. All rights reserved.

THE SINGAPORE MALAY/MUSLIM GROUP (SMG) IN DUBAI: NEAR THE TOP OF THE WORLD FEELING

Ahmad Fuad Abu Bakar

The SMG was formed on 6 February 2006 as an informal non-profit organisation. It was founded by a group of dedicated professionals working and living in the United Arab Emirates (UAE) with a strong desire to volunteer and contribute to the growth and well-being of the Singapore Muslims in the UAE. The founding members were:

- Mr Noor Imambeck
- Dr Ahmad Jaffar
- Mr Syed Hasan Alsagoff
- Mr Ramli Sulaiman
- Mr Zainul Abidin Aljunied
- Mr Ismail Iswan
- Mr Rizal Tan Abdullah
- Mr Ahmad Fuad Abu Bakar

Since its formation, the SMG has grown from strength to strength and has evolved into a mainstream group in the UAE for the Singaporean Muslim community residing in Dubai and other states within the UAE. The SMG has become the centre for social support and networking for both Singaporean Muslims and the expatriate community in the UAE.

The group not only assists newly-arrived Singaporeans settle down in the UAE but at the same time provides assistance to those already residing in the UAE. It is a place where they can exchange experiences and gain social support. More importantly, in line with our Islamic call for the building of a strong *ummah* (community) and the Malay spirit of *gotong-royong*, through our community bonding activities, the SMG has provided Muslim Singaporeans with a sense of belonging and identity in the UAE — one that is deeply rooted in both Islamic and Singaporean Malay culture and traditions.

The SMG initiative also includes networking and linking up with Malay/Muslim organisations, finding opportunities to work together for the betterment of the society both in Singapore and abroad. Similar Singaporean Muslim groups have also indicated their interests to emulate the group's efforts and formed similar groups, such as the SMG–Qatar. This is will further assist the Malay/Muslim community in working towards their overall advancement both in Singapore and internationally.

The SMG is not an "exclusive" club. Although the focus is on Malay/Muslim Singaporeans, the group has also worked closely with other Singapore clubs namely the Singapore Business Council and Singapore Women's Group. Many memorable events such as Singapore Carnival, Singapore National Day Celebration were the result of that close cooperation. SMG members are also free to join other Singapore clubs to cater to their other needs.

Below are some of the activities organised by the group as part of its effort to strengthen ties and improve relations:

- **Ramadan and Hari Raya AidilFitri**

Ramadan and Syawal are important months in the SMG's calendar, when the group would organise annual *iftars* (breaking of fast) and Aidilfitri celebrations for the

Singaporean Muslims in the UAE and also invite Singaporean non-Muslim groups. These events which the SMG have organised have helped foster a greater sense of camaraderie and community spirit among the Singaporean Muslims and also the larger Singaporean population in the UAE. These events are supported and subsidised by the Overseas Singaporean Unit (OSU) in the Prime Minister's Office.

- **Interns Accommodation and JC's Visit**

The SMG also provide accommodation for interns mainly from the Singapore Management University (SMU) and also from other tertiary institutions.

- **SMG-Amanah Charity Work**

As the number of Singaporeans increases in the UAE, the SMG has also taken the opportunity to organise new activities. In 2011, the SMG formalised its charity work under the auspices of a newly-formed sub-group, SMG-Amanah. The subgroup aims to fulfill duties as Muslims and global citizens by organising events to aid and perform charity work. This is a collective effort by Singaporean Muslims in the UAE for the propagation of charitable act. The charity activities span from Africa to China.

- **Self-Enrichment Events**

With regards to self-enrichment, the group has continued to organise talks for the SMG community in Dubai/UAE. Besides speakers from the UAE, the SMG has also invited speakers from Singapore and Malaysia.

- **Annual Breakfast**

Every year during the cooler months, the SMG organises a breakfast gathering. The SMG always see the importance of bringing Singaporeans together. The turmoil in the Middle East emphasised the need for expat community from Singapore to stay in touch with each other and to keep abreast of developments in the community. This will help in situation of emergency and crisis where the need arises to help their fellow citizens.

- **5-Aside Football**

This popular annual event, which is held in conjunction with the celebration of the UAE National Day in December, has now become an important part of the ASEAN community calendar. Spearheaded by the SMG and the Emirates Group Security (EGS) and under the patronage of the Consul General of

Republic of Singapore, the event has developed into an annual charity family occasion where apart from the 5-aside football tournament, the SMG and the EGS organise games and food stalls for the children and ladies attending the event.

- **SMG Youth Wing**

With the increasing number of young Malay/ Muslim Singaporeans professionals coming to the UAE to work, it was felt that it would be good to have a group that could assist fellow Singaporean Malays/ Muslims and other Singaporeans with their transition into a new environment in the UAE and facilitate their

integration into the new society and at the same time maintain roots and links with their home country.

In April 2015, the SMG formalised its youth wing or SMG-Youth. Among other things, the objectives of forming this group are to groom young leaders to

be involved in community work and eventually take over the helm of the SMG leadership and succession.

CHAPTER 39

IN SEARCH FOR THE CANON OF SINGAPORE MALAY POETRY: REFLECTION ON NATURE, RACE, RELIGION AND LOVE*

Hadijah Rahmat

This paper discusses selected poems by three generations of Malay writers in Singapore from the first generation poets who received their vernacular education during British colonial period, before Malayan Independence in 1957; to second generation writers who received Malay education when Singapore was part of Malaysia (1957–1965) who established their poems in 1970s; and the third generation writers who received bilingual education after Singapore became a Republic in the 1980s. These iconic poems embody the aesthetic as well as the cultural and political values of Malay society. It is an early attempt to define and search for the canon of Singapore Malay poetry.

Keywords: Literature; canon; poetry; Singapore; culture; identity; values.

Introduction

Some years ago, I was asked by one English literature professor to identify a few Malay poems written by Singaporean Malay poets which can be regarded as canon. This has led me to reflect on the notions of literary canon and development of Malay poetry.

Modern Malay poetry has a history for about a century since its birth in the early 20th century. However,

*This article first appeared in *Malay Literature* Volume 26, Number 1 (2013). Reproduced with editing.

Malay poetry written by citizens of Singapore since 1965, are relatively young in age, averaging about 45 years old. This length of time after independence is rather short for any nation to develop her national identity despite the strong economic growth and development building rapidly over a few generations. Singapore has inherited many great civilisations from Malay, Indian, Chinese and European worlds. Nevertheless, the development of Singapore's national identity, is still at its early stage, particularly in cultures and the arts.

Therefore, the task of selecting canon Malay poems and poems in other official languages is indeed challenging, especially when canon poem itself firstly must be of a high standard of quality, is sustainable, stable and is well tested in terms of its influence and recognition from audiences and its social contexts. Moreover, a literary work which had already been accepted as canon by a society, would still be revisited and re-evaluated due to changes in society and times.

This was the case for Western literature since 1960s when it was criticised as a collection of books written by "dead white European males" which are not representing the contemporary perspective of a changed Western communities all over the world. For example, Alan Bloom (1987), in his book, *The Closing of the American Mind*, has debunked the existing Western notion of canon of English literature in Europe and America. The contribution of non-white ethnic writers from African–Americans, Hispanic Americans, Asian Americans, Native Americans and non-European writers and female writers who write in English are now given due recognition as a result of this literary debate and re-evaluation. Literary works by feminist and gay authors which were never considered for canon works, have since been accepted and are now being taught in some university courses.

The term 'canon' was first used to refer to "the books of the Bible officially recognised by the Church"; how its meaning has changed and widened to include literary works that have achieved an 'official status' of having high quality and high aesthetic values

(George P. Landow, 2010). The experience of Western literature shows that the concept of literary canon is not static but always changing. This is explained by O'Brien as following:

> *Canon is an evolving creation, not something written in stone*
>
> Sean O'Brien, 2008

Thus, what should be the definition of canon in relation to poetry for Singapore? What are the criteria to be used to select poems by Singapore poets?

> *The literary canon of a country or a group of people is comprised of a body of works that are highly valued by scholars and others because of their aesthetic value and because they embody the cultural and political values of that society*
>
> Thomas J Schoenberg and Lawrence J Trudeau, 2006[1]

Here, the works selected must consist of two values — the aesthetic as well as cultural and political values of its society. Schoenberg and Trudeau have defined literary canon as the "best literary achievement of the culture". This definition recognises the dynamics of literary and cultural processes and complexity of its meanings and significance. This definition is hence adopted as my working definition as it is most suitable and practical for selecting the canon of Singaporean Malay poetry.

Selected Poets

Since 1965 to date, thousands of poems have been written by Singaporean Malay poets.[2] The exact total number of poems produced within this period is unknown as no comprehensive study has been done. Studies on Malay poems in Singapore were done by Masuri S N (1983, 1985), Hadijah Rahmat (1987, 2000, 2004) and by Rasiah Halil (2000).

In comparison to other literary genres, poetry is the most popular and productive. Thousands of poems have been written by numerous poets; however for this article, only 11 poets and 11 poems are selected. These poets have been active in writing for at least two decades within the period of 1965–2000. Their literary works are widely known within the literary fraternity and have received social recognition by the Malay literary awards in Singapore — Hadiah Sastera Singapura (or Anugerah Persuratan). Some poets have been awarded national and regional literary awards such as Anugerah Tun Seri Lanang, Cultural Medallion, Anugerah Mastera and SEA Write Awards. Apart from the literary awards, the stability and sustainability of the author and their works are also taken into consideration. The new writers who appeared only in the last 10 years or so are not included, even though his or her works have shown great potential. Stability and sustainability are critical criteria for this selection.

These poets are also representing three generations of Malay writers in Singapore: the early generation poets who received their vernacular education during British colonial period, before Malayan Independence in 1957 (such as Masuri S N, Suratman Markasan, A Ghani Hamid and Noor SI) and they were active since the 1950s and 1960s; the second generation writers who received Malay education when Singapore was part of Malaysia, 1957–1965 (such as Djamal Tukimin and Mohamad Latif Mohammad) who established their poems in 1970s; and the third generation writers who received bilingual education when Singapore become a Republic (Asmin, Rasiah Halil, Hadijah Rahmat, Johar Buang and Isa Kamari) who began to make an impact in the 1980s. This representativeness of generation of writers and their iconic works is another criterion used besides the poet's stability, sustainability and social recognition. These selection criteria may not be perfect, but they provide an objective, balanced and the best framework to work on given the limited number of poets and space given to the writer.

Selected Poems

Ini Nasi Yang Kusuap
(This Rice that I Eat)

Since the very beginning, Malay literature had emphasised on the role of literature for the development and welfare of society. The social function of traditional literature was continued by modern Malay writers, especially in the 1950s, by a group of young writers from that generation who called themselves Asas '50 and upheld the motto of "Arts for Society" (*Sastera Untuk Masyarakat*). These Asas '50 writers wanted to fight for political independence and was concerned about for the plight of the poor and the underclass, such as the farmers, fishermen and labourers. The struggles and contributions of the working class were highlighted and highly acknowledged. Masuri's poems are the best representation of this literary movement and the new social views that emerged after the Second World War. Masuri's fighting spirit for the cause of the underclass was explicitly manifested in his poem, *Ini Nasi Yang Kusuap* (This Rice that I Eat), as a noble tribute to farmers who struggled in planting and harvesting the *padi* trees to provide rice or basic staple foods needed by society.

Jadi yang kumakan bukan berasal dari nasi
tapi peluh, darah dalam isi mengalir pasti.
jadi yang kutelan bukan berasal dari padi
tapi dari urat, dari nadi seluruh Pak Tani.

(So what I eat is not originally from rice
But from sweat, blood constantly flowing;
So what I swallow is not originally from padi
But from the sinews, the pulse of all peasants.)

This poem was written before 1965, but it should be regarded as canon of Singapore, as it serves as a bridge and historical symbol that reflects the economic, cultural and political relationship between Singapore and Malaysia and other parts of Malay world before 1965. This poem is rather special because of its cultural and historical values, its universal message, and for its aesthetic value. This poem has established Masuri as a pioneer of modern Malay poetry. Interestingly, this poem continues to attract great interest among the younger generation. The poem is widely popular and is being studied in schools in Singapore and Malaysia; and two songs have been composed based on this poetry.[3]

Jalan Permulaan (The Beginning)

Political developments and educational backgrounds determined significantly the development of Malay literature in Singapore. The authors are always sensitive and very concerned about the plight of their community due to Singapore's separation from Malaysia and impact of rapid urbanisation and modernisation which influenced their tradition, culture and identity. This social concern was clearly manifested in the poem, *Jalan Permulaan* (The Beginning), written by a first generation poet, Suratman Markasan. The poet felt a deep sense of loss and expressed it repeatedly, six times in his poem:

Aku kehilangan lautku
Aku kehilangan bukitku
Aku kehilangan diriku.

Aku kehilangan beliaku
Aku kehilangan udara bersih
Aku kehilangan namaku.

(I've lost my sea
I've lost my hill
L've lost my soul.

I've lost my youth
I've lost my clean air
I've lost my self.)

The poem was written in 1979 and described vividly the emotions of the Malay community who were relunctant and find it difficult to leave their life from *kampung* to flat houses. The poem ends with a sense of uncertainty, and a sense of loss of identity, as the poet was not sure about the future of his community, even when he strongly felt that Singapore is truly his country:

Singapuraku
Aku mengerti sekali
Di sini tempatku
Tapi aku tidak tahu bila
Aku akan menemui segala kehilanganku?

(My Singapore
I do indeed understand
Here is my home
But I do not know when
I will regain what I have lost.)

This poem was selected to show the impact of resettlement and urbanisation on the Malays presented in the international seminar, *Britain and Malay World Symposia* at the Royal Asiatic Society, London in 2007.

Melayuku Melayumu (My Malayness Your Malayness)

The plight and predicament of the Malays continue to attract the second generation of Malay poets, represented by Mohamed Latiff Mohammed in his poem, *Melayuku, Melayumu* (My Malayness, Your Malayness):

Telah kutafsir makna Melayuku
Dari mata dan bibir sejarah
Yang luka bagai selendang berdarah
Yang pilu bagai perawan berduka

(I have deciphered the meaning of my Malayness
from the eyes and lips of history
that's wounded like a bloodied shawl
that's downhearted like a deflowered virgin)

This poem presents two types of Malay lives — the Malayness of the poet "Melayuku" (my Malayness) and the Malayness of others "Melayumu" (your Malayness). The interpretation of "Melayu" is rather ambigious. "Melayuku" could refer to Malays in Singapore, while

"Melayumu" might refer to Malay societies beyond Singapore, such as the Malays in the Southeast Asian region and beyond. It could also refer to the Malays within a similar geographical space, but are rather different in their perspective of life (the poet versus others).

In either interpretations, the poem conveys a darker side of feelings of the Malay community in Singapore, who suddenly became a minority after separation of Singapore from Malaysia felt "marginalised", and suffered a great sense of loss because of their economic backwardness and various stresses of modernisation. This social frustration as an alienated minority was expressed intensely by the poet. The feeling is very bitter and murky because of the dark contrasts between the two forms of Malayness:

Mengalirnya Melayumu
Lembut dan terus
Menjadi embun
Dingin mempesona

(The flows of your Malayness
soft and continuous
the dews become
cold and captivating)

Telah kujumpa Melayumu
berjebat dan bertuah
menggenggam tangan membuka dada
mematahkan bianglala
yang melilit pinggang sejarahmu

(I have met your Malayness
in Jebat and Tuah
gripping our hands opening our hearts
like a torn sash
which encircles the waist of history
at the edge of dawn with the distressing dream)

Apart from its social values, the strength of this poem is in its aesthetics. The poet has vividly and effectively employed nature as metaphors to describe the predicament of Malays (*Melayuku*) as follows: "woeful wolf/hurt and tortured/in the belly of cave/dark as coal"; "stuck in mud/dusty and dirty"; "hugged by the savaged city/caressed by the asphalt on the road"; and "a collapsed stage".

This poem is also popular and is always recited at numerous Malay language events in Singapore.[5]

Udara (Air)

In addition to the social problems of their community, national issues are also touched in Malay poetry, for example, life in the cramped, crowded city and stiff competition faced by the population.

Dalam ruang terlalu sempit
Dihembus kembali
Dan setiap hembusan dipadati racunan
Bakal disedut lagi
Berulang dan terus berulang
Hingga pada saatnya
Ada terpaksa dan dipaksa
Untuk mencium bumi.

(In a space cramped too tightly
they breathe out again
and every breath is poisoned
repeating and constantly taking turns
till the moment
that some are forced or are being forced
to kiss the earth.)

Life's struggle or rat race are new national problems faced by all city dwellers of this country, regardless of their race and religion. This social reality and challenges of city life are deemed as necessary, a price that they have to pay for economic development; this urban struggle is being regarded as basic necessity and critical for survival like "udara" (air) to our life:

Di sini, mengalah bererti pasrah
kerana setiap detik adalah perebutan
Antara perut kekalutan

Dengan kemewahan atas injakan
Hingga ada yang tidak punya ruang sama sekali
Untuk bernafas lagi
Pabila udaranya dicuri.

(Here, to lose means surrender
as every moment is rushed
between empty stomachs
and wealth from being stepped upon
till there are those with no space at all
to breathe again
whilst their air is stolen.)

Oleh kaki telah terpijak
kehidupan mesti diperjuangkan
biar bagaimana sesak.
biar bagaimana kotor
udara wajib direbut
untuk bernafas sesaat lagi.

(By the feet that have been stepped upon
life must be contested
no matter how dirty
air must be seized upon
so as to breathe another second.)

This poem won the Anugerah Persuratan in 1979/80. After more than 30 years, its theme is still relevant and might be much more relevant to Singapore today because its population has since increased rapidly. Compared to earlier poems by Suratman and Mohammed Latif which are intense in its emotion, this poem is more guarded in its expression, objective or rather detached observer in discussing common social problem issue.

Bagai Phoenix (Like the Phoenix)

Life's struggle was also the focus by a woman poet, Rasiah Halil. If Asmin had discussed the theme of bio-logical survival of the fittest in *Udara*, Rasiah explored deeper, into personal internal conflicts that are rather heavy and challenging to face. Nevertheless, this internal conflict had been resolved with a positive attitude and perspective, interpreted as God's test and as a learning and maturation process for her. In fact, the poet wanted to rise from the ruins of miseries, following the action taken by the "Phoenix" in Greek Mythology:

Bahawa mereka yang seharusnya menyayang
berwajah tidak peduli dan mendendam, rumah bukan
lagi perlindungan, dan kasih sayang adalah kenangan.

Pelbagai cara Tuhan mengajar manusia
tentang nilai dan erti dewasa
dan bagai phoenix, aku bangkit dari segala duka.

(For they who should have cared
were indifferent and full of vengeance, a home
is no longer a refuge, and love is a memory.
Varied are God's ways in teaching us
the meaning and value of maturity
and like the phoenix, I rise above all miseries.)

Rasiah, the third generation poet who received bilingual education in Singapore, has benefited from her exposure and knowledge of English literature to describe her personal experience and inner struggles, eloquently and effectively. The choice of metaphors from classical Western literature adds uniqueness to her poems compared to other poems by her contemporaries.

Di Tengah Alam (In the Midst of the Universe)

From national issues, the horizon of Malay poetry has widened to universal and global perspective. The global position and the challenge of Malays as a community and citizens of a small nation, was also the focus of Hadijah in her poem, *Di Tengah Alam*, but she is looking it from an international perspective. The poet reflected on her position as an individual from a minority community and a small country, Singapore, who would make an impactful contribution internationally and at the same time strongly upheld her religious belief:

Bagaimana dan bila
manusia seperti aku dari bangsa kerdil
di tengah negara kecil
akan lebih bererti dan disedari di peta dunia
dapat mengukir sebuah bekas di jalanan sejarah
menggantung sebutir kejora di dada cakerawala
sambil mengecap keredhaan Allah!

(How and when will it be possible
a person like me from a minority community
in a small country
will be more significant and known by the world
laying tracks in the pathways of history
fastening the morning star in the universal heart
while appreciating the bounty of Allah.)

The poem was written in 1983 and won the Anugerah Persuratan in 1986. It was a selected text for the GCE 'A' level H2 and H3 papers (19 May 2005).

Seorang Bernama Manusia (Someone Named Humanity)

Nature has been an integral element of Malay poetry since creation of traditional Malay poetry such as *pantun* and *syair*. *Pantun*, for example, uses nature as part of its symmetrical structure and as a foreshadow to convey its message. Hence, nature becomes a traditional element in Malay poetry which is inherited by modern Malay poems, as seen in the many works by the first generation poets such as Noor S I and A Ghani Hamid.

Noor S I in his poem, *Seorang Bernama Manusia* (Someone Named Humanity) used elements of nature such as rainbow, sky and birds as parallelism to human life. Noor S I, A Samad Said, A S Amin and M Ghazali are a group of post-independent modern poets who experimented using new genre of abstract poetry in the 1960s to create their own unique style of expression that was different from poems by poets of Asas '50. They were known as "Penyair Kabur" (Abstract Poets) because Malay literary audience then found it difficult to understand their poems and their message in comparison to works by earlier poets and those before the Second World War.

Apa yang aku pinta
panjatkanlah segala usia
ke puncak kepekaannya
bagai mergastua menghela sayapnya
kelkatu menenggangi lampu tua
memberi makna
dalam warna
pelangi menujuhkalikan indahnya
di mana-mana.

(What I entreat is
the stretching out of every life
to the zenith of sensitivity
like the birds pointing their wings
the night flies disturbing the antique lamp
giving meaning
in colours
of the rainbow with its sevenfold splendor everywhere.

Terkocak (Splashed)

Another first generation poet is A Ghani Hamid, whose works are very close to nature as he uses elements of nature to express his personal feelings and views subtlely. His gentle voice is whispering softly like calm waves, "bisikan ombak yang tenang". His poem, entitled *Terkocak* (Splash), best exemplifies how he effectively combined his feeling with nature[6]:

Riak air tenang
menentang pepohonan di tebing
kuselami dasarnya
kutemui kesepian
kutemani sekitarnya
kutemui satu impian

(Rippling the still water
defying the trees on the bank
I dived to the bottom
and faced loneliness
I befriended the environs
and came upon a dream)

Ketenangan seluas kolam
hijau airnya memanjang
kukucupi bayu lalu
terdengar sebuah lagu
kupetik nadanya
tersua rasa pilu.

(The tranquility of the pond was spread wide
disturbed by a pack of grasshoppers
and a lone straggler at the edge of the water
I touched its wings
thus travellers' tale was whispered
whose ending was uncertain.)

A Ghani Hamid was an early generation poet who had good education in both English and Malay streams which enabled him to write well in both languages. This Tun Sri Lanang Award-winner was also active in visual arts and this added artistic strength to his poetry, and this multiplicity of art forms is manifested in his anthology of poetry, *Petikan Rasa* (2005).[6]

Puisi Syahdu (A Poem of Beauty)

Spiritual and religious issues cannot be separated from Malay poetry. Apart from contemporary social problems, Malay poets also write about spiritual journey as subject of their works. Early experiments in this subject was undertaken by Djamal Tukimin, Noor Hidayat, A Kadir Pandi, and Eunos Asah — the second generation writers. Djamal Tukimin formed a literary group, Grup Gelorasa, which attempted to make changes to literary expression and appreciation, different from the conventional ones done by poets of Asas '50.[7]

Djamal Tukimin made attempts to explore religious themes by combining it with nature and cultural elements. He also uses images of women in his poems, including in his religious poems.[a] Djamal displayed commitment to writing about religious themes. However, it is difficult to select one poem that represents his strengths in religious poems. His poem, "Puisi Syahdu", is chosen because it touches on Islamic educational issues and its aesthetics in its most natural, intimate manners and is less didactic. The poem uses religious phrases and metaphors subtly and indirectly such as "dada langit" (the bossom of the sky), "setiap sujud" (each prostration), "tasbih-menasbih jari langit" (the sky fingers its worry beads), and "bulan sabit terbit di dadanya" (the crescent moon rises in her bosom):

Terbuka lempang dada langit. Kala ini
matahari berkemas menyelam atas buih lautan
kemanisan amat perasa dalam setiap sujud.

(The bosom of the sky is clearly opened. At this time
the man prepares to dive towards the sea's foam
the sweetness is deeply tasted in each prostration)

MRT

Djamal's steps in spiritual journey is followed and even consolidated by another third generation poet, Johar Buang. In his hands, new spiritual and Sufistic poems reaches more prominence. The revival of interest in Islam in Southeast Asian region was significant at the end of the 1970s; hence, resulted in the emergence of interest in Islamic literature and its poetry. Among thousands of spiritual poems produced, Johar's poems are highly commendable, and his niche works in the Sufi poetry have received regional attention and recognition. One of his best and unique poem is entitled MRT, which describe his spiritual journey in the physical or city context, using urban metaphors. This is a rather

---

[a] See his article, "Potret perempuan: Citra dan Proses Kreatif Sang Penyair" in ibid, pp. 296–310.

novel expression, in comparison to other Sufi poetry that tend to use metaphors from nature and cultural elements, such as the sea and boat.

Kuturutkan gerabak ini berlalu
membawa matahatiku
dari Yishun ke Tanah Merah
dari Pasir Ris ke Raffles City
seperti aku pun berlari mencari-Mu
dari Safa ke Marwah
dari masyrik ke maghrib
dari alam malaikut kealam jabarut

(I continue sitting in this moving coach
transporting my consciousness
from Yishun to Tanah Merah
from Pasir Ris to Raffles City
Likewise I ran in search of you
from Safa to Marwah
from the east to the west
from the angelic to perfect dimensions)

This poem was awarded the Literary Award in 1993.

Tasik Rindu (Lake of Longing)

Nature and spiritual elements continue to attract the interest and heart of younger generation of poets in Singapore who were active in 1980s such as Isa Kamari. The third generation poets, even though enjoying higher education in comparison to the earlier generation, were are exposed to more varieties and cosmopolitan life in Singapore but are still motivated to preserve their religious and Malay cultural values. At the same time, they also displayed their inner-most individual voices with refined, gentle and controlled manners.

Isa's poem is selected as it represents latest mixed traditional genre of Malay poetry, formed based on the synthesis of various elements Malay–Islamic art, and contemporary life that is influenced by new technology and existing popular culture. Isa Kamari dedicates his writing by documenting his spiritual experiences in poetry, attempting to revive the Jawi script in his poetry books; and by composing songs based on his poems that would attract a wider audience. He attempts to integrate three forms of literary expressions — writing, reading and singing. His literary approaches and expressions can be regarded as innovative as compared to the conventional approach adopted by previous Malay poets. Nevertheless, Isa's messages and values are still anchored on the religious values upheld by the Malay community. His traditional message is reflected not only in his poems with religious themes that recorded his pilgrimage experience to Mecca, but also in poems about his personal love, in which his values were conveyed subtly and gently. For example, his poem, *Tasik Rindu* (Lake of Longing):

Sebutir embun kautitis
seumur hidupku
lemas ditenggelami
tasik rindu

(A dewdrop that you trickle
my entire life
will be drowned
in the lake of longing)

The poem was awarded Consolation Prize at the Anugerah Persuratan Singapore in 1995.

Conclusions

The above are 11 poems by 11 Singapore Malay poets of various generations that made their sensitive interpretations and insightful reflections on nature, race, religion and love, of their life and surrounding environment. On the whole, their poems uphold ideal religious and cultural values of the Malay society, which have long been rooted in the community's life, and these values are creatively and subtly expressed by the poets employing their own individual poetic style of expression. These major themes and elements are interpreted and given subjective meanings; hence, each poem served additional colours and values to the poetry landscape of Singapore, which on the whole can be acknowledged as "the best literary achievement of a culture over the last 50 years". These selected poems have their own strengths in terms of aesthetic and cultural values and their creation contribute to the development of a strong identity to Malay poetry in Singapore and at the same time enriching its national literature and Malay literature in the region and beyond.

Notes

1. Refer to "Revising the Literary Canon — Introduction", *Twentieth-Century Literary Criticism*. Ed. Thomas J. Schoenberg Lawrence J. Trudeau. Vol. 114. Gale Cengage, 2006. eNotes.com. 2006. 20 August 2010 http://www.enotes.com/twentieth-century-criticism/revising-literary-canon/introduction

2. See the number of literary award winners (1974–1984) in Hadijah Rahmat (1987, 2004).

3. See the songs "Ini Nasi Yang Kusuap" composed by Nuradee and Karmin Abbas.

4. See Hadijah Rahmat, "Portrait of Nation — British Legacy on the Malay Settlement in Singapore", in *Indonesia and the Malay World*, Volume 36, Number 106, November 2008, pp. 359–74(16).

5. Examples are Poetry Recital Competition in Pesta Bahasa dan Budaya 2008 in conjunction with Bulan Bahasa Melayu Singapura 2008, organised by the Executive Committee of Fuchun Community Club, Marsiling and Innova Junior College. See http://www.persadaku.org/pestabahasa08_sajakwajib_PBB08.htmuk

6. See article on A. Ghani Hamid by Hadijah Rahmat, "Nota: A. Ghani Hamid — Sebuah Alunan Ombak dan Kocakan Sepi di Pantai Seni" in *Sastera dan Manusia Melayu Baru* (1998: 258–283) and interview by Hadijah with A. Ghani Hamid (1998: 284–317).

7. "Petikan rasa" (Extracts of feelings) — *A Collection of Poems and Paintings* by A. Ghani Hamid. Published by Asas '50, 2005.

8. For further discussion on the Grup Gelorasa, see Masuri SN, "Puisi Melayu di Singapura" in *The Poetry of Singapore* (1985:22–23); Hadijah, "Sastera Melayu Menjelang Abad ke 21-Cabaran, Kenyataan dan Harapan" in *Sastera dan Manusia Melayu Baru* (1998:178) and Djamal Tukimin, "Membumikan Akar Sejarah Sastera Melayu di Singapura" in *Sejarah Tidak Pernah Luka Kita yang Berduka* (2008: xvii–xx).

9. See his article, "Potret perempuan: Citra dan Proses Kreatif Sang Penyair" in ibid, pp. 296–310.

References

Abdul Ghani Hamid, 2005. *Petikan Rasa — Extracts of Feelings, a collection of Poems and Paintings*, Abdul Ghani Hamid. Singapore: Asas '50.

Djamal Tukimin, 2008. *Sejarah Tidak Pernah Luka, Kita yang Berduka*. Singapura: Pustaka Nasional.

Hadijah Rahmat, 1998. *Sastera dan Manusia Melayu Baru*. Singapore: Persatuan Wartawan Melayu Singapura.

Hadijah Rahmat, Dewani Abbas dan Azhar Ibrahim Alwee, 2004. *Potret Diri Seorang Penyair*. Siri Karya Anugerah Persuratan Singapure 1993–2001, Jilid 5. Singapore: Majlis Bahasa Melayu Singapura.

Isa Kamari, 2006. *Ka'abah*. Malaysia: Ameen Serve Holdings Sdn. Bhd.

Kirpal Singh and Wong Yoon Wah, 2000. *Rhythms — a Singaporean Millennial anthology of Poetry*. Singapore: National Arts Council.

Masuri S N, 1985. "Malay Poetry in Singapore" in *The Poetry of Singapore, Anthology of Asean Literatures*. Edited by Thumboo, Edwin, Wong Yoon Wah, Lee Tzu Peng, Masuri Salikun and Arasu, V.T., published under sponsorship of The ASEAN Committee on Culture and Information.

CHAPTER 40

RESISTING CULTURAL AMNESIA: MALAY LITERATURE OF DIGNIFIED PRESENCE | Azhar Ibrahim

What is important is that men acquire more awareness every day of the need to incorporate themselves into society, and, at the same time, of their importance as motors of that society.

Frantz Fanon

Singapore Malay literature showcases the experiences of ethnic Malays, how they grapple with modernisation, and various challenges affecting the community, such as housing resettlement, structural unemployment, educational opportunities, leadership vacuum, economic hardship, religious resurgence, socio-cultural anomie, the feeling of being marginalised and displaced, and the like.[a] In a political and cultural space where Malay medium discursive site is limited, Singapore Malay literature provides the most visible and viable site for the utterances and engagement of Malay thought, aesthetics and vision. Leading Malay writers, who are at the forefront in taking up Malay issues, have used the literary medium to direct their criticisms and advocacy to the larger Malay/Singapore public. In this process of engagement, they also define what Singapore means to them, while insisting that a dignified presence (*kehadiran/kehidupan yang bermaruah*) is a real challenge, encountered by every member of the community.

---

[a] Shahruddin Maaruf, "Singapore Malay Literature," in Budi Darma, (ed.) *Modern Literature of ASEAN*. (Jakarta: ASEAN Committee on Culture and Information, 2000).

Ismail Hussein notes that modern Malay literature is essentially a people's literature which departs
from the elite-dominated literature of the past.[b] It is
written by the Malay working
class, mostly teachers with a Malay
education background. Their literary repertoires, both in content
and style, articulate peoples' experiences, anxieties, plight, frustrations and hopes. Such themes
suggest strongly that literature
should function socially, as a
receptacle for infusing reflection
and action. This article examines
the contribution of Malay literature in articulating the community's contributions to Singapore.
It argues that there is a central
theme that runs through the writ-
ings of three generations of Singaporean writers: the
emphasis on Malays' dignified presence in Singapore in
the context of a cosmopolitan and multi-ethnic setting.
This theme ensures the Malays to respect their cultural
roots.

The Malay Collection at the National Library Board
has a special focus on language and literature.

Social Function of Malay Literature: Resisting Cultural Amnesia

Singapore Malays are receptive of literature not simply
as an artistic finesse but also as part of cultural, moral
and aesthetical phalanx. Literature functions as a
medium to harken imagination, values and consciousness inasmuch as it is a platform for engagement on
issues affecting the community. It aims to draw attention of the reading public and literary enthusiast, as a
form of cultural response to present predicaments.
Studying Malay literature is crucial in understanding

---

[b] Ismail Hussein. "The New Malaysian Literature — A View," in Syed Muhammad Naguib
al-Attas, *et al.* (eds.) *Bahasa, Kesusasteraan dan Kebudayaan Melayu: Essei-essei Penghormatan
kepada Pendita Za'ba.* (Kuala Lumpur: Kementerian Kebudayaan, Belia dan Sukan, 1976).

Malay society, although it is very much expressed in literary or artistic forms. Most significantly, literary matters have never been given the privilege of pure aesthetical pleasures, nor are they tolerated as purely a receptacle for ideas to be propagated.[c]

Generally, literature or the literary arts (at least in the Malay society) is part of the cultural response to development and progress.[d] The literary medium has been utilised to advocate or call for concerted efforts towards development, by proactive participating in it, galvanising the available resources and strength so that the community is not lagging behind others. The dominant expectation is that the litterateur must take the lead in infusing social and aesthetical consciousness, including being the moral voice to speak against social and cultural apathy, corruptive influences and the struggle for a decent living.[e] However, at the same time, it would be erroneous to say that all Malay literary works in Singapore embraced such paradigms. Nevertheless, one prominent and consistent theme is the need to be on guard against cultural amnesia.[f]

The Challenge of Cultural Amnesia

Essentially, cultural amnesia points to rootlessness and cultural emptiness. Among the litterateur, there is real concern that culture becomes plainly a *heritage,* only to be adorned in special functions and gatherings. In fact, culture here does not just mean the material and manifested dimensions of culture, but also a sense of purpose of living in a community and an identity of collective groupings based on language, cultural

---

[c] A position that many Malay writers have embraced especially those within the Asas '50 circle. Read, Djamal Tukimin. *Sejarah tidak pernah luka kita yang berduka: landskap sastera Melayu Singapura pasca Angkatan 50.* (Singapura: Pustaka Nasional, 2008).

[d] David J Banks. *From Class to Culture: Social Conscience in Malay Novels Since Independence.* (New Haven, Conn.: Yale University Southeast Asia Studies, 1987).

[e] Read, Suratman Markasan, *From the beginning to two streams of social critique = Dari jalan permulaan ke dua jalur kritik social.* (Singapura, 1991).

[f] A theme that I have explored in some details in *Narrating Presence: Awakening from Cultural Amnesia.* (Singapore: The Malay Heritage Foundation, Istana Kg Glam & Select Books, 2014).

heritage and religion. Put simply, cultural amnesia is not simply revolving around identity politics but also implies the condition of having historical and moral lapses. When such a condition persists, one could expect a loss of social commitment, ethical integrity and the abatement of a group's self-esteem and social pride.

Cultural amnesia, which could be engendered by endogenous and exogenous factors, therefore needs to be addressed accordingly. This is exactly a point that several prominent Malay writers have taken up in their writings. Two related dimensions that could be identified in their works, that is, while emphasising on the importance of dignified presence, could only be accomplished if cultural amnesia could be resisted or at least mitigated. To them, a dignified presence is of great importance in the context of living in this cosmopolitan city life, where stiff competition meant that those without social and cultural capital tend to lose out, and remain at the margin. Moreover, in this multicultural setting of diverse religion, ethnicities and languages, the community, being in a minority status, must ensure that they could preserve their culture and tradition in the context of the fast-paced development and modernisation.

Harun Aminurrashid, also known by his pen name *Har, Gustam Negara* and *Atma Jiwa*; was born in Singapore on 8 August 1907 in Kampung Teluk Kurau.

Pioneering Litterateurs

Early modern Malay literature is essentially the literature of the ordinary masses where strong collectivism becomes its hallmark. The Malay litterateur, although more educated than the Malay masses, is not part of the aristocracy. One such figure is Harun Aminurrashid, who became prominent in the pre-Independence period but whose literary career spans into the modern republic of Singapore. Today, he is recognised as one of our literary pioneers. He wrote a number of historical novels like *Panglima Awang* (1965) and *Anak Panglima Awang* (1961) which resurrect memories of the Malays' struggle against the Portuguese colonialists. Harun wrote these historical novels to inject a sense of pride, coupled with the "Nusantara" perspective of history, as well as to counter a

Eurocentric version of history. All these novels, written during the pre-Independence nationalistic period, were meant to instil a sense of historical and cultural pride to the Malay audience. In a way, a cultural history narrated in a fictive form plays a role in infusing such historical consciousness, especially in the context of colonialism where the imagination for the peoples' history remains relegated while the colonial version of history dominates throughout.[g]

One work by Harun worth mentioning is the novel *Simpang Perinang* (1966) [At a Vital Crossroad], where the background was Singapore in the days before intensive industrialisation and development. This novel is a narrative of the resilience of a poor family living on the outskirts of the city. For very long, this family is wrapped in poverty and hunger, with the father doing menial work, while the mother sells *kuih* (Malay cakes) so that she could supplement the family's income. The children were doing well in school and one of them was later offered a job as a teacher. Though this theme may be common, it draws on two important points. First, the narration draws our empathy towards the poor. Second, it challenges the common assumption that the poor Malays are fatalistic and contented with their life with no aspirations to improve their lot.

> "Over the years, I have often been asked: Why do you remain in Singapore? I used to dismiss the question. To me, it needed no answer because it should not have been asked in the first place.
>
> Masuri S N

Another prominent figure in the literary scene is poet Masuri S N who is also one of Singapore's Malay literary pioneers. Masuri has written many poems in

---

[g] Muhammad Haji Salleh. "The uses of history in Harun Aminurrashid's novels", *Nusantara*, Bil. 7 (July 1981) pp. 1–12.

voluminous anthologies and essays, many of which bear a strong social message.[h] Masuri's *Sebelah Kaki Terangkat* [One Leg Lifted] with a subtitle *Diari Seorang Pelajar* [Diary of a Student] is a novelette of will and hope, which is an unpublished manuscript in the holding of the National Library Board. It was written in the early 1970s, against the background of housing resettlement in Singapore. Although Masuri is known for his poems, a craft which he mastered indisputably, this unpublished novelette bears a strong mark of his concerns on the issues of Malays' participation and adjustment in the economy. Masuri, who was also an educator, saw the need to place emphasise on the importance of acquiring education as a means to get out of poverty and climb the social ladder. The targeted audience was obviously the younger readers.

The novelette depicts the lives of the people living in the Malay reserve settlement, many of whom were plagued by poverty and miseries, with their earnings very meagre. Masuri plainly narrates the difficulties facing the people, especially the young who are struggling to complete their education in school, while resisting the temptations of youth which may keep them out of school. Mubarak, the young protagonist, is aware of his family's plight and many others around him. To him, the only way to get out of poverty is to do well in his studies so that he could secure a good job. He has a girlfriend named Rosmah. He likes her very much but he needs to focus on his studies. When Rosmah told him that her father would marry her off to her cousin, Mubarak felt helpless, but Mubarak knows he could not entertain such feelings for too long. He has to build his future and his family. Mubarak, a sensitive but mature young man, is empathic to his surroundings. Poverty through hardship has never been the cause that diminishes the hopes of people like him. The determination to complete his education

---

[h] I have discussed this point, see "Masuri S N Kemanusiaan, Ketukangan dan Kearifan dalam Berkarya," in *Sumbangsih tizkari: buat Masuri S N* Penyunting, Muhammad Bukhari Lubis & Mohamed Pitchay Gani Bin Mohamed Abdul Aziz. (Tanjong Malim: Universiti Pendidikan Sultan Idris, 2009).

echoes many of the hopes of poor families who are convinced that educational qualifications would enable them to attain better jobs and increase their household income. *"Belajar bersungguh-sungguh sehingga mendapat ijazah atau sekurang-kurangnya diploma yang baik dalam sesuatu lapangan profesional.....Tidak ada lain pilihanku. Kerana kalau aku gagal dalam pelajaran sekolahku, lebih-lebih berperangai mengikuti kehendak hati dan nafsuku sendiri, maka masa depanku sudah jelas tertutup."*[i]

Masuri creates such characters to afffirm the importance of self-confidence among youths. The will to sacrifice is imperative. Young men like Mubarak need to make sacrifices. Instead of spending time with his friends and being obsessed with the latest fashion trends, Mubarak spends his time studying at home. This novelette also narrates the anxiety of the *kampung* dwellers to be resettled in the housing estates. Some were doubtful that such plans will work. This novelette is not about lamenting the loss of the village; instead, it documents the process of the Malay community in transition and moving into high-rise housing estates. In all, Masuri creates the character of Mubarak as a young man who is not afraid to enter the modernisation process.

Through the character Mubarak, there is a hope that the community embraces the vitalism of life, and have a will to pursue the living demands of Singapore. Narrating the transition from *kampung* to housing estates, albeit in the literary form, is a form of social memory, which in itself is very important to counter cultural amnesia. Most importantly, the will to strife for a better future is part of a dignified presence. The latter makes the people lend their hands in building the society and nation, and are not simply in the passive mode of begging for assistance and protection.

---

[i] Translation: I must study hard and do well enough in my studies to obtain a degree qualification, or at least a good diploma in a professional industry. I have no other choice. Because if I follow my heart's desire to give in to my temptations and do badly in my studies, then surely my future will be bleak.

Claiming Voices

Apart from Masuri, Mohamed Latiff Mohamed, winner of the Cultural Medallion in 2013, is known for his critical and cynical stance on the plight of the Malays, as shown in his many poems, novels and short stories. One work deserves mention here: a novelette written by Latiff in 1977 entitled *Kota Airmata* (City of Tears).

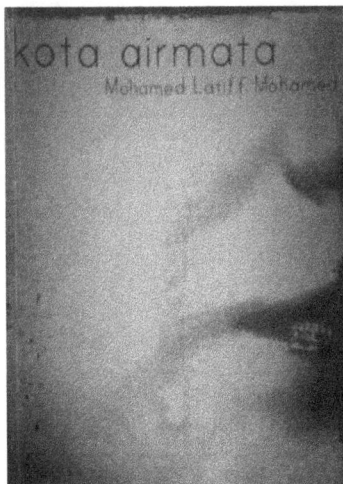

Kota Airmata by Mohamed Latiff Mohamed, Solo Enterprises, Singapore (1977).

Targeting the younger readers, Latiff's novelette narrates another plight of those living in the housing ghettoes, where families are gripped with poverty. The narration of this urban poverty is highly realistic as it is moving. Ani is a young girl who is studying to take her final public examinations. She is worried about raising money for her examination fees. Her mum took up various menial jobs, while her alcoholic father is jobless. Latiff depicts the grim realities of many Malay families living under poverty and the breakdown of its social order. Ani symbolises the plight and the struggle of the community. Ani has no pocket money to bring to school, often returning home hungry as there was also hardly any food at home. The crammed flat is an unconducive place for her to study. Her teacher, Cikgu Majid, often insinuated that Malay families like Ani's pay no attention to their children as they prefer immediate gratification. Such an allegation is of course unfounded as Ani's family is struggling to make ends meet. With no support at home and school, Ani becomes ever more pressured. Her cruel fate becomes aggravated when she met a philanderer, Azmi, who made her pregnant and later abandoned her. Ani was great distraughtly and eventually took her own life.

The day Ani died, nobody weeps nor does anyone even care. While we often boast of this city as pinnacle of development and progress, it is a city of tears for people like Ani and her family. Indeed, many have concluded that Latiff's *Kota Airmata* is a resigned pessimism, not unlike some of his other works.[j] Upon closer reading however, Latiff's masterly narrative schema is

---

[j] Sharifah Maznah Syed Omar. "The Atrophy of Vision and Hope in the Poetry of Mohamed Latiff Mohamed," *Singa, Literature & the Arts in Singapore*, No. 25, December 1992.

not about pessimism but his conviction that the plight of the poor must be part of our social conscience. Ani's tragic end is a lesson. We cannot allow the plight of the community to be in this dead end. Raising such issues of poverty and the plight of the urban poor makes his novelette a serious work of reflection. Abandoning our moral responsibility towards them is also a kind of cultural/social amnesia, a denial of the grim reality around us. His work highlights the failure of the maladjusted person (Ani's drunkard and abusive father); the opportunist (Azmi the Don Juan); blaming-the-victim tendency (Cikgu Majid, Ani's teacher) and the socio-political space bereft of conscience (the city and its inequality in the socio-economic sectors). In all, it is only by our real concern of the poor's plight that we can claim a life of dignified presence. As long as members of our society remain in the state of wretchedness, we cannot boast of our success based on our good work, ethos, merit and discipline.

Assuaging Anxiety

Two decades after Separation, there emerged a group of Malay writers who are now better educated, and are proficient in both Malay and English. Young writers like Rasiah Halil, Isa Kamari, Hadijah Rahmat, and Saeda Buang emerged, along with a few others who contributed to the development of Malay literature in Singapore. Except for Isa who has a background in architectural studies, the rest are academics. This intellectual group is more nuanced in their literary articulations, with deeper philosophical reflections and sociological discernment can be traced.[k] No longer lamenting about the past, they look to the future to redeem this very idea of a dignified presence.

Isa's historical novels is responding to the dominant historical narrative that gives primacy of the colonial version, very much relegating to the indigenous

---

[k] Hadijah Rahmat, "Lukisan Sastera Melayu — Antara Keunggulan dan Kenyataan," in Mohamed Pitchay Gani (ed.) *Sastera Melayu Warisan Jati Diri dan Jagat.* (Singapore: Asas '50 and National Library Board, 2003).

perspectives. For example, his novel *Duka Tuan Bertahta* (2011) is a form of political commentary on various episodes of Singapore history which has direct effect on the Malays, such as the seceding of Singapore to the East India Company by Sultan Hussein Shah and Temenggong Abdul Rahman. But as literary works, it is not simply a counter to the dominant historical narrative, as the focus is to narrate the events and episodes affecting the community from a standpoint of an "insider", though this may not necessarily be factually correct or otherwise. Constraints of space would not allow us to discuss their works in detail except to point out that their works are equally engaging, and they widen the space where issues of the community is taken up in their works, yet maintaining the fictive thrust of a literary piece.

Indeed, the literary realms have been the site where prominent Malay litterateurs are consistently bringing up themes and issues that they consider pertinent to be raised to the community. Another prominent figure is Suratman Markasan, who has taken up the theme of social memory consistently as in his novel *Penghulu Yang Hilang Segala-galanya* (1998) [The Village Headman Who Lost Everything] and several other poems which are critical against policies and practices that relegates the Malay language and the diminishing cultural pride within the community.[1] By writing on such themes, they played the role of the literary intelligentsia as the beacon of social conscience and as the role of persuader of change. Certainly their perspectives and diagnoses may not be comprehensive or valid, but the very persistency in their social engagement in the literary realms is a commendable one.

Annunciating Commitment

Another leading Malay literary figure is the late Muhammad Ariff Ahmad, who has penned a number of

---

[1] Refer Azhar Ibrahim, "Suratman Markasan: Malay Literature and Social Memory," *Biblioasia*, Vol. 10, Issue 1, April–June 2014, pp. 28–33.

literary works, though he was more well-known as a Malay language and cultural expert in Singapore. Not unlike his Asas '50 counterparts, of which he is one of the founding fathers, Ariff's social stance is the need for Malays to embrace progress and to be equally steadfast in preserving their cultural identity.[m] His many essays, such as those compiled in *Mutiara Bijaksana* (2011), are the enumeration of traditional maxims regarded as essential to the ethical consciousness and action. In the spirit that one's commitment to change must be translated to action, Ariff reminds in his poem *Budi* the sacrosanct of altruism, as encapsulated in the concept of *budi*.

> *Pernahkah engkau menabur budi*
> *Atau berkorban dermakan bakti*
> *Kepada ibunda engkau mengabdi*
> *Selama umurmu dikurnia Izzati?*
> *Kalau belum siaplah sekarang!*
> *Aturkan hidupmu dalam budiman*
> *...*[n]

Hadijah Rahmat, in her poem *Cerita Rakyat III* (1992) [The People's Story] envisioned The New Malays (*Melayu Baru*) who are ready to leave behind their agonising past, the era that circumscribed and stunted the growth of Malay personality and character. While some others were lamenting of the loss of the glorious past, Hadijah puts more premium on the future as the basis of new creation.

> *Kita perlu cipta sebuah karya agung seni*
> *Rakaman dan cerminan sebuah perjuangan*
> *Menorak langkah-langkah cemerlang*
> *Menghapus kesesatan*
> *Menangkis latah dan gejala rimba*
> *Dengan kecanggihan ilmu, wahana dan wawasan waja*
> *Dan kentalnya iman dan amal*

---

[m] Read, Mohd Raman Daud, "Tokoh Contoh dalam Pembangunan Nusa" in Rohayah Md.Lani & Juffri Supa'at (eds) Bibliografi Muhammad Ariff Ahmad. (Singapore: NLB, 2012), pp. 239–246.

[n] Juffri Supa'at (ed.) *Sumbangsih Mas: Koleksi Puisi Pilihan* (Singapore: NLB , 2012), p. 32.

Kita pacu tenaga dan rebut keunggulan budi dan cita
Mengukir citra indah bangsa dan manusia
Di panggung jagat raya°

Indeed, Hadijah's enjoinment is very much the hope of many of her generation, including the present, and could be found in various expressions of Malay cultural and artistic repertoires in this island republic.

To sum up, via literary endeavour, Malay litterateur in a way functions as agents for the preservation of language and cultural identity, which have been the cornerstone of cultural ballast. Without these two factors, alongside a discerning historical and moral consciousness, cultural amnesia is a perturbing reality. At one time, the slavish mimicking of Western cultural elements has been objected, fearing that it would lead to rootlessness or cultural amnesia. Today however, the real challenge is not over such superficial trends but the systemic erasure of social memory, underdeveloped historical consciousness and social moral apathy. The very existence of cultural amnesia spells a more precarious situation to the community, as it would mean poor cultural and historical ground, which in turn impairs the visionary outlook. Cultural amnesia could only be dealt with if the community knows the state of affairs of their community, and are prepared to take up the challenges of being the citizens of this modern city-state. Simply put, a debilitating cultural amnesia is a threat to the dignified presence.

Bibliography

Azhar Ibrahim, *Narrating Presence: Awakening from Cultural Amnesia.* Singapore: The Malay Heritage Foundation, Istana Kg Glam & Select Books, 2014.

Azhar Ibrahim, "Suratman Markasan: Malay Literature and Social Memory," *Biblioasia,* Vol.10, Issue 1, April–June 2014, pp. 28–33.

Azhar Ibrahim, "Masuri S.N. Kemanusiaan, Ketukangan dan Kearifan dalam Berkarya," in *Sumbangsih tizkari : buat Masuri S. N.* Penyunting, Muhammad Bukhari Lubis & Mohamed

° Hadijah Rahmat, *Di Tengah Alam.* (Kuala Lumpur: DBP, 2000), p. 35.

Pitchay Gani Bin Mohamed Abdul Aziz. Tanjong Malim : Universiti Pendidikan Sultan Idris, 2009.

Banks, David J. *From Class to Culture: Social Conscience in Malay Novels Since Independence.* New Haven, Conn.: Yale University Southeast Asia Studies, 1987.

Djamal Tukimin. *Sejarah tidak pernah luka kita yang berduka: landskap sastera Melayu Singapura pasca Angkatan 50.* Singapura: Pustaka Nasional, 2008.

Hadijah Rahmat, "Lukisan Sastera Melayu — Antara Keunggulan dan Kenyataan," in Mohamed Pitchay Gani (ed.) *Sastera Melayu Warisan Jati Diri dan Jagat.* Singapura: Asas'50 & NLB, 2003.

Hadijah Rahmat, *Di Tengah Alam.* Kuala Lumpur: DBP, 2000.

Ismail Hussein. "The New Malaysian Literature — A View," in Syed Muhammad Naguib al-Attas, *et al.* (eds.) *Bahasa, Kesusasteraan dan Kebudayaan Melayu: Essei-essei Penghormatan kepada Pendita Za'ba.* Kuala Lumpur: Kementerian Kebudayaan, Belia dan Sukan, 1976.

Juffri Supa'at (ed.) *Sumbangsih Mas: Koleksi Puisi Pilihan* Singapore: NLB, 2012.

Mohd Raman Daud, "Tokoh Contoh dalam Pembangunan Nusa" in Rohayah Md.Lani & Juffri Supa'at (eds) *Bibliografi Muhammad Ariff Ahmad.* Singapore: NLB, 2012, pp. 239–246.

Muhammad Haji Salleh. "The uses of history in Harun Aminurrashid's novels", *Nusantara*, Bil. 7 (Julai 1981) pp. 1–12.

Shahruddin Maaruf, "Singapore Malay Literature," in Budi Darma, (ed.) *Modern Literature of ASEAN.* Jakarta: ASEAN Committee on Culture and Information, 2000.

Sharifah Maznah Syed Omar. "The Atrophy of Vision and Hope in the Poetry of Mohamed Latiff Mohamed," *Singa, Literature & the Arts in Singapore*, No. 25 December 1992.

Suratman Markasan, *From the beginning to two streams of social critique = Dari jalan permulaan ke dua jalur kritik social.* Singapura, 1991.

CHAPTER 41

SELECTED POEMS

Poetry is a distinct literary art form but its role in society is often subjected to interpretation and debate but one of its distinct roles is to engage, influence and inspire readers. With mastery of language, poets are able to motivate and inspire in very few words as compared to for example a novel or a short story. In Singapore, poetry too had played a critical role in nation-building. As Singapore struggled towards nationhood, poetries were used to motivate and inspire the people. Poets use their works to reach out to the community — to uplift spirit in times of distress and discomfort and to lend voice to the downtrodden. Here is a collection of poems by prominent Malay/Muslim poets whose message is as varied as their background.

Ini Nasi Yang Ku Suap
Masuri S N

Melayuku, Melayumu
Mohamed Latiff Mohamed

Jalan Permulaan
Suratman Markasan

Kemahiran Berfikir
Yatiman Yusof

Terlupa
Rasiah Halil

Tasik Rindu
Isa Kamari

Ikrar
Peter Augustine Goh

Ini Nasi Yang Kusuap

Masuri S N

Ini nasi yang kusuap
Pernah sekali menjadi padi harap,
Melintuk dipuput angin pokoknya kerap
Tenang berisi tunduk menatap.
Ini butir nasi yang kukunyah
Sedang kutelan melalui tekak basah,
Jadi dari darah mengalir
Dalam badan gerak berakhir.
Angin kencang mentari khatulistiwa
Membakar raga petani di sawah
Panas hujan dan tenaga masuk kira
Dan nasi yang kumakan campuran dari semua.
Ini budi yang kusambut
Pemberian lumrah beranting dan bertaut,
Ini nasi hasil dari kerja
Kembali pada siapa yang patut menerima.
Jadi yang kumakan bukan berasal dari nasi
Tapi peluh, darah dalam isi mengalir pasti,
Jadi yang kutelan bukan berasal dari padi
Tapi dari urat dari nadi seluruh Pak Tani.

Note: The poet is champion of the underdog — the plight of the poor and the under-class. In this poem, *Ini Nasi Yang Kusuap* (This Rice that I Eat) Masuri is in full praise of the farmers. Their struggles and immense contribution are being explicitly highlighted. This poem is a noble tribute to the farmers and to the working class in general.

Melayuku, Melayumu

Mohammed Latiff Mohammed

telah kutafsir makna Melayuku
dari mata dan bibir sejarah
yang luka bagai selendang berdarah
yang pilu bagai perawan berduka
mengalirnya Melayumu
lembut dan terus
menjadi embun
dingin mempesona
dan Melayuku
bagai riak danau
terkandas di lumpur
berdebu dan kotor.
Melayuku bagai serigala sengsara
sakit dan terseksa
di perut gua
gelap bagai jelaga,
telah kujumpa Melayumu
berjebat dan bertuah
menggenggam tangan membuka dada
mematahkan bianglala
yang melilit pinggang sejarahmu
di hujung senja yang suram mimpinya
dan Melayuku duka rindunya
dipeluk belantara kota
dibelai aspal jalan raya
Melayumu adalah bulan purnama
harum cempaka wangi cendana
Melayuku adalah pelamin yang patah
pusara yang legam
dan malam yang pasrah.

Dewan Sastera, March 1983

Note: This poem is about searching for a lost identity. Post-independent Singapore saw Malay literature in a transition with new thoughts in facing challenges from a perspective of Singaporeans within Nusantara. It was a period of awareness and searching, as Singapore writers and the community compared themselves to their Malay brothers and sisters in neighbouring countries, to find continuity between elements of nationality and culture or ethnicity.

Jalan Permulaan

Suratman Markasan

I
Singapuraku
aku mengerti
di sini darah ibuku tumpah,
di sini tulang-belulangku akan merapuh
di sini anak-anakku membesar
seperti paya terus melebar
di atas batu-bata & pasir-masir bertakhta,
lalu manusia seribu tahun menghamba.

Laut tempatku menangkap ikan
bukit tempatku mencari rambutan
sudah menghutan dilanda batu-bata,
Pak Lasim tak bisa lagi menjadi penghulu
pulaunya sudah dicabut dari peta kepalanya
anak buah sudah terdampar
di batu-bata dan pasir-masir hangat

Aku kehilangan lautku
aku kehilangan bukitku
aku kehilangan diriku.

II
Di hutan padang pasir
anak-anak menggantung kepalanya
mereka mengoyak pasir bagai anjing-anjing
terhendap-hidu di hujung pasir-tandus
mencari sesuatu di dalam tulang-belulang
tanpanya bulan mati, mentari lesu

Antara mereka bersembunyi
di balik huruf kudus aliflammin
dengan kerudung memutih buatan Hadratul-maut
mendakwa dunia sudah di kelengkang syaitan
lalu mereka tidak kenal air dan benci nasi

Dari corong-corong ke langit
tersedu seribu racun
dari sungai ke laut lepas
mengalir seribu ubat bertuba

nafasku berhenti di tenggorok
dan isi laut separuh mati

Aku kehilangan beliaku
aku kehilangan udara bersihku
aku kehilangan namaku.

III
Kemudian
lagu empat menggema lagi
kadang-kadang hilang satu
aku tidak tahu apakah nanti tinggal dua?
akhirnya tinggal satu demi memburu waktu
aku bersatu dengan isteri & anak-anak
pabila kapal mau berangkat lagi

Singapuraku
aku mengerti sekali
di sini tempatku
tapi aku tidak tahu bila
aku akan menemui segala kehilanganku?

Jalan Permulaan, Singapura
Angkatan Sasterawan 50, 1986

Poet's Note: The message I wish to convey in the last stanza of part III of the poem — it is my strongest hope and belief that Malay/Muslim youths will continue to work hard and strive to rediscover and reclaim all that is lost of our community/national identity.

Kemahiran Berfikir

Yatiman Yusof

lahir kita
dianugerahi cairan kelabu
kurnia Maha Esa
Maha Kuasa
lantas kita jadi
makhluk paling luar biasa
di mata yang lain
kitalah raja

tetapi minda adalah anak benih
berkembang apabila dipupuk
bersemarak ketika bertindak
terjana dek pencarian tanpa henti

demikian minda
dalam bertukar pengertian
dalam merenungi laut pengalaman
kita jadi
pemikir kritis
penimbang pragmatis
umat yang terhormat

sayang sekali
andainya permata diri
terbiar dimakan ulat hari
kita tidak lagi bijaksana
kerana minda telah luntur
dan kita hanyalah jadi
oggokan daging
yang hidup membeku

Excerpted from *Percikan Kembara — Antologi Puisi Yatiman Yusof* (1970–2013)
Pustaka Melayu Publisher. First print 2014

Note: The mind is powerful tool and a gift from God. With it we can be the most extraordinary individual. But a great mind needs to be nourished. This poem reminds readers to optimise it, failing which we will be just like pieces of dead meat.

Terlupa

Rasiah Halil

Kita selalu terlupa
di sini pernah bertaut kasih
dalam getir, dalam gusar,
atau riang dalam waktu-waktu santai
tanpa kata-kata iklan
persembahan kaku & pesta pora
kerana perhubungan semula jadi
berpangkalkan hati
minda & nurani yang saling mengerti.

Akar kita lama di sini
rimbun dalam apa pun cuaca
walau ada pohon tumbang sebelum masa
setelah suasana kita bertukar
setelah kehidupan kita berubah
setelah kampung-kampung roboh
setelah laut-laut menjauh
& sekitaran yang kita terbiasa,
muhibah & mesra alam
lenyap atau dikonkritkan keadaan
& kita tercari-cari
ruang legar
keikhlasan
keterbukaan
kebersamaan
pada sebuah kenangan & masa hadapan.

Sebutir benih menjadi pulau
tanpa keikhlasan, kebersamaan,
hanyalah bongkah tanah yang dihias.

7–23 Mei 2011

Poet's Note: This poem recalls the many sacrifices and the sense of togetherness during the earlier times when we faced many difficulties. Yet, with numerous rapid changes that we face, that sense of togetherness seems to slowly erode, as if we are forgetful/*terlupa* (title of the poem) about it. And along with it are values such as sincerity and open-mindedness in our shared spaces. The poem quotes part of a Malay proverb *Kalau asal benih yang baik, jatuh ke laut menjadi pulau* — if you are a good seed/a knowledgeable or skilful person, should you be left out or left to fend for yourself, you will be able to make something of yourself or contribute. You will be an 'island' — self-sustaining and contributing to the common good, although the time taken from being a "seed" to an "island", will be long. But without values such as sincerity and a real sense of togetherness, an island is just a well-decorated piece of land.

Tasik Rindu

Isa Kamari

dalam diam ku kesan gerak
permukaan tasik yang berkaca
ditatang riak minda
begitulah tafakurku padamu

dalam gerak ku genang diam
teratai yang dibuai bayu
dibendung asyik kalbu
begitulah munajatku padamu

embun menitis
mengocak gelora di permukaan
luas kasihmu menebar pusaran syahdu
hidupku dicucuri rahmat
gema dan gerak kudrat
memaut damai di tepian

sebutir embun kau titis
seumur hidupku
lemas ditenggelami
tasik rindu

Poet's Note: This poem was penned by me while on honeymoon on a houseboat at Lake Dal in Kashmir. It is an expression of love to my wife and the Creator.

Ikrar

Peter Augustine Goh

Ini watan kita
yang mesti dibela
oleh setiap yang bergelar warga
tidak kira apa bangsa dan agama
dalam merumahkan setia
kibarkan bendera tercinta
kerana ada bunga kasih berkembang
tertebar harum di balik warna
dalam makna.

Di sini
di bumi bertuah ini
jangan tergeliat lidah
mencipta sejarah luka
juga jangan sesekali kita rebah
terperlus ke dalam lumpur keganasan
menegakkan benang basah
cuba menjadi Jebat
yang kaya dengan dendam kesumat
hilang arah kerana ada luka yang tercabar
ada duka yang tersebar
ada kemanusiaan yang terbakar
ada persaudaraan yang tercemar.

Sungai suasana kian keruh
kerana keliru dengan buruan sendiri
sampai nafsu berkecai di tasik iman
dilanda taufan perasaan bertindih hasutan.

Pantang kita derhaka
pada tanah air merdeka
yang telah dibina dengan
keringat dan air mata
melaknati perit jerih nenek moyang
yang doanya tak pernah tumbang
demi maruah terbilang.

Ini watan kita
yang mesti dibela

tegakkan ikrar tepatilah janji
sebelum terletak nama dan wajah lesu
di akhbar pagi
berulit setia
hapuskan bara sengketa
padamkan api petualang perosak bangsa
robekkan topeng-topeng serigala
yang sentiasa tak terkawal
nafsu derhaka
mencipta huru hara
yang tak pernah direlakan ketersasarannya.

Ini negara kita
rumah kita bumi kita
yang mesti dibela
suara perpaduan mengimbau
sampai ke puncak awan
lalu menjadi kawan
menolak keresahan dan kedurjanaan
terpancang ikrar yang terpahat kukuh di dada
selagi berdenyutnya nadi
hingga ke hujung usia.

First appeared in *Berita Minggu*, 25 July 2004.

Poet's Note: This poem was written as a gentle reminder to all Singaporeans, irrespective of their different race and religion, that we must stand united and always stand by our nation. Singapore is our land, our life, our country. We must be patriotic and never betray, in the good or bad times. Ignorance of this notion will only raise many ugly and unpleasant possibilities and does not augur well with our pledge or vow to be always loyal and true to this beloved nation.

CHAPTER 42

A REFLECTION ON SINGAPORE MALAY POPULAR MUSIC (1965–2015)

Art Fazll

When we talk about 50 years of Singapore Malay music, 1965 to 2015, we cannot ignore the fact that for the first two decades since leaving Malaysia, Singapore remained as the centre of Malay music industry. Almost all the classic songs recorded by legends of the Malay music industry were recorded in Singapore — The Swallows, A Ramlie, Jeffridin, Sharifah Aini, Black Dog Bone, Sweet Charity, M Nasir, Search and Wings, just to name a few.

Like the Malay film industry before it, Singapore became the centre for music mainly due to its ability to provide cutting-edge recording technology of its time and it also has an offering of abundance of homegrown talents — singers, musicians, engineers, record producers and promotional team. Like a honeypot, Singapore also became an attraction to musicians from Indonesia. Zubir Said, the composer of Singapore's national anthem *Majulah Singapura* was one of the many who made Singapore their home.

With all its resplendent colours and sonic offerings, Malay popular music was and is, essentially a dialogue — between tradition and progress, of ethnic identity and modernity. It juggles a juggernaut of syncretic juxtaposition of East–West, modern–traditional. It is an ongoing dialogue throughout the ensuing decades, perhaps a product of a people trying to make sense of things. The music may be modern and Western but the melody is essentially Malay and the lyrics never strayed too far away from the accepted notions and values of the Malay community. Malay popular music has managed somehow, perhaps even unconsciously retained the essence of its "Malayness".

Take for example Pop Yeh Yeh[1] music of the 1960s. Whatever the theory of origin were, whether it was The Swallows, Jefridin and The Siglap 5 or A Ramlie and The Rhythm Boys, the music was an emulative mix of 1960s American surf rock, British invasion pop and psychedelic rock influenced by popular instrumental bands such as The Shadows (UK) and The Ventures (US). The twist was that Malay musicians infused traditional *asli* (Malay traditional song) vocal singing styles to it making it unique. Some of the melodic guitar lines veer into Arabic and Javanese music scales.

Or take the post-1960s "dirtier" sound of Mike Ibrahim and The Nite Walkers. Their music was a cross between American southern rock and post-psychedelic British pop. They wore bell bottoms on the album front covers. But their lyrics dipped into Malay nursery rhymes like *Bang Selebu*, *Cok Cok Gendung* and *Ca Ci Li Ca Ong*. Hence the template has been set. And thus throughout the ensuing decades, be it Ismail Haron and Anita Sarawak's duet albums, Black Dog Bone's disco, the heavy rock of Sweet Charity or Rahimah Rahim's bubblegum pop, Singapore Malay music reflected this essential component.

Nothing was more acute in this desire to express the paradox than Kembara, led by M Nasir. Kembara can be called the quintessential intellectual Singapore Malay rock group. The band's music was labeled as *lagu rakyat*, literally meaning folk songs. Their songs touch on the loss of kampong life like in *Bas No 13*, Malay identity in songs like *Nusantara*, *Kami Orang Melayu* and *Kami Anak Zaman Ini* and materialism in *Duit*. Kembara appealed to urban youths as well as

---

[1] The term *Yeh Yeh* could have been originated in the common refrain "woah, woah, yeah, yeah" used by artistes from the West from the Everly Brothers to Helen Shapiro (Looseley David L., Popular Music in Contemporary France, Berg, Oxford, New York, 2003). In the local music scene, the term Pop Yeah Yeah was never used in its time (1965–1971). The term was coined in the 1980s when there was a sixties music revival in Malaysia. The term used in its active years was *muzik kugiran* (Kumpulan Gitar Rancak) or *Muzik Ago-go*. The term "kugiran" was invented by 1960s Singapore radio presenter by the name of M.I.A. (Mohd Ismail Abdullah).

intellectuals. Its songs were not just sonic delicacies but whose lyrics had meanings coded in metaphors. Kembara's music became the precursor to the "*Nusantara* movement".

In the late 1980s, a sense of cultural consciousness was slowly taking shape within the Malay intelligentsia. It eventually took root in a new movement in Malay music that would be considered as Rennaissance of Malay music. This style came to be known as *Nusantara* music. Amongst its proponents were M Nasir, Rausyanfikir, Zainal Abidin and Nuradee.

Rausyanfikir (meaning thinkers in Persian), a folk rock band consisted of Art Fazil's school friends — the late Esham Jamil and Mohd Khair Mohd Yasin. The term *Nusantara* came from the namesake itself, a geographical location in Southeast Asia known to anthropologists as the Malay World. Malays call the area *Nusantara*, literally meaning "a group of islands". The sound of *Nusantara* music would be that is identified with the use of Indo-Malay elements such as *gendang*, *rebana*, *gambus* and *gamelan* instruments like *bonang*, *kulintang* or the sounds sampled on keyboards. In other words, *Nusantara* music was the Malay offering to the new genre in Western pop music called world music. What set the *Nusantara* music apart from syncretic Malay pop is not just the sonic nuances but also the poetic content of the lyrics which dug into the wealth of Malay folklore, mythology, spirituality, philosophy and poetry.

The late Esham Jamil being flanked by Mohd Khair Mohd Yasin on his right and Art Fazil on his left. Image courtesy of MORO Records © 2015. All rights reserved.

Nusantara music offers a connection to one's roots. It uses modern pop elements but yet infusing ethnic elements. It was so infectious that "Papa Rock" Ramli Sarip, the former frontman of Sweet Charity, switched genre from rock music and released an album in 1990 called *Ihsan*, featuring Singapore-born Khaty Ibrahim. In fact, Ramli Sarip continued to feature *Nusantara* style throughout his subsequent albums such as *Syair Timur* and *Kalam Kasturi*.

The ancient Malay weaponry, crafts and other artifacts such as the *keris* (Malay dagger), the *songket tenun* (a hand-woven fabric in silk or cotton. with gold or silver threads) or even Islamic *khitabs* (books) are important and treasured items that act as important symbols that link the past to the present. Without them, the chain that connects us to the ancient and the traditional would have diminished. In a way, Singapore modern Malay music was perhaps a product of a people trying to make sense of the contemporary, making its way back to the past, finding a link through the arts.

Artists are society's cultural reflectors. Their antenna picks up images, sound, colour and energy and reflects it back in painting, music, theatre and films. Artists have that unique ability to engage individuals in a deep and personal way. Art can help us understand our humanity and the historical conditions we live in. It pushes boundaries, ask questions and create beauty, make a statement, or shines light on issues.

And as all things are, change is constant. New influences such as hip hop and American R&B music began to replace the more roots and rock influences in Malay popular music. What the musicians cannot offer in terms of sonic syncrecity, they offer the lyrical — employing *pantun* (an oral literary form of expression traditionally used among the Malays), *gurindam* (a type of irregular verse forms of traditional Malay poetry) and *syair* (a form of traditional Malay poetry that made up of four-line stanzas or quatrains that conveys a continuous idea from one stanza to the next) in their songs such as music from the likes of Malay hip hop acts such as Ahli Fiqir and Sleeq.

The New Reality and Challenges

The global music business in the second decade of the new millennium is a far cry from its hey days in the yesteryears. The digital onslaught proves a lot tougher for the business. CD sales are neglible and online piracy is uncurbed, even with the availability of legal download sites like iTunes.

The future of Singapore Malay music is uncertain. We are handicapped by market size. The crux of the matter is Malays in Singapore are small in numbers. Malays make up 13.3% (about 512,000) of the total resident population;[2] hence, if we divide the Malay market into subgroups, according to age, taste in music, preferences of style etc., the pie gets smaller.

Legendary artist P Ramlee once said that *"bahasa menunjukkan bangsa"* (language reflects one's race). The decline of usage of Malay language amongst the younger generation is real. Social media has led the younger generation to be more comfortable using English to communicate as compared to the early days. Back then, the local lingua franca was Malay and thus the audience support was national.

Pop music in particular belongs to the youth. The average consumer for music is between the ages of 13–30 years old. If this generation is growing up handicapped in Malay, it would affect the consumption of Malay-based works. (It affects not just music for that matter but also literature, theatre, TV and newspaper.) Malaysia on the other hand has 30 million people, of which 50.1% (about 15 million) are Malays.

In a business that requires mass market, Malaysia is more attractive. Let us be clear here — the larger market has always been in Malaysia. It was the same for Malay cinema during the Golden Age of Malay Cinema in the 1950s. But the game has changed because Singapore is now out of the equation. Malaysian artists can now record their music in new hi-tech studios in Kuala Lumpur.

The economic reality has for decades driven Singapore artistes across the Causeway. Malay entertainment industry in Singapore in the 1970s started off with a sense of uncertainty. Shaw Brothers' Malay Film

---

[2] http://www.amp.org.sg/edisi/data/Publications/3rd%20Convention%20Journal/Section%209%20-%20Demographic%20Study.pdf

Productions and Cathay Films had begun to stop making movies. Actors, producers, directors and even musicians who wanted to carry on in show business moved to Kuala Lumpur where Merdeka Studio and RTM were newly created.

For an industry to thrive, it needs not just the artists but also the intelligentsia to contribute in stimulating interest. The Malay media in Singapore could play an important role in this. Concert reviews, music critique and regular write-ups on homegrown entertainment activities such as album launches and even trivia gossips would be helpful in sustaining interest in local music.

Perhaps it is worth considering bringing back the regular television shows dedicated to music, like *Pesta Pop* and *Hiburan Minggu Ini* to regenerate the local audience interest. Efforts like Radio Ria 89.7 FM's *Singa Maksima* slot where they play only Singapore music are commendable. It has proven to be successful in creating a following amongst the local listeners. Now, new homegrown acts are getting the much needed exposure.

Today, Malaysia's music market is said to be worth $100 million. That is a sweet, lucrative calling to draw Singapore talents away from a small local Malay market. What lies ahead for Singapore Malay artistes is a road with no clear path. The concern is that in the future the outflow of revenue in royalties paid to foreign music played on Singapore radio would be followed by the outflow of Singapore Malay talents hopping on the next bus to KL on a one-way ticket. Success stories like actor Aaron Aziz and composer M Nasir serve to remind Singapore Malay talents that the grass is greener on the other side.

However, migration brings in a whole set of other issues. Not everyone has the means to do so effectively. The alternative would be to stay and hold the fort. Perhaps instead of focusing on the 500,000 Malays, local Malay artistes could look at the bigger picture — the ever-growing 5.5 million citizens of Singapore. This would mean that Malay artistes would have to work within the mainstream "Channel 5" market, i.e., the

English-speaking Singaporeans. Malay artistes could thrive at being bilingual.

Najib Ali is one such exemplary artist. His unique personality as Asia Bagus' zany host earned him fame all over Asia in the mid-1990s. The late Iskandar Mirza Ismail, whose parents were part of the Malay film fraternity in the 1950s, was well known for his contributions to music at national and international level. He received the Cultural Medallion Award for his services in 2008. Although his Malay works were fairly limited, Iskandar is still the pride of the community. Indie bands comprising of mostly Malay musicians like The Pinholes and The Full Pledge Munkees have taken such steps by releasing albums in English and singles in Malay. Recently, these bands have toured Canada and Japan respectively. It has to be said that apart from Taufik Batisah, Sezairie Sezali and a handful of others, most Malay pop artistes are working solely within the Malay corner of the entertainment industry.

In the 1970s, the mainstream entertainment on television was dominated by names such as Kartina Dahari, Julie Sudiro and Rahimah Rahim. They were renowned with the English-speaking crowd. It has to be said that Malays are also conspicuously absent in mainstream media as newscasters, current affairs programme hosts, radio presenters and actors. Malay actors in local English dramas tend to be casted in stereotype roles. There need to be a rethinking to address this imbalance.

Malay music doyenne, the late Kartina Dahari, a familiar and elegant face and voice on local Malay television and radio from the 1960s to the 1980s. Photo courtesy of Salleh Sariman © 2015. All Rights Reserved.

Singapore Malay film industry is considered long gone when the batch of Jalan Ampas actors and directors "took the midnight KTM train to Kuala Lumpur". It happened when Shaw Brothers and Cathay Films closed their Malay film production unit. There have been efforts to revive the local Malay film industry but it has largely been a start-stop affair.

We have to accept the fact that with the shrinking of the creative Malay market in Singapore, the output of new original works will relatively be lesser. This is the reality of the economics of demand and supply. Malays like other Singaporeans are attracted and seduced by "foreign goods".

In the future, it is most likely that Malay entertainment products would be coming in from Malaysia and Indonesia. This is already happening with films. However, a thriving and inclusive Singapore entertainment industry will create a new playing field for local Malay talents. It also has a great potential to create a more cohesive and inclusive national identity and prevent the marginalisation of an already marginal artistic community in a shrinking community.

CHAPTER 43

VISUAL ART DEVELOPMENTS | Syed Muhd Hafiz
WITHIN THE MALAY COMMUNITY | Bin Syed Nasir

All Malay artists in Singapore now have their own
association, "Angkatan Pelukis Aneka Daya" (APAD).
A motto that would become their objective
and guidance in their future activities was also adopted
by the artists at the inauguration. The motto says
"Secipta Mencipta"

(Together We Create).[a]

With the above declaration at the inauguration of APAD and the subsequent declaration of Singapore's Independence in 1965, it
is generally assumed that visual arts culture or Malay
artists only emerged in the same period. This is an
issue of terminology, especially if one thinks in terms
of the nation–state framework. It is important to
understand that other socio-political factors, for
example, the separation of Singapore from Malaysia,
also had an effect on the development of the Malay artists here, just as how it affected the local literary developments, as exemplified by the history of Asas '50.

However, for the purposes of this brief essay here,
it is important to note that prior to the formation of
APAD, there was already a vibrant visual arts scene
amongst the Malay community here with individuals
like Aman Bin Ahmad (Pak Man) who had his studio at
Allenby Road[b] and Suri Bin Mohyani (Cikgu Suri), a

[a] Abdul Ghani Hamid, *An Artist's Note*, (Singapore: Angkatan Pelukis Aneka Daya, 1991), p. 13.
[b] Sulaiman Jeem and Abdul Ghani Hamid, *Aktivis Melayu/ Islam di Singapura*, (Singapore: Persatuan Wartawan Melayu Singapura, 1997), p. 84.

founding member of the Singapore Arts Society in 1949.[c] Alongside pioneering artists like Mahat Bin Chaadang (C Mahat), M Sawoot and Haji Sulaiman Haji Sulaimi, these artists were already active in the pre-APAD days and not to forget, existing in the Malayan context as exemplified in the formation of an earlier association, *Persekutuan Pelukis Melayu Melaya* (Society of Malay Artists, Malaya) which included artists from the rest of the Peninsula, like M Salehuddin and Abu Bakar Ibrahim.[d]

Further evidence of the vibrant art scene amongst the Malay artists here, were also outlined in an essay by Sudar Majid, in the inaugural issue of an art journal published by the Singapore Art Society in 1954.[e] Though brief, his essay hinted at the apparent conservatism of some of the Malay artists back then, especially with regards to figurative depictions. While this essay is too brief to list down the full arguments of figurative representation in art *vis-à-vis* the Islamic tradition, Sudar's essay did highlight two important points in tracing the early visual art development of Malay artists.

The first point was the establishment of the Sultan Idris Training College in Tanjung Malim, Perak in 1922, where 'fundamental painting was first taught to the Malays'.[f] The second point was the familiarisation with 'Western methods and techniques' in order to make progress. Some might argue against the latter point by questioning the adoption of "Western methods" or "Western techniques", or even delve further into notions of progress. However, what was clear at that time was the recognition of the Malay artists' contribution to the local art scene. An example was Cikgu Suri's solo exhibition at the then British Council Gallery situated along Stamford Road in January 1956. Officiated by the then

---

[c] Latiff Mohidin and Adibah Amin (translator) *Line: Latiff Mohidin from Point to Point*, (Kuala Lumpur: Dewan Bahasa dan Pustaka, 1993), p. 30.

[d] Abdul Ghani Hamid, *Kegiatan Kolektif Pelukis-Pelukis Melayu Malaya*, (Singapore: Angkatan Pelukis Aneka Daya, 1990), p. 2.

[e] Sudar Majid, "The Malay Artist," *The Singapore Artist: Journal of the Singapore Art Society*, Vol. 1, No. 2 (December 1954): pp. 3–9.

[f] *Ibid*, p. 7.

Minister for Communications and Works, Mr Francis Thomas, the exhibition featured 60 paintings. Subsequently, a few months after the exhibition, Cikgu Suri embarked on his art studies at the National Art School, Sydney under a UNESCO scholarship.[g]

While APAD's development as an art society continued in showcasing the activities of Malay artists in Singapore, there were also other Malay artists that were active outside the framework of APAD. This is not to suggest some kind of counter movement or narrative but more than anything else, the surrounding art landscape in the region was also shifting in accordance to newer attitudes in collectivism and experimentations with regards to art-making.

In 1972, Iskandar Jalil was awarded the Colombo Plan scholarship to continue his studies in Ceramic Engineering in Japan. Almost a solitary figure in promoting the medium of ceramics back then, Iskandar's role as an educator also helped him established a huge following of students who continue to both, teach and practice ceramics. Deservedly, Iskandar was awarded the Cultural Medallion in 1988 by the Singapore government and more recently, the Order of the Rising Sun (Gold Rays with Rosette) an award bestowed by the Emperor of Japan for his contribution towards the cultural exchange and mutual understanding between Singapore and Japan.[h]

The same year also saw Yusman Aman — originally from Malaysia — whose abstract *batik* painting "Rhythm in Blue" was chosen to be printed on a 50-cent stamp as part of a series of four postage stamps alongside other artists namely Seah Kim Joo, Thomas Yeo and Chen Wen Hsi.[i] Together with Jaafar Latiff and Sarkasi Said, these artists successfully pushed the *batik* medium beyond the craft tradition. It should be noted too that Iskandar and Jaafar played pivotal roles in the

---

[g] Sulaiman Jeem and Abdul Ghani Hamid, *Aktivis Melayu/Islam Singapura*, (Singapore: Persatuan Wartawan Melayu Singapura, 1997), p. 396.

[h] Press Release, "Conferment of the Order of the Rising Sun, Gold Rays with Rosette on Mr Iskandar Jalil", 29 April 2015, The Embassy of Japan in Singapore.

[i] Press Release, "First Exhibits for Proposed Postal Museum", 6 July 1972, Singapore Government Press Statement.

nascent years of the Baharuddin Vocational Institute (BVI), Singapore's first tertiary-level school dedicated towards "manual and applied arts", in the late 1960s. BVI's Applied Arts department produced many designers and craftsmen for the next two decades till its gradual absorption into Temasek Polytechnic in 1990.

The 1970s–1980s period heralded a renewed vigour towards art-making in the region and this laid the ground for what is now known as the development of contemporary art. 1974 saw Malaysian artists Redza Piyadasa and Sulaiman Esa collaborating in an exhibition titled "Towards a Mystical Reality" at the Dewan Bahasa dan Pustaka, Kuala Lumpur, as their response towards the prevailing adoption of the Western framework in art-making. The subsequent year saw a group of young Indonesian artists organising an exhibition "Seni Rupa Baru" (New Art Indonesia) at the Taman Ismail Marzuki in Jakarta, in response to the dominance of traditional art forms, i.e., painting, in their national art competition. Both these exhibitions featured new modes of art-making which included installation art, graphic illustrations and the utilisation of everyday objects in their artworks.

Singapore too had similar artistic developments and towards the end of the 1980s, an artist "colony" known as the Artists Village was established by local artist Tang Da Wu. He was influential to the younger generation of local artists which included young Malay artists like Zai Kuning and Faizal Fadil. Zai's work "Installing Memory" and Faizal's work "Three Thermos Flasks", produced in 1992 and 1991 respectively, raised significant debates about artistic production *vis-à-vis* the increasing urbanisation of Singapore.

In the same year that Artists Village was formed, an exhibition titled "Trimurti" was organised at the Goethe Institute in Singapore by three young artists from the Nanyang Academy of Fine Arts, namely S Chandrasekaran, Goh Ee Choo and Salleh Japar. A collaborative exhibition which aimed to infuse culturally-specific approaches towards art-making, Salleh's Muslim background and his readings on spirituality influenced his installation and mixed-media works produced in the exhibition.[j]

Salleh's and Zai's new approaches towards art-making, just to mention a few artists, preceded a new generation of Malay artists who seem to have announced themselves to a wider audience, and not necessarily framed by their ethnicity. These sentiments were professed in an exhibition curated by Khairuddin Hori in 2003 titled "Berita Harian". Most of the artists featured "preferred the conceptual route" in an attempt to move beyond the "...traditional markers of Malay ethnicity — craft and folk art for instance."[k]

At the international level, Salleh's inclusion in Singapore's inaugural participation at the Venice Biennale in 2001, marked a significant contribution to Singapore's art history. In 2007, sonic or sound sculptor artist Zulkifle Mahmod's selection for the 52nd edition of the Venice Biennale was another milestone as he presented his work titled 'Sonic Dome: An Empire of Thoughts' at the prestigious international exhibition.[l]

Singapore's Malay artists continue to be active participating in both the local and international art scenes, and the past 50 years have seen successive generations of artists making their presence felt to the local arts audience. If there is one observation that can be made from this very brief survey of Malay artists in Singapore, it is their continued resilience in contributing towards the cultural identity of Singapore, despite their minority status and the increasing challenges of market forces in the local art scene.

---

[j] T. K. Sabapathy (ed.), *Trimurti and Ten Years After*, exh. cat. (Singapore: Singapore Art Museum, National Heritage Board, 1998).

[k] In 2003, an exhibition curated by Khairuddin Hori showcased nine 'current generation' Malay artists featuring installations, sound installations, computer animation and video art. The exhibition was held at the Substation Gallery and featured works by the late Juliana Yasin, Zulkifle Mahmod, Harman Hussin, Khairuddin Hori, Ridzuan Saari, Gene Sha Rudyn, Ismail Ishak, Rizman Putra and Sukaimi Sukri. "Berita Harian: Press Release" http://biotechnics.org/1beritaharian.html (accessed 18 February 2016).

[l] Press Release — "Singapore at 52nd Venice Biennale", 6th February 2007, National Arts Council and Singapore Art Museum.

All images in this section courtesy of the National Heritage Board.

Suri Bin Mohyani Kampong Kuchai (Lorong 3, Geylang) **1951** Watercolour on Paper
Collection of National Gallery Singapore

Mohd Salehudin Malay House, Malacca *c.* **1960** Oil on Canvas

Sarkasi Said Tzee Fish **1978** Batik
Collection of National Gallery Singapore

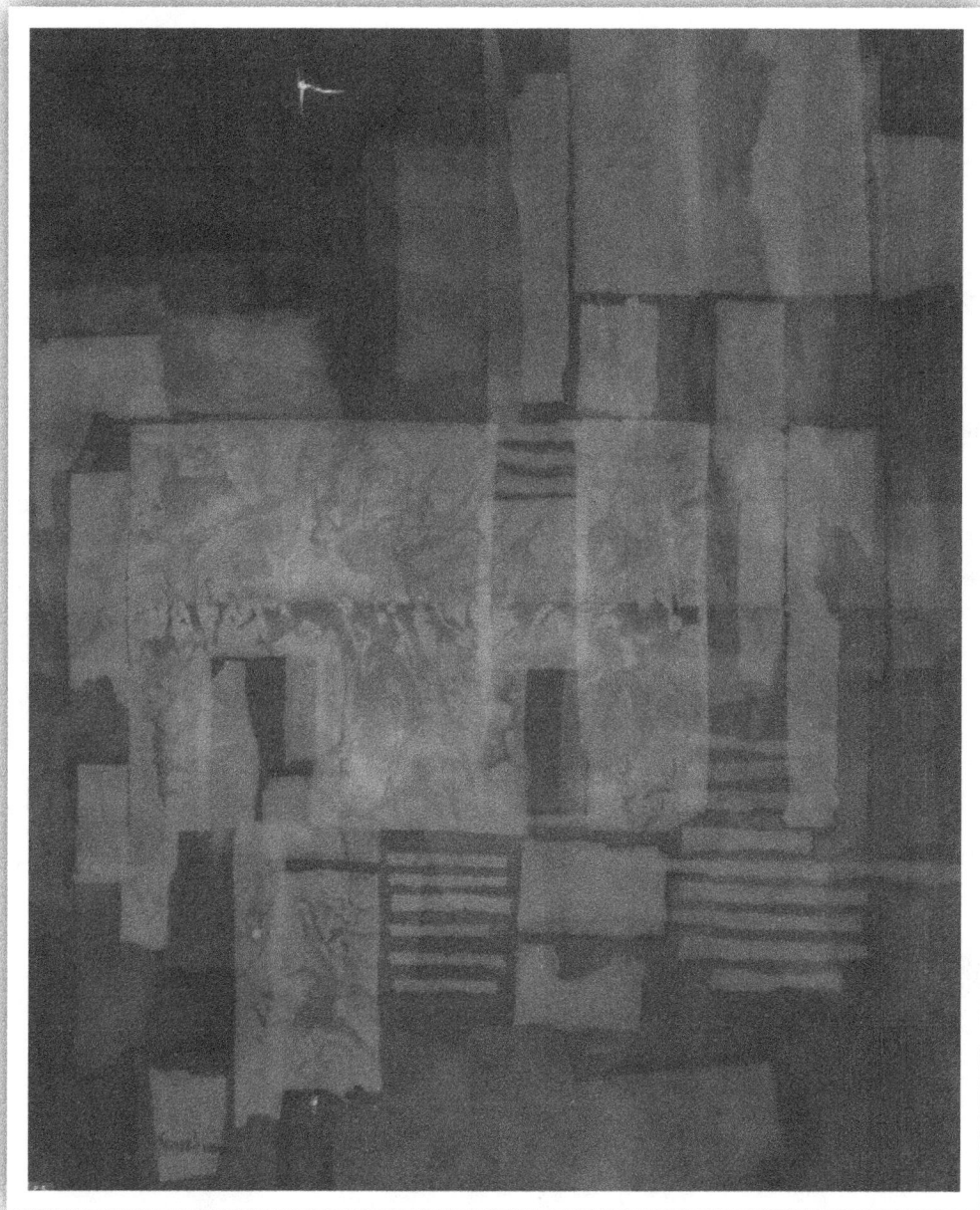

Yusman Aman Rhythm in Blue **1972** Batik
Collection of National Gallery Singapore

Jaafar Latiff Wandering Series 8/79 **1979** Batik on Cloth
Collection of National Gallery Singapore
Gift of the Artist

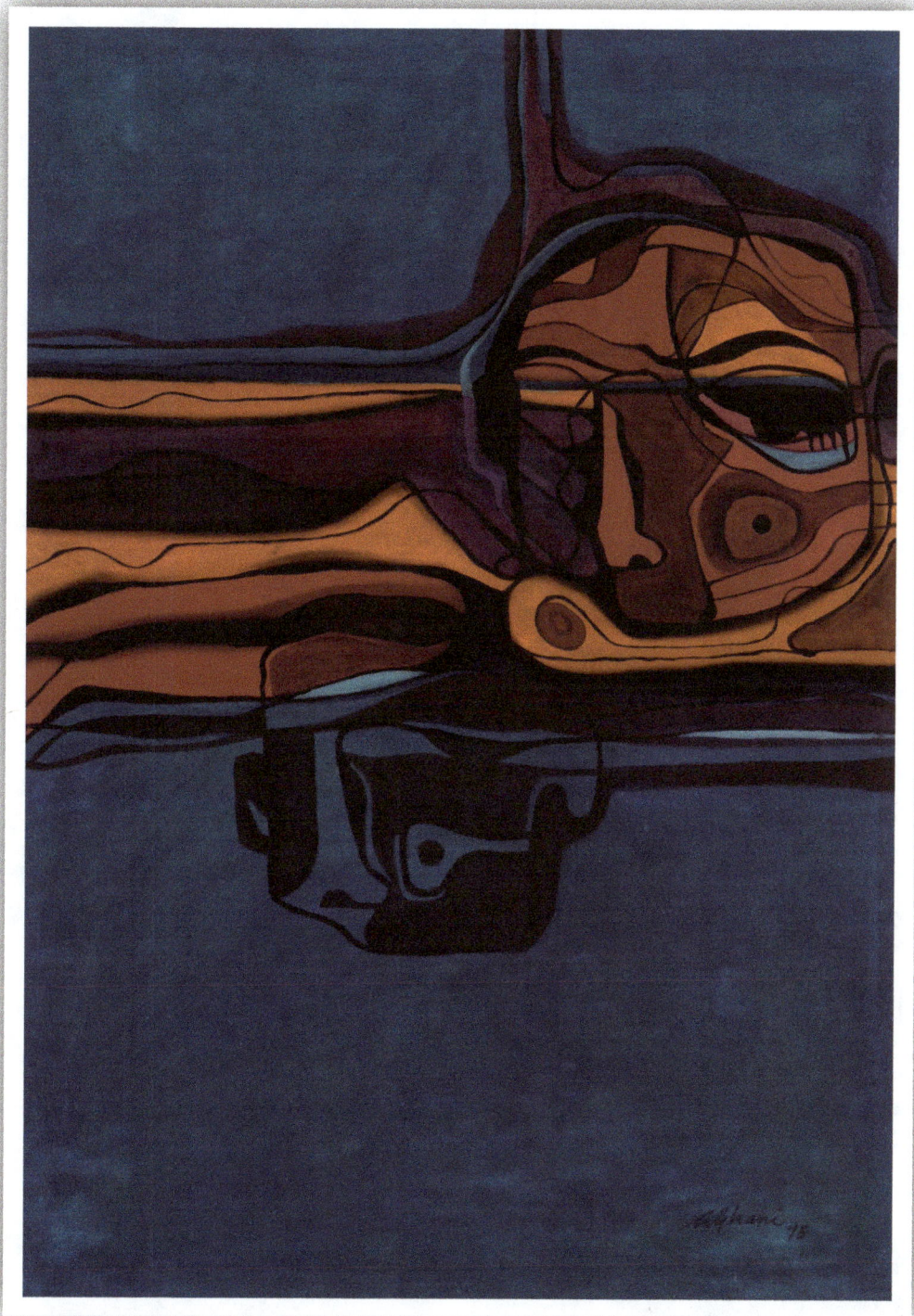

Abdul Ghani Hamid The Face in Meditation **1975** Oil on Canvas
Collection of National Gallery Singapore
Gift of the Artist

M. Faizal Fadil Study of Three Thermos Flasks **1991** Aluminium
Collection of Singapore Art Museum

Zai Kuning Installing Memory **1992** Mixed Media
Collection of Singapore Art Museum

Iskandar Jalil Jawi Script Vessel *c.* **1960s** Stoneware Clay
Collection of the Artist

Salleh Japar Mechanised Learning **1993** Mixed Media
Collection of Singapore Art Museum

PART 2

Icons, Pioneers and All

THE NUSANTARA ETHNIC COMMUNITIES OF SINGAPORE — JAVANESE, BAWEANESE, MINANGS AND BANJARESE

Aidi Abdul Rahim

T he Singapore Malays is not a homogenous group in terms of ethnicity. In Singapore's context, Malay is used as race category by the government, and as an ethnic group identifier of the people originally indigenous to early Singapore (Temasek). When Raffles landed in Singapore, there were already Malays and the Orang Laut (consisting of the Orang Kallang, Orang Seletar, Orang Selat and Orang Gelam) inhabiting under the Johore-Riau-Lingga Sultanate on the island. When Singapore was annexed by the British as a trading post, ethnic groups (such as the Javanese, Baweanese, Minangs, Bugis, Banjarese) from other parts of the archipelago (or the Nusantara i.e., the multi-ethnic groups existing in the islands of Sumatra, Java, Celebes, Kalimantan, that includes, Brunei, Southern Philippines, Southern Thailand and the Malay peninsula) came here in search of employment, trading opportunities and a better life. These ethic groups had, in fact, been traversing around the region well before Raffles,

Native sampan, Singapore.

Photo credit: Art and Picture Collection, The New York Public Library. New York Public Library Digital Collections. Public domain. Last accessed 31 March 2016.

arrived. Though coming from geographically different parts of the Nusantara, these ethnic groups were tied together quite closely based on culture, language and religion. Over time, the various ethnic groups became "Malaynised" by adopting Malay as the main lingua-franca among the Nusantara ethnic groups, when they inter-married between the Malays and the other ethnic groups, and shared a common religion. In post-independent Singapore, the identification of the non-Malay Nusantara ethnic groups became less evident, as many preferred to or simply identified themselves as Malays. The push factor was the Singapore government's policy to promote and categorise the major races into the CMIO (Chinese-Malay-Indian-Others) model as a foundation for racial harmony and multiculturalism that guides government policies and political institutions. There is current interest among the various non-Malay Nusantara ethnic groups to revive some of their cultural art forms, language usage in raising historical awareness. Some of these cultural activities and talks have been supported by the Malay Heritage Centre (Taman Warisan Melayu) located in Kampung Gelam, together with the involvement of local community-based associations which include the Persatuan Jawa al-Masakin, Persatuan Bawean Singapura, and the Persatuan Minang Singapura.

The Javanese

Waves of Javanese migrants came from the island of Java after the establishment of Singapore as a British trading post in 1819. The Javanese are thought to be the largest Nusantara ethnic group that migrated to Singapore in the 19th century. During the initial wave, many Javanese migrants were believed to have been craftsmen and merchants, and they established their trading area in Kampung Java (somewhere between Arab Street and Haji Lane today). The Javanese craftsmen worked in metal and leather crafts, while the merchants traded in cloth, spices, religious texts and other goods.

In the 1825 census, there were 38 Javanese recorded residing in Singapore, and in 1891, the recorded numbers was 8,541. There were both push and pull factors that attracted Javanese immigration into Singapore. The Javanese faced tough economic conditions imposed by the Dutch Colonial government; there was a population explosion in Java leading to a scarcity of arable land to feed the people, and rising poverty. At the same time, there was an active recruitment of Javanese to work as contract labour in large-scale plantation farms and the mining industry opened by the British and capitalist class. The Javanese were viewed also as an alternative substitute of labour to the Chinese and Indians. It was thought that since they shared the same religion as the Malays, the Javanese were able to assimilate easily with the Malays.

There were other factors to explain the Javanese migration to Singapore. In the late 19th century to mid-20th century, Singapore was the staging post for the *haj* pilgrimage from Southeast Asia to Mecca, and many Javanese pilgrims went to the *haj* via Singapore. The Dutch Colonial government was adamant in imposing travel restrictions on pilgrims from the Dutch East Indies traveling directly to Mecca. During this period, between 2000 to 7000 Javanese pilgrims undertook the *haj* annually via Singapore. To pay for the Haj trip, some of these Javanese pilgrims would find work here for months, or sometimes years, to pay for their fare. Upon returning from the *haj*, some would settle in Singapore for a few years to settle their debts. During the Japanese Occupation, 10,000 Javanese were brought in by the Japanese as conscript labour. When the war ended, some returned to Java, some migrated to Malaya, and a few stayed on in Singapore.

When Singapore achieved independence, many of the Javanese who lived here had assimilated with the larger Malay community and consequently, the Javanese too lost their proficiency in their mother tongue. The increasing importance of English education, enlightened Islamic religious reforms, and the passing-away of the pioneer immigrant generation also contributed towards the erosion of many cultural

A Javanese lady sits and poses, c. 1900.

Photo credit: *Photographic Views of Singapore* (PDF), Singapore, G. R. Lambert & Company. Public domain.

and traditional practices that were part of the Javanese ethnic identity.

Kampung Jawa or Kampung Java was the first Javanese settlement established, and it was thought that its close proximity to Arab Street was because many Javanese formed the crew of Arab-owned vessels that operated out of Java. Other areas where the Javanese settled in the 19th century included, Kampung Tempei (near today's Coronation Road), Kampung Chantek (near Binjai Park), Kampung Pachitan (near Kembangan), and various other settlements along Bukit Timah Road. Kampung Java Road, which links Bukit Timah to Newton Circus, was so named due to the large number of Javanese living along that trunk road. In these areas, the Javanese lived alongside the other ethnic communities. There is less Javanese spoken in Singapore homes now, except when relatives from across the Causeway visits; there will be some smattering heard over a short period of time among the elderly. Indeed, many will acknowledge that they may have a Javanese or other non-Malay lineage (such as Boyanese and Minang), but with the prevalence of inter-marriages between Malays and other ethnic groups, they typically identify themselves as Malays. Culturally, the Javanese have a rich artistic tradition that includes dance, *wayang kulit*, and the *gamelan* ensemble. These traditions are slowly being eroded by the decreasing pool of practitioners, competing interests, and the lack of exposure to such cultural art forms among the younger generation.

Two Javanese dancers, c. 1860–1890.

Photo credit: Gift of M. A. D. de Josselin de Jongh-Laman Trip, Aerdenhout. Public domain via Rijksmuseum.

The Baweanese (or Boyanese)

They were originally from the island of Bawean, located north of present-day Surabaya, and migrated to Singapore in the late 19th century until the end of the World War Two, settling along the banks of Sungei Rochor between Jalan Besar and Syed Alwi Road. In the 1849 census, it was recorded there were 763 Boyanese, and in 1950, there were about 24,000 of them. The Baweanese in Singapore were initially employed in the construction of the Serangoon Road Race Course at

Farrer Park. Subsequently, many of them stayed on as horse trainers and drivers. Their migration to Singapore is partly due to their tradition of *merantau*, a rite of passage where young men would leave their homes in search of work opportunity overseas (similar to the Minang community practice enforced on their young men), and in the 1900s, the taxation policy imposed by the Dutch forced many indigenous people of the Dutch East Indies to leave home to avoid paying taxes.

Many who came here to work were young men and supported themselves living in communal houses known as *pondoks*. A *pondok* or ponthuk was a lodging house, which primarily provided housing for the newly-arrived Baweanese. The *pondok* also served the role of a social institution similar to the Chinese clan association. The Baweanese could go to the *pondoks* for work recommendations or community activities. These *pondoks* were located around Singapore, such as at the Minto Road ponthuk, Adam Communal House in Ann Siang Hill, Teluk Dalam Communal House in Dixon Road, and Dedawang Communal House in Sophie Road. In the 1900s, there was a Baweanese settlement within the town limit called Kampung Kapor, or Lime Village, which was located about a kilometre to the North-West of Kampung Boyan. In fact, many of the *pondoks*

Pulau Seking had one of Singapore's earliest Malay settlements. These early inhabitants were from the Johore-Riau Archipelago, and were namely Suku Bintan, Orang Selat and Orang Laut. http:// eresources.nlb.gov.sg/infopedia/articles/SIP_239_2005-01-19.html. Photo courtesy of Salleh Sariman © 2016. All rights reserved.

were located in the Kampung Kapur area. A Baweanese landmark in Kampung Kapor was the Masjid Bawean (or Bawean Mosque) built in 1932, which was located at Weld Road but was demolished in the 1980s for a road widening project. The last *pondok* in Singapore was the Pondok Peranakan Gelam Club, originally located at 64 Club Street in Telok Ayer. In the 1930s to 1960, this large pre-war shop house served as a communal home for about 200 Baweanese immigrants to married couples, singles and children. The fact that the Baweanese and the Javanese shared the same religion and were closely related racially, both were able to mix freely and even intermarried with the Malays. In time, this caused the differences between them to be less obvious, and more Baweanese and Javanese began identifying themselves as Malays.

The Minangs

The majority of Minang people that came to Singapore were from Pariaman and Agam in Western Sumatra. A unique character of this ethnic group is their practice of *Adat Pepatih* or matrilineality i.e., lineage and inheritance are handed down via the mothers. The other tradition that the Minang is associated with is *merantau* — a rite of passage where young men leave their homes to find employment and trading opportunities, and to gain knowledge and experience. The community is guided by the philosophy that advocates their people to integrate and to adhere to the lifestyle and practices of the new homeland in which they settled, while retaining the Minangkabau culture and traditions at the same time. Notable Singaporean personalities from this community are Yusof Ishak (the first President of Singapore), Zubir Said (the composer of the Singapore national anthem), Eunos Abdullah (the "father" of modern Malay journalism), Lieutenant Adnan Saidi (the hero of the Bukit Chandu/Pasir Panjang battle during the World War Two) and Yazid Wandly (a music director at Cathay Kris Films and music arranger for the song *Gurindam Jiwa*). The Minang community is known to be savvy traders and are typically engaged in businesses. They are well-known for their culinary dish, the *nasi padang*. Those involved in the *nasi padang* business can

Malay women sitting *bersimpuh*, a traditional way of sitting with feet tucked to the side, c. early 20th century. Photo reproduced with permission from Malay Heritage Centre © 2016. All rights reserved.

be found around the vicinity of the Kampung Gelam and Geylang Serai areas.

The Banjarese

The Banjar people originated from the southern and eastern coasts of Kalimantan, Borneo around the town of Banjarmasin. The Banjarese tend to be self-employed, working as either farmers or businessmen. However, those who migrated to Singapore were well-known as jewel cutters, polishers and dealers in the region. Those in the jewellery trade had their shops in and around Arab Street up till the late 1960s. The Banjarese who were in the jewellery trade were also involved in the purchase and development of landed property in the city area. Some Banjarese personalities of the past active in this business were the late *Orang Kaya* (Rich Man) Haji Osman Haji Abu Naim, Haji Mahmood Haji Abdul Rahim, Haji Ismail Haji Osman and Haji Hassan Haji Mohd Salleh. The Banjarese community also notably contributed in Singapore's Islamic religious scholarly field; these included Singapore's first Mufti (1969 to 1972), the late Ustaz Mohd Sanusi Mahmood, and religious scholars, Syekh Muhammad Arshad Al-Banjari, Syekh Muhammad Nafis Al-Banjari, and Syekh Abdur Rahman Shiddiq.

The Banjarese make up a very small percentage of the Malay population in Singapore. In 1931, they numbered 445 out of a total Malay population of 65,104 (0.7%). In 1947, they formed only 0.3% of the population. This dropped to 0.2% in 1957 and 0.1% in 1970. By 1980 and 1990, the total numbers could not be determined, probably because the Banjarese have effectively assimilated into the Malay community, but according to a Berita Harian report (October 2014), it was estimated to be about 1% of the total Malay population.

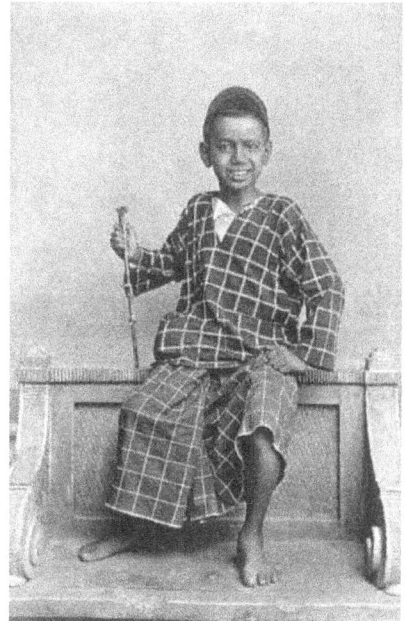

A grinning Malay boy sits and poses, c. 1900.

Photo credit: *Photographic Views of Singapore* (PDF), Singapore: G. R. Lambert & Company. Public domain.

CHAPTER 45

THE BUGIS OF SINGAPORE | Sarafian Salleh

Throughout history, Singapore has been an important calling station between India and West Asia in general and the Far East. Its geographical location at a crossroads of the East and West has contributed to its success as a trading port. The Bugis and several other seasoned traders like the Arabs and Chinese have long recognised Singapore as a city and they knew it was destined to be the future economic hub because of its geographical advantage.

In the year 1820,[a] the first massive wave of Bugis traders commanded by Arung Belawa, a Bugis Prince from Tanjung Pinang, arrived in Singapore. The arrival of Arung Belawa marked a monumental event and was documented in the local papers. He came with several family units totalling approximately 500 members, comprising mostly women and children. They wanted to settle in Singapore following disputes between Arung Belawa and the

Bugis, Singapoor.

Photo credit: The Miriam and Ira D. Wallach Division of Art, Prints and Photographs: Photography Collection, The New York Public Library. New York Public Library Digital Collections. Accessed March 31, 2016. http://digitalcollections.nypl.org/items/510d47dd-cc79-a3d9-e040-e00a18064a99

---

[a] Orang Bugis amat giat dalam dagangan, *Berita Harian*, 9 November 1982, p. 5, Singapore.

Dutch Governor in Tanjung Pinang.[b] Several waves arrived during the monsoon period. The Bugis immigrants brought with them various commodities ranging from spices, opium to precious metals. Their experience in commerce had led to an impressive economic growth during the first 30 years of British colonisation.

The Bugis have played an important role in the inter-island trade during Raffles' time. Trading activities in Singapore occurred around two seasons, the junk[c] season and the phinisi season.[d] The Chinese came in junks to import their goods in transit at warehouse or *gudang* for exports by the Bugis and other merchants. Most of the Bugis sea traders migrated back home after the Dutch declared Makassar a free port in 1847 and by 1860, the Bugis population in Singapore was reduced to less than 1000. Those who decided to stay became Singapore citizens.

The Bugis have assimilated well into the multi-cultural society Singapore and some even adopted Malay as their ethnic group. As time progressed, their industrious character had put them amongst equals in various fields of profession. Despite regarding themselves as Singaporeans now, there are few who still uphold the cultural tradition of the Bugis — a poetic legacy that embraces the root of origin, sculpturing a worthwhile character towards excellence in whatever he does in

A phinisi sailing near Makassar.

Photo credit: Collectie Stichting Nationaal Museum van Wereldculturen, Dr. W.G.N. (Wicher Gosen Nicolaas) van der Sleen (Fotograaf/photographer). Wikimedia commons. https://commons.wikimedia.org/wiki/File:COLLECTIE_TROPENMUSEUM_Een_prauw_met_volle_zeilen_op_zee_bij_Makassar_TMnr_10027859.jpg?fastcci_from=7785504&c1=7785504&c2=6399867&d1=15&d2=15&s=200&a=and

[b] Raja Ali Haji bin Raja Ahmad, Taufat Al Nafis, 1865.

[c] The Junk refers to the Chinese Traders from China. The Singapore River: A Social History, 1819–2002.

[d] The phinisi refers to the traditional Indonesian two-masted sailing ship. It was mainly built by the Konjo tribe, a sub-ethnic group of Bugis-Makassar mostly residents at the Bulukumba regency of South Sulawesi.

life. They have left a distinct mark in the history of Singapore with evidence of their legacy on local stamps, currencies, street names and popular landmarks such as Bugis Junction and Bugis MRT train station. Popular key figures of Bugis descent in Singapore are Haji Ambok Sooloh bin Haji Omar, a prominent Malay businessman, philanthropist and one of the founders of the Malay newspaper Utusan Melayu and Dr Abdul Samad bin Daeng Pagak, the first Malay doctor in Singapore, just to mention a few.

CHAPTER 46

THE ARABS IN SINGAPORE | Al-Wehdah Arab
Association of
Singapore

T he Arabs of Southeast Asia came, almost exclusively, from the Hadhramaut, that region in
what is modern-day Yemen. They can trace their
presence and their place in Singapore back to the
arrival of Raffles and perhaps even before this. In the
Arab Association's 46th anniversary publication in
1992, then Deputy Prime Minister Lee Hsien Loong
paid tribute to the contribution of the Arab community
in Singapore's history:

*The Arabs are one of the smallest communities in Singapore, numbering about
6000. Yet it has retained its identity and contributed significantly to Singapore society. Several members of the community have distinguished themselves in various
fields...I note that the Arab Association will be studying how it can transmit values
and impart the heritage to the younger members. These values will help to give
younger members of your community the cultural ballast necessary to develop and
prosper in a rapidly changing society like ours. I commend the Association for taking
this initiative..."*

For a long time, Singapore's Arab community held
significant positions — in the religious life of the
Muslim community, in social standing and in terms of
financial and commercial strength. The religious leadership they offered can be measured by the teachers
they brought to Singapore and by the madrasahs that
were established and the *wakaf* land dedicated for
mosques and charitable purposes.

In 1992, an article by Ameen Ali Talib, Helmi Talib
and Khaled Talib identified loss of identity, a loss of the

Arabic language, a loss of culture, religious status and economic status as key areas needing to be tackled by the Arab community. They reasoned that another significant area, that of education was "adequately addressed by other Muslim organisations of which the Arab community is a part". They quoted Ibn Khaldun as saying "it was natural for a person to adopt the genealogy of another race". Such people, they said, and a new home and become absorbed into a new life. In time, they will forget their past. The fact that Arab emigration to Southeast Asia in the past has been identified as "almost entirely a male phenomenon" led to a lot of intermarriage with local women. Fathers might have conversed with their children in Arabic, but most mothers spoke Malay and the command of Arabic by the next generation weakened.

The Arab Association of Singapore, also known as Al-Wehdah Al-Arabiah Bi Singhafura, was registered officially as a voluntary organisation on the 11 November 1946. The objectives then were to promote and enhance *syiar* Islam as well as the use of the Arabic language to all. A group photo of some members of Al-Wehdah taken at their clubhouse at Lorong Engku Aman c. 1950s.

Back in 1995, Al-Wehdah organised a seminar titled Singapore Arabs in the 21st century. A paper by Professor Syed Farid Alatas picked up again the subject of identity as being at the heart of the problems of the future of the Arabs in Singapore. "Singapore Arabs have to decide who they want to be," he said.

The Singapore Arab Association, Al-Wehdah, was officially registered as a voluntary society on 11 November 1946. In the 1950s its home was at 891 Geylang Road. In the 1970s, it was at Block 21, 432 Chai Chee Road and in 1989, came the move to its present site in Lorong 37, Geylang.

Promoting peace and togetherness through Samrah Al Wehdah, an Arabic traditional dance. Images courtesy of Al-Wehdah Arab Association of Singapore © 2016. All rights reserved.

CHAPTER 47

A BRIEF ON SINGAPORE INDIAN MUSLIMS | Raja Mohamad Maiden

The contribution to our nation by Muslims who hail from the Indian Sub-continent deserves serious study. They have contributed in diverse areas of local life including but not limited to trade and commerce, social philanthropy, language and education, food and arts, law, politics and nation building, to name a few.

In the Singapore context, anyone with roots from the sub-continent, whether North, South, East or West — the latter two renamed with the partition of India — are considered as Indian Muslims. Although the most visible group is from South India and speak Tamil or sometimes Malayalam, many through interracial marriages and socio-economic reasons have become "Malayanised" and accepted Malay as their mother tongue.

The former President of Singapore, Mr S R Nathan was the Guest-of-Honour at the Official Opening of the Nagore Dargah Indian Muslim Heritage Centre.

Regardless of this social evolution this small community has always punched above its weight and has made notable contributions to Singapore since they began arriving ashore almost two hundred years ago.

In the book *Crossing the Bay of Bengal*, author Sunil S Amrith notes that the "Tamil Muslims of the

Coramandel Coast, created an enduring web of culture and commerce around the Indian Ocean. They more than any other group, focused on the region around the Bay of Bengal where their network was deepest and widest". The crossing of the Bay of Bengal is one key factor for the arrival of Indian Muslims to Singapore amongst many others.

The Singapore Indian Muslims, regionally, if not globally, have specialised in some trades or skills. These include book-selling, ship-chandling, spice trading, textile and gems, literary arts, and religious philanthropy.

The presence of Indian Muslims in Southeast Asia can be traced as far back as 1400 according to Sunil Amrith's book. In Singapore however, the development of some of the more significant religious trusts or *wakaf* gives us a good indication of their presence here. For example, the *wakaf* Jamae Chulia setup by Tamil Muslim merchants hailing from "Coramondel Coast of South India" was established in 1826 or 190 years ago.

Interestingly, nestled within Raffles Place, Robinson Road and Shenton Way are Chulia Street, Mosque Street, Kadayanallur Street and Malabar Street. These markers are testament to how this community was significantly present and dwelled at the busy business districts since their early days in Singapore. Chulia is a term used to commonly identify the Tamil Muslims.

The Nagore Dargah Indian Muslim Heritage Centre is an institution with more than 180 years of history. The centre is located at the site of the Nagore Dargah shrine, which was built between 1828 and 1830 by early immigrants from South India. The shrine was gazetted as a national monument in 1974. In 2013, it underwent a year-long upgrading process. It was officially opened as Nagore Dargah Indian Muslim Heritage Centre by President S R Nathan on 29 May 2011.

In Singapore, the Indian Muslims continue to contribute and still have an almost monopolistic presence in some trades, an example would be money-changing business, butchery and some niche culinary trades such as the beloved "prata and mee goreng" stalls are still operated mostly by Tamil Muslims. Although it may seem small, this demonstrates their resilient and entrepreneurial spirit of wanting to be self-sufficient and enterprising.

Local Indian Muslims today have adopted a Singaporean identity unlike their pioneers who still maintain strong ties to South India. Although one may still find many Indian Muslim centric organisations in Singapore still identifying themselves through the name of the village or town they may have originally come from, their roles and objectives have evolved reflect the Singapore identity in nature. Some of the significantly large Indian Muslim organisations in Singapore are:

(a) Singapore Kadayanallur Muslim League
(b) Singapore Tenkasi Muslim Welfare Society
(c) United Indian Muslim Association
(d) Koothanallur Association of Singapore

In total, there are close to some 20 Indian Muslim centric organisations in Singapore representing not just the Tamil but also the Malayalam and Urdu-speaking Indian Muslims here. The umbrella body Federation of Indian Muslims represents them all.

Today, Singapore Indian Muslims continue to do well and contribute to Singapore's growth story in many ways. Being equal beneficiaries of the merito-cratic system in Singapore, we have Indian Muslims doing well in both public services and private enterprises.

Singapore is also the only country in the world which has a heritage centre dedicated to the Indian Muslims namely the Nagore Dargah Indian Muslim Heritage Centre located at 140 Telok Ayer Street. This is a very significant institution for the small community to share their rich history and legacy with fellow Singaporeans and the rest of the world.

THE STORY OF SINGAPURA

The British used to propagate the idea that the history of Singapore started in 1819 with the arrival of Stamford Raffles but there is now irrefutable evidence that shows Singapore was already a busy entrepôt under the Johor-Riau sultanate where Arab and Indian dhows, Buginese schooners and Chinese junks were already making it their port-of-call. Across the history of the Southeast Asian region, Singapore has been referred to by a variety of names, such as "*Puluozhong*", "*Temasek*" and "*Singapura*".

Puluozhong

A Chinese historical account of Singapore in the third century refers to the island as *Puluozhong* (蒲羅中). It is derived from the Malay words "*pulau*" which means island and "*ujong*", which means at the end.

Temasek

In 1365, Singapore was called Temasek in the epic Javanese poem "*Nagarakretagama*". Temasek means "sea town" in Malay. The poem is recognised today as the most important piece of literature ever written during the Majapahit era. Chinese trader Wang Dayuan, who visited Singapore around 1330, wrote the earliest first-hand account of Singapore's history, referring to Singapore as "*Danmaxi*"(淡马锡), a Mandarin version of "Temasek".

Singapura

"*Sejarah Melayu*" or "The Malay Annals" paints the most captivating picture of how Singapore came to have its present name. Legend has it that Sang Nila Utama, then ruler of Palembang (the capital city of the ancient kingdom of Srivijaya), made an unexpected landing in Temasek. While seeking shelter from the storm, he sighted an animal on the island that appeared to be a lion. He declared the island's new name to be "Singa Pura", which means "Lion City" in Malay. It replaced Temasek as the common name for the island by the end of the 14th century. It was because of this ruler's keen foresight that Singapore was later established as a trading post and settlement, due to its naturally strategic location along the Straits of Malacca.

Bibliography

Kwa Chong Guan, Derek Heng, Tan Tai Yong, *Singapore: A 700-Year History — From Emporium to World City*, National Archives of Singapore, 2009. E-version: http://www.nas.gov.sg/1stCab/700YrBook/index.html. Last accessed 3 April 2016.

John Leyden, *Malay Annals*, a translation with an introduction by Sir Thomas Stamford Raffles, 1821.

John N. Miksic, *Singapore and the Silk Road of the Sea, 1300–1800*, co-published with National Museum of Singapore, NUS Press, 2013.

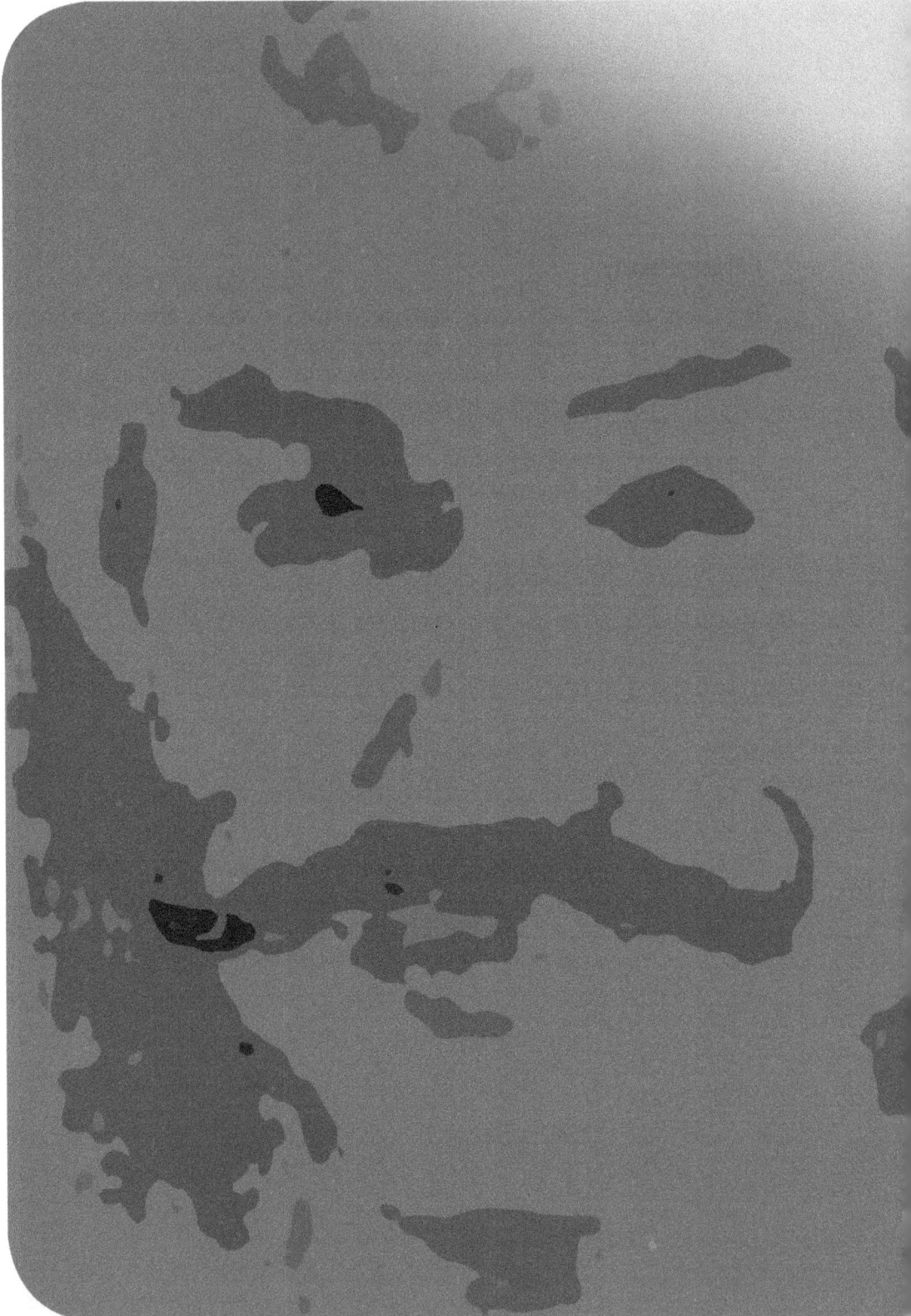

THE STORY OF SANG NILA UTAMA, WHO STAYED AT BENTAN[a]

SANG Nila Utama remained at Bentan highly enamoured of his wife, Wan Sri Bini. On a day, however, after a long time had elapsed, he was seized with a desire of going to divert himself to Tanjong Bemban, and wishing to carry his young wife along with him, he asked permission of his mother-in-law, the Queen Paramisuri Secander Shah. The queen remonstrated with him, asking what was the need to go to Bemban to divert himself, a place where there was neither elk, nor hog-deer, neither deer nor porcupine, where there was neither variety of fish in the sea, nor sea-flowers on the rocks, where as there was every kind of fruit and flower in the garden.

Sang Nila Utama however declared that he had viewed all the streams of Bentan till he was tired; that he had been informed that Tanjong Bemban was a very fine place, and therefore he wished to visit it, and that if he did not obtain permission he wished he might die sitting, die standing, die in every possible kind of way. The princess finding him so obstinate, told him there was no necessity for dying; he might go and take his pleasure. She then ordered Indra B'hupala and Aria B'hupala to prepare for the trip.

Sang Nila Utama accordingly proceeded with his princess to embark in a galley with three masts, accommodated with a cabin and couch, provided with musquito curtains, together with canoes, cooking apparatus, and apparatus for bathing; and a variety of other canoes in company, and arrived at Tanjong Bemban, where they landed to recreate themselves on the sands, and amused themselves by gathering sea-flowers from the rocks. The princess sat under an aloe (Pandan) tree, and all the females of rank around her, delighted with viewing the amusements of her attendants; one of whom brought an oyster, another a cupang (species of oyster), another a bari

---

[a] An English translation of *Sejarah Melayu*[a] by Dr John Leyden with an introduction by Sir Thomas Stamford Raffles. This book was published in 1821. *Sejarah Melayu* (or The Malay Annals), is a Malay literary work believed to have been commissioned by a Regent of Johor in 1612.

(species of oyster), another pulled a wild plantain, another the butan leaf to prepare a salad; another collected agar-agar (dulse), for making a relish. Others adorned themselves with the tertam flower, the turn flower and sangey-bre flower, according to their different kinds. Some sportively pursued each other, and their feet being caught by the rotan creepers, they tumbled down and again springing up pursued their course.

Sang Nila Utama, with the men went a hunting, and found great plenty. A deer started before Nila Utama, and he pierced it with his lance through the back. It continued its flight however, and he pursued it and pierced it through and through, so that it died. Then Sang Nila Utama reached a stone of great height and size, on which he mounted and viewed the opposite shore, with its sands white as cotton; and enquiring what sands were these which he saw, Indra B'hupala informed him they were the sands of the extensive country of Tamasak.

The prince immediately proposed to visit them, and the minister agreeing, they went immediately on shipboard. But as they were passing over, they were caught in a severe storm, and the vessels began to leak, and the crews were unable, after repeated exertions, to throw out the water. They were accordingly compelled to throw overboard the greater part of the baggage in the vessel, which however reached the bay. The water nevertheless continued to gain ground, and every thing was thrown overboard till nothing now remained but the diadem. Then the master addressed the Prince Sang Nila Utama, stating, that the vessel could not support the weight of the diadem; and that if it was not thrown overboard, the vessel could not be relieved. The prince ordered the diadem to be thrown overboard, when the storm ceased and the vessel rose in the water, and the rowers pulled her ashore, and Sang Nila Utama with his attendants, immediately landed on the sands, and went to amuse themselves on the plain near the mouth of the river Tamasak.

There they saw an animal extremely swift and beautiful, its body of a red colour, its head black and its breast white, extremely agile, and of great strength, and its size a little larger than a he-goat. When it saw a great many people, it went towards the inland and disappeared. Sang Nila Utama enquired what animal was this, but none could tell him, till he enquired of Damang Lebar Dawn, who informed him that in the histories of ancient time, the singha or lion was described in the same manner as this animal appeared. This is a fine place which contains so fierce and powerful an animal. Then Sang Nila Utama directed Indra B'hupala to go and inform his mother-in-law, that he should not return; but that if she loved him she should send him people, elephants, and horses, to enable him to form a settlement in the country of Tamasak. Then Indra B'hupala returned to Bentan, and informed Paramisuri Secander Shah of all the circumstances, which had occurred, and the resolution of Sang Nila Utama. The Queen said, "very well, wherever my son chooses to reside, I shall not oppose him." She accordingly sent people, and elephants, and horses, too numerous to be mentioned; and thus Sang Nila Utama settled the country of Tamasak, named it Singhapura, and reigned over it, and was panegyrized by Bat'h, who gave him the name of Sri Tri-buana.

He reigned long over Singhapura, and had two sons, both of them very handsome; the elder of whom was termed Raja Kichil-besar, or the young great Raja; and the younger Raja Kichil Muda, the young little Raja. At last Raja Paramisuri Secander Shah and Damang Lebar Dawn both died, and the son of Damang Lebar Dawn became raja of Bentan, with the title of Tun Talani, and his offspring have the title of Talani Bentan, and have the privilege of eating in a large hall, and their rice and betel are all served up by persons who bear the tatampan, (or yellow gold cloth on their shoulder,) according to the practice of rajas. The country of Singhapura is of great extent, and frequented by merchants innumerable from every quarter, and its ports are very populous.

RIVER MERCHANTS, BRONZE SCULPTURE BY AW TEE HONG

Alexandre Laurie Johnston,[a] seen here negotiating with a Chinese trader and a Malay chief, while the Indian and Chinese coolies were loading goods onto a bullock cart. The sculpture is the work of Aw Tee Hong — a Singaporean artist who is known for his oil paintings of the old Singapore River as well as for numerous public sculptures themed towards Singapore heritage.

---

[a] Alexander Laurie Johnston, (b. Dumfriesshire, South Scotland – d. 19 February, 1850, Bluehill, Kircudbright, Scotland). A former ship's owner/captain, Merchant, Businessman, Magistrate, Justice of Peace, arrived in Singapore in 1820. One of the earliest and much-liked settlers, he was the first Magistrate and Justice of Peace, appointed by Sir Stamford Raffles, who also made him one of the first Trustees of the Singapore Institution (later Raffles Institution).

CHAPTER 48

ISKANDAR JALIL

It was just a dialogue,
then a conversation,
but now it is a sacred conversation.
Nothing can interrupt this private talk
Between clay and me!

Iskandar Jalil

I skandar Jalil is Singapore's foremost Master Potter and leading ceramist. His numerous accolades include the Cultural Medallion (1988), the Public Service Star (2012), and as well as being the first Singapore artist to receive the prestigious Order of the Rising Sun, Gold Rays with Rosette conferred by the Emperor of Japan in 2015, for his contributions in building cultural exchange and mutual understanding between Japan and Singapore through pottery for more than 40 years.

His academic achievements include two Colombo Plan Scholarships: the first to India for textile studies (1966), and next to Japan to study ceramic engineering in 1972 at the Tajimi City Pottery Design and Technical Centre. He then worked as an educator at the former Baharuddin Vocational Institute, and subsequently at Temasek Polytechnic's School of Design. He was also an external examiner for the MARA Institute of Technology in Malaysia, and Curtin University in Australia.

Iskandar is an art ambassador for Singapore, having actively participated in 34 group art and ceramic exhibitions locally and overseas in Malaysia, New Zealand, Cambodia, Korea, Taiwan, Hong Kong, Sweden and Japan. Separately, he has also held 12 solo exhibitions.

Iskandar is well-known for being an active champion of the arts. In the 1990s, he served as an arts advisor to the National Arts Council (NAC) and was a committee member of the Creative Arts Centre at the National University of Singapore and the Singapore Art Museum. He is committed to promote pottery as more than just an art form to the wider community. He is passionate in championing a ceramics culture here; from something that is perceived as a niche leisurely pursuit to one that is worthy to be accepted as part of the society's fabric. Iskandar explains: "There needs to be a culture where we live and breathe pottery, where it is part of our lives; for example, books on pottery should be readily available, funding and support of pottery schools and communities, exhibitions and programmes should be strong, and so, too, the demand for ceramics." People's value of ceramics need to go beyond the functional aspects of its purpose and move towards accepting the aesthetic value inherent in the form, and as a repository of a people's history and culture.

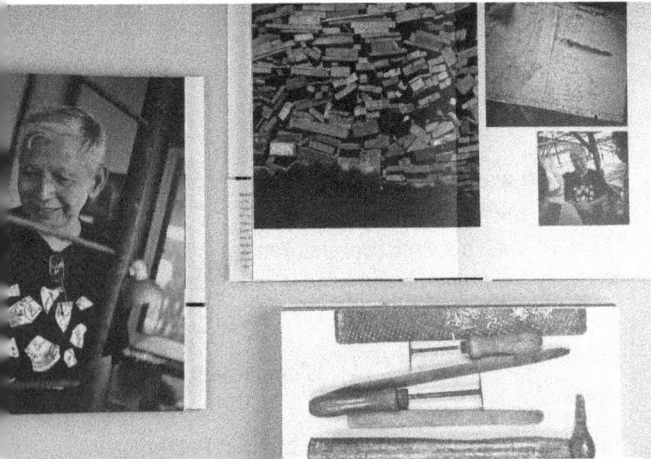

The master potter at work. Photo excerpted from Iskandar Jalil's latest publication, *Iskandar Jalil: Images of My Pottery Travels*. Photo courtesy of Bureau for the Advancement of Lifestyle and Longevity and Success © 2015. All Rights Reserved. Credit also go to the photographers, Ernest Goh (book) and Sam Chin (folio).

Highly textured ceramics in earthy brown, blue and turquoise glazes are characteristic of Iskandar's style. His works of clay marry the Japanese discipline and philosophy with subtle use of Southeast Asian and Islamic motifs. His characteristic or "signature" works possess simple but strong structures with highly tactile and rich surfaces; his vessels often feature branches for handles and deploy clays unique to particular locales or regions. His works range from utilitarian bread and butter pieces, and art works that incorporate an often present blue-oxide colour, which later came to be known as "Iskandar Blue".

Some of his works can be viewed at the MRT wall mural at Tanjong Pagar Station (1998), the Changi Airport Terminal Two (1990) wall mural, and at the Marina Barrage for the Public Utilities Board (PUB) (2004). Some of his works are found in the private collections belonging to the Sultan of Brunei, President George Bush, President Wee Kim Wee and the Governor of Hong Kong.

He believes in creating his works with honesty and humility, and creates one-off pieces rather than produce large numbers of items for profit. As a representative of Singapore's first generation of potters, Iskandar believes he must concentrate on laying the foundations and setting the standards for future potters. He mentors a group of ceramic artists who formed the group Temasek Potters since 2010, to exchange ideas about art and clay, and create greater awareness and appreciation of pottery.

One of Iskandar's elegant works on the cover of the limited edition of *Iskandar Jalil: Images of My Pottery Travels*. Photo courtesy of Bureau for the Advancement of Lifestyle and Longevity and Success © 2015. All Rights Reserved. Credit also go to the photographers, Ernest Goh (book) and Sam Chin (folio).

"I am happy that I managed to raise pottery to a national level and for it to be recognised as an art. From here, I am confident my students — and their students — will continue to sow and nurture a pottery culture we can be proud of."

Image courtesy of Ernest Goh © 2015. All rights reserved.

"The distorted is beautiful."

Iskandar Jalil
The Straits Times
23 March 2015

Source:
http://www.sg.emb-japan.go.jp/JCC/invite_iskandarjalil_
2015.html
https://www.tribute.sg/artist-profile-iskandar-jalil
https://en.wikipedia.org/wiki/Iskandar_Jalil
http://singaporemagazine.sif.org.sg/the-potter-s-touch

CHAPTER 49

CIKGU MUHAMMAD ARIFF AHMAD | Mohd Raman Daud

Cikgu Haji Muhammad Ariff Ahmad — recipient of the Cultural Medallion in 1987 and the Tun Seri Lanang Award in 1993 for literary excellence. He was one of the founding members of Asas '50, the Singapore Writers' Movement, the first literary association which represented the voices of the community and one which utilised literature as a thrust towards independence for the Malaya in 1957. Image: Book cover — *Perjalanan MAS — Memoir Muhammad Ariff Ahmad*, Angkatan Sasterawan 50, 2003.

When Deputy Prime Minister and Secretary–General of the National Trades Union Congress (NTUC) Mr Ong Teng Cheong visited Al-Muttaqin Mosque in 1984, he was introduced to Cikgu[a] Muhammad Ariff Ahmad, the chairman of the mosque.

"I have known him ever since he taught me Malay at Gan Eng Seng Primary School," said Mr Ong (1936–2002), who later became Singapore's fifth and first directly elected President of Singapore from 1993 to 1999.

A former teacher and later a Malay Language lecturer at the Singapore Teachers' Training College from 1959 to 1979, Cikgu Ariff, also known by his pen name MAS, has taught Malay Language and Literature to many students, including non-Malays.

According to Madam Chan Maw Woh, a retired journalist and Chinese–Malay lexicographer, Cikgu Ariff was instrumental in introducing Angkatan Sasterawan '50 (The Singapore Writers' Movement '50 or better known as Asas '50) to Malayan Chinese writers or Mahua[b] writers later referred to as Sinhua writers. She and her husband, Professor Yang Quee Yee, along with

---

[a] *'Cikgu'* is teacher in Malay.

[b] *Mahua* authors are usually Chinese immigrants who came to Malaya and Singapore in the 20th century, and developed and wrote their own literature, termed as "mahua" literature or "overseas Chinese" literature.

Cikgu Muhammad Ariff Ahmad seated centre (wearing tie) with fellow teachers and students at Sekolah Melayu Ponggol, c.1957. Image courtesy of Muhammad Ariff Ahmad © 2015. All rights reserved.

graduates of Nantah's[c] Malay Studies Department in the 1950s to 1960s, such as Dr Tan Tan Sen, Dr Li Chuan Siu and Dr Liaw Yock Fang, remain close friends with Cikgu Ariff till today.

"I have had many discussions with them on the role of the Malay language in a multiracial setting. We exchanged notes and ideas during Singapore's formative years of nation-building," recalled Cikgu Ariff.

Asas '50 was formed by 19 founding members at the compounds of Cikgu Ariff's house on Henderson Road and was the first literary association formed in post-war Malaya. Turning 91 on 6 December 2015, Cikgu Ariff passed away on 23 March 2016.

Asas '50 was among many organisations which organised the three Malay Language and Literary Congresses[d] in 1952, 1954 and 1956.

---

[c] Nantah is now Nanyang Technological University.

[d] The very first Malay Language and Literary Congress was first convened to unite all organisations in Malaya, Singapore and North Borneo and to reach the final decision on the improvement of Malay language and literature, and to defend the rights of authors, literary minders and linguists. (http://melayuonline.com/eng/culture/dig/1905/the-malayan-first-language-and-literature-congress)

The most impactful was the third Malay Language and Literary Congress (Kongres Bahasa Ke-3) under the initiation of Asas '50[e] in 1956. It called upon the people of Malaya to acknowledge the critical role of the Malay language as a unifying language for communication and development.

Its call had attracted several groups of Chinese students, teachers and activists who held discussions with the working committee of the Congress. The period was abuzz with Malaya getting its independence from the British.

There was large support from people from all walks of life for the Malay language to become the working National Language of the newly-independent country. To Cikgu Ariff, that moment was a turning point for the Malay language.

Asas '50 was Singapore's first literary body to organise the pioneering Singapore Writers' Gathering (Pertemuan Penulis Singapura) in 1977. It was an historic attempt to understand the concerns of Singapore writers across ethnic lines.

In the same year, it held the first Regional Malay Literati Conference (Pertemuan Sasterawan Nusantara) — a move that helped to normalise the relationship among Malay writers in the region after the bitter Sukarno-led Confrontation period (1963–1965).

Cikgu Ariff was the point man to usher the important role of the Malay language. He was tasked by the PAP-led government to help Pak Zubir Said[f] refine the lyrics of Singapore's National Anthem, 'Majulah Singapura' (Onward Singapore).

He was also involved in what was considered "social engineering" to uplift the position of the Malay language, when the Malay Language and Cultural Agency was formed under the Ministry of Culture in 1964.

His novelette, *Sarah Pengarang Kecil* (Sarah, the Budding Author), was used as a textbook in secondary

Memoir
YANG QUEE YEE
PENYUSUN KAMUS ANAK PENOREH

Dr Yang Quee Yee — feted by both the Chinese and Malays for his effort in promoting and instilling a level of mutual understanding and tolerance especially during the turbulent 1960s where racial tension was rife in Malaysia and Singapore.

He was conferred the Nanyang Distinguished Alumni Award Recipient in 2008. Image: Book cover — *Memoir Yang Quee Yee: Penyusun Kamus Anak Penoreh*, UKM: Bangi, 2005.

---

[e] http://asas50.com/about/
[f] Zubir Said (1907–1987) was the composer of Singapore's national anthem "Majulah Singapura".

My writing is very much social commentary. All my life, my writing has been social commentary. Culture builds mankind — that is my overall theme. But I try not to be didactic. I just deliberate on the problem, hopefully opening minds and making people aware of their choices, but allow the reader to decide."

Muhammad Ariff
Narratives: Notes on a Cultural Journey:
Cultural Medallion Recipients,
1979–2001

Cikgu Muhammad Ariff Ahmad, seated centre,
was an active member of MENDAKI. Image courtesy
of Yayasan MENDAKI © 2015. All rights reserved.

schools and for the teaching of the Malay language to non-Malay adults.

"I was unaware that *Sarah Pengarang Kecil* had been translated into Mandarin until a Chinese friend pointed it out to me," said Cikgu Ariff, who has himself translated Sun Tzu's *The Art of War*.

Being a culturist, Cikgu Ariff is an ardent advocate for the formation of a National Culture, with each major ethnic group contributing to the common domain or space.

"For example, today, we enjoy our rich legacy of food — be it nasi lemak or chicken rice. We have to strengthen our common interests and acknowledge our differences with wisdom and sensitivity," he said.

His two children's books, *Menangkap Perompak Mini Gang* (To Catch the Mini Gang Robbers, 1973) and *Pipi Kirinya Tercalar* (His Scarred Left Chin, 1974), featured three boys who are close buddies — Mamat, Ah Soon, and Namasivayam. Their sense of camaraderie that went beyond ethnicity and religion is the main message of these children stories.

For more than four decades, Cikgu Ariff's wisdom has been highly sought after in many national committees and advisory boards such as the Malay Traditional Music Advisory Committe with the National Arts Council, and the Malay Heritage Foundation.

He is probably the most decorated Malay gentleman with many awards and accolades under his belt, including the Cultural

Medallion Award (1987), the Tun Sri Lanang Award by the Malay Language Council in 1993, the title of "Pendeta" (The Sage) given to him by Majlis Pusat in 1999, and an honorory "Doctor of Literature" from his alma mater, Sultan Idris Education University in 2006.

The highest accolade in his honour has to be from Nanyang Technological University, which has established the Doctor Muhammad Ariff Ahmad (MAS) Malay Studies Endowment Fund in 2010 — the first of its kind in Singapore's universities. The Muhammad Ariff Ahmad (MAS) Postgraduate Scholarship and Research Grant are dedicated to support further research in the field of Malay Studies, to follow in the footsteps Cikgu Ariff's contributions that have been pivotal in shaping and advancing Malay Studies in Singapore and the region.

In 1959, when Singapore achieved self-government, the Government asked for the song Majulah Singapura to be made into a national anthem. Pak Zubir (seated fourth from the left) asked for Cikgu Muhammad Ariff's (seated fourth from the right) views on the lyrics and he was asked to choose simple and meaningful words for the lyrics so that the song could easily be understood and sung by the many races in Singapore. Image courtesy of Puan Rohana Zubir © 2015. All rights reserved.

Muhammad Ariff Ahmad
1924–2016

Jalan, jalan
Walk, walk

Jalan dan jalan ...
Walk and walk ...

Jangan berhenti separuh jalan,
Do not stop halfway;

Biar sampai ke hujung jalan,
Walk right to the end

Sampai matlamat jalan kesampaian,
Until you fulfil the objective of your walk

atau sampai tak boleh jalan!
Or until you cannot walk anymore!

This poem was written by Cikgu Ariff back in 1949 while on board a train from Tanjung Malim, Perak back to Singapore to start his teaching career. The inspiration came from a guard who had given the green signal and shouted "Jalan" (go). As he journeyed to Singapore, he wrote the poem on a State Express 555 cigarette box. The poem had been his philosophy in his life.

Cikgu Ariff has never stopped writing and imparting his knowledge even when his health took a toll. When he was confined to his home, many still sought his advice. Not only did he teach language but also Malay culture, tradition and literature.

One of the book's editors, Mr Zainul Abidin, paid him a visit on 5 February to seek permission to use some of his photos. His memory of the photos was still vivid. Not only was permission granted, he was given a copy of his book, *Perjalanan MAS*. That is the nature of Pendeta Muhammad Ariff Ahmad, also known as MAS — the father of Singapore's Malay linguistics, a pioneering *bahasawan* (linguist), *budayawan* (cultur-alist) and *sasterawan* (writer).

Among his many contributions and accolades, he co-founded the Malay-language literary association Angkatan Sasterawan '50 in 1950. His works of social commentary spanned across all literary genres including poetry, short story, novel, children's and educational literature, essay and drama. He received the Southeast Asia Write Award and the Tun Sri Lanang Award in 1993. In 1987, he received the Cultural Medallion for his contributions to literature in Singapore. Cikgu Ariff passed away in Singapore at the age of 91 on 23 March 2016.

Syair Tamanan Arif
(for Almarhum Muhammad Ariff Ahmad)

Tuan Puan Saudari Saudara
Inilah untaian merakam jasa
Mahu dilafaz bukannya segera
Diaturkan syair moga bermakna

Syair gubahan mengenang jasa
Pendeta guru padanya kita
Meninggal lalu buat selama
Wasiat ilmunya kandil budaya

Itulah Cikgu Ariff Ahmad
Banyak berjasa meniup tekad
Bahasa budaya pedoman iktikad
Itulah guru penyuluh ruh dan jasad

Marhum berpulang kehadrat Tuhan
Jasa ilmunya pahala bekalan
Rahmatan Tuhan moga tercurahkan
Kepada sang guru kita berinsafan

Bermula ASAS'50 diasas Cikgu
Itulah tirai sastera bertugu
Membangun kesedaran jagoan berseru
Berkhidmat ke bangsa tiadakan jemu

Segak orangnya bersongkok baldu
Tangkas menulis beringat menderu
Tulisan jawinya cantik membiru
Siapa menyaksikan tiadakan ragu

Banyak guru lama dan baru
Sepulau menuntut kepadanya Cikgu
Itulah pendeta Bahasa Melayu
Hukum dan saraf jangan dilalu

Orangnya santai bicaranya santun
Langgamnya sering disisip pantun
Nahu dan tatabahasa siap dilantun
Ingatannya luas boleh menggerun

Menimbun buku ditulis sudah
Cereka dan ilmu senarai bertambah
Kalau sarat tak dapat dipecah
Jumpalah Cikgu dicarikan penyudah

Wahai saudara watan dan ikhwan
Disingkap hidupnya sangat gunawan
Menjadi pemula sampai akhiran
Tiada menyepi tiada gundahan

Usianya panjang menjadi saksi
Dari berpisah ke Merdeka sendiri
Singapura berubah datang dan pergi
Cikgu juga tergolong sebagai pendiri

Inilah istimewa anak negeri
Jasa menimbun pada pertiwi
Menulis mengajar supaya mandiri
Agar tak kekok waktu berdiri

Persuratan dan budaya sedia dikaji
Lama dan baru mahu ditatapi
Cermat menulis diperiksa teliti
Itulah sosok guru mithali

Seisi negeri dan rantauan tetangga
Kenali beliau budayawan berjasa
Dikalungkan penghormatan bukan diminta
Inilah tokoh banggaan kita

UPSI menggelar Doktor Kehormat
Padanya Cikgu pengiktirafan keramat
Guru Melayu rasanya didaulat
Jasa mendidik bangsa dan umat

Beberapa karya ditinggalkan Cikgu
Membaca mengupas jangankan tak mau
Kalau memimpin itulah perlu
Budaya bahasa dibangun baru

Itulah pati penggerak maju
Cikgu menunjuk patutlah ditiru
Teladan beliau seyogia dipacu
Bahasa terbangun harus dituju

Arif Budiman laungan pendidikan
Itulah mau dijadikan pedoman
Cikgu Ariff antara teladan
Inilah ikhtiar yang harus diusahakan

Tamanan Arif syair bernama
Mengingatkan jasa guru bangsa
Berpulang Cikgu tekad bermula
Menyudahkan amanat dan kerjanya

Alfateha dibaca melafaz akhir
Susunan saya bukanpun mahir
Mengenang Cikgu jasawan kabir
Inilah pantun penutup syair

Telok Belangah disebut-sebut
Tempat bermukim Dato' Temenggung
Jasamu Tuan bergunung berlaut
Secarik ilmu budi tertanggung

Dr Azhar Ibrahim Alwee
Malay Studies Department
National University of Singapore

23 March 2016
First appeared in *Berita Harian*, 27 March 2016. Reproduced with permission.

CHAPTER 50

SOM SAID AND SRI WARISAN | Marina Yusof

Madam Som Said in her younger days. Photo courtesy of Som Said

Sri Warisan is a performing arts company founded by renowned Cultural Medallion recipient, Madam Som Said.

Madam Som Said is a Cultural Ambassador for Singapore and has been recognised for her work with children, winning the National Youth Service Award in 1979. She received the Cultural Medallion in 1987 and the Public Service Medal in 1992 for her contributions to dance. In 2007, she received the Anugerah Warisan Kencana by The Malay Heritage Centre, Singapore. She is a choreographer for Instant Asia, a dramatic dance presentation of Singapore's diverse cultural heritage. As Cultural Ambassador for Singapore, she has been involved in creating dance productions unique to Singapore's cultural heritage. As part of an international goodwill exchange programme, the Republic of Singapore has commissioned her to promote the multi-cultural and multi-ethnic performances in many parts of the world such as Russia, Egypt, United Arab Emirates, India, Germany, Nepal, Italy, New Zealand, Korea, Canada and Australia. Som Said continues to share her love for dance with Sri Warisan, which she founded in 1997.

Sri Warisan is one of the pivotal forces in Singapore's Malay dance scene. Blending rich traditional forms with contemporary techniques is Sri Warisan's trade-mark. Its performers are trained to excel in multi-disciplinary art forms such as dance, music, theatre and multi-media.

Madam Som Said's (second from left) dancing days at Sriwana. Photo courtesy of Som Said Copyright © 2015 Som Said. All rights reserved.

From a humble beginning of a dancer, Madam Som Said now leads young dance enthusiasts who want to move towards professionalism in their craft. Photo courtesy of Som Said Copyright © 2015 Som Said. All rights reserved.

Currently, Sri Warisan is being led by Mr Adel Ahmad. Together with 30 performing artists and with more than 200 students as members, the company is committed to developing professionalism in the performing arts that reach out to children, youths and adults. Each year, Sri Warisan performs at more than 200 local events and 10 overseas festivals. Its instructors conduct more than 3000 courses and workshops at schools. In 2011 and 2012, Sri Warisan had conducted an intensive Traditional Malay Dance and Music Masterclass for the cast of the Musical Disney LION KING in Singapore and Hamburg, Germany respectively. Since 1997, Sri Warisan's activities include:

- Participating in more than 70 international events and festivals in Belgium, Brunei, Canada, China, France, Greece, Holland, India, Indonesia, Israel, Italy, Japan, Korea, London, Malaysia, Nepal, Philippines, Spain, Thailand, Turkey and the United States of America.
- Staging more than 40 local productions with the support of the National Arts Council (NAC) Singapore. This includes the mega-production, *Onak Samudera — The Untold Dance Journey* in 2014, *Bendahara — A Betrayal* in 2012, *Lagenda Tun Fatimah*, to commemorate Som's 40th year in the arts scene, *Lagenda Raden Mas* in March 2008, *Towkay Wayang — A Musical* in 2009 and *Anak Wayang Dance Theatre* in 2010.
- Participating in major local events such as WOMAD, Singapore Arts Festival, NAC–Shell Art Reach, IMF 2006, Chingay 2007, National Day Parade 2008, APEC Summit 2009, Heritage Festival 2010 and the Singapore Youth Olympic Games (SYOG) 2010.
- Supporting community projects by organisations such as The Singapore Children Society, Metta

Welfare Association, Hindu Endowments Board, Jamiyah Singapore Muslim Missionary Society and Peoples Association.

- Providing arts education and enrichment to students at more than 300 schools through the NAC–Arts Education Programme.
- Collaborating with arts organisations such as Bhaskar Arts Academy, Chinese Opera Institute, Majlis Pusat, Perkumpulan Seni, Jigri Yaar Bhangra Academy, Singapore Indian Fine Arts Society, YF Performing Arts Troupe, Sriwana, Temple of Fine Arts, Singapore Dance Theatre and Singapore Chinese Orchestra.

No blood ties but "I see them as my parents".

Madam Noriza A Mansor
Winner, The Straits Times
Singaporean of the Year 2015

THE STRAITS TIMES SINGAPOREAN OF THE YEAR AWARD

Madam Noriza A Mansor was awarded The Straits Times Singaporean of the Year in February 2016. The inaugural award, in partnership with UBS Singapore, seeks to honour the positive impact made by Singaporeans and celebrate the triumph of the human spirit.

In October 2014, she made the headlines in October 2014 when she went to help a total stranger, an elderly, Mr Tan Soy Yong, 76, who had soiled himself while grocery shopping.[1] Many would flinch from the stench but that did not stop the bedsheet promoter from reaching out to help the elderly man. Not only did she clean off the faeces on Mr Tan, she even bought him a new pair of shorts and even accompanied him home.

Her win was decided after a public vote and deliberation by a 15-judge panel. The decision to present her with the award was due to her selfless act, undeterred by barriers of age, gender, race or language. The award was presented by Prime Minister Lee Hsien Loong and it comes with a trophy and $20,000 in cash.

But her care and concern for Mr Tan did not stop there. Since then, she has been regularly spending her days off visiting Mr Tan and his wife, Madam Lee Bee Yian, both 76, even after they were hospitalised and moved into nursing homes.[2] Madam Noriza's story is one of pure and unadulterated act kindness.

---

[a] http://www.straitstimes.com/singapore/good-samaritan-helps-to-clean-faeces-off-elderly-man-in-toa-payoh. Last accessed 2 April 2016.

[b] http://www.straitstimes.com/singapore/no-blood-ties-but-i-see-them-as-my-parents#xtor=CS1-10. Last accessed 2 April 2016.

CHAPTER 51

OUR PIONEERS

Singapore was not built by leaders alone but by ordinary Singaporeans as well — the men and women who had sacrificed for one another and for the nation. Here's a collection of stories of seven pioneers sharing heartwarming stories of their personal struggle and experience. These articles first appeared online on the official SG50 website, contributions from ordinary Singaporeans, as a tribute to the pioneer generation.

FATHER TO 1000 CHILDREN | Cikgu Abdul Rahman bin Omar

It's 3 am. A young man sits by a rusty kerosene lamp, his head buried in books. Tonight, he's busy translating Science textbooks into Malay, figuring out how best to convert complex diagrams into something a little more inspiring and easier to understand. It doesn't matter that his day will be starting again at 6 am. Or that riding the bumboat to Pulau Tekong, where he teaches, with a light head from insufficient sleep, will not be very pleasant. To a 20-year-old Abdul Rahman Bin Omar, it is just another day.

> My first students were the kampung boys I grew up with. And they're still my friends."

He was just 18 years old when he acted upon his teacher's advice and started teaching. A young man with a genuine hunger for knowledge, he was clever and ambitious, but also grounded and humble. These traits made him well liked among his peers. By a lucky twist of fate, the first school he was assigned to was in his village. Kampung Gemuruh Malay School was located in the heart of the picturesque fishing village of Kampung Gemuruh[a] — where one of Changi Airport's runways now stands. Abdul Rahman remembers walking into class on his first day as a teacher. All his nerves dissolved when he saw his new students for the first time — they were none other than his old *kampung* buddies. His ties with the villagers meant that they listened to him and respected him. Seeing the change in his childhood friends and the real effect the school had on the community made the hard work worth it and encouraged him to push harder. Twice a week, he attended night classes at the Teacher's College at Patterson Road, convinced that further certification would make him better at his job. In 1964, he left his *kampung* school and ventured to Pulau Tekong for a new teaching post.

Stepping into unknown territory was a challenge he took on with verve. A new syllabus had to be taught, and no child could be allowed to fall behind. Armed with renewed vigour and teaching materials that he had diligently sourced on his own, Abdul Rahman took a bumboat from Changi Jetty to Pulau Tekong every school morning, come rain or shine. On the island, he would take another 15-minute *kampung* taxi ride to reach the school — just in time for the 7 am class. For to Abdul Rahman, teaching was not just a job, it was a responsibility.

As long as I can teach, I'll teach. As long as I can impart knowledge, I will."

Fifty years on, he still finds new ways to make his lessons memorable and inspiring. He loves taking

---

[a] The actual name of the village is Kampung Ayer Gemuruh hence the actual name of the school is Kampung Ayer Gemuruh Malay School.

classes and treats each student like his own grandchild. To Abdul Rahman, the challenge isn't just moulding a child's mind, but in moulding the person a child becomes. "You're the final bastion before they become teenagers — when they decide for themselves what to do with what they're taught." The job may sometimes be thankless, but Abdul Rahman seeks no gratitude. As he says, "The greatest satisfaction is in doing all that you can, not for the rewards, but for the pure act of doing."

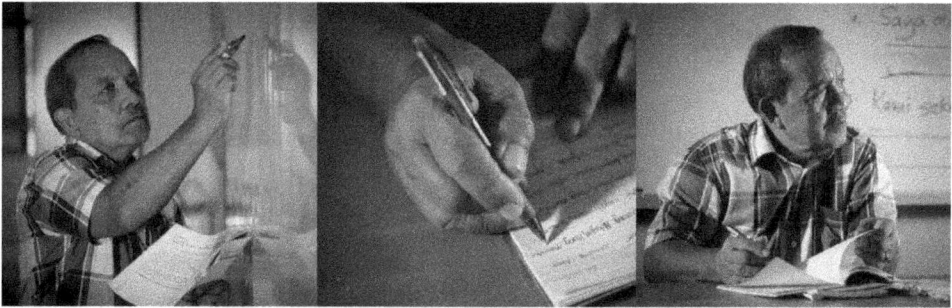

Article first appeared in: https://www.sg/SG50/Pioneer%20Generation/PG%20Story/Cikgu%20 Abdul%20Rahman%20Bin%20Omar-141124-063806.aspx. Reprinted with permission.

Story and images submitted by Cikgu Abdul Rahman bin Omar.

It is a hot, sticky May evening in 1951. Jalan Besar Stadium is packed with 15,000 fans. All eyes are on Rahim Omar, the left winger who's flying across the pitch on his debut for Singapore's national football team. He is as nimble as a dancer. He kicks the ball and it shoots through the right pocket of the net for what is to be Singapore's only goal of the game. Unfortunately, it is a day when Singapore goes on to suffer a 4-1 defeat to Indonesia. Yet for 14-year-old Majid Ariff, Rahim's superlative goal is so inspirational that he aspires to do the same for his country one day. Of course, what he doesn't yet know is that he is destined to become one of the nation's sporting icons.

> Play *bola* and you can *cari makan*. You can travel and see the world."

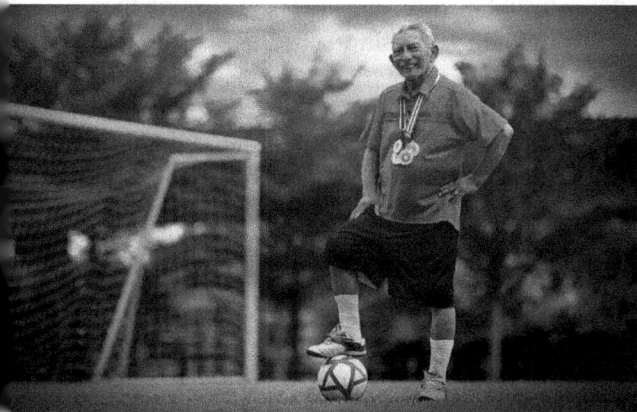

Majid was diligent, and believed that anything could be achieved with hard work and the right spirit. As a young boy, he played for the *kampung* football team and made the occasional trip to Johor to play the odd game. Winning or losing didn't matter, nor did going hungry in order to afford new football boots. He was driven by his ambition to one day don his national team's jersey. Every breath was dedicated to the pursuit of that goal.

In one year, you'll be on the National Team."

Like his idol Rahim Omar, Majid trained at the old football pitch at Farrer Park. He did it alone, barefoot, using an old tyre rim tied to a tree as a target. He played for the Royal Engineer Civilian Association (RECA) football team. In fact, that was the only reason he had a job there as his team depended on him. He trained with them twice a week. But Majid didn't just want to be good. He wanted to be the best. And that would take much more practice. Seven nights a week of practice, to be exact. It was raining the night a stern-looking Chinese man approached him mid-training. The Chinese man turned out to be national coach, Choo Seng Quee, who had been watching Majid for some weeks. Impressed by the boy's talent and dedication, the coach offered him a chance to train with the team. He had to work hard, but Majid was no stranger to that. He had been working to help his mother ever since he had dropped out of school at 13.

He trained for four hours every day, seven days a week. Circuit training. Stamina training. Circuit training again. Time off-pitch was spent learning how to use what he'd learned. How to think as quickly as his feet moved. To be strategic about his ball placement. And to lead. Two days shy of his first anniversary of starting to train, he was drafted into the national team. In his first big league game, in the very stadium where he had first dared to dream it, he helped his new team beat his former club, RECA, 17-0.

His work ethic never waned as his star power grew. Together with the region's football giants, The Asian All Stars, he played a series of exhibition matches in

In Hong Kong, they still call me the 'Stallion.'"

Malaysia and Singapore against English clubs. It was 1966, and to the players from the former colonial outposts, these weren't mere friendlies. He skipped the social parties for more hours of training. To a man who dedicated his life to the game, rewards off the pitch meant little to him.

His career ended on yet another rainy day. In a Malaysia Cup match against Kelantan, Majid took a rough tackle that split his knee open. He would never play football again. But his love for the sport never ended and he continued in the game in various guises, most notably as a mentor to young, upcoming players.

"You can learn how to be good. But greatness requires heart.

Life has a way of coming full circle. Every Saturday morning at the football field in ITE East, an elderly man casts a watchful eye over a group of young footballers. He calls it "paying it forward." Those who know him will tell you that Majid just can't stop working. In 1980, just as Choo Seng Quee did with him decades earlier, he took a young midfielder under his wing. That youngster went on to become another national legend. His name? Fandi Ahmad.

Article first appeared in: https://www.sg/SG50/Pioneer%20Generation/PG%20Story/Majid%20Ariff-141121-090640.aspx. Reprinted with permission.

Story and images submitted by Majid Ariff.

THE BEST SONGBIRDS ARE ALWAYS CAGED | Masadi Masdawi

I t is March 1964. Singapore is in the midst of the Indonesian Konfrontasi. Bombs are exploding and a 12-hour curfew is in place. A young policeman is on his sixth night of foot patrol, guarding the beaches around Siglap with his partner. As the two officers begin their reconnaissance, it starts to rain, and they run to a shack for cover. A stern voice booms from within, demanding the password reserved for Gurkhas and other uniformed officers. Trembling, 22-year-old Masadi Masdawi utters the secret code.

The strongest weapon is love."

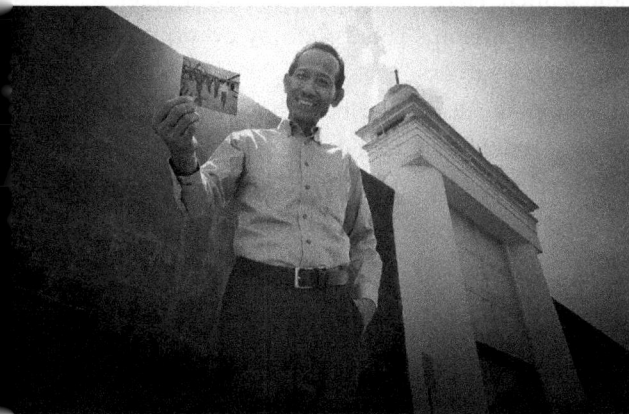

Masadi spent four more years in the police force before transferring to the Prison Department — a job he presumed would be less dangerous than policing the streets. But his very first day taught him the foolhardiness of that assumption. When he walked past the cells on his wing, his new charges, already labelled "career criminals", glared at him threateningly; flexing their muscles as they did so to show off their tattoos and *parang* scars.

But Masadi knew that underneath their bravado, the men were human too, and had lives and loves beyond the prison walls. Over time, he built up a rapport with the inmates, and came to know each one by name. He talked to them about their worries, their grievances, and treated them with compassion. In doing so, he won the respect of the prisoners and the admiration of his superiors. In 1984, he was promoted to Superintendent of the now defunct Jalan Awan Prison, home to society's most hardened criminals.

Every man is capable of change."

The inmates of his new prison were unruly; tougher than those he had encountered in his previous post. He knew that it would take more than just a few chats to get through to them, and opted for a more strategic approach. He assigned several officers to interview the prisoners about their well-being and overall conditions in the jail. Scouring through the subsequent reports his officers produced, it was clear to him that the inmates simply yearned for something to do to break the monotony of prison life.

But first, he wanted to give the inmates something to lift their spirits. He organised a concert and had famous jazz musicians Tony Castillo and Suzanna Two perform at the prison's basketball court. The event went without a hitch. That would be the first of sunnier days in Jalan Awan Prison. "This is not my event. It is ours. Let's make it a success."

Masadi had no musical experience, but his fixation with music as a redemptive tool continued long after that special concert in Jalan Awan Prison. Masadi was later transferred to Selarang Park, and there he became the inmates' choir leader, warden and friend all rolled into one.

He was asked by the Director of the Singapore Prison Service to form a musical troupe capable of performing for the delegates of the annual Association of Southeast Asian Nations meeting. He gathered all the inmates who could play musical instruments, and together he and his band of 'misfits' trained day and night.

For six months, their days were peppered with music theory classes, jam sessions and choreography practice. During this time, the prisoners bonded, learned discipline and regained their self-confidence. The troupe called themselves "Golden Melodies".

"They taught me how to sing.

The performance was a success. Masadi led Golden Melodies in shows island-wide, and they went on to win the national music competition "Clash of the Bands". It was the proudest moment in Masadi's 35-year career.

For the man who aimed only to "help others help themselves", Masadi has enjoyed numerous personal returns. For one, he has learned how to sing. And he has gained countless friends, whose personal successes are testament to his belief that "Every man can change."

Article first appeared in: https://www.sg/SG50/Pioneer%20Generation/PG%20Story/Masadi%20Masdawi-150130-045852.aspx. Reprinted with permission.

Story and images submitted by Masadi Masdawi.

THE VOICE THAT MOVED
1000 MEN

Retired Captain
Shamsudin
Shadan

S ix contingents of the People's Defence Force (PDF) are around the corner and 1,000 soldiers march out onto the Padang. Each soldier is a paragon of perfection. Their uniforms are starched and immaculately pressed. Their boots shine. And not a smudge is to be found on their belt buckles. Reaching their allocated positions, they march in place, before simultaneously coming to attention.

"Semula (All over again)!" commands Regimental Sergeant Major (RSM) Shamsudin bin Shadan from the top of the City Hall steps. Without complaint, the soldiers march quickly back to their starting positions. They were half a beat off, Shamsudin notes. And that simply won't do for Singapore's first National Day Parade. He bellows the command for them to march out again, for the 28th time that afternoon.

Don't waste your life. Spend it doing something useful."

Shamsudin endured a difficult childhood. His father was kidnapped by the Communist Party of Malaya and his mother died when he was only nine years old. With no siblings or relatives, he had to learn how to fend for himself. He would go to school, as well as work odd jobs to earn his keep. It was hard to take lessons in the morning, labour at construction sites in the afternoon, and run errands in the evening. But the hardship forged in him a steely determination and discipline, qualities that would serve him well throughout his life. When Shamsudin was 17 years old, his father was released from internment. In hopes of a better life, they decided to move from Malaysia to Singapore. They had nowhere to live, so they stayed at the British Army Camp barracks. There, Shamsudin started his career in the Army on the lowest rung — a peon sending letters to various parts of the camp. It was a humble job, but he strove to do his best. He excelled in his role and caught the eye of the camp's Commanding Officer, who took a liking to him and gave him more responsibilities.

If they didn't fear me, I wasn't doing my job."

Through hard work and diligence, he worked his way up from being a Private in the Singapore Volunteer Corps, then in the People's Defence Force, to the position of Warrant Officer. Dubbed the "King of the Parade Square," he was known for his commanding, ear-piercingly loud voice and presence. His reputation as a fierce taskmaster preceded him. Nothing escaped his sharp steely eyes on the parade square. Shamsudin also believed in leading by example. Just as he set high standards for others, he also held himself to the highest scrutiny.

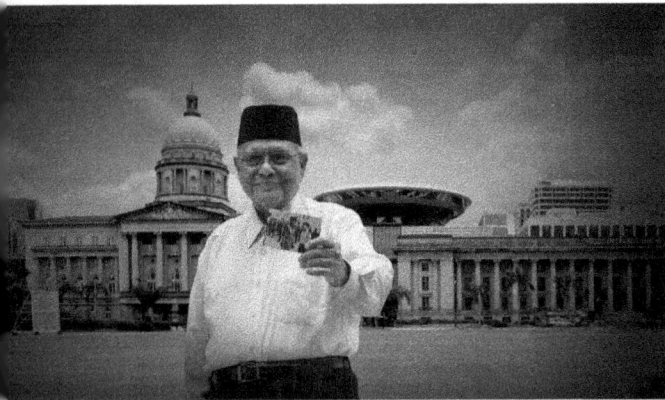

Following the spilt from Malaysia, the country's leaders organised the first National Day Parade. Shamsudin was given the responsibility of putting together a competent marching contingent in just 50 days. The significance of the event was not lost on him. There was an atmosphere of despondency and a great degree of uncertainty about the country's future, and Shamsudin knew that a stirring performance would instil a sense of much needed pride in the newly born nation. So he refused to settle for mediocrity. He made his troops do the drills. Again and again. The Army had to be perfect — for the people, for Singapore.

On 9 August 1966, the crowds lined the streets near City Hall, cheering soldiers on as they marched past with consummate precision. Shamsudin had done his job.

"Always believe that you can do anything.

In 1976, Shamsudin was among the first batch of warrant officers to be given officer commissions. He eventually retired in 1987 at the rank of Captain, after 29 years of giving the army his all. He still feels an immense sense of pride when he watches the National Day parades. "I can see how much the nation and the Army has grown," he muses.

Article first appeared in: https://www.sg/SG50/Pioneer%20Generation/PG%20Story/
Retired%20Captain%20Shamsudin%20bin%20Shadan-141124-051334.aspx.
Reprinted with permission.

Story and images submitted by Retired Captain Shamsudin Shadan.

SOME MEN WILL NEVER FIGHT FOR ANYTHING. WHAT TERRIBLY DULL LIVES THEY MUST LEAD

Syed Abdul Kadir

The elderly man stares into the mirror. He tilts his head slightly and examines the scar still visible above his left brow. Even after all these years, his heart still holds a special place for the Cuban who gave him that scar at the Munich Olympics, and the match that would be the biggest disappointment in his life. It was never about the loss. It was more that the referee had overlooked the foul head-butt and thrown in the towel for him. To a fighter like Syed Abdul Kadir, there is nothing worse than a technical knockout.

All that I know, I learned with a smile."

He grew up in Potong Pasir and, like most boys in the area, went to school at St. Andrew's. He was just nine years old when a free ticket to an international boxing meet introduced the young boy to the gentleman's sport. His school offered an after-school boxing program and, young and impressionable as he was, Kadir would stay behind every afternoon, observing the training and shadowing the older boys' moves.

His coach began by giving the young boy drills to perform. A few months later, Kadir was allowed to participate in the school championships, competing in the light featherweight class that he would dominate for decades.

As a young, hungry fighter, Kadir was unstoppable. Hearing that the Eurasians had a natural flair for the sport, he travelled to Katong to train with them on weekends. Alongside the young Eurasian boys, he practiced shadow boxing, skipping and circuit training.

> Be fast enough so they can't catch you. But keep smiling, so that even in defeat, they can never hate you."

He was only 23 years old when he represented Singapore for the third time at the Southeast Asian Peninsular (SEAP) Games. Asia's best boxer and the defending SEAP champion was a strapping young man called Vanla Dawla from Myanmar. It was said that he had been brought down from the mountains, where men were born warriors. Vanla was a fearsome opponent, undefeated for two years. The day before he was to fight Vanla, Kadir was having dinner when his opponent's coach approached his table and offered this remark, "Eat more; you're going to need it tomorrow." Kadir then went on to defeat Vanla.

> Heart — either you have it or you don't."

In 1969, he was offered a professional boxing career in Australia if he would change his passport. But this eight time medal winner wanted then as much as now to be remembered as a true Singaporean.

At 66, his days still begin as they did when he first donned a pair of boxing gloves — with a 10-kilometre run at 5 am. His hunger for the sport is as fervent as his first foray in the ring; and the scar above his brow is the champ's reminder that what doesn't kill you makes you stronger.

Article first appeared in: https://www.sg/SG50/Pioneer%20Generation/PG%20Story/ Syed%20Abdul%20Kadir-141121-091320.aspx. Reprinted with permission.

Story and images submitted by Syed Abdul Kadir.

NEVER RUN FROM YOUR DUTIES | Mdm Timah Haji Abdul Rashid

Timah Haji Abdul practices the falsetto notes with earnestness for she knows her upcoming performance will be an important one. She likes singing, but is a shy child who prefers athletics to performing on stage. Nevertheless, she averts her eyes from her running shoes and concentrates on her song. When 9 August 1965 comes, she will sing her heart out for President Yusof Ishak, at Singapore's first National Day Parade.

I felt the most liberated when I was running."

The eighth of ten siblings, Timah exhibited a natural flair for all track and field sports, particularly running and hurdling. Had she the opportunity to chase her dreams, she would have become an athlete. But life has a way of running off-course sometimes. She came from a large family and felt obliged to help her parents out in any way she could.

In her teens, she hung up her running shoes and put her feet to the sewing machine pedal instead. To supplement the household

income, Timah sewed *baju kurungs* and curtains for their neighbours. Instead of pursuing her dreams, she pursued a better life for her family.

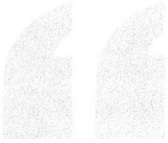

"My colleagues are my second family".

After stints as a factory operator, Timah became a storekeeper at Tan Tock Seng Hospital in 1995. She was responsible for mending and cleaning the linen in the hospital. It was a physically-demanding job, one typically undertaken by male staff. Stacks of linen had to be loaded and unloaded from 10-foot high shelves, and even some of the taller, sturdier staff struggled. But the petite Timah would not let the magnitude of the work overpower her.

When the deadly respiratory virus known as SARS broke out in 2003, Timah proved herself an invaluable member of the hospital team. Many were fearful to be around anyone suffering from the contagious virus, or anything they had come into contact with. But Timah didn't run away from her duties.

Instead, she clocked in more hours at work to help the staff cope. With the spike in patient numbers came an extra demand for linen. She washed bedding and towels used by SARS patients. It was brave of her, because while stringent precautions were taken, there was still a risk of infection. Despite her fears, Timah wanted to do everything possible to help with the day-to-day operations of the hospital.

Today, the Senior Storekeeper manages a team of six. Her favourite aspect of the job cannot be quantified — it's in simple acts of human kindness. "I feel like a mother at work, too," she says.

Article first appeared in: https://www.sg/SG50/Pioneer%20Generation/PG%20Story/
Mdm%20Timah%20Bte%20Haji%20Abdul%20Rashid-150130-045710.aspx.
Reprinted with permission.

Story and images submitted by Madam Timah Haji Abdul Rashid.

REBEL WITH A GREEN CAUSE | Haji Wansi

Haji Wansi descends the staircase leading to his secret garden, tucked away in the Clementi heartland near the disused railway tracks. A piece of paper carelessly nailed onto a signboard attracts his attention. It is a letter from the authorities. The patch of land is being reclaimed by the state. Urban farmer Haji Wansi reads the notice over and over again and resolves to do what he can within the law to save the garden that he and the urban farmers have worked on for years.

" Above all else, becoming a fire fighter taught me about brotherhood."

Haji spent almost 30 years in the Fire Department, first as a fireman and later as a paramedic. He joined on the recommendation of a friend, who told him about free bus rides and movies; privileges afforded to fireman at that time. He didn't get to take advantage of as many freebies as he hoped, but he found himself part of a band of brothers who would become his lifelong friends.

In his career as a fire fighter, Haji was involved in relief efforts during defining episodes like the fire at the squatter settlement in Bukit Ho Swee in 1961, which in addition to fatalities and injuries, left 16,000 people homeless. He was also on duty on 10 March 1965, the day a bomb exploded at MacDonald House, killing three people and injuring scores more; and again on 21 November 1972, when a fire razed the Robinson department store, claiming nine lives.

Working side by side with other men and women from the police force, fire department and paramedic teams during such incidents taught Haji the importance of *gotong-royong* — roughly translated to mean working together, or mutual aid — a principle that has guided him throughout his life.

I enjoy the freedom of farming. It reminds me of the good old kampung days."

One day while out walking, Haji came across what he would come to consider his secret garden in Clementi. Farmers, mostly senior citizens, were pottering around little plots, tending to crops of brinjal, cucumber, chilli and winter melon. Who knew the neglected piece of railway land would prove to be so fertile? Haji marked out his own plot and laboured for hours on end. Soon, what started as a hobby became a way of life.

The garden provided a truly organic source of produce. But it also provided them a source of release. The community of farmers was close, and they each chipped in to share costs for tools and equipment. Over tea in the shade of the trees, they'd trade advice and gossip. On weekends, the rustic space transformed into a chill-out spot where multiple generations of local families came to spend the afternoon.

But the farmers had no authorisation to use the land. A few residents in the neighbourhood complained about burning leaves and mosquito breeding, prompting the authorities to respond with an eviction notice.

Haji, together with his band of green-thumbed cohorts, wrote to the local MP in the hope of reaching a compromise that would keep the community garden open, legally.

A middle ground was indeed finally reached. The land was rented from the state and converted into a more modern community farm. With the new deal came more amenities like a footbath, water points and a tool shed — partly thanks to private donors.

Haji and the Clementi farmers now rent the space on a yearly basis, but they still feel that it is very much theirs. They're still reaping the rewards of the seeds they planted 20 years ago. They share an unbreakable bond and, thanks to the success of their project in a patch of wasteland in Clementi, town councils in other estates across the island are initiating and encouraging community farming.

Article first appeared in: https://www.sg/SG50/Pioneer%20Generation/PG%20Story/Haji%20Wansi-150130-050158.aspx. Reprinted with permission.

Story and images submitted by Haji Wansi.

Icons & Achievers

Every story of success defines a community. Success has many faces and this is a list of individuals in the Malay/ Muslim community who has made positive impact — inspirational individuals with the motivation and determination to make a difference. But success is so much more than just achievements; it is also about values and attitudes. Much as we have tried, the list is by no means exhaustive. We hope readers can draw from their inspiration and motivation from and to reflect on their own potential and possibilities.

LAW

Professor Ahmad Ibrahim (1916–1999)
Professor Ahmad Ibrahim was born on 12 May 1916. In 1936, he received a Queen's Scholarship to study at St. John's College, Cambridge University and in 1939, with first class honours in Economics and Law. While at Cambridge, he received the George Long Prize for Roman Law, and was exhibitioner, scholar and McMahon Law student of St. John's College. He then obtained the Certificate of Honour in the Bar Final exams at Middle Temple, London, and was called to the bar in November 1941.

In Singapore, he was appointed a Singapore Magistrate in 1946, a District Judge and Magistrate in 1955, and later became Singapore's first State Advocate General (1959) and Singapore's first Attorney–General in 1966.

Widely considered as an expert on Muslim law, he drafted the Administration of Muslim Law Act (AMLA), which revamped the Syariah Court's jurisdiction, and established the Islamic Religious Council of Singapore (MUIS).

He was also a key player in the merger talks between Singapore and Malaysia in the early 1960s, being the legal expert in the Singapore delegation to the Malaysia Talks in London (1963) which discussed the country's independence from the British. He then worked in Malaysia for the Faculty of Economics and Administration and subsequently as Dean of the Faculty of Law at the University of Malaya (UM) from 1969 to 1983, and then as Sheikh and Dean of Kulliyyah of Laws at the International Islamic University Malaysia (UIA) from 1983 to 1999. He has written extensively on Islamic law and the legal system in Singapore and Malaysia.

He was awarded the Honorary Degree of Doctor of Laws (LL.D) from the then-University of Singapore (now National University of Singapore) in 1995. While in Malaysia, he was presented with the Johan Mangku Negara (JMN) by His Majesty the Yang-dipertuan Agung of Malaysia, the Darjah Yang Mulia Pangkuan Negara (DMPN) with the title of Datuk, by the Yang-dipertuan Negeri of Pulau Pinang, as well as the Panglima Setia Mahkota (PSM) by His Majesty the Yang-dipertuan Agung, with the title of Tan Sri.

POLITICS

Abdul Rahim Ishak (1925–2001)
Abdul Rahim Ishak was the Member of Parliament for Siglap (1963–1984), Minister of State for Education (1965–1968), and Senior Minister of State for Foreign Affairs (1972–1981). He was also the younger brother of Singapore's first President, Yusof Ishak.

Abdullah Tarmugi
Abdullah Tarmugi was Minister for Community Development, Youth and Sports (1994–2000), and the Minister-in-Charge of Muslim Affairs (2000–2002). He was also the Deputy Speaker of Parliament from 1989 to 1993, before becoming the Speaker of Parliament (2002–2011).

Ahmad Ibrahim (1927–1962)
Ahmad Ibrahim was the elected Member of Parliament for Sembawang in 1959, and was subsequently appointed Minister for Health and Minister for Labour. His legacy is remembered via schools, a mosque and a road that carries his name.

Ahmad Mattar (Ahmad bin Mohammed Mattar)

As Minister-In-Charge of Muslims Affairs (1977–1994), Ahmad Mattar spearheaded the formation of the Mendaki Foundation. He was also the Minister for the Environment and oversaw the passing of stricter environmental laws and the implementation of a smoking ban in public areas. He retired from politics in 1993.

Baharuddin Mohammed Ariff (1933–1961)

Baharuddin Ariff began his political career after being known as an incisive journalist for Utusan Melayu, where he contributed thought-provoking articles concerning labour union strikes and unrest. Unfortunately, he died in April 1965 at the young age of 28, just four months before Singapore's independence. To honour his contributions, Singapore's first vocational school, the "Baharuddin Vocational Institute" was named after him.

Eunos Abdullah (Mohammed Eunos bin Abdullah) (1876–1933)

Eunos Abdullah was touted as the father of modern Malay journalism. He also championed the progress of the Malay community during the period of colonial rule, which drove him to switch to politics. He was also the president of Kesatuan Melayu Singapore in 1926, a quasi-political Malay organisation set up in colonial Malaya to look after the interests of the Malays. To commemorate his legacy, the government named one of its residential districts "Eunos".

Halimah Yacob

Halimah Yacob graduated from the then University of Singapore on a MUIS Scholarship with an honours degree in Law in 1978. She was called to the bar in 1981 and attained her Masters in Law from National University of Singapore (NUS) in 2001.

Halimah is a trailblazer, championing the interests of women and workers. She began her career in NTUC as a legal officer and later became the director of its legal services department in 1992. In 1999, she was made the Director of the Singapore Institute of Labour Studies (SILS), now known as the Ong Teng Cheong (OTC) Institute, and was the Assistant Secretary-General of NTUC and secretary of the NTUC Women's Committee. She was also the first Singaporean to be elected into the International Labour Organization (ILO) as a deputy member representing its workers' group. At one of the ILO conferences, a German member congratulated her for being not only the first Southeast Asian woman, but also the first Muslim woman to be a spokesperson for workers.

She began her political career when she won a seat in Jurong GRC in the 2001 General Elections. She also served as Minister of State in the Ministry of Social and Family Development. She then became the first female Speaker of Parliament in January 2013. She is the longest-serving female Malay/Muslim politician in the ruling People's Action Party (PAP).

The politician and unionist champions social issues such as training for older and less-skilled workers, caring for the elderly and mentally ill, and providing flexible working arrangements to improve work-life balance. She has served on various boards including being an advisor for the National Council of Social Services, for the Housing and Development Board, the Tripartite Alliance on Fair Employment Practices, the Tripartite Workgroup on Enhancing Employment Choices for Women, and MENDAKI Sense.

Halimah was named Berita Harian Achiever of the Year in 2001, and Her World Magazine's "Woman of the Year" in 2004 in recognition of her contributions to society.

Harun Abdul Ghani (1939–2005)

Harun Abdul Ghani was the first elected Member of Parliament for Hong Kah (1996–2000). A former teacher, he is most remembered for laying the groundwork to tackle the drug problem in the Malay community by setting up rehabilitation centres and campaigning against drug abuse. He retired from active politics in 2002.

Othman Wok
Othman Wok was a former Minister for Social Affairs and a Member of Parliament for Pasir Panjang (1963–1977). He was a prominent Malay journalist with Utusan Melayu and was awarded the Anugerah Tokoh Wartawan Dunia Melayu (2008) in recognition of his contributions to Malay journalism. He was also involved in the implementation of the Administration of Muslim Law Act (AMLA), the Mosque Building Fund (MBF) and the management of *Haj* services through the Singapore Pilgrimage Office under the Ministry of Social Affairs.

Rahmat Kenap (1963–1980)
Rahmat Kenap was a former Member of Parliament for Geylang Serai from 1963 to 1980. His win at the General Elections was the slimmest when he polled 6,711 to win a 900-vote majority for the People's Action Party (PAP). He was also Chairman of the Singapore Telephone Board Workers' Union from 1959 to 1963.

Sahorah Ahmat
Sahorah Ahmat won the Siglap seat for PAP in a six-cornered contest in the 1959 Legislative Assembly elections. It is also little known that she had saved the PAP from defeat in 1961, when Chan Chee Seng, Member of Parliament for Jalan Besar, persuaded her to leave her hospital bed to travel by ambulance to the Legislative Assembly Hall to cast her vote for the PAP; and as a result, the PAP survived a no-confidence vote by a majority of one.

Sidek Saniff
Sidek Saniff was an educator, a Malay language and literature activist, and a politician. He was a graduate of the Sultan Idris Training College and the University of London. He began his career as a teacher from 1953 to 1980. Sidek began involving himself in politics as a Member of Parliament for Kolam Ayer/Jalan Besar in 1976, and subsequently for Eunos/Aljunied GRC. He also held important positions in the government, having been appointed as Senior Minister of State for Education (1996), and Senior Minister of State for the Environment, until he retired in 2002.

His contributions to the field of Malay language and literature were recognised by many in the community. Among some of his contributions to the Malay community include being responsible for the conceptualisation of the *Anugerah Persuratan*, an award given to Malay literary arts figures in Singapore by the Malay Language Council (Majlis Bahasa Melayu Singapura). He also suggested the bi-annual celebration of the *Anugerah Persuratan* to make way for the Malay Language Month celebrations. The Malay Language Month is now celebrated annually since 2013. He also planned for and advocated for the use of *Bahasa Melayu Baku* in Singapore, as well as being instrumental in opening the gateway for Malay Language teachers in Singapore to enter Universiti Malaya (UM) from 1993.

He was also awarded the Anugerah Dewan Kehormatan PERSILAT in 1977, the Friend of Labour Award from NTUC in 1997, the Anugerah Tokoh Guru KGMS in 2002 as well as the Anugerah Tokoh Suluh Budiman UPSI in 2003.

Yaacob Ibrahim
Dr Yaacob Ibrahim is the Minister for Communications and Information (since 2011), the Minister-in-Charge of Muslim Affairs (since 2002) and the Minister-in-Charge of Cyber Security (since 2015). Before joining politics, he was an engineer and an academic at Cornell University in the US and at NUS. He is active in community service and has served in AMP, Jamiyah, MUIS, and has been the Chairman of Yayasan MENDAKI since 2002. He was MP for Jalan Besar GRC (1997–2011) and for Moulmein–Kallang GRC (2011–2015). He is currently MP for Jalan Besar GRC (Kolam Ayer).

Yatiman Yusof

Yatiman Yusof was a teacher, journalist and editor for Berita Harian and Berita Minggu (1978–1984) before going into politics and serving as a Member of Parliament from 1984 to 2006. He has held appointments as Parliamentary Secretary and Senior Parliamentary Secretary for the Ministry of Foreign Affairs, and served as Senior Parliamentary Secretary for the Ministry of Information, Communications and the Arts.

Haji Ya'acob bin Mohamed (1925–1989)

Haji Ya'acob bin Mohamed (b. 25 January 1925, Kelantan, Malaya – d. 11 October 1989, Singapore) was a former politician (Senior Minister of State, Prime Minister's Office) and diplomat. He was a staunch advocate of Malay interests in Singapore and played a key role in winning Malay support for the People's Action Party (PAP) in the early 1960s.

SCIENCE & TECHNOLOGY

Dr Abdul Razakjr Omar

In 2005, Dr Abdul Razakjr Omar was the first Malay heart specialist in Singapore. In 2008, he was appointed head of the Committee for Community Health, a committee setup by the Health Promotion Board to raise awareness on health-related issues plaguing the Malay community. His research is widely published in international journals and a regular contributor to Berita Minggu's health column. In 2013, he was awarded the Berita Harian Achiever of the Year for his contributions and achievements.

Associate Professor Aziz Nather (Abdul Aziz bin Mohammed Nather)

Associate Professor Aziz Nather, a renowned expert in bone research and tissue banking, is a recipient of the Public Service Medal in 1995. He also won the Berita Harian Achiever of the Year Award in 2000. He is the author of numerous scientific research articles and book chapters on topics such as bone and allograft transplantation and biological and biomechanical properties of bone and ligament allografts.

Dr Azlinda Anwar

Dr Azlinda Anwar was the first Malay female scientist doing research work at the prestigious Johns Hopkins Singapore. With a doctorate in microbiology, she was also a recipient of the Young Scientist Award conferred by the National University Hospital and the National Medical Research Council in 2001.

Dr Jackie Ying

Professor Jackie Ying is currently the executive director of the Institute of Bioengineering and Nanotechnology (IBN), under the Agency of Science, Technology and Research (A*STAR). She was born in Taipei, Taiwan and came to study in Singapore when she was seven. She specialises in the field of nanostructured materials and devices, and has more than 130 patents issued or pending. Through her organisation's Youth Research Programme, she reached out to more than 60,000 students and teachers in Singapore to encourage the study of chemical engineering.

Dr Mansoor Abdul Jalil

Dr Mansoor Abdul Jalil was the first Malay/Muslim Singaporean to obtain first-class honours degree in Physics from the University of Cambridge in 1993. He has also won the Singapore Youth Award for Science and Technology (2003) and the Young Researcher Award (2009). He was the first recipient of Berita Harian's Jauhari Award in 1999.

Nur Syakirah Mohammed Said

Nur Syakirah Mohammed Said is currently an undergraduate in Singapore Management University's School of Information Systems. She was the best student for Temasek Polytechnic's Diploma in Digital Forensics and was cited by Minister in-charge of Cyber Security Dr Yaacob Ibrahim as a good example of the contributions of Malay/Muslims in the infocomm technology sector.

Dr Rufaihah Abdul Jalil
Dr Rufaihah Abdul Jalil is an Assistant Professor in the Department of Surgery in National University of Singapore (NUS). She also heads the Regenerative Medicine Laboratory as a Senior Research Scientist under the Singapore-Technion Alliance for Reasearch Technology Programme. Her research focuses on the use of bioengineering and stem cell technologies for tissue engineering and regenerative medicine applications, particularly in the field of cardiac restoration in patients with cardiovascular-related diseases. Dr Rufaihah has won several Young Investigator Awards for studies conducted and presented in various scientific conferences. She also won the Junior Chamber International Ten Outstanding Young Persons of the World, Singapore Honoree under the Science/Technology Category for her contributions in the scientific field. She also founded Granada Academy, an initiative that aims to bridge the Malay/Muslim-Science gap, and inspire Malay/Muslim children and youths to pursue science and engineering as career options.

Sarah Salim
Sarah Salim was an Art, Design, and Media graduate from Nanyang Technological University (NTU) currently working at IDA as an information designer involved in the creation of two mobile apps — Beeline and data.gov. Beeline is a mobile app that enables commuters to pre-book rides on express private bus routes while data.gov is the government's one-stop portal to publicly-available data sets from 70 public agencies.

Dato Syed A. M. Alsagoff
Dato Syed A.M. Alsagoff was one of the founding members of Singapore Anti-Tuberculosis Association (SATA).

ACADEMIC

Adil Hakeem Bin Mohammad Rafee
Adil Hakeem first made headlines when he emerged as the top PSLE student in 2005 with an aggregate of 282. He made the news again in 2013 when he became the first Malay student to be awarded the President's Scholarship in 44 years. He is currently an undergraduate at Yale University.

Ahmad Abdurrahman
Ahmad Abdurrahman was one of the first few former madrasah student who was offered a place in the Yong Loo Lin School of Medicine. He was selected from a group of students from the polytechnic route.

Amalina Ridzuan
Amalina Ridzuan was another former *madrasah* students to be offered places in the Yong Loo Lin School of Medicine at the National University of Singapore (NUS).

Ismail Ibrahim
Ismail Ibrahim was the first Malay student to be awarded the President's Scholarship in 1967/8.

Dr Mohamad Farid bin Harunal Rashid
Dr Mohamad Farid was the top PSLE student in 1990 with an aggregate of 285, and later received the Prime Minister's Book Prize in 1991 and 1995. He is currently a medical oncologist at the National Cancer Centre Singapore.

Murshidah Albakri
Murshidah Albakri, a student from Madrasah Al Ma'arif Al-Islamiah was the school's top scorer for the GCE 'O' Level examinations in 2015, having scored nine 'A's. Overall, 2015 was a good year for students from the *madrasah* stream as many students emerged from national level examinations with impressive results.

Natasha Nabila Muhamad Nasir
Natasha Nabila, a Malay student from St. Hilda's Primary School, achieved a score of 294 in the 2007 Primary School Leaving Examinations (PSLE), setting the record for the highest attained score for PSLE.

Nur'Izzah Mohamad Afandi
Nur'Izzah Mohamad Afandi was the first recipient of the Malay Heritage Foundation (MHF) Prize for her interest in studying the Malay culture in Singapore. The award is given to encourage more research into Malay heritage.

UNIFORMED GROUPS

Colonel Anwar Abdullah
Colonel Anwar Abdullah is the Director of Operations, Singapore Civil Defence Force, Singapore. High points in his career include his involvement in 2003 in one of the worst bush fire operations affecting the states of New South Wales and Canberra in Australia that tragically killed four residents in Canberra. As part of SCDF overseas humanitarian assistance, he led SCDF team to assist in the post-earthquake search and rescue operations on the island of Nias, Indonesia in April 2005 (where Singapore Rescue Team successfully rescued two casualties alive from the concrete rubbles) and in Yogyakarta in Central Java in August 2006. He was also involved in the Nicoll Highway collapse incident in Singapore in 2004, where he was awarded a state commendation medal for his efforts.

Brigadier–General Ishak Ismail
Brigadier-General Ishak Ismail is the first Malay to attain the rank of brigadier-general in the Singapore Armed Forces after 28 years of being in service. His promotion marked a milestone in Malay's efforts to be fully accepted in the military.

Captain Muhammad Azlan Abdul Latiff
Captain Muhammad Azlan has been a Super Puma helicopter pilot with the RSAF for eight years.

Captain Muhammad Iskandar Dzulfadhli Abdul Rahman
Captain Muhammad Iskandar has been a F-15SG fighter jet pilot with the RSAF for seven years.

Colonel Zakir Hamid
Zakir Hamid was the first Malay/Muslim air force pilot to earn his wings with the elite Republic of Singapore Air Force in 1992, and as of 2015, is the highest-ranking Malay officer in the RSAF after being promoted to Colonel.

Domain Commander (Air) Zuraidah Abdullah
Zuraidah graduated from Nanyang Technological Institute (now Nanyang Technological University) in 1985 with a degree in Civil Engineering.
     She was a teacher for a while before deciding to join the Singapore Police Force under a direct entry scheme for university graduates, when she saw an advertisement that said "Every day (with the Force) is different" and realised that was what she wanted. She was the first Malay graduate and the sixth woman to join the police force through the scheme.

Zuraidah was posted to the Queenstown Police Division (currently Clementi Police Division) and then to Traffic Police. She soon became a Head of Operations at the Central Police Division, and she was one of three women officers appointed by the police force. She was also the first Malay/Muslim woman officer appointed as a Land Division commander in charge of the Jurong Police Division, which was the largest of six police land divisions.

Zuraidah was then seconded to Yayasan MENDAKI as its Chief Executive Officer from 2007 to 2009. She also became the first woman to be appointed as a Council Member of the Islamic Religious Council of Singapore (MUIS).

In 2010, she returned to the Police Force and became the Commander of the Police Training Command, and was then promoted to the rank of Senior Assistant Commissioner of Police in 2013, the third highest level possible in the force. Zuraidah is the first woman to achieve this position. Recently, she was also appointed as the Commander of the Airport Police Division. She is also the chairperson of the Malay Heritage Foundation, and a member of the National Library Board.

Some of the awards she has received include the Commissioner Police's High Commendation Award (1991) and Her World magazine's "Woman of the Year" (2015).

SPORTS

Aqilah Sudhir

Aqilah Sudhir was a gold medal winner at the Commonwealth Youth Games (2008) for the 10-metre air rifle girls' event. The shooter also won a bronze medal at the 2009 SEA Games in Vietnam as well as a bronze and gold medal in the 2010 Commonwealth Games in India.

Fandi Ahmad

A former Singapore international footballer, Fandi Ahmad is regarded as one of Singapore's most successful football players. He has played for clubs in Singapore, Malaysia, Indonesia and the Netherlands, before he began coaching football teams in Singapore, Malaysia and Indonesia. In 2011, he returned to Singapore and now runs the Fandi Ahmad F-17 Academy, as well as recently launching his own football club, the Fandi Ahmad Football Club, to groom young local football talents.

As a child, Fandi showed an interest in football and constantly persuaded his father, former national goalkeeper Ahmad Wartam, to bring him to watch Malaysia Cup matches and also to the training sessions. A teacher at his school recommended that he join the Milo Soccer Scheme for talented young footballers, but his first application was unsuccessful. When Fandi started training with the Kaki Bukit Constituency Sport Club in his teens, his then-coach Abdullah Yusoff, encouraged him to try for the Milo Soccer Scheme again, and he succeeded this time.

At the age of 15, Fandi became the first team-player for Kaki Bukit in the National Football League Division 1, the highest level of club football at that time. Dubbed "Singapore's schoolboy soccer sensation" by local press, Fandi was vice-captain of the Singapore Under-16 national team that won the Lion City Cup Youth tournament in 1977. He captained the team in 1978, and they went on to retain the Lion City Cup. In the same year, Fandi became the youngest footballer to represent Singapore in a national training tour of Russia. He was also the first player from the Milo Scheme to make it to Singapore's national team.

Fandi's talent attracted attention from football teams abroad, with him eventually signing a one-year contract with Indonesian club Niac Mitra. In 1983, he signed a two-year contract with Dutch team FC Groningen, and became the first Singaporean player to player to play and score in a European Cup competition. In 1999, Fandi was voted into Groningen's Hall of Fame as one of the club's 25 best players. He then returned to Southeast Asia in 1985 to play for clubs in Malaysia and also the Singapore national team.

In his illustrious career, Fandi has won 101 caps, scored 55 goals, and won three SEA Games silver medals. Fandi was named the Football Association of Singapore's Footballer of the Year in 1981. He was also awarded the Public Service Medal in 1994 for captaining Singapore to the Malaysian League and Cup trophies, and in 1999, he was ranked sixth on the list of Singapore's 50 Greatest Athletes of the Century by The Straits Times. Fandi is a popular player noted for his talent, humility and love for the game.

Majid Ariff

Majid Ariff is a former National Football player and is considered by many to be one of the most talented footballers in Singapore. He is the only Singaporean to play for the Asian All-Stars team in 1966, and in the same year, Majid helped the national team finish fourth in the Bangkok Asian Games. He was also one of two Singaporeans among the top 116 Asian footballers to be nominated for Asia's Footballer of the Century Award in 1998 (the other being his protégé Fandi Ahmad). Majid is passionate about the sport is always willing to share his passion and skills with the younger generation.

Mardan Mamat

Mardan Mamat is a golfer who is the first Singaporean to win a European tour event, winning first place at the 2004 Indian Open as well as the 2006 Osim Singapore Masters. He was awarded the Berita Harian Achiever of the Year Award in 2006.

Nurulasyiqah Mohammad Taha

Although born with Spinal Muscular Atrophy, which confines her to a wheelchair, Nurulasyiqah leads an active life. She clinched two gold medals in the Boccia event at the 7th ASEAN Para Games. The Singapore Youth Award recipient was also the first local Boccia player to compete in the Paralympics.

Saiyidah Aisyah Mohammed Rafa'ee

Saiyidah Aisyah won a gold medal at the 27th Southeast Asian Games in the women's lightweight rowing category held in Myanmar in December 2013. She was awarded the Berita Harian Inspiring Young Achiever Award in 2014.

Shamsul Maidin

In the 2006 World Cup in Germany, Shamsul Maidin was the main official, breaking George Suppiah's 32-year record of being the only Singaporean to officiate at the world's biggest sports competition. An illustrious career saw him officiate the 2005 FIFA Confederations Cup, the 1996, 2000 and 2004 AFC Asian Cups as well as the 2001 and 2003 FIFA World Youth Championship. He was the only non-African referee to officiate at the 2006 African Cup of Nations. In January 2016, he was appointed the new AFC Director of Referees.

Sheikh Alauddin

Dubbed the "silat king", Sheik Alauddin won Singapore's first gold medal at the Pencak Silat World Invitational Championships held in Den Haag, the Netherlands (1990). He was also a multiple medallist of the SEA games, having won gold medals at the 1993 and 1995 SEA Games. He was also a three-time winner of the Coach of the Year title in 2000, 2002 and 2003. He was inducted into the Singapore Sports Council Hall of Fame for his contributions to silat (Malay art of self-defence) in Singapore.

Zainal Abidin Abdul Malek

Zainal Abidin Abdul Malek was Singapore's undisputed squash champion from 1977 to 1986, having won the national title five times, the East Asia title six times and the Japan Open title for two consecutive years (1985–1986). He also won the Penang Open title in 1989 by beating then-world champion Ross Norman of New Zealand in the finals.

ARTS

Jaafar Latiff

Jaafar Latiff was a self-taught visual artist known for his acrylic works and his innovation in batik painting by introducing abstract art into batik painting. He was also a lifelong arts educator and taught in various educational institutions including Baharuddin Vocational Institute, LASALLE College of the Arts and the Nanyang Academy of Fine Arts. His works has been exhibited internationally and they can be found in public spaces in Singapore such as Orchard MRT station and Changi Airport.

Khairullah Rahim

Khairullah Rahim, a LASALLE College of the Arts graduate and recipient of the Future Leadership Scholarship, is an artist who is formally trained in the field of painting but also incorporates other mediums such as sculpture, installation and video in his works. He has participated in various exhibitions and have had his works showcased in exhibitions and art fairs abroad such as in Malaysia, Taiwan, Hong Kong, USA and Japan. He won first prize in the Singapore Land Authority (SLA) painting competition in 2009, and was also the top four finalists and recipient of the People's Choice Award at the CLIFTONS Art Prize 2010 competition organised by CLIFTONS, Australia. In 2013, he was invited to extend his research and practice at an artist-in-residence programme organised by YOUKOBO Art Residency Programme, Japan, and INSTINC Gallery, Singapore. He is currently a part-time teacher at LASALLE College of the Arts.

S. Mohdir (Mohamed Abdul Kadir) (1936–2010)

Mohamed Abdul Kadir or better known as S. Mohdir was a highly sought-after batik painting instructor to many schools in Singapore. He was also one of APAD's founding members, serving as Honorary Secretary and subsequently, as its second President from 1984 to 1991.

Nadiputra (Almahdi Al-Haj Ibrahim)

Playwright, director, producer and actor Nadiputra is considered by many as the reigning patriarch of Malay theatre. He has been involved in drama for more than 30 years, and has written more than 300 plays for stage, radio and television. He was the founder of now-defunct children's theatre, Teater Nadi (1985), and served as President of Sriwana (1978–1988). He also received the Cultural Medallion in 1986, and the Anugerah Tun Seri Lanang in 2013.

Sarkasi Said

Sarkasi Said is an internationally-acclaimed Singaporean batik painter. Going by his artist name 'Tzee', he was exposed to the world of batik very early on, when he helped his Javanese grandmother sell batik in a time when it was a highly sought after artistic commodity. He began to develop a serious interest in batik art after observing that foreign artists had featured batik painting techniques in their works, and was inspired to return to his roots.

Sarkasi was self-taught, and through the years, perfected his skills often through observation and experimentation. He also travelled extensively throughout Indonesia to improve his skills. He later developed a distinctively bold artistic style and unconventional wax-resist batik printing techniques, which he is now well-known for.

He was dubbed the "Baron of Batik" when he rose to prominence after his portrayal of the Singapore orchid was chosen as the main design element for the "Singapore National Dress" (the nationwide search for the design was organised by the National Trade Union Congress (NTUC) in the 1970s). In 2003, he set a Guinness World Record for the world's longest batik painting when he produced a 103.9-metre long batik artwork.

Sarkasi's works have been exhibited in Southeast Asia, the USA, France and Japan. His works can be found in public and private collections, including that of the National Museum of Singapore, and are displayed at Serangoon MRT Station as well as the Singapore Airlines Silver Kris Lounge at the Changi Airport. He also sits on the board of several art committees such as the National Art Council's (NAC) Arts Advisory Panel and Singapore's Modern Art Society.

He also frequently donates his paintings to charitable organisations, and volunteered to teach art classes at a drug rehabilitation centre. Kevin Lee, one of his students at the Khalsa Crescent Drug Rehabilitation Centre, had his first batik painting exhibition in November 1993.

Sarkasi often uses his art to promote local culture and sees the popularity of his works as a way of promoting the traditional art of batik to a larger audience by making it contemporary through fusing new techniques and ideas while preserving the traditional touch.

MUSIC

Ahmad Ja'afar (1919–2009)
Musician and composer Ahmad Ja'afar was the lead conductor of the Singapore Broadcasting Corporation Orchestra for over ten years. He wrote songs for movies produced by Cathay Keris Film, a Malay film company in the 1950s, and created some of the most memorable all-time favourite Malay songs such as *Selamat Hari Raya* and *Ibu*. He was awarded the Public Service Star (1970) and the Cultural Medallion (1981) for his tremendous contributions to the world of Malay music.

Art Fazil
Folk singer-songwriter Art Fazil writes and sings in Malay and English. His English single "Sometimes When I Feel Blue" won the Top English Pop Song award at the 1995 COMPASS Awards. The only non-British songwriter in the Edinburgh Fringe Festival songwriting competition, his compositions "Monsoon Rain" and "Karma Train" won awards in 1997. He was awarded a COMPASS Scholarship in 2000 to pursue a postgraduate diploma in continuing professional development at the Guildhall School of Music and Drama in London. His recent Malay song, "Rilek Brader", a collaboration with Malaysian comedian Imuda in 2013, was a social media hit that garnered more than one million views on YouTube.

Iskandar Mirza Ismail (1956–2014)
Iskandar Mirza Ismail was a multitalented and versatile musician, having worked as a composer, arranger, conductor, producer, music director, performer and educator and was known for his ability to work across different musical genres. He was engaged by Warner Taiwan for 15 years to write and produce songs for Chinese artistes, and did the musical arrangements for stage musicals such as Sing to the Dawn (1996) and Chang & Eng (1997). He was also dedicated in nurturing musical talents of the next generation, participating in the annual ChildAid charity concert to raise funds for the Budding Artists Funds for seven years. He was awarded the Berita Harian Achiever of the Year (2003) and the Cultural Medallion (2008) in recognition of his contributions to the local music scene.

Kartina Dahari (1941–2014)
Kartina Dahari, an award-winning Malay songstress known as the "Queen of Keroncong", was the first Malay singer in Singapore to record in English. In 2009, she

was awarded the Perdana Emas, an award given out by local Malay entertainment awards ceremony Pesta Perdana, and in 2010, she was given the Artistic Excellence Award at the 15th Compass Awards (Composers and Authors Society of Singapore).

Kassim Masdor (1938–2014)
Kassim Masdor was instrumental in the development of modern Malay music in Singapore. Making his name as a musician and arranger in the golden era of Malay films in the 1950s–1960s, he soon became one of the foremost Malay music composers in the Singapore music industry for more than half a century. He won the Best Song Award at the Third Malay Film Festival (1982). He also received a Lifetime Achievement Award from the Association of Malay Singers, Composers and Professional Musicians (PERKAMUS) in 2002.

M. Nasir (Mohamad Nasir Mohamad)
Singapore-born M Nasir is a multi-talented and award-winning singer, composer, actor and director. In 1994, he won a record-breaking four awards out of five nominations at the Juara Lagu, a competition organised by Malaysian television channel TV3, for his song *Tanya Sama Itu Hud-hud* (Best Pop Rock Song, Best Performance and Overall Best Song of the Year) and Bonda (Best Irama Malaysia Song). In 1997, he won Best Film in TV3's Anugerah Skrin for his directed film *Merah*. Now based in Malaysia, he was conferred the Honorary Degree of Doctor of Philosophy (Creative Industries Management) by Universiti Utara Malaysia in 2014 for his contributions to the music industry.

Ramli Sarip
Affectionately known as "Papa Rock", Ramli Sarip is the best-selling Malay recording artiste in Singapore. He first made popular the Malay rock scene in Singapore and Malaysia together with his band, Sweet Charity, in the 1970s. He is credited to be the first Malay rock singer to hold two solo concerts at the Istana Budaya in Kuala Lumpur. He was also awarded the COMPASS Artistic Excellence Award in 1998.

Riduan Zalani
Drummer and percussionist Riduan Zalani embarked on his artistic journey from the age of seven. As a passionate ambassador of Malay traditional music, Riduan consistently pushes boundaries to create new blends of modern and traditional Malay music. Riduan has taken his music around the world, representing Singapore in renowned music festivals round the world including Moomba Festival and World of Music, Arts and Dance (WOMAD). In 2011, he co-founded NADI, a traditional Malay music band comprising 27 volunteer youth members. He was awarded the Goh Chok Tong Promise Award in 2006 and the Singapore National Day Silver Award in 2009 for his achievements in putting Malay music on the world stage. Riduan is also a proud receipient of the Singapore Youth Award 2013. In his spare time, Riduan conducts motivational talks at organisations such as the Singapore Boys' Home and volunteers with the Spastic Children's Association of Singapore.

Taufik Batisah
Taufik Batisah is a singer-songwriter and music producer who was the first winner of Singapore Idol. He won the Most Popular Male Artiste Award at regional music award show Anugerah Planet Muzik (2006, 2008-2009). He also received the Singapore Youth Award for Arts and Culture, awarded by the National Youth Council for his achievements in the music industry and for being a role model to the younger generation (2008). His composition *Usah Lepaskan* was awarded the top Malay song with the highest royalties by COMPASS. He has represented Singapore on international platforms such as at the Singapore Day 2009 event in London, the ASEAN-Korea Commemorative Summit in Korea, in Seoul under the invitation of the Ministry of Culture, Sports and Tourism of Korea, and once again at the first ABU TV Song Festival 2012 held at the KBS Concert Hall in Seoul, where he performed Usah Lepaskan alongside high-profile music talents from the region.

Wandly Yazid
Wandly Yazid was a respected and acclaimed composer, arranger and musician known for his contributions to the film and music industry in Singapore and Malaysia. A versatile and prolific composer and arranger of Malay film music from the 1940s to the 1960s, his best known work is the theme song for the 1966 classic Malay film *Gurindam Jiwa*. He was also an accomplished watercolour artist and oil painter. He received a Meritorious Award from the Composers and Authors Society of Singapore (COMPASS) in 2001.

Zaidi Sabtu-Ramli
A graduate of LASALLE College of the Arts, Zaidi Sabtu-Ramli is a composer. He was recently given the opportunity to lead the Banda Henrique Marques Orchestra in a world premiere performance at Teatro Vitoria in Sao Paolo, Brazil. He is also a part of the newly-formed Singapore Sounds Orchestra specialising in music written and arranged by Singaporeans and performed by Singaporeans.

MEDIA

Aaron Aziz
Television and movie actor Aaron Aziz has appeared in many local and Malaysian television series and films. Widely popular in Singapore and Malaysia, his most recent movie KL Gangster is the highest-grossing movie in Malaysian box office history. He has also ventured into business with his own production and management company, Aaron Aziz Productions, and is also a co-owner of concept café Kidz & Crème in Malaysia.

Bani Buang (1929–1996)
Director and producer Bani Buang was regarded as the father of modern Malay drama. He directed and produced numerous Malay plays and was a co-founder of the Malay theatre group Perkumpulan Seni. He also headed the Malay Drama Unit in the then Radio Television Singapore (RTS). He received the inaugural Cultural Medallion (1979) for his contributions to theatre in Singapore.

Basir Siswo
Basir Siswo started his career at the then Singapore Broadcasting Corporation (SBC). He was the producer and host for a Malay current affairs programme Tinjauan. He was promoted to Vice President (Programming) — an appointment he held for eight years. In 2006, he joined the Aljazeera News Network, a Doha-based broadcaster as a Senior Editor. In 2012, he joined ASTRO Measat Broadcast Net work as its Consultant (Factual Programming).

Faisal Ishak
Malaysia-based Faisal Ishak is a well-known Singaporean television producer and film director. He produced several popular children's TV series in Singapore such as Ya Alif and K14. He is the director of many popular and critically-acclaimed TV series and movies such as Nur Kasih and Juvana.

Khairul Anwar Salleh
Khairul Anwar Salleh is the Vice President of Malay Customer Business in MEASAT Broadcast Network Systems Sdn Bhd for the Astro broadcasting service in Malaysia. Known within the industry as "The Awards Show Director", he has helmed several popular television productions, and also created and conceptualised many award shows that continue to run till today, such as the Anugerah Planet Muzik for Singapore and the Anugerah Industri Muzik for Malaysia.

Najip Ali
Most well-known as the crazy host of talent show Asia Bagus, celebrity host Najip Ali is currently the Creative Director of Dua M Pte Ltd, a TV production company that conceptualises TV programmes for Singapore and the region as well as producing award-winning productions such as Kopi O Teh Tarik and Popumentari.

Yusnor Ef (Mohamed Noor Mohamed Yusofe)
Yusnor Ef's stage name was given to him by the film legend P Ramlee. He is highly regarded as lyricist, having penned hundreds of song hits set to music by P Ramlee and Zubir Said, and performed and recorded by artists such as Anita Sarawak and P Ramlee. He is also a Malay-language educator, TV producer, entertainment historian, screenwriter and film expert. He founded PERKAMUS (Association of Malay Singers, Composers and Professional Musicans) in 1992, and still serves as its president. He was also awarded the Cultural Medallion in 2011.

Zakiah Halim
Zakiah Halim has more than 28 years of experience in the broadcasting industry. Recently, she was promoted to the position of Senior Vice President of the Malay Broadcast Division at Mediacorp Pte Ltd. She also serves in committee and advisory boards such as the Malay Language Council and the Advisory Panel of SIM University's Malay Language Programme.

LITERATURE

Abdul Ghani Hamid (1933–2014)
Abdul Ghani Hamid is a multi-talented individual who has works published in both English and Malay, and as a painter, he has participated in more than 60 exhibitions since 1950. He founded the Angkatan Pelukis Aneka Daya (APAD), and was the recipient of the Anugerah Tun Seri Lanang (1997), the Southeast Asia Write Award (1998) and the Cultural Medallion (1999).

Alfian Sa'at
Alfian Sa'at is a Singaporean author and playwright, and writes more widely in English. He won the Golden Point Award for Poetry (2001) and the National Arts Council Young Artist Award for Literature (2001).

Djamal Tukimin
Djamal Tukimin is a playwright, poet, and essayist who is a major figure in the Singapore Malay performing arts and literary scenes. He has also played a key role in archiving the works of Singapore writers, and his published research into the post-war history of modern Malay theatre is now regarded as a standard reference source. In 2007, he was awarded the highest Malay literary award in Singapore, the Tun Seri Lanang Award, in recognition of his contribution to regional and local arts development.

Hadijah Rahmat
Hadijah Bte Rahmat is an Associate Professor and the Deputy Head of the Asian Languages and Cultures Academic Group, Nanyang Technological University. A bilingual author, she writes poetry, short stories, plays, literary essays, academic papers and children's books. She is also actively involved in the Malay literary community and has served in the Malay Language Council Committee since 2001.

Harun Aminurrashid (Harun Mohd Amin) (1907–1986)
One of the pioneers of Malay literature in Singapore, Harun Aminurrashid was the editor of numerous Malay newspapers and magazines. He was awarded the

Certificate of Merit for the Dictionary of International Biography, London in 1968, to commemorate his contributions to Malay literature.

Isa Kamari
Isa Kamari is a Malay writer, both known in the Malay and the English literary scene, with seven of his novels being translated into English. He was awarded the Southeast Asia Write Award (2006), the Cultural Medallion (2007) and the Anugerah Tun Seri Lanang (2009).

Masuri S. N. (1927–2005)
A pioneer in modern Malay poetry, Masuri was a highly prolific poet, having composed more than 1000 poems in his lifetime. He was also a founding member of Angkatan Sasterawan '50 (Asas '50), an important Malay literary organisation in the development Malay literature, and headed the organisation from 2001 to 2005. Masuri was also awarded the Public Service Star (1963) and an Honorary Doctor of Letters from the Sultan Idris University, Malaysia.

Mohammed Latiff Mohammed
Mohamed Latiff Mohamed is a prolific writer and has won accolades such as the Mont Blanc-NUS Centre for the Arts Literary Award (1998); the Southeast Asia Write Award (2002); the Tun Seri Lanang Award (2003); and the Singapore Literature Prize in 2004, 2006 and 2008; and the Cultural Medallion (2013). He was also the vice-president of the Angkatan Sasterawan '50 (Asas '50).

Muhammad Ariff Ahmad (1924–2016)
Muhammad Ariff Ahmad was a highly respected Malay language and cultural luminary, having received numerous awards such as the Cultural Medallion (1987), the SEA Write Award (1993), the Anugerah Tun Seri Lanang (1993) and the Public Service Star (2000). He was a founding member of Angkatan Sasterawan '50 (Asas '50), an important Malay literary organisation in the development Malay literature, and was often regarded as an expert in Malay language, literature and culture.

Noor Hasnah Adam
Noor Hasnah Adam is an educator, a poet and a short story writer. She received numerous awards for her works including the Second Prize in the Golden Point Awards for "Anak Harimau" (Tiger's Cub) in 2001 and the Goh Chok Tong Youth Promise Award (Distinction) in 2008 for her contributions in literature, education and her excellent academic performance at the University of Malaya, having graduated with First Class Honours in Malay Studies.

Suratman Markasan
Suratman Markasan is a prolific author who is also an educator, poet, and essayist. He has received the Southeast Asia Write Award (1989), the Mont Blanc-NUS Centre for the Arts Award (1997), the Tun Seri Lanang Award (1999), the Nusantara Literary Award (1999), and the Cultural Medallion (2011). He was also an active member of the Angkatan Sasterawan '50 (Asas '50) and the Singapore Malay Teachers' Union.

COMMUNITY, SOCIAL WORK & PHILANTHROPY

Che Zahara Binte Noor Mohammed (1907–1962)
Che Zahara Noor Mohammed was the founder of Singapore's first Muslim women's welfare organisation, the Malay Women's Welfare Association (MWWA) in 1947, the first of its kind to offer shelter to destitute women and orphans. Che Zahara had campaigned to change the legal age for girls to get married, from nine years old previously to 16. In 1955, Che Zahara represented Singapore at the World Congress

of Mothers in Switzerland, and worked with the Singapore Council of Women to establish the Women's Charter of Singapore, enarted by Parliament in 1961.

Haji Abu Bakar Maidin (1927–2013)

Haji Abu Bakar Maidin won the Berita Harian Achiever of the Year Award in 2004 for his outstanding contributions to community services as the President of Jamiyah, one of the largest Muslim welfare organisations in Singapore, for 30 years. He was also chairman of the Education Trust Fund (ETF) working committee, a fund-raising initiative to fund pre-school education of needy children.

Hajjah Fatimah Binte Sulaiman (Est 1754–1852)

Businesswoman and philanthropist Hajjah Fatimah Sulaiman was one of the earliest traders in the history of modern Singapore. She donated the land where her house stood in Kampong Gelam, and provided funds for the construction of a mosque, Masjid Hajjah Fatimah, which is now gazetted as a national monument in 1973. She also donated generously to help the needy in Singapore, and built houses to shelter the destitute.

Khatijun Nissa Siraj

Khatijun Nissa Siraj was one of the founders of the Young Women's Muslim Association (now known as PPIS) in 1952. The group's effort in advocating for laws to better protect Muslims eventually led to the formation of the Syariah Court in 1958. Khatijun became the first female counsellor at the Syariah Court in 1960. Her exposure to the problems faced while in that position led her to start the Muslim Women's Welfare Council, providing charity, welfare, and legal and medical advice to Muslim women.

Ridzwan Dzafir (1927–2011)

Affectionately known as "Mr ASEAN" or "Pak Wan", Ridzwan Dzafir was a stellar civil servant best known for his extensive experience in trade. He was also actively involved in leading the Malay/Muslim community in his capacity as the President of the Islamic Religious Council of Singapore (MUIS), having restructured it into a professional organisation with a clear mission of leading Malay/Muslim Singaporeans to excellence in all fields; as the CEO of self-help group MENDAKI in 1990, restructuring the organisation and its programmes by bringing economic and socio-cultural matters under its purview; as well as chairing the working group which established the Malay Heritage Centre in Kampong Gelam in 1999 and becoming the Chairman of the Malay Heritage Foundation which manages the centre.

Beginning his career in the civil service as a junior customs officer, Ridzwan soon rose in ranks to become the Director-General of the then Trade Development Board (now known as International Enterprise Singapore). He was also instrumental in the setting up of the Singapore High Commission in Kuala Lumpur, and the Singapore Embassy in Jakarta when the country became independent. He continued to head the Trade Development Board till 1999, and led the Singapore team to ASEAN's senior economic officials meetings. Ridzwan played an important role promoting Singapore's free trade agenda, and was highly involved in the negotiations that resulted in the establishment of the ASEAN Free Trade Area (AFTA) and the Common Effective Preferential Tarriff (CEPT) scheme. He also frequently participated in Singapore's delegations to the General Agreement on Tariffs and Trade — GATT (now known as the World Trade Organization) meetings.

Locally, he was awarded the Public Administration Medal (Gold) in 1981, the Public Service Star (1990) and the Meritorious Service Award (1993) and the Exemplary Award from the Bawean Association of Singapore (1999) for his contributions to the nation and community. His other awards include the Royal Decoration of the Order of the White Elephant (2nd class) from the government of Thailand in 1984, the Grand Cross of the Order of the Liberator General San Martin from the government of Argentina in 1987, the Order of Bernardo O'Higgins Gran Cruz from the government of Chile (1996).

After his passing, Prime Minister Lee Hsien Loong wrote of his significant contributions in his letter to Ridzwan's widow Mushrifah. It was Pak Wan that had "persuaded successful Malays to help fellow Malays in need." Other government and community leaders followed suit and paid tribute to his contributions to Singapore's trade, and his work with the Malay/Muslim community.

Syed Ali Redha Alsagoff (1928–1998)
Dubbed "Father of Scholarships", Syed Ali Redha Alsagoff was concerned with the large number of poor Malay/Muslim students who failed to continue their education. In 1965, he rallied more than 73 organisations and founded LBKM, The Prophet Muhammad's Scholarship Fund Board, an organisation that offers financial assistance to needy students. He will always be remembered as the founder of the Prophet Muhammad's Birthday Memorial Scholarship Fund Board (LBKM). Apart from leading LBKM for 30 years since its inception in 1965, he also rendered his services in many other areas, from politics to education and religious studies and from community work to business and other fields. In the course of a lifetime of service, Syed Ali received many awards and accolades, including the "Kesatria Mangku Negara" (K.M.N.) by Malaysia's King on 3rd June 1965, when Singapore was still part of the Malaysian Federation. He also received the Public Service Medal. In 1995, he was awarded LBKM's highest honour, "Jasa Gemilang".

Zulkifli Baharuddin
Zulkifli Baharuddin won the Berita Harian Achiever of the Year award in 2005, when he helmed humanitarian organisation, Mercy Relief, growing it into an internationally-recognised organisation with financial support from both local and international businesses. He was also a popular Nominated Member of Parliament (NMP) from 1997 to 2001.

RELIGIOUS LEADERS

Abu Bakar Hashim (1934–2005)
A graduate of Al-Azhar University with a Masters in Islamic Law, Ustaz Abu Bakar Hashim was appointed as Registrar at the Registry of Muslim Marriages, and in 1984, he was appointed as President of the Syariah Court for 10 years. Seeking to rectify rising divorce rates among Malay/Muslim marriages, Ustaz Abu Bakar pioneered the Marriage Preparatory Course, and made it compulsory for all Singaporean Muslims who intended to get married. For his contributions, he was awarded the Anugerah Jasa Cemerlang by MUIS in 1994.

Ahmad Sonhadji Mohamad Milatu (1922–2010)
Ahmad Sonhadji Mohamad Milatu was a prominent religious scholar who played a critical role in the development of Islamic education and the nurturing of *ulamas* in Singapore and the region. He was one of the founding members of PERGAS. He also authored an instructional book on Islamic prayers *Mari Sembahyang* (Let's Pray), used by most Muslim Singaporeans and has also been reprinted and translated into various languages such as Korean and Sinhalese. He was awarded the Public Service Medal (1988) and the Anugerah Jasa Cemerlang (1992) by MUIS for his contributions.

Ahmad Zuhri Mutammim (1905–1985)
Ahmad Zuhri Mutammim was a prominent religious leader instrumental in the founding of PERGAS (Singapore Islamic Scholars and Religious Teachers Association) in 1954, and served as its first president. With Kiyai Zuhri, as he was affectionately known, at the helm of PERGAS, the organisation convinced the government to include Islamic religious subject in Malay schools and to pay its teachers. To this day, PERGAS continues his mission of protecting Islamic educators and Muslim education. In 2014, Prime Minister Lee Hsien Loong announced in his National Day Rally speech

that Madrasah Al-Irsyad Al-Islamiyah was to be renamed Madrasah Irsyad Zuhri Al-Islamiah, in honour of Kiyai Zuhri's contributions.

Alfian Yasrif bin Kuchit
Alfian Yasrif Kuchit was the Syariah Court's youngest President. He holds a bachelor's degree in Syariah from the International Islamic University Malaysia and a Master's in Law from University of Columbia, US.

Embek Ali (1929–2008)
Ustaz Embek Ali was one of the founders of PERDAUS, a Muslim organisation dedicated to community development through the organisation of religious development and human capital development programmes. He is best known for helming efforts to eradicate deviant religious teachings in Singapore and has compiled his findings in the book *Noktah Hitam: Ajaran Sesat di Singapura* (The Black Dot: Deviant Teachings in Singapore).

Ustaz Mohamad Hasbi Hassan
Ustaz Hasbi has been President of the Singapore Islamic Scholars and Religious Teachers Association (PERGAS) since 2003. He is also the co-founder and co-chairman of the Religious Rehabilitation Group (RRG), an organisation that was awarded the Berita Harian Achiever of the Year Award in 2014. He also serves on the MUIS Fatwa Committee as well as the Asatizah Recognition Board. He graduated with Bachelor's degree in Islamic Theology from Al-Azhar University in Cairo, Egypt.

Dr Mohamed Fatris Bakaram
Dr Mohamed Fatris Bakaram is currently the Mufti at the Islamic Religious Council of Singapore (MUIS). An alumni of Madrasah Aljunied, he went on to the Al-Azhar University in Cairo, Egypt. He has a Master's in Islamic Education from the International Islamic University Malaysia, and a PhD in Islamic Studies at Britain's University of Birmingham in 2010.

Mohammad Alami Musa
Alami Musa served as President of MUIS from 2003 to 2013. He is currently the Head of Studies in Inter-Religious Relations in Plural Societies at the S. Rajaratnam School of International Studies (RSIS) at Nanyang Technological University (NTU). He is also the Non-Executive President of MUIS, Non-Resident Ambassador to Algeria and the Honorary Business Representative for Middle East and North Africa for International Enterprise (IE).

Ustaz Syed Abdillah Ahmad Al-Jufri (1938–2003)
A well-known and respected *ulama*, Ustaz Syed Abdillah started his career as a teacher with the Ministry of Education (MOE). He was tasked by MOE to set up the curriculum and write the textbook for Islamic Religious Knowledge in the early 1980s, when Islamic Religious Knowledge was a school subject and was one of the components of Religious Studies for upper secondary students. In 1999, he was appointed President of the Singapore Islamic Scholars and Religious Teachers Association (PERGAS). He was one of the longest serving members of the MUIS Fatwa Council. Also a prolific author, he has written, co-authored and translated many books, and wrote numerous articles and Friday sermons.

Ustaz Tarmizi Wahid
An alumni of Madrasah Aljunied Al-Islamiah, he graduated with a diploma in Islamic Jurisprudence from MARSAH, an Islamic higher institution in Malaysia and received the Mufti of Johor award upon completing his studies there. In 2006, he graduated with a degree in Islamic Law from the Al-Azhar University in Cairo, Egypt. He then worked for MUIS in the Office of the Mufti. He is now the founder and co-owner of Safinah Institute, an organisation providing quality Islamic education for adults.

BUSINESS & ENTREPRENEURSHIP

Aziza Ali
Businesswoman, food consultant and cookbook author Aziza Ali was the first Malay lady recognised with opening Singapore's first Malay restaurant and bringing fine dining for the Malay cuisine to Singaporeans. Opened in 1979 on Emerald Hill Road, Aziza Restaurant was Singapore's first fine-dining Malay restaurant, and was patronised by Dione Warwick and James Ingram. Known for its specialty dish of spicy beef rendang, Aziza Restaurant won Singapore Tourism Board's Best Dining Experience (1996), and she was invited to cook the dishes served at the restaurant all around the world for more than 13 years. In 2011, Aziza was also appointed one of the judiciary council members of the prestigious Culinary Institute of America (CIA). She has authored a few books, "Aziza's Creative Malay Cuisine" and "Sambal Days, Kampong Cuisine" and is currently working on other book projects. Aziza is also a self-taught artist — she has produced more than 160 paintings, and designs and sells her own handmade jewellery.

Haji Hashim Haji Abdullah (1900–1968)
The bookstore started by Haji Hashim Haji Abdullah, now popularly known as Kedai Haji Hashim (Haji Hashim's Bookstore), still in business at Joo Chiat Complex is Haji Hashim's second bookstore. In its prime, the bookstore distributed books to local schools as well as to countries in the region. Today, it continues his legacy as a haven of knowledge for the Malay community, and is still held in high regard by the Malay/Muslim community.

Mohamed Salleh Marican
Mr Mohamed Salleh Marican is the founder, Chairman and Managing Director of the Second Chance Properties Ltd, a retail and property group. His company is the first Malay/Muslim-owned firm to be listed on the Singapore Exchange (SGX) Main Board. A businessman with 33 years of retail experience, his stores "First Lady" and "Golden Chance", specialising in traditional Malay wear and gold respectively, have become a household name in the Malay community. He is also the winner of the Berita Harian Achiever of the Year Award in 2011.

Po'ad Mattar
Po'ad Mattar was appointed as a Member of the Public Service Commission in February 2004. An accountant by training, Mr Mattar had held various positions in Deloitte & Touche before becoming its Senior Partner in 2002. He retired from this position on 28 Feb 2006. He served as a Director of MediaCorp TV Singapore Private Limited (formerly Television Corporation Singapore) between 1994 and 1999. From 1992 to 2003, he was a member of the Ngee Ann Polytechnic Council. He was also a Board member of the Public Utilities Board from 1 Apr 2001 to 31 Mar 2007 and was a director of its wholly-owned subsidiary, PUB Consultants Private Limited from 1 Apr 2004 to 31 Mar 2010. Currently he is a member of the Council of Presidential Advisers and a Pro-Chancellor of the National University of Singapore. In addition, he sits on the Board of Directors of listed companies, Hong Leong Finance Limited and Tiger Airways Holdings Limited, as well as on the Board of Directors of unlisted companies, Keppel Offshore & Marine Ltd and NIE International Private Limited.

Sa'at Ismail
Sa'at Ismail is the creative director of Silicon+, a communications company offering services for branding and marketing exercises, with a diverse portfolio of clientele ranging from healthcare, finance, education and the public service. With the passion

and dedication towards his work, multi award-winning Silicon+ is one of Singapore's leading communications company.

Suhaimi Salleh

Suhaimi Salleh is the CEO of SSA Consulting Group, a company that offers professional services in management consulting, public accounting and assurance and estate planning. His company was recognised as one of the top 1000 SMEs in Singapore in 2010 and 2011. He is also active in community service, and is constantly invited to speak at major conferences in Singapore and the region. He is the current President of LBKM Scholarship Fund Board.

Accolades

Winners of the Berita Harian Achiever of the Year Award
Hadiah Jauhari

1999 - Dr Mansoor Abdul Jalil, lecturer with the Department of Electrical Engineering at the National University of Singapore (NUS)

2000 - Professor Aziz Nather, director at the Tissue Bank and consultant with the Department of Orthopaedic Surgery at NUS

2001 - Madam Halimah Yacob, Assistant Secretary General of NTUC

2002 - Mr Iskandar Jalil, master potter

2003 - Mr Iskandar Mirza Ismail, veteran composer

2004 - Haji Abu Bakar Maidin, a veteran of social service

2005 - Mr Zulkifli Baharudin, Chairman of Mercy Relief

2006 - Mr Mardan Mamat, millionaire golfer

2007 - Mr Ashley Isham, fashion designer

2008 - Datuk Mohd Zain Abdullah, accomplished businessman in the shipping industry

2009 - Madam Som Binte Mohamed Said, cultural ambassador

2010 - Mr Shafie Shamsudin, Chief Executive Officer of Carrefour Indonesia

2011 - Mr Mohamed Salleh Marican, Chairman and Managing Director of SCP

2012 - Mr Suhaimi Rafdi, Chief Executive Officer, Cathay Organisation

2013 - Dr Abdul Razakjr Omar, Cardiologist

2014 - Religious Rehabilitation Group (RRG)

2015 - Alami Musa, President MUIS

Berita Harian Inspiring Young Achiever Award

2013 - Mr Adil Hakeem Mohd Rafee

2014 - Saiyidah Aisyah Mohammed Rafa'ee

2015 - Amalina Ridzuan and Mr Ahmad Abdurrahman Hanifah Marican

2015 Pioneer Generation Achiever Award Winners

Dr Muhammad Ariff Ahmad, Malay language Cultural specialist
Shaikh Syed Isa Semait, former Mufti of Singapore
Sarkasi Said, batik artist

Cultural Medallion
Malay Winners

1979 - Bani Buang (Theatre)
1981 - Ahmad Jaafar (Music)
1986 - Nadiputra (Theatre)
1987 - Muhd Ariff Ahmad (Literary Arts)
1988 - Iskandar Jalil (Visual Arts)
1999 - Abdul Ghani Bin Abdul Hamid (Literary Arts)
2007 - Isa Kamari (Literary Arts)
2008 - Iskandar Mirza Ismail (Music)
2010 - Suratman Markasan (Literary Arts)
2011 - Yusnor Ef (Music)
2011 - Halimah Bte Jaafar (Theatre)
2013 - Mohamed Latiff Mohamed (Literary Arts)

Institution of the Young Artist Award
Malay winners

1992 - Jamaludin Jalil (Dance)
1993 - Osman Bin Abdul Hamid (Dance)
1995 - Mohamed Noor Bin Sarman (Dance)
2001 - Alfian Bin Sa'at (Literary Arts)
2008 - Aidli Mosbit (Theatre)
2012 - Zizi Azah bte Abdul Majid (Theatre)

*From 2013, recipients of the Cultural Medallion and Young Artist Award will no longer be categorised according to art forms.

2013 - Bani Haykal
2013 - Siti Khalijah Zainal
2015 - Riduan Zalani

Malay/Muslim Organisations

Just like government agencies, Malay/Muslim Organisations (MMOs) play equally important roles in helping the Malay/Muslim community as the young nation grapples with post-independence turmoil and uncertainty. Each organisation brings its particular expertise, experience and also reaches out to its own segment of the community collectively by working together in the spirit of *gotong-royong*. As the nation progresses, the MMOs will continue to evolve and innovate to meet the community's requirements and expectations. This list highlights the contributions of the various organisations in areas such as education, social welfare, arts and culture.

JAMIYAH (EST. 1932)

The society was founded in 1932 by Moulana Abdul Aleem Siddiqui, the Roving Ambassador of Peace from Meerut, India together with other religious leaders in Singapore and Malaya at that time. JAMIYAH was then known as the All-Malaya Muslim Missionary Society with branches in the various states of Malaysia. After Separation from Malaysia, the name was changed to the Muslim Missionary Society Singapore or Jamiyah Singapore. Jamiyah aims to be the promoter of missionary, education, knowledge and welfare for the Muslim community and mankind. Besides propagating and defending the teachings of Islam and the well-being of Muslims, they also endeavor to promote inter-faith and multiracial harmony and provide welfare services for the benefit of the community regardless of race or religion.

Jamiyah has made a valuable contribution to the Malay/Muslim community. It has focused on education as the foundation for social mobility. They established a Jamiyah kindergarten, child care centres and a Jamiyah Business School. In addition, it has three student care centres that provide care, supplementary enrichment programmes, tuition and recreational activities for students aged 7 to 16 years old. It also operates four homes: for the less fortunate, orphans and disadvantaged children at Darul Ma'awa, residential nursing care for the aged sick at Darul Syifaa, substance abusers at Darul Islah and destitute seniors at Darul Takrim. A free medical clinic and legal advice for the needy is also available led by a team of volunteer doctors and lawyers. For their members, Jamiyah holds religious education forums for the general public and also organises the weekend *madrasah* classes at the Jamiyah Education Centre and offer diploma and degree programmes on Islamic Studies through collaboration with external universities. With respect to Islamic issues, Jamiyah is non-confrontational in its propagation of Islamic values. It generally prefers to engage the relevant authorities through letters on issues of concern to the community.

Jamiyah is well-known for their close collaboration and strong partnership with other volunteer organisations of other ethnic groups and faiths such as with the Singapore SOKA Association, Singapore Christian Home, The Church of Jesus Christ of the Latter-day Saints, Buddhist Lodge, Inter-Religious Organisation to organise festive celebrations for the less fortunate. Jamiyah leaders are also a strong advocate of strengthening friendship bonds and has done so with the Taoist Federation of Singapore and the Loyang Tua Pek Kong Temple in conjunction with the Lunar New Year.

4PM PERSATUAN PERSURATAN PEMUDA PEMUDI MELAYU (EST. 1948)

Being known as 4PM (pronounced Empat-P-M), coming from the initials of the organisation's name in Malay, Persatuan Persuratan Pemuda Pemudi Melayu, which has four Ps and one M, it began as a youth development society within the Malay/Muslim community just after World War II. Hanifa S. Kanoo, Mohd Yatim Dohon, Syed Ja'afar Almenor, Hussein Bin Mohd Ali and Tengku Abdullah Bin Tenku Omar were the main initiators in the setting up of 4PM who saw the importance of education in the development and success of the Malay community. The association's main focus during its formative years was, therefore, on education and the promotion of the Malay language. During the initial years of 4PM's formation, they trail blazed by establishing a community school at Kampong Serangoon Kecil and a second school, Sekolah Serangoon Kechil.

But 4PM is iconic for organising its namesake debates, the annual *Bahas 4PM* or 4PM Debates which is an inter-school debate competition targeted at primary and secondary school students to promote the use of the Malay language. But the annual debates did not have a continuous run since its inception and was revived in

1993 by 4PM as an annual event for pre-university students from junior colleges, polytechnics and *madrasah* instead.

Their motto of "unite and serve" has been the guiding principle in their approach towards community work. 4PM envisions offering holistic community engagement services in areas that cover social welfare, youth development, literacy, mentoring, and casework management. Working with both youth leaders and youths-at-risk, the services rendered include the setting up of a debating academy to train future debaters, professional counseling and social work services for at-risk children, youths and families and a mentoring and school social work programme for ITE students to help them grow, develop and inculcate in them the values for lifelong, independent learning and an entrepreneurial spirit. Lately, 4PM has been known for their multiracial community service "Ramadhan On Wheels (ROW)" which fosters the spirit of helping the less fortunate by involving the large 4PM volunteers to either deliver donated food provisions, sponsoring new clothes, do a home make-over, or spring cleaning for low income families. Since its inception in 2000, ROW has assisted more than 2000 Singaporean families and built a 7000-strong volunteer force of all races and faiths. Volunteers come from private organisations, schools and tertiary institutions, government departments, as well as social groups. The ROW event generally happens in the month of Ramadhan, the Muslim fasting month, but 4PM is now extending the ROW service period beyond a month to enable a more in-depth delivery of volunteer services to meet the different needs of the client group.

PPIS/ SINGAPORE MUSLIM WOMEN'S ASSOCIATION (EST. 1952)

Since its inception in 1952, PPIS or Singapore Muslim Women's Association has been conducting various services, talks, activities, courses and programmes for Malay/Muslim women in their bid to empower them. Sixty-three years ago, a group of 22 like-minded women came together to set up PPIS, with the vision to create opportunities for women's advancement and progress; and to address the needs and interest of women in their role towards building strong families.

In the first decade, the founding members took it upon themselves to bring irresponsible husbands to court for alimony, implemented social programmes, and organised courses such as sewing, cooking, floral arrangements and literacy programmes for other women so that they can earn some money and be less dependent on their husbands.

Today, PPIS has evolved into a professionally-managed, non-profit Muslim women social service organisation with an approved IPC status. They have more than 180 full-time staff running 14 centres island-wide and a 100-strong active volunteer group. PPIS has reached out to more than 300,000 clients through its service centres over the years. Commonly, PPIS runs two core community services; namely social services and child development services. These involve working with underprivileged families and children from the low-income group, who have low education and low self-esteem. They also assist single parents and their children and those who might have gone through traumas and have difficulties moving on in life.

The PPIS services offered include: the running of six full-day childcare services; organising courses for couples who are remarrying; providing a one stop centre on pre-marital marriage counseling for young and minor couples; a support centre for families and children facing death or divorce; a before-and-after-school care service and offering professional consultancy on family therapy and the training of support professionals that work with their Malay/Muslim clients.

MUHAMMADIYAH ASSOCIATION (EST. 1957)

The association was set up by a group of students from Madrasah Raudatil Atfal and students of the late Ustaz Abdul Rahman Harun, Ustaz Rijal Abdullah and Ustaz Amir Esa.

The advent of Muhammadiyah was inspired by the spirit to appreciate and implement the exhortation of the Al-Quran as follows: "Let there arise out of you a band of people inviting to all that is good, enjoining what is right and forbidding what is wrong. They are the ones to attain felicity." (Surah Ali-Imran, 3:104). This verse behest all believers to organise themselves and call upon mankind to kindness by doing what is good and forbidding what is wrong.

The aims and objectives of Muhammadiyah are as follows:

- To revive the correct teachings of Islam and be a missionary movement
- To function as an agent of social change
- To be a center of Islamic knowledge

The Muhammadiyah operates on the following principles: Upholding and implementing (wherever possible) Islamic values, culture and the way of life in accordance with the Qur'an and the Sunnah; the belief in the unity of Allah as manifested in all facets of life including matters relating to living in a secular country, our role in a multireligious society and our duties as ordinary citizens; fostering greater unity and co-operation among the wider Muslim *ummah*.

Besides conducting Islamic religious study classes for youths and adults, they also run an Islamic college offering Diploma and Bachelor degree programmes, a madrasah that emphasises Islamic values in character development and prepares students for the GCE 'O' level examinations, a kindergarten and also run funeral and pilgrimage services. The Association also manages a welfare home for male teens who were abused and neglected and those who are beyond parental control. The Muhammadiyah Welfare Home has been gazetted as a "Place of Safety", 'Juvenile Rehabilitation Centre' and 'Place of Temporary Care and Protection' by the state authority.

PERGAS (EST. 1957)

PERGAS (Singapore Islamic Scholars and Religious Teachers Association) envisions a "Religious Leadership that is Credible, Integrated and Contributing towards the Development of The Community". They are dedicated to nurture religious teachers who will not only be missionaries but also develop into intellectual and community leaders. The Association is an independent, self-funded entity that relies on its own investments and contributions from the Muslim community. PERGAS is more than just an association of *ulama* or scholars and religious teachers, but over the years, their role has been perceived as "guardians" or "guarantors" of the local Muslim community in addition to being spiritual and intellectual guides. PERGAS believes they should play the role of the "moral anchor" or the "conscience" of the Singaporean Muslim community.

The role of the Islamic scholars and religious teachers (*asatizah*) have transformed to serve the increasing expectations and higher education levels of the Malay/Muslims community and the ever changing *dakwah* landscape in Singapore; from traditional leadership roles, to assuming more versatile roles that contribute towards shaping positive public opinion of the Muslim community.

As an organisation that "Upholds the legacy of the Prophet", PERGAS strives to participate actively in Singapore's civil society. They have done so through public engagement on issues pertaining to the Muslim community, *viz.* the Compulsory Education (2000); the *hijab* or *tudung* issue in National Schools (2002); Jemaah Islamiah Arrest (2002/03); Casino and Gambling Proposals (2004); Israeli aggression on Palestine (2008); Danish cartoon caricature (2007); Homosexual and Gay rights (2008); Innocence of the Muslim Movie (2012), Gaza Crisis (2012); Myanmar Rohingya Mass Killing (2013); Merciless Killing in Rabaah (2013); Tudung Issue in the Uniform Service (2013); Health Promotion Board FAQ on Sexuality (2014). Since 2006, PERGAS has also been entrusted by MUIS to administer the Asatizah Recognition Scheme; a scheme set up to stamp out deviant religious teachings. Additionally, PERGAS executive committee members have been invited to sit as core members on the MUIS Fatwa Legal Committee.

PERDAUS (EST. 1963)

PERDAUS (Association of Adult Religious Class Student of Singapore) has a 52-year history of providing welfare, educational and leadership development services to the community. Their mission is to inspire consciousness, nurture lives, empower families and build communities. This organisation was founded by students of the late Syed Abdillah Balfakeh — former principal of Madrasah Aljunied Al-Islamiah; the late Ustaz Haji Daud Ali, the late Kyai Haji Ahmad Zohri Mutamin and the late Kyai Haji Mohd Fadhullah Suhaimi. The formation of PERDAUS was in response to the rapid growth and interest in adult Islamic knowledge instruction in the 1950s to 1960s to make the learning of Islamic religion more systematic and organised.

Today, PERDAUS has expanded its community services by providing child care services, organising *madrasah* classes for children and teenagers; offering certificate and advanced Islamic Studies programmes for young working adults and organising the annual *qurban* ritual and adult religious classes. The organisation provides spiritual upliftment and Islamic education programmes to members of the public, similar to other religious-based Muslim organisations here, to equip the community with critical knowledge and skills in the development of a virtuous and progressive society. In the 1980s, PERDAUS was the forefront of educating and fighting against deviant Islamic teachings found in the Singaporean Muslim community. In the late 1980s and early 1990s, PERDAUS was seen as the most vocal Muslim organisation in Singapore participating in public debates. When it came to promoting "Islamic" values, it was perceived as a "conservative" organisation even though then their members averaged 30 to 40 years old. PERDAUS had positioned itself to be the new voice in Islam in Singapore's public sphere as the leaders then felt that other (Muslim) religious organisations were perceived to be too close to the government and thus cannot speak freely in public debates. PERDAUS's leaders projected Islam as a "rational" religion where there are spaces for contested interpretation to exist.

Of note, PERDAUS started Mercy Relief in 2003, a non-profit organisation that has been actively involved in many fundraising and humanitarian relief programmes. Mercy Relief has brought together many different races to perform humanitarian relief work. Today, Mercy Relief is an independent organisation in its own right with its own board of directors.

LBKM (EST. 1965)

The Prophet Muhammad's Birthday Memorial Scholarship Fund Board, or its Malay initials — LBKM — as it is better known, served as the premier bursary-disbursing institution for the community ever since its inception.

LBKM was formed in 1965 based on the vision of one man, Syed Ali Redha Alsagoff, the founder President, a successful businessman and community leader; and together with the support of representatives from 73 local Malay/Muslim organizations from Singapore and Malaysia, he rallied the community to set-up an institution to provide financial support to needy students to enable them to pursue their education to the highest levels. LBKM's mantra is "no one should be deprived of furthering one's education because of financial difficulty" and the financial assistance come in the form of bursaries, scholarships and research funding.

Since 1966, LBKM bursaries have been awarded to students from primary to postgraduate levels and for both secular and religious education. In 1966, the first 18 recipients received a total of $3,900 in bursaries. In 2015, 1,412 students received bursaries totaling S$1.6 million. Over a span of 50 years (1966–2015), over S$19 million worth of bursaries and study grants have been disbursed to more than 24,000 students with one in four recipients from the religious education stream.

In 2010, LBKM introduced the LBKM Prestigious Scholarship for undergraduate and postgraduate students studying at any one of the world's top 10 universities ranked by the Times Higher Education World University Rankings and the QS World University Rankings. As of 2014, five undergraduate and seven postgraduate students have been awarded the scholarship. In 2015, a new category, merit scholarship for undergraduate and post graduate was introduced.

Fund-raising activities initially came from direct donations from members of the public, annual Flag Day, and later through the organising of Gala Dinners, the hosting of charity Golf Tournaments, Maulud and Ramadhan Appeals, the Annual Rites of Sacrifice, Walkatons and Telepol. The LBKM also benefits and receives strong support and generosity from their donors and sponsors that include major local corporations such as HSBC Insurance Singapore, Luxasia Foundation, Prima Limited, PropNex, SSA Consultants, Syed Mohamed Traders, Tak Products, Tan Chin Tuan Foundation and Thye Hua Kwan Moral Society who have contributed generously to their bursary funds.

MAJLIS PUSAT (MP)/CENTRAL COUNCIL OF MALAY CULTURAL ORGANIZATIONS SINGAPORE (EST. 1969)

It is an umbrella body of 31 Malay organisations that was setup in 1969 to give voice and act as a collective effort towards self-help within the Malay community. To achieve this role, the central body became the coordinator of activities for its affiliated members so that resources are efficiently and effectively deployed to improve the community in the fields of education, language, culture, spiritual upliftment and economy. The other role MP played was to be the unofficial voice of the community representing Malay concerns and interests to issues and policies to respective government agencies.

During the early years after independence, MP worked towards uplifting the educational status of the community and did so by organising tuition classes for upper secondary and pre-university students with the Singapore Malay Teachers' Union collaboration. They were also involved in organising dialogue sessions and visits to those who stilled lived in the kampungs about national development programmes and the impact of the changing economy viz. high-rise living, national service. In the 1980s, there were 46 Malay and Muslim grassroots organisations under the MP umbrella but the numbers dropped in the early 1990s to 38 affiliates who are involved in the culture, arts, literary development, community service, welfare, youth and sports.

PERTAPIS (EST. 1970)

Pertapis's principal activity is the running of welfare projects designed to address some of the social challenges faced by the community. Their vision is to be the model social service provider for the community. Their welfare services are targeted to help the recovery of the substance abuser, support poor and needy families and the elderly destitute; shelter neglected and abused children from broken families and the rehabilitation of girls and women. In 1984, a Welfare Trust Fund was established with the objective of providing monthly household provisions to help the poor, elderly, destitute and needy families. The programme relies mainly on donations from kind-hearted individuals and charitable and corporate organisations. Each recipient receives rations comprising of rice, sugar, condensed milk, noodles, sardines and other daily necessities.

Other community activities that Pertapis provides includes offering moral education classes for young Muslims (by Pertapis Community Services Limited) and the provision of early childhood and kindergarten classes (under their Kiddy Campus franchise). They have also ventured into social enterprise to assist their halfway house tenants with vocation-cum-work therapy by offering male hairdressing services, digital art printing and household and corporate moving services. Like similar organisations, Pertapis faces the challenge of attracting committed volunteers and talented staff and in generating adequate funds to support the operations of their five welfare homes and community services.

HIMPUNAN BELIA ISLAM (HBI)/MUSLIM YOUTH ASSEMBLY (EST. 1972)

HBI was formed in 1972 as a Salafi/Sunni organisation with the motto, "To strive and defend the purity of Islamic teachings so as to create a society of firm believers who establish befitting acts". Of note, HBI is also a founder member of the Yayasan MENDAKI, the Malay/Muslim community self-help established in 1982. In 1985, HBI changed their orientation to become a Shia organisation after deep research and investigation on the Ahlul Bayt (People of the House [of the Prophet Muhammad]) school of thought and has since then, moved forward to promote the principles of Amar Bil Ma'ruf, Nahi anil Munkar (enjoining good and forbidding wrong). In 2014, there are about 200 registered HBI members and about 4000 Twelver Shias who are mostly ethnic Malays in Singapore.

Despite being a minority in the minority Muslim community, the Shia community is relatively vibrant. The Madrasah Az-Zahra is a weekend institution that provides comprehensive Shi'ah Ithna 'Ashari Islamic education to students of ages 7 to 19 years. The *madrasah* also occasionally organise functions to commemorate important Islamic dates such as the Martyrdom of Imam Husain A.S. and the birth anniversary of Imam Ali A.S. Every month, the Welfare Committee organises a grocery run that includes products such as rice, milk, sugar and vouchers that are given to needy families within the community. Representatives from the welfare bureau also conduct visits to the sick in hospitals or at their homes. HBI have actively collaborated with Pertapis and Jamiyah as part of the Community Leadership Forum (CLF) to organise visits and provide support to disadvantaged Malay/Muslim families. HBI members also have been active participants in 2009 Prophet Muhammad's Birthday Celebration Procession that featured representatives from other Muslim organisations in Singapore too.

DARUL ARQAM (EST. 1973)

Muslim Converts' Association of Singapore was conceived in the early 1970s as a body to provide religious guidance, welfare and support to those reverting or converting to Islam. In those days, they were known as Kumpulan Saudara Baru (New Brethren Group) and was formed with the purpose of providing a space for new Muslim converts to get together and develop the fraternal, religious and social relationships among themselves. The other alternate named associated with the Association is "Darul Arqam" which in Arabic stands for "House of Arqam". "Arqam" or Abu Abdullah Arqam bin Abi al-Arqam, was an early convert to Islam during the first three years of Prophet Muhammad's prophethood in Makkah and he had allowed his house to be used for the learning and propagation of Islam. The name of "Darul Arqam" thus, seems appropriate and it was officially established in 1980 as the newly-formed Muslim Converts' Association of Singapore.

The Association provides Islamic religious courses in English and Mandarin and basically deals with welfare, Islamic guidance and rendering financial and counselling assistance to the new converts. On top of these roles, the Association also functions as the official centre to coordinate all new conversions to Islam and to represent the interests of all Muslim converts residing in Singapore.

An early contribution of Darul Arqam to the larger Muslim community here is the organising of religious talks by Muslim and non-Muslim scholars from abroad. This is part of their *dakwah* or missionary strategy to shift local Muslim perceptions of the religion from a conservative and ritualistic orientation to one that also appeals to the intellect and is able to relate to modernity.

MKAC (EST. 1990)

The Muslim Kidney Action Association (MKAC) was founded as a non-profit social service organisation for the benefit of the chronically-ill members of the community that includes those suffering from kidney and organ failure patients and their families.

MKAC's approach in providing assistance to its clients is to offer a holistic support to both the kidney patient and their families, depending on the financial needs and circumstances of the family. MKAC has officers and Befriender volunteers that visit MKAC patients to provide targeted assistance, caseworker advocacy, financial subsidies and household assistance. For the families, of kidney patients, there are regular support group sessions that allows interaction with other kidney patients and family members to learn, exchange experiences and provide a social support network. Children of kidney patients have the opportunity to be coached and tutored in their school work to achieve better grades and to improve their confidence. Such support and assistance to children of kidney patients is critical because on-going treatments and the uncertainty of a stable family income takes a toll on the emotional, mental and physical strength of school children. As such, these children are also given life skills training by a group of dedicated MKAC mentors and friends to develop their resilience, confidence and self-esteem. On top of these, beneficiaries of MKAC are provided with skills upgrading programmes in sewing, making glass flowers and baking to help them consider starting a small business and to enhance their employment prospects.

Today, MKAC continues to focus on helping to improve the quality of life of kidney patients and their families via subsidies, enrichment programmes and family and community bonding sessions. These efforts are not exclusively limited to Muslims. MKAC has broadened operations to include an enrichment centre for the school-going children of kidney patients, a shelter for the homeless and the recent launch of a transport service to ferry kidney patients from their homes to the dialysis centre and then send them back home after dialysis.

MKAC is a registered charity with the Commissioner of Charities and a Full Member of the National Council of Social Services. Since 2004, MUIS has entrusted

MKAC to manage the affairs of 300 Muslim kidney patients who are MUIS *zakat* recipients. Through this authority, MUIS has empowered MKAC to disburse *zakat* funds to 30 of the 300 kidney patients as a form of financial assistance for the direct benefit of kidney patients.

MERCY RELIEF (EST. 2003)

Headquartered in Singapore, Mercy Relief was established in 2003 to respond to human tragedies and disasters in Asia–Pacific.

Today, they are Singapore's leading independent disaster relief agency with dedicated leadership, capacity building expertise and an affiliate network operating across the entire disaster management cycle.

Mercy Relief provides emergency aid within 72 hours of an appeal in the aftermath of a disaster. Their longer-term sustainable development projects aim to uplift and empower communities in five key areas: water and sanitation, shelter, sustainable livelihoods, healthcare and education. For the past decade, Mercy Relief has responded to more than 56 human tragedies with more than $32.5 million in relief across 24 countries. They have implemented more than 50 sustainable development initiatives and impacted an aggregate of over two million lives.

ADAM ASSOCIATION

ADAM Association was formed in 2004 to fill a critical gap in addressing issues faced by men in Singapore. It has previously carried out many activities aimed at improving the family nucleus through empowering family leaders with knowledge and aptitude to foster a close-knit family circle. The acronym ADAM was derived from Association for Devoted and Active FamilyMen.

AIN SOCIETY

Ain Society was founded in 2000 by 12 activists who resided in Woodlands mainly to serve the residents in that area. As it grew in confidence, its target group has widened not only to the residents in the north, but also island-wide. 'Ain' means 'eyes' in Arabic. It is chosen to symbolise as the 'eyes' of the community to foresee and address social problems in the community especially among the youths and disadvantaged families. The tag line 'Love, Care, Concern' has recently been added to their corporate logo.

CASA RAUDHA WOMEN HOME

Casa Raudha Women Home was officially founded in 2008, with a primary goal to provide temporary shelter and new beginnings for women who were victims of domestic violence and abuse. Now entering its fifth year, Casa Raudha has come a long way from the small office it once occupied in a building along Sims Avenue to its current site today. Although Casa Raudha initially started out as an organisation whose aim was to provide refuge for mistreated Muslim women and children, the shelter welcomes women and their children of all races and religion that require protection.

CLUB HEAL

Club HEAL has been registered with the Registry of Societies on 13 February 2012 by a group of like-minded individuals who have a strong passion in helping people with mental illness and their family members lead a fulfilling and stigma-free life. They run a psychiatric rehabilitation day care service in which psycho-education and supportive counseling to persons with mental illness and their families are provided.

They also provide outreach programs to them and the general public.
While the Club Heal day rehabilitation service caters to the needs of Muslims, they welcome anyone experiencing mental illness, regardless of race or religion.

HIRA SOCIETY

HIRA Society was established as a registered society under the Registrar of Societies on 14 March 2013 and has been accorded the Charity Status on 20 May 2013. At the start, HIRA was greatly involved with the socio-economic development of the Muslim community by organising events with local bodies in order to contribute to the development of the society. HIRA Society was set up as a Voluntary Welfare Organisation (VWO) with the intention of targeting the ex-drug addicts and families who face financial, emotional, accommodation and other related issues.

CONCLUSION

CONCLUSION

MALAY/MUSLIM COMMUNITY — GETTING READY FOR SG100

Norshahril Saat

In 2015, Singaporeans mourn the loss of their founding Prime Minister, Mr Lee Kuan Yew, but at the same time, celebrate the country's achievements for the last 50 years of independence. The Malay/Muslim community can also be proud by what it has achieved: It played its part in contributing to the country's success, and will continue to do so. The articles in *Majulah! 50 Years of Malay/Muslim Community in Singapore* highlight the community's achievements and future challenges in politics, education, religion, arts, literature and economics. The publication of this book this year is timely; since we have concluded the SG50 celebrations, in 2016, we should contemplate on the future challenges, as we move towards SG100. The following paragraphs highlight my vision for the Malay/Muslim community and the role they can continue to play as Singapore progresses into a mature, developed country. These are mainly my critical reflections and in many ways idealistic. My hope is to generate intellectual stretching within the community, especially our youths, as we write the next course of Singapore's success story.

Undeniably, Singapore developed from the third world country — when it gained independence in 1965 — to a developed country within three decades. Many works have discussed this tremendous achievement, and it is not within the scope of this book to do so. Both of Lee Kuan Yew's memoirs, *The Singapore Story* and *From Third World to First*: *1965–2000* serve as good starting points to understand the challenges our pioneers faced in building Singapore.[a] In 2015, there are also many publications which mark Singapore's Jubilee celebration that highlight similar themes.

---

[a] Lee Kuan Yew, *Memoirs of Lee Kuan Yew: The Singapore Story*, (Singapore: Singapore Press Holdings; Times Editions, 1998); Lee Kuan Yew, *Memoirs of Lee Kuan Yew, From Third World To First The Singapore Story:1965–2000* (Singapore Press Holdings; Times Editions, 2000).

Yet, what are the challenges that the country will face after it achieved developed status? The signs are already there: greater polarisation in society, both inter-ethnic and intra-ethnic; stronger calls for freedom of expression; deeper involvement of civil society *vis-á-vis* the state in public discourse; and starker incorporation of global cultures and fashion by locals. Is the Malay/Muslim community ready for these challenges?

As we reflect on ways to improve the conditions of our community, we naturally look back at our pioneers. Two outstanding pioneers highlighted in this book are Encik Yusof Ishak and Pak Zubir Said.[b] Their contributions transcend the community and they are national icons: Encik Yusof as the Republic's first president, and Pak Zubir as the composer of the national anthem. The two icons embody the community's devotion and loyalty to the state. They had the option to move to Malaysia, but chose to stay and struggle as minorities. Even though other Singapore Malays could not match the scale of Encik Yusof's and Pak Zubir's, contributions, they have been part of mainstream Singapore. For example, they serve National Service steadfastly, participate with gusto at Singapore's National Day celebrations, and contribute in many ways that keep Singapore's economy tick. I am confident the community will continue to strive in ensuring Singapore's success and urge the state to recognise their efforts.

Readiness to Change

However, any reflections about the future through thinking of the past only would not suffice. Contemporary challenges are different from what the pioneer generation faced. Existing challenges will also evolve and the process of fine-tuning policies to meet them will be never-ending. In the last 50 years, the Singapore government had made several important decisions, including reversing past ones to meet new challenges. For example, in the 1980s, the government implemented the "Stop at Two" policy to reduce population growth, ensuring sustainable demography crucial for the development of a young nation back then. Couples were allowed to have at most two children, in order to reduce the size of the family significantly. Today, in the likelihood that the country is facing a greying population, the government encourages couples to have three or more children. Singaporeans generally welcome the government's readiness to change its policies; yet, the effect of such changes will be limited because values among Singaporeans have changed, which are now similar with those of other developed countries.

To illustrate further, the government under Prime Minister Lee Hsien Loong allowed for casinos to operate in Singapore, even though it is a sensitive subject for many religious groups. This episode shows how policies need to change for the

---

[b] See earlier chapters on both individuals. See also Norshahril Saat, *Yusof Ishak: Singapore's First President* (Singapore: ISEAS, 2015).

country's survival. It was also under the current government that the government has moved to the left of the political spectrum, by implementing the Pioneer Generation scheme, to help senior citizens cope with retirement, even though the term "welfarism" was a taboo in the past.

Thus, policies and approaches to problems change, but the biggest challenge is how the government communicates it to the public. In other words, one cannot predict what the conditions it will be in the next 50 years, but what the community needs to do is to be constantly vigilant of global trends and opportunities, and ready to tweak their positions.

Can the Malays Change?

Readiness to change positions and strategies does not mean compromising religious values and Malay traditions. In sociology, the concept of tradition allows for change if a practice appears redundant. There will always be extreme thinking which says religion is obsolete as the community progresses. On the contrary, religious values such as hard work, equality and justice, accountability, progress, discipline remain relevant, though they have to be operationalised in ways to meet contemporary challenges.

However, the community needs to move away from old debates, especially in the religious traditions. Today, we still hear questions being raised by some religious elites regarding the validity of *maulid* (celebration of Prophet's birthday) or visitations to graves in Islam. These are centuries old debates that can never be resolved. I also concur with Habib Syed Hassan Al-Attas (see chapter 21) of the need to move the discourse away from rituals. Rather Malays/Muslims should think how they can best serve in modernising Singapore.

To be sure, by overemphasising on religious rituals, the community struggles to grapple with alternative lifestyles of modern living. Their solutions to issues concentrate on rightness or wrongness (*halal* and *haram*), rather than accepting differences in plural society. In this aspect, the religious elites, alongside other community leaders must play their part to discuss the problems. They should refrain from rhetorically saying that Islam has solutions for all problems and ignore the contributions of non-Muslims towards progress. The community needs a holistic approach in solving problems and the religious elites need to involve social scientists, doctors, engineers, lawyers and other professionals.

The community may pride itself with more Malays/Muslims doing well in education and these include *madrasah* graduates. Many more from the community are doing Masters and PhDs. However, the community has to raise standards for success beyond academic achievements. Also, it has to relook at different modes of learning beyond what is taught in religious schools today. Today, the Ministry of Education has made a bold move not to name top PSLE (Primary School Leaving Examinations) achievers, a practise that analysts once said promote elitism. The

Malay/Muslim community should do the same as well and highlight achievers in other fields: sports, arts, politics and others. Furthermore, I believe as the community approaches its next SG50, it has to judge success or leaders based on the quality of their ideas.

Lastly, my vision for SG100 is there will not be another book which celebrates the achievements of Malays/Muslims in Singapore. I may not be living long enough to witness 2065, but I hope future generations will realise the vision set out by our fore fathers: to build a multiracial society, regardless of race, language, or religion. SG100 should no longer be a celebration of the success of the Malay/Muslim community between 2015 and 2065, but of Singaporeans!

TRUST ME WHEN I SAY THAT SOCIAL COHESION IN SINGAPORE WILL BE A CONTINUING CHALLENGE | Zainul Abidin Rasheed

The last 50 years have been extraordinary for Singapore and for the Malay/Muslim community. Despite the odds, we have emerged as a model of development for many, including other developed countries.

However, there are still many uncertainties. The global economy is going through a period of stress, and challenges are aplenty. Singaporeans should expect to face many trials and tribulations in the horizon. Notwithstanding the economic miracle of Singapore's first 50 years of independence, our leaders are quick to point out that if there is a single most important factor for those achievements, it is our social cohesion.

It is reassuring to know that many among the younger generation, including my co-editor, Dr Norshahril, see themselves as part of a future that is race blind.

Personally, I find it interesting, and gratifying when, those of my children's generation, tell me to stop talking about multiculturalism and race because it would only accentuate the divide which we Singaporeans have been concerned about all the time.

> *Stop telling us about your grandfather stories, about race riots and race politics. We are Singaporeans first and we are now race and colour blind.*

These are strong words. I am more sanguine and measured in my approach to race relations. Perhaps it is because of my own personal experience, my life through the early Singapore history of post-independence, fraught with the challenges of communism, communalism, and race politics.

In August 2009, 50 years after self-government, in response to a question in Parliament, related to the Singapore Pledge, whether it was time for Singapore to move beyond race and treat everyone as equal, Founding Prime Minister, the late Mr Lee Kuan Yew delivered one of his last major speeches in Parliament, and sought to bring Parliament "back to earth". Mr Lee reminded everyone what our starting point was, our foundation and that "if we do not recognise where we started from, and that these are our foundations, we will fail". Our pledge therefore serves as both an aspiration and a reminder. We have seen what we can do and achieve as a nation, and that everything we have achieved had come through rising to the challenges.

The Malay/Muslim community went through these same challenges. From a low base in educational and economic foundation, we persevered and worked hard to overcome the challenges with the aid of community's self-help and Malay/Muslim-friendly government programmes, and avoiding any controversial affirmative action policies. Slowly but surely, the community made progress. Much more effort and creative programmes are needed and indeed provided through the various channels for self-reliance, self-improvement and incentive-linked programmes, for inclusive development.

The challenges ahead in terms of attaining better performance in education, gaining better skills sets, and to be better prepared for the future socioeconomic needs, to me, are easier to overcome than to ensure that social cohesion is preserved and enhanced. No doubt, we have to continue to work towards having a better understanding among Singaporeans, especially between the majority–minority groups, about what the common aspirations are, including sensitive issues such as the *tudung* (head-scarf) and the Malay/Muslim presence and role in the SAF. The Malay/Muslim community looks forward to a better understanding of "Work-in-Progress" in these issues, and more open discussions are perhaps needed so as to remove any doubt about any perceived lack of trust. However, we do have a good and strong foundation for us to build on, despite the stark challenges we see around us in terms of race and inter-civilisational relations that have bedevilled the region and the world today.

When I was first appointed Senior Parliamentary Secretary (Foreign Affairs), I asked Mr Goh Chok Tong, whether he trusted me and if he did, why not appoint me to defence? He said if he did not, he would not have brought me in and appointed me as office holder in the first place. Today, not only do we have two Malay/Muslim Ministers in Cabinet (an issue always in the Malay/Muslim community's and Singaporeans' mind whether the community was only good enough to have one 'representational', if not token, Minister) but also a Minister of State for Defence. Was it a matter of right place, right time, or level of trust, or capabilities? Perhaps, I was just not the right man for the job, but I am delighted with the progress we have made.

Looking forward for the next 50 years, one challenge will be whether the Malay/Muslim community will be viewed as Singaporeans first rather than a distinct minority. The community must continue to do its part and contribute to the growth of our nation.

The Malay/Muslim community is already an integral part of Singapore and we strive to be a model community, proud of its past, realistic about the challenges of multicultural living in secular Singapore, an unsettling troubled world, and even more proud to be a real and active contributor towards SG100.

Majulah Singapura!

APPENDIX

SELECTED LITERATURE

In this digital age, physical books are still an important medium for the dissemination of information or purely for leisure. We have listed here a collection of books that directly and indirectly touch on the Malay/Muslim community here in Singapore — both fiction and non-fiction. These books are meant to give readers a source of further reading if they want to know more about the community. The order of the books is not in any particular order of preference or merit.

Batas Langit – Mohamed Latiff Mohamed, Pustaka Nasional Pte Ltd. (2002).

Poverty and political conflicts in the early 1960s, which colour the lives of Adi and the Malay community during that time, are portrayed in this novel.

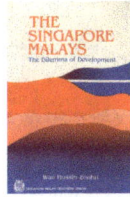

The Singapore Malays – The Dilemma of Development – Wan Hussin Zoohri, Singapore Malay Teachers' Union (1990).

This 1986/90 paper gives useful background information on the Singapore Malay community, and the political and educational policies and factors which have influenced its development since early colonial times.

Memeluk Gerhana – Isa Kamari, Al-Ameen Serve Holdings (2007).

A poignant coming-of-age tale set in Singapore in the 1960s and 1970s. This book is a trip down memory lane for those born and who grew up in those years – familiar songs, games and TV programmes, interspersed with key events in the Lion City and the world.

A Salute to Singapore – In Celebration of Singapore's 25 Years of Nationhood. Text by Anthony Lawrence; captions by Richard Lim, Times of Singapore (1984).

A unique pictorial journey of Singapore through the lens of 42 world's leading photographers as the nation celebrates its 25th anniversary.

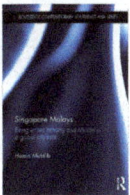

Singapore Malays: Being Ethnic Minority and Muslim in a Global City-State – Hussin Mutalib, Routledge (2012).

This book presents holistic and extensive analysis of the "Malay Muslim story" in Singapore. Comprehensively and convincingly argued, the author examines their challenging circumstances in the fields of politics, education, social mobility, economy, leadership, and freedom of religious expression.

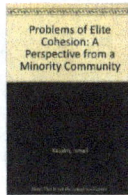

Problems of Elite Cohesion: A Perspective from a Minority Community – Ismail Kassim, Singapore University Press (1974).

This book is a theoretical case study of the problems of elite cohesion in Singapore as seen from the perspective of the Malay minority community.

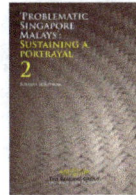

Problematic Singapore Malays – Sustaining a Portrayal – Suriani Suratman, Leftwrite Center in collaboration with the Reading Group Singapore (2010).

This monograph is about the portrayal of the Malays by the government, as found in the mainstream media in Singapore. Through a survey of newspaper reports from the period of the 1960s to the 1990s, this paper argues the sustained reproduction of "the problematic Malays"

The Singapore Dilemma – Lily Zubaidah Rahim, Oxford University Press. Kuala Lumpur (1998).

This book examines the factors that have contributed to the persisting socio-economic marginality of the Singapore Malay Community. It proposes that this problem requires a national solution as it is organically connected to the social, economic, and political challenges confronting the multi-ethinic island republic.

Making the Difference: Ten Years of MENDAKI, Yayasan Mendaki (1992).

This is a publication to commemorate the 10th anniversary of MENDAKI. It details the development of the self-help group of the Singapore Malay/Muslim community.

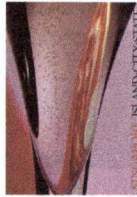

Singapore: Island, City, State, Times Editions (1990).

Singapore's unique status as an island, city and state is being beautifully defined by a series of beautifully-captured photographs and write-ups by well-known individuals in this commemorative book for Singapore's 25th anniversary.

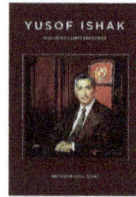

Yusof Ishak: Singapore's First President - Norshahril Saat, ISEAS–Yusof Ishak Institute (2015).

Published in 2015, the book is a biography of Singapore's first President, Yusof Ishak.

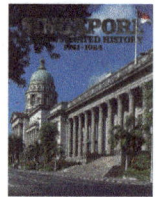

Singapore: An Illustrated History (1941-1984) – Daljit Singh and V T Arasu, Ministry of Culture, Singapore (1984).

This book presents the history of Singapore from 1941 to 1984 in pictures and a short accompanying narrative.

Faith, Authority And The Malays: The Ulama in Contemporary Singapore – Norshahril Saat, Select Publishing (2015).

This book examines the nature of religious life among the Malays of Singapore by researching into the nature of the religious elite and the basis of their authority or legitimacy.

Potret Puisi Melayu Singapura – Isa Kamari, Select Publishing (2014).

In addition to celebrating the intellectual tradition of a past generation of Singaporean Malay thinkers, social and cultural activists, this series provides unique insights and perspectives into the lived-experience and collective memories of the Malay community in Singapore. context, community and

Narrating Presence: Awakening From Cultural Amnesia – Azhar Ibrahim, Select Publishing (2014).

Narrating Presence: Awakening from Cultural Amnesia investigates and raises questions on the background and social-historical conditionings that have shaped and coloured Malay thinking and world view, from the past to contemporary thought, through its literary heritage and letters.

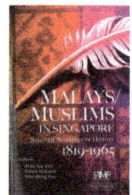

Malays/Muslims in Singapore Selected Readings in History 1819-1965 – Khoo Kay Kim, Elinah Abdullah and Wan Meng Hao (Eds.), Association of Muslim Professionals (AMP) and Pelanduk Publications (2006).

Works on the history of the Singapore Malay/Muslim community from 1819 to 1965 are few. This volume seeks to contribute to the literature by providing readers with a macro view of the chronological development of the Singapore Malay/Muslim community over this 150-year period.

Malay Heritage Centre/ Taman Warisan Melayu – Malay Heritage Centre/The Malay Heritage Foundation/ National Heritage Board (2014).

The Malay Heritage Centre underwent a major transformation and reopened in 2012 boasting a permanent exhibition that focus on the history of Kampong Gelam and showcase an interesting collection of artifacts from the National Collection and the Malay community. This book encapsulated the essence of the galleries.

Malay Heritage of Singapore – Lau, Aileen T. & Dr. Bernhard Platzdasch (Eds.), Suntree Media (2010).

Malay life and culture on Singapore island can be traced back to the 7th century and it has of course always formed a basic factor in Singapore's history and development. The 16 sections in this extensively illustrated volume by specialists, and together, they explore the many dimensions of the Malay heritage.

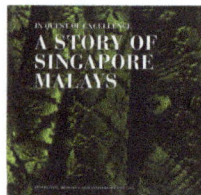

In Quest of Excellence: A Story of Singapore Malays – Saat A. Rahman and Thusitha de Silva (2002).

A book that captures the essence of the Malay community living in cosmopolitan Singapore. As MENDAKI celebrates its 20th anniversary, the book also traces the past and present challenges of the Malay community as well as the aspirations for the future.

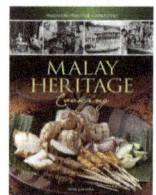

Malay Heritage Cooking - Singapore Heritage Cookbooks – Rita Zahara, Marshall Cavendish (2012).

The Singapore Heritage Cookbook series documents and preserves the cultural and culinary heritage of the different ethnic groups in Singapore through recipes passed down from generation to generation.

Paradigma Melayu Singapura – Sidek bin Saniff, Taman Bacaan Pemuda Pemudi Melayu Singapura (2010).

A collection of the author's political views and speeches on the development of the Malay/Muslim community.

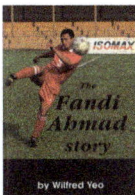

The Fandi Ahmad Story – Wilfred Yeo, Brit Aspen Publishing (1993).

A book that tells the story of Singapore's favourite footballing son — Fandi Ahmad — his early years and to his peak when he played for a Dutch football club FC Gronigen.

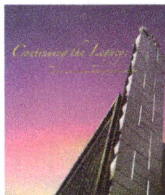

Continuing the Legacy: 30 Years of the Mosque Building Fund in Singapore, The Islamic Religious Council of Singapore (MUIS).

This book is a special publication commemorating 30 years of achievement made by MUIS and the Muslim community through the establishment of this fund.

Muslims in Singapore: A Shared Vision, Published for Majlis Ugama Islam Singapura by Times Editions (1994).

This publication highlights the developments of the Muslim community in Singapore covering the history and heritage of Singapore Muslims.

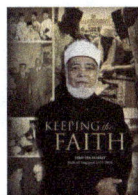

Keeping the Faith- Syed Isa Semait, Mufti of Singapore 1972–2010 – Syed Zakir Hussain, Straits Times Press (2012).

His role to forge a Singapore Muslim identity has helped the community to thrive in a multireligious, modern and cosmopolitan Singapore. Mufti Syed Isa has played a very significant role in providing, leadership and inspiration in enhancing the bond of relationship, among the many faith communities for the greater good of Singapore, and beyond.

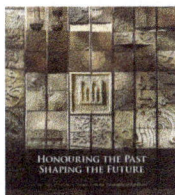

Honouring the Past, Shaping the Future: The MUIS Story – 40 years of building a Singapore Muslim Community of Excellence – Anthony Green, Majlis Ugama Islam Singapura (MUIS).

The book charts MUIS' humble beginnings from just seven people in three tiny offices at the old Empress Place government building, to an organisation with a 130-strong staff occupying its own 11-storey building.

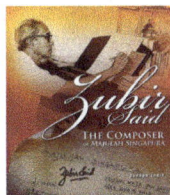

Zubir Said, the Composer of Majulah Singapura – Rohana Zubir, Institute of Southeast Asian Studies (2012).

This book, which includes numerous photographs, documents, musical scores and articles, as well as a CD of a selection of Zubir Said's compositions, vividly reveals one of Singapore's leading composers as family man, friend, composer and mentor. It also accords Zubir Said his rightful place in the history of Singapore.

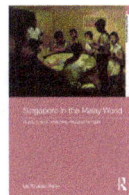

Singapore in the Malay World: Building And Breaching Regional Bridge – Lily Zubaidah Rahim, Routledge (2009).

Relations between Singapore and her immediate Malay neighbours have been perennially fraught with tension and misunderstanding. In making sense of this complex relationship, Lily Rahim explores the salience of historical animosities and competitive economic pressures, and Singapore's Janus-faced security and foreign economic policy orientation and 'regional outsider' complex.

Muslims of Singapore (in Arabic) – The Islamic Religious Council of Singapore (MUIS).

In brief essays and more specific photographic illustrations, this book describes some aspects of Muslim Singaporeans' religious, socio-economic and cultural life from the perspective of social change and transition.

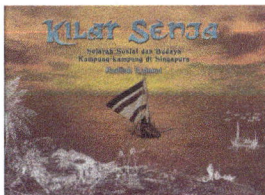

Kilat Senja - Sejarah Sosial dan Budaya Kampung-Kampung di Singapura – Hadijah Rahmat, HS Yang Publishing (2005).

A seminal work by Prof Hadijah Rahmat on Singapore's kampungs. It is a labour of love based on the author's extensive fieldwork conducted in the 1980s. It contains information gleaned from her interviews with elderly residents and is thus a record of settlement and social histories of kampungs in Singapura that would otherwise have been lost entirely.

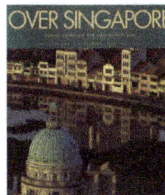

Over Singapore: Aerial Views of the Island Republic – Simon Tay and Guido Alberto Rossi, Archipelago Press (1993).

Photographer Guido Alberto Rossi unveils the many layers of juxtapositions of Singapore in an aerial photographic essay as writer Simon Tay guides the reader through Singapore's urban and rural landscape.

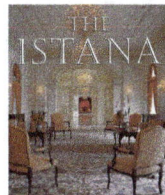

The Istana – K. K. Seet and Peter Mealin, Times Editions (2000).

This volume traces the history of the Istana back to its early incarnation as the Government House, the first of which was built on Bukit Larangan (Fort Canning) in 1823. It documents both the events and lively anecdotes involving its illustrious occupants.

Di Sebalik Tabir — Masuri S N – Dr Pitchay Gani Aziz dan Dr Azhar Ibrahim, National Library Board (2016).

A collection of yet-to-be-published poems by the legendary poet Masuri S. N.

Singapura: Kotaku, Kampung Halamanku — 新加坡：我的城市我的家园

A collection of the representative works of 30 important Singaporean poets who write in Malay and Chinese.

Perjalanan MAS — Memoir Muhammad Ariff Ahmad – Muhammad Ariff Ahmad and Mohd Raman Daud (ed.), Angkatan Sasterawan '50 (2007).

An autobiography of Muhammad Ariff Ahmad, one of Singapore's prominent personality in Malay language, literary works, and culture in Singapore.

Memories & Musings – Wan Hussin Zoohri, 2016.

A former politician reflects on his early life, career, his role as a politician and years of community service. Wan Hussin Zoohri tells the story of a kampung boy who rose through the ranks to become a Member of Parliament in his own words.

Warisan Kita – Julina Khusaini (ed.) and Joey Tan (writer), Taman Warisan Melayu (2015).

A book that records the making of the Warisan Kita mural — a collaborative art project involving more than 170 participants from all walks of life, both Singaporeans and tourists. It is curated by potters and ceramic artists from Jalan Bahar Clay Studios and Temasek Potters.

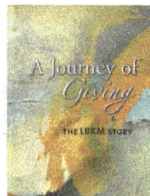

A Journey of Giving – The LBKM Story – Hidayah Amin, Lembaga Biasiswa Kenangan Maulud (2016).

This book chronicles Lembaga Biasiswa Kenangan Maulud (Prophet Muhammad's Birthday Memorial Scholarship Fund Board)'s 50-year history from 1965 to 2015.

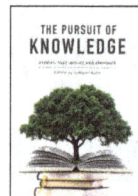

The Pursuit of Knowledge – Stories that Inspire and Empower – Hidayah Amin (ed.), Centre for Research on Islamic and Malay Affairs (RIMA) for Lembaga Biasiswa Kenangan Maulud (LBKM) (2016).

This book is a collection of eight real-life stories of ordinary Singaporeans who struggled to pursue their dreams and ambitions.

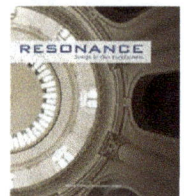

Resonance: Songs of Our Forefathers – Kwek Leng Joo et al. and G. Uma Devi, Preservation of Monuments Board (2009).

Featuring 24 of Singapore's National Monuments, PMB's photography book introduces both iconic and lesser known monuments through the artistic expressions of a team of photographers led by avid photographer Kwek Leng Joo.

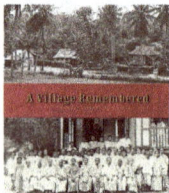

A Village Remembered — Kampong Radin Mas 1800s-1973 – Ibrahim Tahir (ed.) Singapore: OPUS Editorial Private Limited (2013).

Remembering Kampong Radin Mas records the memories of the residents from the kampung who were resettled in 1973. The book explores what life was like in the kampung — the spirit of gotong-royong that had the villagers rallying to help one another; diminishing traditional cultural practices; and the happy times shared by village folk when life was simpler.

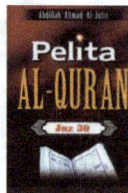

Pelita Al-Quran – Syed Abdillah Al-Jufri, Pustaka Nasional (2003).

A series dedicated to the translation of the Quran, based on compilation of lecture notes by Syed Abdillah, a well-known and respected ulama in Singapore.

Mari Sembahyang (Laki-Laki) – Ahmad Sonhadji Mohamad (1957).

Well illustrated with line drawings, this book was the pioneering literature in the teaching of Islamic prayer. The book has both Malay and Arabic text. This book has been translated into English, Mandarin, Tamil, Sinhala and Korean and has inspired the publications of many other books on prayers that we find today both locally or overseas.

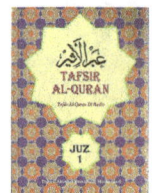

Tafsir 'Abr Athir – Ahmad Sonhadji Mohamad (1960).

Still a *magnum opus* when it comes to reference on the translation of the Quran It has a total of 30 volumes and constitutes the collection and compilation of lectures by Ahmad Sonhadji on radio in Singapore over the years. This effort took up to 20 years to complete, and was published gradually until its completion in 1981.

SG50 MALAY/MUSLIM COLLECTION

The Malay/Muslim community does not want to be left behind in celebrating and commemorating Singapore's golden jubilee. A flurry of publications sprang up each with its own distinct perspective and presentation with topics ranging from postcard art, to language and entrepreneurship. Here's a display of a potpourri of publications commemorating Singapore's 50th birthday.

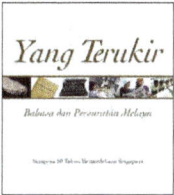

Yang Terukir – Bahasa dan Persuratan Melayu Sempena 50 Tahun Kemerdekaan Singapura

Malay Language Council under the National Heritage Board **(NHB)**

Perintisku, Singapuraku

Yayasan MENDAKI and MUIS

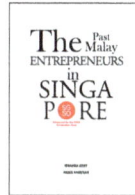

The Past Malay Entrepreneurs in Singapore

Ibrahim Ariff and Andik Marina

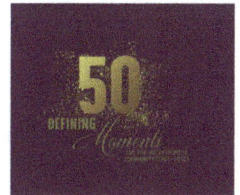

50 Defining Moments –For the Malay/Muslim Community (1965-2015)

Association of Muslim Professionals (AMP) and Berita Harian

SG50Kita A Year of Caring, Sharing, Giving

SG50Kita

Postcard Stories

Yayasan MENDAKI

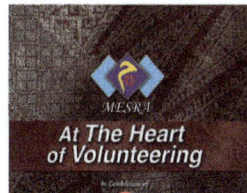

MESRA – At the Heart of Volunteering

People's Association Malay Activity Executive Committee (MAEC)/MESRA

2015 MENDAKI Policy Digest SG50 Special Edition

Yayasan MENDAKI

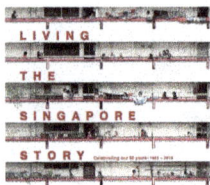

Living the Singapore Story

National Library Board

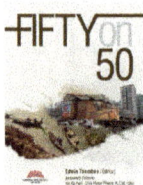

Fifty on 50

National Arts Council of Singapore

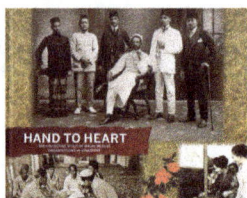

Hand to Heart - The Collective Spirt of Malay/Muslim Organisations in Singapore

National Heritage Board

Majulah! 50 Years of Malay/ Muslim Community in Singapore

World Scientific Publishing Company

1. OVERVIEW

Today, Malays make up 13.3% of the Singapore Resident Population, the second largest ethnic group after the Chinese (74.3%);[a] and 98.7% of Malays in Singapore are Muslims.[b]

2. HOUSING

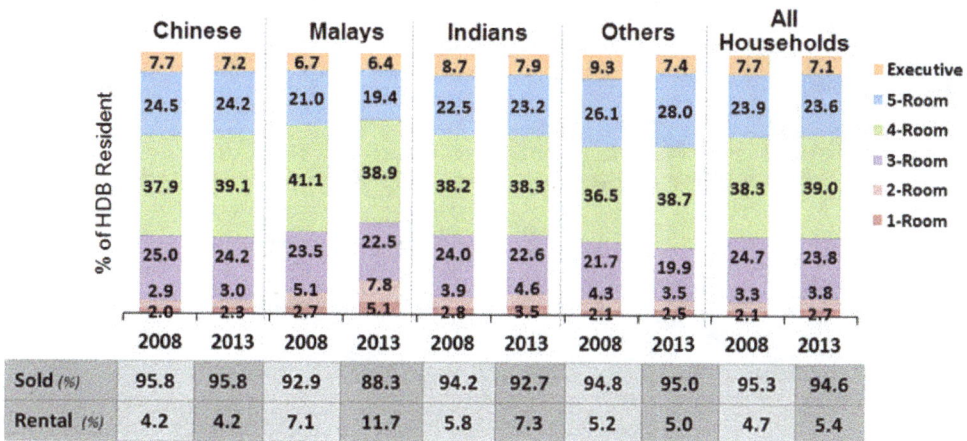

	Chinese		Malays		Indians		Others		All Households		
	2008	2013	2008	2013	2008	2013	2008	2013	2008	2013	
Executive	7.7	7.2	6.7	6.4	8.7	7.9	9.3	7.4	7.7	7.1	
5-Room	24.5	24.2	21.0	19.4	22.5	23.2	26.1	28.0	23.9	23.6	
4-Room	37.9	39.1	41.1	38.9	38.2	38.3	36.5	38.7	38.3	39.0	
3-Room	25.0	24.2	23.5	22.5	24.0	22.6	21.7	19.9	24.7	23.8	
2-Room	2.9	3.0	5.1	7.8	3.9	4.6	4.3	3.5	3.3	3.8	
1-Room	2.0	2.3	2.7	5.1	2.8	3.5	2.1	2.5	2.1	2.7	

% of HDB Resident

	Chinese		Malays		Indians		Others		All Households	
	2008	2013	2008	2013	2008	2013	2008	2013	2008	2013
Sold (%)	95.8	95.8	92.9	88.3	94.2	92.7	94.8	95.0	95.3	94.6
Rental (%)	4.2	4.2	7.1	11.7	5.8	7.3	5.2	5.0	4.7	5.4

Figure 1: HDB Home Ownership by Ethnicity

Source: HDB Household Survey 2013 (Public)

3. EDUCATION

A. Academic Performance

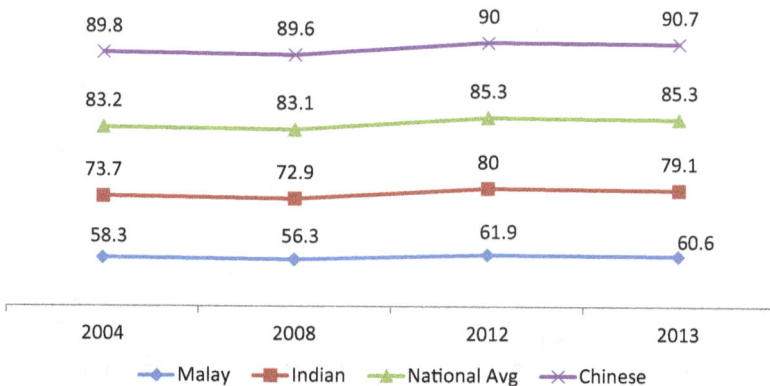

	2004	2008	2012	2013
Chinese	89.8	89.6	90	90.7
National Avg	83.2	83.1	85.3	85.3
Indian	73.7	72.9	80	79.1
Malay	58.3	56.3	61.9	60.6

Malay — Indian — National Avg — Chinese

Figure 1: PSLE students who scored A*–C in Mathematics (%)

Source: MOE (Public)

---

[a] DOS Population Trends, 2014.

[b] DOS, 2012.

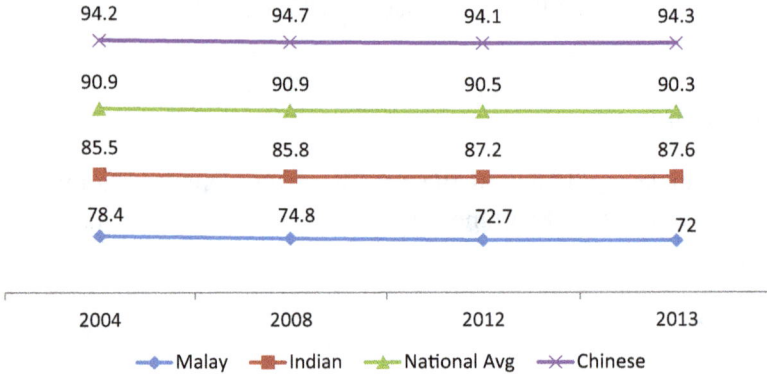

Figure 2: PSLE students who scored A*–C in Science (%)

Source: MOE (Public)

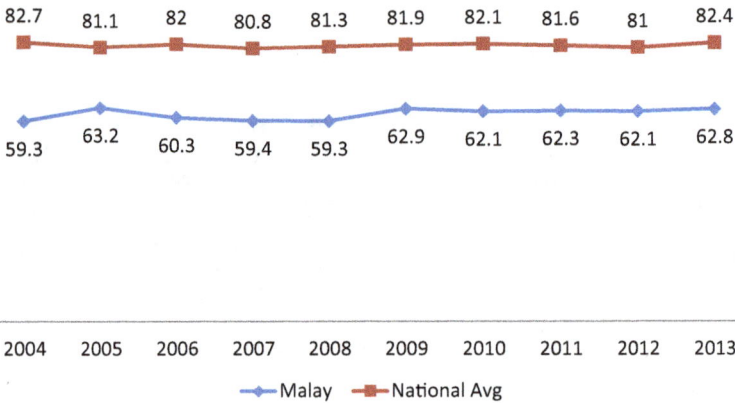

Figure 3: GCE 'O'-Level with at least 5 'O'-Level Passes (%)

Source: MOE (Public)

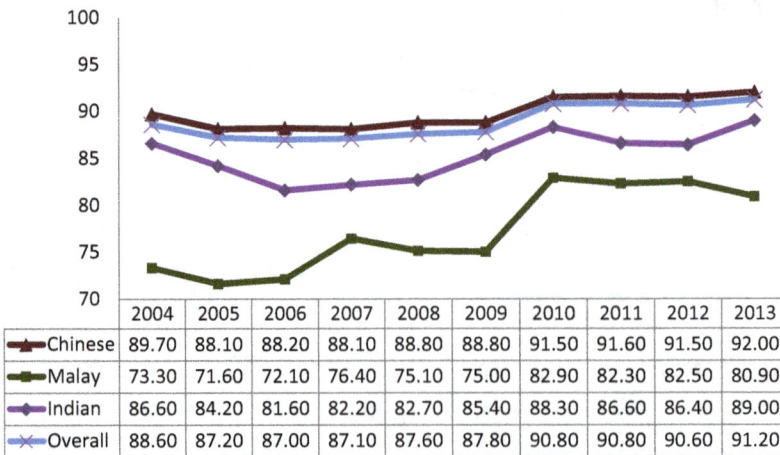

	2004	2005	2006	2007	2008	2009	2010	2011	2012	2013
Chinese	89.70	88.10	88.20	88.10	88.80	88.80	91.50	91.60	91.50	92.00
Malay	73.30	71.60	72.10	76.40	75.10	75.00	82.90	82.30	82.50	80.90
Indian	86.60	84.20	81.60	82.20	82.70	85.40	88.30	86.60	86.40	89.00
Overall	88.60	87.20	87.00	87.10	87.60	87.80	90.80	90.80	90.60	91.20

Figure 4: Students with at least 3 'A'-level Passes, and Pass in GP, 2004 to 2013 (%)

Source: MOE (Public)

B. P1 Cohort Data

1. More Malay P1 cohort students have been admitted to post-secondary institutions, over the past 10 years.

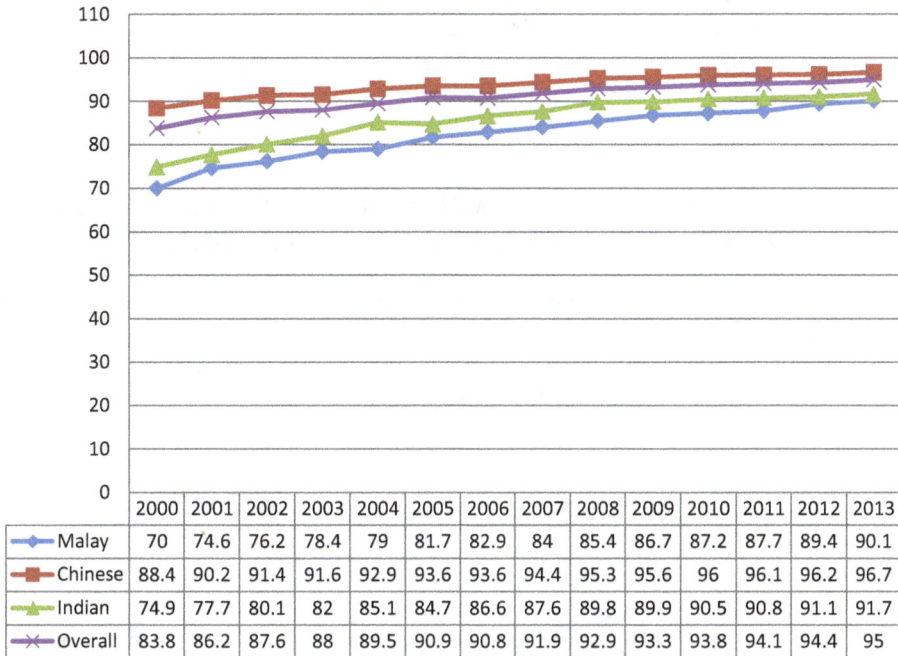

	2000	2001	2002	2003	2004	2005	2006	2007	2008	2009	2010	2011	2012	2013
Malay	70	74.6	76.2	78.4	79	81.7	82.9	84	85.4	86.7	87.2	87.7	89.4	90.1
Chinese	88.4	90.2	91.4	91.6	92.9	93.6	93.6	94.4	95.3	95.6	96	96.1	96.2	96.7
Indian	74.9	77.7	80.1	82	85.1	84.7	86.6	87.6	89.8	89.9	90.5	90.8	91.1	91.7
Overall	83.8	86.2	87.6	88	89.5	90.9	90.8	91.9	92.9	93.3	93.8	94.1	94.4	95

Figure 5: Percentage of P1 Cohort Admitted to Post-Secondary Education Institutions

Source: MOE (Public)

Note: Figures include participation in Junior Colleges, Millennia Institute, Polytechnics, Institute of Technical Education (ITE), LaSalle College of the Arts, Nanyang Academy of Fine Arts and other private education institutions, and take into account students who have left the country.

6. SOCIAL INDICATORS

A. Drug Abuse and Crime Rates

2. Malays form the largest group, about 51.4% of the total drug abusers caught in 2014. Malays are also over-represented among new abusers.

Table 1: Total abusers by ethnic group for 2011–2014

	2009	2010	2011	2012	2013	2014
Chinese	1036	1050	1109	1099	1259	946
Malay	1158	1376	1603	1773	1710	1586
Indian	374	403	539	567	541	497
Others	48	58	75	68	71	56

Source: MHA (Public)

Table 2: New abusers by ethnic group for 2011–2014

	2009	2010	2011	2012	2013	2014
Chinese	543	531	379	327	411	299
Malay	496	588	577	568	513	585
Indian	136	173	141	166	155	146
Others	25	35	31	31	31	28

Source: MHA (Public)

B. Trend in Minor Marriages (where one/both parties were below 21 years at point of Marriage under AMLA)

3. Muslim minor marriages have generally been on a downward trend for the past 10 years. 5

Number of Muslim Minor Marriages

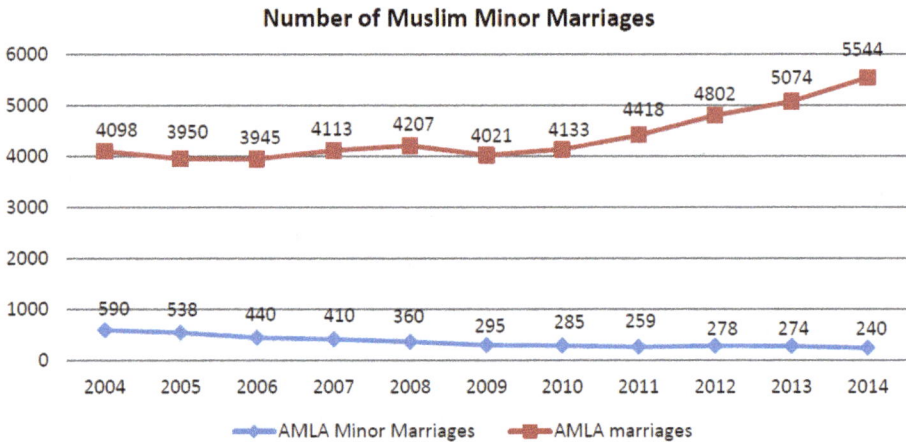

Figure 6: Trend in Minor Marriages, 2004–2014

Source: ROMM (Public)

Table 3: Trend in Minor Marriages from 2004–2014

	'04	'05	'06	'07	'08	'09	'10	'11	'12	'13	'14
AMLA minor marriages	590	538	440	410	360	295	285	259	278	274	240
Total AMLA marriages	4098	3950	3945	4113	4207	4021	4133	4418	4802	5074	5544
% of minor marriages to AMLA marriages	14.4	13.6	11.1	10.0	8.6	7.3	6.9	5.9	5.8	5.4	4.3

Source: ROMM (Public)

C. Trend in Muslim Divorces Involving Minor Marriages (where one/both parties were below 21 years at time of Marriage under AMLA)

4. Muslim divorces involving minor marriages have also generally been on a downward trend for the past 10 years.

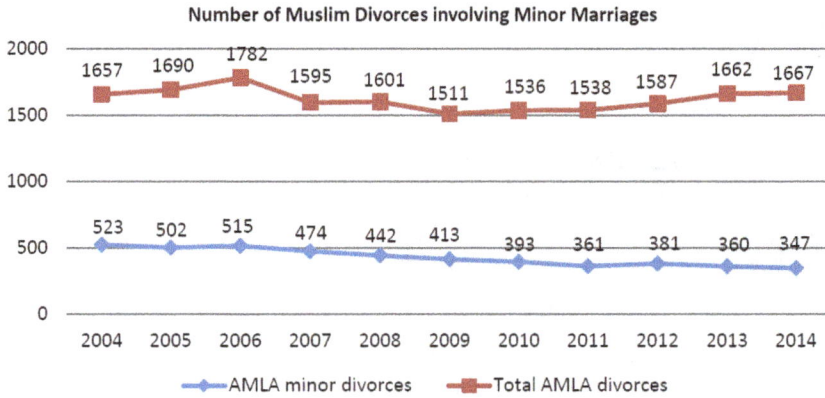

Number of Muslim Divorces involving Minor Marriages

Figure 7: Trend in Divorces Involving Minor Marriages, 2004–2014

Source: SYC (Public)

Table 4: Trend in Muslim Divorces Involving Minor Marriages from 2004–2014 (figure excludes revocation)

	'04	'05	'06	'07	'08	'09	'10	'11	'12	'13	'14
Divorces involving minor mar.	523	502	515	474	442	413	393	361	381	360	347
Total AMLA divorces	1,657	1,690	1,782	1,595	1,601	1,511	1,536	1,538	1,590	1,662	1,667
Proportion (%)	32%	30%	29%	30%	28%	27%	26%	23%	24%	22%	21%

Source: SYC (Public)

D. Trend in Muslim Remarriages

5. The number of Muslim remarriages has been increasing steadily for the past 10 years from 1352 in 2004 to 1444 in 2014.

Number of Muslim Remarriages

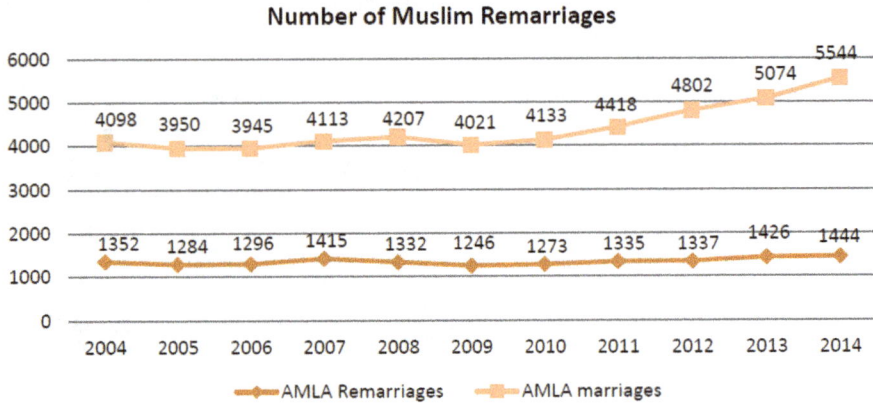

Figure 8: Trend in Muslim Remarriages, 2004–2014

Source: ROMM (Public)

Table 5: Trend in Muslim Remarriages from 2004–2014

	'04	'05	'06	'07	'08	'09	'10	'11	'12	'13	'14
AMLA remarriages	1352	1284	1296	1415	1332	1246	1273	1335	1337	1426	1444
Total AMLA marriages	4098	3950	3945	4113	4207	4021	4133	4418	4802	5074	5544
% of remarriages to AMLA marriages	33.0	32.5	32.9	34.4	31.7	31.0	30.8	30.2	27.8	28.1	26

Source: ROMM (Public)

E. Trend in Muslim Divorces Involving Remarriages

6. Muslim divorces involving remarriages have generally been on a downward trend for the past 10 years.

Number of Divorces involving Remarriages

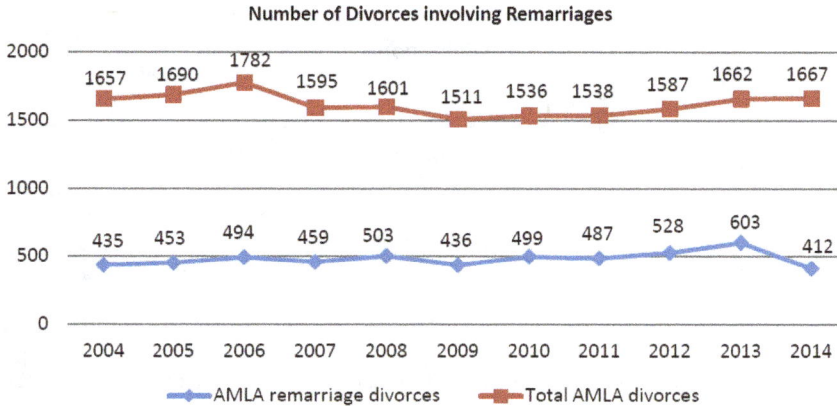

Figure 9:   Trend in Divorces Involving Remarriages, 2004–2014

Source: SYC (Public)

Table 6:   Trend in Muslim Divorces Involving Remarriages from 2004-2014 (figure excludes revocation)

	'04	'05	'06	'07	'08	'09	'10	'11	'12	'13	'14
Divorces involving remarriage	435	453	494	459	503	436	499	487	528	603	412
Total AMLA divorces	1,657	1,690	1,782	1,595	1,601	1,511	1,536	1,538	1,590	1,662	1,667
Proportion (%)	26%	27%	28%	29%	31%	29%	32%	32%	33%	36%	25%

Source: SYC (Public)

7. SOCIAL ASSISTANCE

A. *Zakat*

7. *Zakat* collection has been increasing in the past few years. This has allowed MUIS to regularly revise its qualifying criterion, so as to gradually allow more to qualify for assistance through *zakat*. Overall in 2014, 5,432 families were assisted compared to 5,263 families in 2013 (these include the monthly and one-off assistance rendered).

Table 7:   *Zakat* Collection, 2007–2014

Zakat Collection ($ in mil)

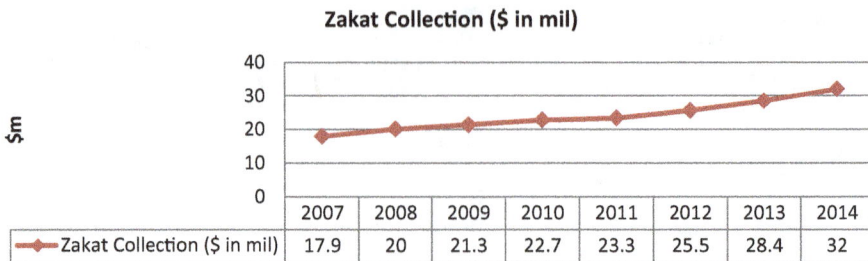

	2007	2008	2009	2010	2011	2012	2013	2014
Zakat Collection ($ in mil)	17.9	20	21.3	22.7	23.3	25.5	28.4	32

Source: MUIS (Public)

Table 8:   Number of *zakat* recipients who receive monthly assistance, 2007–2014

Monthly Zakat Recipients

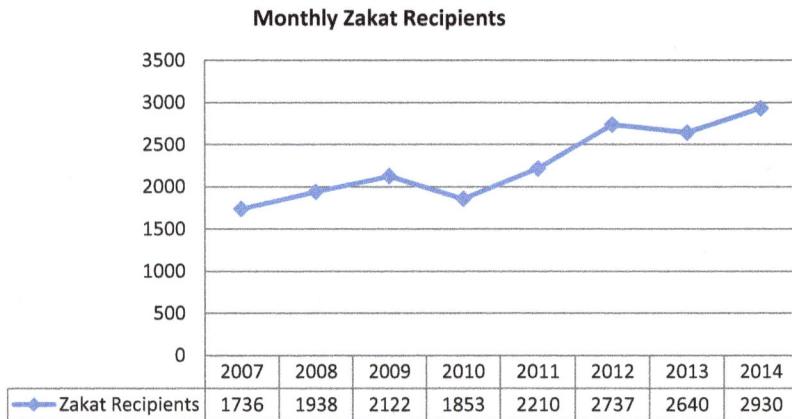

	2007	2008	2009	2010	2011	2012	2013	2014
Zakat Recipients	1736	1938	2122	1853	2210	2737	2640	2930

Source: MUIS (Public)

8. The $2.5M MUIS Progress Fund was first announced in 2010. In 2012, a top-up of $2.0 million was made to Progress Fund bringing the total allocation to $2.9 million. This was done in anticipation of an economic downturn. The current utilisation of the Progress Fund is shown below.

Table 9:   Utilisation of Progress Fund (as at 2014)

No	Type of Programme	Allocated Budget	Actual Expenditure	No. of Beneficiaries
1	Islamic Education (Mosque *madrasah*/ aLIVE)	$800,000	$855,303	2780
2	Madrasah Financial Assistance Scheme (PROMAS)	$488,000	$490,669	361
3	Supportive academic programmes for children of *zakat* recipients	$300,000	$14,110.00	65
4	Befrienders' management framework	$112,000	$127,497	665
5	Training grants for *zakat* recipients (in event of economic downturn)	$300,000	—	—
	Total	$2,000,000	$1,487,579	3871

Source: MUIS (Public)

8. HEALTH

A. State of the Health of the Community

9. The National Health Survey, conducted every six years, found that Malays had the highest prevalence of hypertension (28%), high total cholesterol (22.6%) and obesity (24%).

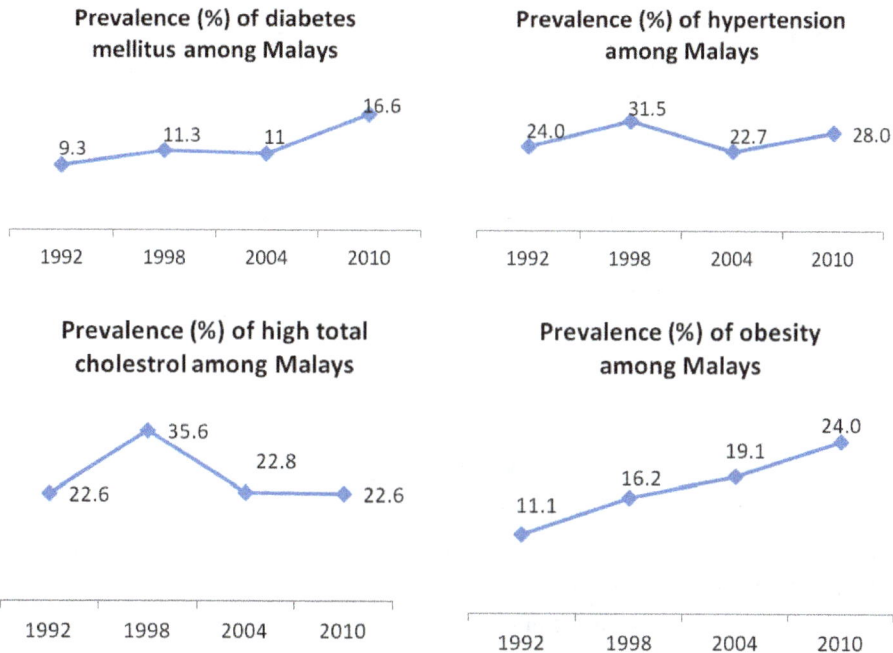

Prevalence (%) of diabetes mellitus among Malays

16.6

11.3   11

9.3

1992   1998   2004   2010

Prevalence (%) of hypertension among Malays

31.5

24.0   22.7   28.0

1992   1998   2004   2010

Prevalence (%) of high total cholestrol among Malays

35.6

22.8

22.6   22.6

1992   1998   2004   2010

Prevalence (%) of obesity among Malays

24.0

19.1

16.2

11.1

1992   1998   2004   2010

Figure 10: Prevalence of (i) diabetes mellitus, (ii) hypertension; (iii) total high cholesterol; and (iv) obesity among Malays.

Source: National Heath Survey 2010 (Public)

B. Prevalence of Abdominal Fatness, Daily Smoking, and Leisure-Time Regular Physical Exercise

10. The Survey also found that Malays had high prevalence of abdominal fatness and daily smoking. Malays, however, had the lowest prevalence of leisure-time regular physical exercise. The mosques are working with the Health Promotion Board to encourage and promote healthy lifestyles within the community.

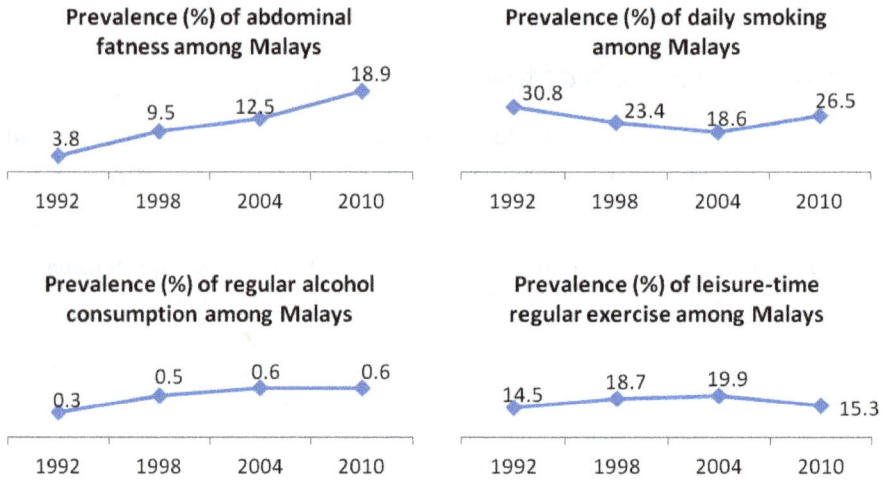

Prevalence (%) of abdominal fatness among Malays

3.8 · 9.5 · 12.5 · 18.9
1992 · 1998 · 2004 · 2010

Prevalence (%) of daily smoking among Malays

30.8 · 23.4 · 18.6 · 26.5
1992 · 1998 · 2004 · 2010

Prevalence (%) of regular alcohol consumption among Malays

0.3 · 0.5 · 0.6 · 0.6
1992 · 1998 · 2004 · 2010

Prevalence (%) of leisure-time regular exercise among Malays

14.5 · 18.7 · 19.9 · 15.3
1992 · 1998 · 2004 · 2010

Figure 11: Prevalence of (i) abdominal fatness, (ii) daily smoking; (iii) regular alcohol consumption; and (iv) regular exercise among Malays.

Source: National Health Survey 2010 (Public)

C. Mental Health

11. The WHO defines mental health as "not just absence of mental disorder. It is defined as a state of well-being in which every individual realises his or her own potential, can cope with the normal stresses of life, can work productively and fruitfully, and is able to make a contribution to her or his own community". The level of mental health of a person at any point of time is affected by multiple social, psychological, and biological factors. Stressful work conditions, gender discrimination, social exclusion and unhealthy lifestyle could result in poor mental health. Among ethnic groups, Indians (11.5%) had the lowest prevalence of mental health compared to Malays (13%) and Chinese (13%).

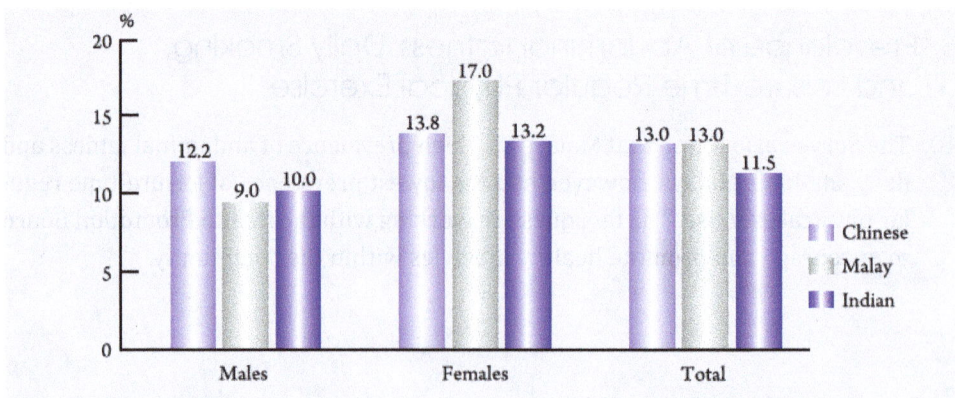

Figure 12: Prevalence of poor mental health among Singapore residents by ethnicity and gender

Source: National Health Survey 2010 (Public)

ACKNOWLEDGMENTS

Pulau Pandan jauh ke tengah,
Gunung Daik bercabang tiga;
Hancur badan dikandung tanah,
Budi yang baik dikenang juga.

Pandan Island far in midst,
With the three peaked Mount Daik;
While the body decomposes in earth,
Good deeds remain to be remembered.

The editors and publisher would like to express their profound thanks to all those who in their institutional, professional or personal capacities have contributed and provided valuable support and assistance in making this publication possible, through their research, writing, granting of permissions, supply of information and creative works. Inevitably some names will be missed out unintentionally for which the editors and publisher would like to apologise.

Abdul Rohim Sarip · Adilah Adnan · Albakri Ahmad · Amatul Jameel Suhani · Andik Marinah · **Angkatan Sasterawan '50** · Arfah Ibrahim · **Association of Muslim Professionals (AMP)** · **Berita Harian/Berita Minggu** · **Bureau for the Advancement of Lifestyle and Longevity and Success (www.thebureau.com.sg)** · Cikgu Abdul Rahman B Omar · Ernest Goh · Erfi Anugrah · Family of the late Masuri S N · Habib Syed Hassan Al Attas · Haji Wansi · Hanna Taufiq Siraj · Hazri Munawar · Herman Cher Main · Ibrahim Ariff · Idris Rashid Khan Surattee · **ISEAS–Yusof Ishak Institute** · Ismiati Ismail · Iylia Nurliyana · Jamsari Ahmad · Jihan Ali Abdat · Khalid Basharahil · Lai Yoke Lan · Lim Yan Hoon · Madam Timah Haji Abdul Rashid · Majid Ariff · **Majlis Bahasa Melayu Singapura** · **Malay Youth Literary Association (4PM)** · Masadi Masdawi · Mas'udin Syarifuddin · **MESRA/MAEC** · **Ministry of Communications and Information** · **Ministry of Culture, Community and Youth** · **Ministry of Finance** · Mohd Anuar Yusop · **MORO Records** · Muhd Fahrur Razi A Hamid · **MUIS** · Mun Chor Seng · Mustafa Izzuddin, Dr · **National Archives of Singapore** · **National Library Board** · Nick Jassmin Hew · Nidyah Sani · Noor Aisha Abdul Rahman, Assoc Prof · Noormah Azizi · Pendeta Dr Muhammad Ariff Ahmad · **People's Association** · Dr Pitchay Aziz · **Prime Minister's Office** ·

Puan Noor Aishah Mohd Salim · Puan Sri Dr Rohana Zubir · **Religious Rehabilitation Group (RRG)** · Rizal Anwardeen · Sabariah Ramilan · Salleh Sariman · Sallim Abdul Kadir · Sam Chin · Samri Badi · Sarafian Salleh · **SG50 Kita** · Shamsudin Shadan (Captain, Ret) · Shila Yatiman · **Singapore Malay Chamber of Commerce and Industry** · Siti Zalinah Adam · Som Said · **Stallion Media** · Suziyana Hamid · Syed Abdul Kadir · **Taman Warisan Melayu and Malay Heritage Foundation** · Tan Chor Koon · **Tanoti Sdn Bhd** · **The Singapore Malay/Muslim Group (SMG)** · Winda Guntor · **Yayasan MENDAKI** · Yeong Yoon Yin · Zalman Ali · Zuraidah Abdullah

Special Mention

Prime Minister Lee Hsien Loong
Minister Heng Swee Keat
Minister Dr Yaacob Ibrahim

EPILOGUE

"

Today we sang *Majulah Singapura* proudly. To still do so in
50 years' time, let us work together as one united people,
regardless of race, language or religion,
for the happiness, prosperity and progress of our nation."

Prime Minister Lee Hsien Loong
National Day Message
9 August 2015

SG50 and Beyond

www.ingramcontent.com/pod-product-compliance
Lightning Source LLC
Chambersburg PA
CBHW051426290326
41932CB00049B/3255